THE MKTG SOLUTION

Visually Engaging Textbook

Online Study Tools

Tear-Out Review Cards

Interactive Ebook

Special Note To Students

It is important to begin reading this text with one thing in mind: *This business course does not have to be difficult* . We have done everything possible to eliminate the problems that students encounter in a typical class. All the features in each chapter have been evaluated and recommended by instructors with years of teaching experience. In addition, business students were asked to critique each chapter component. Based on this feedback, the text includes the following features:

- *Learning objectives* appear at the beginning of each chapter.
- *Inside Business* is a chapter-opening case that highlights how successful companies do business on a day-to-day basis.
- *Margin notes* are used throughout the text to reinforce both learning objectives and key terms.
- *Boxed features* highlight how both employees and entrepreneurs can be successful.
- *Spotlight* features highlight interesting facts about business and society and often provide a real-world example of an important concept within a chapter.

STUDENT RESOURCES:

- Interactive Quizzing
- Flashcards
- Animated Visual Summaries
- Audio Chapter Summaries
- End-of-Chapter Questions
- Marketing Math Tutorials
- Videos with Assignments
- Marketing Plan & Worksheets
- Cases and Exercises

INSTRUCTOR RESOURCES:

- NETA Test Bank
- Basic and Expanded Set of NETA PowerPoint Slides
- Media Guide
- Instructor's Manual
- Instructor Prep Cards

Students sign in at **www.nelson.com/student**

Instructors sign in at **www.nelson.com/instructor**

" The online learning is great and the review cards in the back make test review easy! "

– Kyle McConnell, Student

MKTG, Third Canadian Edition

by Charles W. Lamb, Joe F. Hair, Carl McDaniel, Harish Kapoor, Janice Shearer, Marc Boivin, and Richard Appleby

Vice President, Editorial Higher Education:
Anne Williams

Publisher:
Amie Plourde

Marketing Manager:
David Stratton

Developmental Editors:
Lacey McMaster, Toula Di Leo

Photo Researcher/Permissions Coordinator:
Julie Pratt

Senior Production Project Manager:
Imoinda Romain

Production Service:
Shruti Chopra, MPS Limited

Copy Editor:
Dawn Hunter

Proofreader:
MPS Limited

Indexer:
PJ Heim

Design Director:
Ken Phipps

Managing Designer:
Franca Amore

Interior Design:
Cathy Mayer

Cover Design:
Trinh Truong

Cover Image:
Trinh Truong

Compositor:
MPS Limited

Library and Archives Canada Cataloguing in Publication

Lamb, Charles W., author

MKTG / by Charles W. Lamb, Joe F. Hair, Carl McDaniel, Harish Kapoor, Janice Shearer, Marc Boivin, and Richard Appleby.—Third Canadian edition.

Title from cover.

Revision of: MKTG / Lamb ... [et al.].—2nd Canadian ed.— Toronto :

Nelson Education, [2012], ©2013.

Includes bibliographical references and index.
ISBN 978-0-17-653091-4 (pbk.)

1. Marketing—Textbooks.
2. Marketing—Management—Textbooks. I. McDaniel, Carl D., author II. Shearer, Janice, author III. Kapoor, Harish, author IV. Hair, Joe F., author V. Boivin, Marc, author VI. Appleby, Richard (Marketer), author VII. Title. VIII. Title: Marketing.

HF5415.L34 2015   658.8
C2014-906361-X

ISBN-13: 978-0-17-653091-4
ISBN-10: 0-17-653091-6

BRIEF CONTENTS

Ljupco Smokovski/Shutterstock.com

CONTENTS

© Alyaksandr Stzhalkouski/Alamy

Part 1
MARKETING— LET'S GET STARTED

1 AN INTRODUCTION TO MARKETING   2

2 THE MARKETING ENVIRONMENT, SOCIAL RESPONSIBILITY, AND ETHICS   14

Miikka Skaffari/Getty Images

Part 2
ANALYZING MARKETING OPPORTUNITIES

5 MARKETING RESEARCH   68

© Blue Jean Images/Alamy

© iStockphoto.com/Jan Tyler

6 CONSUMER DECISION MAKING   88

Gena73/Shutterstock.com

Part 3
PRODUCT DECISIONS

Part 4
PRICING DECISIONS

Andrey Armyagov/Shutterstock.com

Part 5
DISTRIBUTION DECISIONS

14 RETAILING 254

Jeff Whyte/ Shutterstock.com

Part 6
PROMOTION DECISIONS

Artpose Adam Borkowskit/Shutterstock.com

© Kristoffer Tripplaar/Alamy

Part 7
MANAGING THE CUSTOMER

ValeStock/Shutterstock.com

Chapter 1

An Introduction to Marketing

Marketing, in my mind, is invaluable and underrated by most people.[1]

—Brett Wilson

After you finish this chapter, go to www.nelson.com/student *for* **STUDY TOOLS**. ------→

1-1 WHAT IS MARKETING?

Marketing **is a word that elicits much opinion and discussion.** It is often defined by what it is not rather than by what it actually is. Marketing is one of the most misused words in business today. It is often reduced to a few words that are attached to the activities of marketing: sales, advertising, and promotion.

Sometimes marketing is seemingly written off entirely: "Marketing is dead." Kevin Roberts, CEO of Saatchi & Saatchi (top advertising agency)[2]

Could this be true? Do we not need to worry about marketing anymore? Far from it. Without marketing, there is no customer. Most departments in a firm—whether accounting or finance or operations—are internally focused on achieving goals related to their functional area. Marketing's sole focus is on the customer and understanding what makes them tick. Without marketing to identify a customer to create revenues and profit, there is no need for an accounting department or manufacturing facility.

1-1a What Is Marketing?

Marketing is about understanding the **needs** of the customer. No other aspect of business has this focus. Marketing helps to shape the products and services of a firm, based on an understanding of what the customer is looking for. Marketing is about engaging in a conversation with that customer and guiding the delivery of what is required to satisfy those needs.

And this engagement is the focus of this edition of *MKTG*. The chapters you will read will help chronicle this new era in marketing. From fresh observations in areas like business-to-business marketing and product development, to an update on the innovative chapter on social media—*MKTG3* will chronicle this new focus.

Kevin Roberts was in fact not speaking of the demise of marketing in the provocative quote, but rather its rebirth. He

marketing the activities that develop an offering in order to satisfy a customer need

need a state of being where we desire something that we do not possess but yearn to acquire

MARKETER SETH GODIN: *Marketing is the name we use to* DESCRIBE THE PROMISES *a company makes, the story it tells, the authentic way it delivers on that promise.*[4]
WRITER MILAN KUNDERA: *Business has only two functions:* MARKETING AND INNOVATION.[5]
DILBERT: *Marketing isn't a real thing, is it? It's mostly guessing.*[6]

implored marketing practitioners to change the way in which marketing is applied. He tasked his audience with seeing marketing differently and moving marketing from "interruption to interaction."[3]

Marketing is becoming a conversation with the customer rather than a distraction. Companies are finding innovative ways in which to lead this conversation, and with access to more tools (Twitter, Facebook), consumers are now, more than ever, able to talk back.

Marketing is not dead. Marketing is constantly changing, along with the customer it continually strives to better understand. We are heading into a new era of marketing—one that is reflective of the digital, online, and engaged world around us. Without marketing, there is no understanding this world.

1-2 THE EVOLUTION OF MARKETING

The misconceptions surrounding marketing come from the evolution of how marketing has been used in firms for more than a century. In their seminal article in the *Journal of Public Policy and Marketing*, renowned researchers William Wilkie and Elizabeth Moore described how today's marketing has resulted from many shifts in both the field of marketing and society. The authors note that the past century of marketing thought "has experienced periodic shifts in dominance of prevailing modes of thinking."[7] Numerous terms and ideologies are used to describe these shifts in thinking, and below are a few of the orientations in marketing that have been part of these periodic shifts. It is important to investigate some prior perspectives on marketing to provide a better understanding of how marketing is perceived today and why there is so much confusion around what truly constitutes marketing.

1-2a The Production Orientation

The **production orientation** focuses on marketing as a messenger. Marketing is seen as a way to let customers know about products and assumes that those customers will beat a path to the producer's door.

This perspective can best be described as the "field of dreams" orientation, thanks to the movie of the same name in which a character states, "if you build it, they will come." The production orientation focuses on products because of a lack of product options in the marketplace. Companies are free to create whatever products they deem appropriate, and customers have to accept what is offered.

© Stocksearch/Alamy

Henry Ford of the Ford Motor Company once stated, "Any customer can have a car painted any colour that he wants, so long as it is black." Ford was describing the line of Model T cars that were available to the customer. His perspective is a great example of the production orientation way of thinking.

1-2b The Sales Orientation

The **sales orientation** is highlighted by the increased power of customer choice. Companies no longer simply produce a product and expect willing customers to be waiting to buy whatever they are selling. Sales techniques were established and evolved to convince consumers to buy, giving consumers choice and ensuring companies focused on creating market share and building sales volume in a highly competitive environment.

Sales pitches are encouraged under this orientation, in which savvy salespeople use their understanding of human nature to convince customers to purchase their products. Answer the door at home to a company using the sales orientation, and you may see a well-dressed person attempting to sell vacuum cleaners or encyclopedias.

The need to coax the customer is paramount in the sales orientation. Behind this belief, companies place resources, specifically sales materials (brochures, print ads, etc.) that are used in great quantities to encourage sales of their products. Companies respond to a marketplace with more competition by overwhelming customers with promotional activities that focus on the hard sell.

Lambert/Archive Photos/Getty Images

Today, some companies still believe in the importance of hard selling to customers. Companies are still using aggressive sales tactics to entice customers, which is why consumers associate marketing with selling and why marketing is often considered intrusive.

The majority of companies and marketers do not subscribe to a marketing approach heavy only on selling. While sales makes up an important part of the marketing offering, it is only one part of the promotional tools available to today's marketer. Management thinker and innovator Peter Drucker put it best: "There will always, one can assume, be a need for some selling. But the aim of marketing is to make selling superfluous. The aim of marketing is to know and understand the customer so well that the product or service fits him and sells itself. Ideally, marketing should result in a customer who is ready to buy."[8]

1-2c The Marketing Company Orientation

The **marketing company orientation** is highlighted by the coordination of marketing activities—advertising, sales, and public relations—into one department in an organization. Much of how a marketing department is organized is based on the need to include those elements. The job of this department is to better understand the customer rather than just trying to sell to them.

As society evolves and consumers become more sophisticated, products and services previously seen as exclusive and out of reach are now seen as possible purchases. In this orientation, customers are grouped into market segments, with marketing professionals tasked with understanding their customer before making their move.

A term that is important in many orientations, and very much so in a marketing company orientation, is the *marketing concept*. The marketing concept focuses on linking the needs of customers with the competencies of an organization seeking to meet those needs.

The bringing together of selling, segments, and other aspects of marketing can be seen in the hugely successful television show *Mad Men*, about advertising firms on Madison Avenue. What the show also chronicles is the early stages of consumer cynicism

sales orientation hard selling to the customer, who has greater choice thanks to more competition in the marketplace

marketing company orientation a strong emphasis on the marketing concept and development of a more comprehensive approach to understanding the customer

toward marketing as a company activity. Characters in the show are shown creating ads that make cigarettes seem healthy while simultaneously using alcohol as creative lubricant.

In bringing the elements of the marketing company orientation together, it becomes clear that marketing and persuasion are intermixed. Marketing professionals focus on how to be shrewder about convincing customers to buy. Emotions are tied to basic-need products, higher-order benefits are attached to everyday products, and the customer is as much of a target of focus as the product.

1-2d Societal Marketing Orientation

It is apparent when we distill the marketing concept down to a basic idea (give customers what they want) that its pursuit can have potentially unsavoury consequences (what if what they want isn't good for them?). Dealing with this challenge created the **societal marketing orientation**, where looking at not only what the customer wants but also what society wants becomes a dual emphasis.

Societal marketing examines the longer-term impacts on the customer and the environment when customers seek to satisfy needs. New movements, such as recycling and waste reduction, sought out companies' solutions to deal with greater consumerism. Health issues relating to product use are at the forefront of this orientation, with greater awareness of the safety and dietary issues attached to products.

The Kobal Collection at Art Resource, NY.

"YOU *are the* PRODUCT. *You*— FEELING *something. That's what sells.*"
—Don Draper (*Mad Men*)[9]

This orientation brings a greater government involvement in consumer needs and wants. Thanks to better customer education and extremely strict promotional restrictions, sales of products like cigarettes have dropped drastically. Industries and companies are placing an emphasis on self-regulation before more strict government involvement created bottom-line and public relations issues.

A signpost for change in societal marketing was the Happy Meal. McDonalds' signature meal has long been a target for critics who argue that the fast-food giant has used it to attract young customers. In 2011, the Happy Meal began to offer more nutritious options, such as yogurt and a "mini" size of fries (31 grams). In 2012, apple slices were offered as a replacement for french fries. In 2013, McDonald's announced it would provide health information on the Happy Meal boxes that touts healthier food choices.

MARKETING CONCEPT

The marketing concept includes the following:

»» Focusing on customer wants and needs so that the organization can distinguish its offerings from those of its competitors

»» Integrating all the organization's activities, including production, to satisfy customers' wants

»» Achieving long-term goals for the organization by satisfying customers' wants and needs legally and responsibly

David Paul Morris/Getty Images

McDonald's, it would appear, is constantly attempting to address public concerns about how and what it promotes to children. A recent study by the Robert John Wood Foundation showed that McDonald's most often targeted children with toys and movie tie-ins, rather than food. McDonald's has attempted to deal with the criticism by making changes to the Happy Meal, while also advertising the fact that 10 cents from every Happy Meal goes to charities like the Ronald McDonald House.

1-2e Relationship Marketing Orientation

Today, the relationship marketing orientation is about developing a real and sustainable relationship

RICE KRIS...IS

While most people don't think of arsenic as part of a healthy diet, the substance is present in many food products consumers buy and use—most notably, apple juice and rice. Two types of arsenic appear in the air, water, and soil—organic and inorganic. Organic arsenic goes through the human body rather quickly and has been deemed relatively harmless. Inorganic arsenic, which comes from many pesticides used on crops, has a toxicity level that over time can pose a cancer risk.

Consumer Reports, a U.S. consumer advocate group, recently conducted a study of rice samples and found high levels of inorganic arsenic in many popular products—from Rice Krispies to Gerber baby food. But there is no real benchmark as to what constitutes a high level of arsenic, as there are no federal standards in the United States or Canada.

Health Canada notes on its website that arsenic levels in food sold in Canada are "generally very low" and there is no need for consumers to "change dietary habits to reduce exposure to arsenic."

However, some countries are taking more drastic steps to deal with the issue. Denmark's Veterinary and Food Administration told parents to stop giving children

Tutti Frutti/Shutterstock.com

rice cakes and rice milk because of the unacceptable levels of inorganic arsenic. Thus, grocery stores in Denmark pulled many rice-related products off the shelves, causing great concern over the safety of rice products.

With greater awareness of food safety issues, and better technology to test for potential carcinogens in products, it is likely there will be more stories like this one. Interestingly, the story of Denmark's arsenic rice warning did not create much buzz in Canada—even though Canadian rice consumption increased by 73 percent between 2002 and 2012.

Sources: Associated Press, "Rising Levels of Arsenic in Rice 'Could Be Toxic and Pose Cancer Risk (accessed September 19, 2012), www.dailymail.co.uk/news/article-2205633/Rising-levels-ARSENIC-rice-toxic-pose-cancer-risk–NO-federal-standards-allowed-food.html#ixzz3AlS6cbOx (accessed September 2013); Consumer Reports, "Arsenic in Your Food," November 2012, www.consumerreports.org/cro/magazine/2012/11/arsenic-in-your-food/index.htm (accessed September 2013); Health Canada, "Arsenic," November 3, 2008, www.hc-sc.gc.ca/fn-an/securit/chem-chim/environ/arsenic-eng.php (accessed September 2013); and USA Rice Federation, "Media Resources," May 23, 2014, http://riceinfo.com/media-resources/ (accessed August 17, 2014).

with the customer. As Kevin Roberts (he of the "marketing is dead" proclamation) said, marketing has to go from "interruption to interaction."[10] This phrase means that marketing can no longer look for a one-off sale; marketing has to focus on taking steps to truly engage with the customer. Engagement is the focus of this orientation, aided by the use of two essential customer-based strategies: customer satisfaction and relationship marketing.

CUSTOMER SATISFACTION

Customer satisfaction is the customer's evaluation of a good or service in terms of whether that good or service has met the customer's needs and expectations. Failure to meet a customer's needs and expectations results in the customer's dissatisfaction with the good or service.[11] Keeping current customers satisfied is just as important as attracting new customers—and a lot less expensive. One study showed that reducing customer attrition by just 5 to 10 percent could increase annual profits by as much as 75 percent.[12] A 2 percent increase in customer retention has the same effect on profits as cutting costs by 10 percent.[13] Firms that have a reputation for delivering high levels of customer satisfaction tend to do things differently from their competitors. When top management is obsessed with customer satisfaction, employees throughout the organization are more likely to understand the link between how they perform their job and the satisfaction of customers. The culture of such an organization focuses on delighting customers rather than on selling products.

RELATIONSHIP MARKETING

Relationship marketing is a strategy that focuses on keeping and improving relationships with current customers. This strategy assumes that many consumers and business customers prefer to keep an ongoing relationship with one organization rather than to switch continually among providers in their search for value. Disney is a good example of an organization focused on building long-term relationships with its customers. Disney managers understand that their company creates products and experiences that become an important part of peoples' lives and memories. This understanding has made Disney a leader in doing

"right by the customer"—starting with the front-line cast members who interact directly with the public and encompassing all employees in all departments, who assess each decision based on how it will affect the customers and their relationship with the Disney brand.

CUSTOMER RELATIONSHIP MANAGEMENT

An important result of the relationship marketing orientation has been the concept of customer relationship management (CRM). While born as a data-mining system to help marketers understand each customer on an individual level, CRM best serves the ultimate goal of meeting the needs of customers and building relationships.

A key aspect of relationships—and any CRM system—is trust. To build trust, companies have to be willing to share their stories with customers and listen to and act on what customers desire. Doing this has not always been possible when companies use data mining from various sources, but it is possible with social and mobile marketing.

Creating a 24/7/365 relationship with customers is now possible, if companies are willing to plug in to the online world, an arena not only for exchange but also for true communication.

In the days of Henry Ford, door-to-door salesmen, and real-life Mad Men, there was never the opportunity to understand and target individual customers. However, this goal is now possible. Just head to a popular social media site, and you will find an interactive world with endless potential.

The final chapter of this text on CRM (Chapter 19) will pull all the pieces together and show the possibility of truly evolving from "interruption to interaction."

1-3 KEY MARKETING TERMS

Now that we have seen the past and given an indication of the future of marketing, it is important to cover some of the fundamental aspects of marketing that every student of marketing should know. These ideas will form the basis of all remaining chapters and will provide you with the necessary tools to discuss and learn about marketing.

1-3a Exchange

One desired outcome of marketing is an **exchange**—people giving up one thing to receive another thing they would rather have. Normally, we think of money as the medium of exchange. We "give up" money to "receive" the goods and services we want. Exchange does not, however, require money. Two people may barter or trade such items as baseball cards or oil paintings.

CUSTOMER VALUE Customer value is the relationship between benefits and the sacrifice necessary to obtain those benefits. Customer value is not simply a matter of high quality. A high-quality product that is available only at a high price will not be perceived as good value, nor will bare-bones service or low-quality goods selling for a low price. Instead, customers value goods and services that are of the quality they expect and are sold at prices they are willing to pay. Value can be used to sell both a Mercedes-Benz and a $3 frozen dinner.

MARKET SEGMENTS Market segments are groups of individuals, families, or companies that are placed together because it is believed that they share similar needs. As we saw in the discussion of the evolution of marketing earlier in this chapter,

exchange people giving up one thing to receive another thing they would rather have

customer value the relationship between benefits and the sacrifice necessary to obtain those benefits

THE FORCE IS WITH DISNEY

A recent example of Disney's relationship marketing was the case of an eight-year-old boy with autism who visited Disney World's Hollywood Studios theme park in Florida in June 2013. The boy, Josiah, had been looking forward to participating in the Jedi Training Academy—and just as he was to enter the stage to "fight" Darth Vader, the Florida skies opened up, and the rest of the event was rained out. Josiah was crestfallen,

Courtesy of Sharon Edwards and David Piggott

and his mother was worried he would retreat into his own world. The mother, Sharon Edwards, rushed over to the Disney employee playing the "Jedi Master" and explained the situation. The actor, David Piggott, told her in a hushed voice to meet him at the side of the building.

David, still in character as the Jedi Master, handed Josiah a lightsaber signed by Darth Vader. Josiah was ecstatic; he had gone from devastation to elation in minutes thanks to a kind act by this Disney employee.

Sharon decided she had to share this experience, so she wrote a post in her blog (which can be seen here: http://writeshesays.wordpress.com/2013/06/13/the-most-beautiful-ruined-moment/) describing their encounter with an employee who went beyond his duty to make a memorable moment for her son. Soon, the blog was being passed around social media and on autism family support websites, and within days her blog had over 200,000 views. As word spread, new media began to get involved, and the story travelled around the world. Sharon had been worried that the publicity from this incident might get David Piggott (the Jedi Master) in trouble for not following protocol. Instead, Disney responded by saying that it will be using this incident as an example of "good customer relations."

Sources: John I. Carney, "A Jedi Master and the Blog Side of the Force," *Times-Gazette*, June 19, 2013, www.t-g.com/story/1979291.html (accessed September 2013); and Sharon Edwards, "The Most Beautiful Ruined Moment," June 13, 2013, http://writeshesays.wordpress.com/2013/06/13/the-most-beautiful-ruined-moment/ (accessed September 2013).

WHEN SALES CONTINUE TO FALL, ACKNOWLEDGE THE CONSUMER AND RESPOND ACCORDINGLY

In the previous edition of this book, we discussed the tale of Kodak and how it had moved from being an industry leader to a firm searching for a new identity. In the same chapter, a few pages on, was an example of a company that was a Canadian success story: Research In Motion. How times have changed!

Kodak is emerging from bankruptcy protection with a sharp focus on serving business with digital imaging and packaging printing. Meanwhile, Research In Motion—renamed BlackBerry Ltd.—is laying off staff and being bought out by another firm, with the company and its parts potentially being sold off.

What's different now? Kodak was able to look at its business, realize its strengths, and develop a new direction focused squarely on a consumer group with specific needs Kodak could satisfy.

Research In Motion focused too much on its platform and security features, and forgot about the customer. The makers of the BlackBerry failed to see that consumers, not businesses, would lead the smartphone market in the future. Consumers were looking for touch screens and a fully interactive communication device. RIM gave consumers keyboards and security features they did not ask for.

© iStockphoto.com/Graffizone

In the end, the title of this box from the previous edition of this textbook still holds true: When sales continue to fall, acknowledge the consumer and respond accordingly.

CONDITIONS OF EXCHANGE

An exchange can take place only if the following five conditions exist:

1. At least two parties are involved.

2. Each party has something that may be of value to the other party.

3. Each party is capable of communication and delivery.

4. Each party is free to accept or reject the exchange offer.

5. Each party believes it is appropriate or desirable to deal with the other party.

Source: Philip Kotler, *Marketing Management*, 11th ed. (Upper Saddle River, NJ: Prentice-Hall, 2003), 12.

To target specific market segments, much has to be done to research the lives, trends, and needs of a particular group. Later in the book, we will look at how marketing research (Chapter 5), consumer decision making (Chapter 6), and business marketing (Chapter 7) help provide the necessary tools to develop strong market segments (Chapter 8).

BUILDING RELATIONSHIPS Attracting new customers to a business is only the beginning. The best companies view new-customer attraction as the launching point for developing and enhancing a long-term relationship. Companies can expand their market share in three ways: attracting new customers, increasing business with existing customers, and retaining current customers. Building relationships with existing customers directly addresses two of the three possibilities and indirectly addresses the other.

segmentation has gone from not being done at all to being done at an almost individual level. Market segments form the core of marketing efforts because they represent the source of customer needs.

Marketers interested in customer value

▶▶ offer products that perform

▶▶ earn trust through loyalty programs

▶▶ avoid unrealistic pricing by communicating clearly

▶▶ give consumers the facts and the opportunity to learn more

▶▶ offer an organization-wide commitment to service and after-sales support

▶▶ partner with consumers to co-create experiences that consumers want

MARKETING MIX The marketing mix—also known as the 4Ps of marketing—refers to product, price, place, and promotion. Each of the 4Ps must be studied and developed to create a proper strategy to go after a market segment:

▶▶ **PRODUCT** relates to the tangible and intangible aspects of a company's offering. A product could be a can of soup or a virtuoso ballet performance; both companies will need to look at what needs are being satisfied and how to best package all of the aspects of the offering so that the consumer will be satisfied.

▶▶ **PRICE** relates to the quantifying of a value in exchange for a company's offering. Competition is a significant issue here, as are customer perception and economic factors. Setting the right price is all about taking those factors into consideration and making the best decision that satisfies the bottom line and the customer.

▶▶ **PLACE** relates to much of the behind-the-scenes activities of making an offering available to the customer. This is the world of channels and logistics, where decisions made on how to get a company's product to market could be more important than the product itself.

▶▶ **PROMOTION** relates to what most people believe marketing to be about. These are the most visible activities of marketing, the ones that get into the news and the faces of customers. Trying to find the right balance of what techniques to use (including advertising) is a constant challenge, as is keeping a consistent feel and look.

1-4 WHY MARKETING MATTERS

Given that this chapter started out by proclaiming the death of marketing, the question that begs to be asked is, *Why does marketing matter?* Here are a few compelling reasons.

1-4a Marketing Is Part of Every Company

No matter what discipline in business you choose to pursue, you will have customers. If you do not concern yourself with the customer, you will cease to have any (just ask Blackberry).

All companies, from multinationals to independent consultants, need to be customer focused. We know now that marketing provides this customer focus; therefore, understanding marketing means understanding your customer.

Successful companies have a strong understanding of the importance of marketing. Apple, the incredibly successful technology firm, created a three-point marketing philosophy when it was founded in 1977. The first point of that philosophy is the most telling: "Empathy—we will truly understand [the customer's] needs better than any company." This fundamental belief lies at the core of many successful organizations, including Apple.[14]

1-4b Marketing Is a Rewarding Career

Marketing can provide both financial and personal rewards. Marketing graduates have the flexibility of seeking employment in any industry, profit or non-profit, public or private. This is because there is an inherent need for marketing in any organization that has a customer—whether final consumers or businesses customers.

A search on the Canadian job site WowJobs.ca for the terms "employment in marketing" came back with some interesting findings:

- Average salaries in jobs in marketing are 10 percent higher than the national salary average in all other job areas.
- Job titles include marketing manager, marketing coordinator, and marketing project officer.
- Responsibilities include developing marketing strategies, conducting market and product research, controlling the marketing budget, and writing and coordinating online marketing content.
- Jobs in marketing are available across Canada, and in firms ranging in size from small startups to multinational corporations.[15]

To excel and advance in the field of marketing, strong communication and analytical skills are essential. Now that we know that marketing forms a fundamental part of any organization, a good marketer will understand the importance of working with other departments to ensure customer needs are met. As well, managers in marketing will deal constantly with uncertainty, so being able to analyze diverse and often divergent information will be key in becoming a successful marketing professional.

1-4c Marketing Provides an Important Skill Set

Even if your career aspirations are not in the field of marketing, you will still need to sell yourself to a future employer. Skills developed when learning marketing—how to understand needs, research trends, create an offering, and communicate benefits—all relate back to a person's job search.

Brett Wilson (pictured), who was quoted on the first page of this chapter on his views on marketing, is a successful Canadian entrepreneur and former panelist on the television show *Dragons' Den*. He has noted the importance of marketing as part of the skill set of any aspiring businessperson. When asked about his best business advice, Wilson stated, "Study

QMI Agency

marketing, entrepreneurship, and philanthropy. The incredible relevance of these courses merits mention. You cannot over-study these life-enhancing courses at any stage in your career."[16]

1-4d Marketing Is Part of Everyday Life

The tasks in marketing, as we have seen in this chapter, go well beyond a simple advertisement or sales call. Marketing includes important tasks that may not always be associated with marketing—such as distribution—that ensure that the products are on store shelves or delivered from a favourite website.

Being informed about marketing means being an informed consumer. Most Canadians' lives are full of activities and tasks (see figures below) that will have them confronting marketing messages from numerous organizations. By learning about marketing, you will be better able to discern a good message from a bad one and hold those companies that are targeting you to a higher standard.

You now have the necessary background and understanding of marketing. Turn the page to start learning about what marketing has to offer.

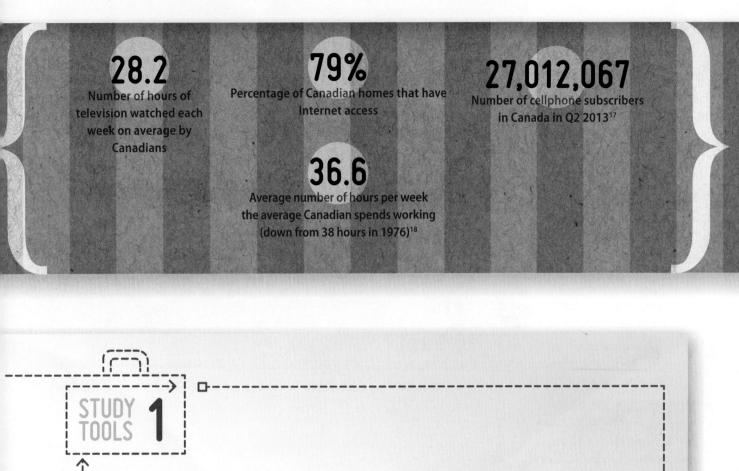

28.2

Number of hours of television watched each week on average by Canadians

79%

Percentage of Canadian homes that have Internet access

27,012,067

Number of cellphone subscribers in Canada in Q2 2013[17]

36.6

Average number of hours per week the average Canadian spends working (down from 38 hours in 1976)[18]

STUDY TOOLS 1

LOCATED AT BACK OF TEXTBOOK

☐ *Tear-Out Chapter Review Card*

LOCATED AT WWW.NELSON .COM/STUDENT

☐ *End-of-Chapter Questions*
☐ *Interactive Flashcards*
☐ *Audio and Visual Summaries*
☐ *Quizzes*
☐ *Additional Cases*

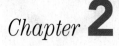

Chapter **2**

The Marketing Environment, Social Responsibility, and Ethics

Although managers can control the marketing mix, they cannot control elements in the external environment.

After you finish this chapter, go to www.nelson.com/student *for* **STUDY TOOLS.** ▢┈┈┈┈┈➔

2-1 THE EXTERNAL MARKETING ENVIRONMENT

An extremely important decision made by marketing managers is the creation of the marketing mix. Recall from Chapter 1 that a marketing mix is the unique combination of product, place (distribution), promotion, and price strategies. (The marketing mix is also addressed in Chapter 3.) The marketing mix is, of course, under the firm's control and is designed to appeal to a specific group of potential buyers—the target market. A **target market** is a defined group of potential customers that managers feel is most likely to buy a firm's product.

Over time, managers alter the marketing mix to keep pace with the changing composition of the target market brought on by the changes in the environment in which consumers live, work, and make purchasing decisions. Also, as markets mature, some new consumers become part of the target market; others drop out. Those who remain may have different tastes, needs, incomes, lifestyles, and buying habits than the original target consumers.

Controllable and uncontrollable variables affect the target market, whether it consists of consumers or business purchasers. Although managers can control the marketing mix, they cannot control elements in the external environment that continually mould and reshape the target market. Managers can shape and reshape the marketing mix to influence the target market. That is, managers react to changes in the external environment and attempt to create a more effective marketing program.

target market
a group of people or organizations for which an organization designs, implements, and maintains a marketing mix intended to meet the needs of that group, resulting in mutually satisfying exchanges

2-1a Understanding the External Environment

Unless marketing managers understand the external environment, the firm cannot intelligently plan for the future. Thus, many organizations assemble a team of specialists to continually collect and evaluate environmental information, a process called *environmental scanning*. The goal in gathering the environmental data is to identify future market opportunities and threats.

2-1b Environmental Management

No one business is large enough or powerful enough to create major change in the external environment. Marketing managers, therefore, are basically adapters rather than agents of change. A firm is not always completely at the mercy of the external environment, however. Sometimes a firm can influence external events—for example, through extensive lobbying. When a company implements strategies that attempt to shape the external environment within which it operates, it is engaging in **environmental management**.

The factors within the external environment that are important to marketing managers can be classified as social, demographic, economic, technological, political and legal, and competitive.

2-2 SOCIAL FACTORS

Social change is perhaps the most difficult external variable for marketing managers to forecast, influence, or integrate into marketing plans. Social factors include our attitudes, values, and lifestyles. Social factors influence the products people buy, the prices paid for products, the effectiveness of specific promotions, and how, where, and when people expect to purchase products.

2-2a Marketing-Oriented Values

A *value* is a strongly held and enduring belief. Our values are key determinants of what is important and not important, what actions we take or do not take, and how we behave in social situations. Our values are typically formed through our interactions with family, friends, and other influencers, such as teachers, religious leaders, and politicians. The changing environment can also play a key role in shaping our values. Four basic values strongly influence attitudes and lifestyles of Canadian consumers:

- ⟫ **SELF-SUFFICIENCY:** Every person should stand on his or her own two feet.
- ⟫ **UPWARD MOBILITY:** Success should come to anyone who gets an education, works hard, and plays by the rules.
- ⟫ **WORK ETHIC:** Hard work, dedication to family, and frugality are moral and right.
- ⟫ **FAIRNESS:** No one should expect to be treated differently from anybody else.

These core values hold for a majority of Canadians today and have led to the perception that Canadians are trustworthy, family oriented, conservative, and increasingly eco-conscious. Canadian society is known to be tolerant and respectful of other cultures.

Values also influence our buying habits. Today's consumers are demanding, inquisitive, and discriminating. No longer willing to tolerate products that break down, we insist on high-quality goods that save time, energy, and often calories. Shoppers rank the characteristics of product quality as (1) reliability, (2) durability, (3) easy maintenance, (4) ease of use, (5) a trusted brand name, and (6) a low price. As shoppers, we are also concerned about nutrition and want to know what's in our food, and many of us have environmental concerns.

2-2b The Growth of Component Lifestyles

Canadian consumers today are piecing together **component lifestyles**. A lifestyle is a mode of living; it is the way we decide to live our lives. In other words, we choose products and services that meet our diverse needs and interests rather than conforming to traditional stereotypes.

In the past, a person's profession—for instance, banker—defined his or her lifestyle. Today, a person can be a banker and also a gourmet cook, a fitness enthusiast, a dedicated single parent, and an Internet guru. Each of these lifestyles is associated with different goods and services and represents a target audience. Component lifestyles increase the complexity of consumers' buying habits. The unique lifestyles of every consumer can require a different marketing mix.

2-2c Families Today

The Vanier Institute of the Family defines the family today as "any combination of two or more persons who are bound together over time by ties of mutual consent, birth and/or adoption or placement and who, together, assume responsibilities for variant combinations of some of the following:

▸▸ **Physical maintenance and care of group members**

▸▸ **Addition of new members through procreation or adoption**

▸▸ **Socialization of children**

▸▸ **Social control of members**

▸▸ **Production, consumption, distribution of goods and services**

▸▸ **Affective nurturance—love"[1]**

Despite a great deal of media coverage on the changing role of the family, it isn't so much the *role* of the family that has changed but the *makeup* of the family. Canadian families have an unprecedented level of diversity. Some men and women are raising children on their own without a partner; others are living together unmarried, with or without children; and gay and lesbian couples are caring for each other and raising children together. In addition, some adult children are following a trend of returning to the nest and living with their parents, and an increasing number of people are living alone.[2] Families today still demonstrate how, as individuals, we accept responsibility for each other.[3]

The Vanier Institute of the Family, "Definition of Family," http://www.vanierinstitute.ca/definition_of_family#.Umhz7Pkqhng Accessed October 22, 2013.

We face significant challenges in how we carry out our family responsibilities. For families today, two key resources are required—time and money—and they are both in short supply. To meet financial obligations it is common for couples to work and, even, in some case, hold multiple jobs. This situation results in further time poverty and affects the consumption choices that a family makes. The recent developments in technology combined with the time poverty of Canadian families has led to an increase in the use of social media not only as a communication tool but also as an information-gathering tool. Decision makers in families are increasingly using the Internet to do chores, plan trips, research products, find health information, read the news, seek out specials, and get coupons or participate in group savings. Consumers freely share the information they find with everyone in their personal networks.

demography the study of people's vital statistics, such as their age, race and ethnicity, and location

2-3 DEMOGRAPHIC FACTORS

Another variable in the external environment and one extremely important to marketing managers is demography—the study of people's vital statistics, such as their age, race and ethnicity, and location. Demographics are significant because they are strongly related to consumer behaviour in the marketplace.

We turn our attention now to a closer look at age groups, their impact, and the opportunities they present for marketers. Why does tailoring the merchandise to particular age groups matter? One reason is that each generation enters a life stage with its own tastes and biases, and tailoring products to what customers value is key to sales. The cohorts have been named tweens, Generation Y, Generation X, and baby boomers. You will find that each cohort group has its own needs, values, and consumption patterns.

2-3a Tweens and Teens

Canada's tweens, now often referred to as Gen-Zers, are preadolescents and early adolescents (ages 9 to 14). With attitudes, access to information, brand consciousness, technical sophistication well beyond their years, and purchasing power to match, these young consumers increasingly represent an attractive segment for marketers of all kinds of products.

The number of tweens who own cellphones has increased significantly over the years, with cellphone ownership among the 11- to 14-year-old age

group reaching 69 percent. This age group represents the fastest-growing segment in the cellphone market.[4] Add to this the dollar amounts that parents will spend on their tweens, and one grasps the importance and potential of this market. Tweens overwhelmingly (92 percent) recognize television commercials for what they are—just advertising—and indicate that they tune out ads simply because they are boring. Despite tweens' tech-savvy attitude, major social network sites, such as Facebook, are off limits to tweens under age 13 because of privacy and safety concerns. A recent statement from Facebook about its intention to open the site to preteens was met with alarm by parents and policymakers alike.[5]

Teens, those ages 15 to 19, represent just over 2.1 million people in Canada. As a group, they are extremely important to marketers because they wield significant purchasing power and are key influencers in family purchases. Teenagers are avid shoppers, spending on fashion, makeup, food, and entertainment. They are computer savvy, heavy users of social media, and active digital music and movie downloaders.

2-3b Generation Y

Those designated by demographics as **Generation Y** were born between 1979 and 1994. They are about 6.4 million strong in Canada. And though Gen-Yers represent a much smaller group than the baby boomers, whose birthdates span nearly 20 years, they are plentiful enough to put their own footprints on society.

Gen-Yers range from 30-somethings to those early in their careers or partway through postsecondary school. Those starting their careers are making major purchases, such as cars and homes; at the very least, they are buying computers, smartphones, DVDs, and gaming devices. Gen-Yers are socially responsible. A survey conducted by Leger Marketing found a growing attitude among young Canadians of expecting their employer to be aware of their impact on the environment and one-third reported they would quit their job over the environmental policies of their company.[6] Gen-Yers have been referred to as "trophy kids" as a result of their high expectations in the workforce and their increased sense of entitlement, which leads to a

Yuri Arcurs/Shutterstock.com

desire for a better work–life balance. This is the generation that was rewarded for participation in a sport—not just when their team won! Most Gen-Yers are the children of baby boomers and so are sometimes referred to as echo boomers. Because of economic necessity, many baby boomers in Canada are working well into their retirement age, thus shrinking the employment opportunities for Gen-Yers. As a result, Gen-Yers are facing unstable employment opportunities and struggling to establish themselves professionally. Gen-Yers are more likely to be entrepreneurial. They have grown up in the face of a global financial crisis and significant meltdown in the financial markets. They are thus able to work with an uncertainty that other generations can't. They have the ability to network and can use social media to their advantage. They have seen people all around them forced out of work and are able to reinvent themselves as freelancers or consultants. Those Gen-Yers who have financial means tend to spend lavishly on luxury products.[7]

Researchers have found Gen-Yers to be

▸ **IMPATIENT:** Because they have grown up in a world that has always been automated, it's no surprise that they expect things to be done now.

▸ **FAMILY ORIENTED:** Gen-Yers had relatively stable childhoods and grew up in a very family-focused era, so they tend to have a stronger family orientation than the generation that preceded them.

▸ **INQUISITIVE:** Gen-Yers tend to want to know why things happen, how things work, and what they can do next.

▸ **OPINIONATED:** Today's youth have been encouraged to share their opinions by their parents, teachers, and other authority figures. As a result, Gen-Yers feel that their opinions are always needed and welcomed.

▸ **DIVERSE:** Gen Y is the most ethnically diverse generation the nation has ever seen, so they're much more accepting overall of people who are different from themselves.

▸ **GOOD MANAGERS OF TIME:** Their entire lives have been scheduled—from playgroups to soccer camp to Little League—so they've picked up a knack for planning along the way.

▸ **SAVVY:** Having been exposed to the Internet and 24-hour cable TV news at a young age, Gen-Yers are not easily shocked. They're much more aware of the world around them than earlier generations were.[8]

daily life, which include everything from housecleaning to dog walking to lawn care. Because of demands on their time, Gen-Xers spend much more on personal services than any other age group.[10] Many Gen-Xers work from home.

Gen-Xers face the reality, however, that the generation ahead of them, having experienced a financial recession, which started in late 2007, may opt not to retire, thereby affecting the Gen-Xers' ability to maximize their income. In addition, as an impending pension crisis looms, the Gen-Xers may find themselves funding the retirement years of the baby boomers. Although Gen-Xers are making and spending money, companies still tend to ignore them, focusing instead on the larger demographic groups—the baby boomers and Gen-Yers.

2-3d Baby Boomers—A Mass Market

Baby boomers make up the largest demographic segment of today's Canadian population. There are nine million **baby boomers** (persons born between 1947 and 1965). The oldest have already turned 65 years old. With average life expectancy increasing, more and more Canadians over the age of 50 consider middle age to be a new start on life. People now in their 50s may well work longer than any previous generation; more men and women, given better health and uncertain economic cycles, are staying in the workforce longer than they ever have.

The boomers' incomes will continue to grow as they keep working, especially those born toward the end of the cohort. In general, baby boomers are active and affluent, but a subsegment of boomers worry about the future and their own financial security.[11] Many retired boomers suffered major losses to their retirement savings during the financial crisis of 2008 that started in the banking sector. Younger baby boomers who are still employed are facing the financial challenges of high debt, reduced incomes, and the need to support their adult

---

Generation Y are known to be the driving force behind the spending on luxury brands, increasing spending on luxury fashion by 33 percent, travel by 74 percent, and fine dining by 102 percent.[9]

▸▸ **CONNECTED:** Gen-Yers use social networks, such as Facebook and Twitter, for both communication and commerce.

2-3c Generation X

Generation X—people born between 1966 and 1978—consists of more than 7 million consumers across Canada. It is the first generation of latchkey children—products of dual-career households or, in roughly half of the cases, of divorced or separated parents. Gen-Xers have been bombarded by multiple media since their cradle days; thus, they are savvy and cynical consumers.

Their careers launched and their families started, Gen-Xers are at the stage in life when a host of demands are competing for their time—and their budgets. As a result, Gen X spending is quite diffuse: food, housing, transportation. Time is at a premium for harried Gen-Xers, so they're outsourcing the tasks of

CANADIANS ON THE MOVE

THE PRIMARY URBAN DESTINATIONS IN CANADA ARE TORONTO, MONTREAL, CALGARY, AND VANCOUVER.

children who are still struggling to be self-sufficient after the recession years.[12] Nielsen research indicates that over the next decade, Canadian households will be smaller. With a tougher economy, those smaller households will spend less, and the shrinking economy will affect the salaries of the Gen-Yers and Gen-Xers. Marketers must change their focus from youth to the boomers. They are a powerful demographic (as they have always been) with a spending power of more than $1 trillion.

2-3e Population Shifts in Canada

Canada is a large country with a relatively small population that was, historically, spread out between rural and urban areas. Since the mid-1970s, however, the population has shifted out of rural areas so that now almost 80 percent of Canadians are considered to be urban dwellers. The majority of this 80 percent live in census metropolitan areas (CMAs), regions defined by Statistics Canada as comprising one or more municipalities situated around a major urban core, with a total population of at least 100,000.[13]

According to Statistics Canada, between 2006 and 2011, the Canadian population grew by 5.9 percent to 33.47 million, and it passed the 35 million mark in 2012. More than 50 percent of the Canadian population lives in four major urban regions in Canada: the Golden Horseshoe in Ontario, Montreal and surrounding area, British Columbia's Lower Mainland, and the Calgary–Edmonton corridor. A Statistics Canada study observed that new parents and those between the ages of 25 and 44 were more likely than any others to move from an urban central municipality to a surrounding municipality or suburb.[14] Approximately 90 percent of Canada's 6.8 million immigrants live in large metropolitan areas, and 63.4 percent of them live in the three large urban centres of Toronto, Montreal, and Vancouver.[15] As a result, these urban core areas are the focus of many marketing programs by firms that are interested in reaching a large national yet very multicultural market.

2-4 GROWING ETHNIC MARKETS

As anyone who lives and works in Canada will know, the population of our country is becoming more diverse. As a result, we are all being exposed to the languages, music, foods, and customs of a host of other cultures. The diversity will increase as more immigrants come to Canada. Given our relatively small population, immigration is an important source of the population growth needed to sustain and improve our economic growth. Each year, nearly 250,000 immigrants arrive in Canada. Close to three-quarters of these arrivals are classified as members of visible minorities.

Statistics Canada projects that by 2017, the visible minority population of Canada will be close to 7 million people and will account for 20 percent of the country's population.[16] And, if current trends continue, by that same year, fully 75 percent of this visible minority population will live in Toronto, Vancouver, or Montreal (see Exhibit 2.1).[17] This multicultural environment will present both challenges and opportunities for firms developing marketing programs in these regions. Both domestic and international firms will need to adapt to this marketing reality.

Exhibit 2.1

VISIBLE MINORITY POPULATION IN SELECTED MAJOR CANADIAN CITIES

	2017
Vancouver	51.0%
Toronto	50.5
Calgary	23.6
Ottawa	27.4
Edmonton	17.5
Montreal	19.4
Winnipeg	15.7
Windsor	21.4
Kitchener	15.1
Hamilton	14.5%

Source: Adapted from the Statistics Canada publication *Visible minority population in selected census metropolitan areas, Canada, 2011*, National Household Survey 2011, http://www12.statcan.gc.ca/nhs-enm/2011/as-sa/99-010-x/2011001/tbl/tbl2-eng.cfm

2-4a Ethnic and Cultural Diversity

Multiculturalism refers to peaceful and equitable coexistence of different cultures, rather than one national culture, in a country. More than 200 different languages are spoken in Canada and the trend in Canada is toward greater multiculturalism.

The largest urban centres or census metropolitan areas in Canada experience the greatest impact of multiculturalism. The 2011 census revealed that 5.8 million Canadians, or 17.5 percent of the population, speaks at least two languages at home. This number is up from the 14.2 percent counted in the 2006 census. Most of the 5.8 million bilingual Canadians speak English and an immigrant language, such as Punjabi or Mandarin, and about 1.4 million Canadians are bilingual in English and French.[18] This finding has major implications for any marketing program. Companies such as CIBC and Sears Canada have altered their advertising campaigns to reflect their changing customer profile and to provide information in other languages. The service sector, in particular, has had to adapt quickly to this change in Canada's demographic makeup. A visit to a local bank or hospital in any urban centre will demonstrate the different needs that must be met in a culturally diverse population and the variety of languages that the services should be offered in. Consider, for example, that the City of Toronto reports that more than 100 different languages are spoken in the city.[19]

© Ken Seet/Corbis

As our immigrant population increases, many firms are either adapting or developing marketing plans to attract these segments. The World Cup of Soccer in 2010 saw Coke launch a World Cup anthem that became a number one iTunes hit in 17 countries. The song, by Somalian-Canadian rapper K'naan and his label, A&M Octone Records, was the musical centrepiece of Coca-Cola's 160-country global marketing theme and it worked.[20] The song "Wavin' Flag" crossed cultures. Marketers in Canada today are challenged to do the same. The cultural diversity of our country and the trend to multiculturalism will require multicultural marketing right at home. More than 20 percent of the visible minority population is under 15 years of age. This group will have a great impact in the decade ahead. Many of these young people can understand and converse in multiple languages and have adapted elements of numerous cultures into their lifestyle. These cultures influence their response to marketing messages and ultimately determine their buying behaviour. What does being a Canadian really mean to a marketer?

Recent immigrants to Canada are tech savvy. Young people from various cultures use the Internet for accessing information and making purchases, which has spawned new strategies for using the Internet to reach the diverse youth markets. Every cultural group has access to websites that cater to their specific culture—everything from social networks, products, and events to links to their native country. These culture-specific websites present opportunities for firms to target specific ethnic groups.

2-5 ECONOMIC FACTORS

In addition to social and demographic factors, marketing managers must understand and react to the economic environment. The three economic areas of greatest concern to most marketers are consumers' incomes, inflation, and recession.

2-5a Consumers' Incomes

As disposable (or after-tax) incomes rise, more families and individuals can afford the "good life." The median total family income in Canada was $76,000 in 2013; that means half of all Canadian households earned less than and the other half earned more than that amount.[21]

Education is the primary determinant of a person's earning potential. According to Human Resources and Skills Development Canada, the benefits of higher education include higher earnings, greater savings and assets, higher growth in earnings, and higher income during retirement. In addition, higher education reduces the risk of experiencing low income and unemployment. The benefits of higher education are consistent across all provinces.[22] Along with willingness to buy, or ability to buy, income is a key determinant of target markets. The marketer who knows where the money is knows where the markets are. If you are seeking a location for a new Louis Vuitton retail store, a brand that caters to high-income–earning consumers, you would probably concentrate on areas where residents have incomes that are significantly higher than the median. In Canada, 25.2 percent of households spend more than 30 percent of their income on shelter, far exceeding the affordable housing standards. Once many Canadians have paid for their essential living expenses, they are left with little or no spare cash. As a result, many Canadians have turned to credit to buy the things they want. Credit gives middle- and lower-income consumers the financial flexibility that only the rich used to enjoy. Since the 1990s, the median income for Canadian households has risen less than median household spending. How can the typical family afford to live? The result has been an increase in household debt. The average Canadian is now $1.63 in debt for every dollar they earn.[23] This situation has led to the growth of off-price retailers and the demand by Canadian shoppers for low prices. Debt, of course, means that consumers must eventually use their income to make interest payments instead of buying more goods and services. Too much debt can ultimately lead to financial ruin.

2-5b Purchasing Power

Rising incomes don't necessarily mean a higher standard of living. Increased standards of living are a function of purchasing power. **Purchasing power** is measured by comparing income to the relative cost of a set standard of goods and services in different geographic areas, usually referred to as the cost of living. Another way to think of purchasing power is income minus the cost of living (i.e., expenses). In general, a cost-of-living index takes into account the costs of housing, food and groceries, transportation, utilities, healthcare, and miscellaneous expenses, such as clothing, services, and entertainment. The cost of living is generally higher in major urban markets. For example, a worker living in Toronto must earn nearly three times as much to have the same standard of living as someone in Sydney, Nova Scotia.

When income is high relative to the cost of living, people have more discretionary income. That means they have more money to spend on nonessential items (in other words, on wants rather than needs). This information is important to marketers for obvious reasons. Consumers with high purchasing power can afford to spend more money without jeopardizing their budget for such necessities as food, housing, and utilities. They also have the ability to purchase higher-priced necessities, such as a more expensive car, a home in a more expensive neighbourhood, or a designer handbag versus a purse from a discount store.

2-5c Inflation

Inflation is a measure of the decrease in the value of money, generally expressed as the percentage reduction in value since the previous

Women are important to marketers because they control about 80 percent of the spending in the household.

Morgan Lane Photography/Shutterstock.com

Ljupco Smokovski/Shutterstock.com

The SUBJECTIVE VALUE *a buyer places on the product is* KEY *in determining purchase.*

year, which is the rate of inflation. Thus, in simple terms, an inflation rate of 5 percent means 5 percent more money is needed today to buy the same basket of products that was purchased last year. If inflation is 5 percent, you can expect that, on average, prices have risen about 5 percent over prices in the previous year. Of course, if pay raises are matching the rate of inflation, then employees will be no worse off in terms of the immediate purchasing power of their salaries.

Inflation pressures consumers to make more economical purchases and still maintain their standard of living. When managers create marketing strategies to cope with inflation, they must realize that, despite what happens to the seller's cost, buyers will not pay more for a product than the subjective value they place on it. No matter how compelling the justification might be for a 10 percent price increase, marketers must always examine the impact of the price increase on demand. Many marketers try to hold prices level as long as is practical. (See Chapter 12 for more information on the strategies marketers use during periods of high inflation.)

2-5d Recession

A **recession** is a period of economic activity characterized by negative growth. More precisely, a recession occurs when the gross domestic product falls for two consecutive quarters. The recession that began in December 2007 affected Canada less than the rest of the world. Statistics Canada's official report on the 2008–2009 slump shows it was a recession that was milder than two previous economic dips.

Canada experienced a recession that was less severe and shorter than in the other G7 nations, and our financial institutions ended up in a much better position than those in the United States, where many required government aid to stay afloat. The effects of the 2008 recession are still being felt in terms of high unemployment rates as the imbalances sparked by the event remain unaddressed.[24] However, rich Canadians report being financially better off after the 2008 recession than before.[25] To cope during the recession, many consumers switched to store brands, which on average cost less than manufacturers' brands. More consumers are using coupons than ever before. Group coupon sites are springing up all over. In a recession, consumers consider the price–value relationship deliberately before making purchases.

2-6 TECHNOLOGICAL FACTORS

Technology is a critical factor in every company's external environment. Our ability, as a nation, to maintain and build wealth depends in large part on the speed and effectiveness with which we invent and adopt machines and technologies that lift productivity. External technology is important to managers for two reasons. First, by acquiring a technology, a firm may be able to operate more efficiently or create a better product. Second, a new technology may render existing products obsolete, as in the case of the traditional film-based camera being replaced by digital camera technology. Staying technologically relevant requires a great deal of research and a willingness to adopt new technologies.

2-6a Research

Canada excels at both basic and applied research. **Basic research** (or pure *research*) attempts to expand the frontiers of knowledge but is not aimed at a specific, pragmatic problem. Basic research aims to confirm an existing theory or to learn more about a concept or phenomenon. For example, basic research might focus on high-energy physics.

Top 10 Tech Trends: Straight from 5 Top Tech VCs, http://www.forbes.com/sites/roberthof/2012/05/22/the-top-10-tech-trends-according-to-5-top-tech-vcs/ accessed Oct. 27, 2013

Applied research, in contrast, attempts to develop new or improved products. Canada is dramatically improving its track record in applied research. For example, the recently rejuvenated auto industry in Ontario is well positioned to release electric cars in the very near future.

2-6b Technology and the Future of Businesses

Of all the external environmental forces, technology is the fastest changing with, perhaps, the most significant impact on businesses. New technologies will create not only new industries but also new ways to develop products, compete, and meet customer needs. A panel discussion hosted in Silicon Valley by Churchill Club[26] listed the top ten tech trends for 2013; here are five of them:

1. *Wearable computing.* Products like Google Glass and Pebble Smartwatches will record our lives and provide a more immersive experience.

2. *The "right-now" economy.* Consumers are moving away from "plan ahead" to "right now." Products like Twitter, Waze, and Uber allow people to plan and do things in real time.

3. *Deus ex machina*: As we use machines, they will learn and become smarter. For example, Nest Thermostats are learning thermostats that overtime learn the habits of a household and adjust the temperature accordingly.

4. *The individual revolution.* Products and services geared towards individual self-sufficiency will increase. There is speculation that in the future consumers will be able to manufacture products they need by using 3-D printing.

5. *Personalized medicine.* Developments in biomedicine and technology combined will result in cheap, highly personalized medicines that are more effective.

Technology will also shape how existing businesses gather information and compete with each other. We'll revisit this topic later in the chapter.

2-7 POLITICAL AND LEGAL FACTORS

Every aspect of the marketing mix is subject to laws and restrictions. It is the duty of marketing managers or their legal assistants to understand these laws and conform to them because failure to comply with regulations can have major consequences for a firm. Sometimes just sensing trends and taking corrective action before a government agency acts can help avoid the negative effects of regulation.

Marketers must balance caution with risk. It is all too easy for a marketing manager—or sometimes a lawyer—to say no to a marketing innovation that actually entails little risk. For example, an overly cautious lawyer could hold up sales of a desirable new product by warning that the package design could prompt a copyright infringement suit. Thus, marketers need a thorough understanding of the laws established by the various levels of government and regulatory agencies to govern marketing-related issues.

2-7a Federal Legislation

The federal legislation affecting how business is conducted in Canada is administered by the **Competition Bureau**, an independent agency of Industry Canada. This bureau encompasses several branches and is responsible for enforcing laws covering such areas as bankruptcy, trade practices, competition, credit, labelling and packaging, copyrights, hazardous products, patents, and trademarks.[27] Some of the specialized federal legislation that affects businesses and business dealings are listed in Exhibit 2.2.

2-7b Provincial and Territorial Laws

In Canada, our constitution divides legal jurisdictions between the provincial or territorial legislatures and the federal government, thus allowing each level of government to legislate in the areas for which it has been given responsibility. For example, Québec's Bill 101 restricts the use of the English language in certain advertising and promotion material. A national company, such as Tim Hortons, may have to alter its advertising and store signage in Québec to be in compliance. Alberta allows the sale of alcoholic beverages by retailers, whereas Ontario has provincially run Liquor Control Board of Ontario (LCBO) outlets. Airlines, on the other hand, are under federal jurisdiction, and the provinces do not have direct powers to regulate airline companies. Marketing managers, especially those working for national companies, must be aware of the differences in each province's and territory's legal environment, and they also need a sound understanding of federal legislation that affects their industry.

Exhibit 2.2

SPECIALIZED FEDERAL LEGISLATION AFFECTING BUSINESS

Legislation	Major Provisions
Competition Act	Encourages free competition and efficiency in the marketplace. It prohibits mergers and governs specific marketing activities, such as misleading advertising, price fixing, predatory pricing, and multilevel marketing fraud.
Consumer Packaging and Labelling Act	Ensures that full information regarding packaging (such as quantity and standard units of weight, volume, or measure) is provided to consumers in both English and French.
Trade-marks Act	Regulates and protects brand names and trademarks.
Textile Labelling Act	Regulates the labelling of consumer textile goods, including clothing, bedding, and carpets.
Food and Drug Act	Monitors the sale of food, drugs, and cosmetics.
Motor Vehicle Safety Act	Regulates the safely standards for the manufacture of motor vehicles.
Personal Information Protection and Electronic Documents Act	Regulates the collection and use of personal information for commercial purposes. It protects the right of privacy of individuals while allowing for personal information to be used for appropriate purposes.
Privacy Act	Includes the ten privacy principles from the National Standard of Canada and outlines other laws and requirements to guide marketers regarding privacy issues.

Source: From ZIKMUND/D'AMICO/BROWNE/DONVILLE. *Effective Marketing*, 1E. © 2008 Nelson Education Ltd. Reproduced by permission. www.cengage.com/permissions.

2-7c **Self-Regulation**

Instead of facing explicit legislation from either the provincial, territorial, or federal governments, many business groups in Canada have formed associations that police themselves. This arrangement is called **self-regulation**. One such association is Advertising Standards Canada (ASC), established by Canada's advertising industry to monitor honesty and fairness in advertising. Advertising is a very visible form of communication strategy, and some firms come under fire from consumer groups regarding deception in their advertising. The ASC provides clear ethical guidelines to both advertisers and advertising agencies in its document "The 14 Clauses of the Canadian Code of Advertising Standards."[28] Another group, the Canadian Association of Broadcasters (CAB), has established a code of ethics for its member television and radio stations. The Canadian Marketing Association (CMA) has made great strides in developing guidelines and ethical practices for its thousands of member marketing firms.

CONSUMER PRIVACY A marketing manager must also be aware of the increasingly important area of consumer privacy, especially because of the vast amounts of data that almost any firm can collect and store by using the latest database technology. Everything from customer information to survey data is valuable to companies, but privacy issues need to be addressed. Firms should be able to justify the type of information they have and how it is to be used. Other issues of note are the security of information storage and the sale or transfer of information to others. Increasingly, and largely as a result of pressure from consumers' groups, governments are looking at developing, or have already developed, privacy legislation.

Canada's federal government, like the governments of many other countries, already has legislation relating to privacy. The Privacy Act (PA) and the Personal Information Protection and Electronic Documents

ASC helps protect Canadians from false messaging in advertising. Because among all the pretty words and pictures – truth matters.

Advertising Standards Canada
adstandards.ca

Act (PIPEDA) were put in place to protect the privacy of our personal information and to ensure that its collection, use, and disclosure are both legal and ethical. The latest protection established by the Canadian Government to improve and protect consumer privacy was established in July 2014 and is referred to as the Canadian Anti-Spam Legislation (CASL). It's intent is to deter the most damaging and deceptive forms of spam from occurring. CASL will be enforced by the CRTC, the Competition Bureau and the Privacy Commissioner. Canadian consumers are concerned about their privacy, but how many are aware of the details of this legislation? Marketers must, therefore, be proactive in ensuring consumer privacy.

2-8 COMPETITIVE FACTORS

The competitive environment encompasses the number of competitors a firm must face, the relative size of the competitors, and the degree of interdependence within the industry. Management has little control over the competitive environment confronting a firm.

2-8a Competition for Market Share and Profits

As Canadian population growth slows, costs rise, available resources tighten, and firms must work harder to maintain both their profits and their market share regardless of the form of the competitive market. Firms often turn to innovative forms of advertising and communication to capture the minds of the target consumer. One such form is social media, a powerful form of communication. Firms also tap into sociocultural trends by using these trends in their communications.

Unlike the old days when companies would painstakingly gather competitive intelligence by reviewing reports, reading newspaper articles, talking with the experts, and gleaning information from the competitors, businesses these days can use technology to collect vast amounts of data from the Internet. For example, in 2012 Nestle created a Digital Acceleration Team to gather competitive intelligence by using sophisticated technological tools located in an office that more closely resembles NASA's mission control centre than a corporate office.[29]

Staff of the Nestle Digital Acceleration Team (DAT) monitor social networks at the company headquarters in Vevey, Switzerland.

NESTLE-ONLINE/WATER REUTERS/Denis Balibouse

2-9 CORPORATE SOCIAL RESPONSIBILITY

Corporate social responsibility is a business's concern for society's welfare. This concern is demonstrated by managers who consider both the long-range best interests of the company and the company's relationship to the society within which it operates. The newest theory in social responsibility is called **sustainability**. This theory refers to the idea that socially responsible companies will outperform their peers by focusing on the world's social problems and viewing them as opportunities to build profits and help the world at the same time. It is also the notion that companies cannot thrive for long (i.e., lack sustainability) in a world where billions of people are suffering and are desperately poor. Thus, it is in business's interest to find ways to attack society's ills.

Another view is that business should focus on making a profit and leave social and environmental problems to nonprofit organizations and government. Economist Milton Friedman believed that the free market, and not companies, should decide what is best for the world.[30] Friedman argued that to the degree that business executives spend more money than they need to—purchasing delivery vehicles with hybrid engines, paying higher wages in developing countries, or even donating company funds to charity—they are spending shareholders' money to further their own agendas. Better to pay dividends and let the shareholders give the money away, if they choose.

Total corporate social responsibility has four components: economic, legal, ethical, and philanthropic.[31] The **pyramid of corporate social responsibility** portrays economic performance as the foundation for the other three responsibilities. At the same time that a business pursues profits (economic responsibility), however, it is also expected to obey the law (legal responsibility); to do what is right, just, and fair (ethical responsibilities); and to be a good corporate citizen (philanthropic responsibility). These four components are distinct but together constitute the whole. Still, if the company doesn't make a profit, then the other three responsibilities are moot.

Stephen Mcsweeny/Shutterstock.com

2-9a Growth of Social Responsibility

The social responsibility of businesses is growing around the world and has become more than simply a fashionable expression. A 2011 sustainability study conducted by MIT's Sloan School of Management and Boston Consulting Group showed that 70 percent of North American corporations have put sustainability permanently on their management agenda. More than 3000 participants in this study also said that sustainability programs lead to profitability for the businesses.[32]

Furthermore, in Canada social responsibility has become increasingly professionalized and integrated across all levels within most organizations. According to Imagine Canada, a national program supporting public and corporate charitable giving, businesses have moved beyond simply writing a cheque to a more engaged and integrated approach to social responsibility that includes in-kind gifts, employee volunteerism, and sponsorships.

Firms are realizing that corporate social responsibility isn't easy or quick. It works only when a firm engages a long-term strategy and effort and the strategy is coordinated throughout the organization. It doesn't always come cheap, and the payoff, both to society and to the firm itself, isn't always immediate. But consumers will patronize firms that are socially responsible.

pyramid of corporate social responsibility a model that suggests corporate social responsibility is composed of economic, legal, ethical, and philanthropic responsibilities and that the firm's economic performance supports the entire structure

green marketing the development and marketing of products designed to minimize negative effects on the physical environment

2-9b Green Marketing

An outgrowth of the social responsibility movement is **green marketing**—the development and marketing of products designed to minimize negative effects on the physical environment. Not only can a company aid the environment through green marketing, but green marketing can often help the bottom line. Environmentally aware consumers tend to earn more and are more willing to pay a premium for green products.

To protect consumers from companies capitalizing on the green movement without substance, the Canadian Competition Bureau launched a guide that provides the business community with green marketing guidelines. While the guide is not law, the Competition Bureau will pursue deceptive environmental claims, fine violators, or remove products from store shelves. The guide suggests that environmental claims should be clear, specific, accurate, and not misleading, and that all environmental claims should be verified and substantiated.

A company known for its green marketing practices is S. C. Johnson & Son. This company developed the Greenlist process, which requires that its

PYRAMID OF CORPORATE SOCIAL RESPONSIBILITY

Four Components of Total CSR or Pyramid of CSR

Philanthropic responsibilities

Ethical responsibilities

Legal responsibilities

Economic performance

CHAPTER 2: The Marketing Environment, Social Responsibility, and Ethics

scientists evaluate all the company's product ingredients to determine their impact on the environment and to reformulate products to reduce that impact.[33] The use of this patented process led to the reformulation of Windex, resulting in a greener and more effective product.

2-10 ETHICAL BEHAVIOUR IN BUSINESS

Social responsibility and ethics go hand in hand. Ethics refers to the moral principles or values that generally govern the conduct of an individual or a group. Ethics can also be viewed as the standard of behaviour by which conduct is judged. Standards that are legal may not always be ethical, and vice versa. Laws are the values and standards enforceable by the courts. Ethics consists of personal moral principles and values rather than societal prescriptions.

Defining the boundaries of ethicality and legality can be difficult. Often, judgment is needed to determine whether an action that may be legal is an ethical or unethical act. Also, judgment is required to determine whether an unethical act is legal or illegal.

Morals are the rules people develop as a result of cultural values and norms. Culture is a socializing force that dictates what is right and wrong. Moral standards may also reflect the laws and regulations that affect social and economic behaviour. Thus, morals can be considered a foundation of ethical behaviour.

Morals are usually characterized as good or bad. *Good* and *bad* have different connotations, including

Manulife Financial and not-for-profit organization Volunteer Canada launched a marketing and social media initiative at www.getvolunteering .ca that was designed to increase the number of Canadian volunteers.

effective and ineffective. A good salesperson makes or exceeds the assigned quota. If the salesperson sells a new stereo or television set to a disadvantaged consumer—knowing full well that the person can't keep up the monthly payments—is the salesperson still considered to be good? What if the sale enables the salesperson to exceed his or her quota?

Good and bad can also refer to conforming and deviant behaviours. Any doctor in Canada who charges extra fees for fast-tracking patients on waiting lists for provincially funded procedures would be considered unprofessional. Such a doctor would not be conforming to the norms and laws of the medical profession or to the laws regarding universal healthcare set by our provincial or territorial legislatures and federal government. Bad and good are also used to express the distinction between criminal and law-abiding behaviour. And finally, different religions define good and bad in markedly different ways. A Muslim who eats pork would be considered bad, as would a fundamentalist Christian who drinks whisky.

2-10a Morality and Business Ethics

Today's business ethics consist of a subset of major life values learned since birth. The values business people use to make decisions have been acquired through family, educational, and religious institutions.

Ethical values are situation specific and time oriented. Nevertheless, everyone must have an ethical base that applies to conduct in the business world and in personal life. One approach to developing a personal set of ethics is to examine the consequences of

TOP 50 SOCIALLY RESPONSIBLE COMPANIES, 2013

For these companies, corporate social responsibility is a key part of the way they do business.

Banks	Retailing
Bank of Montreal	Best Buy Co. Inc.
The Co-Operators Group Ltd.	Loblaw Companies Limited
Desjardins Group	Rona Inc
Royal Bank of Canada	Canadian Tire Corp. Ltd.
TD Bank Group	**Technology**
Vancity (Vancouver City Savings Credit Union)	Accenture plc
Energy & Utilities	Cisco Systems Inc.
Cenovus Energy	Dell Inc.
Suncor Energy Inc.	Intel Corp.
Talisman Energy Inc.	International Business Machines Corp. (IBM)
TransAlta Corp.	SAP Canada Inc.
Food & Beverage	**Telecom/Electronics**
Danone	BCE Inc.
Kellogg Company	Nokia Corp.
Molson Coors Brewing Company	Panasonic Corporation
PepsiCo, Inc.	Sony Corporation
Starbucks Corporation	Telus Corp.
Tim Hortons Inc.	**Textiles, Footwear & Apparel**
Industrials	Adidas
3M Co.	Gildan Activewear
Bombardier, Inc.	Hennes & Mauritz AB
General Electric Company	Nike Inc.
Philips Electronics	Zara (Industria de Diseño Textil SA)
Materials	Gap Inc.
Cascades Inc.	**Transportation & Logistics**
IAMGOLD	BMW
Potash Corp. of Saskatchewan Inc. (PotashCorp)	Canadian National Railway Co.
Teck	Ford Motor Company
	United Parcel Services Inc.
	Volkswagen

Source: Maclean's, The Top 50 Best in class, www.macleans.ca/canada-top-50-socially-responsible-corporations-2013/

code of ethics a
guideline to help marketing
managers and other employees
make better decisions

a particular act. Who is helped or hurt? How long-lasting are the consequences? What actions produce the greatest good for the greatest number of people? A second approach stresses the importance of rules. Rules come in the form of customs, laws, professional standards, and common sense. "Always treat others as you would like to be treated" is an example of a rule.

The last approach emphasizes the development of moral character within individuals. Ethical development can be thought of as having three levels:[34]

▸▸ *Preconventional morality,* the most basic level, is childlike. It is calculating, self-centred, even selfish, and is based on what will be immediately punished or rewarded.

▸▸ *Conventional morality* moves from an egocentric viewpoint toward the expectations of society. Loyalty and obedience to the organization (or society) become paramount. A marketing decision maker at this level would be concerned only with whether the proposed action is legal and how it will be viewed by others.

▸▸ *Postconventional morality* represents the morality of the mature adult. At this level, people are less concerned about how others might see them and more concerned about how they see and judge themselves over the long run. A marketing decision maker who has attained a postconventional level of morality might ask, "Even though it is legal and will increase company profits, is it right in the long run?"

2-10b Ethical Decision Making

Ethical questions rarely have cut-and-dried answers. Studies show that the following factors tend to influence ethical decision making and judgments:[35]

▸▸ **EXTENT OF ETHICAL PROBLEMS WITHIN THE ORGANIZATION:** Marketing professionals who perceive fewer ethical problems in their organizations tend to disapprove more strongly of unethical or questionable practices than those who perceive more ethical problems. Apparently, the healthier the ethical environment, the more likely marketers will take a strong stand against questionable practices.

▸▸ **TOP-MANAGEMENT ACTIONS ON ETHICS:** Top managers can influence the behaviour of marketing professionals by encouraging ethical behaviour and discouraging unethical behaviour.

▸▸ **POTENTIAL MAGNITUDE OF THE CONSEQUENCES:** The greater the harm done to victims, the more likely marketing professionals will recognize the behaviour as unethical.

▸▸ **SOCIAL CONSENSUS:** The greater the degree of agreement among managerial peers that an action is harmful, the more likely marketers will recognize the action as unethical.

▸▸ **PROBABILITY OF A HARMFUL OUTCOME:** The greater the likelihood that an action will result in a harmful outcome, the more likely marketers will recognize the action as unethical.

▸▸ **LENGTH OF TIME BETWEEN THE DECISION AND THE ONSET OF CONSEQUENCES:** The shorter the length of time between the action and the onset of negative consequences, the more likely it is that marketers will perceive the action as unethical.

▸▸ **NUMBER OF PEOPLE TO BE AFFECTED:** The greater the number of persons affected by a negative outcome, the more likely it is that marketers will recognize the behaviour as unethical.

2-10c Ethical Guidelines

Many organizations have become more interested in ethical issues. One sign of this interest is the increase in the number of large companies that appoint ethics officers—from virtually none seven years ago to almost 33 percent of large corporations in 2012. In addition, companies of all sizes have developed a **code of ethics** as a guideline to help marketing managers and other employees make better decisions.

Creating ethics guidelines has several advantages:

▸▸ The guidelines help employees identify the business practices their firm recognizes as being acceptable.

▸▸ A code of ethics can be an effective internal control on behaviour, which is more desirable than external controls, such as government regulation.

▸▸ A written code helps employees avoid confusion when determining whether their decisions are ethical.

▸▸ The process of formulating the code of ethics facilitates discussion among employees about what is right and wrong, which ultimately leads to better decisions.

Businesses must be careful, however, not to make their code of ethics too vague or too detailed. Codes that are too vague give little or no guidance to

It is IN BUSINESS'S INTEREST *to find ways to* ATTACK SOCIETY'S ILLS *and lend a helping hand.*

employees in their day-to-day activities. Codes that are too detailed encourage employees to substitute rules for judgment. For instance, if employees are involved in questionable behaviour, they may use the absence of a written rule as a reason to continue their behaviour, even though their conscience may be telling them otherwise. Following a set of ethical guidelines will not guarantee the "rightness" of a decision, but it will improve the chances that the decision will be ethical.

Although many companies have issued policies on ethical behaviour, marketing managers must still put the policies into effect. They must address the classic "matter of degree" issue. For example, marketing researchers often resort to deception to obtain unbiased answers to their research questions. Asking for a few minutes of a respondent's time is dishonest if the researcher knows the interview will last 45 minutes. Not only must management post a code of ethics, but it must also give examples of what is ethical and unethical for each item in the code. Moreover, top management must stress to all employees the importance of adhering to the company's code of ethics. Without a detailed code of ethics and top management's support, creating ethical guidelines becomes an empty exercise. The Canadian Marketing Association's code of ethics outlines its purpose.

WHAT'S EXPECTED OF CANADIAN MARKETERS

The [Canadian Marketing Association's] Code of Ethics and Standards of Practice ... is designed to establish and maintain standards for the conduct of marketing in Canada.

Marketers acknowledge that the establishment and maintenance of high standards of practice are a fundamental responsibility to the public, essential to winning and holding consumer confidence, and the foundation of a successful and independent marketing industry in Canada.

Members of the Canadian Marketing Association recognize an obligation—to the consumers and the businesses they serve, to the integrity of the discipline in which they operate, and to each other—to practice to the highest standards of honesty, truth, accuracy, fairness, and professionalism.

Source: From Code of Ethics and Standards of Practice, Canadian Marketing Association, www.the-cma.org

$28 Trillion
The amount over which women will have control, in terms of global consumer spending, by 2014[36]

36%
Percentage of consumers who find Facebook most useful for their travel experience

$1 Trillion
Annual spending power of baby boomers

10
The number of years needed to make up lost economic ground if you graduate when the economy is in a recession

Strategic Planning for Competitive Advantage

Chapter **3**

A good strategic plan can help protect and grow the firm's resources.

After you finish this chapter, go to www.nelson.com/student *for* **STUDY TOOLS**. 💼-----→

3-1 THE NATURE OF STRATEGIC PLANNING

Planning in general is the process of anticipating future events and determining strategies to achieve organizational objectives in the future. Planning can take place in an organization at the strategic or tactical levels. **Strategic planning** is the managerial process of creating and maintaining a fit between the organization's objectives and resources and the evolving market opportunities. The goal of strategic planning is long-run profitability and growth. Thus, strategic decisions require long-term commitments of resources. A strategic error can threaten a firm's survival. On the other hand, a good strategic plan can help protect and grow the firm's resources.

Business organizations are increasingly becoming complex, and modern businesses, especially large corporations, constitute a set of diverse business interests spread over several business areas and markets. These diverse businesses within a corporation are linked by common corporate goals and interdependent business strategies that must be coordinated to obtain maximum advantage for the business and its customers. In a large businesses setting, strategic planning is a complex set of activities that takes place at three levels: (1) corporate, (2) business unit, and (3) marketing. The corporate strategic planning takes place at the highest level of an organization and sets the direction and scope of the overall corporation through its mission statement, the identification of key business opportunities and constraints, and the allocation of resources.

Corporate planning leads to objectives for business- and marketing-level planning that address issues related to when, where, how, and against whom to compete. Business planning

planning the process of anticipating future events and determining strategies to achieve organizational objectives in the future

strategic planning the managerial process of creating and maintaining a fit between the organization's objectives and resources and evolving market opportunities

strategic business unit (SBU) a subgroup of a single business or a collection of related businesses within the larger organization

mission statement a statement of the firm's business based on a careful analysis of benefits sought by present and potential customers and an analysis of existing and anticipated environmental conditions

is undertaken at the **strategic business unit (SBU)** level, which is a subgroup of a single business or a collection of related businesses within the larger organization. A properly defined SBU should have a distinct mission and specific target market, control over its resources, its own competitors, and plans independent of the other SBUs in the organization. The goal of business-level planning is to formulate strategies that deal with issues related to the competitive advantage a business intends to achieve through various means—including, for example, the supply chain, strategic partnerships, and the development and capitalization of distinctive competencies. The marketing planning activities are aimed at target market and marketing mix considerations that cover, for example, product lines, branding, pricing, and communication strategies. The corporate planning guides business and marketing planning; however, at the same time the corporate planning is also based on input from the other two lower levels.

Strategic decisions are made at all three levels, whereas tactical decisions are limited to the implementation of marketing plans at the lowest operational level. A **strategic decision** is a decision that is wider in scope and long term in its orientation, whereas a **tactical decision** is narrower in scope and is short term. Strategic decisions affect an organization's long-run course, its allocation of resources, and ultimately its financial success. In contrast, an operating decision, such as changing the package design for Iögo or altering the sweetness of a Kraft salad dressing, probably won't have a big impact on the long-run profitability of the company. What constitutes a long- and short-term orientation is relative and varies from industry to industry. For example, a long-term decision in the auto industry may cover five to seven years, whereas a long-term decision in the high-tech industry may cover two to three years. However, the decisions that an organization makes at the operational and business levels directly link to and flow from the strategic decisions made at the highest level within the organization. For example, an organization might make a strategic decision to increase its presence in a particular market. This decision may result in one of its business units expanding its market share through new product introductions as a result of brand or line extensions.

IÖGO *(pronounced "you go") is a Canadian brand of yogurt. iögo is available in seven lines and comes in over 40 flavours.*

© Helen Sessions / Alamy

How do companies go about developing strategic marketing? How do employees know how to implement the long-term goals of the firm? The answer is a strategic marketing plan that address all three levels of planning (see Exhibit 3.1). The strategic marketing plan is a written document that acts as a guidebook of marketing activities for the marketing manager. In this chapter, you will learn the importance of preparing a strategic marketing plan and the types of information contained in it. Strategic planning begins by setting a company's mission statement.

3-2 CORPORATE PLANNING— DEFINING THE BUSINESS MISSION

The foundation of any marketing plan is the firm's mission statement, which answers the question, "What business are we in?" The way a firm defines its business mission profoundly affects the firm's long-run resource allocation, profitability, and survival. The mission statement is based on a careful analysis of benefits sought by present and potential customers and an analysis of existing and anticipated environmental conditions. The firm's mission statement establishes boundaries for all subsequent decisions,

Exhibit 3.1

ELEMENTS OF A STRATEGIC MARKETING PLAN

objectives, and strategies. As such, a mission statement should focus on the market or markets the organization is attempting to serve rather than on the goods or services offered. Otherwise, a new technology may quickly make the goods or services obsolete and the mission statement irrelevant to company functions.

Business mission statements that are stated too narrowly suffer from **marketing myopia**—defining a business in terms of goods and services rather than in terms of the benefits that customers seek. In this context, *myopia* means narrow, short-term thinking. An example of this would be if the Wm. Wrigley Jr. Company had defined its mission as being a gum manufacturer. (The company actually defines itself as a confectioner.) Alternatively, business missions may be stated too broadly. "To provide products of superior quality and value that improve the lives of the world's consumers" is probably too broad a mission statement for any firm except Procter & Gamble. Care must be taken when stating what business a firm is in. By correctly stating the business mission in terms of the benefits that customers seek, the foundation for the marketing plan is set.

The organization may also need to define a mission statement and objectives for a strategic business unit (SBU). Thus, a large firm, such as Kraft Foods, may have marketing plans for each of its SBUs, which include breakfast foods, desserts, pet foods, and beverages.

3-3 STRATEGIC DIRECTIONS—DESIGNING THE BUSINESS PORTFOLIO

To set an organization's strategic direction, businesses must thoroughly understand their current environment and any potential environment in which they will be operating. This goal is accomplished by conducting a **situation (SWOT) analysis** of an organization's strengths (S) and weaknesses (W) in the context of opportunities (O) and threats (T) that their external environments present.

3-3a Conducting a Situation (SWOT) Analysis

When examining internal strengths and weaknesses, the marketing manager should focus on organizational resources, such as production costs, marketing skills, financial resources, company or brand image, employee capabilities, and available technology. For example, a potential weakness for AirTran Airways is the age of its airplane fleet, which could project an image of danger or low quality. A potential strength is the airline's low

marketing myopia defining a business in terms of goods and services rather than in terms of the benefits that customers seek

situation (SWOT) analysis identifying internal strengths (S) and weaknesses (W) and also examining external opportunities (O) and threats (T)

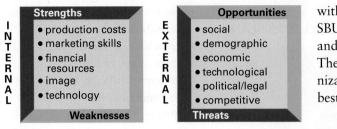

operating costs, which translate into lower prices for consumers. Another issue to consider in this section of the marketing plan is the historical background of the firm—its sales and profit history.

When examining external opportunities and threats, marketing managers must analyze aspects of the marketing environment. This process is called **environmental scanning**—the collection and interpretation of information about forces, events, and relationships in the external environment that may affect the future of the organization or the implementation of the marketing plan. Environmental scanning helps identify business opportunities and threats and provides guidelines for the design of marketing strategy. For example, H&R Block, a tax preparation service, benefits from complex changes in the tax codes that motivate citizens to have their tax returns prepared by a professional. Alternatively, tax-simplification or flat-tax plans would allow people to easily prepare their own returns and would have a dramatic impact on the company's revenues.

The six most often studied macro-environmental forces are social, demographic, economic, technological, political and legal, and competitive. These forces were examined in detail in Chapter 2.

The result of the SWOT analysis is to identify the strategic direction of the firm. This means an organization must decide, based on its strengths and weaknesses, which collection or portfolio of businesses it should operate. One of the popular approaches for business portfolio analysis is the Boston Consulting Group (BCG) portfolio matrix.

3-3b BCG Portfolio Matrix

Recall that large organizations engaged in strategic planning may create strategic business units. Each SBU has its own rate of return on investment, growth potential, and associated risk. Management must find a balance among the SBUs that yields the overall organization's desired growth and profits

with an acceptable level of risk. Some SBUs generate large amounts of cash, and others need cash to foster growth. The challenge is to balance the organization's "portfolio" of SBUs for the best long-term performance.

To determine the future cash contributions and cash requirements expected for each SBU, managers can use the Boston Consulting Group's portfolio matrix. The **portfolio matrix** is a tool for allocating resources among products and strategic business units on the basis of relative market share and market growth rate. Using the portfolio matrix requires classifying each SBU by its present or forecast growth and market share. The underlying assumption is that market share and profitability are strongly linked. The measure of market share used in the portfolio approach is relative market share, the ratio between the company's share and the share of the largest competitor. For example, if a firm has a 50 percent share and its competitor has 5 percent, the ratio is 10 to 1.

Exhibit 3.2 shows a portfolio matrix for a computer manufacturer. The size of the circle in each cell of the matrix represents dollar sales of the SBU relative to dollar sales of the company's other SBUs. The following categories are used in the matrix:

▸ **STARS:** A **star** is a fast-growing market leader. For example, computer manufacturers have

Exhibit 3.2

PORTFOLIO MATRIX FOR A LARGE COMPUTER MANUFACTURER

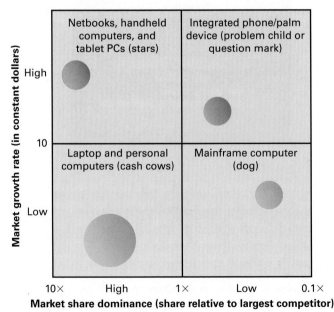

identified subnotebooks, handheld models, and tablets as stars. Star SBUs have large profits but need lots of cash to finance growth. The best tactic is to protect existing market share by reinvesting earnings in product improvement, better distribution, more promotion, and production efficiency. Management must capture new users as they enter the market.

⇉ **CASH COWS:** A cash cow is an SBU that usually generates more cash than it needs to maintain its market share. The product has a dominant share in a low-growth market. Personal computers and laptops are categorized as cash cows in Exhibit 3.2. The strategy for a cash cow is to maintain market dominance by being the price leader and making technological improvements. Managers should not extend the basic line unless they can dramatically increase demand. Instead, they should allocate excess cash to the product categories where growth prospects are the greatest.

⇉ **PROBLEM CHILDREN:** A problem child, also called a question mark, shows rapid growth but poor profit margins. It has a low market share in a high-growth industry. Problem children need lots of cash support to keep from becoming dogs. The strategies are to invest heavily to improve market share, acquire competitors to get the necessary market share, or drop the SBU. Sometimes a firm can reposition a problem child as a star.

⇉ **DOGS:** A dog has low growth potential and a small market share. Most dogs eventually leave the marketplace. For computer manufacturers, the mainframe computer has become a dog. The options for dogs are to harvest or divest.

After classifying the company's SBUs in the matrix, managers must next allocate future resources for each SBU. Four basic strategies can be used:

⇉ **BUILD:** An organization with an SBU that it believes has star potential (probably a problem child at present) may decide to give up short-term profits and use its financial resources to build. Procter & Gamble built Pringles from a money loser to a profit maker.

⇉ **HOLD:** If an SBU is a successful cash cow, a key goal is to preserve market share so that the organization can take advantage of the positive cash flow.

⇉ **HARVEST:** This strategy is appropriate for all SBUs except stars. The goal is to increase the short-term cash return without much concern for the long-run impact. This strategy is especially worthwhile when more cash is needed from a cash cow with unfavourable long-run prospects. For instance, Lever Brothers has harvested Lifebuoy soap for years with little promotional backing.

⇉ **DIVEST:** Getting rid of SBUs with low shares of low-growth markets, such as problem children and dogs, is often a strategically appropriate decision. In 2012, Procter & Gamble divested its Pringle brand of chips to Kellogg Company for $2.7 billion.[1]

3-3c Strategic Alternatives— Developing Growth Strategies

Once an organization decides on the portfolio of businesses, next it must identify opportunities to grow these businesses. To discover a marketing opportunity, management must know how to identify the alternatives. One method for developing alternatives is Ansoff's strategic opportunity matrix (see Exhibit 3.3),

star in the portfolio matrix, a business unit that is a fast-growing market leader

cash cow in the portfolio matrix, a business unit that usually generates more cash than it needs to maintain its market share

problem child (question mark) in the portfolio matrix, a business unit that shows rapid growth but poor profit margins

dog in the portfolio matrix, a business unit that has low growth potential and a small market share

---

BCG—A HISTORY

1963, Boston Consulting Group (BCG) is born.

1968, BCG introduced the growth share matrix, or portfolio matrix.

2012, BCG counted nearly 6200 consultants in 78 offices in 43 countries and generated annual revenue of US $3.7 billion (the company's first month of billings totalled $500).

Source: "America's Largest Private Companies," *Forbes*, as at December 2103, www.forbes.com/companies/boston-consulting-group/ (accessed June 6, 2014).

Exhibit 3.3

ANSOFF'S STRATEGIC OPPORTUNITY MATRIX

	Present Product	New Product
Present Market	**Market Penetration** Starbucks sells more coffee to customers who register their reloadable Starbucks cards.	**Product Development** Starbucks develops new powdered coffee called Via.
New Market	**Market Development** Starbucks opens new stores in India.	**Diversification** Starbucks launches Hear Music and buys Ethos Water.

which matches products with markets. Firms can explore these four options:

» **MARKET PENETRATION:** A firm using the market penetration alternative tries to increase market share among existing customers. If Kraft Foods started a major campaign for Maxwell House coffee by initiating aggressive advertising and offering cents-off coupons to existing customers, it would be following a penetration strategy. Customer databases, discussed in Chapters 4 and 8, would help managers implement this strategy.

» **MARKET DEVELOPMENT:** Market development involves attracting new customers to existing products. Ideally, new uses for old products stimulate additional sales among existing customers while also bringing in new buyers. For example, the growing emphasis on continuing education and executive development by colleges and universities is a market development strategy.

» **PRODUCT DEVELOPMENT:** A product development strategy entails the creation of new products for present markets. In 2013, P&G introduced the new Duracell Quantum battery as part of its strategy to introduce new products.[2] Managers following the product development strategy can rely on their extensive knowledge of the target audience. They usually have a good feel for what customers like and dislike about current products and what existing needs are not being met. In addition, managers can rely on established distribution channels.

» **DIVERSIFICATION:** Diversification is a strategy of increasing sales by introducing new products into new markets. Loblaws in 2013 diversified its grocery businesses by purchasing Shoppers Drug Mart in a $12.4 billion deal.[3] A diversification strategy can be risky when a firm is entering unfamiliar markets, but diversification can be very profitable when a firm is entering markets that have little or no competition.

SELECTING A STRATEGIC ALTERNATIVE

Selecting which alternative to pursue depends on the overall company philosophy and culture. The choice also depends on the tool used to make the decision. Companies generally have one of two philosophies about when they expect profits. Even though market share and profitability are compatible long-term goals, companies either pursue profits right away or first seek to increase market share and then pursue profits.

Companies sometimes make the mistake of focusing on building market share, assuming that profits will follow. The relationship between market share and profits is not always linear and depends on the industry, the company's product mix, and the product life cycle stages the products are at. For example, Apple sold 33.8 million iPhones in its fiscal fourth quarter, which ended September 30, 2013. Those sales represented a 26 percent increase over the preceding year; however, its profits were lower compared with the year before.[4]

3-4 BUSINESS PLANNING FOR COMPETITIVE ADVANTAGE

Once an organization through its corporate planning decides on its business portfolio, then it must find ways to compete in those businesses. At this stage more detailed planning is undertaken at the strategic business unit (SBU) level as to how a business will compete with the end goal of achieving a sustainable competitive advantage. SBUs must identify the **core competencies** that will help them attain sustainable competitive advantage.

3-4a Competitive Advantage

A **competitive advantage** is a set of unique features of a company and its products that are perceived by the target market as significant and superior to the competition. It is the factor or factors that cause customers to patronize a firm and not the competition. Firms may have three types of competitive advantages: cost, product/service differentiation, and niche strategies.

3-4b Cost Competitive Advantage

Cost leadership can result from obtaining inexpensive raw materials, creating an efficient scale of plant operations, designing products for ease of manufacture, controlling overhead costs, and avoiding marginal customers. Having a **cost competitive advantage** means being the low-cost competitor in an industry while maintaining satisfactory profit margins. A cost competitive advantage enables a firm to deliver superior customer value. Walmart is the world's leading low-cost general merchandise store. It offers good value to customers because it focuses on providing a large selection of merchandise at low prices and good

customer service. Walmart is able to keep its prices down because it has strong buying power in its relationships with suppliers.

- Experience Curves
- Efficient Labour
- No-Frills Goods and Services
- Government Subsidies

+ → Cost Competitive Advantage

- Product Design
- Re-engineering
- Production Innovations
- New Methods of Service Delivery

Environmental scanning reveals that specialty cheese consumption in Canada continues to increase year over year. The result is the continued success of specialty cheese stores and more space dedicated to specialty cheeses in retail grocery chain stores.

The Toronto Star/GetStock.com

The EXPERIENCE CURVE *was conceived by the Boston Consulting Group in 1966.*

Costs can be reduced in a variety of ways.

▸ **EXPERIENCE CURVES:** **Experience curves** tell us that costs decline at a predictable rate as experience with a product increases. The experience curve effect encompasses a broad range of manufacturing, marketing, and administrative costs. Experience curves reflect learning by doing, technological advances, and economies of scale. Firms use historical experience curves as a basis for predicting and setting prices. Experience curves allow management to forecast costs and set prices based on anticipated costs as opposed to current costs. The experience curve was conceived by the Boston Consulting Group in 1966.

▸ **EFFICIENT LABOUR:** Labour costs can be an important component of total costs in low-skill, labour-intensive industries, such as product assembly and apparel manufacturing. Many Canadian manufacturers have gone offshore to achieve cheaper manufacturing costs. Many Canadian companies are also outsourcing activities such as data entry and other labour-intensive jobs.

▸ **NO-FRILLS GOODS AND SERVICES:** Marketers can lower costs by removing frills and options from a product or service. WestJet, for example, offers low fares but no seat assignments or meals. Low prices give WestJet a higher load factor and greater economies of scale, which, in turn, mean even lower prices.

▸ **GOVERNMENT SUBSIDIES:** Governments may provide grants and interest-free loans to target industries. Such government assistance enabled Japanese semiconductor manufacturers to become global leaders.

▸ **PRODUCT DESIGN:** Cutting-edge design technology can help offset high labour costs. BMW is a world leader in designing cars for ease of manufacture and assembly. Reverse engineering—the process of disassembling a product piece by piece to learn its components and obtain clues as to the manufacturing process—can also mean savings. Reverse-engineering a low-cost competitor's product can save research and design costs.

▸ **RE-ENGINEERING:** Re-engineering entails fundamental rethinking and redesign of business processes to achieve dramatic improvements in critical measures of performance. It often involves reorganizing from functional departments, such as sales, engineering, and production, to cross-disciplinary teams.

▸ **PRODUCTION INNOVATIONS:** Production innovations, such as new technology and simplified production techniques, help lower the average cost of production. Technologies such as computer-aided design and computer-aided manufacturing (CAD/CAM) and increasingly sophisticated robots help companies, such as Boeing, Ford, and General Electric, reduce their manufacturing costs.

▸ **NEW METHODS OF SERVICE DELIVERY:** Online bill delivery is not only an environmentally friendly alternative but also results in enormous cost savings. Airlines are lowering reservation and ticketing costs by encouraging passengers to use the Internet to book flights and by providing self-service check-in kiosks at the airport.

3-4c Product/Service Differentiation Competitive Advantage

Because cost competitive advantages are subject to continual erosion, product/service differentiation tends to provide a longer-lasting competitive advantage. The durability of this strategy tends to make it more attractive to many top managers. A **product/service differentiation competitive advantage** exists when a firm provides a unique benefit that is valuable to buyers beyond simply offering a low price. Examples include brand names (Lexus), a strong dealer

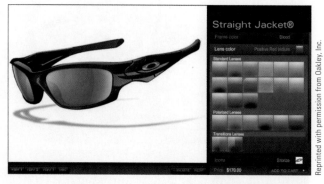

CUSTOMIZE YOUR LOOK WITH OAKLEY!

network (Caterpillar for construction work), product reliability (Maytag appliances), image (Holt Renfrew in clothing), or service (FedEx). A great example of a company with a strong product/service differentiation competitive advantage is Oakley. Oakley's advantage is built around one simple idea—product innovation. This company lets its customers design their own sunglasses at its website, **www.Oakley.ca/custom.**

3-4d Niche Competitive Advantage

A **niche competitive advantage** seeks to target and effectively serve a single segment of the market (see Chapter 8). For small companies with limited resources that potentially face giant competitors, carving out a niche strategy may be the only viable option. A market segment that has good growth potential but is not crucial to the success of major competitors is a good candidate for developing a niche strategy. Many companies using a niche strategy serve only a limited geographic market. Other companies focus their product lines on specific types of products, as is the case with the Canadian company Booster Juice, which specializes in fruit juices, smoothie drinks, and other healthy, nutritious foods.

3-4e Building Sustainable Competitive Advantage

The key to having a competitive advantage is the ability to sustain that advantage. A **sustainable competitive advantage** is an advantage that cannot be copied by the competition. Examples of companies with a sustainable competitive advantage include Rolex (high-quality watches), Harry Rosen stores (customized service), and Cirque du Soleil (top-notch entertainment). Without a competitive advantage, target customers don't perceive any reason to patronize one organization over its competitors.

niche competitive advantage the advantage achieved when a firm seeks to target and effectively serve a single segment of the market

sustainable competitive advantage an advantage that cannot be copied by the competition

NO COMPETITION

It's hard to find a direct competitor for Montreal's Cirque du Soleil, for several reasons:

▸▸ The performers tell a story that goes beyond the acrobatic acts using animals that other circuses focus on.

▸▸ The show employs more than 4000 people from 40 countries.

▸▸ Each stage show has a life of 10 to 12 years.

▸▸ The company runs 19 shows in over 271 cities on every continent except Antarctica, with an annual turnover of US$810 million.

▸▸ More than 300 seamstresses, engineers, and makeup artists sew, design, and build custom materials for exotic shows with such names as Totem, Zarkana, Iris, Amaluna, and its most recent introduction, Michael Jackson: One.

▸▸ The company will perform a special one-night-only original production at the 2015 Pan/Parapan American Games opening ceremony in Toronto.

All that plus an Emmy Award–winning series on Bravo make Cirque du Soleil a tough act to follow. (In marketing terms, that means sustainable competitive advantage has been achieved.)

© Christopher Leggett / Alamy

Source: Cirque du Soleil, "Cirque du Soleil to Create Opening Ceremony for Toronto 2015 Pan Am Games," September 24, 2013, www.toronto2015.org/news/archive/cirque-du-soleil-to-create-opening-ceremony-for-toronto-2015-pan-am-games/74 (accessed June 6, 2014).

The notion of competitive advantage means that a successful firm will stake out a position unique in some manner from its rivals. Imitation by competitors indicates a lack of competitive advantage and almost ensures mediocre performance. Moreover, competitors rarely stand still, so it is not surprising that imitation causes managers to feel trapped in a seemingly endless game of catch-up. They are regularly surprised by the new accomplishments of their rivals.

Companies need to build their own competitive advantages rather than copy a competitor. The sources of tomorrow's competitive advantages are the skills and assets of the organization. Skills are functions, such as customer service and promotion, that the firm performs better than its competitors. Assets include patents, copyrights, locations, and equipment and technology that are superior to those of the competition. Marketing managers should continually focus the firm's skills and assets on sustaining and creating competitive advantages.

Remember, a sustainable competitive advantage is a function of the speed with which competitors can imitate a leading company's strategy and plans. Imitation requires a competitor to identify the leader's competitive advantage, determine how it is achieved, and then learn how to duplicate it.

3-5 MARKETING PLANNING—SETTING THE OBJECTIVES AND IDENTIFYING THE TARGET MARKET

After the corporate level and SBU level, the third level of planning is aimed at developing **marketing strategy**, which involves the activities of selecting and describing one or more target markets and developing and maintaining a marketing mix that will produce mutually satisfying exchanges with target markets.

3-5a Setting Marketing Plan Objectives

Before the details of a marketing plan can be developed, objectives for the plan must be stated. Without objectives, a firm has no basis for measuring the success of its marketing plan activities.

A **marketing objective** is a statement of what is to be accomplished through marketing activities. To be useful, stated objectives should meet several criteria. First, objectives should be realistic, measurable, and time specific. It is tempting to state that the objective is "to be the best marketer of cat food." However, what is "best" for one firm might mean selling 1 million kilograms of cat food per year, whereas another firm might view "best" as having dominant market share. It

JUDGE FOR YOURSELF

Poorly Stated Objectives

▶▶ Our objective is to be a leader in the industry in terms of new-product development.

▶▶ Our objective is to maximize profits.

▶▶ Our objective is to better serve customers.

▶▶ Our objective is to be the best that we can be.

Well-Stated Objectives

▶▶ Our objective is to spend 12 percent of sales revenue between 2012 and 2013 on research and development in an effort to introduce at least five new products in 2013.

▶▶ Our objective is to achieve a 10 percent return on investment during 2012, with a payback on new investments of no longer than four years.

▶▶ Our objective is to obtain customer satisfaction ratings of at least 90 percent on the 2012 annual customer satisfaction survey, and to retain at least 85 percent of our 2012 customers as repeat purchasers in 2013.

▶▶ Our objective is to increase market share from 30 to 40 percent in 2012 by increasing promotional expenditures by 14 percent.

may also be unrealistic for start-up firms or new products to command dominant market share, given other competitors in the marketplace. Finally, by what time should the objective be met? A more realistic objective would be "To achieve 10 percent dollar market share in the cat food market within 12 months of product introduction." Second, objectives must also be consistent with and indicate the priorities of the organization. Specifically, objectives flow from the business mission statement to the rest of the marketing plan.

Carefully specified objectives serve several functions. First, they communicate marketing management philosophies and provide direction for lower-level marketing managers so that marketing efforts are integrated and pointed in a consistent direction. Objectives also serve as motivators by creating goals for employees to strive toward. When objectives are attainable and challenging, they motivate those charged with achieving the objectives. Additionally, the process of writing specific objectives forces executives to clarify their thinking. Finally, objectives form a basis for control; the effectiveness of a plan can be gauged in light of the stated objectives.

3-5b Target Market Strategy

A market segment is a group of individuals or organizations that share one or more characteristics. They therefore may have relatively similar product needs. For example, parents of newborn babies need diapers, receiving blankets, and onesies.

The target market strategy identifies the market segment or segments on which to focus. This process begins with a **market opportunity analysis (MOA)**— the description and estimation of the size and sales potential of market segments that are of interest to the firm and the assessment of key competitors in these market segments. After the firm describes the market segments, it may choose to target one or more of these segments. Marketers use three general strategies for selecting target markets.

Target markets can be selected by appealing to the entire market with one marketing mix, concentrating on one segment, or appealing to multiple market segments using multiple marketing mixes. The characteristics, advantages, and disadvantages of each strategic option are examined in Chapter 8. Target markets could be individuals who are concerned about sensitive teeth (the target of Sensodyne toothpaste) or postsecondary students needing inexpensive transportation (Yamaha Razz scooter).

Any market segment that is targeted must be fully described. Demographics, psychographics, and buyer behaviour should be assessed. Buyer behaviour is covered in Chapters 6 and 7. If segments are differentiated by ethnicity, multicultural aspects of the marketing mix should be examined. If the target market is international, it is especially important to describe differences in culture, economic and technological development, and political structure that may affect the marketing plan. Global marketing is covered in more detail in Chapter 4.

3-6 THE MARKETING MIX

The term marketing mix refers to a unique blend of product, place (distribution), promotion, and pricing strategies (often referred to as the four Ps) designed to produce mutually satisfying exchanges with a target market. The marketing manager can control each component of the marketing mix, but the strategies for all four components must be blended to achieve optimal results. Any marketing mix is only as good as its weakest component. The best promotion and the lowest price cannot save a poor product. Similarly, excellent products with poor placing, pricing, or promotion will likely fail.

Variations in marketing mixes do not occur by chance. Astute marketing managers devise marketing strategies to gain advantages over competitors and best serve the needs and wants of a particular target market segment. By manipulating elements of the marketing mix, marketing managers can fine-tune the customer offering and achieve competitive success.

3-6a Product Strategies

Typically, the marketing mix starts with the product P. The heart of the marketing mix, the starting point, is the product offering and product strategy. Without knowing the product to be marketed, it is difficult to design a place strategy, decide on a promotion campaign, or set a price.

The product includes not only the physical unit but also its package, warranty, after-sale service, brand name, company image, value, and many other factors. A Godiva chocolate has many product elements: the chocolate itself, a fancy gold wrapper, a customer satisfaction guarantee, and the prestige of the Godiva brand name. We buy products not only

market opportunity analysis (MOA) the description and estimation of the size and sales potential of market segments that are of interest to the firm and the assessment of key competitors in these market segments

marketing mix a unique blend of product, place, promotion, and pricing strategies designed to produce mutually satisfying exchanges with a target market

four Ps product, place, promotion, and price, which together make up the marketing mix

implementation
the process that turns a marketing plan into action assignments and ensures that these assignments are executed in a way that accomplishes the plan's objectives

The BEST PROMOTION *and the* LOWEST PRICE
cannot save a POOR PRODUCT.

for what they do (their benefits) but also for what they mean to us (their status, quality, or reputation).

Products can be tangible goods, such as computers; ideas, such as those offered by a consultant; or services, such as medical care. Products should also offer customer value. Product decisions are covered in Chapters 9 and 10, and services marketing is detailed in Chapter 11.

3-6b Place (Distribution) Strategies

Place, or distribution, strategies are concerned with making products available when and where customers want them. Would you rather buy a kiwi fruit at the 24-hour grocery store within walking distance or fly to New Zealand to pick your own? A part of the place P is physical distribution, which involves all the business activities concerned with storing and transporting raw materials or finished products. The goal is to ensure products arrive in usable condition at designated places when needed. Place strategies are covered in Chapters 13 and 14.

3-6c Promotion Strategies

Elements of the promotional mix include advertising, direct marketing, public relations, sales promotion, personal selling, and online marketing. Promotion's role in the marketing mix is to bring about mutually satisfying exchanges with target markets by informing, educating, persuading, and reminding consumers of the benefits of an organization or a product. A good promotion strategy can dramatically increase sales. Good promotion strategies do not guarantee success, however. Despite massive promotional campaigns, much-anticipated movies often have disappointing box-office returns. Each element of the promotion P is coordinated and managed with the others to create a promotional blend or mix. These integrated marketing communications activities are described in Chapters 15, 16, 17, and 18. Technology-driven aspects of promotional marketing are covered in Chapter 5.

3-6d Pricing Strategies

Price is what a buyer must give up to obtain a product. It is often the most flexible of the four marketing mix elements because it is the quickest element to change. Marketers can raise or lower prices more frequently and easily than they can change other marketing mix variables. Price is an important competitive weapon and is very important to the organization because price multiplied by the number of units sold equals total revenue for the firm. Pricing decisions are covered in Chapter 12 and its appendix.

3-7 FOLLOWING UP ON THE MARKETING PLAN

3-7a Implementation

Implementation is the process that turns a marketing plan into action assignments and ensures that these assignments are executed in a way that accomplishes the plan's objectives. Implementation activities may involve

Target market for Lululemon: Educated women (and men) who practise yoga and other activities to reduce stress and lead a healthier life and who also want to look stylish and feel comfortable.

The Canadian Press/Richard Lam

detailed job assignments, activity descriptions, timelines, budgets, and lots of communication. Although implementation is essentially "doing what you said you were going to do," many organizations repeatedly experience failures in strategy implementation. Brilliant marketing plans are doomed to fail if they are not properly implemented. These detailed communications may or may not be part of the written marketing plan. If they are not part of the plan, they should be specified elsewhere as soon as the plan has been communicated.

3-7b Evaluation and Control

After a marketing plan is implemented, it should be evaluated. **Evaluation** involves gauging the extent to which marketing objectives have been achieved during the specified time. Four common reasons for failing to achieve a marketing objective are unrealistic marketing objectives, inappropriate marketing strategies in the plan, poor implementation, and changes in the environment after the objective was specified and the strategy was implemented.

Once a plan is chosen and implemented, its effectiveness must be monitored. **Control** provides the mechanisms both for evaluating marketing results in light of the plan's objectives and for correcting actions that do not help the organization reach those objectives within budget guidelines. Firms need to establish formal and informal control programs to make the entire operation more efficient.

Perhaps the broadest control device available to marketing managers is the **marketing audit**—a thorough, systematic, periodic evaluation of the objectives, strategies, structure, and performance of the marketing organization. A marketing audit helps management allocate marketing resources efficiently.

Although the main purpose of the marketing audit is to develop a full profile of the organization's marketing effort and to provide a basis for developing and revising the marketing plan, it is also an excellent way to improve communication and raise the level of marketing consciousness within the organization. A marketing audit is a useful vehicle for selling the philosophy and techniques of strategic marketing to other members of the organization.

3-8 EFFECTIVE STRATEGIC PLANNING

Effective strategic planning requires continual attention, creativity, and management commitment. Strategic planning should not be an annual exercise, in which managers go through the motions and forget about strategic planning until the next year. It should be an ongoing process because the environment is continually changing and the firm's resources and capabilities are continually evolving.

Sound strategic planning is based on creativity. Managers should challenge assumptions about the firm and the environment and establish new strategies. And above all, the most critical element in successful strategic planning is top management's support and participation.

evaluation gauging the extent to which the marketing objectives have been achieved during the specified period

control provides the mechanisms both for evaluating marketing results in light of the plan's objectives and for correcting actions that do not help the organization reach those objectives within budget guidelines

marketing audit a thorough, systematic, periodic evaluation of the objectives, strategies, structure, and performance of the marketing organization

FOUR CHARACTERISTICS OF A MARKETING AUDIT

▸▸ **COMPREHENSIVE:** covers all major marketing issues facing an organization and not just trouble spots

▸▸ **SYSTEMATIC:** takes place in an orderly sequence and covers the organization's marketing environment, internal marketing system, and specific marketing activities. The diagnosis is followed by an action plan with both short-run and long-run proposals for improving overall marketing effectiveness

▸▸ **INDEPENDENT:** normally conducted by an inside or outside party who is independent enough to have top management's confidence and to be objective

▸▸ **PERIODIC:** for maximum benefit, should be carried out on a regular schedule instead of only in a crisis

Developing a Global Vision

Over the past two decades, world trade has steadily climbed, reaching US$16.7 trillion in 2011.

After you finish this chapter, go to www.nelson.com/student *for* **STUDY TOOLS**. ▭------→

4-1 REWARDS OF GLOBAL MARKETING

Today, global revolutions are under way in many areas of our lives: management, politics, communications, and technology. The word *global* has assumed a new meaning, referring to a boundless mobility and competition in social, business, and intellectual arenas. **Global marketing**—marketing that targets markets throughout the world—has become an imperative for business.

Canadian managers must develop a global vision not only to recognize and react to international marketing opportunities but also to remain competitive at home. Often a Canadian firm's toughest domestic competition comes from foreign companies. Moreover, a global vision enables a manager to understand that customer and distribution networks operate worldwide, blurring geographic and political barriers and making them increasingly irrelevant to business decisions. In summary, having a **global vision** means recognizing and reacting to international marketing opportunities, using effective global marketing strategies, and being aware of threats from foreign competitors in all markets.

In 2011, world trade grew to $16.7 trillion, a 5.2 percent increase over 2010. That was the last year of a 20-year continuous growth period for world trade. In 2012, as a result of Europe's struggling economy, world trade fell by 2 percent and remained sluggish in 2013.[1]

Despite the sluggishness of world trade, it still represents significant opportunities and threats for Canadian business. Countries and companies that were never considered major players in global marketing are now influential, and some of them show great skill. Today's marketers face many challenges to their customary practices. Product development costs are rising, product life is getting shorter, and new technology is spreading around the world faster than ever. But instead of fearing change, marketing winners relish its unrelenting pace.

global marketing marketing that targets markets throughout the world

global vision a recognition of and reaction to international marketing opportunities using effective global marketing strategies and being aware of threats from foreign competitors in all markets

gross domestic product (GDP) the total market value of all goods and services produced in a country for a given period

Adopting a global vision can be very lucrative for a company. Harlequin, one of the world's leading publishers of books targeted at women, was started in Winnipeg, Manitoba, in 1949. Today, it is a multinational publishing company, publishing over 150 books per month, operating around the world with half of its books sold overseas and 95 percent outside of Canada.[2] Another company with a global vision is McCain Foods Limited. McCain is a privately owned company established in 1957 in Florenceville, New Brunswick. McCain employs over 18,000 people worldwide on 6 continents in more than 160 countries. One of McCain's business strategies is to create a single aligned global organization, which has resulted in reported sales of more than $6 billion annually.[3]

Although a company may have a global vision, it doesn't always automatically mean success. Take Research In Motion Ltd. (RIM) as an example. In 2010, RIM initiated conversations with the state-owned fund China Investment Corp. (CIC) to establish a joint venture whereby Beijing agreed to approve RIM as the official supplier of China's wireless operating system. This partnership would have provided RIM with access to the fastest-growing and largest mobile market and a significant advantage over competitors, who until that point had not been able to enter the Chinese market. By 2011, a preliminary understanding was reached; under a licensing agreement between RIM and CIC, a new China-based company would sell Chinese-made phones that would operate on RIM software. Unfortunately, RIM senior executives spent too much time internally debating the China strategy without stewarding CIC, and after two years of debate and no action, the plan was shelved. At the same time, the RIM success story was becoming history.[4]

Global marketing is not, however, a one-way street in which Canadian companies sell their wares and services throughout the world and still have the Canadian market all to themselves. Foreign competition in the domestic market, once relatively rare, is now found in almost every industry. In fact, in many industries, Canadian businesses have lost significant market share to imported products. In electronics, cameras, automobiles, fine china, tractors, leather goods, and a host of other consumer and industrial products, Canadian companies have struggled at home to maintain their market shares against foreign competitors.

4-1a Importance of Global Marketing to Canada

Canada's reliance on international commerce will increase as global markets become easier for Canadian firms to access. Globalization also means that foreign firms will find Canada an appealing market for their products and services. As the world continues to shrink through advances in technology and telecommunications, improved and less costly transportation, and a reduction in trade barriers, the trend toward increased globalization will certainly continue. Canada's future growth will largely depend on our ability to effectively compete in the global marketplace.

In Canada in 2011, exports represented 26 percent of **gross domestic product (GDP)** and imports were 26.6 percent of GDP. Canada's share of the value of global trade has been impacted by the developing countries. In 2011, Canada ranked as the 13th largest exporter and the 11th largest importer. Our largest trading partner, by far, is the United States, which is the destination for 73 percent of our exports and the source of just over 60 percent of our imports.[5] Clearly, the United States is important to our economy and prosperity. However, Canada's overreliance on the United States has led all levels of government to encourage firms of all sizes to seek out new opportunities in almost every region of the world. These efforts are beginning to bear fruit, as Asian economies are increasing their share of trade with Canadian businesses.

A new trend in global trade and marketing is the participation of small and medium-sized firms. Where once the global domain was restricted to large multinationals, today distribution and communications technology has opened the door for all firms, irrespective of size.

THE FEAR OF TRADE AND GLOBALIZATION Protests during meetings of the World Trade Organization, the World Bank, and the International Monetary Fund (three organizations that we will discuss later in the chapter) show that many people fear

EXPORTS AND IMPORTS *account for* 52 PERCENT *of Canada's gross domestic product.*

CANADA'S TOP TEN EXPORT MARKETS, 2013

Country	Export Value (in millions of Canadian dollars)
1. United States	358,199
2. China	20,488
3. United Kingdom	13,970
4. Japan	10,659
5. Mexico	5,386
6. Hong Kong	4,912
7. Netherlands	3,575
8. South Korea	3,502
9. Germany	3,463
10. France	3,039

Design Pics/First Light

Source: Industry Canada, Trade Data Online, 2009–2013, www.ic.gc.ca/app/scr/tdst/tdo/crtr.html%3bjsessionid=0002bjdp54KOQ9ZMl5c0-cJgOIK:-1O0OGVI:-S11FKP?naArea=9999&toFromCountry=CDN&grouped=GROUPED&runReport=true&countryList=TOP&currency=CDN&productType=NAICS&searchType=All&reportType=TE&timePeriod=5%7cComplete+Years (accessed August 2, 2014). Reproduced with the permission of the Minister of Industry, 2014.

world trade and globalization. Protesters' main arguments include the following:

▸▸ Millions of North Americans have lost jobs because of an increase in imports, production being shifted abroad, or the outsourcing of jobs to other countries. Most displaced workers find new jobs—but often for less pay.

▸▸ Millions of others fear losing their jobs, especially at those companies operating under competitive pressure.

▸▸ Employers often threaten to outsource jobs if workers do not accept pay cuts.

▸▸ Service and white-collar jobs are increasingly vulnerable to operations moving offshore.

BENEFITS OF GLOBALIZATION According to traditional economic theory, globalization relies on competition to drive down prices and increase product and service quality. Businesses go to the countries that operate most efficiently and those that have the technology to produce what is needed. Thus, globalization expands economic freedom, spurs competition, and raises the productivity and living standards of people in countries that open themselves to the global marketplace. For less developed countries, globalization also offers access to foreign capital, global export markets, and advanced technology while breaking the monopoly of inefficient and protected domestic producers. Faster growth, in turn, reduces poverty, encourages democratization, and promotes higher labour and environmental standards. Although government officials may face more difficult choices as a result of globalization, their citizens enjoy greater individual freedom. In this sense, globalization acts as a check on governmental power by making it more difficult for governments to abuse the freedom and property of their citizens.

Globalization deserves credit for helping lift many millions out of poverty and for improving standards of living for low-wage families.

4-2 MULTINATIONAL FIRMS

Many large Canadian companies are global marketers, and many have been very successful. A company that is heavily engaged in international trade, beyond exporting and importing, is called a multinational corporation.

multinational corporations companies that are heavily engaged in international trade, beyond exporting and importing

capital intensive using more capital than labour in the production process

Multinational corporations move resources, goods, services, and skills across national boundaries without regard to the country in which the headquarters is located.

Multinationals often develop their global business in stages. In the first stage, companies operate in one country and sell into others. Second-stage multinationals set up foreign subsidiaries to handle sales in one country. In the third stage, they operate an entire line of business in another country. The fourth stage has evolved primarily because of the Internet and involves mostly high-tech companies. For these firms, the executive suite is virtual. Their top executives and core corporate functions may be located in different countries, wherever the firms can gain a competitive edge through the availability of talent or capital, low costs, or proximity to their most important customers. A multinational company may have several worldwide headquarters, depending on the locations of certain markets or technologies.

The role of multinational corporations in developing nations is a subject of controversy. Multinationals' ability to tap financial, physical, and human resources from all over the world and combine them economically and profitably can be of benefit to any country. They also often possess and can transfer the most up-to-date technology. Critics, however, claim that often the wrong kind of technology is transferred to developing nations. Usually, it is **capital intensive** (requiring a greater expenditure for equipment than for labour) and thus does not substantially increase employment. A *modern sector* then emerges in the nation, employing a small proportion of the labour force at relatively high productivity and income levels and with increasingly capital-intensive technologies. In addition, multinationals sometimes support reactionary and oppressive regimes if doing so is in the companies' best interests. Other critics say that the firms take more wealth out of developing nations than they bring in, thus widening the gap between rich and poor nations.

4-2a Global Marketing Standardization

Traditionally, marketing-oriented multinational corporations have used a strategy of providing different product features, packaging, advertising, and so on, in each country where they operate. McDonald's global success is—believe it or not—based on variation rather than standardization. McDonald's

CANADA'S TOP TEN COMPANIES BY REVENUE, 2012

Company	Revenue ($000)
Suncor Energy	38,788,000
Royal Bank of Canada	34,505,000
Power Corp. of Canada	33,027,000
George Weston Ltd.	32,873,000
Imperial Oil	31,189,000
Magna International	31,006,000
Toronto Dominion Bank	30,334,000
Great-West Lifeco	30,115,000
Manulife Financial	30,038,000
Onex Corp	27,511,000

The Canadian Press/Mario Beauregard

changes its salad dressings and provides self-serve espresso for French tastes, bulgogi burgers in South Korea, falafel burgers in Egypt, beer in Germany, and sake in Japan.

In contrast to the idea of tailoring marketing mixes to meet the needs and wants of consumers in different countries, **global marketing standardization** involves producing uniform products that can be sold in the same way all over the world. Communication and technology have made the world smaller so that almost all consumers everywhere want all the things they have heard about, seen, or experienced. Global marketing standardization presumes that the markets throughout the world are becoming more alike, so, by practising uniform production, companies should be able to lower production and marketing costs and increase profits.

Today, many multinational companies use a combination of global marketing standardization and variation. The idea is to determine which product modifications are necessary from country to country while trying to minimize those modifications. While Coca-Cola products are sold in over 160 countries, only three Coca-Cola brands are standardized, and one of them, Sprite, has a different formulation in Japan. Although McDonald's is often considered a good example of a company practising multidomestic standardization, as we just mentioned, it varies its menu for different markets.

Companies with separate subsidiaries in other countries can be said to operate using a multidomestic strategy. A multidomestic strategy occurs when multinational firms enable individual subsidiaries to compete independently in domestic markets. For example, Colgate-Palmolive markets Axion paste dishwashing detergent in developing countries, and La Croix detergent was custom created for the French market. Colgate also uses global standardization, as Colgate toothpaste is marketed the same way globally.

4-3 EXTERNAL ENVIRONMENT FACING GLOBAL MARKETERS

A global marketer or a firm considering global marketing must consider the external environment. Many of the same environmental factors that operate in the domestic market also exist internationally. These factors include culture, economic and technological development, political structure and actions, demographic makeup, and natural resources.

global marketing standardization production of uniform products that can be sold the same way all over the world

4-3a Culture

Central to any society is the common set of values shared by its citizens that determines what is socially acceptable. Culture underlies the family, the educational system, religion, and the social class system. The network of social organizations generates overlapping roles and status positions. These values and roles have a tremendous effect on people's preferences and thus on marketers' options. The sensitivity to a country's culture is critical to a success. Swedish furniture retailer IKEA recently opened its third store in Shanghai, China. Like other multinational retailers, IKEA is hoping to capitalize on the growing Chinese economy and it has done so like no other. IKEA found success in China because it understands the Chinese culture and has adapted its marketing strategy accordingly. IKEA stores show the furniture in small apartment-style displays like the tiny spaces most Chinese families live in. Further, IKEA encourages patrons to sit on the couches and stretch out on the beds in the showrooms. The Chinese customers want to experience true Western culture, and IKEA allows them to do so. The experience has gone so far that bathroom displays have Plexiglas over the toilets so that customers don't forget they are displays and use them.[6]

Language is another important aspect of culture. Marketers must take care in translating product names, slogans, instructions, and promotional messages so as not to convey the wrong meaning. Schweppes

REUTERS/Stringer

Sales success ABROAD *requires a* THOROUGH UNDERSTANDING *of the country's* CULTURE.

Jon Le-Bon/Shutterstock.com

Tonic Water's expansion into the Italian market was challenged because of a campaign that translated the name into "water from the toilet."[7] Free translation software, such as Google Translate, allows users to input text in one language and output in another language. But marketers must still take care!

Each country has its own customs and traditions that determine business practices and influence negotiations with foreign customers. In many countries, personal relationships are more important than financial considerations. Negotiations in Japan often include long evenings of dining, drinking, and entertaining; only after a close a personal relationship has been formed do business negotiations begin.

Making successful sales presentations abroad requires a thorough understanding of the country's culture. Germans, for example, don't like risk and need strong reassurance. A successful presentation to a German client must emphasize three points: (1) the bottom-line benefits, (2) strong service support, and (3) product guarantee. In southern Europe, it is an insult to show a price list. Without negotiating, you will not close the sale. Meanwhile, the English want plenty of documentation for product claims and are less likely to simply accept the word of the sales representative. Compared with managers in other countries, managers in Scandinavian and Dutch companies are more likely to approach business transactions as Canadian managers do.

4-3b Economic and Technological Development

A second major factor in the external environment facing the global marketer is the level of economic development in the countries where it operates. In general, complex and sophisticated industries are found in developed countries, and more basic industries are found in less developed nations. Average family incomes are higher in the more developed countries compared with those in the less developed markets. Larger incomes mean greater purchasing power and demand, not only for consumer goods and services but also for the machinery and workers required to produce consumer goods.

According to the World Bank, the average **gross national income (GNI) per capita** for the world in 2012 was US$10,012. GNI is a country's GDP together with its income received from other countries (mainly interest and dividends) less similar payments made to other countries. The 2012 GDI per capita of Canada was $50,970, just slightly ahead of the United States, which was $50,120. The country with the highest GDI per capita in 2012 was Bermuda at $106,920. Of course, there are many poor countries: Burundi, with a GNI per capita of $240; Ethiopia at $410; and Malawi at $320, for example.[8] GNI per capita is one measure of the ability of a country's citizens to buy various goods and services. A marketer with a global vision can use this data to aid in measuring market potential in countries around the globe.

Not only is per capita income a consideration when going abroad, but so is the cost of doing business in a country. Although it is not the same as the cost of doing business, we can gain insights into expenses by examining the cost of living in various cities. Tokyo is the most expensive place to live in the world. A cup of coffee costs $8.29 while a daily newspaper will set you back over $6.00. In addition to cost of living, one must also consider the personal safety of employees. N'Djamena, the capital and economic hub of the African nation Chad, is the world's eighth most expensive city, but it is also one fraught with violence, further adding to the cost of doing business.[9] Exhibit 4.1 lists the world's most expensive cities to live in.

4-3c The Global Economy

A global marketer today must be fully aware of the intertwined nature of the global economy. The U.S. housing market collapse and speculative financing led to a major global recession in 2008. As the world slowly pulled itself out of the recession, the 2012–2013

Exhibit 4.1
THE WORLD'S MOST EXPENSIVE PLACES TO LIVE IN 2012

City	Monthly Rent Luxury 2 Bedroom ($US)	Cup of Coffee ($US)	Daily Newspaper ($US)
Tokyo, Japan	$4,848	$8.29	$6.38
Luanda, Angola	$6,500	$3.90	$5.46
Osaka, Japan	$3,062	$7.02	$6.38
Moscow, Russia	$4,200	$8.37	$9.78
Geneva, Switzerland	$4,818	$6.57	$4.38
Zurich, Switzerland	$3,614	$6.02	$4.38
Singapore	$3,588	$5.18	$3.59
N'Djamena, Chad	N/A	$3.32	$6.85
Hong Kong	$7,092	$6.83	$3.52
Nagoya, Japan	$2,551	$6.38	$8.42

Source: Rajeshni Naidu-Ghelani, "The World's Most Expensive Places to Live 2012," CNBC, June 12, 2012, http://finance.yahoo.com/news/the-world-s-most-expensive-places-to-live-2012.html?page=all (Accessed August 2, 2014).

Canada and China have a strong trade relationship but a unique one in that is based more on imports versus exports. This situation is more typically seen between a poor developing country and a rich developed country. This flipped trade relationship is a result of Canada's strong resource wealth and China's strong manufacturing ability. Canada imports largely manufactured goods from China, while 25 percent of Canada's exports to China are mineral products.[11]

In a continued effort to diversify our trading partners, Canada is working to improve trade relations with the emerging markets, including the BRIC countries—Brazil, Russia, India, and China.

European economic crisis was being felt everywhere, stifling recovery. The world looks today to economies such as China, India, and Brazil to help jump-start economic growth. The lesson for the global marketer is clear: forecasting global demand and economic growth requires an understanding of what is happening economically in countries around the globe.

DOING BUSINESS IN CHINA AND INDIA

The two countries of growing interest to many multinationals are India and China because of their huge economic potential. They have some of the highest growth rates in the world and are emerging as megamarkets. China and India also have the world's largest populations, two of the world's largest geographic areas, greater linguistic and sociocultural diversity than any other country, and among the highest levels of income disparity in the world—some people are extremely poor whereas others are very rich. Given this scale and variety, there is no average Chinese or Indian customer.

Both India and China have exploded in spending power, particularly in the upper classes. By 2015, China will account for about 20 percent or US$27 billion of global luxury sales. While wealthy Chinese consumers will continue to account for luxury sales, the larger upper-middle class (76 million households by 2015) offer the greatest opportunity, as they demonstrate a desire to purchase luxury goods and services.[10]

4-3d Political Structure and Actions

Political structure is a third important variable facing global marketers. Government policies run the gamut from no private ownership and minimal individual freedom to little central government and maximum personal freedom. As rights of private property increase, government-owned industries and centralized planning tend to decrease. But rarely will a political environment be at one extreme or the other. More often, countries combine multiple elements into a unique political and economic identity. India, for instance, is a republic whose political ideology includes elements of socialism, monopoly capitalism, and competitive capitalism.

A recent World Bank study found that government regulations can have varying effects on different economic sectors, depending on the country's larger political orientation. Regulations can also be effective to varying degrees within a country, depending on the presence of special-interest groups. The conventional wisdom has been that countries with the fewest regulations tend to be most efficient; however, this argument has been increasingly questioned by the rapid rise of centrally planned economies, such as China.

LEGAL CONSIDERATIONS Closely related to and often intertwined with the political environment are legal considerations. Many of the following legal structures are designed to either encourage or limit trade:

» **TARIFF:** a tax levied on the goods entering a country.

» **QUOTA:** a limit on the amount of a specific product that can enter a country. Companies request quotas as a means of protection from foreign competition.

» **BOYCOTT:** the exclusion of all products from certain countries or companies. Governments use boycotts to exclude products from countries with which they have a political dispute.

» **EXCHANGE CONTROL:** a law compelling a company earning foreign exchange from its exports to sell it to a control agency, usually a central bank. A company wanting to buy goods abroad must first obtain foreign currency exchange from the control agency. For instance, Avon Products drastically cut back new production lines and products in the Philippines because exchange controls prevented the company from converting pesos to dollars to ship back to the home office. The pesos had to be used in the Philippines.

» **MARKET GROUPING** (*also known as a common trade alliance*): occurs when several countries agree to work together to form a common trade area that enhances trade opportunities.

» **TRADE AGREEMENT:** an agreement to stimulate international trade. Not all government efforts are meant to stifle imports or investment by foreign corporations. The Uruguay Round of trade negotiations is an example of an effort to encourage trade. The largest Latin American trade agreement is **Mercosur**, which includes Argentina, Bolivia, Brazil, Chile, Colombia, Ecuador, Paraguay, Peru, Uruguay, and most recently Venezuela. The elimination of most tariffs among the trading partners has resulted in trade revenues of over $16 billion annually. The economic boom created by Mercosur will undoubtedly cause other nations to seek trade agreements on their own or to enter Mercosur.

URUGUAY ROUND AND DOHA ROUND

The **Uruguay Round** is an agreement that has dramatically lowered trade barriers worldwide. Adopted in 1994, the agreement has been signed by 148 nations. It is the most ambitious global trade agreement ever negotiated. The agreement has reduced tariffs by one-third worldwide—a move that is expected to raise global income by $235 billion annually. Perhaps most notable is the recognition of new global realities. For the first time, an agreement covers services, intellectual property rights, and trade-related investment measures, such as exchange controls.

A NEW TRADE ORGANIZATION The **World Trade Organization (WTO)** replaced the old **General Agreement on Tariffs and Trade (GATT)**, which was created in 1948. The GATT contained extensive loopholes that enabled countries to avoid the trade-barrier reduction agreements—a situation similar to obeying the law only if you want to! Today, all WTO members must fully comply with all agreements under the Uruguay Round. The WTO also has an effective dispute settlement procedure with strict time limits to resolve disputes.

The trend toward globalization has resulted in the creation of additional agreements and organizations: the North American Free Trade Agreement, the Central America Free Trade Agreement, the European Union, the World Bank, the International Monetary Fund, and the G20, a group of the largest and fastest growing top 20 economies of the world.

NORTH AMERICAN FREE TRADE AGREEMENT

At the time it was instituted, the **North American Free Trade Agreement (NAFTA)** created the world's largest free trade zone. The agreement includes Canada, the United States, and Mexico, with a combined population of 360 million and a combined economy of $6 trillion. Canada, the largest U.S. trading partner, entered a free trade agreement with the United States in 1988, so the main impact of NAFTA was to open the Mexican market to Canadian and U.S. companies. When the treaty went into effect, it removed a web of Mexican licensing requirements, quotas, and tariffs that limited transactions in Canadian and U.S. goods and services.

The real question is whether NAFTA can continue to deliver rising prosperity in all three countries. Canada has certainly benefited from cheaper imports and more investment opportunities abroad.

Although Mexico has thrived under NAFTA, its advantage as a low-cost producer is being lost today to countries such as India and China. American and Canadian businesses complain that Mexico has a dysfunctional judicial system, unreliable power supplies, poor roads, high corporate tax rates, and unfriendly labour relations. These complaints have given companies pause when considering investing in Mexico. Mexico still has a lot to offer, but it must improve its infrastructure.

CANADA AND FREE TRADE AGREEMENTS

Apart from a free trade agreement with the United States and Mexico (NAFTA), Canada is continually improving its mutually beneficial trade relations with other countries. Canada has either signed free trade agreements (FTAs) or is in discussion with many countries worldwide in an effort to increase export/import opportunities.[12]

CANADA'S TOP TEN IMPORT MARKETS, 2013

Country	Import Value (in millions of dollars)
United States	247,824
China	52,731
Mexico	26,727
Germany	15,399
Japan	13,732
United Kingdom	8,433
South Korea	7,338
Italy (incl. Vatican City State)	5,816
France (incl. Monaco, French Antilles)	5,387
Taiwan	4,713

Industry Canada, Trade Data Online, 2009-2013, https://www.ic.gc.ca/app/scr/tdst/tdo/crtr.html?naArea
=9999&searchType=All&productType=NAICS&timePeriod=5%7CComplete+Years&reportType
=TI&toFromCountry=CDN&currency=CDN&countryList=TOP&grouped=GROUPED&runReport=true
(Accessed August 22, 2014). Reproduced with the permission of the Minister of Industry, 2014.

EUROPEAN UNION

One of the world's most important free trade zones is the **European Union (EU)**, which now encompasses most of Europe. More than a free trade zone it is also a political and economic community. It guarantees the freedom of movement of people, goods, services, and capital between member states. It also maintains a common trade policy with outside nations and a regional development policy. The EU represents member nations in the WTO. Recently the EU began moving into foreign policy.

The primary goal of the EU is to create a unified European market. Other goals include instituting a common foreign policy, security policy, and defence policy and a European citizenship, whereby any EU citizen can live, work, vote, and run for office anywhere in the member countries. The EU is creating standardized trade rules and coordinated health and safety standards. Duties, customs procedures, and taxes have been standardized. The standardized rules have helped to create an estimated 2.5 million jobs since 1993.

The European Union currently has 28 member states: Austria, Belgium, Bulgaria, Croatia, Cyrus, Czech Republic, Denmark, Estonia, Finland, France, Germany, Greece, Hungary, Ireland, Italy, Latvia, Lithuania, Luxembourg, Malta, the Netherlands, Poland, Portugal, Romania, Slovakia, Slovenia, Spain, Sweden, and the United Kingdom. There are six official candidate countries: Albania, Iceland, the Republic of Macedonia, Montenegro, Serbia, and Turkey. In addition, the Western Balkan countries of Bosnia-Herzegovina and Kosovo are officially recognized as potential candidates.

The financial crisis experienced in Greece in 2010–2011 demonstrated the challenges of a large currency union where member nations maintain responsibility for their own fiscal policies. Unable to devalue its currency to boost sales of products without injuring other member nations, Greece turned to member states for a bailout. Such situations continue to exist with other member nations as the European economic crisis continues.

The EU is the largest economy in the world, with a GDP of US$18 trillion and a population of over 500 million. The EU is an attractive market with huge purchasing power. But despite the objective of creating a unified European market, many regulations still are not standardized and with more than 15 different languages and individual national customs, Europe will always be far more diverse than North America, and product differences will continue. Marketers thus will not be able to produce a single European product for a generic European consumer.

An entirely different type of problem facing global marketers is the possibility of a protectionist movement by the EU against outsiders. For example, France has a strict quota on Japanese cars to protect French automakers Renault and Peugeot, which would be negatively affected if the quota did not exist.

World Bank an international bank that offers low-interest loans, advice, and information to developing nations

International Monetary Fund (IMF) an international organization that acts as a lender of last resort, providing loans to troubled nations, and also works to promote trade through financial cooperation

Group of Twenty (G20) a forum for international economic development that promotes discussion between industrial and emerging-market countries on key issues related to global economic stability

Despite the country's dire financial situation, Greeks are protesting the austerity measures imposed by the government. Cutbacks to health care in Greece are the largest seen across Europe, affecting huge portions of the population.

THE WORLD BANK AND INTERNATIONAL MONETARY FUND

Two international financial organizations are instrumental in fostering global trade. The **World Bank**, an international bank, offers low-interest loans to developing nations. Originally, the purpose of the loans was to help these nations build infrastructure, such as roads, power plants, schools, drainage projects, and hospitals. Now the World Bank offers loans to help developing nations relieve their debt burdens. To receive the loans, countries must pledge to lower trade barriers and aid private enterprise. In addition to making loans, the World Bank is a major source of advice and information for developing nations.

The **International Monetary Fund (IMF)** was founded in 1945, one year after the creation of the World Bank, to promote trade through financial cooperation and eliminate trade barriers in the process. The IMF makes short-term loans to member nations that are unable to meet their budgetary expenses. It also operates as a lender of last resort for troubled nations. In exchange for these emergency loans, IMF lenders frequently extract significant commitments from the borrowing nations to address the problems that led to the crises. These steps may include curtailing imports or even devaluing the currency.

The **Group of Twenty (G20)** finance ministers and central bank governors was established in 1999 to bring together industrialized and developing economies to discuss key issues in the global economy. The G20 is a forum for international economic development that promotes discussion between industrial and emerging-market countries on key issues related to global economic stability. By contributing to the strengthening of the international financial system, and providing opportunities for discussion on national policies, international cooperation, and international financial institutions, the G20 helps to support growth and development across the globe. The members of the G20 are shown in Exhibit 4.2.

4-3e Demographic Makeup

The three most densely populated nations in the world are China, India, and Indonesia. For marketers, though, that fact alone is not particularly useful; they also need to know whether the population is mostly urban or rural. Countries with a higher population living in urban settings represent more attractive markets. Just

Exhibit 4.2
MEMBERS OF THE G20

Argentina	European Union	Italy	Saudi Arabia
Australia	France	Japan	South Africa
Brazil	Germany	Mexico	Turkey
Canada	India	Republic of Korea	United Kingdom
China	Indonesia	Russia	United States

as important as population is personal income within a country.

Another key demographic consideration is age. A wide age gap separates the older populations of the industrialized countries from the vast working-age populations of developing countries. This gap has enormous implications for economies, businesses, and the competitiveness of individual countries. While Europe and Japan struggle with pension schemes and the rising cost of healthcare, China, Brazil, and Mexico reap the rewards of a demographic dividend: falling labour costs, a healthier and more educated population, and the entry of millions of women into the workforce. The demographic dividend is a gift of falling birthrates, which causes a temporary bulge in the number of working-age people. Population experts have estimated that one-third of East Asia's economic miracle can be attributed to a beneficial age structure. But the miracle occurred only because the governments had policies in place to educate the people, create jobs, and improve health.

4-3f Natural Resources

A final factor in the external environment that has become more evident in the past decade is the shortage of natural resources. Petroleum resources have created huge amounts of wealth for oil-producing countries, such as Norway, Saudi Arabia, and the United Arab Emirates, where both consumer and industrial markets have blossomed. On the flip side, industrial countries, such as Japan, the United States, Canada, and much of Western Europe, experienced an enormous transfer of wealth to the petroleum-rich nations.

Petroleum is not the only natural resource that affects international marketing. A warm climate and lack of water mean that many of Africa's countries will remain importers of foodstuffs. Vast differences in natural resources create international dependencies, huge shifts of wealth, inflation and recession, export opportunities for countries with abundant resources, and even a stimulus for military intervention.

4-4 GLOBAL MARKETING BY THE INDIVIDUAL FIRM

A company should consider entering the global marketplace only after its management has a solid grasp of the global environment. Companies decide to *go global* for a number of reasons. Perhaps the most important reason is to earn additional profits. Managers may feel that international sales will result in higher profit margins or more added-on profits. A second stimulus is that a firm may have a unique product or technological advantage not available to other international competitors. Such advantages should result in major business successes abroad. In other situations, management may have exclusive market information regarding foreign customers, marketplaces, or market situations not known to others. Although exclusivity can provide an initial motivation for international marketing, managers can expect that competitors will catch up with their firm's temporary information advantage. Finally, saturated domestic markets, excess capacity, and potential for economies of scale can also be motivators to go global. Economies of scale mean that average per-unit production costs fall as output is increased.

Many firms form multinational partnerships—called strategic alliances—to assist them in penetrating global markets (strategic alliances will be examined in Chapter 7). Five other methods of entering the global marketplace are, in order of risk, exporting, licensing and franchising, contract manufacturing, the joint venture, and direct investment (see Exhibit 4.3).

Exhibit 4.3

RISK LEVELS FOR FIVE METHODS OF ENTERING THE GLOBAL MARKETPLACE

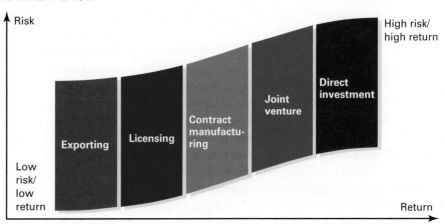

4-4a Exporting

When a company decides to enter the global market, exporting is usually the least complicated and least risky method of entry. **Exporting** is selling domestically produced products to buyers in another country. A company can sell directly to foreign importers or buyers. Exporting is not limited to huge corporations. Smaller Canadian companies have found many export market opportunities for their products and services. A successful Canadian export is icewine. Canada is renowned for our production of high quality icewine, because our climate is ideal for it, and in 2012 over $8.6 million worth of icewine was exported to China alone.[13] The United States is the world's largest exporter. Instead of selling directly to foreign buyers, a company may decide to sell to intermediaries located in its domestic market. The most common intermediary is the export merchant, also known as a **buyer for export**, which is usually treated as a domestic customer by the domestic manufacturer. The buyer for export assumes all risks and sells internationally for its own account. The domestic firm is involved only to the extent that its products are bought in foreign markets.

A second type of intermediary is the **export broker**, who plays the traditional broker's role by bringing buyer and seller together. The manufacturer still retains title and assumes all the risks. Export brokers operate primarily in agricultural products and raw materials.

Export agents, a third type of intermediary, are foreign sales agent-distributors who live in the foreign country and perform the same functions as domestic manufacturers' agents, helping with international financing, shipping, and so on. Export Development Canada provides help for Canadian firms seeking agents or distributors in almost every country. A second category of agents resides in the manufacturer's country but represents foreign buyers. This type of agent acts as a hired purchasing agent for foreign customers operating in the exporter's home market.

4-4b Licensing and Franchising

Another effective way for a firm to move into the global arena with relatively little risk is to sell a licence to manufacture its product to someone in a foreign country. As discussed earlier, RIM was initially willing to license its operating system to CIC as a way to enter the Chinese market. **Licensing** is the legal process whereby a licensor allows another firm to use its manufacturing process, trademarks, patents, trade secrets, or other proprietary knowledge. The licensee, in turn, pays the licensor a royalty or fee agreed on by both parties. Because licensing has many advantages, companies—both big and small—have eagerly embraced the concept.

A licensor must ensure it can exercise sufficient control over the licensee's activities to ensure proper quality, pricing, distribution, and so on. Licensing may also create a new competitor in the long run, if the licensee decides to void the licence agreement. International law is often ineffective in stopping such actions. Two common ways of maintaining effective control over licensees are shipping one or more critical components from Canada or registering patents and trademarks locally to the Canadian firm, not to the licensee. Garment companies maintain control by delivering only so many labels per day; they also supply their own fabric, collect the scraps, and complete accurate unit counts.

Franchising is a form of licensing that has grown rapidly in recent years. Over half of all international franchises are for fast-food restaurants and business services.

4-4c Contract Manufacturing

Firms that do not want to become involved in either licensing or global marketing may choose to engage in **contract manufacturing**, which is private-label manufacturing by a foreign company. The foreign company produces a certain volume of products to specification, with the domestic firm's brand name on the goods. The domestic company usually handles the marketing. Thus, the domestic firm can broaden its global marketing base without investing in overseas plants and equipment. After establishing a solid base, the domestic firm may switch to a joint venture or to direct investment. One company using contract manufacturing is Joe Fresh. To produce good-quality and fashionable garments, Joe Fresh

Yum! Brands' KFC fried-chicken chain has 3700 FRANCHISES IN CHINA, *including a location along the Great Wall.*

contracts production of the goods to factories overseas. The factory collapse in Bangladesh that killed over 300 people in spring 2013 is a poignant example of the risks associated with this retailer's desire for inexpensive production.

4-4d Joint Venture

Joint ventures are similar to licensing agreements. In an international joint venture, the domestic firm either buys part of a foreign company or joins with a foreign company to create a new entity. In 2007, Walmart established a joint venture partnership with Bharti to enter the India market. In October 2013, they announced they were ending their partnership and would now operate as separate businesses.[14] Clearly, the joint venture gave Walmart the much-needed expertise to enter this growing economy.

Joint ventures can be very risky. Many fail; others fall victim to a takeover, in which one partner buys out the other. Sometimes joint venture partners simply can't agree on management strategies and policies. When a joint venture is successful, however, both parties gain valuable skills from the alliance.

4-4e Direct Investment

Active ownership of a foreign company or of overseas manufacturing or marketing facilities is **direct foreign investment.** Direct investors have either a controlling interest or a large minority interest in the firm. Thus, they hold both the greatest potential reward and the greatest potential risk. Sometimes firms make direct investments because they can find no suitable local partners. Also, direct investments avoid the communication problems and conflicts of interest that can arise with joint ventures. Other firms simply don't want to share their technology, which they fear may be stolen or ultimately used against them by a newly created competitor. Toyota Manufacturing Corporation has invested heavily in the manufacturing of its automobiles here in Canada to take advantage of the quality manufacturing occurring in our auto sector.

A firm may make a direct foreign investment by acquiring an interest in an existing company or by building new facilities. It might do so because it has difficulty either transferring some resource to a foreign operation or sourcing that resource locally. One important resource is personnel, especially managers. If the local labour market is tight, the firm may buy an entire foreign firm and retain all its employees instead of paying higher salaries than competitors.

4-5 THE GLOBAL MARKETING MIX

To succeed, firms seeking to enter into foreign trade must adhere to the principles of the marketing mix. Information gathered on foreign markets through research is the basis for the four Ps of global marketing strategy: product, place (distribution), promotion, and price. Marketing managers who understand the advantages and disadvantages of different ways of entering the global market and the effect of the external environment on the firm's marketing mix have a better chance of reaching their goals.

Dick Loek/GetStock.com

Honda Canada's Alliston, Ontario, plant opened in 1986, making it the first plant built in Canada by a Japanese car manufacturer. Alliston now has two more Honda plants supplying cars and engines for Japan, the United States, South America, and other countries.

CANADA'S TOP FIVE EXPORTS, 2013 ($ BILLION)

1. Crude oil and crude bitumen	87.1
2. Motor vehicles for passenger transport (other than buses/public transport)	49.2
3. Gold	17
4. Liquefied petroleum gases	16.7
5. Coal	8.7

Source: Alex Brokaw, "Top 5 Exports: Canada," September 11, 2012, www.minyanville.com/business-news/the-economy/articles/canada-exports-crude-NXY-CNOOC-NXY/9/11/2012/id/43892?page=full (Accessed August 2, 2014).

The first step in creating a marketing mix is developing a thorough understanding of the global target market. Often this knowledge can be obtained through the same types of marketing research used in the domestic market (see Chapter 5). However, global marketing research is conducted in vastly different environments. Conducting a survey can be difficult in developing countries, where telephone ownership is growing but is not always common, and mail delivery is slow or sporadic. Drawing samples that are based on known population parameters is often difficult because of the lack of data. Moreover, the questions a marketer is able to ask may differ in other cultures. In some cultures, people tend to be more private than in Canada and will not respond to personal questions on surveys.

4-5a Product and Promotion

With the proper information, a good marketing mix can be developed. One important decision is whether to alter the product or the promotion for the global marketplace. Other options are to radically change the product or to adjust either the promotional message or the product to suit local conditions.

ONE PRODUCT, ONE MESSAGE The strategy of global marketing standardization, which was discussed earlier, means developing a single product for all markets and promoting it the same way throughout the world. Procter & Gamble uses the same product and promotional themes for Head & Shoulders in China as it does in North America. This advertising brings attention to a person's dandruff problem, which can be an issue in a nation of predominantly black-haired people. Head & Shoulders is one of the best-selling shampoos in China. Global

media—especially satellite and cable TV networks, such as CNN International, MTV Networks, and British Sky Broadcasting—make it possible to beam advertising to audiences unreachable a few years ago. Eighteen-year-olds in Paris often have more in common with 18-year-olds in Halifax than with their own parents. Almost all of MTV's advertisers run unified, English-language campaigns in the 28 nations the firm reaches. The audiences buy the same products, go to the same movies, listen to the same music, and sip the same colas. Global advertising merely works on that premise.

Unchanged products may fail simply because of cultural factors. Any type of war game tends to do very poorly in Germany, even though Germany is by far the world's biggest game-playing nation. A successful game in Germany has plenty of details and a thick rulebook.

© iStockphoto.com/emily2k

TEN BEST GLOBAL BRANDS, 2013

1. Apple
2. Google
3. Coca-Cola
4. IBM
5. Microsoft
6. GE
7. McDonald's
8. Samsung
9. Intel
10. Toyota

Source: Interbrand, "Best Global Brands, 2013," www.interbrand.com/en/best-global-brands/2013/Best-Global-Brands-2013-Brand-View.aspx (Accessed August 2, 2014). Interbrand's Best Global Brands 2013 report is a look at financial performance of the brand, role of brand in the purchase decision process and the brand strength. Go to www.bestglobalbrands.com for more information.

Despite cultural hurdles, numerous multinational firms are applying uniform branding to products around the world. Sometimes the desire for absolute standardization must also give way to practical considerations and local market dynamics. For example, the European version of Diet Coke is known as Coca-Cola Light, as Europeans use the word "light" to denote something low in calories. Sometimes, even if the brand name differs by market, managers can create a strong visual relationship by uniformly applying the brandmark and graphic elements on packaging.[15]

PRODUCT INVENTION In the context of global marketing, product invention can be taken to mean either creating a new product for a market or drastically changing an existing product. For example, to cater to the Japanese market, Nabisco had to remove the cream filling from its Oreo cookies because Japanese children thought the cookies were too sweet. Frito-Lay's most popular potato chip in Thailand is shrimp flavoured.

Consumers in different countries use products differently. For example, in many countries, clothing is worn much longer between washings than in Canada, so a more durable fabric must be produced and marketed. For the Peruvian market, Goodyear developed a tire that differs from its other tire lines; a higher percentage of natural rubber and better treads are needed to handle the tough Peruvian driving conditions.

PRODUCT ADAPTATION Another alternative for global marketers is to slightly alter a basic product to meet local conditions. McDonald's global success is built on this strategy.

Sometimes marketers can simply change the package size. In India, Unilever sells single-use sachets of Sunsilk shampoo for 2 to 4 cents. Unilever's Rexona brand deodorant sticks sell for 16 cents and up. On electronic products, power sources and voltage must be changed. It may be necessary, for example, to change the size and shape of the electrical plug.

MESSAGE ADAPTATION Another global marketing strategy is to maintain the same basic product but alter the promotional strategy. Bicycles are mainly pleasure vehicles in Canada. In many parts of the world, however, they are a family's main mode of transportation. Thus, promotion in these countries should stress durability and efficiency. In contrast, Canadian advertising may emphasize escaping and having fun.

Kit Kat bars are a hit the world over, but Nestlé didn't have much luck selling them in Japan—until it redesigned its message for the teen market. In Japan, the product's name is pronounced *kitto katsu*, which roughly translates to "I hope you win." Fuelling a rumour that Kit Kats bring success at crucial school exams, Nestlé rolled out packages combining the candy with other good-luck charms. Now 90 percent of Japanese school kids say they've heard of Kit Kat bars, and Kit Kat sales have soared 28 percent.[16]

Some cultures view a product as having less value if it has to be advertised. In other nations, claims that seem commonplace by Canadian standards may be viewed negatively or even not allowed. Germany does not permit advertisers to state that their products are the best or better than those of competitors, a description commonly used in Canadian advertising. The hard-sell tactics and sexual themes so common in Canadian advertising are taboo in many countries. Language barriers, translation problems, and cultural differences have generated numerous headaches for international marketing managers.

4-5b Place (Distribution)

Solving promotional and product problems does not guarantee global marketing success. The product still needs to be adequately distributed. Innovative distribution systems can create a competitive advantage for savvy companies. Planes taking tourists by day to Kenya's Nairobi Airport return to their European hubs by night crammed with an average 25 metric tons apiece of fresh beans, bok choy, okra, and other produce that was harvested and packaged just the day before.

In many developing nations, channels of distribution and the physical infrastructure are inadequate. Both inadequate and poorly maintained highways, distribution centres, and storage facilities mean that a significant portion of food products may spoil while being transported from the farm to the market, resulting in higher costs and shortages. A global marketer must consider the impact of such infrastructure issues on their strategy to ensure that they can be competitive.

4-5c Pricing

Once marketing managers have determined a global product and promotion strategy, they can select the remainder of the marketing mix. When creating a final price, exporters must not only cover their production costs but must also consider transportation costs, insurance, taxes, and tariffs. In addition, marketers must also determine what customers are willing to spend on a particular product and ensure that their foreign buyers will pay the price. Because developing nations lack mass purchasing power, selling to them often poses special pricing problems. Sometimes a product can be simplified to lower the price. The firm must not assume that low-income countries are willing to accept lower quality, however. Although the nomads of the Sahara are very poor, they still buy expensive fabrics to make their clothing. Their survival in harsh conditions and extreme temperatures requires this expense. Additionally, certain expensive luxury items can be sold almost anywhere.

4-5d Exchange Rates

The exchange rate is the price of one country's currency in terms of another country's currency. If a country's currency *appreciates*, less of that country's currency is needed to buy another country's currency. If a country's currency *depreciates*, more of that currency will be needed to buy another country's currency.

Appreciation and depreciation affect the prices of a country's goods. If the Canadian dollar depreciates relative to the Japanese yen, Canadian residents will need to pay more dollars to buy Japanese goods. To illustrate, suppose the dollar price of a yen is $0.012 and that a Toyota is priced at 2 million yen. At this exchange rate, a Canadian resident pays $24,000 for a Toyota ($0.012 × 2 million yen = $24,000). If the

dollar depreciates to $0.018 to 1 yen, however, the Canadian resident will have to pay $36,000 for the same Toyota.

As the dollar depreciates, the prices of Japanese goods rise for Canadian residents, so they buy fewer Japanese goods—thus, Canadian imports may decline. At the same time, as the dollar depreciates relative to the yen, the yen appreciates relative to the dollar. This means prices of Canadian goods fall for the Japanese, so they buy more Canadian goods—and Canadian exports rise.

Currency markets operate under a system of **floating exchange rates**. Prices of different currencies float up and down on the basis of the demand for and the supply of each currency. Global currency traders create the supply of and demand for a particular country's currency on the basis of that country's investment, trade potential, and economic strength.

DUMPING Dumping is generally considered to be the sale of an exported product at a price lower than that charged for the same or a like product in the home market of the exporter. This practice is regarded as a form of price discrimination that can potentially harm the importing nation's competing industries. Dumping may occur as a result of exporter business strategies that include (1) trying to increase an overseas market share, (2) temporarily distributing products in overseas markets to offset slack demand in the home market, (3) lowering unit costs by exploiting large-scale production, and (4) attempting to maintain stable prices during periods of exchange rate fluctuations.

Historically, the dumping of goods has presented serious problems in international trade. As a result, dumping has led to significant disagreements among countries and diverse views about its harmfulness. Some trade economists view dumping as harmful only when it involves the use of predatory practices that intentionally try to eliminate competition and gain monopoly power in a market. They believe that predatory dumping rarely occurs and that antidumping rules are a protectionist tool whose cost to consumers and import-using industries exceeds the benefits to the industries receiving protection.

Photodisc/Getty Images

countertrade a form of trade in which all or part of the payment for goods or services is in the form of other goods or services

At Zeniarai Benten shrine, south of Tokyo, worshippers visit a tiny cave where they stoop down and wash their coins and bills in trickling spring water. Cleanse your money here, the saying goes, and it will multiply. The practice is a telling sign of this nation's abhorrence of credit and firm belief in cold, hard cash.

Shizuo Kambayashi/Associated Press

COUNTERTRADE Global trade does not always involve cash. Countertrade is a fast-growing way to conduct global business. In **countertrade**, all or part of the payment for goods or services is in the form of other goods or services. Countertrade is thus a form of barter (swapping goods for goods), an age-old practice whose origins have been traced back to cave dwellers.

One common type of countertrade is straight barter. For example, PepsiCo sends Pepsi syrup to Russian bottling plants and in payment gets Stolichnaya vodka, which is then marketed in the West. Another form of countertrade is the compensation agreement. Typically, a company provides technology and equipment for a plant in a developing nation and agrees to take full or partial payment in goods produced by that plant.

4-6 THE IMPACT OF THE INTERNET

In many respects, "going global" is easier than it has ever been. Opening an e-commerce site on the Internet immediately puts a company in the international marketplace. Sophisticated language translation software can make any site accessible to people around the world. Global shippers, such as UPS, FedEx, and DHL, help solve international e-commerce distribution complexities. Currency conversion software allows companies to post prices in Canadian dollars, then ask their customers what currency they want to use for payment. But despite much advancement, the promises of borderless commerce and the global Internet economy are still being restrained by the old rules, regulations, and habits. For example, Canadians spend an average of $6500 per year by credit card, whereas Japanese spend less than $2000. Many Japanese don't even have a credit card, making it difficult to conduct regular business over the Internet.

4-6a Social Media and Global Marketing

Because Facebook, YouTube, and other social media are popular around the world, firms both large and small have embraced social media marketing. Tim Hortons has over 3000 stores worldwide. To engage its Facebook fans, the company will occasionally post a picture of one of its locations on Facebook and ask its 1.4 million Facebook fans to guess the location. Every time someone makes a guess, Tim Hortons posts a branded message to that fan's news feed. This helps to build awareness of Tim Hortons quickly and exponentially.

Blogs and other social media sites help global marketers gather consumer intelligence quickly to be in a position, on an ongoing basis, to alter and adapt their messages and strategies. Global marketers use social media not only for understanding consumers but also to build their brands as they expand internationally. Zara and Top Shop are two retailers that have entered the Canadian market in the past few years. Because of the power of the Internet, these brands were already well established among a core of Canadians within their target segment, thus leading to success in Canada. The Internet and social media bring every company from every corner of the world into consumers' homes. Even the smallest company today can be a global marketer!

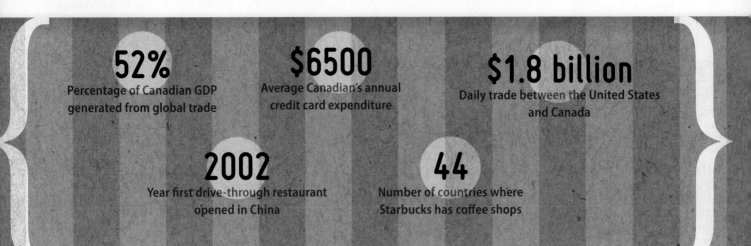

52%
Percentage of Canadian GDP
generated from global trade

$6500
Average Canadian's annual
credit card expenditure

$1.8 billion
Daily trade between the United States
and Canada

2002
Year first drive-through restaurant
opened in China

44
Number of countries where
Starbucks has coffee shops

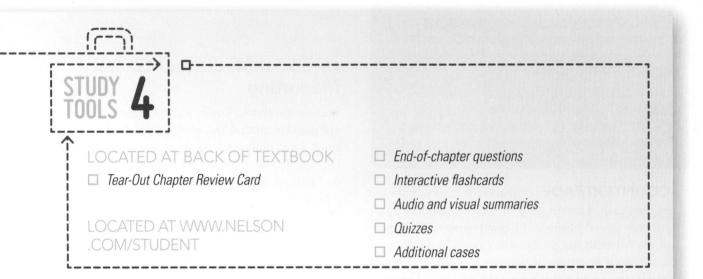

STUDY
TOOLS **4**

LOCATED AT BACK OF TEXTBOOK

☐ *Tear-Out Chapter Review Card*

LOCATED AT WWW.NELSON
.COM/STUDENT

☐ *End-of-chapter questions*

☐ *Interactive flashcards*

☐ *Audio and visual summaries*

☐ *Quizzes*

☐ *Additional cases*

Marketing—Let's Get Started
Part 1 Case

Jammit: Music Lessons at Your Fingertips!

Courtesy of Jammit, Inc. The Jammit trademark and brand are the property of Jammit, Inc.

"I think it very unlikely that I would have ever become President had I not been involved in school music from the time I was 9 until I was 17. It taught me discipline and creativity. It made me see the world in different ways. It made me understand things in different ways."[1]

"I grew up in the northside of Dublin in the beleaguered sixties and seventies—music meant everything to me.... Music is another language in which to express yourself. The feeling from music is liberating. It's the most liberating language of all."[2]

The above quotes from President Bill Clinton and Bono, respectively, demonstrate the belief held by even the most powerful and influential of people that music and music education play a critical role in personal development. Growing evidence suggests that exposure to music contributes to the development of such skills as critical thinking, spatial reasoning, and cognitive development. Further, studies increasingly show that music enhances an individual's social capacity. So it stands to reason, then, that an investment in arts and culture is an investment in a community's economy.

The arts and culture industry in Canada contributes $46 billion to the economy, and it provides more than 600,000 jobs. The arts and culture industry is three times the size of the insurance industry in Canada and twice the size of the forest industry. The music industry is one segment in the arts and culture sector. A study commissioned by Music Canada in 2012 revealed that together independent and major music companies exceeded $398 million in investments and expenditures in Canada. This financial investment resulted in a contribution to Canada's GDP of almost $240 million. Even more startling was the fact that these music companies created more than 4100 jobs, paid out $178 million in wages, and generated almost $44 million in tax revenues.[3]

Canadians love to listen to music. Canada is the seventh-largest music market in the world. Consumption of music and investment in arts and culture is not restricted to individuals for their personal enjoyment. Companies are investing in the arts and culture through sponsorships of events and through investment in music and cultural activities in the workplace as they attempt to create environments that enhance creativity. Communities are investing in cultural product offerings to attract and keep residents.

The Canadian music scene has been dramatically affected by the digitization of music. Downloads continue to dominate, with digital sales growing from just under $60 million in 2007 to just more than $192 million in 2012.[4] Despite the popularity of digital downloads, Canadians continue to attend live performances by their favourite musicians.

Despite the growing evidence in support of the value of an investment in music and the arts to the economic prosperity of a country, investment in music education within the school system in Canada continues to erode. Funding to support music programs in both primary and secondary schools has been cut. Often the music teacher has no music specialist training. These cuts are happening despite much scientific research that shows that exposure to music and music training has a positive impact on children's brains. Studies conducted by Dr. Laurel Trainor, professor of psychology, neuroscience, and behaviour at McMaster University and the director of the McMaster Institute for Music and the Mind, have revealed that young children who take music lessons show different patterns of development and improved memory over those who have not been exposed to music training. Children who take music lessons, whether privately or within the school system, have been found to perform better in a memory test that is correlated with general intelligence skills.[5] An investment in music education, then, is an investment in the creation of a highly skilled workforce.

So, an investment in music education positively influences a child's memory and general intelligence. Music and the arts are an essential economic driver for a community and for the country as a whole. Canadians have embraced the digitization of music but still want to see their favourite musicians live. Can this knowledge be turned into a product?

Introducing Jammit.

In 2012, the Jammit app (available for iOS and Mac and Windows desktops) was launched as a tool for aspiring musicians at all levels to learn, jam, and record their favourite songs. Jammit is the first music software that isolates individual audio tracks from the original multitrack masters of many musicians. The Jammit repertoire of popular music spans the decades from the 1980s to the present. With the Jammit app, each guitar, bass, drum, keyboard, or vocal track within the dense mix of a song can be isolated so that an aspiring musician can learn it. Each isolated track can be looped for repetitive practice

or slowed down for beginners, all without affecting the pitch. The software provides note-for-note and accurate transcriptions of the sheet music. So if you are an aspiring guitar player who would like to play bass for Maroon 5 or a drummer dreaming of playing percussion with Rush, you can live the dream and start jamming as soon as you download the app. Nothing outside of a live concert can get you this close to your favourite musician!

The Jammit app is free to download, and the fee to download any of more than 1000 songs within the Jammit music library is from $2 to $6 per song. The songs are created from the original multitrack master tapes that have individual control over each instrument. The Jammit software gives the user control over the instrument in the mix that they want to isolate to learn to play. Because the Jammit engineers format the content by using the original master recordings, the play-along experience is awesome.[6] Each song in the library is licensed from the rights holders, and everyone is paid accordingly.

Is the Jammit app satisfying a need? We all know learning music is tough. Music education is declining in the school system, and not everyone can afford private lessons. Jammit affordably teaches by allowing the learner to isolate their instrument of choice within a song, and then slow the track down, loop to repeat, or play along with highly talented musicians. Language is learned by hearing and repeating, and learning to play an instrument can happen this way as well. With the extensive and constantly growing library on Jammit, musicians can even play outside their comfort zone and try some jazz even though rock may be their genre of choice.

By offering sheet music in standard notation, Jammit provides an additional interactive learning opportunity. If learners want, they can view the sheet music for the song they are learning. As each note is played, it's highlighted on the staff, offering learners the opportunity to enhance their skill at reading sheet music. For aspiring musicians, the ability to read sheet music is key to success.

An additional feature offered by Jammit is video sharing. Learners can videotape themselves performing and then upload the performance to YouTube for the world to see and critique—performing for the world is a great motivator for improvement. Of course, learners can also upload video for their teachers; Jammit then can act as a conduit for a remote music lesson.[7]

Jammit's target market is aspiring and established musicians, vocalists, music educators, bands, glee clubs, choral groups, singers, and music enthusiasts. Jammit is continually updating its playlist and keeps its users informed through a newsletter and a website.

In the high-tech world in which Jammit competes, innovation is the key to longevity. Many music apps offer the educational aid that Jammit offers, so competition is intense. Jammit's need for constant innovation strains finances but is necessary to remain relevant.

Should Jammit innovate to reach a new target market? Should Jammit extend its line to enhance the product's life cycle? How much should Jammit emphasize the learning tool concept in its positioning? These are just three of the many questions to think about as you strive to ensure that Jammit continues to grow in the highly competitive music app business.

QUESTIONS

1. With information provided in the case and additional reading of resources, such as The Next Big Bang by Music Canada (http://musiccanada.com/resources/research/the-next-big-bang/), complete an external environmental scan of the arts and culture and music industry in Canada.

2. Complete a SWOT analysis for Jammit.

3. Having completed an environmental scan and a SWOT analysis, explain Jammit's competitive advantage.

4. Using the Ansoff strategic opportunity matrix, provide Jammit with some strategic alternatives to address their need to continue to grow in the highly competitive music app business.

Chapter **5** **Marketing Research**

© iStockphoto.com/kasayizg

> "Research is what I'm doing when I don't know what I'm doing."
>
> —Werner von Braun (rocket scientist)

After you finish this chapter, go to www.nelson.com/student *for* **STUDY TOOLS.** 💼------->

5-1 THE ROLE OF MARKETING RESEARCH

Marketing research is about gathering information about customers, their needs, and the marketplace in which they operate. The challenge can be great, as that marketplace is constantly changing, and customers are not always clear (whether intentionally or not) about what their needs are or how they would like them satisfied.

Marketing research is about bringing clarity to unknown aspects of a marketplace. It should not be used simply to try to reinforce a belief, but rather as a means to better understand the connections between marketing actions and customer needs. As famed advertising executive David Ogilvy once said, "Some people use research like a drunkard uses a lamppost: for support, not illumination."[1]

Marketing research is a process, like any other type of research. There is an unknown element—a problem—that needs to be investigated. Investigating the problem requires a plan. There are tools to use to assess the problem and seek out potential solutions—but instead of beakers and lab equipment, marketers use surveys and focus groups. Once those tools have been used to gather data, the data are then processed into information to help solve the problem.

An important note about marketing research is that despite the methodical process, it does not solve the problem on its own. Marketing research is used to help make decisions; it is not the only basis for a decision. It is invaluable in helping companies better understand their customers, the marketplace, and the inherent challenges of meeting customer needs.

How can marketing research information be used to help make decisions? There are three functional roles that marketing research can play in an organization:

1. *Descriptive role*—presenting factual statements. For example, What are the historic sales trends in the industry? What are consumers' attitudes toward a product and its advertising?

marketing research the process of planning, collecting, and analyzing data relevant to a marketing decision

MARKET RESEARCH IN CANADA

The Canadian marketing research industry includes many innovative and leading organizations that are at the fore of industry thought and development. The Marketing Research and Intelligence Association (MRIA) is a nonprofit group that has many of those aforementioned firms as members. The MRIA holds conferences, supports a designation for marketing research professionals, publishes journals and other publications (see *Vue* magazine picture below), and provides overall support for the industry. There are local chapters throughout Canada where industry professionals, academics, and students can meet to learn more about marketing research in Canada. In the statistics at the end of this chapter, you'll see how much it costs for a student

vue
the magazine of the
Marketing Research
and Intelligence
Association

THE BLOG:
INSIDE

to become connected to the marketing research industry in Canada. There are many job opportunities in marketing research, and many leading-edge companies (like Environics and Ipsos) have career opportunities for students who are engaged in and connected to their industry.

---

2. *Diagnostic role*—explaining relationships within data. For example, What is the impact on a product's sales if the colour of the packaging is changed?

3. *Predictive role*—predicting results of a marketing decision (what if?). For example, What is the impact of a new product introduction on market share?

A good marketing research program will attempt to balance these three roles and provide the best information related to the problem.

The best way to understand the role of marketing research is to see it as an overarching activity that supports the many marketing activities of a firm. The American Marketing Association has used the same definition for marketing research for a decade: "Marketing research is the function that links the consumer, customer, and public to the marketer through information—information used to identify and define marketing opportunities and problems; generate, refine, and evaluate marketing actions; monitor marketing performance; and improve understanding of marketing as a process."[2]

This definition shows the impact that marketing research can have when done properly. To conduct marketing research properly, you must understand the process behind it.

5-2 THE MARKETING RESEARCH PROCESS

The marketing research process is a scientific approach to decision-making that maximizes the chance of receiving accurate and meaningful results. Exhibit 5.1

traces the six steps in the research process and provides the basis from which marketing research is undertaken.

5-2a Step 1: Identify the Problem

Identifying the problem is the most important stage of the entire marketing research process. Without a defined problem statement, marketing research will be nothing more than a series of tasks without direction or purpose. This first stage is best explained by a phrase used in information technology: "garbage in, garbage out"; the integrity of the output (results) is dependent on the integrity of the input (the problem).

This means that a researcher should first determine whether there is enough information to clearly define a problem before embarking on the full marketing research process. Decision makers must be able to diagnose the right situation for conducting marketing research. We'll discuss this further in the section

Exhibit 5.1
THE MARKETING RESEARCH PROCESS

1 Identify the problem.

2 Design the research.

3 Collect the data.

4 Analyze the data.

5 Present the report.

6 Provide follow-up.

titled When to Conduct Marketing Research later in the chapter.

The first task in this step is to differentiate between a management decision and a research problem. A management decision is often a big-picture dilemma facing a marketing manager—in other words, what do they need to *do*? A research problem is a statement that identifies what information is to be gathered—in other words, what do they need to *know*? Consider these examples:

» **MANAGEMENT DECISION:** What should be done about a restaurant's slow sales?

» **RESEARCH PROBLEM:** What factors go into a customer's decision to dine at a particular restaurant?

Once this difference has been established, a market researcher can then move forward to create the marketing research objective. A **marketing research objective** is developed to provide insightful decision-making information. It is the specific information needed to solve a marketing research issue. Managers must combine this information with their own experience and other information to make a proper decision.

Marketing research objectives are developed as a series of questions that seek to clarify what decision makers needed to know to make a marketing decision. If the research problem focuses on factors that determine how a customer chooses a restaurant, then some key questions to ask are the following:

» What is the demographic profile of the restaurant's patrons?

» What external factors (time, expense) are influencing the public's willingness to dine out?

» How important is branding to diners in the restaurant industry?

Once these objectives have been created, researchers can then determine the overall approach necessary to meet the research objectives and answer the research question. Marketing research objectives must consider the internal and external environments to ensure that a well-informed decision can be made.

5-2b Step 2: Design the Research

The **research design** specifies how to go about answering the questions and achieving the objectives. This stage is about deciding on the type of study that will be conducted and the tools and techniques that will be used to gather and analyze the collected data. The research design is about creating a roadmap for the research process.

TYPES OF RESEARCH DESIGN To gather the necessary information to answer the research question, a researcher must decide on the type of research design to use. There are two types of research design: exploratory and conclusive.

Exploratory research is done to help explore the problem further, looking for a context in which the research will be conducted. Because the parameters of exploratory research are not always clearly defined, researchers have more flexibility in how the research is conducted. This is a process of informal discovery, where looking for key relationships and variables is more important than making an attempt to solve a research problem. There are a number of different methods of exploratory research: focus groups, expert interviews, literature search, and case studies. Exploratory research uses both secondary research (often in the form of a literature review) and primary research methods.

Conclusive research is, as its name suggests, more focused on developing conclusions and courses of actions. Often conclusive research can help to verify the insights provided by exploratory research—findings from exploratory methods (e.g., focus groups) can help develop conclusive methods (e.g., surveys). Descriptive research uses exclusively primary research methods.

There are two kinds of conclusive research: descriptive and causal. **Descriptive research**, by far the more common type of conclusive research used in business, attempts to describe marketing phenomena and characteristics. **Causal research** focuses on the cause and effect of two variables and attempts to find some correlation between them. This type of conclusive research is used often in academic and research environments.

THE RESEARCH DESIGN PROCESS In deciding on a research design, it should be noted that this is not an "either-or" situation where only one type of research design can be chosen. The best way to consider research design is as a process, described

marketing research objective specific statement about the information needed to solve the research question

research design a plan that specifies how to answer the research question and achieve the research objectives by laying out the research tools and techniques necessary to collect and analyze data

exploratory research an informal discovery process that attempts to gain insights and a better understanding of the management and research problems

conclusive research a more specific type of research that attempts to provide clarity to a decision maker by identifying specific courses of action

descriptive research a type of conclusive research that attempts to describe marketing phenomena and characteristics

causal research a type of conclusive research that focuses on the cause and effect of two variables and attempts to find some correlation between them

in Exhibit 5.2. Researchers should use exploratory research to provide clarity and structure to the problem while also examining if there are existing studies that might help in identifying key variables. Then the researcher can choose, depending on the results of exploratory research, which type of conclusive research (descriptive or causal) will best solve the research problem.

Often researchers will first attempt to solve the problem by using descriptive research methods like surveys. However if there are still outstanding issues or the problem was not solved with descriptive research, then causal research would be used.

5-2c Step 3: Collect the Data

Now that the research design has been chosen, it is time to collect the data by using that design. An important early decision at this stage of the process is what mix of secondary and primary research will be used.

SECONDARY VERSUS PRIMARY RESEARCH The temptation for researchers is to begin collecting their own data to answer their research question. But it is vital that there be an examination of what data already exists.

Secondary data is data that already has been collected by another entity (government, industry association, company). The key thing to remember is that secondary research was collected for another purpose, meaning that it will be very unlikely that secondary data on its

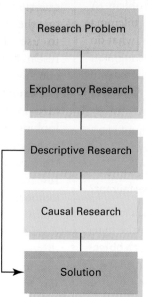

Exhibit 5.2
THE RESEARCH DESIGN PROCESS

Research Problem

Exploratory Research

Descriptive Research

Causal Research

Solution

dcwcreations/Shutterstock.com

own will answer your research question. There are exceptions to every rule, however, as you can see by reading the following example about Campbell's Soup.

Campbell used U.S. government data on nutritional and eating habits and created the famous "Soup is Good Food" campaign. Little else was done in the way of primary research, and the campaign became synonymous with Campbell's Soup for decades.

Much has changed today, however, with Campbell's approach to marketing research. The company recently completed two years of primary research into studying how skin moisture and heart rate change when consumers look at pictures of soup and logo designs. The results of this biometrics research: bigger and clearer pictures of steaming soup and fewer spoons on the packaging of Campbell's Soup products.[3]

Primary research is research that is new and created by the researcher. A number of techniques can be used to generate primary data, all of which can be tailored to meet the specific research needs of an organization. While this research is more expensive and time-consuming than secondary research, it has the distinct advantage of achieving the research objectives specified in step 1 of the research process.

Researchers have to balance the positives and negatives of both secondary and primary research when collecting data:

Advantages of Secondary Data	Disadvantages of Secondary Data
Inexpensive	Collected for another purpose
Clarifies problem	Questionable sources
Fast to collect	Quickly outdated
Advantages of Primary Data	**Disadvantages of Primary Data**
Focuses on solving a specific problem	Expensive
Sources are known	Time-consuming
Results more accurate	Requires specific skills sets

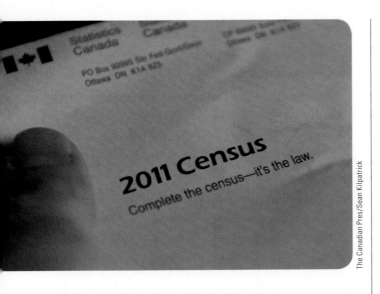

The Canadian Press/Sean Kilpatrick

SECONDARY DATA COLLECTION There are two main sources of secondary data: sources inside the organization conducting the research and external sources that are publicly available, sometimes at a price.

Secondary information originating from within the company includes documents such as annual reports, reports to shareholders, product-testing results (perhaps made available to the news media), the company's own marketing data, and house periodicals prepared by the company for communication to employees, customers, or others. Often this information is incorporated into a company's internal database.

Innumerable outside sources of secondary information also exist. These are principally business data summaries prepared by government departments and agencies (federal, provincial or territorial, and local), such as Statistics Canada. Still more data are available from online journals and research studies available from research and marketing associations, such as the Marketing Research and Intelligence Association (MRIA) and the Canadian Institute of Marketing (CIM).

Trade and industry associations also publish secondary data that can be found in business periodicals and other news media that regularly publish studies and articles on the economy, specific industries, and even individual companies. The unpublished summarized secondary information from these sources includes internal reports, memos, or special-purpose analyses with limited circulation. Economic considerations or priorities in the organization may preclude publication of these summaries. In addition, information on many topics, such as a Nielsen PRIZM segmentation, industry trends, and brands, can be derived from polls, focus groups, surveys, panels, and interviews and is available from such companies as Environics Research Group and other sources online.

Secondary data save time and money if they help solve the researcher's problem. Even if the problem is not solved, secondary data have other advantages. They can aid in formulating a clear research problem and can lead researchers to potential research methods and other types of data needed for solving the problem. In addition, secondary data can pinpoint the kinds of people to approach and their locations, and can serve as a basis of comparison for other data.

The disadvantages of secondary data stem mainly from a mismatch between the researcher's unique problem and the purpose for which the secondary data were originally gathered. For example, a company wanted to determine the market potential for a fireplace log made of coal rather than compressed wood by-products. The researcher found plenty of secondary data on total wood consumed as fuel, quantities consumed in each province and territory, and types of wood burned. Secondary data were also available on consumer attitudes and purchase patterns of wood by-product fireplace logs. The wealth of secondary data provided the researcher with many insights into the artificial-log market. Yet the researchers could not

THE CANADIAN LANDSCAPE OF MARKETING RESEARCH

There are numerous successful and well-known Canadian firms in the field of marketing research. These firms have developed areas of expertise around a successful product or approach to marketing research in Canada: Environics has created 66 lifestyle segments of Canadians called PRIZM C2, Ipsos Canada is known for public opinion polls on public and private affairs, and Leger, The Research Intelligence Group is a Montréal-based marketing research firm that has the inside track on understanding the Québec marketplace.

primary data information that is collected for the first time and is used for solving the particular problem under investigation

Secondary data SAVE TIME AND MONEY *if they help to clarify the researcher's problem.*

locate information on whether consumers would buy artificial logs made of coal.

The quality of secondary data may also pose a problem. Secondary data sources do not often give detailed information that would enable a researcher to assess the data's quality or relevance. Whenever possible, a researcher needs to address these important questions: Who gathered the data? Why were the data obtained? What methodology was used? How were classifications (such as heavy users versus light users) developed and defined? When was the information gathered?

PRIMARY DATA COLLECTION Primary data,
or information collected for the first time, is used for solving the particular issue under investigation. The main advantage of primary data is that they will answer a specific research question that secondary data cannot answer. For example, suppose Pillsbury has two new recipes for refrigerated dough for sugar cookies. Which one will consumers like better? Secondary data will not help answer this question. Instead, targeted consumers must try each recipe and evaluate the taste, texture, and appearance of each cookie.

Moreover, primary data are current and researchers know the source. Sometimes researchers gather the data themselves rather than assigning projects to outside companies. Researchers also specify the methodology of the research. Secrecy can be maintained because the information is proprietary. In contrast, much secondary data is available to all interested parties either for free or for relatively small fees.

Gathering primary data is expensive; costs can range from a few hundred dollars for a limited exploratory study comprising a few focus groups to several million for a nationwide survey research study. Because primary data gathering is so expensive, firms may reduce the number of in-person interviews they conduct and use an online study instead. Larger companies that conduct many research projects might use another cost-saving technique. They *piggyback* studies, or gather data on two different projects by using one questionnaire.

Nevertheless, the disadvantages of primary data gathering are usually offset by the advantages. Gathering primary data is often the only way of helping to solve a research problem. Because of the variety of

THE NEW SOURCE OF SECONDARY DATA: ONLINE

Secondary data research in the past was problematic, with more time spent waiting for data than wading through data. Researchers often had to write to government agencies, trade associations, or other secondary data providers and then wait days or weeks for a reply that might never come. Often, one or more trips to the library were required, and the researcher might find that needed reports were signed out or missing.

Now, however, the rapid development of online secondary data resources has eliminated much of

the drudgery associated with the collection of secondary data. However, a key problem remains: source accuracy.

Students often turn to Google or other search engines as a starting point for secondary research. This can lead them to websites and sources that may or may not be appropriate for a school report. If you would like to start a lively debate in your class about secondary sourcing, just mention Wikipedia!

A good rule of thumb for testing the accuracy of online sources is: **CARS**. This acronym stands for *credibility* (author's credentials), *accuracy* (timeliness), *reasonableness* (balanced and objective argument), and *support* (corroboration of findings).

Source: Robert Harris, "Evaluating Internet Research Sources," Virtual Salt, December 27, 2013, www.virtualsalt.com/evalu8it.htm (accessed August 2, 2014).

techniques now available for research, including surveys, observations, and experiments, primary research can address almost any marketing question.

QUALITATIVE AND QUANTITATIVE RESEARCH

Primary research is collected through either qualitative or quantitative research methods. (See Exhibit 5.3.) Qualitative research is best used when a researcher still needs to clear up aspects of the research problem or requires a better understanding of a research situation. Quantitative research methods are best used when a researcher wants specific numbers and the ability to analyze the data to provide statistical conclusions.

The difference between qualitative and quantitative research methods brings us back to research design (step 2) and the three types of design: exploratory, descriptive, and causal. Exploratory research includes the collection of secondary data and qualitative data collection. Descriptive research seeks to describe phenomena that are observed and collected. Causal research looks for relationships and interactions between variables that are identified before research begins. Both descriptive and causal research are

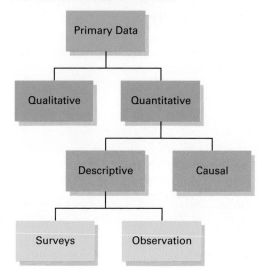

included under quantitative data collection.

QUALITATIVE DATA COLLECTION METHODS

DEPTH INTERVIEWS A **depth interview** involves interviewing people one on one, at their offices or homes, concerning products or services, a process that is very costly. First, individuals must be identified and located, which can be expensive and time-consuming. Once a qualified person is located, the next step is to get that person to agree to be interviewed and to set a time for the interview.

An interviewer must take the time to set up interviews and arrange to have the discussion taped and transcribed. This type of survey requires the very best interviewers because they are frequently conducting interviews on topics that they may not know much about.

FOCUS GROUPS A **focus group** is a small group of recruited participants engaged in a nonstructured discussion in a casual environment. Often recruited by random telephone screening, a small group of individuals possessing desired characteristics form a focus group. These qualified consumers are usually offered a monetary incentive to participate in a group discussion. Compensation can range from around $20 for groups recruited from the general public, to several

© iStockphoto.com/todd olson

depth interview an interview that involves a discussion between a well-trained researcher and a respondent who is asked about attitudes and perspectives on a topic

focus group a small group of recruited participants engaged in a nonstructured discussion in a casual environment

Exhibit 5.3
TYPES OF PRIMARY DATA

- Primary Data
  - Qualitative
  - Quantitative
    - Descriptive
      - Surveys
      - Observation
    - Causal

© McClatchy-Tribune Information Services/Alamy

hundred dollars for participants in more exclusive groups (e.g., senior executives).

The meeting place is usually a room that resembles a typical business meeting room with a large conference table in the centre. The room is equipped with audio and video taping capabilities (which the participants are aware of). One wall of the focus group room has a one-way mirror that allows the client to view the proceedings. A moderator sits at the head of table and leads the discussion with the participants.

The discussion is guided and directed by the moderator, who uses a moderator's guide (a series of questions developed by the researchers) to discuss a variety of topics in an open discussion. Focus groups can be used to gauge consumer response to a product or promotion and are occasionally used to brainstorm new product ideas or to screen concepts for new products.

Focus groups are a popular technique with companies, as the format and discussion are often engaging and entertaining for clients watching the proceedings from behind the one-way mirror. But focus groups should never be confused with quantitative data collection methods like surveys. The unstructured nature of focus group discussions allows for very few conclusive statements. The opinions, no matter how passionately presented in a focus group session, are still those of only a handful of people.

QUANTITATIVE DATA COLLECTION METHODS

SURVEY RESEARCH The most popular descriptive technique for gathering primary data is **survey research**, in which a researcher interacts with people to obtain facts, opinions, and attitudes. Exhibit 5.4 summarizes the characteristics of traditional forms of survey research.

IN-HOME PERSONAL INTERVIEWS Although in-home personal interviews often provide high-quality information, they tend to be very expensive because of the interviewers' travel time and costs. Therefore, in-home personal interviews are rapidly disappearing from North American and European researchers' survey toolboxes. This method is, however, still popular in many countries around the globe.

MALL INTERCEPT INTERVIEWS The **mall intercept interview** is conducted in the common area of a shopping mall or in a market research office within the mall. To conduct this type of interview, the research firm rents office space in the mall or pays

Exhibit 5.4

CHARACTERISTICS OF TRADITIONAL FORMS OF SURVEY RESEARCH

Characteristic	In-Home Personal Interviews	Mall Intercept Interviews	Central-Location Telephone Interviews	Self-Administered and One-Time Mail Surveys	Mail Panel Surveys
Cost	High	Moderate	Moderate	Low	Moderate
Time span	Moderate	Moderate	Fast	Slow	Relatively slow
Use of interviewer probes	Yes	Yes	Yes	No	Yes
Ability to show concepts to respondent	Yes (also taste tests)	Yes (also taste tests)	No	Yes	Yes
Management control over interviewer	Low	Moderate	High	n/a	n/a
General data quality	High	Moderate	High to moderate	Moderate to low	Moderate
Ability to collect large amounts of data	High	Moderate	Moderate to low	Low to moderate	Moderate
Ability to handle complex questionnaires	High	Moderate	High, if computer-aided	Low	Low

a significant daily fee. One drawback is that it is difficult to get a representative sample of the population, as not every consumer type comes to the mall at the same time, and many shoppers are often in a hurry, making them reluctant to participate in a survey. One advantage is the ability of the interviewer to probe when necessary—a technique used to clarify a person's response and ask for more detailed information.

Mall intercept interviews must be brief. Only the shortest interviews are conducted while respondents are standing. Usually, researchers invite respondents to their office for interviews, which are generally less than 15 minutes long. The overall quality of mall intercept interviews is about the same as that of telephone interviews.

Increasingly, marketing researchers are applying computer technology in mall interviewing. One technique that uses this is **computer-assisted personal interviewing**. The researcher conducts in-person interviews, reads questions to the respondent from a computer screen, and directly keys the respondent's answers into the computer. A second approach is **computer-assisted self-interviewing**. A mall interviewer intercepts and directs willing respondents to nearby computers. Each respondent reads questions from a computer screen or iPad and directly keys his or her answers into a computer. The third use of technology is fully automated self-interviewing. Respondents are guided by interviewers or independently approach a centrally located computer station or kiosk, read the questions from a screen, and directly key their answers into the station's computer.

TELEPHONE INTERVIEWS Telephone interviews cost less than personal interviews, but the cost is rapidly increasing because of respondents' refusals to participate. Most telephone interviewing is conducted from a specially designed phone room called a **central-location telephone (CLT) facility**. A phone room has many phone lines, individual interviewing stations, and may include monitoring equipment and headsets. The research firm typically will interview people nationwide from a single location. The Canadian National Do Not Call List (Bill C-37) does not apply to survey research.

Most CLT facilities offer computer-assisted interviewing. The interviewer reads the questions from a computer screen and enters the respondent's data directly into the computer, saving time. Hallmark Cards found that interviewers could administer a printed questionnaire for its Shoebox Greeting cards in 28 minutes. The same questionnaire administered with computer assistance took only 18 minutes. The researcher can stop the survey at any point and immediately print out the survey results, allowing the research design to be refined as necessary.

MAIL SURVEYS Mail surveys have several benefits: relatively low cost, elimination of interviewers and field supervisors, centralized control, and actual or promised anonymity for respondents (which may draw more candid responses). A disadvantage is that mail questionnaires usually produce low response rates because certain elements of the population tend to respond more than others. For example, the Citizen Survey in Kelowna, British Columbia noted that response levels for those 18 to 24 years old were at only 0.4 percent, while this age group actually makes up 11.2 percent of the city's population.[4] The resulting sample may therefore not represent the general population. Another serious problem with mail surveys is that no one probes respondents to clarify or elaborate on their answers.

computer-assisted personal interviewing technique in which the interviewer reads the questions from a computer screen and enters the respondent's data directly into a computer

computer-assisted self-interviewing technique in which the respondent reads questions on a computer screen and directly keys his or her answers into a computer

central-location telephone (CLT) facility a specially designed phone room used to conduct telephone interviewing

Surveys where respondents select an answer from a list or rate the intensity of their response on a scale are relatively easy to evaluate.

Chad McDermott/Shutterstock.com

Mail panels offer an alternative to the one-shot mail survey. A mail panel consists of a sample of households recruited to participate by mail for a given period. Panel members often receive gifts in return for their participation. Essentially, the panel is a sample used several times. In contrast to one-time mail surveys, the response rates from mail panels are high. Rates of 70 percent (of those who agree to participate) are not uncommon.

QUESTIONNAIRE DESIGN

All forms of survey research require a questionnaire. Questionnaires ensure that all respondents will be asked the same series of questions. Questionnaires include three basic types of questions: open-ended, closed-ended, and scaled-response. An **open-ended question** encourages an answer phrased in the respondent's own words. Researchers receive a rich array of information that is based on the respondent's frame of reference (e.g., "What do you think about the new flavour?"). In contrast, a **closed-ended question** asks the respondent to make a selection from a limited list of responses. Closed-ended questions can either be what marketing researchers call *dichotomous* (e.g., "Do you like the new flavour? Yes or No") or *multiple choice*. A **scaled-response question** is a closed-ended question designed to measure the intensity of a respondent's answer.

Closed-ended and scaled-response questions are easier to tabulate than open-ended questions because the response choices are fixed. On the other hand, unless the researcher designs the closed-ended question very carefully, an important choice may be omitted. For example, suppose a food study asked this question:

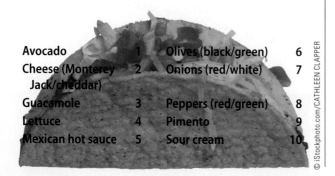

Avocado	1	Olives (black/green)	6
Cheese (Monterey Jack/cheddar)	2	Onions (red/white)	7
Guacamole	3	Peppers (red/green)	8
Lettuce	4	Pimento	9
Mexican hot sauce	5	Sour cream	10

© iStockphoto.com/CATHLEEN CLAPPER

"Besides meat, which of the following items do you normally add to a taco that you prepare at home?" A respondent may then answer, "I usually add a green, avocado-tasting hot sauce" or "I cut up a mixture of lettuce and spinach." How would you code these replies? As you can see, the question needs both an "other" category and a place for respondents to elaborate on their answers.

Good questions address each of the previously set research objectives. Questions must also be clear and concise, and ambiguous language must be avoided. The answer to the question "Do you live within ten minutes of here?" depends on the mode of transportation (maybe the person walks), driving speed, perceived time, and other factors. Language should also be clear. As such, jargon should be avoided, and wording should be geared to the target audience. A question such as "What is the level of efficacy of your preponderant dishwasher soap?" would probably be greeted by blank stares. It would be much simpler to say "Are you (1) very satisfied, (2) somewhat satisfied, or (3) not satisfied with your current brand of dishwasher soap?"

Stating the survey's purpose at the beginning of the interview may improve clarity, but it may also increase the chances of receiving biased responses. Many times respondents will try to provide answers that they believe are "correct" or that the interviewer wants to hear. To avoid bias at the question level, researchers should avoid using leading questions and adjectives that cause respondents to think of the topic in a certain way.

Finally, to ensure clarity, the interviewer should avoid asking two questions in one; for example, "How did you like the taste and texture of the Betty Crocker coffee cake?" This should be divided into two questions, one concerning taste and the other texture.

OBSERVATION RESEARCH

This is another type of descriptive quantitative research, but instead of asking questions to respondents, **observation research** depends on watching what people do. Specifically, it is the systematic process of recording the behavioural patterns of people, objects, and occurrences with or without questioning them. A market researcher uses the observation technique and witnesses and records information as events occur or compiles evidence from records of past events. Carried a step further, observation may involve watching people or phenomena and may be conducted by human

Exhibit 5.5
OBSERVATIONAL SITUATIONS

Situation	Example
People watching people	Observers stationed in supermarkets watch consumers select frozen pizza; the purpose is to see how much comparison shopping people do at the point of purchase.
People watching phenomena	Observers stationed at an intersection count traffic moving in various directions.
Machines watching people	Movie or video cameras record behaviour as in the people-watching-people example above.
Machines watching phenomena	Traffic-counting machines monitor traffic flow.

observers or machines. For example, a machine may be used to track a person's eye movements to see how and what they read in a magazine or on a website. Examples of these various observational situations are shown in Exhibit 5.5.

Two common forms of people-watching-people research are mystery shoppers and one-way mirror observations. **Mystery shoppers** are researchers posing as customers who gather observational data about a store (i.e., are the shelves neatly stocked?) and collect data about customer–employee interactions. The interaction is not an interview, and communication occurs only so that the mystery shopper can observe the actions and comments of the employee. Mystery shopping is, therefore, classified as an observational marketing research method even though communication is often involved. One-way mirror observations allow researchers to see how consumers react to products or promotions.

ETHNOGRAPHIC RESEARCH
Ethnographic research comes to marketing from the field of anthropology. The technique is becoming increasingly popular in commercial marketing research. **Ethnographic research**, or the study of human behaviour in its natural context, involves observation of behaviour and physical setting. Ethnographers, such as Environics, directly observe the population they are studying. As "participant observers," ethnographers can use their intimacy with the people they are studying to gain richer, deeper insights into culture and behaviour—in short, learning what makes people do what they do. Procter & Gamble sends researchers to people's homes for extended periods of time to see how customers do household chores, such as laundry and vacuuming. Cambridge Sound Works, a manufacturer of stereo equipment, assigned researchers to follow a dozen prospective customers for two weeks to determine what was keeping men who wanted a high-end stereo from buying it. (Researchers discovered that the men's wives hated the unsightly appearance of the big, black stereo boxes.)[5] Today, speakers by Sony, Bose, and Bang & Olufsen are smaller with more aesthetically pleasing designs, along with meeting other consumer desires for them to be wireless and even vibration-free.

EXPERIMENTS
An **experiment** is a causal method a researcher can use to gather primary data. The researcher alters one or more variables—price, package design, shelf space, advertising theme, advertising expenditures—while observing the effects of those alterations on another variable (usually sales). The best experiments are those in which all factors are held constant except the ones being manipulated. The researcher can then observe, for example, how sales change as a result of changes in the amount of money spent on advertising.

There are two types of settings for experimental design: laboratory and field. A laboratory environment can be any situation where the researcher can create and control a set of variables to measure. An example of laboratory testing is a test store or simulated supermarket, where shoppers interact in a real or virtual environment that simulates a shopping experience. A field environment is much less controllable than a laboratory; however, field experiments provide a more realistic environment in which a respondent will display relevant behaviours and attitudes.

mystery shoppers researchers posing as customers who gather observational data about a store

ethnographic research the study of human behaviour in its natural context; involves observation of behaviour and physical setting

experiment a method a researcher uses to gather primary data to determine cause and effect

SPECIFYING THE SAMPLING PROCEDURES

Once the researchers decide how they will collect primary data, their next step is to select the sampling procedures to use. A firm can seldom interview or take a census of all possible users of a new product. Therefore, a firm must select a sample of the group to be interviewed. A **sample** is a subset from a larger population.

Several questions must be answered before a sampling plan is chosen. First, the population of interest must be defined. It should include all the people whose opinions, behaviours, preferences, attitudes, and so on are of interest to the marketer. For example, in a study whose purpose is to determine the market for a new canned dog food, the population might be defined to include all current buyers of canned dog food.

After the population has been defined, the next question is whether the sample must be representative of that population. If the answer is yes, a probability sample is needed. Otherwise, a nonprobability sample might be considered (see Exhibit 5.4).

PROBABILITY SAMPLES A **probability sample** is a sample in which every element in the population has a known statistical likelihood of being selected. Its most desirable feature is that scientific rules can be used to ensure that the sample represents the population.

One type of probability sample is a **random sample**—a sample arranged in such a way that every element of the population has an equal chance of being selected as part of the sample. For example, suppose a university is interested in receiving a cross-section of student opinions on a proposed sports complex to be built using student activity fees. If the university can acquire an up-to-date list of all the enrolled students, it can draw a random sample by using random numbers from a table (found in most statistics books) to select students from the list. Common forms of probability and nonprobability samples are shown in Exhibit 5.6.

NONPROBABILITY SAMPLES Any sample in which little or no attempt is made to have a representative cross-section of the population can be considered a **nonprobability sample**. Therefore, the probability of each sampling unit being selected is not known. A common form of a nonprobability sample is the

SIMULATED SHOPPING? THAT'S S.M.A.R.T.

Shoppers at a grocery store would be hard pressed not to notice a Frito Lay product. With brands such as *Doritos, Lay's®, SunChips®, and Tostito's®, Frito-Lay®* is a major player in the snack food aisle at your local grocery store. However, *Frito-Lay* learns about how their customers will act once their carts take them down the snack aisle at the local grocery store by using a virtual grocery store.

In Dallas Texas, *Frito-Lay* operates a 15,000-square-foot simulated shopping environment called the S.M.A.R.T. (Shopper Marketing and Retail Testing) Learning Center. This centre allows *Frito-Lay* to create causal experiments to assess and better understand consumer decisions when it comes to buying items like potato chips and pretzels. The environment at the S.M.A.R.T. is highly customizable, allowing for

Courtesy of PepsiCo Foods Canada

changes to be made to a displays and to aisles without permission from retailers.

Frito-Lay has a state-of-the-art environment to test numerous theories and marketing strategies in a setting that it controls. While the decision to buy snack foods is considered impulse, the effort that goes into where we buy them certainly is not.

Sources: FritoLay, "About Us," 2014, www.fritolay.com (Accessed August 2, 2014); Pamela Forbus and Donna M. Romeo, "Informing Intuition across the Enterprise," Marketing Science Institute, January 1, 2011, www.msi.org/conferences/presentations/informing-intuition-across-the-enterprise/ (accessed August 2, 2014); and John Karolefski, "Simulated Supermarket Helps Frito-Lay Understand Shopper Behavior" CPGMatters, August 2008, www.cpgmatters.com/ShopperInsights0808.html#anchor_110 (accessed August 2, 2014).

convenience sample, which uses respondents who are convenient, or readily accessible, to the researcher—for instance, employees, friends, or relatives.

Nonprobability samples are acceptable as long as the researcher understands their nonrepresentative nature. Because of their lower cost, nonprobability samples are the basis of much marketing research.

TYPES OF ERRORS Whenever a sample is used in marketing research, two major types of error may occur: measurement error and sampling error. **Measurement error** occurs when the information desired by the researcher differs from the information provided by the measurement process. For example, people may tell an interviewer that they purchase Crest toothpaste when they do not. Measurement error generally tends to be larger than sampling error.

Sampling error occurs when a sample does not represent the target population. A sampling error can be one of several types. A nonresponse error occurs when the sample interviewed differs from the sample drawn. This error happens because the original people selected to be interviewed either refused to cooperate or were inaccessible.

Frame error, another type of sampling error, arises when the sample drawn from a population differs from the target population. For instance, suppose a telephone survey is conducted to find out Calgary beer drinkers' attitudes toward Molson Canadian. If a Calgary telephone directory is used as the frame (the device or list from which the respondents are selected), the survey will contain a frame error. Not all Calgary beer drinkers have a phone, others may have unlisted phone numbers, and often young adults have only a cellphone. An ideal sample (for example, a sample with no frame error) matches all important characteristics of the target population to be surveyed. Can you suggest a perfect frame for Calgary beer drinkers?

Random error occurs when the selected sample is an imperfect representation of the overall population. Random error represents how accurately the chosen sample's true average (mean) value reflects the population's true average (mean) value. For example, we might take a random sample of beer drinkers in Calgary

convenience sample a form of nonprobability sample using respondents who are convenient, or readily accessible, to the researcher—for example, employees, friends, or relatives

measurement error an error that occurs when the information desired by the researcher differs from the information provided by the measurement process

sampling error an error that occurs when a sample does not represent the target population

frame error a sample drawn from a population that differs from the target population

random error a type of sampling error in which the selected sample is an imperfect representation of the overall population

Exhibit 5.6
TYPES OF SAMPLES

Probability Samples	
Simple Random Sample	Every member of the population has a known and equal chance of selection.
Stratified Sample	The population is divided into mutually exclusive groups (by gender or age, for example); then random samples are drawn from each group.
Cluster Sample	The population is divided into mutually exclusive groups (by geographic area, for example); then a random sample of clusters is selected. The researcher then collects data from all the elements in the selected clusters or from a probability sample of elements within each selected cluster.
Systematic Sample	A list of the population is obtained—e.g., all persons with a chequing account at XYZ Bank—and a skip interval is obtained by dividing the sample size by the population size. If the sample size is 100 and the bank has 1000 customers, then the skip interval is 10. The beginning number is randomly chosen within the skip interval. If the beginning number is 8, then the skip pattern would be 8, 18, 28, etc.
Nonprobability Samples	
Convenience Sample	The researcher selects the easiest population members from which to obtain information.
Judgment Sample	The researcher's selection criteria are based on personal judgment that the elements (persons) chosen will likely give accurate information.
Quota Sample	The researcher finds a prescribed number of people in several categories—e.g., researcher selects a specific number of business students, arts students, science students, etc., so that each group has a specific number represented in the study. Respondents are not selected on probability sampling criteria.
Snowball Sample	Additional respondents are selected on the basis of referrals from the initial respondents. This method is used when a desired type of respondent is difficult to find—e.g., persons who have taken round-the-world cruises in the last three years are asked to refer others they know that have taken long cruises and could be involved in the research study. This technique employs the old adage "Birds of a feather flock together."

and find that 16 percent regularly drink Molson Canadian beer. The next day we might repeat the same sampling procedure and discover that 14 percent regularly drink Molson Canadian beer. The difference is due to random error. Error is common to all surveys, yet it is often not reported or is underreported. Typically, the only error mentioned in a written report is a sampling error.

Exhibit 5.7

EXAMPLE OF A CROSS-TABULATION OF GENDER AND POPCORN BRAND

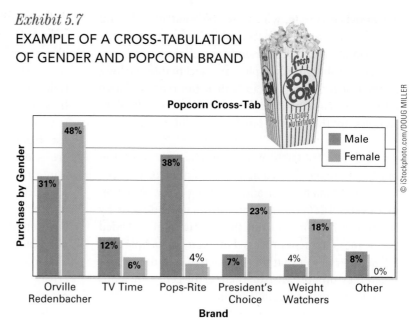

5-2d Step 4: Analyze the Data

After collecting the data, the marketing researcher proceeds to the next step in the research process: data analysis. The purpose of this analysis is to interpret and draw conclusions from the mass of collected data. The marketing researcher tries to organize and analyze those data by using one or more techniques common to marketing research: one-way frequency counts, cross-tabulations, and more sophisticated statistical analysis. Of these three techniques, one-way frequency counts are the simplest. One-way frequency tables simply record the responses to a question. For example, the answers to the question "What brand of microwave popcorn do you buy most often?" would provide a one-way frequency distribution. One-way frequency tables are always used in data analysis, at least as a first step, because they provide the researcher with a general picture of the study's results. A **cross-tabulation** shows the analyst the responses to one question in relation to the responses to one or more other questions. For example, what is the association between gender and the brand of microwave popcorn bought most frequently, as shown in Exhibit 5.7?

Researchers can use many other more powerful and sophisticated statistical techniques, such as hypothesis testing, measures of association, and regression analysis. A description of these techniques goes beyond the scope of this book but can be found in any good marketing research textbook. The use of sophisticated statistical techniques depends on the researchers' objectives and the nature of the data gathered.

5-2e Step 5: Present the Report

After data analysis has been completed, the researcher must prepare the report and communicate the

conclusions and recommendations to management. This is a key step in the process. If the marketing researcher wants managers to carry out the recommendations, he or she must convince the managers that the results are credible and justified by the data collected.

Researchers are usually required to present both written and oral reports on the project. They should begin with a clear, concise statement of the research issue studied, the research objectives, and a complete but brief and simple explanation of the research design or methodology employed, including the nature of the sample and how it was selected. A summary of major findings should come next. The way in which this section is written is very important, as this is the part of the report that will build a case as to how the marketing research will help solve the research problem. Staying away from technical jargon is vital; the report has to be written in an accessible manner for the manager who will be making a decision based on the information provided. The findings can be presented in a number of formats, including cross-tabulations tables, line charts, and flow charts. Having a mix of writing and visuals will keep the attention of the reader and provide for a more compelling presentation than writing alone.

The conclusion of the report should also present recommendations to management. Any research report should present limitations that might have affected the research. These limitations will warn or advise the readers of any issues that could affect the reliability and validity of the research. Awareness of these limitations may also help future researchers and may serve as cautions to managers when making their decision.

Most people who enter marketing will become research users rather than research suppliers. Thus, they must know what items to take note of in a report. As with many items we purchase, quality is not always readily apparent, and a high price does not guarantee superior quality. The basis for measuring the quality of a marketing research report is the research proposal. Did the report meet the objectives established in the proposal? Was the methodology outlined in the proposal followed? Are the conclusions based on logical deductions from the data analysis? Do the recommendations seem prudent, given the conclusions?

5-2f Step 6: Provide Follow-Up

The final step in the marketing research process is to follow up. The way in which follow-up is conducted will depend on whether the marketing researcher was an internal or external provider.

Internal providers of marketing research will have the opportunity for greater interaction and feedback into the report and research efforts. They should be prepared to answer any questions and be available to discuss the project and its ramifications. The internal researcher should keep track of the project that relates to the research. Questions to ask include the following:

▸▸ **Was sufficient decision-making information included?**

▸▸ **What could have been done to make the report more useful to management?**

A good rapport is essential between the internal market researcher and the manager who authorized the project. Often, these individuals must work together on many studies throughout the year.

External marketing research providers will not have the same level of access to the decision makers as someone who works within an organization. For the external provider, managing the client is a very important part of the research process and can ensure that there is the possibility of future work with that client. The external researcher may be asked to be part of implementing aspects of the research report. If they are not part of this process, it is important to agree with the client on a follow-up schedule. Often postreport meetings are included in research contracts, with some meetings occurring years after the final report has been handed in. A fundamental question to ask a client is whether the research has been conducted

properly and accurately. In other words, did the researcher solve the research problem and help in making a management problem clearer?

5-3 THE IMPACT OF TECHNOLOGY ON MARKETING RESEARCH

Technology is pervasive in our lives. You may be reading these words from your laptop, tablet, or cellphone. Marketing research must keep up with technology to meet the needs of both those looking to conduct research and those who would be the subjects of such research.

There are two main areas in which technology and marketing research have combined: online and mobile devices. There are now focus groups online, surveys on cellphones, and virtual repositories of data being used in ways unimaginable a few years ago.

We also must be aware of the public's reduced use of and reliance on tried-and-true marketing research tools, like telephone interviewing and mail surveys. Researchers are scrambling to keep up with a digital revolution that threatens to leave them behind unless they incorporate the new technological reality into their methods and activities.

Let's now look at some of the ways technology is changing marketing research.

5-3a Online Surveys

In 2012, 83 percent of Canadians over the age of 16 used the Internet, compared with 80 percent the year before.[6] Greater Internet access means a larger sample from which to recruit survey respondents. Better online survey tools have been the result of this improved access, and websites like Survey Monkey allow even the most untrained marketing researcher to develop a survey and put it online.

The huge growth in the popularity of Internet surveys is the result of many advantages:

▸▸ **RAPID DEVELOPMENT, REAL-TIME REPORTING:** Internet surveys can be broadcast to thousands of potential respondents simultaneously. Respondents complete surveys simultaneously; then, results are tabulated and posted for corporate clients to view as the returns arrive. Survey results can be in a client's hands in significantly less time than would be required for traditional surveys.

» **DRAMATICALLY REDUCED COSTS:** The Internet can cut costs significantly and provide results in half the time required for traditional telephone surveys. Traditional survey methods are labour-intensive efforts incurring costs related to training, telecommunications, and management. Electronic methods eliminate these costs completely. While costs for traditional survey techniques rise proportionally with the number of interviews desired, electronic solicitations can grow in volume with little increase in project costs.

» **IMPROVED RESPONDENT PARTICIPATION:** Internet surveys take half as much time to complete as phone interviews, can be accomplished at the respondent's convenience (after work hours), and can be much more stimulating and engaging. As a result, Internet surveys enjoy much higher response rates.

» **CONTACT WITH THE DIFFICULT-TO-REACH:** Certain groups—doctors, high-income professionals, top management in Global 2000 firms—are among the most surveyed individuals on the planet and the most difficult to reach. Many of these groups are well represented online. Internet surveys provide convenient "anytime, anywhere" access that makes it easy for busy professionals to participate.

5-3b Online Research Panels

A panel is a group of respondents who agree to be polled by a marketing research firm about a series of products and services. This is not a one-time occurrence like other surveys—panelists are involved over a long period. This method allows research firms to build large pools of individuals who are available to respond quickly to the demands of online marketing research. Internet panels have grown rapidly, with marketing research companies boasting of millions of people in many countries who form their online research panels.

Thanks to the ease of use of online surveys, participants can

Feng Yu/Shutterstock.com. Bank note image used with the permission of the Bank of Canada.

COMPANIES CAN NOW PURCHASE ONLINE FOCUS GROUP SOFTWARE, WHICH CAN COST HUNDREDS OF DOLLARS. THIS COMPARES QUITE FAVOURABLY TO CONVENTIONAL FOCUS GROUPS, WHICH CAN COST THOUSANDS OF DOLLARS.

REASONS FOR THE SUCCESS OF INTERNET MARKETING RESEARCH

» Better and faster decision making through much more rapid access to business intelligence

» Improved ability to respond quickly to customer needs and market shifts

» Follow-up studies and tracking research much easier to conduct and more fruitful

» Reduction of labour- and time-intensive research activities (and associated costs) including mailing, telephone solicitation, data entry, data tabulation, and reporting

complete Internet panels quickly and efficiently. Those participants come from all walks of life. TNS Canada, a marketing and opinion research firm, offers online panels of more than 100,000 Canadians ranging from a teen panel to a doctor panel. TNS boasts over 1 million panel members in the United States and over 500,000 in Europe.[7]

5-3c Online Focus Groups

The exploratory research method of focus groups has also found a home online. A number of organizations are currently offering this new means of conducting focus groups. The process is fairly simple. The research firm builds a database of respondents via a screening questionnaire on its website. When a client comes to a firm with a need for a particular focus group, the firm goes to its database and identifies individuals who appear to qualify. The firm sends an email to these individuals, asking them to log on to a particular site at a particular time scheduled for the group. Like in-person focus groups, firms pay respondents an incentive for their participation.

The firm develops a moderator's guide similar to the one used for a conventional focus group, and a moderator runs the group by typing in questions online for all to see. The group operates in an

CHARITY STARTS ONLINE

Online panels are an effective tool not only for marketing research companies and for-profit firms—charities are now going online to seek out panelists. Charities can gain valuable information from access to online panels, including getting feedback on fundraising programs, determining donor profiles, and assessing the effectiveness of marketing campaigns. Charities can either hire a marketing research firm or create their own panel. Good Works Co. is an Ottawa-based firm that started out helping charities better execute direct mail campaigns. Good Works focuses on helping charities build meaningful long-term relationships with donors by giving them access to online panels. Good Works labels online panels as "a hot new trend in market research." Charities are also being encouraged to create their own online panels. If a charity creates a panel of donors, not only does it have access to potential fundraising sources, but the panel

itself could also be a source of income as external marketing research firms are often looking for stable and dynamic online panels.

Sources: Good Works, "Donor Research," 2014, http://goodworksco.ca/what-we-do/donor-research.aspx (Accessed August 2, 2014); and UKFundrasing, "Three Reasons Why Charities Should Build a Market Research Panel," October 30, 2013, www.fundraising.co.uk/blog/2013/10/30/three-reasons-why-charities-should-build-market-research-panel (accessed August 2, 2014).

environment similar to that of a chat room so that all participants see all questions and all responses. The firm captures the complete text of the focus group and makes it available for review after the group has finished.

5-3d Mobile Marketing Research

Of those Internet users in Canada mentioned previously, 58 percent have accessed the Internet by using a wireless handheld device. A Google survey of 1000 Canadians in 2013 noted that 56 percent of Canadians owned a smartphone, a staggering jump from just 33 percent in 2012.[8]

And it is the increased use of smartphones that has allowed people to complete many more activities with the use of their mobile device. The Google study showed that consumers use their smartphones to research products, seek out information from offline advertisements, and make purchases. More than one-third of respondents in the Google survey stated they would give up their television before giving up their smartphone.

These trends we have just outlined have created a greater focus on conducting marketing research by using customers' mobile devices. Research firms can develop applications that can be downloaded by respondents, which can allow for participation in surveys, focus groups, and panels. Respondents can provide insights through videos, photos, and messages sent from the phone, creating a dynamic and almost instant connection with the respondent. However, this interaction has created concerns over privacy and security of information, prompting the European Society for Opinions and Market Research (ESOMAR) to create a comprehensive set of guidelines relating to mobile marketing research. It has been predicted that smartphone marketing research will become commonplace in developed nations around the world.[9]

5-3e Social Media Marketing Research

With the changes created by the Internet and mobile devices, it is not hard to see how social media might become part of the discussion on technology and marketing research. The online and mobile technologies

> *"If you can't* MEASURE *it, you can't* MANAGE *it."*
> —W. Edwards Deming (business consultant, statistician)[12]

allow for greater communication and sharing among customers.

With two-thirds of Canadians who use the Internet being regular social media users[10] and 78 percent of smartphone users connecting to social media,[11] marketing researchers are beginning to listen. Numerous social media sites can be tapped by marketing researchers, from the more popular (Facebook, Twitter, LinkedIn) to specialized social media networks. There are social media analytical tools that firms are selling to help keep track of all the conversations going on in social media about companies, brands, perceptions, and attitudes—a veritable gold mine for companies and researchers.

The challenge with social media marketing research is trying to find a way to measure the chatter going on in social media. HootSuite provides a means of helping companies manage social media websites and better track what is being said about a brand or marketing campaign. From their Vancouver head office, HootSuite provides companies with a dashboard from which data from a number of social media sites can be tracked and analyzed.

5-3f The Rise of Big Data

With the introduction of the various technologies we have outlined, one of the greatest challenges is how to deal with all the data that are generated from these new sources of information.

This new age of technology has given rise to what is being called "big data." With so much information available to companies and consumers alike, it has become very challenging to figure out what to do with it all. How do you track all those tweets, posts, emails, ads, and other sources of data? Big data is all about how to deliver information from these areas of new technology.

If the claim that 90 percent of all data available today was made in the last two years, it is difficult to imagine how all of it can even be measured, let alone managed. But data analytics firms are trying to do just that—they're attempting to bring structure to this Wild West of data.

The focus is on trying to find the trends in the data and thus finding a way to create strategies around whatever patterns emerge. Consider, for example, the attempts of one of the world's largest software firms—SAP (see SAP-ping Its Strength).

5-4 WHEN TO CONDUCT MARKETING RESEARCH

You don't have to be a rocket scientist to admit you don't know what you don't know. However, too often company decision makers do not heed Werner von Braun's advice when trying to solve a problem.

Marketing research is a process, and the first step in that process is the most important. Understanding the problem is a key to determining what next steps (if any) are necessary. As information is gathered, it may become clear that marketing research may not be necessary. This can only be determined once a researcher has explored the problem. Some firms with big brands and large budgets, like Procter & Gamble, can afford to cut down on the marketing research done to introduce new products in markets where they control a large part of the market share. However,

Courtesy of HootSuite Media Inc.

most firms can benefit from conducting marketing research.

Gathering the right information can require a great deal of time and expense. However, the potential expense to a company when introducing a new product or entering a new market without the right information can be catastrophic. Even if a firm can only afford to do some secondary research, the value of the information to the decision process is immense. With technology making this information more accessible and the data more detailed, it is incumbent upon any business decision maker to include some aspect of the research process in their decision-making process.

Marketers can use information from an external environmental analysis (see Chapter 2) in combination with marketing research data to help in making important strategic decisions. Since competitive advantage is a significant goal in any business, being able to understand other companies can be of great value, especially in highly competitive industries.

Competitive intelligence (CI) helps managers assess their competitors and their vendors and create a more efficient and effective company. Intelligence is analyzed information. It becomes decision-making intelligence when it has implications for the organization. For example, a primary competitor may have plans to introduce a product with performance standards equal to a company's current product but with a 15 percent cost advantage. The new product will reach the market in eight months. This intelligence has important decision-making and policy consequences for management. Competitive intelligence and environmental scanning combine to create marketing intelligence.

We leave this chapter with another look to the stars—this time with the words of the first man on the moon, Neil Armstrong: "Research is creating new knowledge." And we all know what kind of power knowledge can provide.[13]

SAP-PING ITS STRENGTH

SAP, the German-based multinational, is known for creating systems that track accounting, financial, and asset data. But SAP is also in the business of big data and specifically the business of better marketing research, with a new tool called SAP Consumer Insight 365. This new tool uses data analytics to collect reams of data about cellphone users from mobile providers, including location, age, website tracking, and home location. SAP claims the data collected are "privatized and anonymized," and it runs the data through a database program that organizes and structures the results. SAP claims that using SAP Consumer Insight 365 is more effective than using surveys, panels, and applications. Companies can then access the wireless user data and assess the effectiveness of their marketing efforts. For example, a company can introduce a new advertising campaign and then use

Unlocking and Monetizing Mobile Data for Better Consumer Insight

SAP The Best-Run Businesses Run SAP™

SAP's service to determine the number of mentions of their brand or visits to their website that coincide with the timing of the advertising. While there may be concerns over how people's wireless data are being bought and sold, the data being mined will be a tempting buy for companies looking for gold in all that big data.

Sources: Judith Aquino, "SAP's Big Mobile Monetization Plan," AdExchanger, June 18, 2013, www.adexchanger.com/mobile/saps-big-mobile-monetization-plan (accessed August 2, 2014); and "Take Marketing Research to the Next Level with SAP Consumer Insight 365," SAP, 2014, www.sap.com/pc/tech/mobile/software/mobile-services/consumer-insight/index.html (accessed August 2, 2014).

Chapter **6**

Consumer Decision Making

© iStockphoto.com/Paul Piebinga

"The aim of marketing is to know and understand the customer so well the product or service fits him and sells itself."

—Peter F. Drucker

After you finish this chapter, go to www.nelson.com/student *for* **STUDY TOOLS**. ⊡- - - - - - →

6-1 THE IMPORTANCE OF UNDERSTANDING CONSUMER BEHAVIOUR

To create a proper marketing mix for a well-defined market, marketing managers must have a thorough knowledge of **consumer behaviour.** The understanding of consumer behaviour is even more critical given that consumers' product and service preferences are constantly changing. Consumer behaviour describes how consumers make purchase decisions and how they use and dispose of the purchased goods or services. The study of consumer behaviour also includes an analysis of factors that influence purchase decisions and product use.

Understanding how consumers make purchase decisions can help marketing managers in several ways. For example, if a manager knows through research that gas mileage is the most important attribute in an automobile for a certain target market, the manufacturer can redesign the product to meet that criterion. If the firm cannot change the product design in the short run, it can use other marketing elements in an effort to change consumers' decision-making criteria. When Virgin Mobile realized that Gen-Yers were looking for more flexibility and convenience and more value-added services than traditional cellphone plans offered, the company redesigned its marketing strategy to more closely match targeted consumers' needs, wants, and desires. Thus, depending on the amount of time desired and when consumers want access, they can choose from different member plans at different prices.

consumer behaviour how consumers make purchase decisions and how they use and dispose of purchased goods or services; also includes the factors that influence purchase decisions and product use

6-2 THE CONSUMER DECISION-MAKING PROCESS

When buying products, consumers generally follow a series of steps known as the **consumer decision-making process**, shown in Exhibit 6.1. The steps in the process are (1) need recognition, (2) information search, (3) evaluation of alternatives, (4) purchase, and (5) postpurchase behaviour. These five steps represent a general process that can be used as a guide for studying how consumers make decisions. This guideline does not assume that consumers' decisions will proceed in order through all the steps of the process. In fact, the consumer may end the process at any time or may not even make a purchase. The section on the types of consumer buying decisions later in the chapter discusses why a consumer's progression through these steps may vary. Before addressing this issue, however, we will describe each step in the process in detail.

6-2a Need Recognition

The first stage in the consumer decision-making process is need recognition. **Need recognition** occurs when consumers are faced with an imbalance between actual and desired states. This imbalance is triggered when a consumer is exposed to either an internal or an external **stimulus**. *Internal stimuli* are occurrences you experience, such as hunger or thirst. *External stimuli* are influences from an outside source, such as someone's recommendation of a new restaurant, the design of a package, or an advertisement on television or radio.

Marketing managers can create wants on the part of the consumer. A **want** is a particular product or service that the consumer believes could satisfy an unfulfilled need. A want can be for a specific product, or it can be for a certain attribute or feature of a product. For example, if your cellphone runs through the washing machine in your jeans pocket, you'll *need* to buy a replacement and may *want* one with greater speed, 12 mega-pixel camera, voice recognition, and so forth.

A marketing manager's objective is to get consumers to recognize an imbalance between their present status and their preferred state. Advertising and sales promotion often provide this stimulus. By surveying buyer preferences, marketers gain information about consumer needs and wants, which they can then use to tailor their products and services.

Another way marketers create new products and services is by observing trends in the marketplace. IKEA, the home furnishing giant, realized that Generation-Y consumers prefer furniture that is stylish, easy to clean, multifunctional, and portable, so it created a line of products to meet those preferences. One item in the line is a space-saving multifunction desk that can be converted into a dining table; it has wheels so that it can be easily moved.[1]

Consumers recognize unfulfilled wants in various ways. The two most common occur when a current product isn't performing properly and when the consumer is about to run out of something that is generally kept on hand. Consumers may also recognize unfulfilled wants if they become aware of a product that seems superior to the one they currently use. Such is the case with cellphones. With increased options and usage, consumers desire longer battery life for their phones. Cellphone companies have thus replaced batteries with longer-lasting lithium-ion batteries (300 to 500 rechargings), but this still means the batteries will die in one to two years. As the iPhone batteries are nonreplaceable (unless returned to the company, which costs $90), this means the consumer is faced with this inconvenience and expense, as well as emerging new technological features. They are thus faced with a buying decision.

Exhibit 6.1
CONSUMER DECISION-MAKING PROCESS

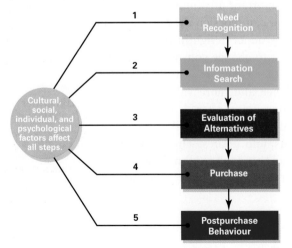

And as you read in Chapter 4, marketers selling their products in global markets must carefully observe the needs and wants of consumers in various regions.

6-2b Information Search

After recognizing a need or want, consumers search for information about the various alternatives available to satisfy it. An information search can occur internally, externally, or both. An **internal information search** is the process of recalling information stored in one's memory. This stored information stems largely from previous experience with a product—for example, recalling whether a hotel where you stayed earlier in the year had clean rooms and friendly service.

In contrast, an **external information search** is the process of seeking information in the outside environment. There are two basic types of external information sources: nonmarketing-controlled and marketing-controlled. A **nonmarketing-controlled information source** is an information source not associated with advertising or promotion. These information sources include personal experiences (trying or observing a new product); personal sources (family, friends, acquaintances, and co-workers who may recommend a product or service); and public sources, such as *Consumer Reports* and other rating organizations that comment on products and services. For example, if you feel like seeing a movie, you may search your memory for past experiences at various cinemas when determining which one to go to (personal experience). To choose which movie to see, you may rely on the recommendation of a friend or family member (personal sources), or you may read the critical reviews in the newspaper or online (public sources). Marketers gather information on how these information sources

work and use this information to attract customers.

On the other hand, a **marketing-controlled information source** originates with marketers promoting the product. Marketing-controlled information sources include mass-media advertising (radio, newspaper, television, and magazine advertising), sales promotion (contests, displays, and premiums), salespeople, product labels and packaging, and the Internet. Many consumers, however, are wary of the information they receive from marketing-controlled sources, believing that most marketing campaigns stress the product's attributes and ignore its faults. These sentiments tend to be stronger among better-educated and higher-income consumers. Social media is being used extensively by consumers to seek product information from both marketer and nonmarketer sources.

The extent to which an individual conducts an external search depends on his or her perceived risk, knowledge, prior experience, and level of interest in the good or service. Generally, as the perceived risk of the purchase increases, the consumer expands the search and considers alternative brands. For example, you would probably spend more time researching the purchase of a laptop or a car than the purchase of an energy drink. A consumer's knowledge about the product or service will also affect the extent of an external information search. A consumer who is knowledgeable and well informed about a potential purchase is less likely to search for additional information and will conduct the search more efficiently, thereby requiring less time to search.

The extent of a consumer's external search is also affected by confidence in one's decision-making ability. A confident consumer not only has sufficient

internal information search the process of recalling information stored in one's memory

external information search the process of seeking information in the outside environment

nonmarketing-controlled information source a product information source not associated with advertising or promotion

marketing-controlled information source a product information source that originates with marketers promoting the product

evoked set (consideration set) a group of the most preferred alternatives resulting from an information search, which a buyer can further evaluate to make a final choice

stored information about the product but also feels self-assured about making the right decision. People lacking this confidence will continue an information search even when they know a great deal about the product. A third factor influencing the external information search is product experience. Consumers who have had a positive prior experience with a product are more likely to limit their search to items related to the positive experience. For example, when planning a trip, consumers are likely to choose airlines with which they have had positive experiences, such as consistent on-time arrivals, and will likely avoid airlines with which they had a negative experience, such as lost luggage.

Finally, the extent of the search is positively related to the amount of interest a consumer has in a product. A consumer who is more interested in a product will spend more time searching for information and alternatives. A dedicated runner searching for a new pair of running shoes may enjoy reading about the new brands available and, as a result, may spend more time and effort than other buyers in deciding on the next shoe purchase.

The buyer's **evoked set** (or **consideration set**) is a group of the most preferred alternatives resulting from an information search, which a buyer can further evaluate to make a final choice. Consumers do not consider all brands available in a product category, but they do seriously consider a much smaller set. Having too many choices can, in fact, confuse consumers and cause them to delay the decision to buy or, in some instances, can cause them to not buy at all.

Brian A Jackson/Shutterstock.com

6-2c **Evaluation of Alternatives and Purchase**

After acquiring information and constructing a set of alternative products, the consumer is ready to make a decision. A consumer will use the information stored in memory and obtained from outside sources to develop a set of criteria. These standards help the consumer to evaluate and compare alternatives. One way to begin narrowing the number of choices in the consideration set is to pick a product attribute and then exclude all products in the set without that attribute. For example, if you are buying a car and live in the mountains, you will probably exclude all cars without four-wheel drive.

Another way to narrow the number of choices is to use cutoffs. Cutoffs are either minimum or maximum levels of an attribute that an alternative must pass to be considered. If your budget for that new car is $25,000, you will not consider any four-wheel drive vehicle above that price point. A final way to narrow the choices is to rank the attributes under consideration in order of importance and evaluate the products on how well each performs on the most important attributes.

If new brands are added to a consideration set, the consumer's evaluation of the existing brands in that set changes. As a result, certain brands in the original set may become more desirable. If you discover that you can get the exact car you want, used, for $18,000 instead of spending $25,000 for a new model, you may revise your criteria and select the used car.

The goal of the marketing manager is to determine which attributes have the most influence on a consumer's choice. Several attributes may collectively affect a consumer's evaluation of products. A single attribute, such as price, may not adequately explain how consumers form their consideration set. Moreover, attributes the marketer thinks are important may not be very important to the consumer. A brand name can also have a significant impact on a consumer's ultimate choice. By providing consumers with a certain set of promises, brands in essence simplify the consumer decision-making process so consumers do not have to rethink their options every time they need something.[2] Following the evaluation of alternatives, the consumer decides which product to buy or decides not to buy a product at all. If he or she decides to make a purchase, the next step in the process is an evaluation of the product after the purchase.

6-2d Postpurchase Behaviour

When buying products, consumers expect certain outcomes from the purchase. How well these expectations are met determines whether the consumer is satisfied or dissatisfied with the purchase. For the marketer, an important element of any postpurchase marketing activity is reducing any lingering doubts that the decision was sound. Eliminating such doubts is particularly important to increase consumer satisfaction with their purchases by providing **decision confirmation** support. The decision confirmation is the reaffirmation of the wisdom of the decision a consumer has made, and such a need is stronger among consumers after making an important purchase.

A failure to confirm one's decision may result in **cognitive dissonance**—also popularly known as buyers' remorse—induced by constant doubt about one's choice. Cognitive dissonance is defined as an inner tension that a consumer experiences after recognizing an inconsistency between behaviour and values or opinions. For example, suppose a consumer is looking to purchase a laptop that has a light weight, long battery life, and a CD-ROM drive and is considering buying either an Apple MacBook Air or a MacBook Pro. In such a situation, where no one alternative is clearly offering all the key attributes the consumer is seeking, either choice is likely to induce cognitive dissonance unless the consumer changes his or her attribute preference.

Consumers try to reduce dissonance by justifying their decision. They may seek new information that reinforces positive ideas about the purchase, avoid information that contradicts their decision, or revoke the original decision by returning the product. In some instances, people deliberately seek contrary information so they can refute it and reduce the dissonance. Dissatisfied customers sometimes rely on word of mouth to reduce cognitive dissonance, by letting friends and family know they are displeased.

Marketing managers can help reduce dissonance through effective communication with purchasers. Postpurchase letters sent by manufacturers and dissonance-reducing statements in instruction booklets may help customers to feel more at ease with their purchase. Advertising that displays the product's superiority over competing brands or guarantees can also help relieve the possible dissonance of someone who has already bought the product. Ultimately, the marketer's goal is to ensure that the outcome meets or exceeds the customer's expectations rather than being a disappointment.[3]

> **decision confirmation** the reaffirmation of the wisdom of the decision a consumer has made
>
> **cognitive dissonance** the inner tension that a consumer experiences after recognizing an inconsistency between behaviour and values or opinions

SURVEY SAYS ...

According to the annual report by the Canadian Radio-television and Telecommunications Commission (CRTC), the average monthly spending of a Canadian household in 2012 on communication was $185. This amount showed an increased spending on wireless and Internet and decreased spending on traditional services like landline phones. The report also said that, in 2012, Canadians watched a little less TV and listened to a little less radio than in the previous years; however, they watched more programs through the Internet and streaming radio. Collectively, the communication industry generated $60 billion in revenues in 2012.

Juice Images/Jupiterimages

SOURCE: CRTC, "Communications Monitoring Report 2013," www.crtc.gc.ca/eng/publications/reports/policyMonitoring/2013/cmr.htm (accessed November 9, 2013).

involvement the amount of time and effort a buyer invests in the search, evaluation, and decision processes of consumer behaviour

routine response behaviour the type of decision making exhibited by consumers buying frequently purchased, low-cost goods and services; requires little search and decision time

limited decision making the type of decision making that requires a moderate amount of time for gathering information and deliberating about an unfamiliar brand in a familiar product category

extensive decision making the most complex type of consumer decision making, used when considering the purchase of an unfamiliar, expensive product or an infrequently purchased item; requires the use of several criteria for evaluating options and much time for seeking information

6-3 TYPES OF CONSUMER BUYING DECISIONS AND CONSUMER INVOLVEMENT

All consumer buying decisions generally fall along a continuum of three broad categories: routine response behaviour, limited decision making, and extensive decision making (see Exhibit 6.2). Goods and services in these three categories can best be described in terms of five factors: level of consumer involvement, length of time to make a decision, cost of the good or service, degree of information search, and the number of alternatives considered. The level of consumer involvement is perhaps the most significant determinant in classifying buying decisions. **Involvement** is the amount of time and effort a buyer invests in the search, evaluation, and decision processes of consumer behaviour.

Frequently purchased, low-cost goods and services are generally associated with **routine response behaviour**. These goods and services can also be called low-involvement products because consumers spend little time on the search and decision before making the purchase. Usually, buyers are familiar with several different brands in the product category but stick with one brand. Consumers engaged in routine response behaviour normally don't

experience need recognition until they are exposed to advertising or see the product displayed on a store shelf. These consumers buy first and evaluate later, whereas the reverse is true for consumers who engage in extensive decision making.

Limited decision making requires a moderate amount of time for gathering information and deliberating about an unfamiliar brand in a familiar product category. It typically occurs when a consumer has previous product experience but is unfamiliar with the current brands available. Limited decision making is also associated with lower levels of involvement (although higher than routine decisions) because consumers expend only moderate effort in searching for information or in considering various alternatives. If a consumer's usual brand is sold out, he or she will likely evaluate several other brands before making a final decision.

Consumers practise **extensive decision making** when considering the purchase of an unfamiliar, expensive product or an infrequently purchased item. This process is the most complex type of consumer buying decision and is associated with high involvement on the part of the consumer. The process resembles the model outlined in Exhibit 6.1. Because these consumers want to make the right decision, they want to know as much as they can about the product category and the available brands. People usually experience cognitive dissonance only when buying high-involvement products. Buyers use several criteria for evaluating their options and spend much time seeking information. Buying a home or a car, for example, requires extensive decision making.

The type of decision making that consumers use to purchase a product does not necessarily remain

Exhibit 6.2

CONTINUUM OF CONSUMER BUYING DECISIONS

	Routine	Limited	Extensive
Involvement	Low	Low to moderate	High
Time	Short	Short to moderate	Long
Cost	Low	Low to moderate	High
Information Search	Internal only	Mostly internal	Internal and external
Number of Alternatives	One	Few	Many

Michael Stuparyk/GetStock.com

constant. If a routinely purchased product no longer satisfies, consumers may practise limited or extensive decision making to switch to another brand. Consumers who first use extensive decision making may then use limited or routine decision making for future purchases. For example, a family may spend a lot of time figuring out that their new puppy prefers hard food to soft, but once they know, the purchase will become routine.

6-3a Factors Determining the Level of Consumer Involvement

The level of involvement in the purchase depends on the following five factors:

- ▸ **PREVIOUS EXPERIENCE:** When consumers have had previous experience with a good or service, the level of involvement typically decreases. After repeated product trials, consumers learn to make quick choices. Because consumers are familiar with the product and know whether it will satisfy their needs, they become less involved in the purchase.

- ▸ **INTEREST:** Involvement is directly related to consumer interests, as in cars, music, movies, bicycling, or electronics. Naturally, these areas of interest vary from one individual to another. A person highly involved in bike racing will be more interested in the type of bike she owns than someone who rides a bike only for recreation.

- ▸ **PERCEIVED RISK OF NEGATIVE CONSEQUENCES:** As the perceived risk in purchasing a product increases, so does a consumer's level of involvement. The types of risks that concern consumers include financial risk, social risk, and psychological risk. First, financial risk is exposure to loss of wealth or purchasing power. Because high risk is associated with high-priced purchases, consumers tend to become extremely involved. Therefore, price and involvement are usually directly related: as price increases, so does the level of involvement. Second, consumers take social risks when they buy products that can affect people's social opinions of them (for example, driving an old, beat-up car or wearing unstylish clothes). Third, buyers undergo psychological risk if they

feel that making the wrong decision might cause some concern or anxiety. For example, some consumers feel guilty about eating foods that are not healthy, such as regular ice cream rather than fat-free frozen yogurt.

- ▸ **SITUATION:** The circumstances of a purchase may temporarily transform a low-involvement decision into a high-involvement one. High involvement comes into play when the consumer perceives risk in a specific situation. For example, an individual might routinely buy canned fruit and vegetables, but for dinner parties shop for high-quality fresh produce.

- ▸ **SOCIAL VISIBILITY:** Involvement also increases as the social visibility of a product increases. Products that are often on social display include clothing (especially designer labels), jewellery, cars, and furniture. All these items make a statement about the purchaser and, therefore, carry a social risk.

6-3b Marketing Implications of Involvement

Marketing strategy varies according to the level of involvement associated with the product. For high-involvement product purchases, marketing managers have several responsibilities. First, promotion to the target market should be extensive and informative. A good ad gives consumers the information they need to make the purchase decision and specifies the benefits and unique advantages of owning the product.

For low-involvement product purchases, consumers may not recognize their wants until they are in the store. Therefore, marketing managers focus on package design so the product will be eye-catching and easily recognized on the shelf. In-store promotions and displays also stimulate sales of low-involvement products. A good display can explain the product's purpose and prompt recognition of a want. Coupons, cents-off deals, and two-for-one offers also effectively promote low-involvement items.

Linking a product to a higher-involvement issue is another tactic that marketing managers can use to increase the sales of a low-involvement product. Although

culture the set of values, norms, attitudes, and other meaningful symbols that shape human behaviour and the artifacts, or products, of that behaviour as they are transmitted from one generation to the next

packaged food may normally be a low-involvement product, reference to health issues raises the involvement level. While the consumption of milk has decreased over the last ten years, the sale of yogurt has gone up, especially Greek yogurt, which has seen its sales increase 10 percent per year since 2010.[4]

6-3c Factors Influencing Consumer Buying Decisions

The consumer decision-making process does not occur in a vacuum. On the contrary, the decision process is strongly influenced by underlying cultural, social, individual, and psychological factors. These factors have an effect from the time a consumer perceives a stimulus through to the time of postpurchase behaviour. Cultural factors, which include culture and values, subculture, and social class, exert the broadest influence over consumer decision making.

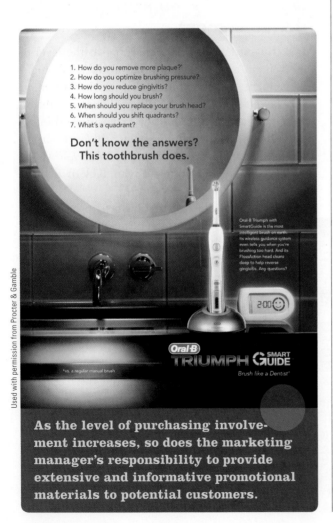

1. How do you remove more plaque?*
2. How do you optimize brushing pressure?
3. How do you reduce gingivitis?
4. How long should you brush?
5. When should you replace your brush head?
6. When should you shift quadrants?
7. What's a quadrant?

Don't know the answers? This toothbrush does.

Oral-B Triumph with SmartGuide is the most intelligent brush on earth. Its wireless guidance system even tells you when you're brushing too hard. And its FlossAction head cleans deep to help reverse gingivitis. Any questions?

*vs. a regular manual brush

Oral-B TRIUMPH SMART GUIDE
Brush like a Dentist*

Used with permission from Procter & Gamble

As the level of purchasing involvement increases, so does the marketing manager's responsibility to provide extensive and informative promotional materials to potential customers.

Social factors sum up the social interactions between a consumer and influential groups of people, such as reference groups, opinion leaders, and family members. Individual factors, which include gender, age, family life-cycle stage, personality, self-concept, and lifestyle, are unique to each individual and play a major role in the type of products and services consumers want. Psychological factors determine how consumers perceive and interact with their environments and influence the ultimate decisions consumers make. They include perception, motivation, learning, beliefs, and attitudes. Exhibit 6.3 summarizes these influences.

6-4 CULTURAL INFLUENCES ON CONSUMER BUYING DECISIONS

Of all the factors that affect consumer decision making, cultural factors exert the broadest and deepest influence. Marketers must understand the way people's culture and its accompanying values, as well as their subculture and social class, influence their buying behaviour.

6-4a Culture and Values

Culture comprises the set of values, norms, attitudes, and other meaningful symbols that shape human behaviour and the artifacts, or products, of that behaviour as they are transmitted from one generation to the next. Culture is the essential character of a society that distinguishes it from other cultural groups.

Culture is pervasive. What people eat, how they dress, what they think and feel, and what language they speak are all dimensions of culture. Culture encompasses all the things consumers do without conscious choice because their culture's values, customs, and rituals are ingrained in their daily habits.

Culture is functional. Human interaction creates values and prescribes acceptable behaviour for each culture. By establishing common expectations, culture gives order to society. Sometimes these expectations are enacted into laws, such as the expectation that drivers will stop at red lights. Other times, these expectations are taken for granted: grocery stores and hospitals are open 24 hours, whereas banks are not.

Exhibit 6.3

FACTORS THAT AFFECT THE CONSUMER DECISION-MAKING PROCESS

Social Factors

Reference groups

Opinion leaders

Family

Buy? **Don't buy?**

Cultural Factors

Culture and values

Subculture

Social class

Individual Factors

Gender

Age and family life-cycle stage

Personality, self-concept, and lifestyle

Consumer Decision-Making Process

Psychological Factors

Perception

Motivation

Learning

Beliefs and attitudes

Hill Street Studios/Blend Images/Jupiterimages

Culture is learned. Consumers are not born knowing the values and norms of their society. Instead, they must learn what is acceptable from family and friends. Children learn the values that will govern their behaviour from parents, teachers, and peers.

Culture is dynamic. It adapts to changing needs and an evolving environment. The rapid growth of technology in today's world has accelerated the rate of cultural change. How we communicate with each other regardless of the geographical distance has changed with the use of Internet and mobile devices. Another factor that contributes to cultural shifts in Canada is our rapidly increasing diversity, which influences our food, music, clothing, and entertainment.

The most defining element of a culture is its **values**—the enduring beliefs shared by a society that

a specific mode of conduct is personally or socially preferable to another mode of conduct. People's value systems have a great effect on their consumer behaviour. Consumers with similar value systems tend to react similarly to various marketing-related inducements. Values also correspond to consumption patterns. For example, Canadians place a high value on convenience as we are thought to be in a time-starved society. This value has created lucrative markets for products such as breakfast bars, energy bars, and nutrition bars that allow consumers to eat on the go.[5] Those values considered central to the Canadian way of life include success, freedom, materialism, capitalism, progress, and youth.

The personal values of target consumers have important implications for marketing managers because values give rise to beliefs that, in turn, are the building blocks of consumer attitude. When marketers understand the core values that underlie the attitudes that shape consumers' buying patterns, they can target their message more effectively.

SOME COMPONENTS OF CANADIAN CULTURE

Custom—Bathing daily

Ritual—Thanksgiving dinner

Value—Success through hard work

Myth—Santa Claus and the Easter Bunny

6-4b Understanding Culture Differences

Underlying core values can vary across cultures. As the Canadian marketplace becomes more culturally diverse and more companies expand their operations globally, the need to understand different cultures becomes more important. A firm has little chance of selling products in a multicultural country like Canada if it does not understand the cultural differences. Like people, products have cultural values and rules that influence their perception and use. Culture, therefore, must be understood before we can understand the behaviour of individuals within the cultural context.

Language is another important aspect of culture that Canadian marketers must consider. In 2011, the proportion of Canadians able to communicate in both English and French declined to 17.5 percent, after reaching a peak of 17.7 percent in 2001. However, it is significant to note that number of Canadians proficient in English and one of the immigrant languages has increased in recent years.[6] This change in language usage has considerable implications for Canadian marketers.

Modern Manners explores the ways in which new technologies, like cellphones, have changed North American culture.

6-4c Subculture

A culture can be divided into subcultures on the basis of demographic characteristics, geographic regions, national and ethnic background, political beliefs, and religious beliefs. A **subculture** is a homogeneous group of people who share elements of the overall culture and also have their own unique cultural elements. Within subcultures, people's attitudes, values, and purchase decisions are even more similar than they are within the broader culture. Subcultural differences may result in considerable variation within a culture in terms of how, when, and where people buy goods and services, and what they buy.

In Canada's multicultural society, French Canadians represent a dominant subculture. While this subculture is mainly based in Quebec, Canada is officially a bilingual nation, and marketers in all regions of the country must be knowledgeable about the language and lifestyle values of the French Canadian subculture. As previously mentioned, it is important to note that the nature of bilingualism in Canada is changing: an increasing proportion of the population is bilingual not in English and French but in English and one of the immigrant languages.

Once marketers identify subcultures, they can design special marketing programs to serve their needs. In response to the growing Asian market, companies have been spending a larger percentage of their marketing budgets advertising to this group. Canadian banks, such as TD Canada Trust and CIBC, have developed marketing campaigns targeting the Asian market, particularly in Vancouver and Toronto. Major league sports teams, such as the Vancouver Canucks and the Toronto Raptors, have used ethnic media outlets, such as Omni Television and CHIN Radio in the Toronto market, in campaigns that target this growing segment of potential fans.

6-4d Social Class

Like other societies, Canada has a class system. A social class is a group of people who are considered nearly equal in status or community esteem, who regularly socialize among themselves both formally and informally, and who share behavioural norms.

One view of contemporary Canadian status structure is shown in Exhibit 6.4. The capitalist executive group comprises the small segment of affluent and wealthy Canadians who are more likely to own their own homes and purchase new cars and trucks and who are less likely to smoke. The most affluent

Exhibit 6.4

INCOME INEQUALITY IN CANADA (YEAR 2010)

Average annual Canadian income = $38,700
Number of top 1% income earners in Canada = 272,600
Minimum income needed to be in top 1% = $191,000
Average income of the top 1% = $381,300
Minimum income needed to be in the top 0.1% = $685,000
Minimum income of the top 0.01% = $2.57 million
Average income of the top 0.01% = $5.11 million

Source: "Who Are Canada's Top 1 Per Cent?" CBC, September 13, 2013, www.huffingtonpost.ca/2013/09/13/canada-1-per-cent_n_3918972.html (Accessed February 20, 2014).

consumers are more likely to attend art auctions and galleries, dance performances, operas, the theatre, museums, concerts, and sporting events.

The majority of Canadians today define themselves as middle class, regardless of their actual income or educational attainment. This phenomenon most likely occurs because working-class Canadians tend to aspire to the middle-class lifestyle while some of those who achieve affluence may downwardly aspire to respectable middle-class status as a matter of principle.

Social class is typically measured as a combination of occupation, income, education, wealth, and other variables. For instance, affluent upper-class consumers are more likely to be salaried executives or self-employed professionals with at least an undergraduate degree. Working-class or middle-class consumers are more likely to be hourly service workers or blue-collar employees with only a high-school education. Educational attainment, however, seems to be the most reliable indicator of a person's social and economic status. Those with university or college degrees or graduate degrees are more likely to fall into the upper classes, while those people with some postsecondary experience fall closer to traditional concepts of the middle class.

Marketers are interested in social class for two main reasons. First, social class often indicates which medium to use for advertising. An insurance company wanting to sell its policies to middle-class families might advertise during the local evening news because middle-class families tend to watch more television than other classes do, but if the company wanted to sell more policies to affluent individuals, it might place a print ad in a business publication such as the *Financial Post*. Second, knowing what products appeal to which social classes can help marketers determine where best to distribute their products.

Education seems to be the most reliable indicator of a person's social and economic status. Those with postsecondary degrees are more likely to fall into the upper classes, while those with some postsecondary experience tend to fall into the middle class.

6-5 SOCIAL INFLUENCES ON CONSUMER BUYING DECISIONS

Most consumers are likely to seek out the opinions of others to reduce their search and evaluation effort or uncertainty, especially as the perceived risk of the decision increases. Consumers may also seek out others' opinions for guidance on new products or services, products with image-related attributes, expensive products, or products where attribute information is lacking or uninformative. Specifically, consumers interact socially with reference groups, opinion leaders, and family members to obtain product information and decision approval.

6-5a Reference Groups

All the formal and informal groups that influence the purchasing behaviour of an individual are that

reference group a group in society that influences an individual's purchasing behaviour

primary membership groups groups with which individuals interact regularly in an informal, face-to-face manner

secondary membership groups groups with which individuals interact less consistently and more formally than with primary membership groups

aspirational reference groups groups that an individual would like to join

norms the values and attitudes deemed acceptable by a group

SOCIAL CLASS AND EDUCATION

Educational Profile	Mean Earnings
Less than high school	$22,698
High school graduates	$28,756
Some college	$26,741
College graduates	$35,180
University graduates, bachelor	$45,793
Master's degree	$56,587
Doctorate degree	$69,267

Source: "Education (Still) Pays, But by How Much?" Martin Prosperity Institute, February 29, 2012, http://martinprosperity.org/2012/02/29/education-still-pays-but-by-how-much/ (Accessed November 9, 2013).

Photodisc/Getty Images

person's **reference groups.** Consumers may use products or brands to identify with or become a member of a group. Consumers observe how members of their reference groups consume, and they use the same criteria to make their own consumer decisions.

Reference groups can be broadly categorized as being either direct or indirect (see Exhibit 6.5). Direct reference groups are face-to-face membership groups that touch people's lives directly. They can be either primary or secondary. **Primary membership groups** include all groups with which people interact regularly in an informal, face-to-face manner, such as family, friends, and co-workers. In contrast, people associate with **secondary membership groups** less consistently and more formally. These groups might include clubs, professional associations, and people who share a religious affiliation.

Consumers are also influenced by many indirect, nonmembership reference groups they do not belong to. **Aspirational reference groups** are those groups that a person would like to join. To join an aspirational group, a person must conform to that group's **norms;** that is, the values and attitudes deemed acceptable by the group. Thus, a person who wants to be elected to public office may begin to dress more conservatively, to match the attire of other politicians. Athletes are an aspirational group for several market segments. To appeal to the younger market, Coca-Cola signed basketball star LeBron James to be the spokesperson for its Sprite and Powerade brands, and Nike signed a sneaker deal with him reportedly worth US$90 million. Coca-Cola and Nike assumed James would encourage consumers to drink Coke brands and buy Nike shoes because they would like to identify with James.[7]

Nonaspirational reference groups, or **dissociative groups,** influence our behaviour because we try to maintain distance from them. A consumer may avoid buying some types of clothing or cars, going to certain restaurants or stores, or even buying a home in a certain neighbourhood to avoid being associated with a particular group.

The activities, values, and goals of reference groups directly influence consumer behaviour. For marketers, reference groups have three important implications: (1) they serve as information sources and influence perceptions; (2) they affect an individual's aspiration levels; and (3) their norms either constrain or stimulate consumer behaviour. Understanding the effect of reference groups on a product is important for marketers as they track the life cycle of their products. Marketers continually face the challenge of identifying the trendsetters in a particular target market. For example, a snowboard

Exhibit 6.5
TYPES OF REFERENCE GROUPS

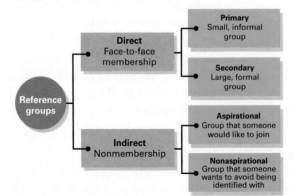

nonaspirational reference groups (dissociative groups) groups that influence our behaviour because we try to maintain distance from them
opinion leader an individual who influences the opinions of others
sociometric leader a low-profile, well-respected collaborative professional who is socially and professionally well connected

manufacturer can determine what is considered cool in the snowboard market by seeking out the trendsetters on their favourite slopes. The unique ways in which these snowboarders personalize their equipment and clothing can be looked on as being desirable and thus may be modified by the influencers who are seeking to express their own individual character. Once the fad look is embraced by the influencers, it has the potential to be adopted by the others in that socio-geographic group. However, as the adoption of the latest trend becomes more common, that trend loses its appeal to the trendsetters, and they seek new ways to express their individualism. The effects of reference groups are especially important both for products that satisfy such visible, unique, socially desirable, high-involvement needs as wine, fashion, and the latest foods, and for personal services, such as spa treatments and vacation destinations and activities. Thus, marketers must understand and track the effects of reference groups on the sales of a product as it moves through its life cycle.

6-5b Opinion Leaders

Reference groups frequently include individuals known as group leaders, or **opinion leaders**—those who influence others. Obviously, it is important for marketing managers to persuade such people to purchase their goods or services.

Opinion leaders are often the first to try new products and services, usually as the result of pure curiosity. They are typically self-indulgent, making them more likely to explore unproven but intriguing products and services. Technology companies have found that teenagers, because of their willingness to experiment, are key opinion leaders for the success of new technologies. Texting became popular with teenagers before it gained widespread appeal. Today, tweeting has become a major means of communication. As a result, many technology companies include tweets in their marketing programs targeted to teens. Recent studies on opinion leaders in the pharmaceutical industry have uncovered the key influencer to be the **sociometric leader**, typically a well-respected collaborative professional who is socially and professionally well connected. These lower-profile individuals have certainly had marketers reflecting on whom they should be marketing to and with.[8]

After identifying potential opinion leaders, marketers will often endeavour to engage these people to support their products. On a wider scale, large companies, groups, associations, and causes will seek out recognized organizations or individuals in sports, business, entertainment, religion, or politics to endorse or support the promotion of their product. The organization's or individual's familiarity,

Mike Powell/Allsport Concepts/Getty Images

attractiveness, credibility, and relative association, can greatly influence a target group. Thus, while Miley Cyrus can influence teens' fashion or desire to go to a summer music event, a promotion featuring Sidney Crosby might influence an athlete or hockey fan, and a local company's support of a new charity fundraiser or disaster relief can influence other companies, communities, and individuals to also support the cause.

6-5c Family

The family is the most important social institution for many consumers, strongly influencing their values, attitudes, self-concepts—and buying behaviour. For example, a family that strongly values good health will have a grocery list distinctly different from that of a family that views every dinner as a gourmet event. Moreover, the family is responsible for the **socialization process**—the passing down of cultural values and norms to children. Because children learn by observing their parents' consumption patterns, they will tend to shop in a similar pattern.

Decision-making roles among family members tend to vary significantly, depending on the types of items purchased. Family members assume a variety of roles in the purchase process. *Initiators* suggest, initiate, or plant the seed for the purchase process. The initiator can be any member of the family. For example, a sister might initiate the product search by asking for a new bicycle as a birthday present. *Influencers* are those members of the family whose opinions are valued. In our example, Mom might function as a price-range watchdog, an influencer whose main role is to veto or approve price ranges. A brother may give his opinion on certain makes of bicycles. The *decision maker* is the family member who actually makes the decision to buy or not to buy. For example, Dad or Mom is likely to choose the final brand and model of bicycle to buy after seeking further information from the sister regarding cosmetic features, such as colour, and after imposing additional parental criteria, such as durability and safety. The *purchaser* (probably Mom or Dad) is the one who actually exchanges money for the product. Finally, the *consumer* is the actual user—the sister, in the case of the bicycle.

Marketers should consider family purchase situations along with the distribution of consumer and decision-maker roles among family members. Ordinary marketing views the individual as both decision maker and consumer. Family marketing adds several other possibilities: sometimes more than one family member or all family members are involved in the decision; sometimes only children are involved in the decision; sometimes more than one consumer is involved; and sometimes the decision maker and the consumer are different people.

6-6 INDIVIDUAL INFLUENCES ON CONSUMER BUYING DECISIONS

A person's buying decisions are also influenced by personal characteristics that are unique to each individual, such as gender; age and life-cycle stage; and personality, self-concept, and lifestyle. Individual characteristics are generally stable over the course of one's life. For instance, most people do not change their gender, and the act of changing personality or lifestyle requires a complete reorientation of one's life. In the case of age and life-cycle stage, these changes occur gradually over time.

6-6a Gender

Physiological differences between men and women result in different needs. Just as important are the distinct cultural, social, and economic roles played by men and women and the effects that these roles have on their decision-making processes. Most car manufacturers have realized that men and women tend to look at different features when purchasing a vehicle. Generally, men gravitate toward gadgets and performance related items, while women prefer to focus on convenience features, such as ease of access, carrying capacity, cup holders, and heated/cooled seats.

Indeed, men and women do shop differently. Studies show that men and women share similar motivations in terms of where to shop—that is, seeking reasonable prices, merchandise quality, and a friendly, low-pressure environment—but they don't necessarily feel the same about shopping in general. Most women enjoy shopping, while most men claim to dislike the experience and shop only out of necessity. Further, men desire simple shopping experiences, such as stores with less variety and more convenience.

Trends in gender marketing are influenced by the changing roles of men and women in society. In October 2007, Satoru Iwata, Nintendo's president, noted that Japanese women had overtaken their male counterparts to become the biggest users of Nintendo's Wii and DS machines, which would have global implications.[9] Certain product categories considered the traditional domain of men are attracting women customers as well. For example, video games have been traditionally targeted at men and boys. A 2013 report by the Entertainment Software Association reports that 55 percent of the video game players in the United States are male and 45 percent are female.[10] Companies must develop new strategies that reflect the changing roles of women at home and work. But other changes also need to be considered by marketers. With recent changes in the views of millennial males to take more active roles in parenting and household duties, males are now at home more, and as of 2010, they comprise a slight majority (at 51 percent) of primary grocery shoppers. This means that products, channels, and promotion need to change to meet the behaviours and needs of the male shopper.[11]

6-6b Age and Family Life-Cycle Stage

The age and family life-cycle stage of a consumer can have a significant impact on consumer behaviour. How old a consumer is generally indicates the products he or she may be interested in purchasing. Consumer tastes in food, clothing, technology, cars, furniture, and recreation are often age related. In a research study by Harris Interactive, the first Youth EquiTrend Study asked 8- to 24-year-olds to rate brands on familiarity, quality, and purchase consideration. The results showed marked differences in age groups. The 8- to 12-year-old tweens listed as their top preferences Nintendo, Doritos, Oreos, and M&Ms. The teens (ages 13 to 17) shifted to Apple, Google, M&Ms, and Oreos. The young adults' choices (ages 18 to 24) were more tech-savvy products, namely Apple, Google, Facebook, and Gatorade.[12]

Ian Dagnall//GetStock.com

Related to a person's age is his or her place in the family life cycle. As Chapter 8 explains in more detail, the *family life cycle* is an orderly series of stages through which consumers' attitudes and behavioural tendencies evolve through maturity, experience, and changing income and status. Marketers often define their target markets in terms of family life cycle, such as "young singles," "young married with children," and "middle-aged married without children." As you can imagine, the spending habits of young singles, young parents, and empty nesters are very different. For instance, the presence of children in the home is the most significant determinant of the type of vehicle that's driven off the new-car lot. Parents are the ultimate need-driven car consumers, requiring larger cars and trucks to haul their children and all their belongings, which explains why sport utility vehicles (SUVs) and minivans were selling at a brisk pace before rising fuel costs became a major consideration when purchasing a vehicle.

Marketers should also be aware of the many non-traditional life-cycle paths that are common today and provide insights into the needs and wants of such consumers as divorced parents, lifelong singles, and childless couples.

6-6c Personality, Self-Concept, and Lifestyle

Each consumer has a unique personality. **Personality** is a broad concept that can be thought of as a way of organizing and grouping the consistency of an individual's reactions to situations. Thus, personality combines psychological makeup and environmental forces. It also includes people's underlying dispositions, especially their most dominant characteristics. Some marketers believe that personality influences the types and brands of products purchased. For instance, the type of car, clothes, or jewellery a consumer buys may reflect one or more personality traits.

Self-concept, or self-perception, is how consumers perceive themselves in terms of attitudes, perceptions, beliefs, and self-evaluations. Although a self-concept may change, the change is often gradual. Through self-concept, people define their identity, which in turn provides for consistent and coherent behaviour.

Self-concept combines the **ideal self-image** (the way an individual would like to be) and the **real self-image** (the way an individual actually perceives himself or herself to be). Generally, we try to raise our real self-image toward our ideal (or at least narrow the gap). Consumers seldom buy products that jeopardize their self-image. For example, a woman who sees herself as a trendsetter wouldn't buy clothing that doesn't project a contemporary image.

Human behaviour depends largely on self-concept. Because consumers want to protect their identity as individuals, the products they buy, the stores they patronize, and the credit cards they carry support their self-image. By influencing the degree to which consumers perceive a good or service to be self-relevant, marketers can affect consumers' motivation to learn about, shop for, and buy a certain brand. Marketers also consider self-concept important because it helps explain the relationship between individuals' perceptions of themselves and their consumer behaviour.

An important component of self-concept is *body image*, the perception of the attractiveness of one's own physical features. For example, a person's perception of body image can be a stronger reason for weight loss than either good health or other social factors.[13] With the median age of Canadians rising, many companies are introducing products and services aimed at aging baby boomers who are concerned about their age and physical appearance. Marketers are also seeing boomers respond to products aimed at younger audiences. For instance, several of the cars designed and targeted at Gen Y have attracted more buyers from the oldest of the baby boom cohort (ages 55 to 64).[14]

Personality and self-concept are reflected in lifestyle. A **lifestyle** is a mode of living, as identified by a person's activities, interests, and opinions. *Psychographics* is the analytical technique used to examine consumer lifestyles and to categorize consumers. Unlike personality characteristics, which can be difficult to describe and measure, lifestyle characteristics are useful in segmenting and targeting consumers. We, as consumers, are ever-changing in terms of our affluence (income and spending focus), where we live (urban, suburban, or rural), and our relationships (family stage or life-stage groups). Lifestyle and psychographic analyses explicitly address the way consumers outwardly express their inner selves in their social and cultural environment. For example, to better understand their market segments, many Canadian companies now use psychographics such as PRIZM, which segments consumers into 66 different groups (e.g., Winner's Circle, a classification to which many of you aspire).[15] Psychographics and lifestyle segmentation are discussed in more detail in Chapter 8.

6-7 PSYCHOLOGICAL INFLUENCES ON CONSUMER BUYING DECISIONS

An individual's buying decisions are further influenced by **psychological factors**: perception, motivation, learning, beliefs, and attitudes. These factors are what consumers use to interact with their world, recognize their feelings, gather and analyze information, formulate thoughts and opinions, and take action. Unlike the other three influences on consumer behaviour, psychological influences can be affected by a person's environment because they are applied on specific occasions. For example, you will perceive different stimuli and process these stimuli in different ways depending on whether you are sitting in class concentrating on the instructor, sitting outside of class talking to friends, or sitting in your dorm room watching television.

6-7a Perception

The world is full of stimuli. A stimulus is any unit of input affecting one or more of the five senses: sight, smell, taste, touch, or hearing. The process by which we select, organize, and interpret these stimuli into a meaningful and coherent picture is called **perception**. In essence, perception is how we see the world around us and how we recognize that we need some help in making a purchasing decision.

People cannot perceive every stimulus in their environment. Therefore, they use **selective exposure**, a process whereby a consumer decides which stimuli to notice and which to ignore. The familiarity of an object, as well as its contrast, movement, intensity (such as increased volume), and smell, are cues that influence perception. Consumers use these cues to identify and define products and brands. The shape of a product's packaging, such as Coca-Cola's signature contour bottle, can influence perception. Colour is another cue, and it plays a key role in consumers' perceptions. Packaged food manufacturers use colour to trigger unconscious associations for grocery shoppers who typically make their shopping decisions in the blink of an eye. Food marketers use green to signal environmental well-being and healthy, low-fat foods, whereas black, brown, and gold are used to convey premium ingredients.[16] The shape and look of a product's packaging can also influence perception.

What is perceived by consumers may also depend on the vividness or shock value of the stimulus. Graphic warnings of the hazards associated with a product's use are perceived more readily and remembered more accurately than less vivid warnings or warnings that are written in text. Sexier ads excel at attracting the attention of younger consumers. Companies such as Calvin Klein and Guess use sensuous ads to "cut through the clutter" of competing ads and other stimuli to capture the attention of the target audience.

Two other concepts closely related to selective exposure are selective distortion and selective retention. **Selective distortion** occurs when consumers change or distort information that conflicts with their feelings or beliefs. For example, suppose you buy a Sony Tablet Xperia. After the purchase, if you receive new information about an alternative brand, such as an Amazon Kindle, you may distort the information to make it more consistent with the prior view that the Tablet is just as good as the Kindle, if not better.

Selective retention is a process whereby consumers remember only information that supports their personal feelings or beliefs. The consumer forgets all information that may be inconsistent. Consumers may see a news report on suspected illegal practices by

perception the process by which people select, organize, and interpret stimuli into a meaningful and coherent picture

selective exposure the process whereby a consumer decides which stimuli to notice and which to ignore

selective distortion a process whereby consumers change or distort information that conflicts with their feelings or beliefs

selective retention a process whereby consumers remember only information that supports their personal beliefs

IS SUBLIMINAL PERCEPTION REAL?

In 1957, a researcher claimed to have increased popcorn and Coca-Cola sales at a movie theatre after flashing "Eat popcorn" and "Drink Coca-Cola" on the screen every five seconds for 1/300th of a second, although the audience did not consciously recognize the messages. Almost immediately, consumer protection groups became concerned that advertisers were brainwashing consumers, and this practice was pronounced illegal in California and Canada. The researcher later admitted to having fabricated the data, and scientists have been unable to replicate the study since. Nonetheless, consumers are still wary of hidden messages that advertisers may be sending. In 2010, BMW Motorcycles was reported to have tested a similar subliminal concept by using flash video in a cinema in Europe. Afterward, patrons who had closed their eyes reported seeing the BMW logo.

KARL B DEBLAKER/UPI/Landov

Source: David Kiley, Video: "BMW Subliminal Ad Burns Logo onto Your Eyelids. Effectiveness in Influencing Customers Has Not Been Determined as of Yet," December 17, 2010, www.autoblog.com/2010/12/17/video-bmw-subliminal-ad-burns-logo-onto-your-eyelids/ (accessed August 28, 2011).

A typical consumer is exposed to more than 2500 ADVERTISING MESSAGES a day but notices only between 11 and 20.

their favourite retail store but soon forget the reason the store was featured on the news.

Which stimuli will be perceived often depends on the individual. People can be exposed to the same stimuli under identical conditions but perceive them very differently. For example, two people viewing a TV commercial may have different interpretations of the advertising message. One person may be thoroughly engrossed by the message and become highly motivated to buy the product. Thirty seconds after the ad ends, the second person may not be able to recall the content of the message or even the product advertised.

MARKETING IMPLICATIONS OF PERCEPTION

Marketers must recognize the importance of cues, or signals, in consumers' perception of products. Marketing managers first identify the important attributes that the targeted consumers want in a product, such as price, social acceptance, or quantity, and then design signals to communicate these attributes. Gibson Guitar Corporation briefly cut prices on many of its guitars to compete with Japanese rivals Yamaha and Ibanez but found instead that it sold more guitars when it charged more. Consumers perceived the higher price as indicating a better-quality instrument.[17]

Marketing managers are also interested in the *threshold level of perception:* the minimum difference in a stimulus that the consumer will notice. This concept is sometimes referred to as the "just-noticeable difference." For example, how much would Apple have to drop the price of its iPad before consumers recognized it as a bargain—$25? $50? or more? One study found that the just-noticeable difference in a stimulus is about a 20 percent change. That is, consumers will likely notice a 20 percent price decrease more quickly than a 15 percent decrease. This marketing principle can also be applied to other marketing variables, such as package size or loudness of a broadcast advertisement.[18]

Another study showed that the bargain-price threshold for a name brand is lower than that for a store brand. In other words, consumers perceive a bargain more readily when stores offer a small discount on a name-brand item than when they offer the same discount on a store brand; a larger discount is needed to achieve a similar effect for a store brand.[19] Researchers also found that for low-cost grocery items, consumers typically do not see past the second digit in the price. For instance, consumers do not perceive any real difference between two comparable cans of tuna, one priced at $1.52 and the other at $1.59, because they ignore the last digit.[20]

Marketing managers who intend to do business in global markets should be aware of how foreign consumers perceive their products. For instance, in Japan, product labels are often written in English or French, even though they may not translate into anything meaningful. Many Japanese associate the foreign words with products that are exotic, expensive, and of high quality.

6-7b Motivation

By studying motivation, marketers can analyze the major forces influencing consumers to buy or not buy products. When you buy a product, you usually do so to fulfill some kind of need. These needs become motives when aroused sufficiently. For instance, you can be motivated by hunger to stop at McDonald's for, say, an Egg McMuffin before an early morning class. **Motives** are the driving forces that cause a person to take action to satisfy specific needs.

Why are people driven by particular needs at particular times? One popular theory is **Maslow's hierarchy of needs**, shown in Exhibit 6.6, which arranges needs in ascending order of importance: physiological, safety, social, esteem, and self-actualization. As a person fulfills each stage to a somewhat satisfied level, a higher-level need becomes more important.

The most basic human needs are *physiological*—that is, the needs for food, water, and shelter. Because these needs are essential to survival, they must be satisfied first. *Safety* needs include security and freedom from pain and discomfort. Marketers sometimes appeal to consumers' fears and anxieties about safety to sell their products.

Consumer math: $1.52 = $1.59

Exhibit 6.6
MASLOW'S HIERARCHY OF NEEDS

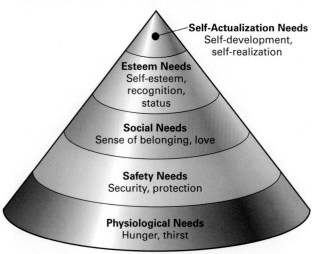

Self-Actualization Needs
Self-development, self-realization

Esteem Needs
Self-esteem, recognition, status

Social Needs
Sense of belonging, love

Safety Needs
Security, protection

Physiological Needs
Hunger, thirst

After physiological and safety needs have been fulfilled, *social needs*—especially love and a sense of belonging—become the focus. Love includes acceptance by one's peers, as well as sexual and romantic love. Marketing managers probably appeal more to this need than to any other. The need to belong is also a favourite of marketers, especially those marketing products to teens. Shoes and clothing brands, such as Nike, Adidas, Hollister, and American Eagle Outfitters, score high with teenagers, who wear these labels to feel and look like they belong to the "in" crowd.

> MORE THAN ONE MOTIVE MAY DRIVE A CONSUMER'S PURCHASE. ASIAN CONSUMERS OFTEN LOOK TO PRODUCTS THAT SATISFY MULTIPLE NEEDS SUCH AS STATUS AND THE VALUE OF FAMILY.

© Blue Jean Images/Alamy

Self-esteem needs are the needs to feel good about ourselves, including self-respect and a sense of accomplishment. Esteem needs also include prestige, fame, and recognition of one's accomplishments. Asian consumers, in particular, are often strongly motivated by status and appearance and are constantly aware of their place in a group, an institution, or society as a whole. The importance of gaining social recognition motivates many Asians to spend freely on premium brands. Indeed, marketers of luxury products, such as Gucci, Louis Vuitton, Prada, BMW, and Mercedes Benz, find that demand for their products is so strong among image-conscious consumers that their sales are generally unaffected by economic downturns. Beyond impressing others, self-esteem needs also motivate us to indulge in purchases that truly reflect who we are.

The highest human need is *self-actualization*. It refers to realizing one's true potential, reaching the point in life at which "people are what they feel they should be." Maslow felt that very few people ever attain this level. Even so, advertisements may focus on this type of need by appealing to consumers' ambition, such as encouraging adults to go back to school, look for better career opportunities, or volunteer for charities that are consistent with their values and goals.

Maslow's hierarchy at a first glance seems to suggest rigid boundaries between different levels, but this would be an over simplification of the theory. Do we need to *fully* meet all our needs at one level before we move to the next higher level? Can an individual try to meet needs at two different levels at the same time? In fact, we do not need to meet all our needs at one level before moving to the next. New university graduates, for example, tend to rent their first apartment (a physiological need) before buying a larger house at a later stage in life. At the same time, the new graduates spend money on clothing to meet their self-esteem needs and making friends and joining dating sites to look for potential mates. This pattern suggests that consumers must realize some level of achievement at one level before moving to the next higher level and effortlessly move between different levels at the same time.

6-7c Learning

Almost all consumer behaviour results from **learning**, which is the process that creates changes in behaviour, immediate or expected, through experience and practice. It is not possible to observe learning directly, but we can infer when it has occurred by a person's actions. For example, suppose you see an advertisement for a new and improved cold medicine. If you go to the store that day and buy that remedy, you have most likely learned something about the cold medicine.

There are two types of learning: experiential and conceptual. *Experiential learning* occurs when an experience changes your behaviour. For example, if the new cold medicine does not relieve your symptoms, you may not buy that brand again. *Conceptual learning*, which is not acquired through direct experience, is the second type of learning. Assume, for example, that you are a heavy bottled-water drinker and you see the advertisement for Brita that appears on this page. You note that the advertisement talks about the water tasting good but, more importantly, the picture of all the empty bottles and the copy gets you thinking about the waste you are creating with the number of empty bottles you toss away. This new learning motivates you to buy the Brita and change your behaviour. You have learned a new behaviour without even trying out the Brita first.

Reinforcement and repetition boost learning. Reinforcement can be positive or negative. For example, if you see a vendor selling frozen yogurt (a stimulus), and you buy it (your response), you may find the yogurt to be quite refreshing (your reward). In this example, your behaviour has been positively reinforced. On the other hand, if you buy a new flavour of yogurt and it does not taste good (negative reinforcement), you will not buy that flavour of yogurt again (your response). Without positive or negative reinforcement, a person will not be motivated to repeat the behaviour pattern or to avoid it. Thus, if a new brand evokes neutral feelings, some marketing activity, such as a price change or an increase in promotion, may be required to induce further consumption. Learning theory is helpful for reminding marketers that concrete and timely actions are what reinforce desired consumer behaviour.

Repetition is a key strategy in promotional campaigns because it can lead to increased learning. Most marketers use repetitious advertising so that consumers will learn their unique advantage over the competition. Generally, to heighten learning, advertising messages should be spread over time rather than clustered together.

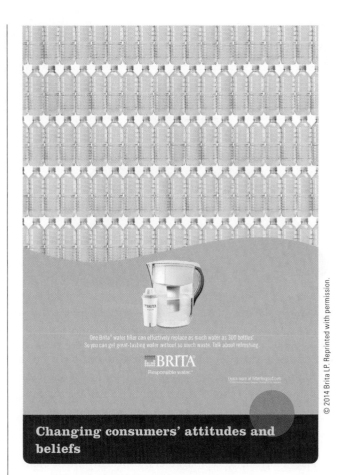

One Brita® water filter can effectively replace as much water as 300 bottles. So you can get great-tasting water without so much waste. Talk about refreshing.

BRITA
Responsible water.™

Learn more at filterforgood.com

© 2014 Brita LP. Reprinted with permission.

Changing consumers' attitudes and beliefs

6-7d Beliefs and Attitudes

Beliefs and attitudes are closely linked to values. A **belief** is an organized pattern of knowledge that an individual holds as true about his or her world. A consumer may believe that Sony's camcorder makes the best home videos, tolerates hard use, and is reasonably priced. These beliefs may be based on knowledge, faith, or hearsay. Consumers tend to develop a set of beliefs about a product's attributes and then, through these beliefs, form a *brand image*—a set of beliefs about a particular brand. In turn, the brand image shapes consumers' attitudes toward the product.

An **attitude** is a learned tendency to respond consistently toward a given object, such as a brand. Attitudes rest on an individual's value system, which represents personal standards of good and bad, right and wrong, and so forth; therefore, attitudes tend to be more enduring and complex than beliefs. For an example of the nature of attitudes, consider the differing attitudes of North American and European consumers toward the practice of purchasing on credit. North Americans have long been enthusiastic about charging goods and services and are willing to pay high interest rates for the privilege of postponing payment. To many European consumers, however, doing what amounts to taking out a loan, even a small one, to pay for anything seems absurd.

CHANGING BELIEFS If a good or service is meeting its profit goals, positive attitudes toward the product merely need to be reinforced. If the brand is not succeeding, however, the marketing manager must strive to change target consumers' attitudes toward it. This change can be accomplished in three ways: (1) changing beliefs about the brand's attributes, (2) changing the relative importance of these beliefs, or (3) adding new beliefs. The first technique is to turn neutral or negative beliefs about product attributes into positive beliefs. For example, many consumers believe that cars with smaller engines (four cylinders versus six cylinders) are less powerful. In 2012, BMW, long known for producing powerful cars, started manufacturing four-cylinder cars, and through its promotions changed public beliefs about small-size engines.

Changing consumers' beliefs about a service can be more difficult because service attributes are intangible. Convincing consumers to switch hairstylists or lawyers or to go to a mall dental clinic can be much more difficult than getting them to change their brand of razor blades. Image, which is also largely intangible, significantly determines service patronage. Service marketing is explored in detail in Chapter 11.

The second approach to modifying attitudes is to change the relative importance of beliefs about an attribute. For example, milk has always been considered a healthy beverage for children and adults. Now, however, dairies are aware of milk's added benefits, primarily the importance of calcium for bone strength, which they now actively promote on their packaging. Marketers can also emphasize the importance of some beliefs over others. The third approach to transforming attitudes is to add new beliefs, such as that breakfast cereal is also a great after-school snack.

6-7e Consumer Behaviour Elements—Working Together

As a result of their environment, individuals change, which, in turn, changes the nature of the goods and services they consume. By using the stages of the buying process to make the best choices, consumers become more experienced. This experience changes the parts of the buying process they use, the degree of effort and time they spend on each stage of buying, and the importance each of the psychological influences in their final buying decision. Effective marketers will carefully study their target markets, noting these changes and the degrees of difference. Then, after understanding the consumers' needs, these marketers can adjust their approach to the various elements in the marketing mix to meet the consumers' needs and help them move through the buying process.

300+
Number of vendors at the spring 2011 fashion week in Toronto

$45,793
Mean income of someone with a bachelor's degree
Levels in Maslow's hierarchy of needs; steps in the consumer decision-making process

$22,698
Mean income of someone with less than a high-school education

Top 1%
Earners in Canada make more than ten times as much as the average Canadian.

11—20
Number of advertising messages a consumer actually remembers each day

2500
Approximate number of advertising messages a typical consumer is exposed to in a day

Chapter **7**

Business Marketing

sheelamohanachandran2010/Shutterstock.com

"Coming together is a beginning. Keeping together is progress. Working together is success."[1]

—Henry Ford

After you finish this chapter, go to
www.nelson.com/student *for* **STUDY TOOLS.** 💼 ------->

7-1 WHAT IS BUSINESS MARKETING?

Describing business marketing is not as simple as inserting the word "business" in front of marketing terms and concluding that this is how it is different from consumer marketing. Business marketing is not just differentiated because of the volume of transactions between businesses, nor is it different because there are unique jobs and career paths in business marketing.

Business marketing *is* marketing. But it is marketing done differently.

Business marketing is often referred to as **business-to-business (B2B) marketing**, and the hyphens between those bolded words are important. Those hyphens represent a connection between two entities, and it is that idea of a connection that is vital to understanding business marketing.

In Chapter 1, you encountered the concept of relationships and learned how successful marketers seek to build relationships with customers over time. The challenge in forming such relationships is to figure out how to create a system to keep track of all those customers (see Chapter 19 on customer relationship management). In business marketing, the number of customers is also the challenge in building relationships—not because there are so many, but the exact opposite: because there are so few.

With limited options to choose from, it becomes important to treat any relationship with care and attention.

Marketing to consumers is often described as creating a marketing mix (recall the four Ps) and delivering it to a consumer. There is a sense that marketing is an activity done separate from the consumer. In business marketing, there needs to be an active interaction between businesses to ensure needs are met. There needs to be trust, mutual respect, and an understanding that even if both parties work together there is still the possibility of achieving one's own company goals.

business-to-business (B2B) marketing the process of matching capabilities between two nonconsumer entities to create value for both organizations and the "customer's customer"; also referred to as *business marketing*

Consumer marketing: Active seller and passive buyer

Business marketing: Active seller and active buyer

7-2 BUSINESS VERSUS CONSUMER MARKETING

In trying to describe marketing of any kind, we'll use examples that you can relate to: a consumer (the buyer) goes into a store and purchases a widely distributed product from a store (the seller). Often the discussion surrounds what the seller can do to better understand the needs of this customer, to determine why the consumer is buying the product, and to figure out how to influence this and future purchases. But what this explanation implies is that the customer is passive, simply waiting to be researched, analyzed, and retained.

In business marketing, neither the seller nor the buyer can afford to be passive. Neither business interest can rely on the other party doing all the work—there needs to be effort and cooperation on both sides of the exchange. This level of cooperation is not yet seen in consumer marketing, but that may change.

Consumer marketing is now seeing a more engaged buyer. Aided by the information and options afforded by technology, specifically the Internet and social media, consumers are taking a more active role in the exchange process of marketing. For example, term life insurance policy premiums were reduced quite significantly with the emergence of online insurance quote websites. Once consumers were given access to choice and information, they became less passive and more willing to actively involve themselves in the role of buyer. KANETIX.ca, a Canadian online insurance comparison website, offers consumers multiple quotes from a variety of insurance providers in Canada. The company philosophy is about empowering consumer choice, even claiming that the X at the end of its brand name represents the X placed on a ballot when voting.[2]

What then has to be created in business marketing is a sense of involved self-interest mixed with mutual benefit. The Canadian Marketing Association, a leading advocate for the marketing community in

Courtesy of KANETIX.ca

Canada, has taken on this approach of mutual benefit when describing business marketing:

> What makes B-to-B different than consumer marketing is the complex nature of *relationships* and *interactions* that form a buying process and customer lifecycle that lasts months or years. It involves a *network* of individuals from buyer, seller, and even third-party partners who have different needs and interests.[3]

The terms provided in this quotation—*relationships, interactions, networks*—are not always ones associated with marketing and need to be explained further. Let's now consider what these terms mean in the context of business marketing.

7-3 THE NETWORK AND RELATIONSHIPS APPROACH TO BUSINESS MARKETING

In looking at business marketing from a network and relationships perspective, one must understand how each of these terms is meant and applied.

7-3a Relationships in Business Marketing

Clearly, relationships are important in marketing, but they are usually the result of greater effort on one side (the seller). In business marketing, business relationships are more complex, as they involve greater commitment from both sides, and thus more company resources and effort. There are two particularly important aspects of such relationships: commitment and trust.

Relationship commitment is a firm's belief that an ongoing relationship with some other firm is so important that it warrants maximum efforts at maintaining it indefinitely.[4] A perceived breakdown in commitment by one of the parties often leads to a reduction in the relationship.

Trust exists when one party has confidence in an exchange partner's reliability and integrity.[5] Some alliances fail when participants lack trust in their trading partners and benefits are not shared. An example of a failed relationship was a partnership between pharmaceutical giant Eli Lilly and a small biotechnology company, Amylin Pharmaceuticals, Inc. The plan was to jointly develop and market a new diabetes drug. However, after Lilly entered into another partnership with a company selling a potentially competing product, Amylin became concerned about the strength of their alliance. A low point in the relationship followed a shouting match between the marketing chiefs from Lilly and Amylin in a hallway following a joint presentation to senior management at Lilly. The main problem: mutual distrust.[6]

The concepts of trust and commitment show the importance of collaboration between entities in a business-to-business relationship. To build and develop a relationship requires a level of cooperation that is not always comfortable for firms used to competing for market share and industry profits. North American firms often believe that laws and regulations are the most important components in maintaining business relationships. However, in many parts of the world, cooperation is a vital part of conducting business. In Japan, for example, exchange between firms is based on personal relationships that are developed through what is called *amae*, or indulgent dependency. *Amae* is the feeling of nurturing concern for, and dependence on, another. Reciprocity and personal relationships contribute to *amae*. Relationships between companies can develop into a *keiretsu*—a network of interlocking corporate affiliates.

7-3b Interaction in Business Marketing

To understand the concept of interaction, we need to go back to Kevin Roberts (recall his quotation from Chapter 1: "Marketing is dead"). In a speech, he mentioned that marketing needed to go from "interruption to interaction."[7] In his view, marketing was too often focused on getting attention through whatever means possible, trying essentially to interrupt consumers from whatever they were doing at the time.

What this interruption approach achieves are a series of one-off transactions, which generate short-term revenue and profits, but little in long-term gain. A long-term perspective is precisely what interaction is about. An interaction can be seen as the culmination of numerous transactions (sales) between two business entities that builds over time. Interaction includes not only transactions but also negotiations, discussions, customizations—anything that is part of the relationship between the two organizations.

An example of transaction versus interaction can be seen with buying versus leasing an automobile. Car companies often prefer to lease vehicles, as evidenced by the many incentive programs offered for leasing vehicles. Through leasing programs, a car company can develop a relationship with the customer over time. If a customer buys a vehicle, on the other hand, the relationship may be limited to warranty issues and may end as soon as the customer drives off the lot.

The Industrial Marketing and Purchasing Group (IMP Group), a leading group of researchers in business marketing, developed an interaction model that provides a good explanation of interaction: "Business exchange cannot be understood as a series of disembedded and independent transactions of given resources—but rather as complex relationships between buying and selling organisations, where what is exchanged is created in interaction."[8]

7-3c Networks in Business Marketing

The Canadian Marketing Association's definition of business marketing describes a "network" of buyers, sellers, and other third parties. This network approach to business marketing takes the interactions and relationships and places them into a bigger context.

> *"I have found no greater satisfaction than achieving success through honest dealing and strict adherence to the view that* FOR YOU TO GAIN, THOSE YOU DEAL WITH SHOULD GAIN AS WELL.*"*[9]
>
> —Alan Greenspan

To understand the network approach, we must note how it differs from two other approaches to business marketing:

▸ **THE SALES APPROACH.** If you look for "B2B marketing" on any search engine, most of the results will focus on sales and selling to companies. The sales approach is focused on generating leads and new business through various persuasion techniques. This approach focuses on what a company has to offer to other firms, but very little time is spent on understanding the problems facing potential customers.

▸ **THE MARKET MANAGEMENT APPROACH.** This approach looks at B2B marketing much like B2C (business-to-consumer) marketing. Develop a product, price it, place it, and promote it—all to a waiting set of customers. This approach focuses on that passive customer and assumes that all customers will have the same needs and will respond in a similar way.

▸ **THE NETWORK APPROACH.** This approach looks at the factors and forces around a firm and the other firms that will have an impact on their business—suppliers, customers, and even competitors. Companies are encouraged to research the external marketplace and by doing so should develop an idea of the forces and challenges facing them and the rest of the companies in their network.

Companies in a network can then develop their relationships through interaction over time. Cooperation gets built into these networks, as it becomes evident that working together can achieve goals that might not have been possible if one firm had tried to work on its own or just on a transaction basis. See Exhibit 7.1 for an example of a representation of a business network.

The concept of business networks is not new. Cooperation and making a profit are not seen as two competing forces in places like Japan and China. As mentioned earlier, in Japan, the concept of *amae* is used in business interaction and denotes mutual dependence and respect, and a network called a *keiretsu* is developed based on *amae*. Within a *keiretsu*, executives may sit on the boards of their customers or their suppliers. Members of a *keiretsu* trade with each other whenever possible and often engage in joint product development, finance, and marketing activity. For example, the Toyota Group *keiretsu* includes 14 core companies and an additional 170 companies that receive preferential treatment. Toyota holds an equity position in many of these 170 member firms and is represented on many of their boards of directors. (See Exhibit 7.2.)

In China, *guanxi* is a term that loosely means "relationships" or "networking," and in business, *guanxi* refers to a network of firms tied together based not only on economic relationships but also on

Exhibit 7.1
A SAMPLE NETWORK MODEL

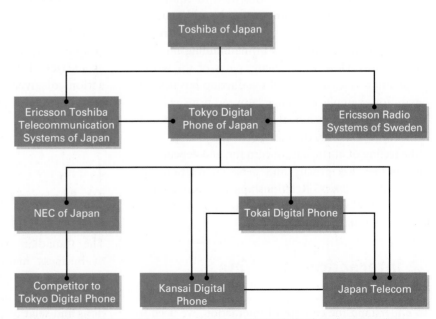

Source: Adapted from Desirée Blankenburg Holm, Kent Eriksson and Jan Johanson, "Creating value through mutual commitment to business network relationships," *Strategic Management Journal*, Vol. 20(5), pp. 467–486, May 1999. Copyright © 1999 John Wiley and Sons, Ltd.

Exhibit 7.2
EVOLUTION OF A NETWORK SUPPLIER MODEL

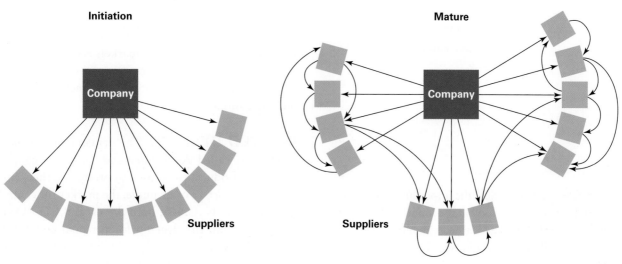

personal relationships. *Guanxi* networks help to distinguish collaborators from competitors and serve to build trust in business relationships.[10] There can be negative aspects to the *guanxi* network model, as it can lead to a group of insiders unwilling to interact with external firms and creating internal rules and regulations that fall outside the law. Many Canadian firms have found that the best way to compete in Asian countries is to form relationships with Asian firms.

The Canadian government created the Networks of Centres of Excellence (NCE) in 1989, but the program has really taken off since a new technology strategy was introduced in 2007. The NCE program brings together government and industry funding to develop networks of organizations to tackle economic and social changes in Canada. Consider some interesting facts about the NCE program:

▸▸ **There was a 160 percent rise in industry contributions to NCE from 2009 to 2012.**

DOWN UNDER PLUNDER

In Australia, a lack of network strength is one of the main reasons why there is no more automobile production Down Under. Car manufactures like General Motors and Ford have been driven out of the Australian markets because of a number of issues, including tariff regulations and labour costs, leaving Toyota in early 2014 as the only manufacturer still producing in Australia. Having only one producer places an incredible strain on the supplier network for car parts in Australia. With fewer cars to be built, suppliers of automobile parts will not be able to sustain their businesses. This lack of sustainability is partly the reason that as of 2018, there will be no

automobile production in Australia. Networks form the backbone of automobile manufacturing, and when that backbone is compromised, not a lot of structure is left.

derived demand demand in the business market that comes from demand in the consumer market

- ▸▸ In 2011–2012, NCEs created 145 new products and filed for 267 patents.

- ▸▸ In 2011–2012, there were 2483 new jobs created as a result of NCE activity.[11]

7-4 FUNDAMENTAL ASPECTS OF BUSINESS MARKETING

Now that we can appreciate the importance of relationships and networks, let's look at the fundamental aspects of business marketing. These aspects highlight the importance of the purchasing relationship between buyer and seller in a business interaction. Without knowledge of the types of buyers, buying situations, products, and services in business marketing, it would be virtually impossible to create a network of strong relationships.

7-4a Types of Demand

Because demand in business markets is driven by comparatively fewer buyers, there are aspects of demand that are important to consider. These include derived, inelastic, and joint demand.

DERIVED DEMAND The demand for business products is called **derived demand** because organizations buy products to be used in producing their customers' products. For example, the market for central processing units (CPUs), hard drives, and CD-ROMs is derived from the demand for personal computers (PCs). These items are only valuable as components of computers. Demand for these items rises and falls with the demand for PCs.

KEEPING THEIR "WITS" ABOUT THE NETWORK

PREVNet is an umbrella network of more than 120 leading Canadian researchers and 60 national youth-serving organizations in Canada. PREVNet's mission is to stop bullying in Canada and to promote safe and healthy relationships for all Canadian children and youth. This network was created through funding from the Government of Canada's Networks of Centres of Excellence (NCE) in 2006, and it has created numerous initiatives, resources, and assessment tools thanks to the cooperation of network members. Faced with the challenge of reducing the incidence of bullying in Canada (Canada ranks 25th out of 36 countries for bullying incidents according to the World Health Organization), PREVNet has connected two of its partner organizations, the Rock Solid Foundation and the Royal Canadian Mounted Police (RCMP), to further promote and disseminate WITS programs, which were first developed in the mid-1990s in Victoria, B.C.

Courtesy of the WITS Program

WITS stands for "Walk away, Ignore, Talk it out, Seek help" and is a program designed to provide skills to children from kindergarten to Grade 3 to deal with bullying and peer victimization. WITS LEADS stands for "Look and listen, Explore points of view, Act, Did it work?, and Seek help," which was created to provide developmentally appropriate strategies and resources to older elementary students so that they may become WITS Leaders in their schools.

Sources: PREVNet, "About Promoting Relationships and Eliminating Violence Network," 2014, www.prevnet.ca/about (accessed August 9, 2014); PREVNet, "WITS: Walk Away, Ignore It, Talk It Out, Seek Help," www.prevnet.ca/projects/wits (accessed August 9, 2014); and WITS Program, "Using Your WITS," www.witsprogram.ca (accessed August 9, 2014).

Because demand is derived, business marketers must carefully monitor demand patterns and changing preferences in final consumer markets, even though their customers are not in those markets. Moreover, business marketers must carefully monitor their customers' forecasts because derived demand is based on expectations of future demand for those customers' products.

Some business marketers not only monitor final consumer demand and customer forecasts but also try to influence final consumer demand. Aluminum producers use television and magazine advertisements to point out the convenience and recycling opportunities that aluminum offers to consumers who can choose to purchase juice and soft drinks in either aluminum or plastic containers.

INELASTIC DEMAND

The demand for many business products is inelastic with regard to price. *Inelastic demand* means that an increase or a decrease in the price of the product will not significantly affect demand for the product.

The price of a product used either in the production of another product or as part of another product is often a minor portion of the final product's total price. Therefore, demand for the final consumer product is not affected. If the price of automobile paint or spark plugs rises significantly—for example, 200 percent in one year—will the price increase affect the number of new automobiles sold that year? Probably not.

JOINT DEMAND

Joint demand refers to the demand for two or more items used together in a final product. For example, a decline in the availability of memory chips will slow the production of microcomputers, which will in turn reduce the demand for disk drives. Likewise, the demand for Apple operating systems exists as long as there is demand for Apple devices. Sales of the two products are directly linked.

FLUCTUATING DEMAND

The demand for business products, particularly for new plants and equipment, tends to be less stable than the demand for consumer products. A small increase or decrease in consumer demand can produce a much larger change in demand for the facilities and equipment needed to make the consumer product. Economists refer to this phenomenon as the **multiplier effect** (or **accelerator principle**).

7-4b Number of Customers

Business marketers usually have far fewer customers than consumer marketers. The advantage is that it is much easier to identify prospective buyers, monitor current customers' needs and levels of satisfaction, and personally attend to existing customers. The main disadvantage is that each customer becomes crucial—especially for those manufacturers that have only one customer. In many cases, this customer is the Canadian government. The success or failure of one bid can make the difference between prosperity and bankruptcy.

© iStockphoto.com/Evgeny Terentyev

joint demand the demand for two or more items used together in a final product

multiplier effect (accelerator principle) the phenomenon in which a small increase or decrease in consumer demand can produce a much larger change in demand for the facilities and equipment needed to make the consumer product

EDUCATION DERIVATION

Here is a quick activity to help you understand derived demand better: Take the textbook you have in your hands (or on your laptop or mobile phone). First, think about all the companies that had to work together for this textbook to have been published. Done? Your list should have included pulp and paper companies, ink producers, binding companies (for the hard copy of the book), the publisher (Nelson, of course!), the companies with pictures in the textbook, and of course the postsecondary institutions (instructors, bookstore). The question that remains is, What is the consumer demand that the demand for a marketing textbook is derived from? (For the answer, see the facts and figures box at the end of the chapter.)

RECIPROCITY *is generally considered a reasonable business practice.*

Jeff Whyte/Shutterstock.com

7-4c Location of Buyers

Business customers tend to be much more geographically concentrated than consumers. For instance, many of Canada's largest B2B buyers are located in or around the large urban centres of Canada: Toronto, Montréal, Calgary, and Vancouver. The oil and gas industry is centred in Alberta, the automotive industry in southwestern Ontario, and the wine industry primarily in British Columbia and southern Ontario.

7-4d Type of Negotiations

Consumers are used to negotiating prices on automobiles and real estate. In most cases, however, Canadian consumers expect sellers to set the price

and other conditions of sale, such as time of delivery and credit terms. In contrast, negotiating is common in business marketing. Buyers and sellers negotiate product specifications, delivery dates, payment terms, and other pricing matters. Sometimes these negotiations occur during many meetings over several months. Final contracts are often very long and detailed.

7-4e Use of Reciprocity

Business purchasers often choose to buy from their own customers, a practice known as **reciprocity**. Once trust is developed in a business network, reciprocity is a natural progression where companies will become each other's best customers. For example, General Motors (GM) buys engines for use in its automobiles and trucks from BorgWarner, which in turn buys many of the automobiles and trucks it needs from GM. This practice is neither unethical nor illegal unless one party coerces the other and the result is unfair competition. The Japanese *keiretsu* and Chinese *guanxi* are good examples of systems that encourage reciprocity.

7-4f Use of Leasing

Consumers normally buy products rather than lease them. But businesses commonly lease expensive equipment, such as computers, construction equipment and vehicles, and automobiles. Leasing allows firms to reduce their capital outflow, acquire a seller's latest products, receive better services, and gain tax advantages.

The lessor, the firm providing the product, may be either the manufacturer or an independent firm. The benefits to the lessor include greater total revenue from leasing compared with selling and an opportunity to do business with customers who cannot afford to buy.

The concept of leasing fits well into the relationships and network model. A lease provides the basis for a long-term interaction, where two firms are reliant on each other for either payment for or use of a leased product.

7-4g Types of Business Products

There are numerous types of business products, and there are different classification systems used for them. (See Exhibit 7.3.) Here are the main categories:

- ‣ **MAJOR EQUIPMENT:** large and expensive purchases that depreciate over time (e.g., buildings, machinery).

- ‣ **ACCESSORY EQUIPMENT:** smaller in size and expense than major equipment, this equipment is more standardized and often sold to consumers as well (e.g., power tools, printers).

- ‣ **RAW MATERIALS:** unprocessed or untapped materials that are extracted or harvested for consumption of further processing (e.g., oil, canola, potash).

- ‣ **COMPONENT PARTS AND MATERIALS:** finished products ready for assembly or requiring very little in the way of further processing to become part of other products (e.g., engines, pulp paper, chemicals).

- ‣ **SUPPLIES:** consumable items that are not part of the final product but provide some solution to a business's needs (pencils, paper, coffee).

BUSINESS SERVICES **Business services** include a number of actions that are not necessarily part of the final product but may have a direct impact on the customer's willingness to buy and maintain a relationship over time. While services can be as basic as hiring janitorial staff to clean an office on a weekend, there are important services that can be provided to customers.

Providing a support or help line for customers to help with or troubleshoot any challenges with a product is one example of an important business service. With the rising importance of leasing options for a number of industries, the product becomes only part of the interaction, as much of the focus is placed on the services that are needed during the leasing period.

Exhibit 7.3
TYPES OF BUSINESS PRODUCTS

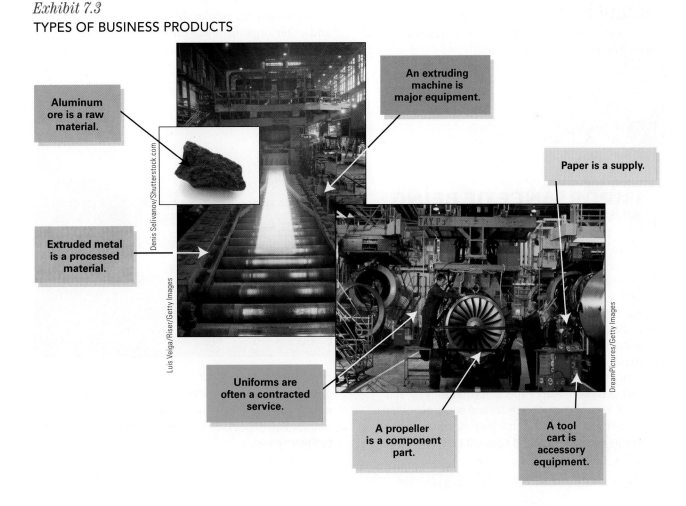

Aluminum ore is a raw material.

An extruding machine is major equipment.

Paper is a supply.

Extruded metal is a processed material.

Uniforms are often a contracted service.

A propeller is a component part.

A tool cart is accessory equipment.

Denis Selivanov/Shutterstock.com

Luis Veiga/Riser/Getty Images

DreamPictures/Getty Images

7-5 CLASSIFYING BUSINESS CUSTOMERS

Now that the major components of business marketing have been identified, it is time to turn our attention to the business customer. While traditional means of segmentation are not as useful in business marketing because of the unique nature of the business customer, there are still means with which to organize and structure business customers.

7-5a Major Categories of Business Customers

The business market consists of four major categories of customers: producers, resellers, governments, and institutions.

PRODUCERS The producer segment of the business market includes profit-oriented individuals and organizations that use purchased goods and services to produce other products, to incorporate into other products, or to facilitate the daily operations of the organization. Examples of producers include construction, manufacturing, transportation, finance, real estate, and food service firms. In the early 2000s, Canada was a major exporter of cars, pulp and paper, and electronics. Today, all those areas of production have lower export numbers. These areas of production have been replaced by oil and gas, minerals, chemicals, and food products.[12]

Producers are often called **original equipment manufacturers (OEMs)**. This term includes all individuals and organizations that buy business goods and incorporate them into the products that they produce for eventual sale to other producers or to consumers. Companies such as General Motors that buy steel, paint, tires, and batteries are said to be OEMs.

RESELLERS The reseller market includes retail and wholesale businesses that buy finished goods and resell them for a profit. A retailer sells mainly to final consumers; wholesalers sell mostly to retailers and other organizational customers. Wholesale trade contributed $71.1 billion to Canada's gross domestic

IMPORTANCE OF BEING MALLEY-ABLE

Malley Industries is a New Brunswick–based company that provides vehicle and product solutions to organizations that carry equipment, cargo, or people. Malley specializes in ambulances, which it sells to customers as far away as Chile. Malley Industries also manufactures wheelchair-accessible conversions and law enforcement vehicles, and produces a broad variety of custom commercial vehicles. As well, it designs and manufactures plastic components, creating unique products that enhance special functionality for end users in the automotive sector and numerous other industries. This company has been successful by meeting clients' varying needs and ensuring that its products

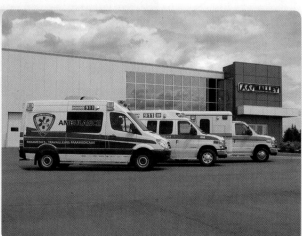

Courtesy of Malley Industries Inc.

exceed customer expectations. Their growth has been through their ability to diversify and develop creative solutions that solve problems for their expanding customer base.

Sources: "Malley Industries," *Canadian Business Journal*, 2014, www.cbj.ca/business_in_action/manufacturing/it_took_20_years_for_malley_industries_to_become_an_overnight_su.html (accessed August 9, 2014) ; and "Malley: About Us," www.malleyindustries.com/about-us/ (accessed August 9, 2014).

product (GDP) in 2011, while retail trade contributed slightly more at $76.9 billion.[13]

Consumer product firms, such as Procter & Gamble, McCain Foods, and Canada Dry Motts, sell directly to large retailers and retail chains and through wholesalers to smaller retail units. Retailing is explored in detail in Chapter 14.

Business product distributors are wholesalers that buy business products and resell them to business customers. They often carry thousands of items in stock and employ sales forces to call on business customers. Businesses that want to buy a gross of pencils or a hundred kilograms of fertilizer typically purchase these items from local distributors rather than directly from manufacturers.

GOVERNMENTS A third major segment of the business market is government. Government organizations include thousands of federal, provincial or territorial, and municipal buying units. They make up what may be the largest single market for goods and services in Canada.

Contracts for government purchases are often put out for bid. Interested vendors submit bids (usually sealed) to provide specified products during a particular time. Sometimes the lowest bidder is awarded the contract. When the lowest bidder is not awarded the contract, strong evidence must be presented to justify the decision. Grounds for rejecting the lowest bid include lack of experience, inadequate financing, or poor past performance. Bidding allows all potential suppliers a fair chance at winning government contracts and helps ensure that public funds are spent wisely.

FEDERAL GOVERNMENT Name just about any good or service and chances are that someone in the federal government uses it. The federal government buys goods and services valued at approximately $16.05 billion per year, making it the nation's largest customer.[14]

Although much of the federal government's buying is centralized, no single federal agency contracts for all the government's requirements, and no single buyer in any agency purchases all that the agency needs. We can view the federal government as a combination of several large companies with overlapping responsibilities and thousands of small independent units.

MUNICIPAL, ACADEMIC, SOCIAL, AND HOSPITALS (MASH) Many of the entities in this category are run by either provincial, territorial, or local governments. These are significant customers in terms of size and scope in the Canadian market: health and social services institutions employ close to 900,000 people, while academic institutions employ over 380,000, and local government accounts for over 600,000 employees.[15]

In Canada, each province and territory sets its own regulations and buying procedures within this municipal, academic, social, and hospitals (MASH) sector. The potential for both large and small vendors is great, however, as more than 6000 municipal clients are spread across all the provinces and territories.

INSTITUTIONS The fourth major segment of the business market consists of institutions that seek to achieve goals other than the standard business goals

Zhong Chen/Shutterstock.com

of profit, market share, and return on investment. Excluding the MASH sector, this segment includes places of worship, labour unions, fraternal organizations, civic clubs, foundations, and other so-called nonbusiness organizations. Many firms have a separate sales force that calls on these customers.

7-5b Classification by Industry

If you are looking for more detail than a general classification of business customers provides, you can look to the NAICS system. The **North American Industry Classification System (NAICS)** is an industry classification system for North American business establishments. The system, developed jointly by the United States, Canada, and Mexico, provides a common industry classification system for the North American Free Trade Agreement (NAFTA) partners. Goods- or service-producing firms that use identical or similar production processes are grouped together. (See Exhibit 7.4.) This makes searching for, and finding, companies that provide products and services in hundreds of different industries across North America more efficient.

NAICS is an extremely valuable tool for business marketers engaged in analyzing, segmenting, and targeting markets. Each classification group is relatively homogeneous in terms of raw materials required, components used, manufacturing processes employed, and problems faced. The more digits in a code, the more homogeneous the group is. Therefore, if a supplier understands the needs and requirements of a few firms within a classification, requirements can be projected for all firms in that category. The number, size, and geographic dispersion of firms can also be identified. This information can be converted to market potential estimates, market share estimates, and sales forecasts. It can also be used for identifying potential new customers. NAICS codes can help identify firms that may be prospective users of a supplier's goods and services. For a complete listing of all NAICS codes, visit **www.naics.com**.

7-6 BUSINESS BUYING BEHAVIOUR

Once you are able to identify your customers, you still have to understand how they make purchase decisions. Learning about the makeup and motivation behind business buying provides excellent insights for marketers on how to create products and services that meet the needs of business customers.

7-6a Buying Centres

A **buying centre** includes all those people in an organization who become involved in the purchase decision. Membership and influence vary from company to company. For instance, in engineering-dominated firms, such as Bell Helicopter, the buying centre may consist almost entirely of engineers. In marketing-oriented firms, such as Toyota and IBM, marketing and engineering have almost equal authority. In consumer goods firms, such as Procter & Gamble, product managers and other marketing decision makers may dominate the buying centre. In a small manufacturing company, almost everyone may be a member.

The number of people involved in a buying centre varies with the complexity and importance of the purchase decision. The composition of the buying group will usually change from one purchase to another and sometimes even during various stages of the buying process. To make matters more complicated, buying centres do not appear on formal organization charts.

Exhibit 7.4
HOW NAICS WORKS

NAICS Level	NAICS Code	Description
Sector	51	Information
Subsector	513	Broadcasting and telecommunications
Industry group	5133	Telecommunications
Industry	51332	Wireless telecommunications carriers, except satellite
Subdivision of industry	513321	Paging

For example, although a formal committee may have been set up to choose a new plant site, such a committee is only part of the buying centre. Other people, such as the company president, often play informal yet powerful roles. In a lengthy decision-making process, such as finding a new plant location, some members may drop out of the buying centre when they can no longer play a useful role. Others whose talents are needed then become part of the centre. No formal announcement is ever made concerning "who is in" and "who is out."

NATURE OF BUYING Unlike consumers, business buyers usually approach purchasing rather formally. Businesses use professionally trained purchasing agents or buyers who spend their entire career purchasing a limited number of items. They get to know the items and the sellers well. Some professional purchasers earn the designation of Certified Purchasing Manager (CPM) after participating in a rigorous certification program.

NATURE OF BUYING INFLUENCE Typically, more people are involved in a single business purchase decision than in a consumer purchase. Experts from fields as varied as quality control, marketing, and finance, as well as professional buyers and users, may be grouped in a buying centre.

ROLES IN THE BUYING CENTRE As in family purchasing decisions, several people may play a role in the business purchase process.

IMPLICATIONS OF BUYING CENTRES FOR THE MARKETING MANAGER Successful vendors realize the importance of identifying who is in the decision-making unit, each member's relative influence in the buying decision, and each member's evaluative criteria. Successful selling strategies often focus on determining the most important buying influences and tailoring sales presentations to the evaluative criteria most important to these buying-centre members. For example, Loctite Corporation, the manufacturer of Super Glue and industrial adhesives and sealants, found that engineers were the most important influencers and deciders in adhesive and sealant purchase decisions. As a result, Loctite focused its marketing efforts on production and maintenance engineers.

7-6b Buying Situations

Business firms, especially manufacturers, must often decide whether to make something or buy it from an outside supplier. The decision is essentially one of economics. Can an item of similar quality be bought at a lower price elsewhere? If not, is

BUSINESS PURCHASING ROLES

» **INITIATOR:** the person who first suggests making a purchase.

» **INFLUENCERS/EVALUATORS:** people who influence the buying decision. They often help define specifications and provide information for evaluating options. Technical personnel are especially important as influencers.

» **GATEKEEPERS:** group members who regulate the flow of information. Frequently, the purchasing agent views the gatekeeping role as a source of his or her power. An administrative assistant may also act as a gatekeeper by determining which vendors schedule an appointment with a buyer.

» **DECIDER:** the person who has the formal or informal power to choose or approve the selection of the supplier or brand. In complex situations, it is often difficult to determine who makes the final decision.

» **PURCHASER:** the person who actually negotiates the purchase. It could be anyone from the president of the company to the purchasing agent, depending on the importance of the decision.

» **USERS:** members of the organization who will actually use the product. Users often initiate the buying process and help define product specifications.

manufacturing it in-house the best use of limited company resources? For example, Briggs & Stratton Corporation, a major manufacturer of four-cycle engines, might be able to save $150,000 annually on outside purchases by spending $500,000 on the equipment needed to produce gas throttles internally. Yet Briggs & Stratton could also use that $500,000 to upgrade its carburetor assembly line, which would save $225,000 annually. If a firm does decide to buy a product instead of making it, the purchase will either be a new task buy, a modified rebuy, or a straight rebuy.

NEW TASK BUY

A **new task buy** is a situation requiring the purchase of a product for the first time. For example, suppose a manufacturing company needs a better way to page managers while they are working on the shop floor. Currently, each of the several managers has a distinct ring, for example, two short and one long, which sounds over the plant intercom when a manager is being paged in the factory. The company decides to replace its buzzer system of paging with hand-held wireless radio technology that will allow managers to communicate immediately with the department initiating the page. This situation represents the greatest opportunity for new vendors. No long-term relationship has been established for this product, specifications may be somewhat fluid, and the buyers are generally more open to new vendors.

If the new item is a raw material or a critical component part, the buyer cannot afford to run out of supply. The seller must be able to convince the buyer that the seller's firm consistently delivers a high-quality product on time.

Eimantas Buzas/Shutterstock.com

MODIFIED REBUY

A **modified rebuy** is normally less critical and less time-consuming than a new buy. In a modified-rebuy situation, the purchaser wants some change in the original good or service. It may be a new colour, greater tensile strength in a component part, more respondents in a marketing research study, or additional services in a janitorial contract.

Because the two parties are familiar with each other and credibility has been established, buyer and seller can concentrate on the specifics of the modification. In some cases, though, modified rebuys are open to outside bidders. The purchaser uses this strategy to ensure that the new terms are competitive. An example is the manufacturing company buying radios with a vibrating feature for managers who have trouble hearing the ring over the factory noise. The firm may open the bidding to examine the price/quality offerings of several suppliers.

STRAIGHT REBUY

A **straight rebuy** is the situation vendors prefer. The purchaser is not looking for new information or new suppliers. An order is placed and the product is provided as in previous orders. Usually, a straight rebuy is routine because the terms of the purchase have been agreed to in earlier negotiations. An example would be the previously cited manufacturing company purchasing, on a regular basis, additional radios from the same supplier.

One common instrument used in straight-rebuy situations is the purchasing contract. Purchasing contracts are used with high-volume products that are bought frequently. In essence, because of the purchasing contract, the buyer's decision making becomes routine and the salesperson is promised a sure sale. The advantage to the buyer is a quick, confident decision, and the advantage to the salesperson is reduced or eliminated competition.

Suppliers must remember not to take straight-rebuy relationships for granted. Retaining existing customers is much easier than attracting new ones.

7-6c Evaluative Criteria for Business Buyers

Business buyers evaluate products and suppliers against three important criteria: quality, service, and price—often in that order.

QUALITY In evaluative criteria, quality refers to technical suitability. A superior tool can do a better job in the production process, and superior packaging can increase dealer and consumer acceptance of a brand. Evaluation of quality also applies to the salesperson and the salesperson's firm. Business buyers want to deal with reputable salespeople and companies that are financially responsible. Quality improvement should be part of every organization's marketing strategy.

SERVICE Almost as much as business buyers want satisfactory products, they also want satisfactory service. A purchase offers several opportunities for service. Suppose a vendor is selling heavy equipment. Pre-purchase service could include a survey of the buyer's needs. After thorough analysis of the survey findings, the vendor could prepare a report and recommendations in the form of a purchasing proposal. If a purchase results, postpurchase service might consist of installing the equipment and training those who will be using it. Postpurchase services may also include maintenance and repairs. Another service that business buyers seek is dependability of supply. They must be able to count on delivery of their order when it is scheduled to be delivered. Buyers also welcome services that help them to sell their finished products. Services of this sort are especially appropriate when the seller's product is an identifiable part of the buyer's end product.

PRICE Business buyers want to buy at low prices—at the lowest prices, in most circumstances. However, when a buyer pressures a supplier to cut prices to a point where the supplier loses money, the supplier is almost forced to take shortcuts on quality. The buyer also may, in effect, force the supplier to quit selling to him or her. The buyer will then need to find a new source of supply.

As we noted in Chapter 2, ethics refers to the moral principles or values that generally govern the conduct of an individual or a group. Ethics can also be viewed as the standard of behaviour by which conduct is judged.

Many companies also have codes of ethics that help guide buyers' and sellers' behaviour. In general, these codes deal both with "doing things right" and "the right thing to do." The Supply Chain Management Association (SCMA) has developed the "SCMA Code of Ethics for Professionals in the Field of Supply Chain Management" to guide Canadian purchasing agents in their dealings with vendors; you can find this code at **www.scmanational.ca.**

SUPPLIER–BUYER RELATIONSHIP The three buying situations described above provide a context to the changing nature of supplier–buyer relationships. While there can be some stability with a straight rebuy, often buyers are looking for the supplier to make adjustments and improvement to maintain the relationship over time. The supplier–buyer relationship has been called "the backbone of economic activities in the modern world." A recent study looked at the supplier–buyer relationship by examining 130 suppliers and the multinational firm with which they were conducting business. It was determined that that average number of years of a supplier–buyer relationship was slightly over six. The suppliers came from different industries and provided different products ranging from machinery and equipment to component parts and materials. The researchers in this study also noted that the more of an identity that suppliers create in their networks, the stronger and more sustainable the relationships become.[16]

7-7 BUSINESS MARKETING ONLINE

The online world presents a great opportunity for business marketing. Given the challenge of trying to find customers and suppliers to create a network of solid relationships, firms are looking online for help. While the possibilities for business marketing online are immense, the B2B world is still trying to find the best way to conduct business online.

The creation and growth of business marketing online followed a pattern similar to that of the Internet. As websites became more advanced and online security was improved, businesses began to conduct business online. The term *e-commerce* (electronic commerce) was attached to the business-to-business world and described the transactions that were taking place between firms via the Internet. Given the sheer volume of products and services exchanged between businesses around the world, the ability to complete transactions online created a buzz.

Huge sales numbers were published, touting an online e-commerce world with billions of dollars changing hands in transactions. In Canada, $122 billion worth of goods and services were sold over the Internet by Canadian businesses in 2012, an amount that has more than doubled since 2007.[17] But this amount, as large as it may seem, makes up only 4 percent of sales of goods and services in Canada. Only 11 percent of Canadian firms were selling online in 2012, a modest increase from 7 percent in 2007.

With new technologies creating excellent online interfaces, it is perplexing why Canadian business-to-business companies do not invest more time and effort to create a stronger online presence. Nine out of ten businesses reported using the Internet in 2012; however, only 45 percent reported having a website. Companies that reported selling to consumers had a much higher likelihood of having a website than businesses focused on selling to other businesses.

These troubling statistics prompted the federal government of Canada to table a report titled "E-Commerce in Canada: Pursuing the Promise." The report highlights many of the statistical trends previously mentioned, and attempts to find a way to get Canadian businesses more engaged in the world of online commerce commerce. According to a study cited in the report, only 15 percent of Canadian companies surveyed used an online presence for marketing purposes.[18] (See Exhibit 7.5 for usage rates of specific B2B marketing tactics.)

The problem? There are several. Most notable is the cost of creating an online presence and the access to funding to make that happen. Other concerns include security issues and the fear of revealing company information online. The government report presented some solutions to the problem, with the focus on improving broadband Internet access and improving online payment systems.[19]

There are many roadblocks for business marketing online in Canada, but there are some trends in the marketplace that might make this move forward a little easier.

7-7a Trends in B2B Online Marketing

A number of new technologies and approaches can help businesses improve online presence and sales.

THE GROWTH OF MOBILE Oracle, a worldwide leader in technology and online solutions for businesses, published its well-known "B2B Commerce Study" based on discussions with world leaders in business marketing online. A main finding from the Oracle report in 2013: almost one-third of respondents in the survey stated an intention to invest in mobile technologies in 2013.[20] Business marketers are beginning to see the power of online applications that are built for phones and tablets, and how building their own application could greatly improve the chances of conducting business online.

IMPORTANCE OF CONTENT MARKETING Borrowing from the business-to-consumer (B2C) market is another solid trend for business marketers. An area of greater importance for B2B marketers online is getting the word out about their company—which is what content marketing is all about. Recently, the B2B Content Marketing Benchmarks Report was published, and it showed that 93 percent of B2B marketers are using content marketing.[21] Much of that content marketing is happening

Exhibit 7.5

TACTICS USED IN B2B MARKETING

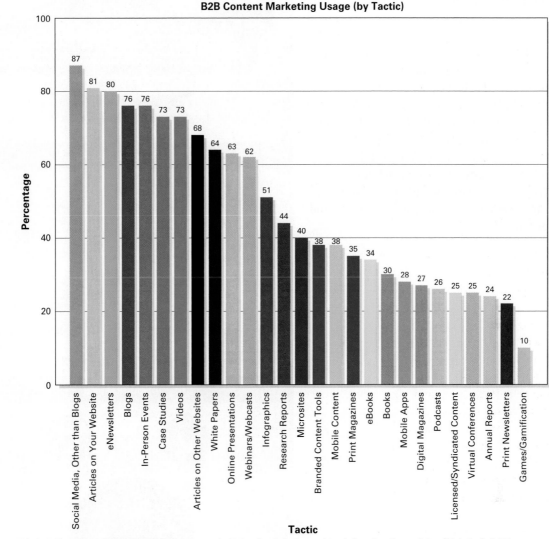

B2B Content Marketing Usage (by Tactic)

Source: www.marketingprofs.com/charts/2013/11759/2014-b2b-content-marketing-benchmarks-budgets-and-trends. Reproduced by permission of MarketingProfs, LLC.

online with B2B online content marketing tools, such as blogs, articles on websites, e-newsletters, videos, and the most popular—social media.

SOCIAL MEDIA GROWTH While many view social media as a consumer-driven phenomenon, it is important to remember that some of the earliest adopters of social media were firms with a strong B2B component: IBM, Sun Microsystems,

and Hewlett Packard. Given the importance of each relationship in business marketing, companies need to put a great deal of time and effort into making sure their social media presence is handled properly.

Recently, CEOs of B2B companies were polled and asked about the importance of social media in online business interactions. Almost eight out of ten CEOs identified the importance of social networks

An area of great importance for B2B marketers online is
GETING THE WORD OUT *about their company.*

and social media as part of an online engagement strategy.[22]

LinkedIn is the most popular social media site for businesses to interact. A recent Forrester Study noted that 40 percent of B2B decision makers use LinkedIn to research and interact with a vendor or business partner. Contrast this with 88 percent of those decision makers using LinkedIn to keep in touch with peers and colleagues.[23] The same Forrester report also encourages business marketers to have a Twitter and Facebook presence. Despite an overwhelming usage by consumers, these social media sites can still be avenues for content marketing and advertising.

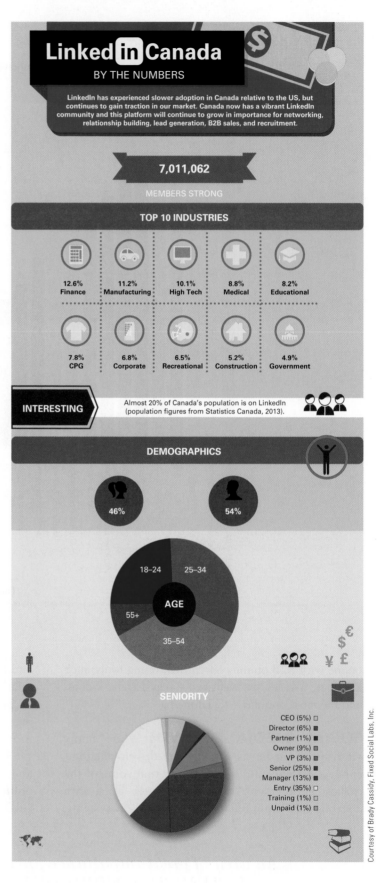

"Coca-Cola doesn't care if it loses a few customers to a rival. However, a company that makes engines for commercial auto fleets CARES DEEPLY *about* EACH *and* EVERY CUSTOMER."

—Paul Gillin (B2B social media strategist)

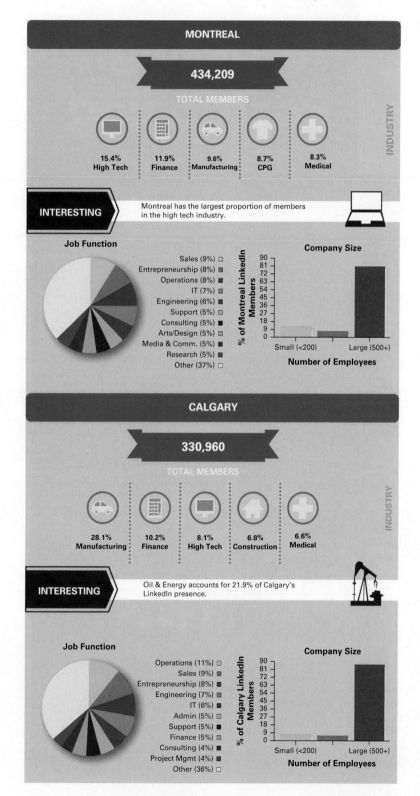

Chapter 8

Segmenting, Targeting, and Positioning

Market segmentation plays a key role in the marketing strategy of almost all successful organizations.

After you finish this chapter, go to
www.nelson.com/student *for* **STUDY TOOLS.** 📋------->

8-1 MARKET SEGMENTATION

The term **market** means different things to different people. We are all familiar with the supermarket, stock market, labour market, fish market, and flea market. All these types of markets share several characteristics. First, they are composed of people (consumer markets) or organizations (business markets). Second, these people or organizations have wants and needs that can be satisfied by particular product categories. Third, they have the ability to buy the products they seek. Fourth, they are willing to exchange their resources, usually money or credit, for desired products. In sum, a market is (1) people or organizations with (2) needs or wants and with (3) the ability and (4) the willingness to buy. A group of people or an organization that lacks any one of these characteristics is not a market.

Within a market, a **market segment** is a subgroup of people or organizations sharing one or more characteristics that cause them to have similar product needs. At one extreme, we can define every person and every organization in the world as a market segment because each is unique. At the other extreme, we can define the entire consumer market as one large market segment and the business market as another large segment. All people have some similar characteristics and needs, as do all organizations.

From a marketing perspective, market segments can be described as being somewhere between the two extremes. The process of dividing a market into meaningful, relatively similar, and identifiable segments or groups is called **market segmentation**. The purpose of market segmentation is to enable the

market people or organizations with needs or wants and the ability and willingness to buy

market segment a subgroup of people or organizations sharing one or more characteristics that cause them to have similar product needs

market segmentation the process of dividing a market into meaningful, relatively similar, and identifiable segments or groups

marketer to tailor marketing mixes to meet the needs of one or more specific segments.

8-2 THE IMPORTANCE OF MARKET SEGMENTATION

Until the 1960s, few firms practised market segmentation. When they did, it was more likely a haphazard effort rather than a formal marketing strategy. Before 1960, for example, the Coca-Cola Company produced only one beverage and aimed it at the entire pop market. Today, Coca-Cola offers more than a dozen different products to market segments on the basis of diverse consumer preferences for flavours and for calorie and caffeine content. Coca-Cola offers traditional pop flavours, energy drinks (such as Powerade), flavoured teas (Heaven and Earth), fruit drinks (Fruitopia), and water (Dasani).

Marketers segment markets for three important reasons. First, segmentation enables marketers to identify groups of customers with similar needs and to analyze the characteristics and buying behaviour of these groups. Second, segmentation provides marketers with information to help them design marketing mixes specifically matched with the characteristics and desires of one or more segments. Third, segmentation is consistent with the marketing concept of satisfying customer wants and needs while meeting the organization's objectives.

8-3 BASES FOR SEGMENTING CONSUMER MARKETS

Marketers use **segmentation bases**, or **variables**, which are characteristics of individuals, groups,

or organizations, to divide a total market into segments. The choice of segmentation bases is crucial because an inappropriate segmentation strategy may lead to lost sales and missed profit opportunities. The key is to identify bases that will produce substantial, measurable, and accessible segments that exhibit different response patterns to marketing mixes.

Markets can be segmented by using a single variable, such as age group, or by using several variables, such as age group, gender, and education. Although a single-variable segmentation is less precise, it has the advantage of being simpler and easier to use than multiple-variable segmentation. The disadvantages of multiple-variable segmentation are that it is often more difficult to use than single-variable segmentation; usable secondary data are less likely to be available; and as the number of segmentation bases increases, the size of the resulting segments decreases. Nevertheless, the current trend is toward using more rather than fewer variables to segment most markets. Multiple-variable segmentation is clearly more precise than single-variable segmentation.

Consumer goods marketers commonly use one or more of the following characteristics to segment markets: geography, demographics, psychographics, benefits sought, and usage rate.

Ermek/Shutterstock.com

8-3a Geographic Segmentation

Geographic segmentation refers to segmenting markets by a region of a country or a region of the world, market size, market density, or climate. Market density means the number of people within a unit of land, such as a census tract. Climate is commonly used for geographic segmentation because of its dramatic impact on residents' needs and purchasing

THREE REASONS TO GO REGIONAL

1. To find new ways to generate sales in sluggish and intensely competitive markets

2. To appeal to local preferences

3. To react quickly to competition

Avon, a brand associated with older generations, is attempting to break into a more youthful market with its Mark brand of beauty products. From their dorms, college and university students sell the brightly coloured makeup in its funky packaging.

behaviour. Snow blowers, water and snow skis, clothing, and air-conditioning and heating systems are products with varying appeal, depending on climate. Not all Pizza Hut restaurants around the world serve the same pizza toppings that are commonly available in Canada. For example, Pizza Hut in Japan offers squid and other seafood toppings so it can meet the regional food preferences of its Japanese customers.

8-3b Demographic Segmentation

Marketers often segment markets on the basis of demographic information because such information is widely available and often relates to consumers' buying and consuming behaviour. Some common bases of **demographic segmentation** are age, gender, income, ethnic background, and family life cycle.

AGE SEGMENTATION Marketers use a variety of terms to refer to different age groups: newborns, infants, preschoolers, young children, tweens, teens, young adults, baby boomers, Generation X, Generation Y, and seniors. Age segmentation can be an important tool, as a brief exploration of the market potential of several age segments illustrates.

demographic segmentation
segmenting markets by age, gender, income, ethnic background, and family life cycle

Through the spending of their allowances, earnings, and gifts, children account for, and influence, a great deal of consumption. Tweens (ages 9 to 14), who comprise approximately 2 million of Canada's total population, have direct spending power of approximately $2 billion, and growing, and an influence over how their families spend another $20 billion.[1] Tweens desire to be kids but also want some of the fun of being a teenager. Many retailers such as Old Navy, American Eagle Outfitters, and Bluenotes serve this market with clothing that is similar in style to that worn by teenagers and young adults.

The teenage market (ages 15 to 19) includes more than 2.1 million individuals,[2] and, like the tweens, this market accounts for substantial purchasing power, most of which is spent on clothing, entertainment, and food. Teens spend an average of 13 hours per week online compared with a weekly average of 19 hours for adults.[3] Magazines specifically designed to appeal to teenage girls include *Teen Vogue, Teen People, CosmoGIRL!, Elle Girl, Seventeen,* and *girlworks.*[4] Clothing marketers such as Ralph Lauren, Guess, DKNY, Dior, Giorgio Armani, and Juicy Couture advertise heavily in these magazines.[5]

The baby boom generation, born between 1947 and 1965, makes up the largest age segment, with 9.6 million people in the group, approximately 29 percent of the entire Canadian population.[6] The Canadian population is the youngest among the G8 countries but has the largest percentage of boomers. The highest percentage of baby boomers in Canada reside in Québec, B.C., and Atlantic Canada.[7] Together, baby boomers and the older generation (seniors) form a large and very lucrative market. Individuals 50 years old and older are continuing to lead active, fully involved lifestyles. Baby boomers represent tremendous current and future market potential for a wide range of products, including retirement properties, health and wellness products, automobiles with features designed for their age group, and other goods and services you might not

TWEENS, *those between the ages of 9 and 14, have a* SPENDING POWER *of* $2.0 BILLION, *and they influence how their families spend another* $20 billion.

THE NISSAN ROGUE. TESTED FOR CITY LIVING.
The award winning Small Urban Crossover with available intuitive All-Wheel Drive,¹ exceptional fuel efficiency and XM™ Satellite Radio² is ready for city living. To learn more about the Nissan Rogue visit **nissan.ca**

SHIFT urban

expect. Not only are baby boomers often nostalgic and eager to continue their active lives, but they now can afford to buy top-of-the-line models of products from their youth. Marketers find it hard to please boomers because of their unique needs and tastes; at the same time, this segment is so varied in its age composition that targeting it as one large market creates marketing problems.[8]

Seniors (those ages 65 and older) are especially attracted to companies that build relationships by taking the time to get to know them and their preferences. Most Canadian seniors, who number nearly 5 million,[9] do not, however, think of themselves as old, or as seniors, despite their demands for traditional seniors' products. Seniors are more likely than younger adults to have the combination of free time, money, and good health that allows them to pursue leisure-time activities, especially education and travel.[10] Mississauga-based Block Drug Company, having realized that today's seniors are healthier and perceive themselves to be younger than any seniors before, launched a very different promotional campaign for its Polident brand of denture cleanser.

Canadian seniors are increasingly using technology to stay in touch with their extended families and to shop for products and services they need; however, the rate of adoption of new technological devices, such as a smartphone—at 29 percent of seniors—is lower than that of the general population.[11]

GENDER SEGMENTATION Marketers of products such as clothing, cosmetics, personal-care items, magazines, jewellery, and footwear commonly continue to segment markets by gender. Many marketers that have traditionally focused almost exclusively on women have now recognized the importance and potential of the male segment. For example, males are increasingly involved in wedding planning—deciding on everything from the site, seating plans, and table decorations to the wedding cake and keepsakes for guests. As men become more involved with their weddings, businesses such as engagement consultants, resorts, and spas are beginning to create special packages designed to attract men.[12]

Brands that have traditionally been targeted to men, such as Gillette razors and Nivea for Men, are increasingly targeting women.[13] The Entertainment Software Association, a trade group, found that women are buying just as much game software as men, resulting in more game companies and websites focusing their marketing efforts on girls and women.[14] Conversely, several Internet sites provide guidance for grooms: the WeddingChannel.com's groom-centric content includes holiday proposal dos and don'ts.[15]

INCOME SEGMENTATION Income is a popular demographic variable for segmenting markets because income level influences consumers' wants and determines their buying power. Many markets are segmented by income, including the markets for housing, clothing, automobiles, and food. For example, in the auto industry, many car manufacturers have two different brands aimed at different income groups, such as Honda and Acura; Nissan and Infiniti; Toyota and Lexus. Honda, Nissan, and Toyota are targeted at relatively lower-income consumers than Acura, Infiniti, and Lexus buyers.

ETHNIC SEGMENTATION Canada is a very culturally diverse country, and Canadian marketers are strongly aware of the multicultural makeup of the market. When considering Canada's ethnic communities, marketers might first focus on French Canadian and English Canadian markets, which are the largest, but they will then consider the other ethnic populations. Many companies are segmenting their markets according to ethnicity, and some marketers are developing unique approaches to sizable ethnic segments.

Recent Canadian surveys also show that English and French bilingualism is on the decline, whereas bilingualism in the form of English and one immigrant language is on the rise.[16]

Tracking ethnic communities is one of a multicultural marketer's most challenging and most important tasks. Some companies have found that segmenting according to the main ethnicities is not precise enough. Nearly one in five Canadian is an immigrant and the emerging society can be termed *postmulticultural*, where immigrants are identifying themselves as Canadian first.[17] For example, a study on the impact of 2010 Vancouver Olympics found that Canadians, regardless of their heritage, showed deep pride in being Canadian first. This means that Canadian marketers will have to adapt their strategies in the coming decade to meet the changing sentiments of the first-generation Canadians.

Regardless of the segment being targeted, marketers need to stay educated about the consumers they are pursuing, convey a message that is relevant to each particular market, use the Internet as a vehicle to educate ethnic markets about brands and products, and use integrated marketing techniques to reinforce the message in various ways.

FAMILY LIFE-CYCLE SEGMENTATION Consumer buying behaviour varies, and the variations are often not sufficiently explained by the

The median Canadian family INCOME is $76,000 per year, while median individual income is $27,600.[18] More than 3.3 million Canadians spend in excess of 30 percent of their incomes on housing.[19]

family life cycle (FLC) a series of stages determined by a combination of age, marital status, and the presence or absence of children

demographic factors of gender, age, and income. The consumption patterns among people of the same age and gender frequently differ because they are in different stages of the family life cycle. The **family life cycle (FLC)** is a series of stages determined by a combination of age, marital status, and the presence or absence of children.

According to the 2011 Canadian census, there are 9.4 million families in Canada. Out of this number,

one-quarter are what are known as the "traditional" families, which include a husband, a wife, and children.[20] The number of same-sex couples increased 42.4 percent between 2006 and 2011 to 64,575, with nearly one-third of them classified as same-sex married couples while others were in common-law relationships.[21]

Exhibit 8.1 illustrates numerous FLC patterns and shows how families' needs, incomes, resources, and expenditures differ at each stage. The horizontal flow shows the traditional family life cycle. The lower

Exhibit 8.1

FAMILY LIFE CYCLE

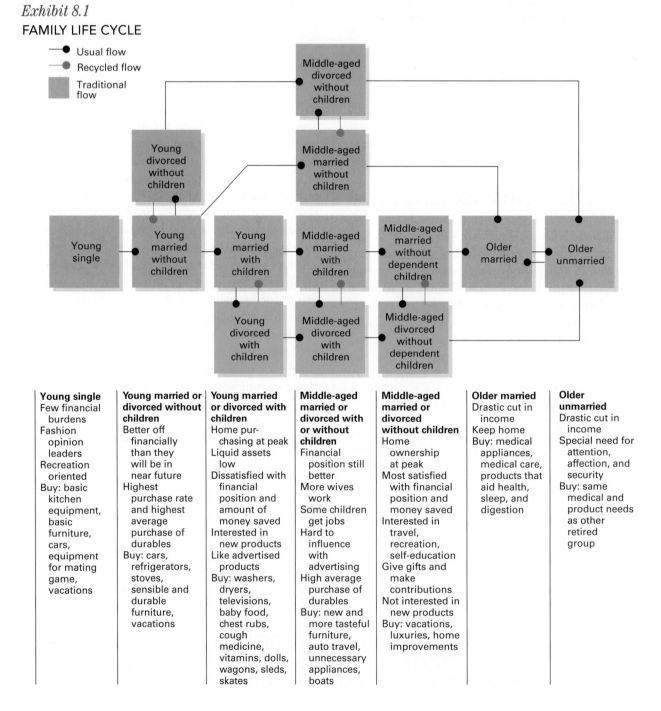

Young single	Young married or divorced without children	Young married or divorced with children	Middle-aged married or divorced with or without children	Middle-aged married or divorced without children	Older married	Older unmarried
Few financial burdens	Better off financially than they will be in near future	Home purchasing at peak	Financial position still better	Home ownership at peak	Drastic cut in income	Drastic cut in income
Fashion opinion leaders	Highest purchase rate and highest average purchase of durables	Liquid assets low	More wives work	Most satisfied with financial position and money saved	Keep home	Special need for attention, affection, and security
Recreation oriented	Buy: cars, refrigerators, stoves, sensible and durable furniture, vacations	Dissatisfied with financial position and amount of money saved	Some children get jobs	Interested in travel, recreation, self-education	Buy: medical appliances, medical care, products that aid health, sleep, and digestion	Buy: same medical and product needs as other retired group
Buy: basic kitchen equipment, basic furniture, cars, equipment for mating game, vacations		Interested in new products	Hard to influence with advertising	Give gifts and make contributions		
		Like advertised products	High average purchase of durables	Not interested in new products		
		Buy: washers, dryers, televisions, baby food, chest rubs, cough medicine, vitamins, dolls, wagons, sleds, skates	Buy: new and more tasteful furniture, auto travel, unnecessary appliances, boats	Buy: vacations, luxuries, home improvements		

part of the exhibit lists some of the characteristics and purchase patterns of families in each stage of the traditional life cycle. The exhibit also acknowledges that about half of all first marriages end in divorce. When young married couples move into the young-divorced stage, their consumption patterns often revert to those of the young-single stage of the cycle. About four out of five divorced persons remarry by middle age and re-enter the traditional life cycle, as indicated in the exhibit by the recycled flow.

At certain points in the life cycle, consumers are especially receptive to marketing efforts. Soon-to-be-married couples are typically considered to be the most receptive because they are making brand decisions about products that could last longer than their marriages. Similarly, young parents are the target of companies promoting baby products, as these parents expect to have higher expenses. A thorough understanding of the FLC can help marketers to design, develop, and successfully sell their products in the most competitive manner.

8-3c Psychographic Segmentation

Age, gender, income, ethnicity, family life-cycle stage, and other demographic variables are usually helpful in developing segmentation strategies, but often they don't paint the entire picture. Demographics provide the skeleton, but psychographics add meat to the bones. **Psychographic segmentation** is market segmentation on the basis of the variables in the box below.

Psychographic variables can be used individually to segment markets or can be combined with other

> **psychographic segmentation** market segmentation on the basis of personality, motives, lifestyles, and geodemographics categories
>
> **geodemographic segmentation** segmenting potential customers into neighbourhood lifestyle categories

PSYCHOGRAPHIC SEGMENTATION VARIABLES

» **PERSONALITY:** Personality is a person's traits, attitudes, and habits. Porsche Cars North America Inc. understood the demographics of the Porsche owner: a fortysomething male university graduate earning over $100,000 per year. However, research discovered that this general demographic category actually included five personality types that more effectively segmented Porsche buyers. As a result, Porsche refined its marketing, and the company's sales rose by 48 percent.[22]

» **MOTIVES:** Marketers of baby products and life insurance appeal to consumers' emotional motives—namely, to care for their loved ones. Using appeals to economy, reliability, and dependability, carmakers such as Subaru and Suzuki target customers by appealing to their rational motives.

» **LIFESTYLES:** Lifestyle segmentation divides people into groups according to the way they spend their time, the importance of the things around them, their beliefs, and socioeconomic characteristics such as income and education.

» **GEODEMOGRAPHICS:**
Geodemographic segmentation clusters potential customers into neighbourhood lifestyle categories. It combines geographic, demographic, and lifestyle segmentations. Geodemographic segmentation helps marketers develop marketing programs tailored to prospective buyers who live in small geographic regions, such as neighbourhoods, or who have very specific lifestyle and demographic characteristics.

variables to provide more detailed descriptions of market segments. One combination approach is the Environics PRIZM C2[23] lifestyle segmentation system that divides the Canadian population into 66 different groups, clusters, or consumer types, all with catchy names. The clusters combine basic demographic data, such as age, ethnicity, and income, with lifestyle information, such as magazine and sports preferences, taken from consumer surveys. For example, the "Kids and Cul-de-Sacs" group comprises upscale, suburban families with a median household income of $68,900 who tend to shop online and visit Disney theme parks. The "Bohemian Mix" cluster refers to professionals aged 22 to 44 with a median income of $38,500, who are likely to shop at the Gap and read *Elle* magazine. The program also predicts the neighbour-hoods across the country to which the clusters are likely to gravitate.

8-3d Benefit Segmentation

Benefit segmentation is the process of grouping customers into market segments according to the benefits they seek from the product. Most types of market segmentation are based on the assumption that related subgroups of people or organizations share one or more characteristics that cause them to have similar product needs. Benefit segmentation is different because it groups potential customers on the basis of their needs or wants rather than some other characteristic, such as age or gender.

Customer profiles can be developed by exam-ining demographic information associated with people seeking certain benefits. This informa-tion can be used to match marketing strategies to selected target markets. The many different types of performance energy bars with various combina-tions of nutrients are aimed at consumers looking for different benefits. For example, PowerBar is designed for athletes looking for long-lasting fuel, while PowerBar Protein Plus is aimed at those who want extra protein for replenishing their muscles after strength training. Carb Solutions High Protein Bars are for those on low-carb diets; Luna Bars are targeted to women who want a bar with soy pro-tein, calcium, and fewer calories; and Clif Bars are for people who want a natural bar made from such ingredients as rolled oats, soybeans, and organic soy flour.[24]

8-3e Usage-Rate Segmentation

Usage-rate segmentation divides a market by the amount of product bought or consumed. Categories vary depending on the product, but they are likely to include some combination of the following: former users, potential users, first-time users, light or irregular users, medium users, and heavy users. Segmenting by usage rate enables marketers to focus their efforts on heavy users or to develop mul-tiple marketing mixes aimed at different segments. Because heavy users often account for a sizable por-tion of all product sales, some marketers focus on the heavy-user segment. Developing customers into heavy users is the goal behind many frequency and loyalty programs.

The **80/20 principle** holds that 20 percent of all customers generate 80 percent of the demand. Although the percentages usually are not exact, the general idea often holds true. For example, in the fast-food industry, heavy users account for only one of five fast-food patrons but represent 60 percent of all visits to fast-food restaurants. Thus, according to an Agriculture and Agri-Food Canada report, heavy users account for $9.36 billion of the $15.6 billion spent on fast food at Canada's 25,000 fast-food restaurants.[25]

8-4 CRITERIA FOR SUCCESSFUL SEGMENTATION

To be useful, a segmentation scheme must produce segments that meet four basic criteria:

1. *Substantiality:* A segment must be large enough to warrant developing and maintaining a special marketing mix. This criterion does not necessarily mean that a segment must have many potential cus-tomers. Marketers of custom-designed homes and business buildings, commercial airplanes, and large computer systems typically develop marketing pro-grams tailored to each potential customer's needs. In most cases, however, a market segment needs many potential customers to make commercial sense.

2. *Identifiability and measurability:* Segments must be identifiable and their size measurable. Data on

the population within geographic boundaries, the number of people in various age categories, and other social and demographic characteristics are often easy to get, and they provide fairly concrete measures of segment size.

3. *Accessibility:* The firm must be able to reach members of targeted segments with customized marketing mixes. Some market segments are more difficult to reach, for example, senior citizens (especially those with reading or hearing disabilities), individuals who don't speak English, and people who are illiterate.

4. *Responsiveness:* Markets can be segmented by using any criteria that seem logical. Unless one market segment responds to a marketing mix differently from other segments, however, that segment need not be treated separately. For instance, if all customers are equally price-conscious about a product, marketers have no need to offer high-, medium-, and low-priced versions to different segments.

8-5 BASES FOR SEGMENTING BUSINESS MARKETS

The business market consists of four broad segments: producers, resellers, government, and institutions (for a detailed discussion of the characteristics of these segments, see Chapter 7). Whether marketers focus on only one or on all four of these segments, they are likely to find diversity among potential customers. Thus, further market segmentation offers just as many benefits to business marketers as it does to consumer-product marketers.

8-5a Company Characteristics

Company characteristics, such as geographic location, type of company, company size, and product use, can be important segmentation variables. Some markets tend to be regional because buyers prefer to purchase from local suppliers, and distant suppliers may have difficulty competing in terms of price and service. Therefore, firms that sell to geographically concentrated industries benefit by locating close to their markets.

Segmenting by customer type allows business marketers to tailor their marketing mixes to the unique needs of particular types of organizations or industries. Many companies are finding this form of segmentation to be quite effective. For example, Rona, one of the largest do-it-yourself retailers in Canada, has targeted professional repair and remodelling contractors in addition to consumers.

A commonly used basis for business segmentation is volume of purchase (heavy, moderate, light). Another is the buying organization's size, which may affect its purchasing procedures, the types and quantities of products it needs, and its responses to different marketing mixes. Many products, especially raw materials, such as steel, wood, and petroleum, have diverse applications. How customers use a product may influence the amount they buy, their buying criteria, and their selection of vendors.

8-5b Buying Processes

Many business marketers find it helpful to segment current and prospective customers on the basis of how they buy. For example, companies can segment some business markets by ranking key purchasing criteria, such as price, quality, technical support, and service. Atlas Corporation developed a commanding position in the industrial door market by providing customized products in just four weeks, which was much faster than the industry average of 12 to 15 weeks. Atlas's primary market is companies with an immediate need for customized doors.

The purchasing strategies of buyers may provide useful segments. Two purchasing profiles that have been identified are satisficers and optimizers. **Satisficers** are business customers who place their order with the first familiar supplier to satisfy their product and delivery requirements. **Optimizers**, on the other hand, are business customers who consider numerous suppliers (both familiar and unfamiliar), solicit bids, and study all proposals carefully before selecting one.

The personal characteristics of the buyers themselves (their demographic characteristics, decision styles, tolerance for risk, confidence levels, job responsibilities, etc.) influence their buying behaviour and thus offer a viable basis for segmenting some business markets. IBM computer buyers, for example, are sometimes characterized as being more risk-averse than buyers of less expensive computers that perform

satisficers business customers who place their order with the first familiar supplier to satisfy their product and delivery requirements

optimizers business customers who consider numerous suppliers, both familiar and unfamiliar, solicit bids, and study all proposals carefully before selecting one

essentially the same functions. In advertising, therefore, IBM stressed its reputation for high quality and reliability.

8-6 STEPS IN SEGMENTING A MARKET

The purpose of market segmentation, in both consumer and business markets, is to identify marketing opportunities. Markets are dynamic, so it is important that companies proactively monitor their segmentation strategies over time. Often, once customers or prospects have been assigned to a segment, marketers think their task is done. After customers are assigned to an age segment, for example, they stay there until they reach the next age bracket or category, which could be 10 years in the future. Thus, the segmentation classifications are static, but the customers and prospects are changing. Marketing managers typically follows these six steps to segment a market based on the criteria described in the previous sections:

1. *Select a market or product category for study.* Define the overall market or product category to be studied. It may be a market in which the firm already competes, a new but related market or product category, or a totally new market or category.

2. *Choose a basis or bases for segmenting the market.* This step requires managerial insight, creativity, and market knowledge. No scientific procedures guide the selection of segmentation variables. However, a successful segmentation scheme must produce segments that meet the four basic criteria discussed earlier in this chapter.

3. *Select segmentation descriptors.* After choosing one or more bases, the marketer must select the segmentation descriptors. Descriptors identify the specific segmentation variables to use. For example, a company that selects usage segmentation needs to decide whether to pursue heavy users, nonusers, or light users.

4. *Profile and analyze segments.* The profile should include the segments' sizes, expected growth, purchase frequency, current brand usage, brand loyalty, and long-term sales and profit potential. This information can then be used to rank potential market segments by profit opportunity, risk, consistency with organizational mission and objectives, and other factors important to the firm.

5. *Select target markets.* Selecting target markets is not a part of the segmentation process but is a natural outcome of the segmentation process. It is a major decision that influences and often directly determines the firm's marketing mix. This topic is examined in detail later in this chapter.

6. *Design, implement, and maintain appropriate marketing mixes.* The marketing mix has been described as product, place (distribution), promotion, and pricing strategies intended to bring about mutually satisfying exchange relationships with target markets. Chapters 9 through 19 explore these topics in detail.

Not all segments are stable over time and dynamic segmentation reflects real-time changes made to market segments based on a customer's ongoing search and shopping behaviours. For example, the chapters.indigo.ca website suggests book titles based on a site visitor's browsing and purchase pattern. Similar segmentation techniques are also used by Netflix.ca. Dynamic segmentation uses advanced mathematical and computer programming techniques to offer highly customized solutions to customers.

8-7 STRATEGIES FOR SELECTING TARGET MARKETS

So far, this chapter has focused on the market segmentation process, which is only the first step in deciding whom to approach about buying a product. The next task is to choose one or more target markets. A **target market** is a group of people or organizations for which an organization designs, implements, and maintains a marketing mix intended to meet the needs of that group, resulting in mutually satisfying exchanges. Because most markets will include customers with different characteristics, lifestyles, backgrounds, and income levels, a single marketing mix is unlikely to attract all segments of the market. Thus, if a marketer wants to appeal to more than one segment of the market, it must develop different marketing mixes. For example, Sunlight Saunas makes saunas that retail at various prices between $1695 and $5595. The company segments its customer base into luxury and health markets based on data it gathers from visits to its website and conversations with potential customers. The same saunas appeal to both market segments, but the different groups require different marketing messages. Three general strategies are used for selecting target markets—undifferentiated, concentrated, and multisegment targeting. Exhibit 8.2 illustrates the advantages and disadvantages of each targeting strategy.

8-7a Undifferentiated Targeting

A firm using an **undifferentiated targeting strategy** essentially adopts a mass-market philosophy, viewing the market as one big one with no individual segments. The firm uses one marketing mix for the entire market. A firm that adopts an undifferentiated targeting strategy assumes that individual customers have similar needs that can be met through a common marketing mix. As such, marketers of commodity products, such as flour and sugar, are likely to use an undifferentiated targeting strategy.

The first firm in an industry sometimes uses an undifferentiated targeting strategy. With no competition, the firm may not need to tailor marketing mixes to the preferences of market segments. At one time, Coca-Cola used this strategy with its single product offered in a single size in a familiar green bottle. Undifferentiated marketing allows companies to save on production and marketing and achieve economies of mass production. Also, marketing costs may be lower when a company has only one product to promote and a single channel of distribution.

Too often, however, an undifferentiated strategy emerges by default rather than by design, reflecting a failure to consider the advantages of a segmented approach. The result is often sterile, unimaginative product offerings that have little appeal to anyone.

Another problem associated with undifferentiated targeting is the company's greater susceptibility to competitive inroads. Coca-Cola forfeited its position as the leading cola seller in supermarkets to Pepsi-Cola in the late 1950s, when Pepsi began offering its cola in several sizes.

Undifferentiated marketing can succeed. A grocery store in a small, isolated town may define all the people who live in the town as its target market. It may offer one marketing mix that generally satisfies everyone. This strategy is not likely to be as effective, however, when a community has three or four grocery stores.

8-7b Concentrated Targeting

Firms using a **concentrated targeting strategy** select a market **niche** (one segment of a market) to target its marketing efforts. Because the firm is appealing to a single segment, it can concentrate on understanding the needs, motives, and satisfactions of that segment's members and on developing and maintaining a highly specialized marketing mix. Some firms find that concentrating resources and meeting the needs of a narrowly defined market segment is more profitable than spreading resources over several different segments.

Small firms often adopt a concentrated targeting strategy to compete effectively with much larger firms. ChickenBurger, a fast-food restaurant in Halifax, describes itself as "destination for families and friends" and refers to itself as a historical destination, thus using a concentrated strategy to compete

undifferentiated targeting strategy a marketing approach that views the market as one big market with no individual segments and thus uses a single marketing mix

concentrated targeting strategy a strategy used to select one segment of a market to target marketing efforts

niche one segment of a market

Exhibit 8.2

ADVANTAGES AND DISADVANTAGES OF TARGET MARKETING STRATEGIES

Targeting Strategy	Advantages	Disadvantages
Undifferentiated targeting	• Potential savings on production/marketing costs	• Unimaginative product offerings
		• Company more susceptible to competition
Concentrated targeting	• Concentrates resources	• Segments too small or changing
	• Can better meet the needs of a narrowly defined segment	• Large competitors may more effectively market to niche segment
	• Allows some small firms to better compete with larger firms	
	• Provides strong positioning	
Multisegment targeting	• Greater financial success	• High costs
	• Economies of scale in producing/marketing	• Cannibalization

against the large fast-food chain restaurants.[26] Similarly, Starbucks became successful by focusing on customers who wanted gourmet coffee products.

Concentrated targeting violates the old adage "Don't put all your eggs in one basket." If the chosen segment is too small or if it shrinks because of environmental changes, the firm may suffer negative consequences. A concentrated strategy can also be disastrous for a firm that is not successful in its narrowly defined target market. For example, before Procter & Gamble introduced Head & Shoulders shampoo, several small firms were already selling antidandruff shampoos. Head & Shoulders was introduced with a large promotional campaign, and the new brand immediately captured over half the market. Within a year, several of the firms that had been concentrating on this market segment went out of business.

8-7c Multisegment Targeting

A firm that chooses to serve two or more well-defined market segments and develops a distinct marketing mix for each has a **multisegment targeting strategy**. Maple Leaf Foods offers many different kinds of bacon, such as regular and salt-reduced bacon. For convenience-seeking consumers, the company has developed Ready Crisp microwaveable bacon. For health-conscious segments, it offers turkey and chicken bacons. Cosmetics companies, on the other hand, seek to increase sales and market share by targeting multiple age and ethnic groups. Maybelline and CoverGirl, for example, market different lines catering to tween girls, teenagers, young adult women, older women, and women in visible minority groups.

Multisegment targeting is used for stores and shopping formats, not just for brands. Marketers at Best Buy have identified five customer segments, which they have personalized by naming them: "Jill," a busy suburban mom; "Buzz," a focused, active younger male; "Ray," a family man who likes his technology practical; "BB4B" (Best Buy for Business), a small-business employer; and "Barry," an affluent professional male who's likely to drop tens of thousands of dollars on a home theatre system.

Multisegment targeting offers many potential benefits to firms, including greater sales volume, higher profits, larger market share, and economies of scale in manufacturing and marketing. Yet it may also involve greater product design, production, promotion, inventory, marketing research, and management costs. Before deciding to use this strategy, firms should compare the benefits and costs of multisegment targeting to those of undifferentiated and concentrated targeting.

Another potential cost of multisegment targeting is **cannibalization**, which occurs when sales of a new product cut into sales of a firm's existing products. In many cases, however, companies prefer to steal sales from their own brands rather than lose sales to a competitor. Marketers may also be willing to cannibalize existing business to build new business.

8-8 ONE-TO-ONE MARKETING

Most businesses today use a mass-marketing approach designed to increase *market share* by selling their products to the greatest number of people. For many businesses, however, a more efficient and profitable strategy is to use **one-to-one marketing** to increase their *share of customers*—in other words, to sell more products to each customer. One-to-one marketing is an individualized marketing method that uses customer information to build long-term, personalized, and profitable relationships with each customer. The goal is to reduce costs through customer retention while increasing revenue through customer loyalty. One of the best-known examples of one-to-one marketing is Dell, which lets buyers customize the computer they order.

The difference between one-to-one marketing and the traditional mass-marketing approach can be compared with shooting a rifle versus a shotgun. If you have good aim, a rifle is the more efficient weapon to use. A shotgun, on the other hand, increases your odds of hitting the target when it is more difficult to focus. Instead of scattering messages far and wide across the spectrum of mass media (the shotgun approach), one-to-one marketers look for opportunities to communicate with each individual customer (the rifle approach).

Though it is much easier to deliver highly customized services, there are several examples of companies that seek active customer participation in the design and delivery of products. For example, through NikeID consumers can customize their shoes and other accessories. Several factors suggest that personalized communications and product customization will continue to expand as more and more companies understand

positioning a process that influences potential customers' overall perception of a brand, a product line, or an organization in general

ONE-TO-ONE *marketers look for opportunities to communicate with each* INDIVIDUAL *customer.*

Stephen Hilger/Bloomberg/Getty Images

why and how their customers make and execute purchase decisions. At the same time, production costs of highly customized product is falling, thus creating a viable business model for companies. At least four trends will lead to the continuing growth of one-to-one marketing:

▸▸ **PERSONALIZATION:** The one-size-fits-all marketing of the past no longer fits. Consumers do not want to be treated like the masses. Instead, they want to be treated as the individuals they are, with their own unique sets of needs and wants. By its personalized nature, one-to-one marketing can fulfill this desire.

▸▸ **TIME SAVINGS:** Consumers will have little or no time to spend shopping and making purchase decisions. Because of the personal and targeted nature of one-to-one marketing, consumers can spend less time making purchase decisions and more time doing the things that are important.

▸▸ **LOYALTY:** Consumers will be loyal only to those companies and brands that have earned their loyalty and reinforced it at every purchase occasion. One-to-one marketing techniques focus on finding a firm's best customers, rewarding them for their loyalty, and thanking them for their business.

▸▸ **TECHNOLOGY:** Advances in marketing research and database technology will allow marketers to collect detailed information on their customers, not just the approximation offered by demographics but specific names and addresses. Mass-media approaches will decline in importance as new technology offers one-to-one marketers a more cost-effective way to reach customers and enables businesses to personalize their messages to customers. With the help of database technology, one-to-one marketers can track their customers as individuals, even if they number in the millions.

One-to-one marketing is a huge commitment and often requires a 180-degree turnaround for marketers who spent the last half of the twentieth century developing and implementing mass-marketing efforts. Although mass marketing will probably continue to be used, especially to create brand awareness or to remind consumers of a product, the advantages of one-to-one marketing cannot be ignored.

8-9 POSITIONING

The development of any marketing mix depends on **positioning**, a process that influences potential overall perception of a brand, a product line, or an

TRINACRIA PHOTO/Shutterstock.com

STANDARD TISSUE

You might think a firm producing a standard product, such as toilet tissue, would adopt an undifferentiated strategy. However, this market has industrial segments and consumer segments. Industrial buyers want an economical, single-ply product sold in boxes of a hundred rolls. The consumer market demands a more versatile product in smaller quantities. Within the consumer market, the product is differentiated with

designer print or no print, cushioned or noncushioned, scented or unscented, economy priced or luxury priced, and single, double, or triple rolls. Fort Howard Corporation, the market share leader in industrial toilet paper, does not even sell to the consumer market.

position the place a product, brand, or group of products occupies in consumers' minds relative to competing offerings

product differentiation a positioning strategy that some firms use to distinguish their products from those of competitors

perceptual mapping a means of displaying or graphing, in two or more dimensions, the location of products, brands, or groups of products in customers' minds

organization in general. **Position** is the place a product, brand, or group of products occupies in consumers' minds relative to competing offerings. Consumer goods marketers are particularly concerned with positioning. Procter & Gamble, for example, markets 11 different laundry detergents, each with a unique position.

Positioning assumes that consumers compare products on the basis of important features. Marketing efforts that emphasize irrelevant features are therefore likely to misfire. Effective positioning requires assessing the positions occupied by competing products, determining the important dimensions underlying these positions, and choosing a position in the market where the organization's marketing efforts will have the greatest impact. For example, Toyota Canada presents its philosophy of continuous improvement in three words—"make things better"—and positions itself as being environmentally friendly. With this positioning, Toyota is using product differentiation to create the perception that its products have very real advantages for the target market.

As the previous example illustrates, **product differentiation** is a positioning strategy that some firms use to distinguish their products from those of competitors. The distinctions can be either real or perceived. Companies can develop products that offer very real advantages for the target market. However, many everyday products, such as bleach, Aspirin, unleaded regular gasoline, and some soaps, are differentiated by such trivial means as brand names, packaging, colour, smell, or secret additives. The marketer attempts to convince consumers that a particular brand is distinctive and that they should demand it over competing brands.

Some firms, instead of using product differentiation, position their products as being similar to competing products or brands. For example, artificial sweeteners are advertised as tasting like sugar, and margarine is touted as tasting like butter.

8-9a Perceptual Mapping

Perceptual mapping is a means of displaying or graphing, in two or more dimensions, the location of products, brands, or groups of products in customers' minds. For example, Levi Strauss has developed for the youth market a range of products that range from different styles of jeans to nylon pants that can be unzipped into shorts. At the same time Levi's has strengthened its position in the adult apparel market by extending the Dockers and Slate brand casual clothing. Exhibit 8.3 presents a perceptual map that shows a positioning map for soft drinks.

8-9b Positioning Bases

Firms use a variety of bases for positioning, including the following:

» **ATTRIBUTE:** A product is associated with an attribute, a product feature, or a customer benefit. Rockport shoes are positioned as an always-comfortable brand that is available in a range of styles from working shoes to dress shoes.

Exhibit 8.3

PERCEPTUAL MAP AND POSITIONING STRATEGY FOR SOFT DRINKS

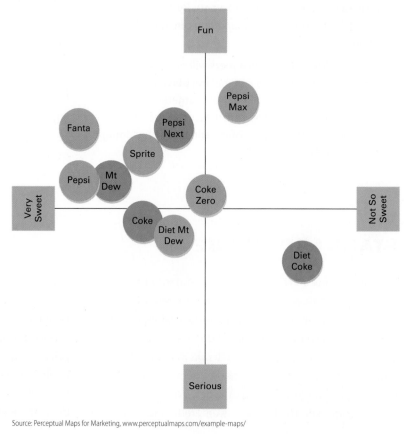

Source: Perceptual Maps for Marketing, www.perceptualmaps.com/example-maps/

repositioning changing consumers' perceptions of a brand in relation to competing brands

▸ **PRICE AND QUALITY:** This positioning base may stress high price as a signal of quality or emphasize low price as an indication of value. Denmark-based Lego uses a high-price strategy for its toy building blocks, whereas Montreal-based Mega Bloks uses a low-price strategy.[27] Similarly, Walmart has successfully followed the low-price and value strategy. Mass merchandiser Target has developed an interesting position that is based on price and quality. It is known as an upscale discounter, sticking to low prices but offering higher quality and design than most discount chains.

▸ **USE OR APPLICATION:** A company can stress a product's uses or applications as an effective means of positioning it with buyers. Snapple introduced a new drink called Snapple-a-Day that is intended for use as a meal replacement.

▸ **PRODUCT USER:** This positioning base focuses on a personality or type of user. Gap Inc. has several different brands: Gap stores offer basic casual pieces, such as jeans and T-shirts, to middle-of-the-road consumers at mid-level prices; Old Navy offers low-priced, trendy casual wear geared to youth and postsecondary-age groups; and Banana Republic is an upscale brand offering fashionable, luxurious business and casual wear to 25- to 35-year-olds[28]

▸ **PRODUCT CLASS:** The objective here is to position the product as being associated with a particular category of products—for example, positioning a margarine brand with butter. Alternatively, products can be disassociated from a category.

▸ **COMPETITOR:** Positioning against competitors is part of any positioning strategy. The Avis rental car positioning as number two exemplifies a company positioning against specific competitors.

▸ **EMOTION:** Positioning that uses emotion focuses on how the product makes customers feel. A number of companies use this approach. For example, Nike's "Just Do It" campaign didn't tell consumers what "it" is, but most got the emotional message of achievement and courage.

It is not unusual for a marketer to use more than one of these bases. A print ad in the "Got Milk?" campaign featuring pop singer Rihanna sporting a milk moustache reads as follows:

> "Drink it in. Pop star? Not exactly. Milk is more my move. Some studies suggest that teens who choose milk instead of sugary drinks tend to be leaner and the protein helps build muscle. So, shut up and drink."[29]

This ad reflects the following positioning bases:

▸ **PRODUCT ATTRIBUTE/BENEFIT:** The emphasis that protein in milk "helps build muscle" describes a product attribute. Choosing milk instead of sugary drinks results in a leaner body, a benefit.

▸ **USE OR APPLICATION:** Rihanna values milk—"milk is more my move."

▸ **PRODUCT USER:** The use of Rihanna, a successful pop music star, shows that milk is not just for kids.

▸ **PRODUCT CLASS (DISASSOCIATION):** The ad differentiates milk from other beverages, showing that milk is healthier than sugary drinks.

▸ **COMPETITOR (INDIRECT):** Rihanna prefers milk over other drinks.

▸ **EMOTION:** The ad conveys an upbeat, contemporary attitude.[30]

8-9c Repositioning

Sometimes products or companies are repositioned to sustain growth in slow markets or to correct positioning mistakes. **Repositioning** refers to changing consumers' perceptions of a brand in relation to competing brands.

Recently, Domino's Pizza engaged in a new repositioning strategy[31] after it realized a negative same-store growth for three years in a row. Its new CMO, Russell Weiner, wondered about how to revitalize the brand and increase sales and decided to focus on transparency in business as a theme to revitalize the brand. This strategy was well timed: most consumers after the 2008–2009 recession were questioning the sincerity of the business's managers in their dealings with consumers.

8-9d Developing a Positioning Statement

Segmenting, targeting, and positioning are key managerial activities that go beyond simply understanding the process of how to complete each task. Marketing managers often fail to develop and communicate effective positioning statements for their products/brands even though they might have developed effective market segments; thus, they fail to state how the business will compete in a given market segment. A positioning statement is also critical for consumers to understand what specific benefits will they obtain from a product. Tybout and Sterthal[32] provide guidelines for crafting a positioning statement:

1. *Targeted consumers:* Develop a brief statement of the target market in terms of their segment description.

2. *Frame of reference:* Develop a statement of the goal for the target market about the product benefit, thus identifying the consumption situations in which the product/brand is to be used.

3. *Point of difference:* Develop a statement asserting why the product/brand being offered is superior.

4. *Reason to believe:* Provide evidence to support the claim provided in the frame of reference.

Following is an excellent positioning statement from Black & Decker for their DeWalt power tools: "To the tradesman who uses his power tools to make a living and cannot afford downtime on the job [target], DeWalt professional power tools [frame of reference] are more dependable than other brands of professional power tools [point of difference] because they are engineered to the brand's historic high-quality standards and are backed by Black & Decker's extensive service network and guarantee to repair or replace any tool within 48 hours [reasons to believe]."[33]

20%
Percentage of customers responsible for 80 percent of a company's demand

6
Number of steps in segmenting a market

2
Number of supermarkets that go out of business for each Walmart supercentre built

13
Average number of hours a teen spends online each week

5 & 11
P&G has identified 5 different segments of detergent users in Canada and 11 in the United States

STUDY TOOLS **8**

LOCATED AT BACK OF TEXTBOOK
☐ *Tear-Out Chapter Review Card*

LOCATED AT WWW.NELSON .COM/STUDENT

☐ *End-of-chapter questions*
☐ *Interactive flashcards*
☐ *Audio and visual summaries*
☐ *Quizzes*
☐ *Additional cases*

The Marketing Environment, Social Responsibility, and Ethics Part 2 Case

Mary Kay, Inc.—Changing Consumer Demographics

Founded in 1963 by Mary Kay Ash and her son, Richard, Mary Kay, Inc. is a company that has long believed in the power of women. The company was founded with a focus on providing personal growth and financial independence to women. Dedicated to making life more beautiful for women, the company emphasized the Golden Rule of "praising people to success" and the principle of placing faith first, family second, and career third. Before her death in 2001, Mary Kay Ash received numerous awards that exemplified her personal beliefs, which were embedded as the heart and soul of the company.

MARY KAY, INC.

Mary Kay, Inc., headquartered in Addison, Texas, develops and manufactures beauty and personal care products for both women and men. The company spends millions of dollars and conducts more than 300,000 product tests to ensure that Mary Kay products meet the highest standards of quality, safety, and performance. Mary Kay doesn't test its products on animals. In fact, Mary Kay is committed to eliminating all animal testing. With products ranging from skin care to makeup to spa and body to fragrances, the company sells products through its direct sales force of more than 3 million independent beauty consultants in countries such as Argentina, Armenia,

Australia, Brazil, Canada, China, the Czech Republic, El Salvador, Finland, Germany, Guatemala, Hong Kong, India, Kazakhstan, Korea, Malaysia, Mexico, Moldova, New Zealand, Norway, the Philippines, Poland, Portugal, the Russian Federation, Slovakia, Spain, Sweden, Taiwan, Ukraine, the United Kingdom, the United States, and Uruguay. The company's worldwide wholesale sales topped $3 billion in 2013.

COSMETICS INDUSTRY AND TRENDS

The Canadian cosmetics industry constitutes a significant part of the $9.4 billion retail industry; its revenues for 2012 were estimated to be $1.7 billion.[1] However, the growth in the cosmetics industry in Canada has been slow since 2008, averaging 0.7 percent per year. Because of this, the competition between cosmetics companies has intensified, putting increased pressure on profit margins. Another significant feature of the cosmetics industry is that a large number of the products sold in Canada are imported. Currently, the figure stands at 94.9 percent, up from 89.2 percent in 2008.[2]

The top three players in the cosmetics industry in Canada are L'Oreal Canada, Inc., Unilever, and Procter &

Gamble. The overall value and volume of the cosmetics products consumers in Canada has remained unchanged, but the industry has witnessed a shift from consumption of prestige to mass-produced brands.[3] This downward pressure on prices has given value-conscious consumers access to prestige products. At the same time, mass brands that were sold exclusively to salons in the past are also becoming available to consumers, thus further increasing pressure on the cosmetics companies. Retail distribution of cosmetic products has also undergone a shift in Canada, with the majority of sales taking place through drug stores rather than through traditional department stores.

BEAUTY AND PERSONAL CARE PRODUCTS AND DIRECT SELLING

While consumers think twice before spending on high-end nonessential items, many beauty and personal care products are considered necessities. At the same time, beauty and personal care products do not have national boundaries—such products are universal and easily available through various retail channels, with direct selling being the predominant retail format. Direct selling is a method of distributing products directly to the consumer via person-to-person selling or party plan selling rather than from permanent retail locations. According to one report, beauty and personal care products are a cornerstone of the direct selling industry and, likewise, direct selling is good for the beauty and personal care products industry. Approximately 40 percent of all the direct sales in Canada are for personal care products that include cosmetics, jewellery, skin care, and so on.[4]

According to the Direct Sellers Association of Canada, an estimated 1.3 million people are involved in direct selling in Canada, with more than 66 million people engaged worldwide. Interestingly, more than 91 percent of direct sellers in Canada are women, and 75 percent of them are married.[5] The predominance of women in the direct selling marketplace has proven especially important for direct sellers like Mary Kay, Inc. Mary Kay has more than 39,000 independent sales directors across the globe, with approximately 575 women achieving this goal in Canada alone.[6]

TARGET MARKET

With women as its primary target market, Mary Kay has stayed abreast of changing buyer behaviour. For example, the company knows that the younger generation expects to touch and experiment with products, so it offers products, shades, packaging, and forms that both enable and encourage the potential user to try something new. Although there are geographic differences among preferences (e.g., Asian women focus on skin care, while Latin American and some European women are more interested in colour cosmetics and fragrances), the company has found that, worldwide, women are more similar than dissimilar in their preferences.

The number of Gen-Y women, between 18 and 25 years of age, is estimated to be 571 million globally, with a buying power of US$170 annually.[7] Mary Kay understands that it must continually refocus its attention on the ever-changing demographics of the market and reposition itself. Given the size and importance of the Gen-Y consumers, Mary Kay is introducing a new line of cosmetic products specifically designed for this segment. Mary Kay introduced four new colours of eye and lip products in 2014 that it expects will be more appealing to younger consumers and keep Mary Kay competitive.[8]

Targeting a younger market also forces Mary Kay to understand the decision-making process involved for Gen-Y consumers, who are very different from the previous market segments that the company targeted. Unlike, their mothers, Gen-Y women are independent, ambitious, socially well connected, and tech-savvy, and see their personal and professional lives differently. These younger women are impatient and headstrong and want to make a real difference in their own lives and the lives of others around them because of their dissatisfaction with the current corporate culture. Technology is fully integrated into all aspects of Gen-Y lives for communication, entertainment, and work. Appealing to this vast segment requires any company to make changes to how it approaches and appeals to consumers. Mary Kay has a unique combination of opportunities and challenges in this regard because of their reliance on direct selling. Gen-Y is short on time, and multitasking is a way of life for them. Direct selling can help time-conscious consumers, and also provides an opportunity to connect personally with them. Today, however, when more and more Gen-Y women are using mobile devices to organize their lives. Mary Kay will have to speak in a language that the Gen-Y segment can relate to. This new language must include words such as *Internet* in general and will have to pay particular attention to Facebook, YouTube, Twitter, WhatsApp, and other mobile communication technologies.

While the company has been successful product-wise with the younger demographic, Mary Kay, Inc. has been particularly astute at tapping into this changing demographic with respect to its independent sales consultants. Approximately one-third of its new sales consultants since 2010 are Gen-Yers, and nearly half of the U.S. sales force is under 35 years of age.[9] The average age of the Mary Kay consultant is now 36, and the company's fastest-growing segment of consultants is the 24- to 35-year-old age group. Because they represent the future of the company, Mary Kay, Inc. can provide these women with the opportunity to meet any goal they are willing to work toward—whether it is additional income or financial independence.[10]

Yet the company recognizes that other direct-selling companies also want to harness the power and dynamic of this age group. These young leaders are known for wanting increased flexibility, unlimited earning power, and the freedom to experiment in their work lives. There is a vast market opportunity for Mary Kay, Inc. in the millennial generation, and the company wants to take advantage of that opportunity to usher in a new era of direct selling of Mary Kay products.

QUESTIONS

1. **What challenges and opportunities do the changing demographics present to Mary Kay?**

2. **How can Mary Kay capitalize on the changing social and cultural environment of its target market to stay competitive?**

3. **How should Mary Kay create a target market?**

4. **How would you position Mary Kay in the Canadian cosmetics market?**

5. **What marketing research techniques can Mary Kay use to measure the attitudes of its consumers?**

Product Concepts

Chapter 9

The product is the starting point in creating a marketing mix.

"Don't find customers for your products, find products for your customers."

—Seth Godin

After you finish this chapter, go to
www.nelson.com/student *for* **STUDY TOOLS.**

9-1 WHAT IS A PRODUCT?

The product offering, the heart of an organization's marketing program, is usually the starting point in creating a marketing mix. Though many marketing mix decisions are made simultaneously, however, a marketing manager cannot determine a price, design a promotion strategy, or create a distribution channel until the firm has a product to sell. Moreover, an excellent distribution channel, a persuasive promotion campaign, and a fair price have no value when the product offering is poor or inadequate.

A **product** may be defined as anything, both favourable and unfavourable, received by a person in an exchange for possession, consumption, attention, or short-term use. It is important to note that not all products received by a someone can be owned by them because a product may be a tangible good (a pair of shoes), a service (a haircut), an idea ("don't litter"), a person (a political candidate or a celebrity), a place (a tourism destination "Inspiring the world to explore Canada"), or any combination of these. Customers can own a tangible product, like a pair of shoes, but they only use a service, such as staying at a hotel. For a tangible good, packaging, style, colour, options, and size are some typical product features. Just as important are such intangibles as service, the seller's image, the manufacturer's reputation, and the way consumers believe others will view the product.

To most people, the term *product* means a tangible good, but services, ideas, persons and places are also defined as products because they can be marketed by organizations. (Chapter 11 focuses specifically on the unique aspects of marketing services.) The marketing process identified in Chapter 1 is the same whether the product marketed is a good, a service, an idea, a person, a place, or some combination of these.

product anything, both favourable and unfavourable, received by a person in an exchange for possession, consumption, attention, or short-term use

business product
a product used to manufacture other goods or services, to facilitate an organization's operations, or to resell to other customers

consumer product
a product bought to satisfy an individual's personal wants

convenience product a relatively inexpensive item that merits little shopping effort

shopping product
a product that requires comparison shopping because it is usually more expensive than a convenience product and is found in fewer stores

9-2 TYPES OF CONSUMER PRODUCTS

Products can be broadly classified as either business or consumer products, depending on the buyer's intentions. The key distinction, as discussed earlier in the book, between the two types of products is their intended use. If the intended use is a business purpose, the product is classified as a business or industrial product. As explained in Chapter 7, a **business product** is used to manufacture other goods or provide services, to facilitate an organization's operations, or to resell to other customers. A **consumer product** is bought to satisfy an individual's personal wants. Sometimes the same item can be classified as either a business or a consumer product, depending on its intended use. Examples include light bulbs, pencils and paper, and computers.

We need to know about product classifications because different products are marketed differently: They are marketed to different target markets, often using different distribution, promotion, and pricing strategies.

Chapter 7 examined seven categories of business products and services: major equipment, accessory equipment, component parts, processed materials, raw materials, supplies, and services. This chapter examines an effective way of categorizing consumer products. Although they can be classified in several ways, the most popular approach includes these four types: convenience products, shopping products, specialty products, and unsought products. This approach classifies products according to how much effort is normally used to shop for them.

9-2a Convenience Products

A **convenience product** is a relatively inexpensive item that merits little shopping effort—that is, a consumer is unwilling to shop extensively for such an item. Candy, pop, small hardware items, and many grocery items fall into the convenience product category.

Consumers buy convenience products regularly, usually without much planning. Nevertheless, consumers do know the brand names of popular convenience products, such as Coca-Cola, Colgate toothpaste, Right Guard deodorant, and Gillette razors like the Venus Breeze. Convenience products normally require

Gillette Venus Breeze SPA

2 in 1
Razor *Plus*
Shave Gel Bars
Rasoir *Plus* barres
de gel à raser

SCENT OF
WHITE TEA
PARFUM DE
THÉ BLANC

1 Razor
rasoir
1 Cartridge with
Shave Gel Bars
cartouche avec
barres de gel à raser

NET WT/POIDS NET .067 OZ (1.9 g)

Courtesy of P&G Canada

wide distribution to be easily accessible to consumers. For example, Dentyne Ice gum is available everywhere, including at Walmart, Shoppers Drug Mart, Shell gas stations, newsstands, and vending machines.

Impulse products are a type of convenience products that consumers purchase without any planning and are usually stocked near the cash registers in stores. For example, candies, single servings of beverages, various fashion and gossip magazines, and unusual knick-knacks fall in this category and are placed near the cash registers for consumers to see and purchase at the last minute.

9-2b Shopping Products

A **shopping product** is a product that requires comparison shopping because it is usually more expensive than a convenience product and is found in fewer stores. Consumers usually buy a shopping product only after comparing different brands' style, practicality, price, and lifestyle compatibility. Shoppers are typically willing to invest some effort in this process to get their desired benefits.

Shopping products can be divided into two types: homogeneous and heterogeneous. Consumers perceive *homogeneous* shopping products as being basically similar in terms of their functions and features—for example, toasters, mixers, and other kitchen appliances tend to be similar. When shopping for homogeneous shopping products, consumers typically look for the lowest-priced brand that has the desired features. For example, consumers might compare Black & Decker, Betty Crocker, and Sunbeam toasters, perceive them to be similar, and select the one with the lowest price.

In contrast, consumers perceive *heterogeneous* shopping products as essentially different in terms of their features, quality, and performance—for example, furniture, clothing, housing, and universities. Consumers often have trouble comparing heterogeneous shopping products because the prices, quality, and features vary so much. The benefit of comparing heterogeneous shopping products is that consumers can find the best product or brand for their needs, a decision that is often highly individual. For example, it can be difficult to compare a small, private university with a large, public university.

9-2c Specialty Products

When consumers search extensively for a particular item with unique characteristics and are very reluctant to accept substitutes, that item is known as a **specialty product**. Specialty products don't have to be expensive; however, most expensive products, such as Patek Philippe watches, Rolls-Royce automobiles, Bose speakers, Ruth's Chris Steak House, and highly specialized forms of medical care are generally considered specialty products. An inexpensive product can also be considered a specialty item if it possesses a unique product or brand attribute; for example, people visiting several Canadian cities may want to try the pastry known as BeaverTails because of their unique taste, presentation, and limited availability.

Marketers of specialty products often use selective advertising to maintain their product's exclusive image. Distribution is often limited to one or a very few outlets in a geographic area. Brand names and quality of service are often very important.

9-2d Unsought Products

A product unknown to the potential buyer or a known product that the buyer does not actively seek is referred to as an **unsought product**. New products fall into this category until consumer awareness of them is increased through advertising and distribution.

Some goods are always marketed as unsought items, especially needed products that we do not like to think about or do not care to spend money on. Insurance, burial plots, and similar items require aggressive personal selling and highly persuasive advertising. Salespeople actively seek leads to potential buyers. Because consumers usually do not seek out this type of product, the company must approach customers directly through a salesperson, direct mail, or direct-response advertising.

9-3 PRODUCT ITEMS, LINES, AND MIXES

Rarely does a company sell a single product. More often, it sells a variety of products. Marketing managers make important decisions regarding the number and type of products a company should sell under a brand name in a given market. A **product item** is a specific version of a product that can be designated as a distinct offering among an organization's products. Campbell's Cream of Chicken Soup is an example of a product item (see Exhibit 9.1).

A group of closely related product items is a **product line.** For example, the column in Exhibit 9.1 titled "Soups" represents one of Campbell's product lines. Different container sizes and shapes also distinguish items in a product line. Diet Coke, for example, is available in cans and various plastic containers. Each size and each container is a separate product item.

An organization's **product mix** includes all the products it sells. All Campbell's products—soups, sauces, frozen entrées, beverages, and biscuits—constitute its product mix. Each product item in the product mix may require a separate marketing strategy. In some cases, however, product lines and even entire product mixes share some marketing strategy components. LG consumer electronics promotes all its products with the same theme of "Life is Good." Companies derive several benefits from organizing related items into product lines.

The product mix of a business organization can be described in terms of product mix width, product line length, depth, and consistency.

Product mix width (or breadth) refers to the number of product lines an organization offers. In Exhibit 9.1, for example, the width of Campbell's product mix is five product lines. **Product line length** is the number of product items in a product line. As shown in Exhibit 9.1, the sauces product line consists of four product items; the frozen entrée product line includes three product items. **Product line depth** refers to the number of types and sizes offered for each product in the line. For example, Campbell's soup offers different sizes of the tomato soups that also come in different flavours.

Firms increase the *width* of their product mix to diversify risk. To generate sales and boost profits, firms spread risk across many product lines rather than depending on only one or two. Firms also widen their product mix to capitalize on established reputations. The Oreo Cookie brand has been extended to include items such as breakfast cereal, ice cream, Jell-O pudding, and cake mix.

Firms increase the *length* and *depth* of their product lines to attract buyers with different preferences, to increase sales and profits by further segmenting the market, to capitalize on economies of scale in production and marketing, and to even out seasonal sales patterns. P&G is adding some lower-priced versions of its namesake brands, including Bounty Basic and Charmin Basic. These brands are targeted to more price-sensitive customers, a segment that Procter & Gamble had not been serving with its more premium brands.[1]

9-3a Adjustments to Product Items, Lines, and Mixes

Over time, firms change product items, lines, and mixes to take advantage of new technical or product developments or to respond to changes in the environment. They may adjust by modifying products, repositioning products, or extending or contracting product lines.

PRODUCT MODIFICATION Marketing managers must decide whether and when to modify

Exhibit 9.1

CAMPBELL'S PRODUCT LINES AND PRODUCT MIX

Width of Product Mix			
Soups	**Sauces**	**Beverages**	**Crackers**
Campbell Broths	Prego	V8	Goldfish
• Beef • Chicken	• Mushroom and Green Pepper • Tomato, Onion and Garlic • Original and more...	• Low Sodium Veg Cocktail • Smooth and Seasoned Cocktail • Berry Blend • Tropical Blend • Fusion Mango and more...	• Cheddar • Giant Goldfish • Cheddar Whole Grain • Cheese Trio • Colours and more...
Campbell Condensed			
• Bean with Bacon • Beef with Vegetable Barley • Cheddar Cheese			
Campbell Gardennay			
• Butternut Squash • Roasted Sweet Pepper Tomato			
Campbell Chunky			
• Chicken Corn Chowder • Chunky Beef			
Campbell Soups on the Go			
• Chicken Noodle • Chunky Sirloin Burger More...			

Product Line Length

existing products. **Product modification** changes one or more of a product's characteristics:

product modification changing one or more of a product's characteristics

planned obsolescence the practice of modifying products so those that have already been sold become obsolete before they actually need replacement

» **QUALITY MODIFICATION:** a change in a product's dependability or durability. Reducing a product's quality may allow the manufacturer to lower the price, thereby appealing to target markets unable to afford the original product. Conversely, increasing quality can help the firm compete with rival firms. Increasing quality can also result in increased brand loyalty, greater ability to raise prices, or new opportunities for market segmentation. Inexpensive ink-jet printers have improved in quality to the point that they can now produce photo-quality images.

» **FUNCTIONAL MODIFICATION:** a change in a product's versatility, effectiveness, convenience, or safety. Tide with Downy combines into one product the functions of both cleaning power and fabric softening.[2]

» **STYLE MODIFICATION:** an aesthetic product change, rather than a quality or functional change. Clothing and auto manufacturers also commonly use style modifications to motivate customers to replace products before they are worn out.

Companies often introduce changes that may focus on one of three types of modifications one at a time or sometimes modifications may include two or more dimensions at the same time. For example, Kleenex might introduce four-ply tissue paper that could be termed a quality modification only. However, suppose that Kleenex introduces a four-ply tissue paper in pink that also comes with or without moisturizer. In this case, the product introduction includes all three types of modifications. The key consideration here is that product modifications are periodically needed to meet changing consumer and competitive demands.

Planned obsolescence describes the practice of modifying products so that those products that have already been sold become obsolete before they actually need replacement. Some argue that planned obsolescence is wasteful; some claim it is unethical. Marketers respond that consumers favour planned obsolescence so that they can acquire products with the latest features and functions. Planned obsolescence is more frequent in some industries than in others. For example, computer and mobile phone manufacturers tend to introduce new models annually to entice consumers into replacing their older version of the products. It has come to be almost an annual ritual for Apple to introduce new versions of the iPhone and systematically phase out older versions, making them less compatible or completely incompatible with the newer operating systems and product accessories.

BENEFITS OF PRODUCT LINES

» **ADVERTISING ECONOMIES:** Product lines provide economies of scale in advertising. Several products can be advertised under the umbrella of the line. Campbell's can talk about its soup being "m-m-good" and promote the entire line.

» **PACKAGE UNIFORMITY:** A product line can benefit from package uniformity. All packages in the line may have a common look and still keep their individual identities. Again, Campbell's soup is a good example.

» **STANDARDIZED COMPONENTS:** Product lines allow firms to standardize components, thus reducing manufacturing and inventory costs. For example, General Motors uses the same parts on many automobile makes and models.

» **EFFICIENT SALES AND DISTRIBUTION:** A product line enables sales personnel for companies such as Procter & Gamble to provide a full range of choices to customers. Distributors and retailers are often more inclined to stock the company's products if it offers a full line. Transportation and warehousing costs are likely to be lower for a product line than for a collection of individual items.

» **EQUIVALENT QUALITY:** Purchasers usually expect and believe that all products in a line are of equal quality. Consumers expect that all Campbell's soups and all Gillette razors will be of similar quality.

REPOSITIONING Repositioning, as Chapter 8 explained, involves changing consumers' perceptions of a brand. Recently, Listerine, known for its antibacterial mouthwash qualities, has introduced, among others, Listerine Whitening Plus Restoring, Listerine Total Care, and Listerine Zero to emphasize its new product positioning in the market. Similarly, Head & Shoulders has repositioned itself away from being a dandruff-only shampoo and introduced 14 different variations to suit different hair care needs. Changing demographics, declining sales, or changes in the social environment often motivate firms to reposition established brands.

PRODUCT LINE EXTENSIONS

A **product line extension** occurs when a company's management decides to add products to an existing product line to compete more broadly in the industry. For example, the Diet Coke line includes multiple extensions: Diet Cherry Coke, Diet Coke with Lemon, and Diet Coke with Lime. Recently, Coca-Cola developed a brand extension for Diet Coke that was

designed to appeal to men ages 18 to 34 who want a lower-calorie drink but see Diet Coke as a woman's drink. The product is called Coca-Cola Zero.[3]

PRODUCT LINE CONTRACTION

Sometimes marketers can get carried away with product extensions (Does the world really need 41 varieties of Crest toothpaste?), and some extensions are not embraced by the market, such as Vanilla Coke. Other times, contracting product lines is a strategic move. Heinz deleted a number of product lines, such as vegetables, poultry, frozen foods, and seafood, to concentrate instead on the products it sells best: ketchup, sauces, frozen snacks, and baby food.[4]

Three major benefits are likely when a firm contracts its overextended product lines. First, resources become concentrated on the most important products. Second, managers no longer waste resources trying to improve the sales and profits of poorly performing products. Third, new product items have a greater chance of being successful because more financial and human resources are available to manage them.

9-4 BRANDING

The success of any business or consumer product depends in part on the target market's ability to distinguish one product from another. Branding is the main tool marketers use to distinguish their products from the competition's.

New specialized formula = functional modification

New design or convenient transportation = style modification

YOUR BRAND'S OVEREXTENDED WHEN . . .

▸▸ some products in the line do not contribute to profits because of low sales or they cannibalize sales of other items in the line.

▸▸ manufacturing or marketing resources are disproportionately allocated to slow-moving products.

▸▸ some items in the line are obsolete because of new product entries in the line or new products offered by competitors.

According to the American Marketing Association (AMA), a **brand** is a name, term, symbol, design, or combination thereof that identifies a seller's products and differentiates them from competitors' products.[5] However, in a broader sense a brand is much more than the name and symbols that a company can create: what a brand stands for also involves consumers and is the sum total of their expectations, feelings, thoughts, and actions that are associated with a brand. This deeper meaning of a brand is created by consumers over time when they hear, experience, and interact with a brand in

brand a name, term, symbol, design, or combination thereof that identifies a seller's products and differentiates them from competitors' products

Companies such as Rolls-Royce, Cross, Xerox, Levi Strauss, Frigidaire, and McDonald's aggressively enforce their trademarks. Rolls-Royce, Coca-Cola, and Xerox even run newspaper and magazine ads stating that their names are trademarks and should not be used as descriptive or generic terms. Some ads threaten lawsuits against competitors that violate trademarks.

Despite severe penalties for trademark violations, trademark infringement lawsuits are not uncommon. Some of the major battles involve brand names that closely resemble an established brand name. Donna Karan filed a lawsuit against Donnkenny, Inc., whose NASDAQ trading symbol—DNKY—was too close to Karan's DKNY trademark.

Companies must also contend with fake or unauthorized brands. Knockoffs of Burberry's trademarked tan, black, white, and red plaid are easy to find in cheap shops all over the world, and loose imitations are also found in some reputable department stores. One website sells a line of plaid bags, hats, and shoes that it says are "inspired by Burberry." Burberry says it spends a couple of million pounds a year running ads in trade publications and sending letters to trade groups, textile manufacturers, and retailers reminding them about its trademark rights. It also sues infringers, works with customs officials and local law enforcement to seize fakes, and scans the Internet to pick up online chatter about counterfeits.[11]

In Europe, you can sue counterfeiters only if your brand, logo, or trademark is formally registered. Until recently, formal registration was required in each country in which a company sought protection. Now, a company can use just one application to register its trademark in all European Union (EU) member countries.

9-5 PACKAGING

Packages have always served a practical function—that is, they hold contents together and protect goods as they move through the distribution channel. Today, however, packaging is also a container for promoting the product and making it easier and safer to use.

9-5a Packaging Functions

The three most important functions of packaging are to contain and protect products, to promote products, and to facilitate the storage, use, and convenience of products. A fourth function of packaging that is becoming increasingly important is to facilitate recycling and reduce environmental damage.

CONTAINING AND PROTECTING PRODUCTS The most obvious function of packaging is to contain products that are liquid, granular, or otherwise divisible. Packaging also enables manufacturers, wholesalers, and retailers to market products in specific quantities, such as kilograms.

Physical protection is another obvious function of packaging. Most products are handled several times between the time they are manufactured, harvested, or otherwise produced and the time they are consumed or used. Many products are shipped, stored, and inspected several times between production and consumption. Some products, such as milk, need to be refrigerated. Others, such as beer, are sensitive to light. Still others, such as medicines and bandages, need to be kept sterile. Packages protect products from breakage, evaporation, spillage, spoilage, light, heat, cold, infestation, and many other conditions.

PROMOTING PRODUCTS Packaging does more than identify the brand, list the ingredients, specify features, and give directions. A package differentiates a product from competing products and may associate a new product with a family of other products from the same manufacturer. Welch's repackaged its line of grape juice–based jams, jellies, and juices to unify the line and get more impact on the shelf.

Packages use designs, colours, shapes, and materials to try to influence consumers' perceptions and buying behaviour. For example, marketing research shows that health-conscious consumers are likely to think that any food is probably good for them as long as it comes in green packaging. Packaging can also influence consumer perceptions of quality and prestige. And packaging has a measurable effect on sales. Quaker Oats revised the package for Rice-a-Roni without making any other changes in marketing strategy and experienced a 44 percent increase in sales in one year.

FACILITATING STORAGE, USE, AND CONVENIENCE Wholesalers and retailers prefer packages that are easy to ship, store, and stock on shelves. They also like packages that protect products, prevent spoilage or breakage, and extend the product's shelf life.

Consumers' requirements for storage, use, and convenience cover many dimensions. Consumers are constantly seeking items that are easy to handle, open, and reclose, and some consumers want packages that

Packaging can also influence consumer PERCEPTIONS OF QUALITY.

are tamperproof or childproof. Research indicates that hard-to-open packages are among consumers' top complaints.[12] Surveys conducted by *Sales & Marketing Management* magazine revealed that consumers dislike—and avoid buying—leaky ice cream boxes, overly heavy or fat vinegar bottles, immovable pry-up lids on glass bottles, key-opener sardine cans, and hard-to-pour cereal boxes. Such packaging innovations as zipper tear strips, hinged lids, tab slots, screw-on tops, and pour spouts were introduced to solve these and other problems. Easy openings are especially important for kids and older consumers.

Some firms use packaging to segment markets. Heinz creates small packages for use with meals on airplanes and in hotels, and sells larger packages of their product to retail outlets that sell to consumers. Differently sized packages appeal to heavy, moderate, and light users. Campbell's soup is packaged in single-serving cans aimed at the seniors and singles market segments. Packaging convenience can increase a product's utility and, therefore, its market share and profits.

FACILITATING RECYCLING AND REDUCING ENVIRONMENTAL DAMAGE One of the most important packaging issues today is compatibility with the environment. Some firms use their packaging to target environmentally concerned market segments. Brocato International markets shampoo and hair conditioner in bottles that are biodegradable in landfills. Products as different as deodorant and furniture polish are packaged in eco-friendly, pump-spray packages that do not rely on aerosol propellants.

9-5b Labelling

An integral part of any package is its label. Labelling generally takes one of two forms: persuasive or informational. **Persuasive labelling** focuses on a promotional theme or logo, and consumer information is secondary. Note that the standard promotional claims—such as "new," "improved," and "super"—are no longer very persuasive. Consumers have been saturated with "newness" and thus discount these claims.

Informational labelling, in contrast, is designed to help consumers make proper product selections and to lower their cognitive dissonance after the purchase. Sears attaches a "label of confidence" to all its floor coverings. This label gives such product information as durability, colour, features, cleanability, care instructions, and construction standards. Most major furniture manufacturers affix labels to their wares that explain the products' construction features, such as type of frame, number of coils, and fabric characteristics. The Consumer Packaging and Labelling Act mandates detailed nutritional information on most food packages and standards for health claims on food packaging. An important outcome of this legislation has been guidelines from Health Canada for the use of such terms as *low fat, light, reduced cholesterol, low sodium, low calorie, low carb,* and *fresh.*

9-5c Universal Product Codes (UPCs)

The **universal product codes (UPCs)** that now appear on most items in supermarkets and other high-volume outlets were first introduced in 1974. Because the numerical codes appear as a series of thick and thin vertical lines, they are often called *bar codes.* The lines are read by computerized optical scanners that match the codes to brand names, package sizes, and prices. They also print information on cash register tapes and help retailers rapidly and accurately prepare records of customer purchases, control inventories, and track sales.

© Kristoffer Tripplaar/Alamy

The Coca-Cola company uses a ONE-BRAND-NAME STRATEGY *in more than 200 countries around the world.*

9-6 GLOBAL ISSUES IN BRANDING AND PACKAGING

When planning to enter a foreign market with an existing product, a firm has three options for handling the brand name:

» **ONE BRAND NAME EVERYWHERE:** This strategy is useful when the company markets mainly one product and the brand name does not have negative connotations in any local market. The Coca-Cola Company uses a one-brand-name strategy in more than 200 countries around the world. The advantages of a one-brand-name strategy are greater identification of the product from market to market and ease of coordinating the promotion from market to market.

» **ADAPTATIONS AND MODIFICATIONS:** A one-brand-name strategy is not possible when the name cannot be pronounced in the local language, when the brand name is owned by someone else, or when the brand name has a negative or vulgar connotation in the local language. The Iranian detergent "Barf," for example, might encounter some resistance in the Canadian market.

» **DIFFERENT BRAND NAMES IN DIFFERENT MARKETS:** Local brand names are often used when translation or pronunciation problems occur, when the marketer wants the brand to appear to be a local brand, or when regulations require localization. Henkel's Silkience hair conditioner is called Soyance in France and Sientel in Italy. The adaptations were deemed to be more appealing in the local markets. Coca-Cola's Sprite brand had to be renamed Kin in Korea to satisfy a government prohibition on the unnecessary use of foreign words.

In addition to making global branding decisions, companies must consider global packaging needs. Three aspects of packaging especially important in international marketing are labelling, aesthetics, and climate considerations. The major concern is properly translating ingredient, promotional, and instructional information on labels. Care must also be employed in meeting all local labelling requirements. Several years ago, an Italian judge ordered that all bottles of Coca-Cola be removed from retail shelves because the ingredients were not properly labelled. In Canada, by law, labelling is required to be bilingual.

Package *aesthetics* may also require some attention. Even though simple visual elements of the brand, such as a symbol or logo, can be a standardizing element across products and countries, marketers must stay attuned to cultural traits in host countries. For example, colours may have different connotations. In some countries, red is associated with witchcraft, green may be a sign of danger, and white may be symbolic of death. Aesthetics also influence package sizes. Pop is not sold in six-packs in countries that lack refrigeration. In some countries, products such as detergent may be bought only in small quantities because of a lack of storage space. Other products, such as cigarettes, may be bought in small quantities, and even single units, because of the low purchasing power of buyers.

Extreme *climates* and long-distance shipping necessitate sturdier and more durable packages for goods sold overseas. Spillage, spoilage, and breakage are all more important concerns when products are shipped long distances or are frequently handled during shipping and storage. Packages may also have to ensure a longer product life if the time between production and consumption lengthens significantly.

9-7 PRODUCT WARRANTIES

Just as a package is designed to protect the product, a **warranty** protects the buyer and provides essential information about the product. A warranty confirms the quality or performance of a good or service. An **express warranty** is a written guarantee. Express warranties range from simple statements—such as "100 percent cotton" (a guarantee of quality) and "complete satisfaction guaranteed" (a statement of performance)—to extensive documents written in technical language. In contrast, an **implied warranty** is an unwritten guarantee that the good or service is fit for the purpose for which it was sold.

Although court rulings might suggest that all products sold in Canada carry an implied warranty, actual warranties do vary depending on the province or territory. At the federal level, protection against misleading warranties is provided under the Competition Act.

In general, products sold must be free from encumbrances (the seller must have clear title to ownership), the descriptions of the product on the package must be accurate, the product must be fit for its intended purpose, and the product must be of reasonable durability.

More than 200
Number of countries where the Coca-Cola brand name is used

20%
Percentage of a brand's revenue that has to come from international sources before it can be considered a global brand

4
Types of consumer products; functions of packaging

1974
The first bar code is scanned in Ohio in the United States. The first product to have a barcode: Wrigley's gum.

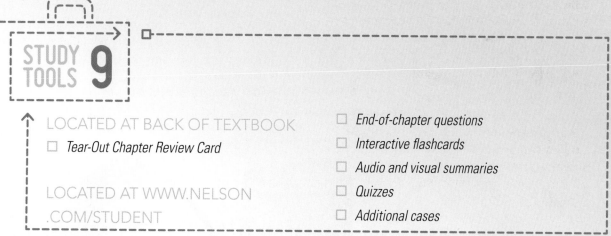

STUDY TOOLS 9

LOCATED AT BACK OF TEXTBOOK
- ☐ Tear-Out Chapter Review Card

LOCATED AT WWW.NELSON.COM/STUDENT

- ☐ End-of-chapter questions
- ☐ Interactive flashcards
- ☐ Audio and visual summaries
- ☐ Quizzes
- ☐ Additional cases

Chapter 10

Developing and Managing Products

Hiroshi Watanabe/Digital Vision/Jupiterimages

Learning Outcomes

10-1 *Explain the importance of developing new products and describe the six categories of new products 167–168*

10-2 *Explain the steps in the new-product development process 169–175*

10-3 *Discuss global issues in new-product development 175*

10-4 *Explain the diffusion process through which new products are adopted 175–177*

10-5 *Explain the concept of product life cycles 177–180*

The average fast-moving consumer goods company introduces 70 to 80 new products per year.

After you finish this chapter, go to www.nelson.com/student *for* **STUDY TOOLS**. 💼 - - - - - - >

10-1 THE IMPORTANCE OF NEW PRODUCTS

New products are important to sustain growth, increase revenues and profits, and replace obsolete items. New-product development and introduction are also important to meet ever-changing consumer wants and are compounded by the development of new technologies and shrinking product life cycles. According to *Forbes* magazine, in 2010 alone approximately 250,000 new products were introduced to the world.[1] At the same time, the new-product development process is replete with failures and high introduction costs. Businesses must introduce new products to stay competitive or risk being pushed out of the market. According to a Boston Consulting Group survey of senior executives, more than two-thirds cite innovation as a priority but 57 percent are dissatisfied with the returns on their innovation investments.[2] It is no wonder. Despite spending huge sums on research and development, most companies have many more failures than successes; however, the companies that succeed in introducing new products reap substantial financial and market rewards. Smucker's, for example, is one of the few companies that enjoy a higher than industry average rate of new-product introductions. Smucker's introduced more than 60 new products in each of 2012 and 2013 and is aiming to introduce more than 100 new products in 2014.[3] Such a rapid rate of new-product introductions resulted in US$530 million in additional sales, 9 percent of the total sales, for Smucker's in 2013.[4] Other companies that do a particularly good job at product innovation include Apple, BMW, P&G, and Samsung.

10-1a Categories of New Products

The term **new product** can be confusing because its meaning varies widely and has several correct definitions. A new product doesn't carry the same level of newness in different markets or companies: a product can be new to the market, new to the

new product a product new to the world, new to the market, new to the producer or seller, or new to some combination of these

Exhibit 10.1
NEW PRODUCT CATEGORIES

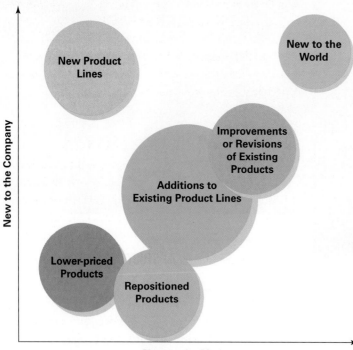

producer or seller, new to the world, or new to some combination of these (see Exhibit 10.1). The degree of newness even for the same product varies from one market to the other and from one company to the next. Based on the degree of newness, new products can be classified into six categories:

» **NEW-TO-THE-WORLD PRODUCTS** *(also called discontinuous innovations)*: These products create an entirely new market. New-to-the-world products represent the smallest category of new products, since few products are seen as completely new by everyone.

» **NEW-PRODUCT LINES:** These products, which the firm has not previously offered, allow the firm to enter an established market. After Procter & Gamble purchased Iams pet food brand, its worldwide sales doubled and profits tripled. The brand moved from the fifth-best-selling pet food brand in the United States to the top spot in less than five years.[5]

» **ADDITIONS TO EXISTING PRODUCT LINES:** This category includes new products that supplement a firm's established line. Examples of product line additions include Huggies Pull-Ups, Pampers Kandoo baby wipes, and other personal care products for kids.

» **IMPROVEMENTS OR REVISIONS OF EXISTING PRODUCTS:** The new and improved product may be significantly or slightly changed. Gillette's Fusion and Fusion Proglide razors are examples of product improvements. Another type of revision is package improvement. The Heinz EZ Squirt Ketchup bottle is short and made from easy-to-squeeze plastic; its needle-shaped nozzle lets small hands use it to decorate food. Most new products fit into the revision or improvement category.

» **REPOSITIONED PRODUCTS:** These are existing products targeted at new markets or new market segments. For example, in 2013 Apple repositioned iPad mini as the baseline product in its iPad product line and termed the existing 9.7-inch (25-centimetre) display version as iPad Air. Similarly, McDonald's has been attempting to reposition its coffee, McCafé, to compete with Tim Hortons.[6]

» **LOWER-PRICED PRODUCTS:** This category refers to products that provide performance similar to that of competing brands at a lower price. Hewlett-Packard LaserJet 3100 is a scanner, copier, printer, and fax machine combined. This new product is priced lower than many conventional colour copiers and much lower than the combined price of the four items purchased separately.

NEW-TO-THE-WORLD PRODUCTS

Ten of the most important new-to-the-world products introduced in the past 100 years:

1. Penicillin
2. Transistor radio
3. Polio vaccine
4. Mosaic (the first graphic Web browser)
5. Microprocessor
6. Black-and-white television
7. Plain paper copier
8. Alto personal computer (prototype of today's PCs)
9. Microwave oven
10. Arpanet network (the groundwork for the Internet)

Source: "Changing the World," *Entrepreneur*, October 2003, 30.

10-2 THE NEW-PRODUCT DEVELOPMENT PROCESS

The management consulting firm Booz Allen Hamilton has studied the new-product development process for more than 30 years. After analyzing five major studies undertaken during this period, the firm concluded that the companies most likely to succeed in developing and introducing new products are those that take the following actions:

» Make the long-term commitment needed to support innovation and new-product development.

» Use a company-specific approach, driven by corporate objectives and strategies, with a well-defined new-product strategy at its core.

» Capitalize on experience to achieve and maintain competitive advantage.

» Establish an environment—a management style, an organizational structure, and a degree of top-management support—conducive to achieving company-specific new-product and corporate objectives.

Exhibit 10.2
NEW-PRODUCT DEVELOPMENT PROCESS

1 New-product Strategy
2 Idea Generation
3 Idea Screening
4 Business Analysis
5 Development
6 Test Marketing
7 Commercialization

New Product

Most companies follow a formal new-product development process, usually starting with a new-product strategy. Exhibit 10.2 traces the seven-step process, which is discussed in this section. The exhibit is funnel-shaped to highlight the fact that each stage acts as a screen. The purpose is to filter out unworkable ideas.

10-2a New-Product Strategy

A **new-product strategy** links the new-product development process with the objectives of the marketing department, the business unit, and the corporation. A new-product strategy must be compatible with these objectives, and, in turn, all three objectives must be consistent with one another.

A new-product strategy is part of the organization's overall marketing strategy. It sharpens the focus and provides general guidelines for generating, screening, and evaluating new-product ideas. The new-product strategy specifies the roles that new products must play in the organization's overall plan and describes the characteristics of products the organization wants to offer and the markets it wants to serve.

As discussed at the beginning of this chapter, companies with successful new-product introduction programs derive a substantial percentage of their total sales from new-product introductions. These companies tend to have tens of new-product ideas at various stages of development at the same as they realize that very few of their ideas will be successful in the market.

10-2b Idea Generation

New-product ideas come from many sources, including customers, employees, distributors, competitors, vendors, research and development (R&D), and consultants.

» **CUSTOMERS:** The marketing concept suggests that customers' wants and needs should be the springboard for developing new products. Many of

> **new-product strategy** a plan that links the new-product development process with the objectives of the marketing department, the business unit, and the corporation

kursatunsal/iStock Editorial/Thinkstock

margins also shrink, resulting in less shelf space for mature items, lower dealer inventories, and a general reluctance to promote the product. Thus, promotion to dealers often intensifies during this stage to retain loyalty.

Heavy consumer promotion by the manufacturer is also required to maintain market share. Cutthroat competition during this stage can lead to price wars. Another characteristic of the maturity stage is the emergence of niche marketers that target narrow, well-defined, underserved segments of a market. Starbucks Coffee targets its gourmet line at the only segment of the coffee market that is growing: new, younger, more affluent coffee drinkers.

10-5d Decline Stage

A long-run drop in sales signals the beginning of the **decline stage.** The rate of decline is governed by how rapidly consumer tastes change or substitute products are adopted. Many convenience products and trendy items lose their market overnight, leaving large inventories of unsold items, such as designer jeans. Others die more slowly. Video rental stores like Blockbuster went out of business and were replaced by Netflix and other forms of digital entertainment.

KODAK'S FIRST CONSUMER CAMERA WAS INTRODUCED IN 1888. LOOK HOW FAR THAT DISCONTINUOUS INNOVATION HAS COME!

Exhibit 10.7

RELATIONSHIPS BETWEEN THE DIFFUSION PROCESS AND THE PRODUCT LIFE CYCLE

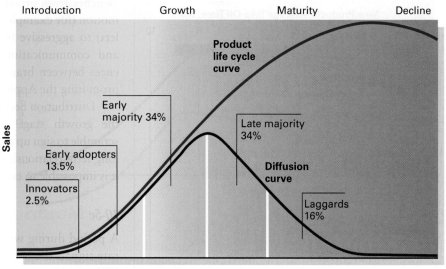

Diffusion curve: Percentage of total adoptions by category
Product life-cycle curve: Time

Some firms have developed successful strategies for marketing products in the decline stage of the product life cycle. They eliminate all nonessential marketing expenses and let sales decline as more and more customers discontinue purchasing the products. Eventually, the product is withdrawn from the market.

Management sage Peter Drucker said that all companies should practise organized abandonment, which involves reviewing every product, service, and policy every two or three years and asking the critical question "If we didn't do this already, would we launch it now?" If the answer is no, it's time to begin the abandonment process.[21]

10-5e Implications for Marketing Management

The product life cycle concept encourages marketing managers to plan so that they can take the initiative instead of reacting to past events. The PLC is especially useful as a predicting, or forecasting, tool. Because products pass through distinctive stages, it is often possible to estimate a product's location on the curve by using historical data. Profits, like sales, tend to follow a predictable path over a product's life cycle.

Exhibit 10.7 shows the relationship between the adopter categories and the stages of the PLC. Note that the various categories of adopters first buy products in different stages of the life cycle. Almost all sales in the maturity and decline stages represent repeat purchasing.

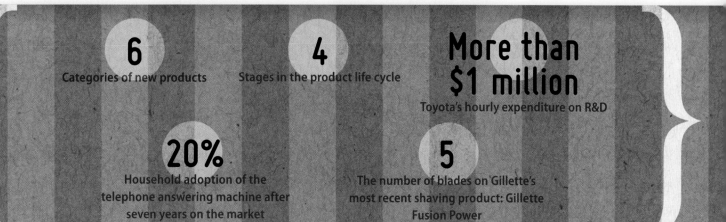

6 Categories of new products

4 Stages in the product life cycle

More than $1 million Toyota's hourly expenditure on R&D

20% Household adoption of the telephone answering machine after seven years on the market

5 The number of blades on Gillette's most recent shaving product: Gillette Fusion Power

STUDY TOOLS 10

↑ LOCATED AT BACK OF TEXTBOOK
☐ *Tear-Out Chapter Review Card*

LOCATED AT WWW.NELSON .COM/STUDENT

☐ *End-of-chapter questions*
☐ *Interactive flashcards*
☐ *Audio and visual summaries*
☐ *Quizzes*
☐ *Additional cases*

Chapter 11 | Services and Nonprofit Organization Marketing

The recent global financial crisis has left many feeling anxious about the world economy but Canadians have taken comfort in the fact that our banks and financial institutions are well run and well regulated. In 2012 the World Economic Forum once again ranked Canadian banks as the soundest in the world.[1]

After you finish this chapter, go to www.nelson.com/student *for* **STUDY TOOLS**.

11-1 THE IMPORTANCE OF SERVICES

A service is the result of applying human or mechanical efforts to people or objects. Services involve a deed, a performance, or an effort that cannot be physically possessed. Today, the service sector substantially influences the Canadian economy. According to Statistics Canada, in 2012 the service sector accounted for 78 percent of all employment.[2] Canadian economic growth continues to be driven by growth in the service sector, with over two-thirds of Canadian GDP coming from by services. The growing service sector is a key area for employment opportunities, representing 75 percent of employment and 90 percent of new job creation.[3] Canadian services are of world-class quality, and our financial services sector is regarded even more highly in the wake of the recent global financial crisis. The demand for services is expected to continue. Much of this demand results from demographics. An aging population will need nurses, home healthcare, physical therapists, and social workers. Demand for information managers, such as computer engineers and systems analysts, will also increase. There is also a growing market for Canadian service companies worldwide.

Whether you are marketing a good or a service, the marketing process discussed in Chapter 1 is the same. In addition, although a comparison of goods and services marketing can be beneficial, in reality it is difficult to distinguish clearly between manufacturing and service firms. Indeed, many manufacturing firms can point to service as a major factor in their success. Take, for example, commodity-based manufacturers, such as the steel industry. In creating a competitive advantage, it is often the service provided throughout the sale that will set one firm apart from another.

service the result of applying human or mechanical efforts to people or objects

Business executives rank the IMPROVEMENT OF SERVICE QUALITY *as one of the most critical challenges facing them today.*

Services have some unique characteristics that distinguish them from goods, and marketing strategies need to be adjusted for these characteristics.

11-2 HOW SERVICES DIFFER FROM GOODS

Services have four unique characteristics that distinguish them from goods. Services are intangible, they are inseparable, they run the risk of being inconsistent, and they cannot be inventoried.

11-2a Intangibility

The basic difference between services and goods is that services have no physical attributes. Because of their **intangibility**, they cannot be touched, seen, tasted, heard, or felt in the same manner that goods can be sensed.

Evaluating the quality of services before or even after making a purchase is harder than evaluating the quality of goods because, compared with goods, services tend to exhibit fewer search qualities. A **search quality** is a characteristic that can be easily assessed before purchase—for instance, the colour of a car or the size of a smartphone. At the same time, services tend to exhibit more experience and credence qualities. An **experience quality** is a characteristic that can be assessed only after use, such as the quality of a meal in a restaurant. A **credence quality** is a characteristic that consumers may have difficulty assessing even after purchase because they do not have the necessary knowledge or experience. Medical and consulting services are examples of services that exhibit credence qualities.

These characteristics also make it more difficult for marketers to communicate the benefits of an intangible service than to communicate the benefits of tangible goods. Thus, marketers often rely on tangible cues to communicate a service's nature and quality. For example, Ronald McDonald House uses the symbol of a house drawn as a child would, with a heart coming out of the chimney, to symbolize the warmth and love provided to families of critically ill children who stay in a Ronald McDonald House.

The facilities that customers visit, or from which services are delivered, are a critical tangible part of the total service offering. Messages about the organization are communicated to customers through such elements as the decor, the clutter or neatness of service areas, and the staff's manners and dress. Think of how you assess the service of a new hairdresser before your first appointment. Undoubtedly, you consider the appearance of both the salon and the hairdresser to get a sense of whether the salon's style suits your needs. This assessment, which is based on the physical surroundings, is critical in your decision to proceed with the appointment.

11-2b Inseparability

Goods are produced, sold, and then consumed. In contrast, services are often sold, and then produced and consumed at the same time. In other words, their production and consumption are inseparable activities. This **inseparability** means that because consumers must be present during the production of services, such as haircuts or surgery, they are actually involved in the production of the services they buy.

Simultaneous production and consumption also means that services normally cannot be produced in a centralized location and consumed in decentralized locations, as goods typically are. Services are also inseparable from the perspective of the service provider. Thus, the quality of service that firms are able to deliver depends on the quality of their employees.

11-2c Inconsistency

One great strength of McDonald's is consistency. Whether customers order a Big Mac in Tokyo or Moscow, they know exactly what they will get. This is not the case with many service firms. Because services depend on a service provider, the quality of the service can reveal **inconsistency**. For example, one day the Winnipeg Jets may have a great game, but in the next game, they may play terribly and lose. Physicians in a group practice or hairstylists in a salon differ in their technical and interpersonal skills. Because services tend to be labour intensive and production and

consumption are inseparable, consistency and quality control can be difficult to achieve.

Standardization and training help increase consistency and reliability. Montréal-based DavidsTea, a tea retailer with 93 Canadian locations and 15 U.S. locations, has capitalized on consumers' love for tea (tea is the second-most consumed beverage in the world and fourth in Canada) by demystifying it and making it fun and modern. To ensure that the consumer is met with knowledgeable staff who can, in fact, demystify tea, the tea ambassadors (sales staff) attend a nine-hour training session and receive on-the-job apprenticeship-like learning to enhance their knowledge of tea. All the customer needs to do is ask for a certain flavour of tea and the tea ambassador will provide recommendations. Once the consumer settles on a flavour, the tea ambassador will then demonstrate how to make the tea at home to ensure a quality cup of tea each time. Tea ambassadors are trained not just in the product but also in the brand's identity and purpose so that at the retail level, on the front line, the brand is delivered with quality and consistency.[4]

11-2d Inventory

The fourth characteristic of services is **inventory**. Services cannot be stored, warehoused, or inventoried. If a service is not consumed, it perishes. If the runs aren't busy at the Fernie Alpine Ski resort, they cannot be stored for the next day or the next busy day. The revenue from the lack of skiers is lost. Yet service organizations are often forced to turn away full-price customers during peak periods.

One of the most important challenges in many service industries is finding ways to synchronize supply and demand. The philosophy that some revenue is

better than none has prompted many hotels to offer deep discounts on weekends and during the off-season. In some service sectors, compensation is based on a commission system in an attempt to not waste inventory cost on idle production capacity.

11-3 SERVICE QUALITY

Because of the four unique characteristics of services, service quality is more difficult to define and measure than the quality of tangible goods. Business executives rank the improvement of service quality as one of the most critical challenges facing them today.

Research has shown that customers evaluate service quality by the following five components:[5]

▸▸ **Reliability:** the ability to perform the service dependably, accurately, and consistently. Reliability refers to performing the service right the first time and every time. This component has been found to be the one most important to consumers. Reliability of delivery will create brand loyalty, which in the highly competitive service industry is coveted. Take, for example, the Vancouver Canucks: consistent on-ice performance will keep the arena stands full and will increase the potential for season ticket sales.

▸▸ **Responsiveness:** the ability to provide prompt service. Examples of responsiveness include returning customers' calls quickly, serving lunch fast to someone in a hurry, or ensuring that the consumer does not have to wait past the appointment time. The ultimate in responsiveness is offering service 24 hours a day, seven days a week.

▸▸ **Assurance:** the knowledge and courtesy of employees and their ability to convey trust. Skilled employees exemplify assurance when they treat customers with respect and when they make customers feel that they can trust the firm. Starbucks refers to employees as partners and provides them with the opportunity to be more than an "employee." Partners are charged with connecting with Starbucks' customers and the community, to become part of something bigger and to inspire positive change in the world around them. Starbucks' baristas hand over millions of cups of coffee a week, and Starbucks' philosophy is that each one of those interactions is a unique connection that can foster good. This belief creates a level of assurance that is second to none.[6]

empathy caring, individualized attention paid to customers

tangibles the physical evidence of a service, including the physical facilities, tools, and equipment used to provide the service

gap model a model identifying five gaps that can cause problems in service delivery and influence customer evaluations of service quality

▸▸ **Empathy:** caring, individualized attention paid to customers. Firms whose employees recognize customers and learn their specific requirements are providing empathy. Again, empowering employees to be partners provides the opportunity for Starbucks' baristas to be empathetic. The emphasis on creating connections is the stimulus for the barista–customer relationship that many Starbucks' baristas and customers have come to enjoy.

▸▸ **Tangibles:** the physical evidence of the service. The tangible parts of a service include the physical facilities, tools, and equipment used to provide the service, and the appearance of personnel. Starbucks' physical facility reinforces its desire to create and foster connections. Starbucks promotes socializing in the restaurants—they are neighbourhood gathering places offering comfortable seating, Wi-Fi, and newspapers. The stores are a haven from the stresses of the day.

Overall service quality is measured by combining customers' evaluations for all five components.

11-3a The Gap Model of Service Quality

A model of service quality called the **gap model** identifies five gaps that can cause problems in service delivery and influence customer evaluations of service quality (see Exhibit 11.1):[7]

▸▸ **GAP 1:** Knowledge gap—the gap between what customers want and what management thinks customers

Exhibit 11.1
GAP MODEL OF SERVICE QUALITY

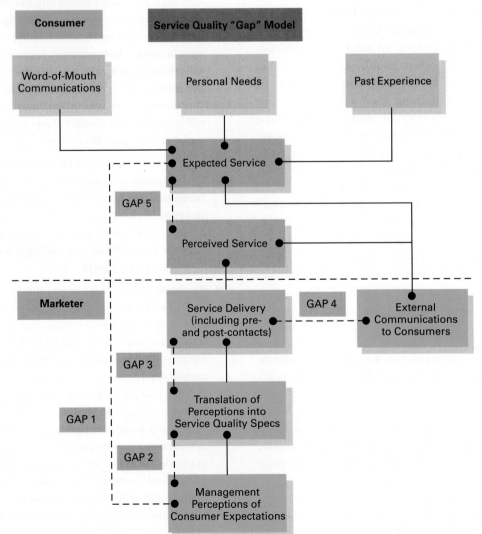

want. This gap results from a lack of understanding or a misinterpretation of the customers' needs, wants, or desires. A consumer's expectations may vary for a variety of reasons, including his or her past experiences and the type of situation. A firm that does little or no customer satisfaction research is likely to experience this gap. To close gap 1, firms must stay attuned to customer wants by researching customer needs and satisfaction. Because employees in a service setting are the service provider, gap 1 can be managed by increasing the interaction and communication between management and employees.

▶▶ **GAP 2:** Standards gap—the gap between what management think customers want and the quality specifications that management develops to provide the service. Essentially, this gap is the result of management's inability to translate customers' needs into delivery systems within the firm. In other words, the gap is a result of management not having provided the appropriate service designs and standards. The reduction in this gap is achieved through the creation of policies and procedures related to the delivery of the service, the establishment of metrics to measure performance on an ongoing basis, and the training and development of employees. As noted in the management of gap 1, employee involvement in the establishment of both the policies and procedures and the metrics is critical for success, as the employee is in constant contact with the customer in the delivery of the service and thus is extremely knowledgeable with respect to customer expectations.

▶▶ **GAP 3:** Delivery gap—the gap between the service quality specifications and the service that is actually provided. If both gaps 1 and 2 have been closed, then gap 3 results from the inability of management and employees to do what should be done. Management needs to ensure that employees have the skills and the proper tools to perform their jobs, including effective training programs and ongoing feedback. Starbucks' management is committed to service quality being paramount, but it recognizes that the quality of the service is as equally dependent on process as it is on their staff's (their partners') performance. To ensure their partners are motivated to live the Starbucks mission, Starbucks' compensation is topnotch. All partners working 20 hours or more a week are offered a benefits package called "Your Special Blend." This benefits package offers health coverage, a tuition reimbursement program, recognition programs, and other important perks. Unquestionably, Starbucks is attempting to create an unparalleled retail environment.[8]

▶▶ **GAP 4:** Communication gap—the gap between what the company provides and what the customer is told it provides. To close this gap, companies need to create realistic customer expectations through honest, accurate communication regarding what they can provide. Communication programs must be managed to ensure messaging reflects what the company can consistently deliver.

▶▶ **GAP 5:** Expectation gap—the gap between the service that customers expect they should receive and the perceived service after the service has been provided. This gap can be positive or negative and clearly influences consumers' perception of service quality. Ongoing research is necessary to understand consumers' perceptions and to manage their expectations. In this age of social media, where peer-to-peer conversations are happening online in real time on a number of online forums, companies must be vigilant in their monitoring of these conversations to ensure timely responses.

When one or more of these gaps is large, service quality is perceived as being low. As the gaps shrink, service quality perception improves.

11-4 MARKETING MIXES FOR SERVICES

Services' unique characteristics—intangibility, inseparability of production and consumption, inconsistency, and inventory—make the marketing of services more challenging. Elements of the marketing mix (product, place, promotion, and pricing) need to be adjusted to meet the special needs created by these characteristics. In addition, effective marketing of services requires the management of four additional Ps: people, process, productivity, and physical environment.

11-4a Product (Service) Strategy

A product, as defined in Chapter 9, is everything a person receives in an exchange. In the case of a service organization, the product offering is intangible and is part of a process or a series of processes. This definition suggests then that the service firm must attempt to make the intangible tangible by providing physical cues of the service quality and positioning. Logos, tag lines, and promotional materials attempt to create tangible evidence of the service offering.

SERVICE AS A PROCESS Two broad categories of things are processed in service organizations: people and objects. In some cases, the process is physical, or tangible; in other cases, the process is intangible. Using these characteristics, service processes can be placed into one of four categories:[9]

» **PEOPLE PROCESSING** takes place when the service is directed at a customer. Examples are transportation services and healthcare.

» **POSSESSION PROCESSING** occurs when the service is directed at customers' physical possessions. Examples are lawn care and veterinary services.

» **MENTAL STIMULUS PROCESSING** refers to services directed at people's minds. Examples are theatre performances and education.

» **INFORMATION PROCESSING** describes services that use technology or brainpower directed at a customer's assets. Examples are insurance and consulting.

Because customers' experiences and involvement differ for each of these types of services processes, marketing strategies may also differ. Take, for example, a season's pass to the games of a Canadian Football League (CFL) team. It is a mental stimulus–processing service where the quality of the product (the service) is very much dependent on the quality of the players and the coaching staff. The game outcome can never be controlled, but the individual clubs can control other aspects of the game to ensure the game attendee has

Fluke Transportation Group is an example of a possession-processing service. This service focuses less on the attractiveness of its physical environment than would a people-processing service, such as a massage therapist, but emphasis is still placed on the logo and the look of the physical cues that represent the company.

Courtesy of Fluke Transportation Group

a positive experience. The half-time shows, the game-day give-aways, the stadium itself, and the food and drink are elements of the product that can be controlled to enhance the service experience.

CORE AND SUPPLEMENTARY SERVICE PRODUCTS The service offering can be viewed as a bundle of activities that includes the **core service**, which is the most basic benefit the customer is buying, and a group of **supplementary services** that support or enhance the core service. For the Grounds Guys Landscape Management franchise network, the core service is residential and commercial grounds care. The supplemental services include irrigation, landscape design, landscape enhancements, snow and ice control, and even outdoor holiday decoration installation.

Grounds maintenance is a highly competitive industry that could be considered a commodity, where purchase decisions are made purely on price, and brand loyalty is fickle. By emphasizing supplemental services and consistently innovating to provide unique, quality services, the Grounds Guys franchise network is able to differentiate itself and grow its market share in the more than 170 markets it operates in throughout Canada and the United States.[10]

Courtesy of The Grounds Guys

THE SERVICE MIX Many service organizations market more than one service. For example, Vancouver City Savings Credit Union, more commonly known as Vancity, is a financial cooperative offering a wide range of banking and investment services to both individuals and organizations. Each service within the organization's service mix represents a set of opportunities, risks, and challenges. Each part of the service mix makes a different contribution to achieving the firm's overall goals. To succeed, each service may also need a different level of financial support. Designing a service strategy therefore means deciding what new services to introduce to which

Courtesy of Vancity

target market, what existing services to maintain, and what services to eliminate.

11-4b Process Strategy

Because services are delivered before or while being consumed, the marketing mix for services includes the strategic decisions surrounding the process. Here, *process* refers to the establishing of standards to ensure the service delivery is consistent and compatible with the service positioning. To establish these processes, the knowledge gap must be reduced through market research that seeks to understand consumer expectations; a process protocol must then be established to ensure the service delivery meets customers' expectations. Process is fluid, which means that customer satisfaction should be evaluated on an ongoing basis and processes should be updated to ensure service delivery continues to meet expectations. The more standardized the delivery, the less likely the need for ongoing evaluation of process.

11-4c People Strategy

The standards gap and the delivery gap must be managed to improve the service. The service is provided by a service provider, but distinguishing between the two is often very difficult. Thus, managing the employee who is the service provider is highly strategic. Strategies include providing incentives, training, and recognition programs that management consistently supports. Employees who are well trained, empowered, and rewarded will deliver on the service promise. Take Moksha Yoga Studios as an example. Founded in Toronto in 2004 by two yoga practitioners, Moksha Yoga has grown into an international company offering a variety of yoga classes in a hot studio. The Moksha method is a series of 40 poses done in a hot room. The studios must follow strict green standards and be committed to offering weekly low-cost classes and community classes to keep the yoga experience affordable for everyone. Moksha studios are independently owned and operated by individuals. To ensure the Moksha brand's positioning is managed across all studios, Moksha owner/operators must meet exacting specifications before being awarded a franchise. They must have taken the 11-month Moksha teacher training program and demonstrate commitment to the Moksha seven pillars. While each studio is unique to reflect the community it is in, the Moksha seven pillars reflect in part, a commitment to service excellence through lifelong learning, healthy living, community service and support, green living, and accessibility for all. These seven pillars form the foundation to ensure that each studio and each yoga class leader delivers on the Moksha Yoga promise.[11]

11-4d Place (Distribution) Strategy

Distribution strategies for service organizations must focus on such issues as convenience, number of outlets, direct versus indirect distribution, location, and scheduling. One of the key factors influencing the selection of a service provider is *convenience*. Hence, the place strategy is important to service firms.

An important distribution objective for many service firms is the *number of outlets* to use or the number of outlets to open during a certain time. Generally, the intensity of distribution should meet, but not exceed, the target market's needs and preferences. Having too few outlets may inconvenience customers; having too many outlets may boost costs unnecessarily. Intensity of distribution may also depend on the image desired. Having only a few outlets may make the service seem more exclusive or selective.

Driven to providing healthcare where families need it most, Ronald McDonald House Southern Alberta (RMHSA) launched the Ronald McDonald Care Mobile in the east Calgary community to improve healthcare accessibility and help reduce health disparities for those most in need. This intensification of availability provided by RMHSA was never more truly appreciated and needed than in the summer of 2013. When floods devastated High River, Alberta, a community a short distance from Calgary, the Ronald McDonald Care Mobile was sent into that community to help healthcare providers whose offices had been destroyed to provide the basic medical care that their patients needed. That took the Ronald McDonald Care Mobile out of the east Calgary market, which meant if RMHSA was to maintain its mission of increasing access to healthcare for families in east Calgary, a second Care Mobile was needed. As a result of the support of the business community in Calgary and Ronald McDonald House Charities Canada, a second Care Mobile became a reality.[12]

The next service distribution decision is whether to distribute services to end-users *directly* or *indirectly* through other firms. Because of the nature of services, many service firms choose to use direct distribution or franchising. Examples include legal, medical, accounting, and personal-care services. The Internet has provided some service providers with the opportunity to intensify their distribution and even to automate part of the service to better satisfy the customer. Most of the major airlines are now using online services to sell tickets directly to consumers, which results in lower distribution costs for the airline companies. Other firms with standardized service packages have developed indirect channels that place the service in more convenient locations for their customers. Bank ATMs located in gas stations and hotel lobbies are a good example of standardizing a service and intensifying distribution by relying on indirect channels.

The *location* of a service most clearly reveals the relationship between its target market strategy and its distribution strategy. For time-dependent service providers, such as airlines, physicians, and dentists, *scheduling* is often a more important factor.

11-4e Physical Evidence Strategy

Closely associated with managing place strategies to maintain service quality is managing the physical evidence surrounding the service delivery. All four categories of service processes can benefit from attention paid to both the physical environment in which the service is being offered and the quality of the equipment used to deliver the service. For example, when you arrive at your dental appointment, old equipment may lead you to question the ability of the dentist to provide the best oral care with the least amount of pain.

McMaster Children's Hospital in Hamilton, Ontario has as its vision "advancing health and integrating care for children and youth through excellence, innovation and partnerships." Phase one of the new Children's Emergency Department was opened in spring 2011, creating a children-only service to treat those aged 18 and under. Physical changes included a Pediatric Clinical Decision Unit, where children who need to be treated in the Emergency Department for several hours are cared for more comfortably; larger treatment rooms to allow for family care at the bedside; and special attention to the decor of the walls from one metre down to enhance the view and involvement of young children and those in wheelchairs. Such attention to physical surroundings further establishes in the minds of the families of sick children that they are in the best place for the care of a child.[13]

11-4f Promotion Strategy

Consumers and business users have more trouble evaluating services than goods because services are less tangible. In turn, marketers have more trouble promoting intangible services than tangible goods. Here are four promotion strategies for services:

▸ **STRESSING TANGIBLE CUES:** A tangible cue is a concrete symbol of the service offering. To make their services more tangible, hotels will turn down beds in the evening and leave a mint on the pillow, ensure concierge staff are attentive, and offer free newspapers outside the room door each morning.

▸ **USING PERSONAL INFORMATION SOURCES:** A personal information source is someone consumers are familiar with (such as a celebrity) or someone they know or can relate to personally. Service firms can set up blogs and stimulate customer interaction on the blogs to generate positive word of mouth. Facebook, Twitter, LinkedIn, and other social media sites are used by service firms in their promotion strategy to capitalize on the potential for consumer discussion around their service offerings. Of course, there is always the possibility of negative word of mouth, which requires a comprehensive and often swift crisis communication plan.

▸ **CREATING A STRONG ORGANIZATIONAL IMAGE:** One way to create an image is to manage the evidence, including the physical environment of the service facility, the appearance of the service employees, and the tangible items associated with a service, such as the firm's website, stationery, and brochures. Medavie EMS Inc., as part of the broader Medavie organization that includes Medavie Blue Cross and is one of the top employers in Atlantic Canada, delivers effective and innovative healthcare, education, and public safety solutions, including EMS systems. Their paramedics offer first-class prehospital care. This level of quality care is demonstrated in all aspects of the company, from the appearance of the ambulances and paramedic uniforms to its website. Medavie EMS Inc. consistently emphasizes quality healthcare in all communication pieces and at all touch points that the consumer may have with Medavie EMS Inc. Medavie

EMS manages ambulance services in several parts of Canada and the United States, including Atlantic Canada, Ontario, Saskatchewan, Alberta, and Massachusetts.[14]

» **ENGAGING IN POSTPURCHASE COMMUNICATION:** Postpurchase communication refers to the follow-up activities that a service firm might engage in after a customer transaction. Emails, letters, and other types of follow-up are excellent ways to demonstrate to the customer that their feedback matters.

11-4g Price Strategy

Considerations in pricing a service are similar to the pricing considerations to be discussed in Chapter 12. However, the unique characteristics of services present special pricing challenges.

First, to price a service, it is important to define the unit of service consumption. For example, should pricing be based on the specific task (such as washing the car) or should it be time based (such as the amount of time it takes to wash the car)? Some services include the consumption of goods. Restaurants charge for the food and drink consumed, not for the table and chairs that have been used.

Second, for services that comprise multiple elements, the issue is whether pricing should be based on a bundle of elements or whether each element should be priced separately. Often a bundle price is used because consumers don't want to pay "extra" for every element in the service, and it is administratively easier for the service company.

Marketers should set performance objectives when pricing each service. Three categories of pricing objectives have been suggested:[15]

» **REVENUE-ORIENTED PRICING** focuses on maximizing the surplus of income over costs. A limitation of this approach is that determining costs can be difficult for many services.

» **OPERATIONS-ORIENTED PRICING** seeks to match supply and demand by varying prices. For example, matching hotel demand to the number of available rooms can be achieved by raising prices at peak times and decreasing them during slow times.

» **PATRONAGE-ORIENTED PRICING** tries to maximize the number of customers using the service. Thus, prices vary with different market segments' ability to pay, and methods of payment (such as credit) are offered to increase the likelihood of a purchase.

A firm may need to use more than one type of pricing objective. In fact, all three objectives may need to be included to some degree in a pricing strategy, although the importance of each type may vary depending on the type of service provided, the prices that competitors are charging, the differing ability of various customer segments to pay, or the opportunity to negotiate price.

11-4h Productivity Strategy

Because services are often tied to a service provider and because the delivery of a service cannot be inventoried if supply exceeds demand, it is critical that the service firm work to manage the supply or the availability of the service without affecting service quality. Such a strategy is often referred to as capacity management. A trip to Florida during your February break is likely much more expensive than the same trip in September. Student demand for holidays to Florida is high in February, and hotels and airlines try to capitalize on the demand. In September, on the other hand, school has just started, and students and families are thus otherwise engaged, so hotels and airlines offer lower prices to stimulate demand. After all, the plane still has to fly despite empty seats, and the hotels are still open despite empty rooms. This method of capacity management is called *off-peak pricing*, and every day we see plenty of examples of it.

11-5 RELATIONSHIP MARKETING IN SERVICES

Many services involve ongoing interaction between the service organization and the customer. Thus, these services can benefit from relationship marketing, the strategy described in Chapter 1, as a means of attracting, developing, and retaining customer relationships. The idea is to develop strong loyalty by

Effective marketing *of services requires the management of an additional* Four Ps: *People, process, productivity, and physical environment.*

NEL

CHAPTER 11: Services and Nonprofit Organization Marketing   191

Relationship marketing is used to ATTRACT, DEVELOP, *and* RETAIN CUSTOMERS. *How likely is it that the customer will use this service* AGAIN?

racorn/Shutterstock.com

© iStockphoto.com/Jan Tyler

creating satisfied customers who will buy additional services from the firm and are unlikely to switch to a competitor. Satisfied customers are also likely to engage in positive word-of-mouth communication, thereby helping to bring in new customers.

Many businesses have found it more cost-effective to hang on to the customers they have than to focus only on attracting new customers.

Services that purchasers receive on a continuing basis (for example, prescriptions, banking, and insurance) can be considered membership services. This type of service naturally lends itself to relationship marketing. When services involve discrete transactions (for example, a movie screening, a restaurant

meal, or public transportation), it may be more difficult to build membership-type relationships with customers. Nevertheless, services involving discrete transactions may be transformed into membership relationships by using marketing tools. For example, the service could be sold in bulk (for example, a subscription to a theatre season or a commuter pass on public transportation). Or a service firm could offer special benefits to customers who choose to register with the firm (for example, loyalty programs for hotels and airlines). While the registration process and subsequent use of the loyalty card at every purchase is designed to reward the consumer for repeat buying, the data gathered by the firm based on each purchase allows for targeted communication with the customer, which serves to further enhance the service–customer relationship. Relationship marketing can be practised at three levels:[16]

▸▸ **LEVEL 1:** Pricing incentives are used to encourage customers to continue doing business with a firm. Frequent flyer programs are an example of level 1 relationship marketing. This level of relationship marketing is the least effective in the long term because its price-based advantage is easily imitated by other firms.

▸▸ **LEVEL 2:** This level of relationship marketing also uses pricing incentives but seeks to build social bonds with customers. The firm stays in touch with its customers, learns about their needs, and designs services to meet those needs. Level 2 relationship marketing is often more effective than level 1 relationship marketing.

▸▸ **LEVEL 3:** At this level, the firm again uses financial and social bonds but adds structural bonds to the formula. Structural bonds are developed by offering value-added services that are not readily available from other firms. Many high-end hotels leave treats in repeat guests' hotel rooms when they celebrate special events, such as a bottle of wine for a couple celebrating an anniversary. Marketing programs like this one have the strongest potential for sustaining long-term relationships with customers.

11-6 INTERNAL MARKETING IN SERVICE FIRMS

The service and the service provider are inseparable. Thus, the quality of a firm's employees is crucial to delivering a consistently superior product and to building long-term relationships with customers. Employees who like their jobs and are satisfied with the firm they work for are more likely to deliver superior service to customers. Their superior service, in turn, increases the likelihood of retaining customers. Thus, it is critical that service firms practise **internal marketing**, which means treating employees as customers and developing systems and benefits that satisfy their needs. To satisfy employees, companies have designed and instituted a wide variety of programs, such as flextime, onsite daycare, investments in wellness, and compassionate care top-up payments. Sunnybrook Medical Centre in Toronto offers the use of a gym as part of the company's employment strategy. With the investment in a gym, the company is investing in its employees' wellness, and the result is employees that are typically healthier, absent less often, and often more productive, efficient, and willing to work a little harder.[17]

11-7 GLOBAL ISSUES IN SERVICES MARKETING

In response to the rebounding of the global economy, Canada's international services exports rose to just over $84 billion in 2012. While Canada continues to trade strongly in services, a services trade deficit persists. In 2012, Canada's imports of services were just over $108 billion. As expected, our largest trading partner (both exports and imports) in services is the United States.[18] The international marketing of services is a major part of global business. To be successful in the global marketplace, service firms must first determine the nature of their core product. Next, the marketing mix elements should be designed to take into account each country's cultural, technological, and political environments.

Because of their competitive advantages, many Canadian service industries have been able to enter the global marketplace. Banks, for example, with their strength in customer service and strong reputations, have done well in the global marketplace.

11-8 NONPROFIT ORGANIZATION MARKETING

A **nonprofit organization** is an organization that exists to achieve some goal other than the usual business goals of profit, market share, and return on investment. Both nonprofit organizations and private-sector service firms market intangible products, and both often require the customer to be present during the production process. Both for-profit and nonprofit services vary greatly from producer to producer and from day to day, even from the same producer.

Canada's nonprofit and voluntary sector is the second largest in the world, behind the Netherlands. In Canada, more than two million people are employed in the nonprofit sector, representing 11.1 percent of the economically active population. The nonprofit sector represents $79.1 billion or 7.8 percent of Canada's gross domestic product (GDP), which is larger than the manufacturing or automotive industries.[19]

The nonprofit sector includes many organizations that support those who are disadvantaged, as well as hospitals, colleges, and universities. If these organizations are removed from the picture, the remaining organizations are what Statistics Canada calls the core nonprofit sector. The core nonprofit sector accounts for about 2.4 percent of GDP, which is more than three times that accounted for by the motor vehicle industry.[20]

11-8a What Is Nonprofit Organization Marketing?

Nonprofit organization marketing is the effort by nonprofit organizations to bring about mutually satisfying exchanges with target markets. Although these organizations vary substantially in size and purpose and operate in different environments, most perform the following marketing activities:

▸▸ **Identifying the customers they want to serve or attract (although they usually use another term, such as clients, patients, members, or donors)**

▸▸ **Explicitly or implicitly specifying objectives**

internal marketing treating employees as customers and developing systems and benefits that satisfy their needs

nonprofit organization an organization that exists to achieve some goal other than the usual business goals of profit, market share, or return on investment

nonprofit organization marketing the effort by nonprofit organizations to bring about mutually satisfying exchanges with target markets

- Developing, managing, and maintaining programs and services

- Deciding on prices to charge (although they may use other terms, such as *fees, donations, tuition, fares, fines,* or *rates*)

- Scheduling events or programs, and determining where they will be held or where services will be offered

- Communicating their availability through both online and offline media vehicles; the nonprofit sector has embraced social media as a fast and relatively inexpensive way to build brand awareness and even to raise the much-needed donations.

11-8b Unique Aspects of Nonprofit Organization Marketing Strategies

Like their counterparts in for-profit business organizations, nonprofit managers develop marketing strategies to bring about mutually satisfying exchanges with their target markets. However, marketing in nonprofit organizations is unique in many ways—including the setting of marketing objectives, the selection of target markets, and the development of appropriate marketing mixes.

OBJECTIVES In the private sector, the profit motive is both an objective for guiding decisions and a criterion for evaluating results. Nonprofit organizations do not seek to make a profit for redistribution to owners or shareholders. Rather, their focus is often on generating enough funds to deliver the service while covering expenses.

Most nonprofit organizations are expected to provide equitable, effective, and efficient services that respond to the wants and preferences of their multiple constituencies, which may include users, donors, politicians, appointed officials, the media, and the general public. Nonprofit organizations place great emphasis on building and maintaining relationships with a variety of constituent groups. Nonprofit organizations cannot measure their success or failure in strictly financial terms.

Managers in the nonprofit sector are challenged to demonstrate achievement of multiple, diverse, and often intangible objectives, which can make performance evaluation difficult.

TARGET MARKETS Two issues relating to target markets are unique to nonprofit organizations:

- **APATHETIC OR STRONGLY OPPOSED TARGETS:** Private-sector organizations usually give priority to developing those market segments that are most likely to respond to particular offerings. In contrast, some nonprofit organizations must, by nature of their service, target those who are apathetic about or strongly opposed to receiving their services, such as vaccinations or psychological counselling.

- **PRESSURE TO ADOPT UNDIFFERENTIATED SEGMENTATION STRATEGIES:** Nonprofit organizations are sometimes forced to adopt undifferentiated strategies (see Chapter 8). Today however, as nonprofits become more sophisticated in their data management, they are recognizing the value of data mining to find like prospects to target with differentiated strategies. While the economies of scale often evident in an undifferentiated strategy may seem appealing, the higher returns (higher response rates, higher average donation) achieved by using a differentiated approach far outweigh the low-cost-per-person reach of an undifferentiated strategy.

POSITIONING DECISIONS Because of the unique issues relating to target markets, positioning decisions are critical to the nonprofit. The mission and vision of the nonprofit must be clearly articulated and communicated through the nonprofit's positioning statement, also referred to as the nonprofit's *value proposition*, which then drives all messaging. Because nonprofit organizations are in competition for donor dollars with many other nonprofits and are often in complementary roles with those offering similar services in the public sector, a single-minded positioning is key to maintaining an accurate perception of the nonprofit among all constituent groups.

PRODUCT DECISIONS Three product-related characteristics distinguish business organizations from nonprofit organizations:

- **BENEFIT COMPLEXITY:** Nonprofit organizations often market complex and emotional behaviours or ideas. Examples include the need to exercise or eat properly and the need to quit smoking. The benefits that a person receives are complex, long term, and intangible, and therefore are more

THIS IS MY SANCTUARY.
THIS IS WHERE HOPE WAITS AROUND EVERY CORNER.
THIS IS WHERE I'M ALWAYS GREETED WITH OPEN ARMS.
THIS IS WHERE MY BODY LANGUAGE SPEAKS VOLUMES.
THIS IS WHERE I'M ALLOWED TO FEEL HURT, WORRIED AND STRESSED.
THIS IS WHERE I CAN GET AWAY FROM THE HURT, WORRY AND STRESS.
THIS IS WHERE MY KIDS CAN BE KIDS. AND SO CAN I.
THIS IS WHERE I PLAY WHATEVER GAME THEY WANT.
THIS IS WHERE I LAUGH AS MUCH AS I CRY.

THIS IS MY RONALD MCDONALD HOUSE.
THIS IS WHERE FAMILIES FIND A HOME AWAY FROM HOME CLOSE TO THEIR SICK CHILDREN.

DONATE AT RMHC.CA

RONALD MCDONALD
HOUSE CHARITIES®
CANADA

Ronald McDonald House Charities® Canada is attempting to message the comfort and the care offered to parents of a sick child with both the words and the visuals in this print ad.

difficult to communicate to consumers. Ronald McDonald House offers a home away from home for families of sick children receiving treatment at area hospitals. This nonprofit enables families to stay close to their child at a very critical time. The benefit is enormous, but unless you have experienced having nowhere to sleep but in your car or in a chair at your child's bedside, how do you fully and accurately communicate the service benefits of Ronald McDonald House?

▸ **BENEFIT STRENGTH:** The benefit strength of many nonprofit offerings is not immediate or is indirect. What are the direct, personal benefits to you of driving within the required speed limit or volunteering at your local hospice, or putting out only one bag of garbage per week? In contrast, most private-sector service organizations can offer customers immediate and direct personal benefits.

▸ **INVOLVEMENT:** The involvement level of the products offered by nonprofit organizations varies greatly by nature of the intangibility of the product and the perceived importance of the product to the target market ("I don't have children so why would I pay attention to the Ronald McDonald House organization?"). Many nonprofit organizations market products that elicit very low involvement ("Prevent forest fires") or very high involvement ("Stop smoking"). The typical range for private-sector goods is much narrower. Traditional promotional tools may be inadequate to motivate adoption of either low- or high-involvement products.

PLACE (DISTRIBUTION) DECISIONS A non-profit organization's capacity for distributing its service offerings to potential customer groups when and where they want them is typically a key variable in determining the success of those service offerings. For example, many universities and colleges have one or more satellite campus locations and offer online courses to provide easier access for students in other areas. Canadian Blood Services has placed a heavy emphasis on mobile donor sites that take the opportunity to donate to the donor's place of business, in essence intensifying distribution.

The extent to which a service depends on fixed facilities has important implications for distribution decisions. Services such as those offered by a community food bank are limited by the space the food bank has to store the food.

PROMOTION DECISIONS Many nonprofit organizations are explicitly or implicitly prohibited from advertising, thus limiting their promotion options. Other nonprofit organizations simply do not have the resources to retain advertising agencies, promotion consultants, or marketing staff. However, nonprofit organizations have a few special promotion resources to call on:

▸ **PROFESSIONAL VOLUNTEERS:** Nonprofit organizations often seek out marketing, sales, and advertising professionals to help them develop and implement promotion strategies. In some instances, an advertising agency donates its services in exchange for potential long-term benefits. Donated services create goodwill, personal contacts, and general awareness of the donor's organization,

public service advertisement (PSA) an announcement that promotes a program of a nonprofit organization or of a federal, provincial or territorial, or local government

reputation, and competency. One such example is john st., a Toronto advertising firm that does creative work for the Canadian-based nonprofit War Child.

» **SALES PROMOTION ACTIVITIES:** Sales promotion activities that make use of existing services or other resources are increasingly being used to draw attention to the offerings of nonprofit organizations. Sometimes nonprofit charities even team up with other companies for promotional activities. Special events are a great way to reach many targets while partnering with both for-profit and nonprofit companies. A perfect example is the Running Room, which offer nonprofits the opportunity to associate with its sponsored runs. Runners can choose to run and raise money for the charity when registering for the run.

» **PUBLIC RELATIONS:** Public relations is a valuable tool for nonprofits. But organizations must ensure that their message is compelling and meaningful. One form of public relations used often by nonprofits is public service advertising. A **public service advertisement (PSA)** is an announcement that promotes a program of a nonprofit organization or of a federal, provincial or territorial, or local government. Unlike a commercial advertiser, the sponsor of the PSA does not pay for the time or space. Instead, these are donated by the medium as a public service.

» **SOCIAL MEDIA:** Nonprofits generally want to promote a message so that people will come together bound by a common goal. Social media can amplify the message by its ability to connect groups of people. Social media allows nonprofits to share their message to build community and to create action. Nonprofits are embracing podcasting, blogging, and social networking because, for very little money, they allow nonprofits to build relationships and engage with their stakeholders. As more and more social media tools are created to make the use of various social media sites easier and increasingly more measureable, nonprofits' ability to maximize the potential of social media for engagement and relationship building will continue.

NONPROFIT MARKETING STRATEGY AT A GLANCE

Objectives

» May be multiple and intangible

Positioning

» Single-minded

Place

» Intensity of distribution

Price

» Objectives
» Nonfinancial pricing
» Indirect payment
» Separation between payers and users
» Below-cost pricing

Target Markets

» Apathetic or strongly opposed
» Pressure to adopt an undifferentiated strategy

Product

» Benefit complexity
» Benefit strength
» Involvement

Promotion

» Professional volunteers
» Sales promotion activities
» Public relations
» Social media

PRICING DECISIONS Five key characteristics distinguish the pricing decisions of nonprofit organizations from those of the profit sector:

▸ **PRICING OBJECTIVES:** The main pricing objective in the profit sector is revenue or, more specifically, profit maximization, sales maximization, or target return on sales or investment. Many nonprofit organizations must also be concerned about revenue. Often, however, nonprofit organizations seek to either partially or fully defray costs rather than achieve a profit for distribution to stockholders. Nonprofit organizations also seek to redistribute income through the delivery of their service. Moreover, they strive to allocate resources fairly among individuals or households or across geographic or political boundaries.

▸ **NONFINANCIAL PRICES:** In many nonprofit situations, consumers are not charged a monetary price but instead must absorb nonmonetary costs. Nonmonetary costs include time and maybe even embarrassment, depending on the service being provided. Habitat for Humanity requires the recipients of a home to contribute sweat equity as part of the price of the building of their new home.

▸ **INDIRECT PAYMENT:** Indirect payment through taxes is common to marketers of free services, such as libraries, fire protection, and police protection. Indirect payment is not a common practice in the profit sector.

▸ **SEPARATION BETWEEN PAYERS AND USERS:** By design, the services of many charitable organizations are provided to those who are relatively poor and are largely paid for by those who are better off financially. Although examples of separation between payers and users can be found in the profit sector (such as insurance claims), the practice is much less prevalent.

▸ **BELOW-COST PRICING:** An example of below-cost pricing is university tuition. Virtually all private and public colleges and universities price their services below their full costs.

6205
The number of bank branches across Canada

78%
The percentage of employment accounted for by the service sector

5
Possible gaps in service quality

$80 million
The amount of money raised by the Ride to Conquer Cancer in Toronto since 2008

52
The number of countries that have a Ronald McDonald House

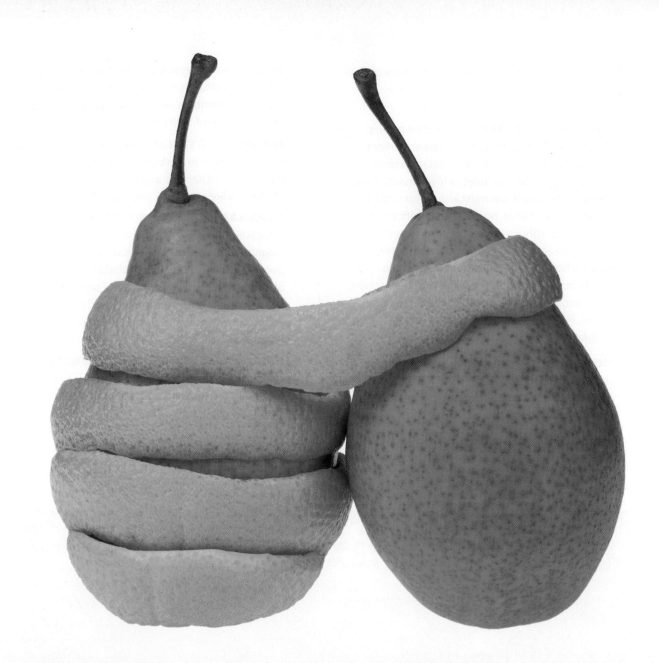

Your online study partner.

www.nelson.com/student

Product Decisions Part 3 Case

Harley-Davidson—Street 750 and Street 500

"We're really not about transportation; it's not about getting from point A to point B. It is about living life the way you choose."

—Mark-Hans Richer, chief marketing officer, Harley-Davidson

Harley-Davidson (HD), founded in 1903, is an iconic American brand deeply associated with motorcycles. The storied history of Harley-Davidson originates from a 3 metre × 4.5 metre (10′ × 15′) shed in Milwaukee, Wisconsin, where William Harley and Arthur Davidson (with Walter and William Davidson) developed the first prototype of the bike, which needed pedal help to climb hills.[1] The prototype was revised, and in 1904 it competed in a Milwaukee motorcycle race held at State Fair Park, placing fourth. In January 1905, ads were placed in the *Automobile and Cycle Trade Journal* to sell HD engines to do-it-yourself customers. This was followed by production of complete motorcycles in April of that year. During World War I, HD provided 15,000 motorcycles to the US military. The success of Harley-Davidson continued and it, along with another U.S. motorcycle company, Indian, was able to successfully weather the Depression and World War II.[2]

Since then, Harley-Davidson has seen its share of ups and down in the motorcycle industry, including major competition and loss of market share to the Japanese motorcycle manufacturers and a series of product quality controversies. However, since 2009 Harley-Davidson has been undergoing major restructuring in its business operations, product lines, and market focus, the results of which are looking very promising. In 2012, the annual sales of HD worldwide were estimated to be US$5.5 billion with an overall sales growth of more than 6 percent. According to Interbrand,[3] the value of the HD brand is US$3.9 billion and the future is looking good.

MOTORCYCLE INDUSTRY TRENDS IN CANADA

More than 103,000 motorcycles, scooters, and all-terrain vehicles (ATVs) were sold in Canada in 2012, costing consumers approximately $1.5 billion.[4] Motorcycles and scooters accounted for 49.1 percent of the total sales, with motorcycles accounting for 48.7 percent or $750 million.[5] According to an estimate for 2012, there were 1085 motorcycle dealers in Canada. Retail motor-cycle sales in Canada grew between 2005 and 2008 from 80,334 units/year to 89,390 units/year. Since then, however, sales declined significantly, reaching only 50,545 units in 2012.[6] Motorcycles with an engine size of 950cc and more accounted for more than half the units sold in Canada in 2012. Given the climate in Canada, motorcycle sales tend to be seasonal, with more than 75 percent of all units sold in the spring and the summer every year. Overall, the recent trends in motorcycle sales point to an uncertain future for the motorcycle industry.

WHO RIDES A HARLEY?

The brand team at Harley-Davidson continually monitors the market and in its recent report has found the following:

▸▸ **The average age of a Harley biker is increasing. The average rider is currently 46 years old, up from 1999** when the average age was 43.4 years.[7] This poses problems for Harley as the pool of older riders, especially from the baby boom generation, is decreasing. Harley is struggling to appeal to the 18-to-34 segment.[8]

▶▶ **Younger riders view Harley-Davidson as an American icon, but to them it represents the 1960s.**

▶▶ **Harleys are for old guys who are trying to be rebellious.**

▶▶ **Harley bikes are outdated and too expensive.**

▶▶ **Harleys aren't what they used to be.**

However, most motorcycle riders admit that Harley provides a unique product experience. The Harley brand team also found that most bike riders agree with the following:

▶▶ **Riding a Harley is an experience and a thrill unlike any other, and it is one that every generation can enjoy.**

▶▶ **No other motorcycle has the feel and sound of the twin-V engine, and nothing else rides as smoothly as a Harley.**

Given these product and brand challenges, Harley has struggled since 2008 to appeal to the younger demographics without much success. The problem is not that younger consumers don't want a bike, but that the prices of the Harley bikes are out of reach for them.

HARLEY-DAVIDSON MARKET-PRODUCT GROWTH STRATEGY

Harley-Davidson has focused on the North American and European markets in the past for the majority of its sales, up to 80 percent of the total revenues. Harley currently offers a wide range of product lines to its consumers in the United States and Canada that include an entry-level line of motorcycles, the Sportster, followed by product lines with larger bikes—Dyna, Softail, V-Rod, Touring, CVO, and Trikes. The U.S. and Canadian markets have matured for heavyweight motorcycles, with engines greater than 900cc, resulting in sluggish sales. The sales for motorcycles in general dropped a whopping 37 percent between 2008 and 2012. To counter this decline, Harley-Davidson is using a two-pronged growth strategy: (1) focus on emerging markets and (2) target the younger demographics in North America.

Harley's entry into India and China, the two most populous and fastest-growing economies, has met with mixed results. Unlike the phenomenal growth for car sales seen in China, Harley has found it very difficult to penetrate the Chinese market given the strict laws governing the purchase and use of motorcycles. Motorcycles are banned in close to 200 cities in China or have very limited access to main roads during the day.[9] China also requires that motorcycles older than 11 years be completely scrapped.[10] This last requirement, combined with the very high prices of Harley-Davidson motorcycles, has deterred leisure riders from entering the motorcycle market.

India, on the other hand, doesn't have such strict laws regarding motorcycles, resulting in Harley focusing more on the Indian market. However, Indian riders also find the prices of Harley motorcycles high, putting most of them out of reach for the majority of bike enthusiasts. Given the price sensitivity and desire for smaller motorcycles, Harley-Davidson has opened its first overseas manufacturing plant in India, where it assembles motorcycles to cut down on some of the product costs.

To better meet the demands of the newer markets and younger demographics in both emerging and North American markets, Harley introduced another line of smaller motorcycles called Street 750 and Street 500 in summer 2014 in India and the United States. These introductions considerably expanded the entry-level product offerings to the younger consumers in all markets. Street motorcycles are designed specifically for the urban riding experience, which is very different from leisure riding covering long distances. Harley's current plan is to use the Indian manufacturing plant to sell its Street bikes in India and to export them to China and other countries, except the North American market. These bikes will be available to Canadian consumers in spring 2015. These smaller motorcycles will be produced in Harley's Kansas plant in the United States. The two products are the first major product design for Harley in the last 13 years.

Critics of Harley's introduction of smaller bikes view it a violation of the Harley brand and a betrayal of the loyal riders who identify themselves with the bigger bikes. However, Harley appears to be evolving, bringing in new and younger customers while still retaining the old loyalists. Harley's strategy will be to draw younger consumers into the showroom to purchase Street or Sportster models and then gradually transition them to more expensive models over the years.

What will the Harley motorcycle of the future look like? In June 2014, Harley announced Project Livewire, its first electric motorcycle, which blends new technologies with environmental consciousness. Project Livewire, if successfully commercialized, will herald Harley's foray into unknown territory.

1. Go to Harley-Davidson Canada's website, review its product lines, and comment on Harley's product mix, product lines, and product-line width.

2. Is the decision to introduce the Street product line a violation of Harley core brand values?

3. Draw a product life cycle (PLC) for Harley-Davidson. What stage of the PLC is Harley-Davidson at?

4. Based on your understanding of Harley's current stage of the PLC, what recommendations would you make to Harley?

Chapter **12** **Setting the Right Price**

"The sole purpose of marketing is to sell more to more people, more often and at higher prices. There is no other reason to do it."[1]

—Sergio Zyman (author)

After you finish this chapter, go to www.nelson.com/student *for* **STUDY TOOLS**.

12-1 THE IMPORTANCE OF PRICE

Price means one thing to the consumer and something else to the seller. To the consumer, price is the cost of something. To the seller, price is revenue, the primary source of profits. In the broadest sense, price allocates resources in a free-market economy.

But price goes beyond the supposed rationality of economics. Price is something that is debated between buyer and seller (as the quotation from Sergio Zyman tells us). Marketing has a large role to play in the determination of price—this is one area where marketing is directly responsible for revenue generation. But there are two aspects of pricing that must be considered: the internal pricing (determined by financial and accounting formulas) and the external pricing determinants (determined by an understanding of marketing and the external environment). Keeping both in mind will ensure that companies establish a price that satisfies not only the bottom line but also the customer.

12-1a What Is Price?

Price is that which is given up in an exchange to acquire a good or service. It is typically the money exchanged for the good or service, but it may also include the time lost while waiting to acquire the good or service.

Consumers are interested in obtaining a reasonable price, which refers to the perceived value at the time of the transaction. The price paid is based on the satisfaction consumers *expect* to receive from a product and not necessarily the satisfaction they *actually* receive. Price can relate to anything with perceived value, not just money. When goods and services are exchanged, the trade is called *barter*.

12-1b The Importance of Price to Marketing Managers

Prices are the key to revenues, which in turn are the key to profits for an organization. **Revenue** is the price charged to customers

price that which is given up in an exchange to acquire a good or service

revenue the price charged to customers multiplied by the number of units sold

multiplied by the number of units sold. Revenue is what pays for every activity of the company: production, finance, sales, distribution, and so on. What's left over (if anything) is **profit**. Managers usually strive to charge a price that will earn a fair profit.

$$\text{Revenue} = \frac{\text{Price}}{\text{Unit}} \times \text{Units}$$

Profit = Revenue − Expenses

To earn a profit, managers must choose a price that is not too high or too low, a price that equals the perceived value to target consumers. If, in consumers' minds, a price is set too high, the perceived value will be less than the cost, and sale opportunities will be lost. Conversely, if a price is too low, the consumer may perceive it as a great value, but the firm loses revenue it could have earned.

Trying to set the right price is one of the most stressful and pressure-filled tasks of the marketing manager, as attested to by the following trends in the consumer market:

▸▸ **Confronting a flood of new products, potential buyers carefully evaluate the price of each one against the value of existing products.**

▸▸ **The increased availability of bargain-priced private and generic brands has put downward pressure on overall prices.**

▸▸ **Many firms are trying to maintain or regain their market share by cutting prices.**

▸▸ **The Internet has made comparison shopping easier.**

In the business market, buyers are also becoming more price sensitive and better informed. Computerized information systems enable organizational buyers to compare price and performance with great ease and accuracy. Improved communication and the increased use of direct marketing and computer-aided selling have also opened up many markets to new competitors. Finally, competition in general is increasing, so some installations, accessories, and component parts are being marketed as indistinguishable commodities.

12-2 THE FOUR-STEP PRICING PROCESS

Now that we know what pricing is and why it is important, we need to look at the process of setting the right price. There is no easy formula here; while there are numbers, there are also considerations that go into setting a price that go beyond numbers.

Exhibit 12.1

STEPS IN SETTING THE RIGHT PRICE ON A PRODUCT

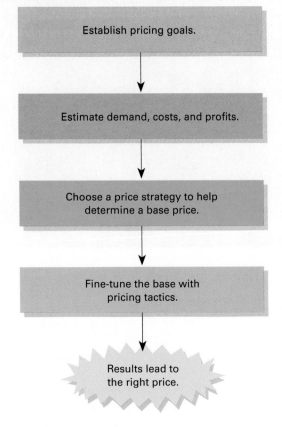

Setting the right price on a product is a four-step process (see Exhibit 12.1):

1. **Establish pricing goals.**

2. **Estimate demand, costs, and profits.**

3. **Choose a price strategy to help determine a base price.**

4. **Fine-tune the base price by using pricing tactics.**

12-2a Step 1—Establish Pricing Goals

The first step in setting the right price is to establish pricing goals. Those goals fall into three categories: profit oriented, sales oriented, and status quo. These goals are derived from the firm's overall objectives. A good understanding of the marketplace and of the consumer can sometimes tell a manager very quickly whether a goal is realistic.

All pricing goals have trade-offs that managers must weigh. A profit-maximization goal may require a bigger initial investment than the firm can commit or wants to commit. A sales-oriented goal, such as reaching the desired market share, often means sacrificing short-term profit, because without careful management, long-term profit goals may not be met. Although meeting the competition is the easiest pricing goal to implement, it can also be short-sighted and costly.

In all situations, when managers set about establishing pricing goals, they must consider the product's demand, costs, profits, and so forth, as it progresses through its life cycle. This process usually means trade-offs occur in terms of meeting the target customer's needs, being competitive, having considerations for changing economic conditions, and meeting the company's overall objectives. What follows is an explanation of the three main pricing objectives and their potential impact on overall company objectives.

PROFIT-ORIENTED PRICING OBJECTIVES

Profit-oriented objectives include profit maximization, satisfactory profits, and target return on investment.

▸▸ **PROFIT MAXIMIZATION:** Profit maximization means setting prices so that total revenue is as large as possible relative to total costs. Profit maximization does not always signify unreasonably high prices, however. Both price and profits depend on the type of competitive environment a firm faces, such as whether it is in a monopoly position (i.e., the firm is the only seller) or in a much more competitive situation. Although this goal may sound impressive to shareholders, it is not good enough for planning.

When attempting to maximize profits, managers can try to expand revenue by increasing customer satisfaction, or they can attempt to reduce costs by operating more efficiently. A third possibility is to attempt to do both. Research has shown that striving to enhance customer satisfaction leads to greater profitability (and further customer satisfaction) than following a cost-reduction strategy or attempting to do both. While it is not always easy to focus on improving both customer satisfaction and productivity, some firms have found a way to be successful (see box below).

SERVICE AND PROFIT LIVING IN HARMONY

Virgin Airlines has entered the airline market with a goal, but it hasn't yet been profitable. The airline is known for its customer service and for providing passengers with a superior experience. It offers Wi-Fi, comfortable seats, and a preflight video (which became an Internet sensation in late 2013) that people actually enjoy watching. Such consumer perks are great for the customer but maybe not for the shareholder. Virgin has yet to show a profit and has had to curtail ambitious plans for growth. So we must ask: Can a company be both service- *and* profit-oriented? There are examples of success, and you need not look further than the airline industry—consider Southwest Airlines in the United States and WestJet in Canada. The key theme for these airlines is putting the customer first. These airlines focus on a service culture where the customer feels valued and receives value at the same time. Just before the Christmas holidays in 2013, WestJet released a video showing customers in Hamilton and Toronto bound for Calgary being asked what they wanted for Christmas. A team of over 150 WestJet employees

Ben Nelms/Bloomberg/Getty Images

took down this information and then scrambled to fulfill all the passengers' holiday wishes by rushing to Calgary malls to find the gifts. Once arriving in Calgary, passengers were awestruck to see their presents coming down the conveyor belt at the airport. The video has received over 30 million hits on YouTube. While the presents may have been a cost for WestJet's bottom line, the potential future revenue from goodwill and customer satisfaction should provide ample future revenue.

Sources: Carmine Gallo, "How Southwest And Virgin America Win By Putting People Before Profit," Forbes, September 10, 2013, www.forbes.com/sites/carminegallo/2013/09/10/how-southwest-and-virgin-america-win-by-putting-people-before-profit/ (accessed August 10, 2014); Matt Richtel, "At Virgin America, a Fine Line Between Pizazz and Profit," The New York Times, September 8, 2013, www.nytimes.com/2013/09/08/business/at-virgin-america-a-fine-line-between-pizazz-and-profit.html?pagewanted=all&_r=0 (accessed August 10, 2014); Virgin America, "Virgin America Safety Video #Vxsafetydance," October 29, 2013, www.youtube.com/watch?v=DtyfiPlHslg (accessed August 10, 2014); "WestJet Airlines Ltd. Performs Christmas Marketing Miracle with Viral Video," Financial Post, December 11 2013, http://business.financialpost.com/2013/12/11/westjet-airlines-ltd-performs-christmas-marketing-miracle-with-viral-video/ (accessed August 10, 2014); and WestJet, "WestJet Christmas Miracle: Real-Time Giving," December 8, 2013, www.youtube.com/watch?v=zlElvi2MuEk (accessed August 10, 2014).

▸ **SATISFACTORY PROFITS:** Satisfactory profits are a reasonable level of profits. Rather than maximizing profits, many organizations strive for profits that are satisfactory to the shareholders and management—in other words, a level of profits consistent with the level of risk an organization faces. In a risky industry, a satisfactory profit may be 35 percent. In a low-risk industry, it might be 7 percent. Satisfactory profits are often connected to corporate social responsibility (CSR), where companies may forgo a blind pursuit of profits to focus on the environment, a safe work environment, and other CSR initiatives. Patagonia, the world-renowned clothing company, focuses sharply on fair labour practices and safe working conditions for all employees throughout the supply chain (www.patagonia.com/ca/patagonia.go?assetid=67372).

▸ **TARGET RETURN ON INVESTMENT:** The most common profit objective is a target **return on investment (ROI)**, sometimes called the firm's return on total assets. ROI measures management's overall effectiveness in generating profits with the company's assets that have come from its investors. The higher the firm's ROI, the better off the firm is. Many companies use a target ROI as their main pricing goal. ROI is a percentage that puts a firm's profits into perspective by showing profits relative to investment.

Generally, firms seek ROIs in the 10 to 30 percent range. In some industries, such as the grocery industry, however, a return of less than 5 percent is common and acceptable. A company with a target ROI can predetermine its desired level of profitability. The marketing manager can use the standard, such as 10 percent ROI, to determine whether a particular price and marketing mix are feasible. In addition, however, the manager must weigh the risk of a given strategy even if the return is in the acceptable range.

SALES-ORIENTED PRICING OBJECTIVES

Sales-oriented pricing objectives are often based on market share.

▸ **MARKET SHARE:** Market share is a company's product sales as a percentage of total sales for that industry. Sales can be reported in dollars or in units of product. Knowing whether market share is expressed in revenue or units is important because the results may differ. Consider four companies competing in an industry with 2000 total unit sales and total industry revenue of $4 million (see Exhibit 12.2). Company A has the largest unit market share at 50 percent, but it has only 25 percent of the revenue market share. In contrast, company D has only a 15 percent unit share but the largest revenue share: 30 percent. Usually, market share is expressed in terms of revenue and not units.

Many companies believe that maintaining or increasing market share is an indicator of the effectiveness of their marketing mix. Larger market shares have indeed often meant higher profits, thanks to greater economies of scale, market power, and the ability to recruit and compensate top-quality management. Conventional wisdom also says that market share and return on investment are strongly related. For the most part they are; however, many companies with low market share survive and even prosper. To succeed with a low market share, companies need to compete in industries with slow growth and few product changes. Ferrari, the Italian sports car manufacturer, is one example of such a

Exhibit 12.2

TWO WAYS TO MEASURE MARKET SHARE (UNITS AND REVENUE)

Company	Units Sold	Unit Price	Total Revenue	Unit Market Share	Revenue Market Share
A	1,000	$1,000	$1,000,000	50%	25%
B	200	4,000	800,000	10%	20%
C	500	2,000	1,000,000	25%	25%
D	300	4,000	1,200,000	15%	30%
Total	2,000		$4,000,000		

> *"We don't have a* MONOPOLY. *We have* MARKET SHARE. *There's a difference."*[2]
>
> —Steve Ballmer (former CEO, Microsoft)

company. Otherwise, companies must compete in an industry that makes frequently purchased items, such as consumer convenience goods.

The conventional wisdom regarding market share and profitability isn't always reliable, however. Because of extreme competition in some industries, many market share leaders either do not reach their target ROI or actually lose money. Procter & Gamble switched from market share to ROI objectives after realizing that profits don't automatically follow as a result of a large market share. Still, for some companies, the struggle for market share can be all-consuming.

The tablet market is on the rise, at the expense of desktops and laptops, and three companies are fighting it out for market share. Apple, with its iPad offerings, continues to lead the way in the tablet marketplace. However, Apple maintains a certain margin on their products, meaning that lower-priced competitors can enter into the market. This is where Samsung and Microsoft come in. Samsung is top in Android tablet sales, with Microsoft making gains. Analysts predict Microsoft will double its share of the tablet market in 2014. But with hundreds of smaller competitors in the marketplace, who knows how long these big three will be able to hold on to their tablet market share.[3]

Research organizations, such as Nielsen and Information Resources, Inc., provide excellent market share reports for many different industries. These reports enable companies to track their performance in various product categories over time.

▸ **SALES MAXIMIZATION:** Rather than strive for market share, companies sometimes try to maximize sales. A firm with the objective of maximizing sales will ignore profits, competition, and the marketing environment as long as sales are rising.

If a company is strapped for funds or faces an uncertain future, it may try to generate a maximum amount of cash in the short run. Management's task when using this objective is to calculate which price–quantity relationship generates the greatest cash revenue. Sales maximization can also be effectively used on a temporary basis to sell off excess inventory.

Maximization of cash should never be a long-run objective because cash maximization may mean little or no profitability.

STATUS QUO PRICING OBJECTIVES Status quo pricing seeks to maintain existing prices or to meet the competition's prices. This third category of pricing objectives has the major advantage of requiring little planning. It is essentially a passive policy.

Often, firms competing in an industry with an established price leader simply meet the competition's prices. These industries typically have fewer price wars than those with direct price competition. In other cases, managers regularly shop competitors' stores to ensure that their prices are comparable.

12-2b Step 2—Estimate Demand, Costs, and Profits

After establishing pricing goals in Step 1, managers should then estimate total revenue at a variety of prices. Next, they should determine the corresponding costs for each price. They are then ready to estimate how much profit, if any, and how much market share can be earned at each possible price. Demand can be estimated by looking at the product life cycle (see Chapter 10).

As a product moves through its life cycle, the demand for the product and the competitive conditions tend to change:

▸ **INTRODUCTORY STAGE:** Management usually sets prices high during the introductory stage of a product. One reason is that the company hopes to recover its development costs quickly. In addition, demand originates in the core of the market (the customers whose needs ideally match the product's attributes) and thus is relatively inelastic. On the other hand, if the target market is highly price sensitive, management often finds it better to price the product at or below the market level.

▸ **GROWTH STAGE:** As the product enters the growth stage, prices generally begin to stabilize for several reasons. First, competitors have entered the market, increasing the available supply. Second, the product has begun to appeal to a broader market, often lower-income groups. Finally, economies of scale are lowering costs, and the savings can be passed on to the consumer in the form of lower prices.

» **MATURITY STAGE:** Maturity usually brings further price decreases as competition increases and inefficient, high-cost firms are eliminated. Distribution channels become a significant cost factor, however, because of the need to offer wide product lines for highly segmented markets, extensive service requirements, and the sheer number of dealers necessary to absorb high-volume production. The manufacturers that remain in the market toward the end of the maturity stage typically offer similar prices. At this stage, price increases are usually cost initiated, not demand initiated. Nor do price reductions in the late phase of maturity stimulate much demand. Because demand is limited and producers have similar cost structures, the remaining competitors will probably match price reductions.

» **DECLINE STAGE:** The final stage of the life cycle may see further price decreases as the few remaining competitors try to salvage the last vestiges of demand. When only one firm is left in the market, prices begin to stabilize. In fact, prices may eventually rise dramatically if the product survives and moves into the specialty goods category, as have horse-drawn carriages and vinyl records.

12-2c Step 3—Choose a Price Strategy

The basic, long-term pricing framework for a good or service should be a logical extension of the pricing goals. The marketing manager's chosen **price strategy** defines the initial price and the intended direction for price movements over the product life cycle (see Exhibit 12.3).

The price strategy sets a competitive price in a specific market segment that is based on a well-defined positioning strategy. Changing a price level from premium to prestige may require a change in the product itself, the target customers served, the promotional strategy, or the distribution channels.

A company's freedom in pricing a new product and devising a price strategy depends on the market conditions and the other elements of the marketing mix. If a firm launches a new item resembling several

Exhibit 12.3
PRODUCT-CYCLE PRICING STRATEGIES

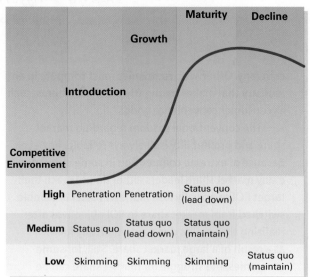

others already on the market, its pricing freedom will be restricted. To succeed, the company will probably need to charge a price close to the average market price. In contrast, a firm that introduces a new product with no close substitutes will have considerable pricing freedom.

A recent study found that only approximately 8 percent of the companies surveyed conducted serious pricing research to support the development of an effective pricing strategy. In fact, 88 percent of companies surveyed did little or no in-depth pricing research. McKinsey & Company's Pricing Benchmark Survey estimated that only about 15 percent of companies do thorough pricing research.[4]

Strategic pricing decisions tend to be made without an understanding of the likely response from either buyers or the competition. Managers often make tactical pricing decisions without reviewing how they may fit into the firm's overall pricing or marketing strategy. Many companies make pricing decisions and changes without an existing process for managing the pricing activity. As a result, many of them do not have a serious pricing strategy and do not conduct pricing research to develop their strategy.[5]

On the other hand, those companies that conduct both research and serious planning for creating a pricing strategy are endeavouring to understand the environment that their product has entered or is currently in. These companies first consider their current product positioning (see Chapter 8), the product's demand and costs, the company's long-term goals, and

As long as demand is greater than supply, SKIMMING *is an* ATTAINABLE STRATEGY.

the product life-cycle stage, and then select from three basic approaches: price skimming, penetration pricing, and status quo pricing.

PRICE SKIMMING
Price skimming is sometimes called a *market-plus approach to pricing* because it denotes a high price relative to the prices of competing products. The term **price skimming**, referring to a high introductory price, often coupled with heavy promotion, is derived from the phrase "skimming the cream off the top." Companies often use this strategy for new products when the product is perceived by the target market as having unique advantages. Often, companies will use skimming and then lower prices over time, known as *sliding down the demand curve.* Hardcover-book publishers, such as HarperCollins, lower the price when books are released in paperback. Other manufacturers maintain skimming prices throughout a product's life cycle.

Price skimming works best when the market is willing to buy the product even though it carries an above-average price. Firms can also effectively use price skimming when a product is well protected legally, when it represents a technological breakthrough, or when it has in some other way blocked the entry of competitors. Managers may follow a skimming strategy when production cannot be expanded rapidly because of technological difficulties, shortages, or constraints imposed by the skill and time required to produce a product. As long as demand is greater than supply, skimming is an attainable strategy.

A successful skimming strategy enables management to recover its product development costs quickly. Even if the market perceives an introductory

price as being too high, managers can lower the price. Firms often feel it is better to test the market at a high price and then lower the price if sales are too slow. Successful skimming strategies are not limited to products. Well-known athletes, lawyers, and hairstylists are experts at price skimming. Naturally, a skimming strategy will encourage competitors to enter the market.

PENETRATION PRICING
Penetration pricing is at the opposite end of the spectrum from skimming. **Penetration pricing** means charging a relatively low price for a product initially as a way to reach the mass market. The low price is designed to capture a large share of a substantial market, resulting in lower production costs. If a marketing manager has decided that the firm's pricing object is to obtain a large market share, then penetration pricing is a logical choice.

Penetration pricing does mean lower profit per unit. Therefore, to reach the break-even point, the company requires a higher volume of sales than needed under a skimming policy. The recovery of product development costs may be slow. As you might expect, penetration pricing tends to discourage competition.

A penetration strategy tends to be effective in a price-sensitive market. Price should decline more rapidly when demand is elastic (demand for a product is price sensitive) because the market can be expanded in response to a lower price. Also, price sensitivity and greater competitive pressure should lead either to a stable low price or to a lower initial price and then a later, relatively slow decline in the price.

© Anatolii Babii / Alamy

Apple has added a twist to the skimming strategy. Rather than introducing their products at a high price and then lowering their prices later, Apple stakes out a price and then maintains and defends that price by significantly increasing the value of their products in future iterations. For example, over the past six years, the average sales price of the iPhone has remained remarkably stable with the subsidized price remaining at $200 and the unsubsidized price hovering around $650.[6]

Although Walmart is typically associated with penetration pricing, other chains have also done an excellent job of following this strategy. Dollar stores, those bare-bones, strip-mall chains that sell staples at cut-rate prices, are now the fastest-growing retailers in North America. Dollar chains can locate their small stores right in downtown neighbourhoods, where their shoppers live. Parking is readily available, and shoppers can be in and out in less time than it takes to hike across a jumbo Walmart parking lot.[7]

If a firm has a low fixed-cost structure, and each sale provides a large contribution to those fixed costs, penetration pricing can boost sales and provide large increases in profits—but only if the market size grows or if competitors choose not to respond. Low prices can attract additional buyers to the market. The increased sales can justify production expansion or the adoption of new technologies, both of which can reduce costs. And, if firms have excess capacity, even low-priced business can provide incremental dollars toward fixed costs.

Penetration pricing can also be effective if an experience curve will cause costs per unit to drop significantly. The experience curve proposes that per-unit costs will decrease as a firm's production experience increases. Manufacturers that fail to take advantage of these effects will find themselves at a competitive cost disadvantage relative to others that are further along the curve.

The big advantage of penetration pricing is that it typically discourages or blocks competition from entering a market. The disadvantage is that penetration means gearing up for mass production to sell a large volume at a low price. If the volume fails to materialize, the company will face huge losses from having built or converted a factory to produce the failed product.

Penetration pricing can also prove disastrous for a prestige brand that adopts the strategy in an effort to gain market share and fails. When Omega—once a more prestigious brand than Rolex—was trying to improve the market share of its watches, it adopted a penetration pricing strategy that destroyed the watch's brand image by flooding the market with lower-priced products. Omega never gained sufficient share on its lower-priced and lower-image competitors to justify destroying its brand image and high-priced position with upscale buyers.

STATUS QUO PRICING The third basic price strategy a firm may choose is status quo pricing, also called *meeting the competition* or *going-rate pricing*. It means charging a price identical to or very close to the competition's price.

Although status quo pricing has the advantage of simplicity, its disadvantage is that the strategy may ignore demand or cost, or both. If the firm is comparatively small, however, meeting the competition may be the safest route to long-term survival.

12-2d Step 4—Use a Price Tactic

After managers have set pricing goals, estimated demand, costs, and profits, and chosen a pricing strategy, they should set a base price. A **base price** is the general price level at which the company expects to sell the good or service. The general price level is correlated with the actions taken in the first three steps of the price-setting process. Once a base price has been

DOLLAR STORES ARE PROFITABLE

Great Canadian Dollar Store started in B.C. in 1993 and by 2014 had grown to nearly 100 locations across Canada. Claiming to have found a niche by selling products for between $1 and $3, the Great Canadian Dollar Store offers those low prices while also providing good customer service.

QMI Agency

determined, a series of price tactics are offered to help fine-tune the base price to make sure it satisfies the company and customer.

Fine-tuning techniques are short-run approaches that do not change the general price level. They do, however, result in changes within a general price level. These pricing tactics allow the firm to adjust for competition in certain markets, meet ever-changing government regulations, take advantage of unique demand situations, and meet promotional and positioning goals. Fine-tuning pricing tactics include various sorts of discounts, geographic pricing, and other pricing tactics.

DISCOUNTS AND ALLOWANCES
A base price can be lowered through discounts and allowances. Managers use the various forms of discounts to encourage customers to do what they would not ordinarily do, such as paying cash rather than using credit, taking delivery out of season, or performing certain functions within a distribution channel.[8] The following are the most common tactics:

▸ **QUANTITY DISCOUNTS:** When buyers are charged a lower unit price when buying either in multiple units or at more than a specified dollar amount, they are receiving a **quantity discount**. A **cumulative quantity discount** is a deduction from list price that applies to the buyer's total purchases made during a specific period; it is intended to encourage customer loyalty. In contrast, a **noncumulative quantity discount** is a deduction from list price that applies to a single order rather than to the total volume of orders placed during a certain period. It is intended to encourage orders in large quantities.

▸ **CASH DISCOUNTS:** A **cash discount** is a price reduction offered to a consumer, an industrial user, or a marketing intermediary in return for prompt payment of a bill (for example, 2/10, net 30). Prompt payment saves the seller carrying charges and billing expenses and allows the seller to avoid bad debt.

▸ **FUNCTIONAL DISCOUNTS:** When distribution channel intermediaries, such as wholesalers or retailers, perform a service or function for the manufacturer (for example, setting up retail displays or extending credit), they must be compensated. This compensation, typically a percentage discount from the base price, is called a **functional discount (or trade discount)**. Functional discounts vary greatly from channel to channel, depending on the tasks performed by the intermediary.

▸ **SEASONAL DISCOUNTS:** A **seasonal discount** is a price reduction for buying merchandise out of season (for example, buying new ski equipment in March and accepting delivery in July). It shifts the storage function to the purchaser. Seasonal discounts also enable manufacturers to maintain a steady production schedule year-round.

VALUE-BASED PRICING
Value-based pricing, also called *value pricing*, is a pricing strategy that has grown out of the quality movement. Instead of determining prices on the basis of costs or competitors' prices, value-based pricing starts with the customer, considers the competition, and then determines the appropriate price. The basic assumption is that the firm is customer driven, seeking to understand the attributes customers want in the goods and services they buy and the value of that bundle of attributes to customers. Because very few firms operate in a pure monopoly, however, a marketer using value-based pricing must also determine the value of competitive offerings to customers. Customers determine the value of a product (not just its price) relative to the value of alternatives. In value-based pricing, therefore, the price of the product is set at a level that seems to the customer to be a good price compared with the prices of other options.

Because of Walmart's strong market entry into groceries, rival supermarkets are adopting value-based pricing as a defensive move. Shoppers in competitive markets are

Aquir/Shutterstock.com

quantity discount a unit price reduction offered to buyers buying either in multiple units or at more than a specified dollar amount

cumulative quantity discount a deduction from list price that applies to the buyer's total purchases made during a specific period

noncumulative quantity discount a deduction from list price that applies to a single order rather than to the total volume of orders placed during a certain period

cash discount a price reduction offered to a consumer, an industrial user, or a marketing intermediary in return for prompt payment of a bill

functional discount (trade discount) a discount to wholesalers and retailers for performing channel functions

seasonal discount a price reduction for buying merchandise out of season

value-based pricing setting the price at a level that seems to the customer to be a good price compared with the prices of other options

seeing prices fall as Walmart pushes rivals to match its value prices. Numerous regional grocery chains have switched to value pricing. In the past, they offered weekly specials to attract shoppers and then made up the lost profit by keeping nonsale prices substantially higher. Now, Costco and Walmart have conditioned consumers to expect inexpensive goods every day.[9]

GEOGRAPHIC PRICING Because many sellers ship their wares to a nationwide or even a worldwide market, the cost of freight can greatly affect the total cost of a product. Sellers may use several different geographic pricing tactics to moderate the impact of freight costs on distant customers. The following methods of geographic pricing are the most common:

▸ **FOB ORIGIN PRICING:** FOB origin pricing, also called FOB factory or FOB shipping point, is a price tactic that requires the buyer to absorb the freight costs from the shipping point ("free on board"). The farther buyers are from sellers, the more they pay, because transportation costs generally increase with the distance merchandise is shipped.

▸ **UNIFORM DELIVERED PRICING:** If the marketing manager wants total costs, including freight, to be equal for all purchasers of identical products, the firm will adopt uniform delivered pricing, or postage stamp pricing. With uniform delivered pricing, the seller pays the actual freight charges and bills every purchaser an identical, flat freight charge.

▸ **ZONE PRICING:** A marketing manager who wants to equalize total costs among buyers within large geographic areas—but not necessarily in all of the seller's market area—may modify the base price with a zone-pricing tactic. Zone pricing is a modification of uniform delivered pricing. Rather than using a uniform freight rate for its total market, the firm divides it into segments or zones and charges a flat

freight rate to all customers in a given zone. Honda, for example, has standardized freight charges on its vehicles, which are based on costs from the point of origin to a specific region.

▸ **FREIGHT ABSORPTION PRICING:** In freight absorption pricing, the seller pays all or part of the actual freight charges and does not pass them on to the buyer. The manager may use this tactic in intensely competitive areas or as a way to break into new market areas.

▸ **BASING-POINT PRICING:** With basing-point pricing, the seller designates a location as a basing point and charges all buyers the freight cost from that point, regardless of the city from which the goods are shipped. Thanks to several adverse court rulings, basing-point pricing has waned in popularity. Freight fees charged when none were actually incurred, called phantom freight, have been declared illegal.

OTHER PRICING TACTICS Unlike geographic pricing, other pricing tactics are unique and defy neat categorization. Managers use these tactics for various reasons—for example, to stimulate demand for specific products, to increase store patronage, and to offer a wider variety of merchandise at a specific price point. Other pricing tactics include a single-price tactic, flexible pricing, professional services pricing, price lining, leader pricing, bait pricing, odd–even pricing, price bundling, and two-part pricing.

▸ **SINGLE-PRICE TACTIC:** A merchant using a single-price tactic offers all goods and services at the same price (or perhaps two or three prices).

Zone Pricing
shipped to Kelowna: $10
shipped to Toronto: $20

khz/Shutterstock.com

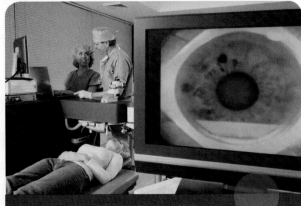

Professional services pricing

HuntStock/Photolibrary

Netflix is an example of a single-price tactic where for $8.99 per month, members can watch unlimited movies and TV episodes on their TVs and computers. Dollar stores are another example of retailers using the single-price tactic.

Single-price selling removes price comparisons from the buyer's decision-making process. The retailer enjoys the benefits of a simplified pricing system and minimal clerical errors. However, continually rising costs are a headache for retailers that follow this strategy. In times of inflation, they must frequently raise the selling price.

▸ **FLEXIBLE PRICING:** Flexible pricing (or variable pricing) means that different customers pay different prices for essentially the same merchandise bought in equal quantities. This tactic is often found in the sale of shopping goods, specialty merchandise, and most industrial goods except supply items. Car dealers and many appliance retailers commonly follow the practice. It allows the seller to adjust for competition by meeting another seller's price. Thus, a marketing manager with a status quo pricing objective might readily adopt the tactic. Flexible pricing also enables the seller to close a sale with price-conscious consumers.

The obvious disadvantages of flexible pricing are the lack of consistent profit margins, the potential ill will of high-paying purchasers, the tendency for salespeople to automatically lower the price to make a sale, and the possibility of a price war among sellers.

▸ **PROFESSIONAL SERVICES PRICING:** Professional services pricing is used by people with lengthy experience, training, and often certification by a licensing board—for example, lawyers, physicians, and family counsellors. Professionals typically charge customers at an hourly rate, but sometimes fees are based on the solution of a problem or performance of an act (such as an eye examination) rather than on the actual time involved.

Those who use professional pricing have an ethical responsibility not to overcharge a customer. Because demand is sometimes highly inelastic (demand for a product will not change when there is a rise or a reduction in price), there may be a temptation to charge what the market will bear.[10]

▸ **PRICE LINING:** When a seller establishes a series of prices for a type of merchandise, it creates a price line. Price lining is the practice of offering a product line with several items at specific price points. The Limited may offer women's dresses at $40, $70, and $100, with no merchandise marked at prices between those figures. Instead of a normal demand curve (a curve that represents the relationship between price and quantity demanded) running from $40 to $100, The Limited has three demand points (prices). Theoretically, the curve exists only because people would buy goods at the in-between prices if it were possible to do so.

Price lining reduces confusion for both the salesperson and the consumer. The buyer may be offered a wider variety of merchandise at each established price. Price lines may also enable a seller to reach several market segments. For buyers, the question of price may be quite simple: all they have to do is find a suitable product at the predetermined price. Moreover, price lining is a valuable tactic for the marketing manager because the firm may be able to carry a smaller total inventory than it could without price lines. The results may include fewer markdowns, simplified purchasing, and lower inventory-carrying charges.

Price lines also present drawbacks, especially if costs are continually rising. Sellers can offset rising costs in three ways. First, they can begin stocking lower-quality merchandise at each price point. Second, sellers can change the prices, although frequent price line changes may confuse buyers. Third, sellers can accept lower profit margins and hold quality and prices constant. This third alternative has short-run benefits, but its long-run handicaps may drive sellers out of business.

▸ **LOSS LEADER PRICING:** Loss leader pricing is selling a product near or even below cost in the hope that shoppers will buy other items once they are in the store. This type of pricing appears weekly in the newspaper advertising of supermarkets. Leader pricing is normally used on well-known items that consumers can easily recognize as bargains. The goal is not necessarily to sell large quantities of leader items but to try to appeal to customers who might shop elsewhere.[11]

Leader pricing is not limited to products. Health and fitness clubs often offer a one-month free trial as a loss leader.

flexible pricing (variable pricing) different customers pay different prices for essentially the same merchandise bought in equal quantities

price lining offering a product line with several items at specific price points

leader pricing (loss-leader pricing) a product is sold near or even below cost in the hope that shoppers will buy other items once they are in the store

Slavoljub Pantelic/Shutterstock.com

odd–even pricing (psychological pricing) odd-numbered prices connote bargains, and even-numbered prices imply quality

price bundling marketing two or more products in a single package for a special price

unbundling reducing the bundle of services that comes with the basic product

▸▸ **ODD–EVEN PRICING:** Odd–even pricing (or **psychological pricing**) means using odd-numbered prices to connote a bargain and even-numbered prices to imply quality. For years, many retailers have priced their products in odd numbers—for example, $99.95—to make consumers feel they are paying a lower price for the product.

▸▸ **PRICE BUNDLING:** Price bundling is marketing two or more products in a single package for a special price. For example, Microsoft offers suites of software that bundle spreadsheets, word processing, graphics, electronic mail, Internet access, and groupware for networks of microcomputers. Price bundling can stimulate demand for the bundled items if the target market perceives the price as a good value.

Hotels and airlines sell a perishable commodity (hotel rooms and airline seats) with relatively constant fixed costs. Bundling can be an important income stream for these businesses because the variable cost tends to be low—for instance, the cost of cleaning a hotel room. Therefore, most of the revenue can help cover fixed costs and generate profits.

Bundling has also been used in the telecommunications industry. Companies offer local service, long-distance service, DSL Internet service, wireless, and even cable TV in various menus of bundling. Telecom companies use bundling as a way to protect their market share and fight off competition by locking customers into a group of services. For consumers, comparison shopping may be difficult since they may not be able to determine how much they are really paying for each component of the bundle. A related price tactic is **unbundling**, or reducing the bundle of services that comes with the basic product. To help hold the line on costs, some stores require customers to pay for gift wrapping.

Clearly, price bundling can influence consumers' purchase behaviour. But what about the decision to consume a particular bundled product or service? Some of the latest research has focused on how people consume certain bundled products or services. According to this research, the key to consumption behaviour is how closely consumers can link the costs and benefits of the exchange.[12] In complex transactions, such as a holiday package, it may be unclear which costs are paying for which benefits. In such cases, consumers tend to mentally downplay their upfront costs for the bundled product, so they may be more likely to forgo a benefit that's part of the bundle, such as a free dinner.

PENNY FOR YOUR TACTIC?

While it is a very common pricing tactic, odd-even pricing might be running into a problem—the death of the penny. In early 2013, the Royal Canadian Mint officially stopped producing the Canadian one-cent coin. This means that retailers have had to make changes to their prices, at a cost of more than $100,000 for some large organizations (that's a lot of pennies!). Rounding has also become an issue, as prices that were using odd pricing of 99 cents may be rounded up if customers are not paying with credit, debit, or cheque. The Royal Canadian Mint has put out information on these changes, but it is still something that both companies and consumers will have to get used to. Odd pricing might become even odder as the new penny-less reality takes hold.

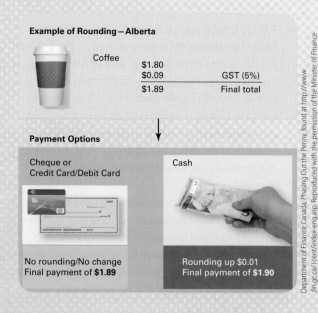

Example of Rounding—Alberta

Coffee	$1.80	
	$0.09	GST (5%)
	$1.89	Final total

Payment Options

Cheque or Credit Card/Debit Card
No rounding/No change
Final payment of **$1.89**

Cash
Rounding up $0.01
Final payment of **$1.90**

Department of Finance Canada, Phasing Out the Penny, found at http://www.fin.gc.ca/1cent/index-eng.asp. Reproduced with the permission of the Minister of Finance Canada, 2014.

Sources: John Rieti, "5 Odd Questions about the Death of the Penny," *CBC News*, February 1, 2013, www.cbc.ca/news/canada/5-odd-questions-about-the-death-of-the-penny-1.1353684 (accessed August 11, 2014); and Royal Canadian Mint, "Phasing Out the Penny," www.mint.ca/store/mint/learn/phasing-out-the-penny-6900002#.UtQ7oRZ23ww (accessed August 11, 2014).

two-part pricing
charging two separate
amounts to consume a single
good or service

Similarly, when people buy season's tickets to a concert series, sporting event, or other activity, the sunk costs (price of the bundle) and the pending benefit (going to see the events) become decoupled. The result is a reduced likelihood of consumption of all the events over time. Researchers found that theatregoers who purchased tickets to four plays were only 84 percent likely to use their first-play tickets and only 78 percent likely to use any given ticket across the four plays.[13]

If one of the plays in the bundle is *Wicked*, however, that might change things. Although the production eventually grossed $1.3 million a week in New York and broke box office records in Toronto, *Wicked* was not an instant success. Despite the show's initially low consumer awareness, producer Marc Platt was convinced that if he could just get people in the door, they would find the performance completely captivating. So he cut ticket prices by 30 percent and watched as patrons began to make repeat ticket purchases during intermission.

Theatregoers who purchase tickets to a single play are almost certain to use those tickets. This behaviour is consistent with the idea that in a one-to-one transaction (i.e., one payment, one benefit), the costs and benefits of that transaction are tightly coupled, resulting in strong sunk cost pressure to consume the pending benefit.

A theatre manager might expect a no-show rate of 20 percent when the percentage of season's ticket holders is high, but a no-show rate of only 5 percent when the percentage of season's ticket holders is low. When a theatre has a high number of season's ticket holders, a manager can oversell performances and maximize the revenue for the theatre.

The physical format of the transaction also figures in. A ski lift pass in the form of a booklet of tickets strengthens the cost–benefit link for consumers, whereas a single pass for multiple ski lifts weakens that link.

Although the price bundling of services can result in a lower rate of total consumption of that service, the same is not necessarily true for products. Consider the purchase of an expensive bottle of wine. When the wine is purchased as a single unit, its cost and eventual benefit are tightly coupled. As a result, the cost of the wine will be significant, and a person will likely reserve that wine for a special occasion. When the wine is purchased as part of a bundle (e.g., as part of a case of wine), however, the cost and benefit of that individual bottle of wine will likely become decoupled, reducing the impact of the cost on eventual consumption. Thus, in contrast to the price bundling of services, the price bundling of physical goods could lead to an increase in product consumption.

▸▸ **TWO-PART PRICING:** Two-part pricing means charging two separate amounts to consume a single good or service. Health and fitness clubs charge a membership fee and then a flat fee each time a person uses certain equipment or facilities.

Consumers sometimes prefer two-part pricing because they are uncertain about the number and the types of activities they might use, such as at an amusement park. Also, the people who use a service most often pay a higher total price. Two-part pricing can increase a seller's revenue by attracting consumers who would not pay a high fee even for unlimited use.

© KATHY WILLENS/ASSOCIATED PRESS

Pricing Decisions Part 4 Case

Net Loss to Net Gain—Netflix

On Tuesday July 12, 2011, Jessie Becker, VP of marketing for Netflix, published a short blog posting on the company's website. The content of this post would cause such a stir that Netflix would lose 800,000 subscribers and 77 percent of its stock price in 4 months.[1]

What unadvised or insulting topics were included in this post? Did Ms. Becker lose her sense of judgement and state something unthinkable? No, it was neither of these scenarios. Ms. Becker simply announced a price change for Netflix's services.

Netflix began in 1997, with co-founders Reed Hastings and Marc Randolph starting up a company to offer a new choice in movie rentals. Pricing was always a consideration and the two co-founders worked on a number of systems for pricing until coming up with an unlimited rental service for one low monthly subscription price.

The number of monthly subscribers began to grow, enticed by one price for all DVD rentals and delivery to customers' homes. Netflix made an initial public offering (IPO) in May 2002 with 600,000 subscribers. By the end of 2010, Netflix had 20 million subscribers, an increase of 63 percent from 2009.

The growth of Netflix had more to do with what consumers liked about Netflix than it did with what consumers hated about the video rental business in general. Netflix offered one set price for rentals from a website, and those rentals were sent to the consumer's front door. The big business of video rental was much different: consumers had to go to the store, pick out a movie that was available, and then return that movie to that same store. Netflix had one other huge advantage in the eyes of customers: no late fees.

Video rental stores long relied on late fees not only as a source of revenue but also as a way to ensure that the most valuable commodity in the store (the new release movie) was available to customers. Prices of new releases were often much higher than older movies, and customers seemed willing to pay this increased price, but only if there were copies available on store shelves.

As Netflix began to get traction in the marketplace, competitors in brick-and-mortar video rentals spaces began questioning this late fee pricing policy. In 2006, Canadian video rental store Rogers began a "no-late-fee" policy, in attempt to compete with online companies like Netflix. This policy lasted less than a year, and in 2007, Rogers introduced a "pay-per-day" policy where a consumer could be charged up to $4 extra in late fees (or, as they called them, "incentives") when a past-due new rental was returned.[2]

The industry leader at the time, Blockbuster, was among the first rental stores to institute a no-late-fee policy in 2005. This was a complete turnaround for a company that had benefited greatly from these "incentives" in the past. In fact, in 2000, Blockbuster made $800 million in late fees, which accounted for 16 percent of its overall revenue.[3]

Clearly, the video rental industry was reeling from the entry of companies like Netflix into the marketplace, with their simple and up-front pricing policies. Netflix was also the clear leader in providing movie rentals for companies. But Netflix had a problem. It didn't actually want to rent DVDs at all. It wanted to be an online streaming company only.

In November 2010, Netflix made its first move, changing its pricing to shift to the desired business model. In a post on the Netflix website, similar to the one in 2011 mentioned earlier, Netflix announced those pricing changes and introduced an online streaming option.

That first post included a table of the price changes that clearly showed an attempt to use pricing as a disincentive to customers ordering DVDs to move them to the streaming option. However, Netflix increased the more popular options (one or two DVDs at a time) by only one dollar, while the price of a limited plan of two DVDs a month stayed the same. The new unlimited no DVDs plan was also introduced at a flat rate of $7.99 per month.[4]

To entice customers to try the streaming options, Netflix offered DVDs as a $2 add-on to the price of streaming. This was touted as a good deal for customers and had customers flocking to the $9.99 "all-you-can-eat" streaming and DVD option. Mission accomplished? Not really.

Only a year later, that now infamous July 2011 post on Netflix explained a less than advisable pricing change. Netflix did not change the price for the unlimited streaming option ($7.99), but it did remove the $2 option for DVDs by mail entirely. Instead, Netflix offered a "new" and "lowest price ever" option for an unlimited number of DVD rentals. However, Netflix did not offer any grandfathering of new prices, which quickly angered and alienated their core customer base.

Citing financial constraints and the "long life that we think DVDs by mail will have," Netflix set out to change its product by using a drastically different pricing strategy. The result was near catastrophic. Thousands of angry comments from Netflix customers can still be seen on the original blog post (visit it here: **http://blog.netflix.com/ 2011/07/netflix-introduces-new-plans-and.html**). Most responses were from customers feeling misled by Netflix; many more were from people stating their intent to end their relationship with the firm. Consumers felt they had not been consulted or warned about the price change. Most saw this as a greedy price grab by a faceless corporation.

Comments like this one were common:

"Netflix, I have been one of your biggest supporters, getting my parents, friends and other family members signed up, but I can no longer promote a company that does this to its customers. I have been loyal a long time and it's a shame that you disrespect and undervalue your customers so much. —Brett, Ohio"[5]

Hundreds of thousands of customers ended their subscriptions; Netflix's stock price took a hit over a few months. Was it possible to recover from such a disaster?

Luckily for Netflix, it was. The company took a huge gamble that online streaming of movie and television shows was the future, and, in fact, it was. After only a few months, statistics showed that 75 percent of new Netflix customers were choosing only the streaming option, with no interest in ordering DVDs by mail.[6] For the company, the logistics of mailing out hundreds of thousands of DVDs had been far too complicated, and now the bandwidth in the online world was there to rescue it.

Netflix began repairing their relationship with customers, and over the next few years, it improved its streaming offerings. It added a new "Just for Kids" tab to the online site in fall 2011 and stabilized the price for the streaming option, keeping it the same for close to three years.[7]

In 2014, Netflix sent a letter to shareholders hinting at a new price change. Netflix had been working on new pricing options for months, looking at different options. The company was very clear that it had learned its lesson from its previous experience, noting that no changes would happen right away. In the statement to shareholders, Netflix stated that when the new price went into effect, existing clients would not face those changes immediately. The company even went to the extent of bolding part of a sentence stating that there would be a grandfathering of existing clients and their plans.[8]

A **bold** statement indeed.

QUESTIONS

1. Go to the Netflix website and find the 2011 price change blog post. Rewrite the blog post in a way that would better reflect the needs of customers. Be sure to include your pricing strategy in your post.

2. For Netflix's new proposed pricing increase, choose a pricing tactic from Chapter 12 and apply it to a new pricing approach for Netflix.

3. Discuss the use of odd–even pricing for Netflix in this case. Describe how this strategy could still be used after the abolishment of the penny in Canada.

4. Create a market segment for Netflix users based on price sensitivity. Describe the current Netflix customer and then describe a potential customer segment. Be sure to use all your segmentation tools from Chapter 8.

Chapter **13** **Marketing Channels and Supply Chain Management**

Fuse/Thinkstock

The term channel is derived from the Latin word *canalis*, which means "canal."

After you finish this chapter, go to www.nelson.com/student *for* **STUDY TOOLS**. ☐------→

13-1 THE NATURE OF MARKETING CHANNELS

13-1a A Plea for Place—The Forgotten P

Now that the market has been segmented, the product or service has been created, and the price has been determined, what's left? We need to promote the product to the customer. But there's still another significant element missing—one that is often forgotten—distribution. Sometimes referred to as the forgotten P, place is an element of the marketing mix that focuses on getting a finished product to the end customer.

Why is place often forgotten? Perhaps because the activities involved in distribution do not seem to coincide with what most people think constitutes marketing. When we create a product, find a price, and promote it, these are activities normally associated with marketing. In addition, as consumers we see the products, look at the prices, and are exposed to the promotions—but we rarely see anything to do with distribution.

Aside from a retail employee stocking a shelf or a transportation truck with a large company logo passing by, people are not often exposed to what distribution can provide. And what it can provide is significant—a source of competitive advantage that is unrivalled by any of the other three Ps of the marketing mix. It is becoming increasingly difficult to gain a competitive advantage based on product, price, or promotion. Because of constant innovation and technology transfer, products have a hard time standing out from each other. Thanks to globalization, firms can find cheap means of production for their product, thus keeping prices within a competitive range. Oversaturation of the marketplace with constant communication with and promotion to customers has left many customers seeking a way to distance themselves from the promotional noise.

Place can work in concert with the other three Ps, helping determine the price or provide insights into the best packaging. There are many ways in which place can help with the other elements of the marketing mix. But it is important to first understand what makes the P of place work.

Channels of distribution can achieve competitive advantage through a thoughtful strategy that takes advantage of several trends:

▸ **Continual push for growth in most companies**

▸ **Increased power of retailers**

▸ **Greater role of information technology**

Ultimately, the main reason that place can be a source of competitive advantage is that if done right, a well-operated channel of distribution is very hard to emulate.

13-1b The Marketing Channel and Intermediaries Defined

A **marketing channel** (also called a **channel of distribution**) is a business structure of interdependent organizations that reach from the point of product origin to the customer, whose purpose is to move products to their final consumption destination. In other words, a marketing channel is a set of interdependent organizations that ease the transfer of ownership as products move from producer to business user or consumer. Marketing channels represent the *place* or *distribution* function in the marketing mix (product, price, promotion, and place). The marketing channel is all about getting the right product to the right place at the right time.

Many different types of organizations participate in marketing channels. **Channel members** (also called *intermediaries* and *resellers*) comprise all parties in the marketing channel that negotiate with one another, buy and sell products, and facilitate the change of ownership between buyer and seller as they move products from the manufacturer into the hands of the final consumer. An important aspect of marketing channels is the joint effort of all channel members to create a

continuous and seamless supply chain. The **supply chain** is the connected chain of all the business entities, both internal and external to the company, that perform or support the marketing channel functions.

13-1c How Intermediaries Help the Supply Chain

As products move through the supply chain, channel members facilitate the distribution process through three key actions: providing specialization and division of labour, overcoming discrepancies, and providing contact efficiency.

PROVIDING SPECIALIZATION AND DIVISION OF LABOUR According to the concept of specialization and division of labour, breaking down a complex task into smaller, simpler tasks and then allocating them to specialists will both create greater efficiency and lower average production costs. Manufacturers achieve economies of scale through producing large quantities of a single product.

Marketing channels can also attain economies of scale through specialization and division of labour by aiding producers who lack the motivation, financing, or expertise to market directly to end-users or consumers. In some cases, as with most consumer convenience goods, such as pop, the cost of marketing directly to millions of consumers—taking and shipping individual orders—makes no sense.

For this reason, producers hire channel members, such as wholesalers and retailers, to do what the producers are not equipped to do or what channel members are better prepared to do. Channel members can do some things more efficiently than producers because they have built good relationships with their customers. Therefore, their specialized expertise enhances the overall performance of the channel.

OVERCOMING DISCREPANCIES Marketing channels also aid in overcoming discrepancies of quantity, assortment, time, and space created by economies of scale in production. For example, assume that Quaker Oats can efficiently produce its Aunt Jemima instant pancake mix at a rate of 5000 units in a typical day. Not even the most ardent pancake fan could consume that amount in a year, much less in a day. The quantity produced to achieve low unit costs has created a **discrepancy of quantity**, which is the difference between the amount of product produced and the amount an end-user wants to buy. By storing the product and distributing it in the appropriate amounts, marketing channels overcome quantity discrepancies by making products available in the quantities that consumers desire.

Mass production creates not only discrepancies of quantity but also discrepancies of assortment. A **discrepancy of assortment** occurs when a consumer does not have all the items needed to receive full satisfaction from a product. For pancakes to provide maximum satisfaction, several other products are required to complete the assortment. At the very least, most people want a knife, a fork, a plate, butter, and syrup. Even though Quaker is a large consumer-products company, it does not come close to providing the optimal assortment to go with its Aunt Jemima pancakes. To overcome discrepancies of assortment, marketing channels assemble in one place many of the products necessary to complete a consumer's needed assortment.

A **temporal discrepancy** is created when a product is produced but a consumer is not ready to buy it. Marketing channels overcome temporal discrepancies by maintaining inventories in anticipation of demand. For example, manufacturers of seasonal merchandise, such as Christmas or Halloween decorations, operate year-round, despite consumer demand being concentrated only during certain months of the year.

Furthermore, because mass production requires many potential buyers, markets are usually scattered over large geographic regions, creating a **spatial discrepancy**. Often global, or at least nationwide, markets are needed to absorb the outputs of mass producers. Marketing channels overcome spatial discrepancies by making products available in locations convenient to consumers. For example, if all the Aunt Jemima pancake mix is produced in Peterborough, Ontario, then the Quaker Oats Company must use an intermediary to distribute the product to other regions of Canada.

PROVIDING CONTACT EFFICIENCY The third need fulfilled by marketing channels is the contact efficiency provided by reducing the number of stores customers must shop in to complete their purchases. Suppose you had to buy your milk at a dairy and your meat at a stockyard. You would spend a great deal of time, money, and energy shopping for just a few groceries. Supply chains simplify distribution by cutting the number of transactions required to move products

discrepancy of assortment the lack of all the items a customer needs to receive full satisfaction from a product or products

temporal discrepancy a product is produced but a customer is not ready to buy it

spatial discrepancy the difference between the location of a producer and the location of widely scattered markets

CANADA'S SUPPLY CHAIN—MUST-SEE TV

Canada's immense size and low population density are causes for concern for any company setting up a distribution channel. Because of this spatial discrepancy, the economies of scale so coveted in marketing channels become very difficult to achieve with so much ground to cover. Add to this Canada's unpredictable climate and you have a very challenging market in which to create a successful marketing channel and supply chain system. However, these challenges are not bad news to everyone. Discovery Canada has a popular show called *Highway Thru Hell* that chronicles the work of a heavy-vehicle towing company in Hope, British Columbia. The show revolves around

Courtesy of Great Pacific Media Inc.

the rescue of large transport trucks carrying out channel and supply chain functions on treacherous roads in bad weather on highways in British Columbia. The show's premiere in 2012 attracted the largest audience in Discovery Canada's history. It would seem that people are in fact interested in channels and supply chain after all!

Sources: *Highway Thru Hell*, Discovery Canada, http://highwaythruhell.discovery.ca (accessed August 3, 2014); and "Big Wrecks and Big Guys Fill Screen in TV's *Highway Thru Hell*," *The Province*, August 28, 2013, http://blogs.theprovince.com/2013/08/28/big-wrecks-and-big-guys-fill-screen-in-tvs-highway-thru-hell/ (accessed August 3, 2014).

Martin Good/Shutterstock.com

from manufacturers to consumers and by making an assortment of goods available in one location.

Consider the example illustrated in Exhibit 13.1. Four consumers each want to buy a new LED television. Without a retail intermediary, such as Future Shop, television manufacturers JVC, Zenith, Sony, Toshiba, and RCA would each have to make four contacts to reach the four buyers who are in the target market, for a total of 20 transactions. However, when Future Shop acts as

an intermediary between the producer and customers, each producer makes only one contact, reducing the number of transactions to nine. Each producer sells to one retailer rather than to four customers. In turn, customers buy from one retailer instead of from five producers. Information technology has enhanced contact efficiency by making information on products and services easily available over the Internet. Shoppers can find the best bargains without physically searching for them and can also search for ratings and feedback on products without having to visit the store.

13-2 CHANNEL INTERMEDIARIES AND THEIR FUNCTIONS

Channel intermediaries must find a way to work together while simultaneously achieving their business goals and objects. Intermediaries in a channel will have to negotiate with one another, decide on terms of ownership transfer between buyers and sellers, and coordinate the physical movement of products from the manufacturer to the final consumer.

What separates intermediaries is the fundamental idea of ownership or title. *Taking title* means that an

Exhibit 13.1

HOW MARKETING CHANNELS REDUCE THE NUMBER OF REQUIRED TRANSACTIONS

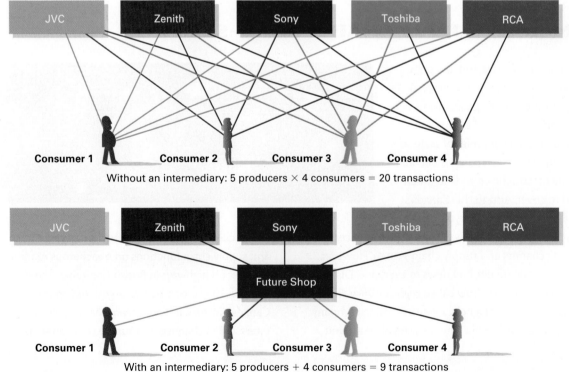

intermediary made the decision to own the merchandise and control the terms of the sale—for example, price and delivery date. Retailers and merchant wholesalers are examples of intermediaries that take title to products in the marketing channel and resell them. **Retailers** are firms that sell mainly to consumers and business customers. Retailers will be discussed in more detail in Chapter 14.

The main characteristics that determine what type of intermediary should be used by a manufacturer (producer) are as follows:

▸ *Product characteristics*, which may require a certain type of wholesaling intermediary, include whether the product is standardized or customized, the complexity of the product, and the gross margin of the product. For example, a customized product, such as insurance, is sold through an insurance agent or broker who may represent one or multiple companies. In contrast, a standardized product, such as a chocolate bar, is sold through a merchant wholesaler that takes possession of the product and reships it to the appropriate retailers.

▸ *Buyer considerations* that affect the wholesaler choice include how often the product is purchased and how long the buyer is willing to wait to receive the product. For example, at the beginning of the school term, a student may be willing to wait a few days for a textbook if it means paying a lower price by ordering online. Thus, this type of product can be distributed directly. But if the student waits to buy the book until right before an exam and needs the book immediately, the student will need to purchase it for full price at the school bookstore or pay even more by adding on high shipping charges to have it delivered immediately from an online site.

▸ *Market characteristics* that determine the wholesaler type include the number of buyers in the market and whether they are concentrated in a general location or are widely dispersed. Chocolate bars and textbooks, for example, are produced in one location and consumed in many other locations. Therefore, a merchant wholesaler is needed to distribute the products. In contrast, in a home sale, the buyer and seller are localized in one area, which facilitates the use of an agent or a broker relationship.

13-2a Channel Functions Performed by Intermediaries

Retailing and wholesaling intermediaries in marketing channels perform several essential functions that enable the flow of goods between producer and buyer. The three basic functions that intermediaries perform are summarized in Exhibit 13.2.

Exhibit 13.2

MARKETING CHANNEL FUNCTIONS PERFORMED BY INTERMEDIARIES

Type of Function	Description
Transactional functions	*Contacting and promoting:* Contacting potential customers, promoting products, and soliciting orders
	Negotiating: Determining how many goods or services to buy and sell, type of transportation to use, when to deliver, and method and timing of payment
	Risk taking: Assuming the risk of owning inventory
Logistical functions	*Physically distributing:* Transporting and sorting goods to overcome temporal and spatial discrepancies
	Storing: Maintaining inventories and protecting goods
	Sorting: Overcoming discrepancies of quantity and assortment
	Sorting out: Breaking down a heterogeneous supply into separate homogeneous stocks
	Accumulating: Combining similar stocks into a larger homogeneous supply
	Allocating: Breaking a homogeneous supply into smaller and smaller lots ("breaking bulk")
	Assorting: Combining products into collections or assortments that buyers want available at one place
Facilitating functions	*Researching:* Gathering information about other channel members and customers
	Financing: Extending credit and other financial services to facilitate the flow of goods through the channel to the final consumer

Although individual members can be added to or deleted from a channel, someone must still perform these essential functions. They can be performed by producers, end-users or consumers, channel intermediaries such as wholesalers and retailers, and sometimes by nonmember channel participants. For example, if a manufacturer decides to eliminate its private fleet of trucks, it must still move the goods to the wholesaler. This task may be accomplished by the wholesaler, which may have its own fleet of trucks, or by a nonmember channel participant, such as an independent trucking firm. Nonmembers also provide many other essential functions that may at one time have been provided by a channel member. For example, research firms may perform the research function; advertising agencies may provide the promotion function; transportation and storage firms, the physical distribution function; and banks, the financing function.

13-3 TYPES OF MARKETING CHANNELS

A product can take many routes to reach its final customer. Marketers search for the most efficient channel from the many alternatives available. Marketing a consumer convenience good, such as gum or candy, differs from marketing a specialty good, such as a Coach handbag. The next sections discuss the structures of typical and alternative marketing channels for consumer and business-to-business products.

13-3a Channels for Consumer Products

Exhibit 13.3 illustrates the four ways manufacturers can route products to consumers. Producers use the **direct channel** to sell directly to customers. Direct-marketing activities—including telemarketing, mail-order and catalogue shopping, and online shopping—are a good example of this type of channel structure. Direct channels have no intermediaries. Producer-owned stores and factory outlet stores—such as Danier Leather and Rocky Mountain Chocolate Factory—are examples of direct channels. Direct marketing and factory outlets are discussed in more detail in Chapter 14.

By contrast, an *agent/broker channel* is fairly complicated and is typically used in markets characterized by many small manufacturers and many retailers that lack the resources to find each other. Agents or brokers bring manufacturers and wholesalers together for negotiations, but they do not take title to merchandise. Ownership passes directly to one or more wholesalers and then to retailers. Finally, retailers sell to the ultimate consumer of the product. For example, a food broker represents buyers and sellers of grocery products. The broker acts on behalf of many different producers and negotiates the sale of their products to wholesalers that specialize in foodstuffs. These wholesalers in turn sell to grocers and convenience stores.

Most consumer products are sold through distribution channels similar to the other two alternatives: the retailer channel and the wholesaler channel. A *retailer channel* is most common when the retailer is large and can buy in large quantities directly from the manufacturer.

BREAKING BULK

The term *breaking bulk* (see Exhibit 13.2) came from shipping, where it referred to extraction of some part of the cargo on a ship. Cargo could be in the form of barrels, crates, and boxes on a ship, and when the ship reached a port, breaking bulk involved pulling off a certain amount of that cargo for distribution. This would have been an arduous and back-breaking task. Today, a marketing channel intermediary (usually a wholesaler) buys a large amount of a product and the breaks the bulk of its purchase in preparation for resale to its own customers. However, intermediaries have access to machinery and technology that the tea bulk breakers would have marvelled at.

Dmitry Kalinovsky/Shutterstock.com

Exhibit 13.3

MARKETING CHANNELS FOR CONSUMER PRODUCTS

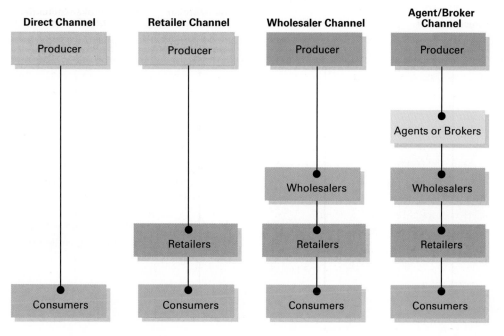

Direct Channel	Retailer Channel	Wholesaler Channel	Agent/Broker Channel
Producer	Producer	Producer	Producer
			Agents or Brokers
		Wholesalers	Wholesalers
	Retailers	Retailers	Retailers
Consumers	Consumers	Consumers	Consumers

Walmart, Sears, and car dealers are examples of retailers that often bypass a wholesaler. A *wholesaler channel* is commonly used for low-cost items that are frequently purchased, such as candy, gum, and magazines.

13-3b Channels for Business and Industrial Products

As Exhibit 13.4 illustrates, five channel structures are common in business and industrial markets. First, direct channels are typical in business and industrial markets. For example, manufacturers buy large quantities of raw materials, major equipment, processed materials, and supplies directly from other manufacturers. Manufacturers that require suppliers to meet detailed technical specifications often prefer direct channels. The direct communication required between Chrysler Canada and its suppliers, for example, along with the tremendous size of the orders, makes anything but a direct channel impractical. The channel from producer to government buyers is also a direct channel. Since much government buying is done through bidding, a direct channel is attractive.

Companies selling standardized items of moderate or low value often rely on *industrial distributors*. In many ways, an industrial distributor is like a supermarket for organizations. Industrial distributors are wholesalers and channel members that buy and take title to products. Moreover, they usually keep inventories of their products and sell and service them. Often,

FOOD BROKER MATCHMAKER

Let's say that you come up with a great new food product. You have sold it at farmer's markets to rave reviews, but now you want to go further and expand your market. A possible method would be to use the services of a food broker. Here are some questions you should ask any prospective food broker:

▸▸ May I see a list of your major clients?

▸▸ What are your five largest retail accounts?

▸▸ Do you have any products similar to mine?

▸▸ Are there brokers in your firm familiar with this line of products?

Brokers will be looking for a product that will get them sales volume and a level of commitment from you that is shown by the research you have done on the marketplace. So where can you get this advice? Any provincial or territorial agriculture or food ministry in Canada.

Source: "Food Brokers," Alberta Agriculture and Rural Development, April 2003, www1.agric.gov.ab.ca/$department/deptdocs.nsf/all/agdex590 (accessed August 3, 2014).

Exhibit 13.4

CHANNELS FOR BUSINESS AND INDUSTRIAL PRODUCTS

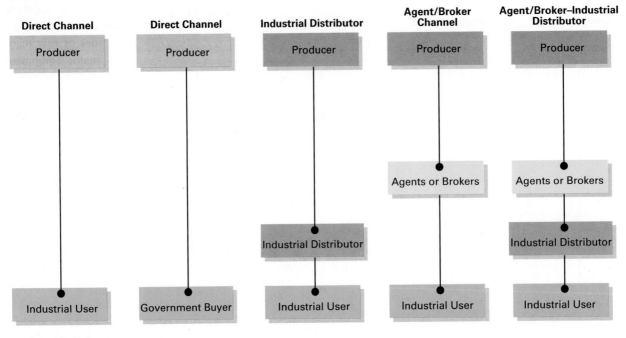

REVERSE AUCTIONS

Another form of online business exchange is the reverse auction. Instead of the buyers doing the bidding, in a reverse auction the seller is the bidder. A buyer in a reverse auction will post a request for bidding on a product or service they require. The bidding is then opened to a group of selected (preapproved) sellers who offer their product or service at an initial bid price, then continue rebidding until they are the lowest bidder and win the business; or they quit bidding because they can no longer lower their bid price. Reverse auctions are competitions between firms bidding to the lowest possible price to secure a business transaction with a buyer. You can see on the graphic to the right that the price is going down rather than up, as in a traditional auction. Reverse auctions are used for purchasing large amounts of business products. The greatest benefit for businesses is that by using reverse auctions, companies can reach 98 percent of the suppliers in a particular field, compared to only about 25 percent in other methods of exchange.

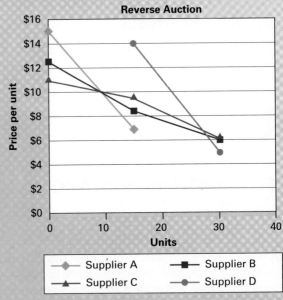

Source: Courtesy of Ion Wave Technologies, Inc.

Sources: Olivia Korostelina, "Online Reverse Auctions: A Cost-Saving Inspiration for Businesses," March 17, 2012, *Dartmouth Business Journal*, http://dartmouthbusinessjournal.com/2012/03/online-reverse-auctions-a-cost-saving-inspiration-for-businesses/ (accessed August 23, 2014); and "What Are Reverse Auctions?" Reverse Auctions, 2008, www.reverseauctions.com/index.html (accessed August 23, 2014).

small manufacturers cannot afford to employ their own sales force. Instead, they rely on manufacturers' representatives or selling agents to sell to either industrial distributors or users, such as Sysco.

The Internet has enabled virtual distributors to emerge and thereby has forced traditional industrial distributors to expand their business model. Many manufacturers and customers are bypassing distributors and going direct, often online. Companies looking to drop the intermediary from the supply chain have created exchanges. Retailers use the Worldwide Retail Exchange to make purchases (that in the past would have required telephone, fax, or face-to-face sales calls), and, in so doing, save approximately 15 percent in their purchasing costs. Finally, a third type of Internet marketplace is a private exchange. Private exchanges allow companies to automate their supply chains while sharing information only with select suppliers. Dell, IBM, and Hewlett-Packard, for example, use private exchanges to manage their inventory supplies and save on distribution and freight costs.[1]

13-3c Alternative Channel Arrangements

Rarely does a producer use just one type of channel to move its product. It usually employs several different or alternative channels, which include multiple channels, nontraditional channels, and strategic channel alliances.

MULTIPLE CHANNELS When a producer selects two or more channels to distribute the same product to target markets, this arrangement is called **dual distribution** (or **multiple distribution**). As more people have access to the Internet and embrace online shopping, an increasing number of retailers are choosing to use multiple distribution channels. For example, companies such as Roots, which includes Roots Home Design, Roots Business to Business, and Roots Yoga, sell in-store, online, and through catalogues.

NONTRADITIONAL CHANNELS Often nontraditional channel arrangements help differentiate a firm's product from the competition. Nontraditional channels include the Internet, mail-order channels, and infomercials. Although nontraditional channels may limit a brand's coverage, for a producer serving a niche market, they provide a way to gain market access and customer attention without having to establish channel intermediaries.

Nontraditional channels can also provide another avenue of sales for larger firms. For example, vending machines, which are often associated with dispensing pop, snacks, or cash, are taking on new roles. A British publisher sells short stories through vending machines in the London Underground. Instead of the traditional book format, the stories are printed like folded maps, making them an easy-to-read alternative for commuters. A California company called Medbox recently signed an agreement with a lab in Canada licensed by Health Canada to provide marijuana via vending machines. However, Canadian law would prohibit anyone wanting to purchase marijuana for medical reasons to access the vending machines directly. Only licensed sellers of marijuana could access the Medbox vending machines, and they would then ship the product to the customer. Medbox vending machines are already being used at doctors' offices and hospitals in California. The company believes that the Canadian market provides a significant growth opportunity for the firm.[2]

Julie Pratt

STRATEGIC CHANNEL ALLIANCES
Companies often form **strategic channel alliances**, which are cooperative agreements between business firms to use one of the manufacturer's already established channels. Alliances are used most often when the creation of marketing channel relationships may be too expensive and time-consuming. Starbucks contracted with Pepsi to develop and bottle a Starbucks brand of ready-to-drink (RTD) coffee. The resulting Frappuccino and Doubleshot were an immediate success. Today, the Pepsi Bottling Group is still the sole distributor for Starbucks RTD beverages, and Starbucks has continued access to the thousands of outlets where Pepsi is sold.[3] Strategic channel alliances are proving to be more successful for growing businesses than for mergers and acquisitions. This success is especially true in global markets where cultural differences, distance, and other barriers can prove challenging.

13-4 MAKING CHANNEL STRATEGY DECISIONS

Devising a marketing channel strategy requires several critical decisions. Supply chain managers must decide what role distribution will play in the overall

dual distribution (multiple distribution) the use of two or more channels to distribute the same product to target markets

strategic channel alliances cooperative agreements between business firms to use one of the manufacturer's already established distribution channels

marketing strategy. In addition, they must be sure that the channel strategy chosen is consistent with product, promotion, and pricing strategies. In making these decisions, marketing managers must determine which factors will influence the choice of channel and the appropriate level of distribution intensity.

13-4a Factors Affecting Channel Choice

Supply chain managers must answer many questions before choosing a marketing channel. The final choice depends on their desired distribution channel objectives in terms of coverage, costs, and control of their products. To determine the final choice means first analyzing several factors that often interact with each other. These factors can be grouped as market factors, product factors, and producer factors.

MARKET FACTORS Among the most important market factors affecting the choice of distribution channel are target customer considerations. Specifically, supply chain managers should answer the following questions: Who are the potential customers? What do they buy? Where do they buy? When do they buy? How do they buy? Additionally, the choice of channel depends on whether the producer is selling to consumers or to industrial customers. Industrial customers tend to buy in larger quantities and often require more customer service than consumers. For example, Toyota Industrial Equipment manufactures the leading lift truck used to move materials in and out of warehouses and other industrial facilities. Its business customers buy large numbers of trucks at one time and require additional services, such as data tracking on how the lift truck is used.[4] In contrast, consumers usually buy in very small quantities and sometimes do not mind if they receive little or no service, such as when shopping in discount stores like Walmart and Target.

The geographic location and the size of the market are also important in channel selection. As a rule, if the target market is concentrated in one or more specific areas, then direct selling through a sales force is appropriate. When markets are more widely dispersed, intermediaries would be less expensive. The size of the market also influences channel choice. Generally, larger markets require more intermediaries. For instance, Procter & Gamble has to reach millions of consumers with its many brands of household goods. As a result, it needs many intermediaries, including wholesalers and retailers.

PRODUCT FACTORS Products that are more complex, customized, and expensive tend to benefit from shorter and more direct marketing channels. These types of products sell better through a direct sales force. Examples include pharmaceuticals, scientific instruments, airplanes, and mainframe computer systems. On the other hand, the more standardized a product is, the longer its distribution channel can be and the greater the number of intermediaries that can be involved. For example, with the exception of flavour and shape, the formula for chewing gum is about the same from producer to producer. Chewing gum is also very inexpensive, so the distribution channel for gum tends to involve many wholesalers and retailers.

The product's life cycle is also an important factor in choosing a marketing channel. In fact, the choice of channel may change over the life of the product. As products become more common and less intimidating to potential users, producers tend to look for alternative channels. Brokerhouse Distributors, a leading wholesale supplier in Canada, started out selling vending machines, but now offers customers an array of products. Instead of just selling machines that dispense chocolate bars or cans of pop, Brokerhouse provides the hospitality industry in Canada with everything from professional milk frothers to water coolers.[5]

Another factor is the delicacy of the product. Perishable products, such as vegetables and milk, have a relatively short lifespan. Therefore, they require fairly short marketing channels. Today, consumers' desire for fresh (often organic) produce and other farm products has led to a renewed growth across Canada in farmers' markets and in businesses delivering these products from the farm directly to consumers' homes.

MaximImages/GetStock.com

The Canadian Press/JAE C. HONG

ZOOMSYSTEMS PROVIDES IN-STORE RETAIL SOLUTIONS (OTHERWISE KNOWN AS VENDING MACHINES) THAT DISPENSE EVERYTHING FROM HEADPHONES TO ESPRESSO.

PRODUCER FACTORS Several factors pertaining to the producer itself are important to the selection of a marketing channel. In general, producers with large financial, managerial, and marketing resources are better able to use more direct channels. These producers have the ability to hire and train their own sales force, warehouse their own goods, and extend credit to their customers. Smaller or weaker firms, on the other hand, must rely on intermediaries to provide these services. Compared with producers that have only one or two product lines, producers that sell several products in a related area are able to choose channels that are more direct. Their sales expenses then can be spread over more products.

A producer's desire to control pricing, positioning, brand image, and customer support also tends to influence channel selection. For instance, firms that sell products with exclusive brand images, such as designer perfumes and clothing, usually avoid channels in which discount retailers are present, preferring instead to sell their wares only in expensive stores to maintain an image of exclusivity. Many producers have opted to risk their image, however, and test sales in discount channels. Well-recognized brands will work directly with discount retailers like Dollarama to get overstock and discontinued items on to a Dollarama shelf.[6]

13-4b Levels of Distribution Intensity

Organizations have three options for intensity of distribution: intensive distribution, selective distribution, or exclusive distribution.

INTENSIVE DISTRIBUTION

Intensive distribution is a form of distribution aimed at maximum market coverage. **Coverage** refers to ensuring product availability in every outlet where potential customers might want to buy it. If buyers are unwilling to search for a product (as is true of convenience goods and operating supplies), then the product must be very accessible to buyers.

Most manufacturers pursuing an intensive distribution strategy sell to a large percentage of the wholesalers willing to stock their products. Retailers' willingness (or unwillingness) to handle items tends to control the manufacturer's ability to achieve intensive distribution. For example, a retailer already carrying ten brands of gum may show little enthusiasm for carrying one more brand.

SELECTIVE DISTRIBUTION Selective distribution is achieved by screening dealers and retailers to eliminate all but a few in any single area. Because only a few are chosen, the consumer must seek out the product. For example, when Heeling Sports Ltd. launched Heelys, thick-soled sneakers with a wheel embedded in each heel, the company needed to create demand. It hired a group of 40 teens to perform Heelys exhibitions in targeted malls, skate parks, and college and university campuses across the country. The company then made the decision to avoid large stores, such as Sears, preferring instead to distribute the shoes only through selected mall retailers and skate and surf shops, where the Heelys could be positioned as "cool and kind of irreverent."[7] Heelys are available only in bricks-and-mortar retail stores in Ontario but can be purchased online via Amazon.ca.

Selective distribution strategies often hinge on a manufacturer's desire to maintain a superior product image so as to be able to charge a premium price.

EXCLUSIVE DISTRIBUTION The most restrictive form of market coverage is **exclusive distribution**, which is a form of distribution that involves only one or a few dealers within a given area. Because buyers may have to search or travel extensively to buy the product, exclusive distribution is usually confined to consumer specialty goods, a few shopping goods, and major industrial equipment. Sometimes, exclusive territories are granted by new

intensive distribution a form of distribution aimed at having a product available in every outlet where target customers might want to buy it

coverage ensuring product availability in every outlet where potential customers might want to buy it

selective distribution a form of distribution achieved by screening dealers to eliminate all but a few in any single area

exclusive distribution a form of distribution that involves only one or a few dealers within a given area

channel power a marketing channel member's capacity to control or influence the behaviour of other channel members

channel control one marketing channel member intentionally affects another member's behaviour

channel leader (channel captain) a member of a marketing channel who exercises authority and power over the activities of other channel members

channel conflict a clash of goals and methods among distribution channel members

companies (such as franchisers) to obtain market coverage in a particular area. Limited distribution may also serve to project an exclusive image for the product.

Retailers and wholesalers may be unwilling to commit the time and money necessary to promote and service a product unless the manufacturer guarantees them an exclusive territory. This arrangement shields the dealer from direct competition and enables it to be the main beneficiary of the manufacturer's promotion efforts in that geographic area. In an exclusive distribution, channels of communication are usually well established because the manufacturer works with a limited number of dealers rather than many accounts.

Exclusive distribution also takes place within a retailer's store rather than a geographic area—for example, when a retailer does not sell competing brands. Mark's partners with manufacturers to produce its Dakota and WindRiver lines, brands sold only in its stores.

13-5 HANDLING CHANNEL RELATIONSHIPS

A marketing channel is more than a set of institutions linked by economic ties. Social relationships play an important role in building unity among channel members. A critical aspect of supply chain management, therefore, is managing the social relationships among channel members to achieve synergy. The basic social dimensions of channels are power, control, leadership, conflict, and partnering.

13-5a Channel Power, Control, and Leadership

Channel power is a channel member's capacity to control or influence the behaviour of other channel members. **Channel control** occurs when one channel member intentionally affects another member's behaviour. To achieve control, a channel member assumes channel leadership and exercises authority and power. This member is termed the **channel leader**, or **channel captain**. In one marketing channel, a manufacturer may be the leader because it controls new-product designs and product availability. In another marketing channel, a retailer may be the channel leader because it wields power and control over the retail price, inventory levels, and postsale service.

The exercise of channel power is a routine element of many business activities in which the outcome is often greater control over a company's brands. Apple started its line of retail stores because management was dissatisfied with how distributors were selling the company's computers (i.e., with its lack of control). Macintosh computer displays were often buried inside other major retail stores, surrounded by personal computers running Microsoft's more popular Windows operating systems. To regain channel power, Apple hired a retail executive to develop a retail strategy that relied heavily on company-owned stores reflecting Apple's design sensibilities. This has been further enhanced in the creation of a new position at Apple: senior vice president of retail and online stores.[9]

13-5b Channel Conflict

Inequitable channel relationships often lead to **channel conflict**, which is a clash of goals and methods among distribution channel members. In a broad context, conflict may not be bad. Often it arises because staid, traditional channel members refuse to keep pace with the times. Removing an outdated intermediary may result in reduced costs for the entire supply chain. The Internet has forced many intermediaries to offer online services, such as merchandise tracking and inventory availability.

Conflicts among channel members can be due to many different situations and factors. Often, conflict arises because channel members have conflicting goals, as was the case with Apple and its distributors. Conflict can also arise when channel members fail to fulfill expectations of other channel members—for example, when a franchisee does not follow the rules set down by the franchiser or when communications channels break down between channel members. Further, ideological differences and different

Apple store SALES dropped by 3.3 percent in September 2013 and by 9.6 percent in June 2013. The reason? A BETTER DISTRIBUTION NETWORK was pushing sales to third-party resellers.[8]

perceptions of reality can also cause conflict among channel members. For instance, some retailers, believing the customer is always right, may offer a very liberal return policy. Conversely, some wholesalers and manufacturers may feel that people often try to get something for nothing or don't follow product instructions carefully. These differing views of allowable returns will undoubtedly conflict with those of retailers.

Conflict within a channel can be either horizontal or vertical. **Horizontal conflict** is a channel conflict that occurs among channel members on the same level, such as two or more different wholesalers or two or more different retailers that handle the same manufacturer's brands. This type of channel conflict is found most often when manufacturers practise dual or multiple distributions. Horizontal conflict can also occur when channel members feel that other members on the same level are being treated differently by the manufacturer, such as only some channel members receiving substantial discounts.

Many regard horizontal conflict as healthy competition. Much more serious is **vertical conflict**, which occurs between different levels in a marketing channel, most typically between the manufacturer and wholesaler or the manufacturer and retailer. Producer-versus-wholesaler conflict occurs when the producer chooses to bypass the wholesaler and deal directly with the consumer or retailer.

Dual distribution strategies can also cause vertical conflict in the channel, such as when high-end fashion designers sell their goods through their own boutiques and luxury department stores. Similarly, manufacturers experimenting with selling to customers directly over the Internet create conflict with their traditional retailing intermediaries. Producers and retailers may also disagree over the terms of the sale or other aspects of the business relationship.

13-5c Channel Partnering

Regardless of the locus of power, channel members rely heavily on one another. Even the most powerful manufacturers depend on dealers to sell their products; and even the most powerful retailers require the products provided by suppliers. In sharp contrast to the adversarial relationships of the past between buyers and sellers, contemporary management emphasizes the development of close working partnerships among channel members. **Channel partnering**, or **channel cooperation**, is the joint effort of all channel members to create a supply chain that serves customers and creates a competitive advantage. Channel partnering is vital if each member is to gain something from other members. By cooperating, retailers, wholesalers, manufacturers, and suppliers can speed up inventory replenishment, improve customer service, and reduce the total costs of the marketing channel.

Channel alliances and partnerships help supply chain managers create the parallel flow of materials and information required to leverage the supply chain's intellectual, material, and marketing resources. The rapid growth in channel partnering is due to new technology and the need to lower costs. Collaborating channel partners meet the needs of customers more effectively, thus boosting sales and profits. Forced to become more efficient, many companies are turning formerly adversarial relationships into partnerships.

13-6 MANAGING THE SUPPLY CHAIN

A supply chain consists of a group of companies working together to produce, handle, and distribute products to an end customer. Many modern companies are turning to supply chain management to gain a competitive advantage. The goal of **supply chain management** is to coordinate and integrate all the activities performed by supply chain members into a seamless process, from the source to the point of consumption, ultimately giving supply chain managers total visualization of the supply chain, both inside and outside the firm. The philosophy behind supply chain management is that by visualizing the entire supply chain, supply chain managers can maximize strengths and efficiencies at each level of the process to create a highly competitive, customer-driven supply system that is able to respond immediately to changes in supply and demand.

Supply chain management is mostly customer driven. In the mass-production era, manufacturers produced standardized products that were pushed down through the supply channel to the consumer. In today's

horizontal conflict a channel conflict that occurs among channel members on the same level

vertical conflict a channel conflict that occurs between different levels in a marketing channel, most typically between the manufacturer and wholesaler or between the manufacturer and retailer

channel partnering (channel cooperation) the joint effort of all channel members to create a supply chain that serves customers and creates a competitive advantage

supply chain management a management system that coordinates and integrates all the activities performed by supply chain members into a seamless process, from the source to the point of consumption, resulting in enhanced customer and economic value

just-in-time production (JIT)
a process that redefines and simplifies manufacturing by reducing inventory levels and delivering raw materials just when they are needed on the production line

order processing system a system whereby orders are entered into the supply chain and filled

Borrowed from the Japanese, **just-in-time production (JIT)**, sometimes called *lean production*, requires manufacturers to work closely with suppliers and transportation providers to get necessary items to the assembly line or factory floor at the precise time they are needed for production. For the manufacturer, JIT means that raw materials arrive at the assembly line in guaranteed working order "just in time" to be installed, and finished products are generally shipped to the customer immediately after completion. For the supplier, JIT means supplying customers with products in just a few days, or even a few hours, rather than weeks. For the ultimate end-user, JIT means lower costs, shorter lead times, and products that more closely meet the consumer's needs. For example, Zara, a European clothing manufacturer and retailer with more than 1770 stores in 86 countries, uses the JIT process to ensure that its stores are stocked with the latest fashion trends. Using its salespeople to track which fashions are selling fastest, the company can increase production of hot items and ship them to its stores in just a few days. Because Zara stores do not maintain large inventories, they can respond quickly to fashion trends and offer their products for less, giving Zara a distinct advantage over more traditional retailers, such as the Gap, that place orders months in advance.[13]

13-6e Order Processing

The order is often the catalyst that sets the supply chain in motion, especially in build-to-order environments. The **order processing system** processes the requirements of the customer and sends the information into the supply chain via the logistics information system. The order goes to the manufacturer's warehouse. If the product is in stock, the order is filled and arrangements are made to ship it. If the product is not in stock, it triggers a replenishment request that finds its way to the factory floor.

Proper order processing is critical to good service. As an order enters the system, management must monitor two flows: the flow of goods and the flow of information. Good communication among sales representatives, office personnel, and warehouse and shipping personnel is essential to accurate

Marcin Balcerzak/Shutterstock.com

Today's companies rely on sophisticated software to help them control inventories.

order processing. Shipping incorrect merchandise or partially filled orders can create just as much dissatisfaction as stockouts or slow deliveries. The flow of goods and information must be continually monitored so that mistakes can be corrected before an invoice is prepared and the merchandise shipped.

Order processing is becoming more automated through the use of computer technology known as **electronic data interchange (EDI)**. The basic idea of EDI is to replace the paper documents that usually accompany business transactions, such as purchase orders and invoices, with electronic transmission of the needed information. A typical EDI message includes all the information that would traditionally be included on a paper invoice, such as product code, quantity, and transportation details. The information is usually sent via private networks, which are more secure and reliable than the networks used for standard email messages. Most importantly, the information can be read and processed by computers, significantly reducing costs and increasing efficiency. Companies that use EDI can reduce inventory levels, improve cash flow, streamline operations, and increase the speed and accuracy of information transmission. EDI also creates a closer relationship between buyers and sellers.

Retailers such as Walmart and the Bay have become major users of EDI because logistics speed and accuracy are crucial competitive tools in the overcrowded retail environment. EDI works hand in hand with retailers' *efficient consumer response* programs to ensure the right products are on the shelf, in the right styles and colours, at the right time, through improved techniques for tracking inventory, ordering, and distribution.

13-6f Inventory Control

The **inventory control system** develops and maintains an adequate assortment of materials or products to meet a manufacturer's or a customer's demands. Inventory decisions, for both raw materials and finished goods, have a big impact on supply chain costs and the level of service provided. If too many products are kept in inventory, costs increase—as do risks of obsolescence, theft, and damage shrinkage. If too few products are kept on hand, then the company risks product shortages, angry customers, and ultimately lost sales. The goal of inventory management, therefore, is to keep inventory levels as low as possible while maintaining an adequate supply of goods to meet customer demand.

Managing inventory from the supplier to the manufacturer is called **materials requirement planning (MRP)**, or **materials management**. This system also encompasses the sourcing and procurement operations, signalling when raw materials, supplies, or components will need to be replenished for the production of more goods. The system that manages the finished goods inventory from manufacturer to end-user is commonly referred to as **distribution resource planning (DRP)**.

Both inventory systems use various inputs, such as sales forecasts, available inventory, outstanding orders, lead times, and mode of transportation to be used, to determine what needs to be done to replenish goods at all points in the supply chain. Marketers identify demand at each level in the supply chain, from the retailer back up the chain to the manufacturer, and use EDI to transmit important information throughout the channel.

As you would expect, JIT has a significant impact on reducing inventory levels. Because supplies are delivered exactly when they are needed on the factory floor, little inventory of any kind is needed, and companies can order materials in smaller quantities. Those lower inventory levels can give firms a competitive edge through the flexibility to halt production of existing products in favour of those gaining popularity with consumers. Savings also come from having less capital tied up in inventory and from the reduced need for storage facilities. At the retail level, the reduced need for storage space allows for more extensive use of the retail store's area (its real estate space) for the display of more products to their customers.

13-6g Trends in Supply Chain Management

Several technological advances and business trends affect the job of today's supply chain manager. Three of the most important trends are advanced computer technology, outsourcing of logistics functions, and electronic distribution.

ADVANCED COMPUTER TECHNOLOGY

Advanced computer technology has boosted the efficiency of logistics dramatically with tools such as

electronic data interchange (EDI) information technology that replaces the paper documents that usually accompany business transactions, such as purchase orders and invoices, with electronic transmission of the needed information to reduce inventory levels, improve cash flow, streamline operations, and increase the speed and accuracy of information transmission

inventory control system a method of developing and maintaining an adequate assortment of materials or products to meet a manufacturer's or a customer's demand

materials requirement planning (MRP) (materials management) an inventory control system that manages the replenishment of raw materials, supplies, and components from the supplier to the manufacturer

distribution resource planning (DRP) an inventory control system that manages the replenishment of goods from the manufacturer to the final consumer

outsourcing (contract logistics)
a manufacturer's or supplier's use of an independent third party to manage an entire function of the logistics system, such as transportation, warehousing, or order processing

electronic distribution a distribution technique that includes any kind of product or service that can be distributed electronically, whether over traditional forms, such as fibre-optic cable, or through satellite transmission of electronic signals

automatic identification systems (auto ID) using barcoding and radio-frequency technology, communications technology, and supply chain software systems that help synchronize the flow of goods and information with customer demand. At Amazon.com's state-of-the-art distribution centres, sophisticated order systems use computer terminals to guide workers through the picking and packing process. Radio-frequency technology, which uses radio signals that work with scanned bar codes to identify products, directs Amazon's workers to the exact locations in the warehouse where the product is stored. These supply chain technology tools have resulted in a 70 percent improvement in operational efficiency.[14]

Many companies use radio-frequency identification (RFID) tags in shipments to Walmart stores. RFID tags are chips attached to a pallet of goods that allow the goods to be tracked from the time they are packed at the manufacturing plant until the consumer purchases them. Benefits include increased revenue for Walmart because the shelves are always full and reduced inventory management costs because time spent counting items and overstocking are minimized.[15]

OUTSOURCING LOGISTICS FUNCTIONS

External partners are becoming increasingly important in the efficient deployment of supply chain management. **Outsourcing**, or **contract logistics**, is a rapidly growing segment of the distribution industry in which a manufacturer or supplier uses an independent third party, such as SDV Logistics, to manage an entire function of the logistics system, including transportation, warehousing, and order processing. To focus on their core competencies, some companies choose to turn their logistics functions over to firms with expertise in that area. Partners create and manage entire solutions for getting products where they need to be, when they need to be there. Because a logistics provider is focused, clients receive service in a timely, efficient manner, thereby increasing customers' level of satisfaction and boosting their perception of added value to a company's offerings.

Third-party contract logistics allow companies to cut inventories, locate stock at fewer plants and distribution centres, and still provide the same service level or even better. The companies can then refocus investment on their core business. In the hospitality industry,

RFID tags can be attached to pallets of products or to individual items, such as CLOTHING TAGS.

© A3508 Rolf Vennenbernd/dpa/Corbis

Sysco negotiates with suppliers to obtain virtually everything that a hotel might need in terms of food and beverages. By relying on Sysco to manage many aspects of the supply chain, hotels such as Fairmont Hotels & Resorts and Intercontinental Hotels Group can concentrate on their core function—providing hospitality.[16] Many firms are taking outsourcing one step further by allowing business partners to take over the final assembly of their product or its packaging in an effort to reduce inventory costs, speed delivery, or better meet customer requirements.

ELECTRONIC DISTRIBUTION Electronic distribution is the most recent development in the logistics arena. Broadly defined, **electronic distribution** includes any kind of product or service that can be distributed electronically, whether over traditional forms, such as fibre-optic cable, or through satellite transmission of electronic signals. Online sites like iTunes and eTrade have built their business models around electronic distribution.

13-7 DISTRIBUTION CHALLENGES IN WORLD MARKETS

With the spread of free-trade agreements and treaties, global marketing channels and management of the supply chain have become increasingly important to corporations that export their products or manufacture abroad.

13-7a Developing Global Marketing Channels

Manufacturers introducing products in global markets must decide which type of channel structure to use. Using company salespeople generally provides more control and is less risky than using foreign intermediaries. However, setting up a sales force in a foreign country also involves a greater commitment, both financially and organizationally.

Channel structures and types abroad may differ from those in North America. For instance, the more highly developed a nation is economically, the more specialized its channel types. Therefore, a marketer wanting to sell in Germany or Japan will have several channel types to choose from. Conversely, developing countries, such as India, Ethiopia, and Venezuela, have limited channel types available: typically, these countries have few mail-order channels, vending machines, or specialized retailers and wholesalers.

13-7b Global Logistics and Supply Chain Management

One of the most critical global logistical issues for importers of any size is coping with the legalities of trade in other countries. Shippers and distributors must be aware of the permits, licences, and registrations they may need to acquire and, depending on the type of product they are importing, the tariffs, quotas, and other regulations that apply in each country. This multitude of different rules is why multinational companies are committed to working through the World Trade Organization to develop a global set of rules and to encourage countries to participate.

Transportation can also be a major issue for companies dealing with global supply chains. Uncertainty regarding shipping usually tops the list of reasons that companies, especially smaller ones, resist international markets. In some instances, poor infrastructure makes transportation dangerous and unreliable. And the process of moving goods across the borders of even the most industrialized nations can still be complicated by government regulations. To make the process easier, Wide Range Transportation Services operates a 3700-square-metre (40,000-square-foot) facility in Grimsby, Ontario, between Hamilton and Buffalo, New York. It offers brokerage, warehousing, fleet, and logistics services to help its clients reduce costs and save time shipping goods across the border.[17] The company uses technology similar to E-ZPass (an electronic toll collection system used extensively in the Eastern United States) to automate border crossings. The new system sends short-range radio signals containing information on the load to tollbooths, weigh stations, and border crossings. If the cargo meets requirements, the truck or train receives a green light to go ahead. Questionable cargo is set aside for further inspection. Transportation industry experts say the system can reduce delivery times by more than three hours.[18]

14
Canada's place in the Global Rankings of Logistics Performance by the World Bank[19]

6 in 10
Number of firms in a 2013 IT industry study that stated the incidence of channel conflict is increasing[20]

15.9%
Average annual rate of growth for Apple retail stores from 2002 to 2013[21]

1996
The first year of the strategic alliance between Pepsi and Starbucks to distribute Starbucks ready-to-drink coffee[22]

3
Number of levels of distribution intensity: intensive, selective, and exclusive

Canadian retailers ring up more than $40 billion in sales each month!

After you finish this chapter, go to www.nelson.com/student *for* **STUDY TOOLS.** ⌐ - - - - - →

14-1 THE ROLE OF RETAILING

Retailing—all the activities directly related to the sale of goods and services to the ultimate consumer for personal, nonbusiness use—has enhanced the quality of our daily lives. When we shop for groceries, hairstyling, clothes, books, and many other products and services, we are involved in retailing. The millions of goods and services provided by retailers mirror the needs and styles of Canadian society.

Retailing affects all of us directly or indirectly. The retailing industry is one of the largest employers; in 2012 over 2 million people were employed by over 200,000 Canadian retailers, representing just over 12 percent of the working population.[1] More than 200,000 Canadian retailers employ over 12 percent of the working population. This number has decreased somewhat from previous years, as Canadian retailers are continuing to invest in productivity measures that reduce labour costs, in an attempt to increase profit margins in the face of intensified competition because of the increasing presence of foreign retailers, such as Target and Nordstrom, and their continued investment in online retailing. The Canadian economy is heavily dependent on retailing. **Retailers** ring up over $465 billion in sales annually, about 6.5 percent of the gross domestic product (GDP).[2] On a per capita basis, retail sales in Canada reached US$13,000 in 2011, which was, for the first time, equivalent to per capita retail sales in the United States.[3] Although most retailers are quite small, a few giant organizations dominate the industry (see Canada's Top Retailers).

retailing all the activities directly related to the sale of goods and services to the ultimate consumer for personal, nonbusiness use

retailer the market intermediary that sells goods and services to the final consumer

independent retailers retailers owned by a single person or partnership and not operated as part of a larger retail institution

chain stores stores owned and operated as a group by a single organization

franchises relationships in which the business rights to operate and sell a product or service are granted by the franchiser to the franchisee

14-2 CLASSI-FICATION OF RETAIL OPERATIONS

A retail establishment can be classified according to its ownership, level of service, product assortment, and price. Specifically, retailers use the last three variables to position themselves in the competitive marketplace. (As noted in Chapter 8, positioning is the strategy used to influence how consumers perceive one product in relation to all competing products.) These three variables can be combined in several ways to create distinctly different retail operations. Exhibit 14.1 lists the major types of retail stores discussed in this chapter and classifies them by level of service, product assortment, price, and gross margin.

14-2a Ownership

Retailers can be broadly classified by form of ownership: independent, part of a chain, or franchise outlet. Retailers owned by a single person or partnership and not operated as part of a larger retail institution are **independent retailers**. Around the world, most retailers are independent, operating one or a few stores in their community. Local florists and ethnic food markets typically fit this classification.

Chain stores are owned and operated as a group by a single organization. Under this form of ownership, many administrative tasks are handled by the home office for the entire chain. The home office also buys most of the merchandise sold in the stores. Gap and Starbucks are examples of chains.

Franchises, such as Subway and Quiznos, are owned and operated by individuals but are licensed by a larger supporting organization. The franchising approach combines the advantages of independent ownership with those of the chain store organization.

CANADA'S TOP RETAILERS

Ranking in Canada	Ranking Global	Name of Company	Dominant Operational Format	Retail Revenue 2011 (US$ millions)	# of countries of operation
1	31	Alimentation Couche-Tard Inc.	Convenience	32,868	10
2	32	Loblaw Companies Limited	Hypermarket/supermarket/superstore	30,978	1
3	53	Empire Company Limited/Sobeys	Supermarket	17,353	1
4	83	Metro Inc.	Supermarket	11,923	1
5	92	Shoppers Drug Mart Corporation	Drug Store/Pharmacy	10,788	1
6	96	Canadian Tire Corporation, Limited	Other Specialty	10,387	1
7	189	RONA Inc.	Home Improvement	4,887	1
8	226	Hudson's Bay Company	Department Store	4,087	1
9	239	Liquor Control Board of Canada	Other Specialty	3,902	1

Source: "Global Powers of Retailing 2014: Retail Beyond Begins," Deloitte, www2.deloitte.com/content/dam/Deloitte/global/Documents/Consumer-Business/dttl_CB_Global-Powers-of-Retailing-2014.pdf (accessed August 4, 2014).

Exhibit 14.1
TYPES OF STORES AND THEIR CHARACTERISTICS

Type of Retailer	Level of Service	Product Assortment	Price	Gross Margin
Department store	Moderately high to high	Broad	Moderate to high	Moderately high
Specialty store	High	Narrow	Moderate to high	High
Supermarket	Low	Broad	Moderate	Low
Convenience store	Low	Medium to narrow	Moderately high	Moderately high
Drugstore	Low to moderate	Medium	Moderate	Low
Full-line discount store	Moderate to low	Medium to broad	Moderately low	Moderately low
Discount specialty store	Moderate to low	Medium to broad	Moderately low to low	Moderately low
Warehouse clubs	Low	Broad	Low to very low	Low
Off-price retailer	Low	Medium to narrow	Low	Low
Restaurant	Low to high	Narrow	Low to high	Low to high

14-2b Level of Service

The level of service that retailers provide can be classified along a continuum, from full service to self-service. Some retailers, such as exclusive clothing stores, offer high levels of service. They provide alterations, credit, delivery, consulting, liberal return policies, layaway, gift wrapping, and personal shopping. Other retailers, such as factory outlets and warehouse clubs, offer virtually no services.

14-2c Product Assortment

The third basis for positioning or classifying stores is by the breadth and depth of their product line. Specialty stores—for example, Maison Birks—have the most concentrated product assortments, usually carrying single or narrow product lines but in considerable depth. On the other end of the spectrum, full-line discounters typically carry broad assortments of merchandise with limited depth. For example, Costco carries automotive supplies, household cleaning products, and athletic wear. Typically, though, it carries a very limited selection of running shoes. In contrast, a specialty running store, such as The Running Room, carries a seemingly endless variety of running shoes for every foot and body type.

Other retailers, such as factory outlet stores, may carry only part of a single line. Nike stores sell only certain items of its own brand. Discount specialty stores, such as Best Buy and Toys "R" Us, carry a broad assortment in concentrated product lines, such as electronics and toys.

David Cooper/Toronto Star via Getty Images

14-2d Price

Price is a fourth way to position retail stores. Traditional department stores and specialty stores typically charge the full suggested retail price. In contrast, discounters, factory outlets, and off-price retailers use low prices as a major lure for shoppers.

The last column in Exhibit 14.1 shows the typical **gross margin**—the amount of money the retailer makes as a percentage of sales after the cost of goods sold is subtracted. The level of gross margin and the price level generally match. For example, a traditional jewellery store has high prices and high gross margins of approximately 50 percent. Gross margins can decline as a result of markdowns on merchandise during sale periods and price wars among competitors, when stores lower their prices on certain items in an effort to win customers.

14-3 MAJOR TYPES OF RETAIL OPERATIONS

Traditionally, retail stores have been of several distinct types, with each offering a different product assortment, type of service, and price level, according to its customers' shopping preferences. A recent trend, however, has retailers experimenting with alternative formats that make it difficult to categorize them by using the traditional classifications. For instance, supermarkets are expanding their nonfood items and services. Loblaw

Companies Limited has been highly successful with the launch of the Joe Fresh brand, which has expanded from clothing into accessories and makeup. Discounters like Walmart have added groceries, drugstores are becoming more like convenience stores, and department stores are experimenting with smaller stores. Nevertheless, many stores still fall into one of the basic types.

14-3a Department Stores

A **department store** is a store housing several departments under one roof. It usually carries a wide variety of shopping and specialty goods, including apparel, cosmetics, housewares, electronics, and sometimes furniture. Purchases are generally made within each department rather than at one central checkout area. Each department is treated as a separate buying centre to achieve economies in promotion, buying, service, and control. Each department is usually headed by a **buyer**, a department head who selects the merchandise for his or her department and may also be responsible for promotion and for personnel. For a consistent, uniform store image, central management sets broad policies about the types of merchandise carried and price ranges. Central management is also responsible for the overall advertising program, credit policies, store expansion, customer service, and so on. Large independent department stores are rare today. Most are owned by national chains. Canada's department store market is dominated by Sears and Hudson's Bay Co. Sears Canada Inc. is currently in the process of executing a strategic turnaround plan as it struggles to maintain market share in Canada. The department store sector is hurting as the retail landscape evolves and new entrants, such as discount retailer Target and high-end fashion retailer Nordstrom, offer the Canadian consumer more choices.

Hudson's Bay Co. was founded in 1670 and is North America's longest continually operated company. It operates 90 Hudson's Bay department stores in Canada, making it the largest department store chain in the country. In addition, it operates 69 Home Outfitters stores in Canada, which are home specialty superstores. In the United States, Hudson's Bay Co. operates Lord & Taylor, a department store with 48 locations. Just recently, Hudson's Bay Co. acquired Saks Fifth Avenue. The Saks acquisition brings together three strong retail brands under one

The Canadian Press/Fred Lum/The Globe and Mail

The Canadian Press/Graham Hughes

company. Hudson's Bay Co. intends to launch Saks into the Canadian retail landscape.[4] In January 2014, Hudson's Bay Co. sold its flagship downtown Toronto location to Cadillac Fairview Corp. The Hudson's Bay Co. will lease the location back and reopen as the first Saks Fifth Avenue store in Canada.

The $1.8 billion takeover of 220 Zellers stores by Target (USA) in 2011 and the opening of 124 Target stores in Canada in 2013 caused quite a stir in the Canadian retail environment. Canadian consumers embraced the entry of Target into Canada, as they expected to be offered great product selection and competitive prices. However, surveys completed six months after the retailer's launch indicated that these expectations had not been met. Target, while building a Canadian-specific supply chain and hiring and training thousands of employees, had trouble maintaining consistent inventory in stores, and consumers found the prices high. While the Target opening drew curious shoppers, the subsequent letdown caused by inventory and pricing issues resulted in consumers returning to Walmart and other retailers.

14-3b Specialty Stores

Specialty store formats allow retailers to refine their segmentation strategies and tailor their merchandise to specific target markets. A **specialty store** is not only a type of store but also a method of retail operations—namely, specializing in a given type of merchandise. Examples include children's clothing, baked goods, and pet supplies. A typical specialty store carries a deeper but narrower assortment of specialty merchandise than a department store. Generally, specialty stores' knowledgeable sales clerks offer more attentive customer service. The format has become very powerful in the apparel market and other areas. In fact, consumers buy more clothing from specialty stores than from any other type of retailer. Lululemon and MEC are examples of successful chain specialty retailers.

In specialty outlets, consumers usually consider price to be secondary. Instead, a store's popularity is determined by distinctive merchandise, the store's physical appearance, and the calibre of the staff. Because of these stores' limited product line and their attention to customers, manufacturers often favour introducing new products in small specialty stores before moving on to larger retail and department stores.

14-3c Supermarkets

Canadian consumers spend about a tenth of their disposable income in **supermarkets**. Supermarkets are large, departmentalized, self-service retailers that specialize in food and some nonfood items. Supermarkets have experienced declining sales in recent years, some of which has resulted from increased competition from discounters like Walmart and Costco. But demographic and lifestyle changes have also affected the supermarket industry, as families eat out more or are just too busy to prepare meals at home.

Conventional supermarkets are being replaced by bigger *superstores*, which are usually twice the size of supermarkets. Superstores meet the needs of today's customers for convenience, variety, and service by offering one-stop shopping for many food and nonfood needs, in addition to many services—including pharmacies, flower shops, salad bars, in-store bakeries, takeout food sections, sit-down restaurants, health food sections, dry-cleaning services, shoe repair, photo processing, and banking. Some even offer family dentistry or optical shops, and many now have gas stations. This tendency to offer a wide variety of nontraditional goods and services under one roof is called **scrambled merchandising**.

To stand out in an increasingly competitive marketplace, many supermarket chains are tailoring their marketing strategies to appeal to specific consumer segments. Most notable is the shift toward *loyalty marketing programs* in which repeat customers use their frequent shopper cards to earn discounts or gifts. After frequent shopper cards are scanned at the checkout, they help supermarket retailers electronically track shoppers' buying habits to aid their customer relationship management (CRM) programs.

14-3d Drugstores

Drugstores stock pharmacy-related products and services as their main draw, but they also carry an extensive selection of over-the-counter (OTC) medications, cosmetics, health and beauty aids, seasonal merchandise, specialty items such as greeting cards and a limited selection of toys, and even refrigerated convenience foods. As competition has increased from

specialty store a retail store specializing in a given type of merchandise

supermarkets large, departmentalized, self-service retailers that specialize in food and some nonfood items

scrambled merchandising the tendency to offer a wide variety of nontraditional goods and services under one roof

drugstores retail stores that stock pharmacy-related products and services as their main draw

convenience store a miniature supermarket, carrying only a limited line of high-turnover convenience goods

discount store a retailer that competes on the basis of low prices, high turnover, and high volume

full-line discount stores retailers that offer consumers very limited service and carry a broad assortment of well-known, nationally branded hard goods

mass merchandising a retailing strategy using moderate to low prices on large quantities of merchandise and lower levels of service to stimulate high turnover of products

supercentres retail stores that combine groceries and general merchandise goods with a wide range of services

specialty discount stores retail stores that offer a nearly complete selection of single-line merchandise and use self-service, discount prices, high volume, and high turnover

mass merchandisers and supermarkets that have their own pharmacies, drugstores have added such services as 24-hour open drive-through pharmacies and low-cost health clinics staffed by nurse practitioners. Drugstores are also selling more food products, including perishables.

Consolidations in the Canadian retail sector have recently made headlines. In June 2013, Sobeys announced a deal to acquire Safeway Inc.'s Canadian assets, and in July 2013, Loblaw Companies Ltd. announced a definitive agreement to acquire Shoppers Drug Mart. These consolidations improve the competitiveness of the two food giants in the face of increasing grocery product competition from Walmart and Target. The purchase by Sobeys will provide them with a stronger presence in Western Canada, and the acquisition of Shoppers Drug Mart by Loblaw gives Loblaw a better presence in urban areas and an improved health and beauty aid product line. Shoppers Drug Mart will keep its name and operate as a separate company with access to Loblaw's extensive network of food suppliers and the President's Choice line of products. This will allow Shoppers Drug Mart to continue to evolve a strategy of increasing their product mix, especially in the area of fresh food items.[5]

14-3e Convenience Stores

A **convenience store** can be defined as a miniature supermarket, carrying only a limited line of high-turnover convenience goods. There are 23,000 convenience stores in Canada generating over $39 billion in sales each year.[6] These self-service stores, such as Quickie Convenience, Circle K, Alimentation Couche–Tard, and Mac's Convenience, are typically located near residential areas, and many are open 24 hours, seven days a week. Convenience stores offer exactly what their name implies: a convenient location, long hours, and fast service. However, prices are almost always higher at a convenience store than at a supermarket. Thus, the customer pays for the convenience.

In response to recent heavy competition from gas stations and supermarkets, convenience store operators have changed their strategy. They have expanded their offerings of nonfood items with health and beauty aids, and some have added upscale sandwich and salad lines and more fresh produce. Some convenience stores are even selling pizzas, hot dogs, and tacos that are prepared in the store.

14-3f Discount Stores

A **discount store** is a retailer that competes on the basis of low prices, high turnover, and high volume. Discounters can be classified into four major categories: full-line discount stores, specialty discount stores, warehouse clubs, and off-price discount retailers.

FULL-LINE DISCOUNT STORES Compared with traditional department stores, **full-line discount stores** offer consumers very limited service and carry a much broader assortment of well-known, nationally branded hard goods, including housewares, toys, automotive parts, hardware, sporting goods, and garden items, in addition to clothing, bedding, and linens. As with department stores, national chains dominate the discounters. Full-line discounters are often called mass merchandisers. **Mass merchandising** is the retailing strategy whereby retailers use moderate to low prices on large quantities of merchandise and lower levels of service to stimulate high turnover of products.

Supercentres combine a full line of groceries and general merchandise with a wide range of services, including pharmacy, dry cleaning, portrait studios, photo finishing, hair salons, optical shops, and restaurants—all in one location. For supercentre operators such as Walmart and Target, food is a customer magnet that sharply increases the store's overall volume, while taking customers away from traditional supermarkets. To be successful in Canada, Target has recognized that they need to draw consumers into their stores by building awareness of their competitive grocery pricing.

SPECIALTY DISCOUNT STORES Another discount niche includes the single-line **specialty discount stores**—for example, stores selling sporting goods, electronics, auto parts, office supplies, housewares, or toys. These stores offer a nearly complete selection of single-line merchandise and use self-service, discount prices, high volume, and high turnover to their advantage. Hudson's Bay Co. is competitive in this niche with their Home Outfitters stores. Specialty discount stores are often termed **category killers** because they heavily dominate their narrow merchandise segment. Examples include Best Buy in electronics, Staples in office supplies, and IKEA in home furnishings.

Category killers have also emerged in other specialty segments, creating retailing empires in highly fragmented markets. For instance, the home improvement industry, which for years was served by professional builders and small hardware stores, is now dominated by Home Depot, Lowes, and Rona. Category-dominant retailers like these serve their customers by offering a large selection of merchandise, stores that make shopping easy, and low prices every day, which eliminates the need for time-consuming comparison shopping.

WAREHOUSE MEMBERSHIP CLUBS

Warehouse membership clubs sell grocery products and merchandise items. The product mix is generally quite wide and the items are often sold in bulk at discounted prices in exchange for a membership fee. Merchandise is displayed without any frills and inventory turns over quickly. Currently, the leading store in this category is Costco, with over 640 stores worldwide and over 71 million members throughout their global reach.

OFF-PRICE RETAILERS

An **off-price retailer** sells brand name merchandise at considerable discounts. Off-price retailers buy manufacturers' overruns, closeouts on lines, or orders from manufacturers that department stores may have cancelled at or below cost. They may also absorb goods from bankrupt stores, irregular merchandise, and unsold end-of-season output. Much off-price retailer merchandise is first-quality, current goods and because of strong buying policies and relationships, the merchandise in many off-price retailers is continually fresh and trendy. Consumers have come to enjoy the "thrill of the hunt" in buying from off-price retailers, which offer an exciting shopping experience that they can return to regularly. Today, there are dozens of off-price retailers. One of the best known in Canada is Winners, and a recent entrant is Marshall's. Off-price

retailers have done very well as their strong value proposition has resonated with the consumer.

Factory outlets are an interesting variation on the off-price concept. A **factory outlet** is an off-price retailer that is owned and operated by a manufacturer. Thus, it carries one line of merchandise—its own. Each season, 5 to 10 percent of a manufacturer's output does not sell through regular distribution channels because it consists of close-outs (merchandise being discontinued), factory seconds, and cancelled orders. By operating factory outlets, manufacturers can regulate where their surplus is sold, and they can realize higher profit margins than if they disposed of the goods through independent wholesalers and retailers. Factory outlet malls typically locate in out-of-the-way rural areas or near vacation destinations. Most are situated 10 to 15 kilometres from urban or suburban shopping areas so that the manufacturers don't alienate their department store accounts by selling the same goods virtually next door at a discount.

On August 1, 2013, Toronto Premium Outlets opened, offering consumers 25 to 65 percent savings on some of North America's leading brands and designers. Located in Halton Hills, it operates

Niloo/Shutterstock.com

category killers specialty discount stores that heavily dominate their narrow merchandise segment

warehouse membership clubs limited-service merchant wholesalers that sell a limited selection of brand-name appliances, household items, and groceries to members, small businesses, and groups

off-price retailer a retailer that sells brand-name merchandise at considerable discounts

factory outlet an off-price retailer that is owned and operated by a manufacturer

QMI Agency

as a 50/50 partnership between Calloway and Simon Property Group Inc. The Premium Outlets offer fashion-conscious shoppers high-quality brands in a unique outdoor setting. Canadian consumers are very familiar with Premium Outlets as they are often a destination for cross-border shoppers. While the discounts and retailers may be the same, the layout and experience are unique to the Canadian market, and consumers from all over Ontario have made Halton Hills a popular destination.[7]

14-3g Restaurants

Restaurants straddle the line between retailing establishments and service establishments. Restaurants do sell tangible products—food and drink—but they also provide a valuable service for consumers in the form of food preparation and food service. Most restaurants could even be defined as specialty retailers, given that most concentrate their menu offerings on a distinctive type of cuisine—for example, Swiss Chalet and Starbucks coffee shops.

As a retailing institution, restaurants deal with many of the same issues as more traditional retailers, such as personnel, distribution, inventory management, promotion, pricing, and location. Restaurants and food-service retailers cover the spectrum from those offering limited service and inexpensive food, such as fast-food chains and the local snack bar, to those that offer sit-down service and moderate to high prices, such as The Keg or a local trendy French bistro.

14-4 NONSTORE RETAILING

The retailing methods discussed so far are in-store methods, requiring customers to physically shop at stores. In contrast, **nonstore retailing** is shopping without visiting a store. Because consumers demand convenience, nonstore retailing is currently growing faster than in-store retailing. The major forms of nonstore retailing are automatic vending, direct retailing, direct marketing, and electronic retailing.

14-4a Automatic Vending

A low-profile yet important form of retailing is **automatic vending**, the use of machines to offer goods for sale—for example, the vending machines dispensing pop, candy, and snacks typically found in cafeterias and office buildings. Food and beverages account for about 85 percent of all sales from vending machines. Consumers are willing to pay higher prices for products from a convenient vending machine than for the same products in a traditional retail setting, resulting in a strong gross margin of over 50 percent.

Retailers constantly seek new opportunities to sell via vending machines. Many vending machines today also sell nontraditional kinds of merchandise, such as videos, toys, stickers, sports cards, office-type supplies, disposable cameras, and even Apple products and other electronics. In addition, in response to our cashless society, vending machines are now equipped to accept debit, credit, and mobile payments. They are becoming increasingly more interactive with digital screens and video cameras. These "smart" machines can prompt consumers to buy additional products, run advertisements, and track users' purchases to offer frequency discounts. By 2018, it is estimated that there will be over two million of these types of vending machines in the North American market.[8]

14-4b Direct Retailing

In **direct retailing**, representatives sell products door-to-door, office-to-office, or in at-home sales parties.

© jeremy sutton-hibbert / Alamy

VENDING MACHINES *are now even equipped to accept* MOBILE *payments!*

Companies such as Avon and The Pampered Chef have used this approach for years, and both have typically hired women as direct sellers and targeted women as their primary customers. Although most direct sellers, like Silpada Jewelry, still encourage the "party" method, the realities of the marketplace have forced them to be more creative in reaching their target customer. Direct sales representatives now hold sales opportunities in offices, parks, libraries, and other common locations. Others hold informal open houses where shoppers can drop in at their convenience to make a purchase. Many direct retailers are also turning to direct mail, the telephone, and social media to reach their target customer.

14-4c Direct Marketing

Direct marketing, sometimes called **direct-response marketing**, refers to the techniques used to get consumers to make a purchase from their home, office, or other nonretail setting. Those techniques include direct mail, catalogues and mail order, telemarketing, and electronic retailing. Shoppers using these methods are less bound by traditional shopping situations. Time-strapped consumers and those who live in rural or suburban areas are most likely to be direct-response shoppers because they value the convenience and flexibility provided by direct marketing.

DIRECT MAIL Direct mail can be the most efficient or the least efficient retailing method, depending on the quality of the mailing list and the effectiveness of the mailing piece. By using direct mail, marketers can precisely target their customers according to demographics, geographics, and even psychographics. Good mailing lists come from an internal database or are available from list brokers.

Direct mailers are becoming more sophisticated in targeting the right customers. By using statistical methods to analyze census data, lifestyle and financial information, and past purchase and credit history, direct mailers can pick out those most likely to buy their products.

CATALOGUES AND MAIL ORDER Consumers can now buy just about anything through the mail, from the mundane to the outlandish. Although women comprise the majority of catalogue

shoppers, the percentage of male catalogue shoppers has recently soared, as both women and men view shopping via catalogues, whether via mail order or online, as more time efficient than a trip to the mall.

Successful catalogues are usually created and designed for highly segmented markets. The print catalogue industry in Canada is nowhere near as developed as in the United States, and the Internet has certainly made the catalogue less necessary. The IKEA print catalogue is the world's most widely distributed commercial publication. Over 5 million are distributed to Canadian homes each year, and they are highly anticipated. Canadians use the catalogue as a way to gather information about the vast number of items carried in an IKEA store before a store visit. Those not located near an IKEA store (there are 12 stores in Canada) use the catalogue in combination with the IKEA website to place their orders. In 2013, the IKEA website attracted over 1 billion visitors. The catalogue and the website are excellent companion tools to aid in making purchase choices at IKEA. In 2014 the catalogue was enhanced by the inclusion of digital content. With the IKEA Catalogue App that the consumer has downloaded onto their smartphones or tablets they can learn more about certain items that have been digitally enhanced within the catalogue by scanning the item with the App. This allows the consumer to view the item on their smartphone or tablet in 3D and even place the item into their own homes.[9]

Martin Good/Shutterstock.com

TELEMARKETING Telemarketing is the use of the telephone to sell directly to consumers. It consists of outbound sales calls, usually unsolicited, and inbound calls, which are usually customer orders made through toll-free 800 numbers or fee-based 900 numbers.

Rising postage rates and decreasing long-distance phone rates have made *outbound* telemarketing an attractive direct-marketing technique. *Inbound* telemarketing programs, which use 800 and 900 numbers, are mainly used to take orders, generate leads, and provide customer service. Inbound 800 telemarketing has successfully supplemented direct-response TV, radio, and print advertising for more than 25 years.

14-4d Electronic Retailing

Electronic retailing includes the 24-hour, shop-at-home television networks and online retailing.

SHOP-AT-HOME NETWORKS The shop-at-home television networks are specialized forms of direct-response marketing. The shows on these networks display merchandise, with the retail price, to home viewers. Viewers can phone in their orders directly on a toll-free line and shop with a credit card. The shopping channel can use the power of demonstration, reminders of product benefits from the host, and repeated encouragement to buy in a controlled setting, eliminating the need to train and manage sales staff. The shop-at-home industry has quickly grown into a billion-dollar business with a loyal customer following. The best-known shop-at-home network is The Shopping Channel. In 2013, The Shopping Channel underwent a makeover and rebranding, including a revamped logo, a change in the studio sets and on-air look, and an online presence and new shipping policies. Consumers now experience the TV shopping channel across multiple platforms and can buy online via mobile tablets and social media apps.[10]

ONLINE RETAILING For years, shopping at home meant looking through catalogues and then placing an order over the telephone. For many people today, however, shopping at home now means turning on a computer, surfing retail websites, and using the click of a mouse to select and order products online. **Online retailing**, or *e-tailing*, is a type of shopping available to consumers who have personal computers and access to the Internet.

Online retailing has exploded in the last several years as consumers have found this type of shopping convenient and, in many instances, less costly. Consumers can shop without leaving home, choose from a wide selection of merchants, use shopping comparison services to search the Web for the best price, and then have the items delivered to their homes. By 2018, online spending in Canada will account for 8 percent of overall retail, or $33.8 billion. The popularity of online retailing is leading traditional bricks-and-mortar retailers to set up dedicated Canadian websites and encouraging U.S. retailer websites to offer shipping to Canada. In 2013, retailers such as Macy's started shipping to Canada with prices displayed in Canadian dollars and very reasonable shipping rates. Despite the increase in the number of Canadian retailers offering online options, online commerce in Canada is significantly less than that in the United States. The key impediment is the high cost of shipping in Canada due to our small population and large geography. The greater number of retailers in the United States, with greater product selection and very competitive shipping rates, is leading many Canadians to shop on foreign sites.[11]

As the popularity of online retailing grows, it is critical that retailers offer their products online and that their stores, websites, and catalogues be integrated. Customers expect to find the same brands, products, and prices whether they purchase online, on the phone, or in a store. This form of retailing, referred to as **omni channel retailing**, is key to success. For example, Joe Fresh, the highly success Loblaw Companies apparel line, has launched online shopping, offering free shipping on orders over $50.

14-4e M-commerce

M-commerce (mobile e-commerce) enables consumers who have wireless mobile devices to connect to the Internet and shop. Essentially, m-commerce goes beyond text message advertisements to allow consumers to purchase and pay for goods and services by using wireless mobile devices, such as smartphones and tablet computers. M-commerce users adopt the new technology because it saves time and offers more convenience in a greater number of locations. Consumers want choice when it comes to payment options, and Canadian consumers are ready for it. In a study conducted by MasterCard, Canadians ranked high on in-store mobile payment readiness. Canadian consumers are leading the way in the acceptance of and use of MasterCard's Tap & Go contactless payment technology. It appears that the technology has been well accepted because it is quick, secure, and simple to use.[12] Smartphones can also assist in the buying process. Smartphone apps allow the consumer to price compare at store level, read reviews, and receive immediate price deals.

14-5 FRANCHISING

A **franchise** is a continuing relationship in which a franchiser grants to a franchisee the right to operate a business or to sell a product. The **franchiser** originates the trade name, product, methods of operation, and so on. The **franchisee**, in return, pays the franchiser for the right to use its name, product, or business methods. A franchise agreement between the two parties usually lasts for 10 to 20 years, at which time the agreement can be renewed if both parties are agreeable. In Canada franchised businesses account for 40 percent of retail sales and 10 percent of Canada's GDP. There are over 78,000 franchise units

across Canada directly employing over 1 million people annually.[13]

To be granted the rights to a franchise, a franchisee usually pays an initial, one-time franchise fee. The amount of this fee depends solely on the individual franchiser. In addition to this initial franchise fee, the franchisee is expected to pay royalty fees, usually in the range of 3 to 7 percent of gross revenues. The franchisee may also be expected to pay advertising fees, which usually cover the cost of promotional materials and, if the franchise organization is large enough, regional or national advertising. The cost to purchase a McDonald's franchise varies depending on whether the franchise is bought from McDonald's or from a McDonald's owner/operator, but generally $500,000 of nonborrowed personal resources are required for an individual to be considered for a franchise, and 25 percent must be paid as a cash down payment, with the remaining paid within seven years. While owning a franchise, the franchisee pays McDonald's a 4 percent service fee based on monthly gross sales performance and a monthly base rent that is a percentage of monthly gross sales. Recently franchisees have expressed frustration that on top of the monthly fees, more and more operating costs are being shifted to them, as McDonald's Corporation revamps both the restaurants and the menus to meet an increasingly competitive marketplace.[14]

Two basic forms of franchises are used today: product and trade name franchising and business format franchising. In *product and trade name franchising*, a dealer agrees to sell certain products provided by a manufacturer or a wholesaler. This approach has been used most widely in the auto and truck, pop bottling, tire, and gasoline service industries. For example, a local tire retailer may hold a franchise to sell Michelin tires.

Business format franchising is an ongoing business relationship between a franchiser and a franchisee. Typically, a franchiser sells a franchisee the rights to use the franchiser's format or approach to doing business. This form of franchising has rapidly expanded since the 1950s through retailing, restaurant, food-service, hotel and motel, printing, and real estate franchises.

franchise a relationship in which the business rights to operate and sell a product are granted by the franchisor to the franchisee

franchiser the originator of a trade name, product, methods of operation, and so on, that grants operating rights to another party to sell its product

franchisee an individual or a business that is granted the right to sell a franchiser's product

FAST-FOOD FRANCHISES TO OWN IN CANADA

Franchise	Number of Canadian Locations	Cost to Open	Corporate Fees: Monthly Royalty–Gross Sales	Corporate Fees: Monthly Advertising Fee–Gross Sales
Taco Bell	200	$1.3 million–$2.5 million	5.5%	4.5%
Harvey's	240+	$575,000–$975,000	Monthly royalty of 5% of gross sales and monthly advertising fee of 4% of gross sales	
Burger King	290+	$1.2 million–$2.2 million	Monthly royalty of 4.5%	4%
Wendy's	368	$2.2 million–$2.5 million	4%	4%
Country Style	490	$325,000–$360,000	4.5%	3.5%
Dairy Queen	580+	$800,000–$1.3 million	4%	5%
Pizza Pizza	692	$100,000–$450,000	4%	6%
KFC	700	$1.2 million	5%	5%
A&W	753	$900,000–$1.2 million	2.5% net sales	2.5% net sales
McDonald's	1,400+	$296,000–$445,000	4%	
Tim Hortons	3,295	$480,000–$515,000	4.5%	4%

Source: Jason Buckland, "Best Fast Food Franchises to Own in Canada," MSN Money, September 23, 2013, http://money.ca.msn.com/small-business/gallery/best-fast-food-franchises-to-own-in-canada#image=14 (accessed August 4, 2014).

14-6 RETAIL MARKETING STRATEGY

Retailers must develop marketing strategies that are based on overall goals and strategic plans. Retailing goals might include more traffic, higher sales of a specific item, a more upscale image, or heightened public awareness of the retail operation. The strategies that retailers use to obtain their goals might include a sale, an updated decor, or a new advertisement. The key tasks in strategic retailing are defining and selecting a target market and developing the retailing mix to successfully meet the needs of the chosen target market.

14-6a Defining a Target Market

The first task in developing a retail strategy is to define the target market. This process begins with market segmentation, one of the topics of Chapter 8. Successful retailing has always been based on knowing the customer.

Determining a target market is a prerequisite to creating the retailing mix. Target markets in retailing are often defined by demographics, geographics, and psychographics. For instance, Hudson's Bay Co. believes that luxury shoppers—particularly high-income-earning, middle-aged women—are leaving Canada to shop. In an effort to keep luxury shoppers' retail spending in Canada, as noted earlier, the Hudson's Bay Co. recently purchased Saks, the American luxury goods retailer. Hudson's Bay Co. plans to open seven full-line Saks stores in Canada.[15]

14-6b Choosing the Retailing Mix

Retailers combine the elements of the retailing mix to come up with a single retailing method to attract the

© simon Jonathan webb / Alamy

target market. The **retailing mix** consists of six Ps: the four Ps of the marketing mix (product, place, promotion, and price) plus presentation and personnel (see Exhibit 14.2).

The combination of the six Ps projects a store's image, which influences consumers' perceptions. Using these impressions of stores, shoppers position one store against another. A retail marketing manager must ensure that the store's positioning is compatible with the target customers' expectations. As discussed at the beginning of the chapter, retail stores can be positioned on three broad dimensions: service provided by store personnel, product assortment, and price. Management should use everything else—place,

presentation, and promotion—to fine-tune the basic positioning of the store.

THE PRODUCT OFFERING

The first element in the retailing mix is the **product offering**, also called the *product assortment* or *merchandise mix*. Retailers decide what to sell on the basis of what their target market wants to buy. They base their decisions on a number of variables including past sales, fashion trends, customer requests, competition, and other sources. Analysis of sales within local areas assists retailers in ensuring that the product mix within individual locations suits the shoppers in that area. Data mining uses complex mathematical models to help retailers make better product mix decisions. Target, Walmart and other retailers use data mining to determine which products to stock at what price, how to manage markdowns, and how to advertise to draw target customers. The data they collect in CRM (customer relationship management) databases allows manufacturers and retailers to gain better insight into who is buying their products and how to build relationships with them so as to hopefully be rewarded with customer loyalty. Shoppers Drug Mart's successful points program is a brilliant tool that collects shopping data that is mined to enhance Shoppers Drug Mart's ability to build relationships with the consumer and improve the consumer's shopping experience with Shoppers Drug Mart.

Developing a product offering is essentially a question of the width and depth of the product assortment. *Width* refers to the assortment of products offered; *depth* refers to the number of different brands offered within each assortment. Price, store design, displays, and service are important to consumers in determining where to shop, but the most critical factor is merchandise selection. This reasoning also holds true for online retailers. Amazon.com, for instance, offers considerable width in its product assortment with millions of different items, including books, music, toys, videos, tools and hardware, health and beauty aids, electronics, and software. Conversely, online specialty retailers, such as 1-800-Flowers.com and Joefresh.com, focus on a single category of merchandise, hoping to attract loyal customers with their larger depth of products at lower prices and better customer

retailing mix a combination of the six Ps—product, place, promotion, price, presentation, and personnel—to sell goods and services to the ultimate consumer

product offering the mix of products offered to the consumer by the retailer; also called the product assortment or merchandise mix

Exhibit 14.2
THE RETAILING MIX

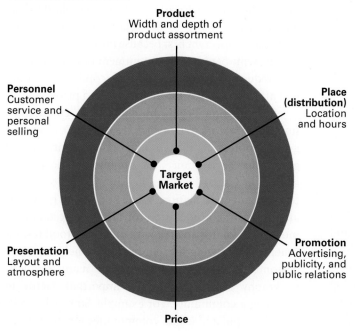

Product
Width and depth of product assortment

Place (distribution)
Location and hours

Promotion
Advertising, publicity, and public relations

Price

Presentation
Layout and atmosphere

Personnel
Customer service and personal selling

Target Market

WITH A NARROW PRODUCT LINE, ONLINE RETAILING CAN ALLOW THE RETAILER TO REACH A GLOBAL MARKET.

service. Many online retailers purposely focus on single-product-line niches that could never garner enough foot traffic to support a traditional bricks-and-mortar store. For instance, caterpillarbaby.com is a family-run online store that provides cloth diapers and accessories for new parents. With such a narrow product line it makes much more sense to offer the product online, thereby reaching a global target market while keeping overhead low.[16]

After determining which products will satisfy target customers' desires, retailers must find sources of supply and evaluate the products. When the right products are found, the retail buyer negotiates a purchase contract. The buying function can either be performed in-house or be delegated to an outside firm. The goods must then be moved from the seller to the retailer, which means shipping, storing, and stocking the inventory. The trick is to manage the inventory, both by cutting prices to move slow goods and by keeping adequate supplies of hot-selling items in stock. As in all good systems, the final step is to evaluate the entire process to seek more efficient methods and eliminate problems and bottlenecks.

PROMOTION STRATEGY Retail promotion strategy includes advertising, public relations and publicity, and sales promotion. The goal is to help position the store in consumers' minds. Retailers design intriguing ads, stage special events, and develop promotions aimed at their target markets. Today's grand openings are a carefully orchestrated blend of advertising, merchandising, goodwill, and glitter. All the elements of an opening—press coverage, special events, media advertising, and store displays—are carefully planned.

Retailers' advertising is carried out mostly at the local level. Local advertising by retailers usually provides specific information about their stores, such as location, merchandise, hours, prices, and special sales. In contrast, national retail advertising generally focuses on image. Hudson's Bay Co. emphasizes product mix and pricing in national newspaper inserts and flyers on a weekly basis with radio support using Vice Chairman Bonnie Brooks as the spokesperson. Advertising campaigns also take advantage of cooperative advertising, another popular retail advertising practice. Traditionally, marketers paid retailers to feature their products in store mailers, or a marketer developed a TV campaign for the product and simply tacked on several retailers' names at the end. Today advertising makes use of a more collaborative trend by integrating products such as Tide laundry detergent or Coca-Cola into the actual campaign. Another common form of cooperative advertising involves the promotion of exclusive products. For example, Target hires famous trendy designers for temporary partnerships, during which they develop reasonably priced product lines available exclusively at Target.

THE PROPER LOCATION The retailing axiom "location, location, location" has long emphasized the importance of place to the retail mix. The location decision is important first because the retailer is making a large, semi-permanent commitment of resources that may reduce its future flexibility. Second, the location will affect the store's future growth and profitability.

Site location begins by choosing a community. Important factors to consider are the area's economic growth potential, the amount of competition, and geography. For instance, the population and income growth in Calgary has resulted in millions of square feet of retail construction. While population growth is an important consideration for fast-food restaurants, most also look for an area with other fast-food restaurants because being located in clusters helps to draw customers for each restaurant. For many retailers, geography remains the most important factor in choosing a community. For example, Starbucks seeks densely populated urban communities for its stores.

After settling on a geographic region or community, retailers must choose a specific site. In addition to growth potential, the important factors are neighbourhood socioeconomic characteristics, traffic flows, land costs, zoning regulations, and public transportation. A particular site's visibility, parking, entrance and exit locations, accessibility, and safety and security issues are also considered. Additionally, a retailer should consider how its store would fit into the surrounding environment. For example, the Hudson's Bay Co. would be unlikely to locate one of its seven new Saks stores next to a Dollarama.

Retailers face one final decision about location: whether to have a freestanding unit or to become a tenant in a shopping centre or mall.

FREESTANDING STORES An isolated, freestanding location can be used by large retailers, such as Best Buy or Target, and sellers of such shopping goods as furniture and cars because they are known as destination stores. **Destination stores** are stores consumers seek out and purposely plan to visit. An isolated store location may have the advantages of low site cost or rent and no nearby competitors. On the other hand, it may be difficult to attract customers to a freestanding location, and no neighbouring retailers are around to share costs.

Freestanding units are increasing in popularity as retailers strive to make their stores more convenient to access, more enticing to shop in, and more profitable. More and more retailers are deciding not to locate in pedestrian malls. Perhaps the greatest reason for developing a freestanding site is greater visibility. Retailers often feel they get lost in huge shopping centres and malls, but freestanding units can help stores develop an identity with shoppers. Also, an aggressive expansion plan may not allow time to wait for the shopping centre to be built. Drugstore chains, such as Shoppers Drug Mart, have been determinedly relocating their existing shopping centre stores to freestanding sites, especially street corner sites for drive-through accessibility.

SHOPPING CENTRES Shopping centres began in the 1950s when Canadians started migrating to the suburbs. The first shopping centres were *strip malls*, typically located along busy streets. They usually included a supermarket, a variety store, and perhaps a few specialty stores. Next, *community shopping centres* emerged, with one or two small department stores, more specialty stores, a couple of restaurants, and several apparel stores. These community shopping centres provided off-street parking and a broader variety of merchandise.

Regional malls offering a much wider variety of merchandise started appearing in the mid-1970s. Regional malls are either entirely enclosed or roofed to allow shopping in any weather. Most are landscaped with trees, fountains, sculptures, and the like to enhance the shopping environment. They have hectares of free parking. The *anchor stores* or *generator stores* (often major department stores) are usually located at opposite ends of the mall to create heavy foot traffic.

According to shopping centre developers, *lifestyle centres* are emerging as the newest generation of shopping centres. Lifestyle centres typically combine outdoor shopping areas that comprise upscale retailers and restaurants, plazas, fountains, and pedestrian streets. They appeal to retail developers looking for an alternative to the traditional shopping mall, a concept rapidly losing favour among shoppers.

RETAIL PRICES Another important element in the retailing mix is price. Retailing's ultimate goal is to sell products to consumers, and the right price is critical in ensuring sales. Because retail prices are usually based on the cost of the merchandise, an essential part of pricing is efficient and timely buying.

Price is also a key element in a retail store's positioning strategy. Higher prices often indicate a level of quality and help reinforce the prestigious image of retailers, as they do for Harry Rosen and Maison Birks. On the other hand, discounters and off-price retailers, such as Target and Winners, offer good value for money. There are even stores, such as Dollarama, that use a single-price-point strategy aimed at getting customers to make impulse purchases through what analysts call the "wow" factor—the excitement of discovering that an item costs only a dollar.

PRESENTATION OF THE RETAIL STORE

The presentation of a retail store helps determine the store's image and positions the retail store in consumers' minds. For instance, a retailer that wants to position itself as an upscale store would use a lavish or sophisticated presentation.

The main element of a store's presentation is its **atmosphere**, the overall impression conveyed by a store's physical layout, decor, and surroundings. The atmosphere might create a relaxed or busy feeling, a sense of luxury or of efficiency, a friendly or cold attitude, a sense of organization or of clutter, or a

ValeStock/Shutterstock.com

Layout also includes the placement of products in the store. Many technologically advanced retailers are using a technique called *market-basket analysis* to analyze the huge amounts of data collected through their point-of-purchase scanning equipment. The analysis looks for products that are commonly purchased together to help retailers find ideal locations for each product. Walmart uses market-basket analysis to determine where in the store to stock products for customer convenience. Kleenex tissues, for example, are in the paper-goods aisle and beside the cold medicines.

The following factors are the most influential in creating a store's atmosphere:

▸ **EMPLOYEE TYPE AND DENSITY:** Employee type refers to an employee's general characteristics—for instance, being neat, friendly, knowledgeable, or service oriented. Density is the number of employees per thousand square feet of selling space. Whereas low employee density creates a do-it-yourself, casual atmosphere, high employee density denotes readiness to serve the customer's every whim.

▸ **MERCHANDISE TYPE AND DENSITY:** A prestigious retailer, such as Harry Rosen, carries the best brand names and displays them in a neat, uncluttered arrangement. Discounters and off-price retailers often carry seconds or out-of-season goods crowded into small spaces and hung on long racks by category—tops, pants, skirts, etc.—creating the impression that "We've got so much stuff, we're practically giving it away."

▸ **FIXTURE TYPE AND DENSITY:** Fixtures can be elegant (rich woods), trendy (chrome and smoked glass), or consist of old, beat-up tables, as in an antiques store. The fixtures should be consistent with the general atmosphere the store is trying to create.

▸ **SOUND:** Sound can be pleasant or unpleasant for a customer. Music can entice customers to stay in the store longer and buy more or eat quickly and leave a table for others. It can also control the pace of the store traffic, create an image, and attract or direct the shopper's attention.

▸ **ODOURS:** Smell can either stimulate or detract from sales. Research suggests that people evaluate merchandise more positively, spend more time shopping, and are generally in a better mood when an agreeable odour is present. Retailers use fragrances as an extension of their retail strategy.

fun or serious mood. HMV Music stores, targeted to Generation Y consumers, use a recording studio feel.

The layout of retail stores is a key factor in their success. The goal is to use all of the store's space effectively, including aisles, fixtures, merchandise displays, and non-selling areas. In addition to making shopping easy and convenient for the customer, an effective layout has a powerful influence on traffic patterns and purchasing behaviour. IKEA uses a unique circular store layout, which encourages customers to pass all of a store's departments to reach the checkout lanes. The shopper thus is exposed to all of IKEA's merchandise assortment.

TRADING UP *means persuading customers to* BUY A HIGHER-PRICED ITEM *than they originally intended to buy.*

Over 800 stores! More than 100 eating establishments! Nine major attractions! Spanning the area of 48 city blocks, the West Edmonton Mall is North America's largest entertainment and shopping centre.

▸ **VISUAL FACTORS:** Colours can create a mood or focus attention and therefore are an important factor in atmosphere. Red, yellow, and orange are considered warm colours and are used when a feeling of warmth and closeness is desired. Cool colours, such as blue, green, and violet, are used to open up closed-in places and create an air of elegance and cleanliness. Many retailers have found that natural lighting, either from windows or skylights, can lead to increased sales. Outdoor lighting can also affect consumer patronage.

PERSONNEL AND CUSTOMER SERVICE

People are a unique aspect of retailing. Most retail sales involve a customer–salesperson relationship, if only briefly. When customers shop at a grocery store, the cashiers check and bag their groceries. When cus-

tomers shop at a prestigious clothier, the sales clerks may assist in the fitting process, offer alteration services, wrap purchases, and even offer a glass of champagne. Sales personnel provide their customers with the amount of service prescribed in the retail strategy of the store.

Retail salespeople serve another important selling function: they persuade shoppers to buy. They must therefore be able to persuade customers that what they are selling is what the customer needs. Salespeople are trained in two common selling techniques: trading up and suggestion selling. Trading up means persuading customers to buy a higher-priced item than they originally intended to buy. To avoid selling customers something they do not need or want, however, salespeople should take care when practising trading-up techniques.

Suggestion selling, a common practice among most retailers, seeks to broaden customers' original purchases with related items. For example, if you buy a new printer at Staples, the sales representative will ask whether you want to purchase paper, a USB cable, or extra ink cartridges. Suggestion selling and trading up should always help shoppers recognize true needs rather than sell them unwanted merchandise.

Providing great customer service is one of the most challenging elements in the retail mix because customer expectations for service are so varied. What customers expect in a department store is very different from their expectations for a discount store. Customer expectations also change. Ten years ago, shoppers wanted personal one-on-one attention. Today, most customers are happy to help themselves as long as they can easily find what they need.

Customer service is also critical for online retailers. Online shoppers expect a retailer's website to be easy to use, products to be available, and returns to be simple. Online retailers need to design their sites to give their customers the information they need, such as what's new and what's on sale, and consider using suggestive selling. On JoeFresh.com when a purchase choice is made, a recommendation of complementary items is offered to upsell the shopper.

14-7 NEW DEVELOPMENTS IN RETAILING

In an effort to better serve their existing customers and to attract new customers, retailers are constantly adopting new strategies. As Canadians continue to

Tyler McKay/Shutterstock.com

Apple stores use large, open tables to display company products, making it easier for visitors to play with them.

adopt online shopping and as U.S. retailers continue to move into the Canadian market, Canadian retailers have to evolve their retail strategy. Many big-box retailers are moving to smaller stores. Best Buy for example has launched Best Buy Mobile—smaller stores to more intimately service the customer. It is not only big-box stores that are pursuing the "small is better" strategy. Department stores and supermarkets are considering how to create smaller, more intimate environments. Hudson's Bay Co. is creating stores within stores with some of their strong brands, such as TopShop, and Loblaw is even offering in-store sit-down restaurants in some of their banner stores.

80%
Percentage of retailers that have fewer than 10 employees

$40 billion
Canadian retail sales per month

$411
Average amount the Canadian family spends on groceries per month

-4.7%
Decline in retail sales in convenience stores between July 2012 and July 2013

12%
Percentage of all Canadian employment that is in the retail sector

$34 billion
Predicted online yearly retail sales by 2018

Distribution Decisions Part 5 Case

Grand Theft Digital

Cue an opening scene: "A grizzled man named Michael walks out of his house and to his car. He proceeds to drive wildly right into his front gate, smashing the front end of his car. He then drives recklessly through the streets, running over stop signs and pedestrians and causing head-on collisions. Michael then jumps out of his car, starts kicking the rear bumper of another vehicle, and then beats the driver of this vehicle senseless and steals the car. In this stolen vehicle, Michael proceeds to T-bone another car, then drives away without remorse or a second thought."

Is this the crazed plot of a low-budget action movie? The actions of an unfeeling sociopath? No, the above scene describes late-night TV host Conan O'Brien playing the video game *Grand Theft Auto V* (GTA V).

In a segment on his show called "Clueless Gamer," O'Brien plays new video game releases. In late 2013, he tried out GTA V. And if you think the scene above is eye opening, watch the rest of his nine-plus minutes of mayhem in this world of Grand Theft Auto **(www .youtube.com/watch?v=EB_XX_IM8io)**.

GTA V is the fifth installment of the hugely successful video game series developed by Rockstar Games. The world of GTA is equal parts disturbing and exhilarating. Gamers take on the persona of a character in the game and can follow the storyline to achieve successes and complete the game. But it is really in open play (like O'Brien's aforementioned exploits) that many people find excitement, albeit often through darker and antisocial exploits. People can shoot guns, drive recklessly, and commit unspeakable acts that if committed in real life would land them in jail. Often these actions go unnoticed and mostly unpunished, as the seemingly lawless worlds created by Rockstar Games encourage anarchy and mayhem.

Stefanie Keenan/Getty Images

This type of violence, although in digital form, has alarmed some people, with concern being focused on the impact on children playing games with such explicit and violent content. There is debate about how video game violence translates to the real world.

However, if you think that this dystopian world, created by Rockstar Games, would be shunned by gamers, you would be dead wrong. GTA V was released on September 17, 2013, and *on that day* it accumulated $800 million in sales.[1] Compare this with the highest grossing movie for 2013, *Iron Man 3,* which had

© Jeffrey Blackler / Alamy

$408 million in sales over four months.[2] With sales pushing it into the top five video games of all time (Tetris is #1), GTA V is a smashing success.

The reviews have been even more impressive than the sales. Ratings of 5 out of 5 or 10 out of 10 were common on video game rating sites. *The Globe and Mail* called it "perfect" and maybe the "best game ever."[3] Much of the praise goes to the quality of graphics and the story in GTA V. Reviewers and gamers marvel at the ease of play, realism in movement, and engrossing gameplay environment.

These sales numbers and reviews all point to a rosy picture for the video game industry. But in the distribution of this game lie some interesting challenges for the industry.

The publisher and distributor of the GTA series is Take Two Interactive. The company made a rather controversial decision in choosing a September 2013 launch date for GTA V. The reason? Two new video game consoles were about to be released later on that fall: PlayStation 4 and Xbox One. Why would Take Two not wait a few weeks? Mostly because millions of gamers already had the older consoles (PlayStation 3 and Xbox 360). But also because the gaming console may no longer be the means by which gamers will play games like GTA V.

In February 2014, when there was still no version of GTA V for PlayStation 4 or Xbox One, Take Two Interactive's CEO Strauss Zelnick was asked why. His response was, "If that is where the consumers are, absolutely [we'll release the game on those platforms]. But we wouldn't drive them there. We are not in the hardware business. We don't have a dog in that hunt; we just want to be where the consumer is."[4]

And where the consumer seems to be more and more is online. In its 2013 report, the Entertainment Software Association of Canada (ESAC) noted that while traditional gaming consoles are still predominant, mobile gaming sales have taken an increasing share of industry revenue, and digital distribution channels are "more prevalent than before."[5]

Digital distribution in video games is much like digital distribution of music. Video games are distributed in a digital format from seller to buyer, with no need for a physical product (game cartridge, CD, etc.). Video games have been available for digital distribution for many years, but it was not until there was widespread and affordable bandwidth capabilities for downloading that digital options were feasible for most gamers.

Now, many video game companies have gone into the digital gaming business. Electronic Arts has Origin (**www.origin.com**), and for smaller developers there is Steam (**http://store.steampowered.com**). Even console developers have gotten into the business, including Microsoft with Xbox LIVE (**www.xbox.com/en-ca/live**).

Digital distribution includes accessing games via a PC, mobile phone, tablet, or video game console. The system of digitally distributing games is a serious threat to video game retailers, who rely on gamers visiting their stores to purchase not only games but also other video game and electronic products. If consumers can buy games in the comfort of their own homes or on their smartphones while on the bus, there is no need to visit a bricks-and-mortar retailer.

Market research firm DFC Intelligence, a leader in research on interactive entertainment, has predicted that by 2018, 75 percent of game software revenue will come from digital distribution.[6]

But it is not only retailers that might be left behind by this digital revolution; video game publishers might also have to adjust their business models. In the past, video game developers (like Rockstar Games) relied on video game publishers (like Take Two Interactive) to distribute their video games. Now any developer of video games can create its own digital gaming store or use an existing digital gaming site.

A few weeks after GTA V hit the stores, Rockstar Games announced that the game could be downloaded from Xbox Live. Gamers on PlayStation could use the PlayStation Store to buy GTA V right from the release date. Gamers on Xbox 360 were encouraged to use the digital download option, especially after Rockstar warned users not to install the "play" disk onto the hard drives of the Xbox 360 console. This was due to issues with the Xbox 360's ability to stream the data from the hard drive and the "play" disk at the same time.[7]

In early March 2014, Rockstar games released an update to the hugely successful GTA V game. But it was not a PlayStation 4 or Xbox One version. It was called The Business Update and was only available in digital form through Xbox Live and the PlayStation Store. In The Business Update, gamers have access to new attire, cars, and weapons to use in the game.[8] It would seem that digital is becoming the new normal in video games, and it would be a crime if companies in the industry do nothing to address it.

QUESTIONS

1. **Create a SWOT for Rockstar Games, with a focus on the *Grand Theft Auto* series of games.**

2. **Read the ESAC industry report on the video game industry in Canada (http://theesa.ca/wp-content/uploads/2013/10/Essential-Facts-English.pdf). Compare the information provided on the market segments of gamers identified in the report with your knowledge of market segmentation. Create a market segment for the current gamer as identified in the ESAC report.**

3. **Create a new channel system that would best describe the digital distribution system for video games.**

4. **Describe how the retailers in the video game channel system could mitigate the challenges presented by digital distribution.**

Chapter 15

Marketing Communication

Robert Churchill//iStock./Thinkstock

Good promotion campaigns create positive memories and feelings that influence behaviour over time to encourage us to alter our behaviour in some way at a later date.

After you finish this chapter, go to www.nelson.com/student *for* **STUDY TOOLS**.

15-1 THE ROLE OF PROMOTION IN THE MARKETING MIX

Few goods or services, no matter how well developed, priced, or distributed, can survive in the marketplace without effective **promotion**—communication by marketers that informs, persuades, reminds, and connects potential buyers to a product or service for the purpose of influencing their opinion or eliciting a response.

Promotional strategy is a plan for the use of the elements of promotion (the promotional mix elements): advertising, public relations, sales promotion, personal selling, direct-response communication, and social media. As Exhibit 15.1 shows, the marketing manager determines the goals of the company's promotional strategy in light of the firm's overall goals for the marketing mix—product, place (distribution), promotion, and price. Using these overall goals, marketers combine the elements of the promotional strategy (the promotional mix) to form a coordinated plan. The promotion plan then becomes another integral part of the marketing strategy for reaching the target market.

The main function of a marketer's promotional strategy is to convince target customers that the goods and services offered provide a competitive advantage over the competition. Take, for example, the beer Stella Artois, which is distributed in Canada by Labatt Brewing Company. To create a niche for this beverage in a highly competitive marketplace, the brewer has repositioned Stella Artois to focus on the heritage and quality of the Belgian beer. Communication centres on their brewing roots dating back to 1366 ("We were brewing beer in Belgium before Belgium was Belgian") and reinforces quality ("Master Brewers required. 600 years' experience

promotion communication by marketers that informs, persuades, reminds, and connects potential buyers to a product for the purpose of influencing an opinion or eliciting a response

promotional strategy a plan for the use of the elements of promotion: advertising, public relations, personal selling, sales promotion, direct-response communication, and social media

needed"). With this repositioning, Stella Artois continues to use the symbol of the "chalice-like" glass that a cold Stella should be served in. The symbol unites past advertising with the current repositioning, reinforcing the brand's heritage and quality with its style.[1] This is clearly a unique strategy that demonstrates Stella Artois's **competitive advantage**. Promotion is a vital component of the marketing mix, informing consumers of a product's benefits and thereby positioning the product in the marketplace.

15-2 MARKETING COMMUNICATION

Promotional strategy is closely related to the process of communication. Communication is the process by which we exchange or share meanings through a common set of symbols. When a company develops a new product, changes an old one, or simply tries to increase sales of an existing good or service, marketers use promotion programs to communicate information about the firm and its products to potential customers and various publics.

Exhibit 15.1
ROLE OF PROMOTION IN THE MARKETING MIX

Communication can be divided into two major categories: interpersonal communication and mass communication. **Interpersonal communication** is direct, face-to-face communication between two or more people. When communicating face to face, each person can see the other's reaction and can respond almost immediately. A salesperson speaking directly with a client is an example of an interpersonal marketing communication.

Mass communication involves communicating a concept or message to large audiences. A great deal of marketing communication is directed to consumers as a whole, usually through a mass medium, such as television or magazines. When a company uses mass communication, it generally does not personally know the people with whom it is trying to communicate. Furthermore, the company is unable to respond immediately to consumers' reactions to its message. Any clutter from competitors' messages or other distractions in the environment can reduce the effectiveness of the mass-communication effort.

15-2a The Communication Process

Marketers are both senders and receivers of messages. As *senders*, marketers attempt to inform, persuade, remind, and connect with the target market to adopt a particular course of action. As *receivers*, marketers attune themselves to the target market so they can develop the appropriate messages, adapt existing messages, spot new communication opportunities, and connect with the target audience. In this way, marketing communication is a two-way, rather than one-way, process. The two-way nature of the communication process is shown in Exhibit 15.2.

THE SENDER AND ENCODING The **sender** is the originator of the message in the communication process. In an interpersonal conversation, the sender may be a parent, a friend, or a salesperson. For an advertisement or press release, the sender is the company or organization. It can sometimes be difficult to tell who the sender of a promotional message is, especially in the case of bold, avant-garde advertisements. Sometimes advertisers intentionally obscure their identities in the hopes of building buzz around the message.

Encoding is the conversion of the sender's ideas and thoughts into a message, usually in the form of words or signs. The Maison Birks campaign used the new logo, the revamped stores, and visual imagery from Canadian nature, together with the new tagline "Discover Birks in

Exhibit 15.2
COMMUNICATION PROCESS

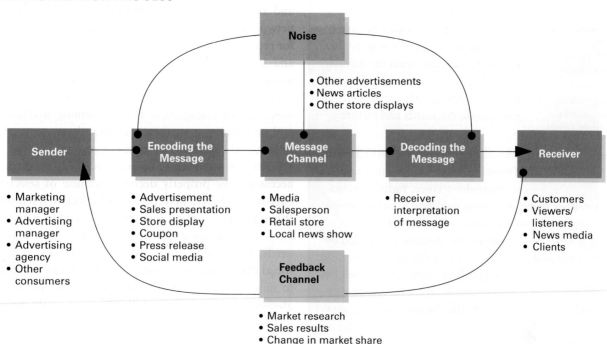

Noise
- Other advertisements
- News articles
- Other store displays

Sender
- Marketing manager
- Advertising manager
- Advertising agency
- Other consumers

Encoding the Message
- Advertisement
- Sales presentation
- Store display
- Coupon
- Press release
- Social media

Message Channel
- Media
- Salesperson
- Retail store
- Local news show

Decoding the Message
- Receiver interpretation of message

Receiver
- Customers
- Viewers/listeners
- News media
- Clients

Feedback Channel
- Market research
- Sales results
- Change in market share
- Social media

HOW DO YOU BUILD NEW LIFE IN A BRAND THAT HAS STOOD THE TEST OF TIME?

Birks, the iconic Canadian jewellery retailer, rebranded in an attempt to set itself apart from other jewellery retailers and brands. The rebranding included a name change to Maison Birks and a new jewellery collection that emphasized more diverse product designs. In addition, new stores were opened under the Maison Birks name. These stores featured the Maison Birks brand exclusively and were designed with an open-concept environment to make the process of jewellery buying less intimidating for the consumer. Remaining Birks retail locations were revamped and renamed. The Birks logo was updated to include their new name, and it continued to emphasize the iconic blue boxes in which all Birks products are packaged. Advertising to support the revamp featured the tagline "Discover Birks in all its purity." This tagline was chosen to demonstrate the essence of the restage—including the fact that the retailer uses only Canadian diamonds in its products and that the new stores will only carry the Maison Birks brand.

Source: Jorda Twiss, "Birks Channels Heritage for Rebrand," Strategy, August 2013, http://strategyonline.ca/2013/08/16/birks-channels-heritage-for-rebrand/ (accessed September 14, 2013).

the brand out to purchase. Heavy sampling, introductory consumer advertising, cents-off campaigns, and couponing are also all part of a pull strategy.

Rarely does a company use a pull or a push strategy exclusively. Instead, the mix will usually emphasize one of these strategies. For example, pharmaceutical companies generally use a push strategy, through personal selling and trade advertising, to promote their drugs and therapies to physicians. Sales presentations and advertisements in medical journals give physicians the detailed information they need to prescribe medication to their patients. Most pharmaceutical companies supplement their push promotional strategy with a pull strategy targeted directly to potential patients through advertisements in consumer magazines and on television.

15-7 INTEGRATED MARKETING COMMUNICATIONS

Ideally, marketing communications from each promotional mix element (advertising, public relations, sales promotion, personal selling, direct-response communication, and social media) should be integrated—that is, the message reaching the consumer should be the same regardless of whether it is from an advertisement, a salesperson in the field, a magazine article, a Facebook fan page, or a coupon in a newspaper insert.

Consumers do not think in terms of the six elements of promotion. Instead, everything is an "ad." The only people who recognize the distinctions among these communications elements are the marketers themselves. So, unfortunately, when planning promotional messages, some marketers treat each of the promotion elements separately, failing to integrate the communications efforts from one element to the next.

To prevent this disjointed communication from happening, companies today have adopted the concept of **integrated marketing communications (IMC)**. IMC is the careful coordination of all promotional messages—traditional advertising, public relations,

sales promotion, personal selling, direct-response communication, and social media—for a product or service to ensure the consistency of messages at every contact point where a company meets the consumer. Following the concept of IMC, marketing managers carefully work out the roles that various promotional mix tools will play in the communications strategy. The timing of promotional activities is coordinated, and the results of each campaign are carefully monitored to improve future use of the promotional mix tools.

In 1988, Nike's ad agency Weiden+Kennedy created the infamous tagline "Just do it." From its inception, the tagline has appeared on every Nike ad, whether it was a print ad or a television commercial. "Just do it" became Nike and Nike became "Just do it." The tagline is easy to remember, and it has meaning for everyone from elite athletes to average consumers. It transcends cultures and speaks boldly about the brand. It even became the motivational message for the salesforce—get out and "Just do it." To celebrate the 25-year history of the tagline, Nike launched its Possibilities campaign. The campaign includes a 90-second television ad featuring world-famous athletes inspiring viewers to push themselves beyond the norm to be their best. Nike+ challenges were made available through social media. The Nike+ running app, for example, allows runners to set a new distance goal and to invite friends to join them in the challenge. It tracks progress and keeps runners motivated by allowing them to see how they rank among their friends. For three weeks during the Possibilities campaign launch, Nike ran a Nike+ contest for runners that allowed them to log their Nike+ miles toward winning a memorable running experience. All who participated in various Nike+ challenges were encouraged to tweet their challenge and progress through #justdoit. After more than 25 years, "Just do it" continues to inspire people to reach beyond their comfort level. The Possibilities campaign provided the inspiration, the tools, the products, and the services to make it happen and to let the world know.[11] Nike continues to demonstrate mastery in integrated marketing communication.

The IMC concept continues to grow in popularity for several reasons. First, the proliferation of thousands of media choices and the continued use of

360b/Shutterstock.com

social media by all age groups has made communication a more complicated task. Instead of promoting a product through only mass-media options, such as television and magazines, promotional messages today can appear in a variety sources. Rarely will a marketer use all promotional tools; rather, he or she will assess the media consumption behaviour of the target customer and then create a promotion mix that is appropriately varied and integrated. Further, the mass market has been fragmented. The traditional broad market groups that marketers promoted to in years past have been replaced by selectively segmented markets requiring niche marketing strategies that rely on well-integrated communication campaigns. Finally, marketers have slashed their advertising spending in favour of promotional techniques that generate immediate sales responses and those that are more easily measured. Online advertising has thus earned a bigger share of the budget because of its measurability, the immediacy of feedback, and its success at engaging the individual consumer.

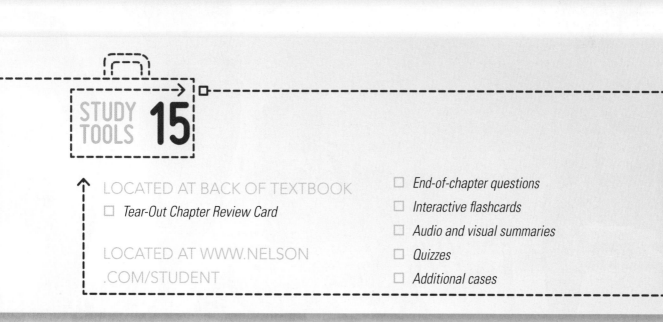

$100 billion
Dollar value of Facebook

1988
The year the Nike slogan "Just do it" was launched

1000
The number of Xbox One consoles given away in the Win Every Hour contest by PepsiCo Canada and Microsoft to support the launch of Xbox One

$3 billion
Value Canadian online revenue exceeded in 2012

$3.5 billion
TV's advertising revenue in 2012

STUDY TOOLS 15

LOCATED AT BACK OF TEXTBOOK
☐ *Tear-Out Chapter Review Card*

LOCATED AT WWW.NELSON.COM/STUDENT

☐ *End-of-chapter questions*
☐ *Interactive flashcards*
☐ *Audio and visual summaries*
☐ *Quizzes*
☐ *Additional cases*

Chapter 16

Advertising, Public Relations, and Direct Response

Cultura RM/Richard Iwordy/Getty Images

"Good advertising does not just circulate information. It penetrates the public mind with desires and belief."

—Leo Burnett

After you finish this chapter, go to
www.nelson.com/student *for* **STUDY TOOLS.** ᏟᎵ------→

16-1 WHAT IS ADVERTISING?

In Chapter 1, we learned that marketing is about understanding the needs of the customer. It helps to shape a business's products and services, based on an understanding of what the customer is looking for. We learned that marketing is about engaging in a *conversation* with that customer, and guiding the delivery of what is required to satisfy those needs. *Advertising is the conversation.*

In 1935, advertising legend Leo Burnett, who launched what became one of the most successful advertising agencies in the world, said this of advertising: "The sole purpose of business is service. The sole purpose of advertising is explaining the service that the business renders."[1] He also said, "Advertising says to people, 'Here's what we've got. Here's what it will do for you. Here's how to get it.'"[2] Advertising is indeed the conversation with the consumer, and Burnett must have got it right, for his agency helped launch many of the brands and brand icons that we still revere today: Maytag and the Lonely Maytag Repair Man, Frosted Flakes and Tony the Tiger, Pillsbury and the Pillsbury Doughboy. In Chapter 15, we defined *advertising* as any form of impersonal, paid communication in which the sponsor or company is identified. It is a popular form of promotion, especially for consumer packaged goods and services, for both its entertainment value and persuasiveness. This popularity is clearly evidenced by the anticipation surrounding the television commercials featured during the Super Bowl. Companies have come to see the Super Bowl as one of the biggest media events that bring people together; thus, they are willing to pay over US$4 million for a 30-second spot. Consumers eagerly anticipate seeing these commercials, which receive almost as much promotion prior to the Super Bowl itself. To see some of the commercials featured during the Super Bowl, go to **www.superbowl-commercials.org**.

Closer to home, the Alberta Gaming and Liquor Commission's Responsibly campaign demonstrates the power of advertising to bring about social change through awareness and education.

advertising response function a phenomenon in which spending for advertising and sales promotion increases sales or market share up to a certain level but then produces diminishing returns

The campaign is aimed at male and female drinkers ages 18 to 24. Each advertisement depicts fictional wine, beer, and vodka products that come in packages of two for women and three for men, according to the national guidelines for low risk liquor consumption. The ads (radio, billboard, transit, and restaurant and bar posters) drive the reader to the website **EnjoyResponsibly.ca** in the hopes of educating the target audience about *responsible* and *moderate* drinking.[3]

16-1a Advertising and Market Share

Today's most successful brands of consumer goods, such as Pillsbury products or Frosted Flakes, were built long ago by heavy advertising and marketing investments. Today's advertising dollars are spent on maintaining brand awareness and market share. The challenge for marketers has always been to determine the most appropriate advertising budget. As a percentage of sales, established brands like Frosted Flakes generally spend proportionally less on

To capitalize on a continually growing trend toward healthy baking with healthier ingredients, Robin Hood launched line extensions to its All Purpose Flour called Nutri Flour Blend. To make storage more convenient, new packaging accompanied the line extensions. Print, television, and social media are being used to used communicate the new products.

advertising than new brands, but whether you are marketing an established product or a new product, marketers must be aware of the phenomenon of the **advertising response function**. The advertising response function helps marketers establish the most effective dollar amount to spend on advertising. The advertising response function demonstrates that there exists a diminishing return from advertising spending. That is, sales or market share tend to level off or begin to decrease no matter how much is spent on advertising. Marketers need to measure the incremental value of spending additional money on advertising versus sales increase to ensure the greatest return on investment.

16-1b The Effects of Advertising on Consumers

Advertising affects consumers' daily lives, informing them about products and services and influencing their attitudes, beliefs, and ultimately their purchases. Advertising affects the TV programs people watch, the content of the newspapers they read, the politicians they elect, the medicines they take, and the toys their children play with. Consequently, the influence of advertising on the Canadian socioeconomic system has been the subject of extensive debate in nearly all corners of society.

Though advertising cannot change consumers' deeply rooted values and attitudes, advertising may succeed in transforming a person's negative attitude toward a product into a positive one. For instance, serious or dramatic advertisements are more effective at changing consumers' negative attitudes. Humorous ads have been found to increase the viewer's involvement in the ad, thereby increasing the impact of the advertisement's message.[4] Advertising also reinforces positive attitudes toward brands. When consumers have a neutral or favourable frame of reference for a product or brand, advertising often positively influences them. When consumers are already highly loyal

Julie Pratt

Alberta Gaming and Liquor Commission

to a brand, they may buy more of it when advertising and promotion for that brand increase.[5] This behaviour explains why to this day Kellogg's continues to advertise Frosted Flakes with Tony the Tiger—to reinforce and remind their loyal customers "to get a sweet crunchy start to your morning with oven-toasted flakes as part of a nutritious breakfast. They're gr-r-reat!"[6]

Advertising can also affect the way consumers rank a brand's attributes. For example, Travel Manitoba recently launched a new campaign to increase tourism in Manitoba (of the ten provinces, Manitoba ranks seventh in tourism). The campaign entitled 'Manitoba: Canada's Heartbeat,' is designed to reinforce the uniqueness of Manitoba. While some may feel the television ads simply reinforce the obvious, there is a general lack of awareness of what Manitoba has to offer, and advertisers hope that the emotional messages in these ads will correct that.[7]

16-2 MAJOR TYPES OF ADVERTISING

The firm's promotional objectives determine the type of advertising it uses. If the goal of the promotion plan is to improve the image of the company or the industry, **institutional advertising** may be used. In contrast, if the advertiser wants to enhance the sales of a specific good or service, **product advertising**, which promotes the benefits of a specific good or service, is used.

16-2a Institutional Advertising

Historically, advertising in Canada has been product oriented. Today, many companies market multiple products and need a different type of advertising. Institutional advertising, or corporate advertising, promotes the corporation as a whole and is designed to establish, change, or maintain the corporation's identity. It usually does not ask the audience to do anything but maintain a favourable attitude toward the advertiser and its goods and services. Ideally, this favourable attitude will transfer to the products being marketed by the company, thereby creating a competitive advantage over other companies.

Advocacy advertising is a form of institutional advertising in which an organization expresses its views on a particular issue or cause. Companies have increased their investment in advocacy advertising, as the benefits of publicly supporting social issues and causes that their target consumer is committed to has proven valuable. During the 2013 holiday season, the LCBO (Liquor Control Board of Ontario) once again ran its Deflate the Elephant campaign, which demonstrates solutions to dealing with holiday guests who are intending to drink and drive. The television campaign was accompanied by a strong social media presence and a contest promoted both in LCBO retail stores and online. In addition to solutions to prevent guests from drinking and driving, the **deflatetheelephant.com** website featured over 50 nonalcoholic drinks and a forum for visitors to share ideas on responsible entertaining and preventing impaired driving.[8]

16-2b Product Advertising

Unlike institutional advertising, product advertising promotes the benefits of a specific good or service. The product's stage in its life cycle often determines whether the product advertising used is pioneering advertising, competitive advertising, or comparative advertising.

PIONEERING ADVERTISING Pioneering advertising is intended to stimulate primary demand for a new product or product category. Heavily used during the introductory stage of the product life cycle, pioneering advertising offers consumers in-depth information about the benefits of the product class. Pioneering advertising also seeks to create interest. Pharmaceutical companies often use pioneering advertising.

COMPETITIVE ADVERTISING Firms use competitive or brand advertising when a product enters

Liquor Control Board of Ontario

DRINKING AND DRIVING SHOULD NEVER BE THE ELEPHANT IN THE ROOM.

SPEAK UP. YOU COULD SAVE A LIFE.

DEFLATE THE ELEPHANT

BILL GREENBLATT/UPI/Newscom

To achieve awareness of the new Budweiser Black Crown, Anheuser-Busch launched the product with a 30-second ad during the 2013 Super Bowl: "You have people who are, by behaviour, tuning into that telecast, watching the game but also there to watch the advertising. That, we think, creates a powerful combination for us to launch innovation."[9]

Todd Oren/Getty Images

A SodaStream commercial featuring Scarlett Johansson was banned from Fox's 2013 Super Bowl coverage because the spot ends with Johansson saying, "Sorry, Coke and Pepsi." The controversy created by the taunting of Coke and Pepsi and Fox's decision to ban the ad actually worked in favour of SodaStream, as just before the airing of the Super Bowl, the banned commercial was viewed over a million times on YouTube.[10]

the growth phase of the product life cycle and other companies begin to enter the marketplace. Instead of building demand for the product category, the goal of **competitive advertising** is to influence demand for a specific brand. During this phase, promotion often becomes less informative and, instead, appeals more to emotions. Advertisements may begin to stress subtle differences between brands, with heavy emphasis on building recall of a brand name and creating a favourable attitude toward the brand. Automobile advertising has long used very competitive messages, drawing distinctions on the basis of such factors as quality, performance, and image.

COMPARATIVE ADVERTISING Comparative advertising directly or indirectly compares two or more competing brands on one or more specific attributes. Some advertisers even use comparative advertising against their own brands. Products experiencing sluggish growth or those entering the marketplace against strong competitors are more likely to employ comparative claims in their advertising.

Before the 1970s, comparative advertising was allowed only if the competing brand was veiled and unidentified. In 1971, the Federal Trade Commission (FTC) in the United States fostered the growth of comparative advertising, claiming it provided consumers with useful information. The Competition Act in Canada prohibits advertisers from falsely describing competitors' products and allows competitors to sue if ads represent their products or brand names in an incorrect or false manner. Advertising Standards Canada guidelines also prevent advertisers from making false claims about their own products.

16-3 CREATIVE DECISIONS IN ADVERTISING

Advertising strategies are typically organized around an advertising campaign. An **advertising campaign** is a series of related advertisements focusing on a common theme, slogan, and set of advertising appeals. It is a specific advertising effort for a particular product that extends for a defined period of time.

Before any creative work can begin on an advertising campaign, it is important to determine what goals or objectives the advertising should achieve. An

advertising objective a specific communication task that a campaign should accomplish for a specified target audience during a specified period

advertising appeal a reason for a person to buy a product

unique selling proposition a desirable, exclusive, and believable advertising appeal selected as the theme for a campaign

advertising objective is the specific communication task that a campaign should accomplish for a specified target audience during a specified period. The objectives of a specific advertising campaign often depend on the overall corporate objectives, the product being advertised, and, according to research, where the consumer is with respect to product adoption. Where the consumer is in the AIDA process (see Chapter 15) helps to determine whether the advertising objective is to create awareness, arouse interest, stimulate desire, or create a purchase.

The DAGMAR approach (Defining Advertising Goals for Measured Advertising Results) establishes a protocol for writing advertising objectives. According to this method, all advertising objectives should precisely define the target audience, the desired percentage change in a specified measure of effectiveness, and the time frame during which that change is to occur.

Once the advertising objectives are defined, creative work can begin on the advertising campaign. Specifically, creative decisions include identifying product benefits, developing and evaluating advertising appeals, executing the message, and evaluating the effectiveness of the campaign.

16-3a Identifying Product Benefits

A well-known rule of thumb in the advertising industry is "Sell the sizzle, not the steak." In other words, the advertising goal is to sell the benefits of the product, not its attributes. An attribute is simply a feature of the product, such as in the case of SodaStream where the added bubbles and flavour are the attributes. The resulting benefit is less sugar and fewer bottles, which is the message brought home by Johannson in the controversial commercial discussed earlier.

Marketing research and intuition are usually used to unearth the perceived benefits of a product and to rank consumers' preferences for these benefits.

16-3b Developing and Evaluating Advertising Appeals

An **advertising appeal** identifies a reason for a person to buy a product. Developing advertising appeals, a challenging task, is generally the responsibility of the creative people in the advertising agency. Advertising appeals typically play off consumers' emotions or address consumers' needs or wants.

Advertising campaigns can focus on one or more advertising appeals. Often the appeals are quite general, thereby allowing the firm to develop a number of subthemes or minicampaigns using both advertising and sales promotion. Several possible advertising appeals are listed in Exhibit 16.1.

Choosing the most appropriate appeal normally requires market research. Criteria for evaluation include desirability, exclusiveness, and believability. The appeal first must make a positive impression on and be desirable to the target market. It must also be exclusive or unique; consumers must be able to distinguish the advertiser's message from competitors' messages. Most important, the appeal should be believable. An appeal that makes extravagant claims not only wastes promotional dollars but also creates ill will towards the advertiser.

The advertising appeal selected for the campaign becomes what advertisers call its **unique selling proposition**. The unique selling proposition usually becomes the campaign's slogan. Tim Hortons' advertising campaign aimed at coffee drinkers carries the slogan "Always Fresh. Always Tim Hortons." Effective slogans often become so ingrained that when consumers hear the slogan, they can immediately conjure up images of the product.

Exhibit 16.1
COMMON ADVERTISING APPEALS

Profit	Informs consumers whether the product will save them money, make them money, or keep them from losing money
Health	Appeals to those who are body conscious or who want to be healthy
Love or Romance	Appeals to the consumer, setting the product apart in a competitive category often used to sell cosmetics and perfume, it appeals to emotions
Fear	Effectively encourages engagement, but as a powerful appeal technique, advertisers need to exercise care when using this type of appeal
Admiration	Often leads to the use of celebrity spokespeople in advertising
Convenience	Communicates how the product or service will save time or money, is easier or simpler to use.
Fun and Pleasure	Are often the key to advertising vacations, beer, amusement parks, and more
Vanity and Egotism	Are used most often for expensive or conspicuous items such as cars and clothing
Environmental Consciousness	Centres on protecting the environment and being considerate of others in the community

16-3c Executing the Message

Message execution is the way an advertisement portrays its information. Again, the AIDA plan (see Chapter 15) is a good blueprint for executing an advertising message. Any ad should immediately draw the attention of the reader, viewer, or listener. The advertiser must then use the message to hold interest, create desire for the good or service, and ultimately motivate a purchase.

The style in which the message is executed is one of the most creative elements of an advertisement. Exhibit 16.2 lists examples of executional styles used by advertisers. Executional styles often dictate what type of media is used to employ to convey the message. Scientific executional styles lend themselves well to print advertising, where more information can be conveyed. Testimonials by athletes are one of the more popular executional styles.

Injecting humour into an advertisement is a popular and effective executional style. Humorous executional styles are more often used in radio and television advertising than in print or magazine advertising where humour is less easily communicated. Humorous

ads are typically used for lower-risk, low-involvement, routine purchases. Humorous ads can be effectively used to reinforce a brand's unique personality or to break through the clutter to ensure that the advertisement stands out and is remembered. Advertisers must exercise caution,

Exhibit 16.2

TEN COMMON EXECUTIONAL STYLES FOR ADVERTISING

Slice of Life	Depicts people in settings where the product would normally be used.
Lifestyle	Shows how well the product will fit in or enhance the consumer's lifestyle.
Spokesperson/ Testimonial	Can feature a celebrity, a company official, or a typical consumer making a testimonial or endorsing a product. Galen Weston appears in television ads with regular consumers, promoting the launch of the new PC Plus program.
Fantasy	Creates a fantasy for the viewer built around use of the product. Carmakers often use this style to let viewers fantasize about how they would feel speeding around tight corners or down long country roads in their cars.
Humorous	Advertisers often use humour in their ads to break through the clutter and be memorable.
Real/Animated Product Symbols	Creates a character that represents the product in advertisements. The Telus animals have become product symbols.
Mood or Image	Builds a mood or an image around the product, such as peace, love, or beauty. J'adore by Dior perfume ads present the iconic fragrance as the ultimate expression of femininity, luxury, and sexuality through the use of beautiful actresses and images.
Demonstration	Shows consumers the expected benefit. Many consumer products use this technique. Tide laundry detergent is famous for demonstrating how their product will clean clothes whiter and brighter.
Musical	Conveys the message of the advertisement through song.
Scientific	Uses research or scientific evidence to depict a brand's superiority over competitors.

medium the channel used to convey a message to a target market

media planning the series of decisions advertisers make regarding the selection and use of media, allowing the marketer to optimally and cost-effectively communicate the message to the target audience

After the Super Bowl, consumers are asked to vote on their favourite ads, and the rankings are then posted on various sites. While not entirely scientific, this survey does provide marketers with a sense of the ability of different ads to generate awareness and arouse interest.

however, when using humour. They must ensure that it is the brand that is remembered, not the humour itself.

Sometimes a company will modify its executional styles to make its advertising more relevant or to make it stand out among competitive advertisements. While the emotional style used by Travel Manitoba, discussed earlier in the chapter, is a new strategy designed to achieve awareness of Manitoba's unique culture and landscape, the approach appears similar to that being used by Newfoundland and Labrador Tourism. One wonders if it will indeed stand out.

16-3d Postcampaign Evaluation

Evaluating an advertising campaign can be a demanding task. How can one be sure that the change in product awareness, sales, or market share is solely the result of the advertising campaign? Many advertising campaigns are designed to create an image. How does one measure whether the intended image has been created? So many variables shape whether a product or service has achieved its objectives that determining the true impact of the advertising campaign is often impossible. Nonetheless, marketers spend considerable time studying advertising effectiveness and its probable impact on sales, market share, or awareness.

Testing ad effectiveness can be done either before or after the campaign. Before a campaign is released, marketing managers use pretests to determine the best advertising appeal, layout, and media vehicle. After advertisers implement a campaign, they use several monitoring techniques to determine whether the campaign has met its original goals. Even if a campaign has been highly successful, advertisers still typically do a postcampaign analysis to identify how the campaign might have been more efficient and which factors contributed to its success.

16-4 MEDIA DECISIONS IN ADVERTISING

A major decision for advertisers is the choice of **medium**—the channel used to convey a message to a target market. **Media planning**, therefore, is the series of decisions advertisers make regarding the selection and use of media, allowing the marketer to optimally and cost-effectively communicate the message to the target audience. Specifically, advertisers must determine which types of media will best communicate the benefits of their product or service to the target audience and when and for how long the advertisement will run.

Media selection is affected by the target market and the promotional objectives, as well as by the advertising appeal and execution decisions. Both creative and media decisions are made at the same time. Creative work cannot be completed without knowing which medium will be used to convey the message to the target market. In many cases, the advertising objectives dictate the medium and the creative approach to be used. For example, if the objective is to demonstrate how fast a product operates, the best medium to show this action is likely a commercial that is shown on television, in theatres, on social media, or all of these.

In 2012, Canadian advertisers spent roughly $15 billion on media, with $12.5 billion of that accounted for by major media. Online content is now a component of most traditional media publishers, but if you consider just traditional television advertising (i.e., remove online content from television advertising), television revenue accounts for 27.8 percent of all media expenditures. The Internet is close behind at 24.7 percent. Exhibit 16.3 outlines reported media spending by distribution channel.[11]

While advertising revenue increased slightly between 2011 and 2012, the net gain was a result of increased expenditures in Internet advertising. Search and display advertising spending continues to dominate advertisers' Internet investment, but in 2012, mobile ad spending saw the largest year-to-year increase, with almost 100 percent growth.

Exhibit 16.3
SHARE BY DISTRIBUTION CHANNEL

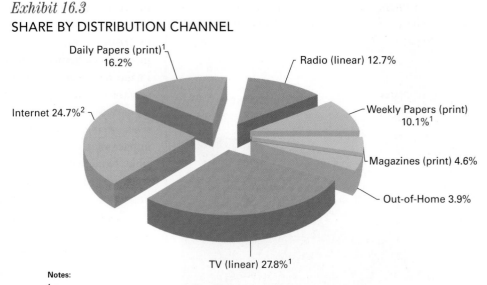

Daily Papers (print)[1] 16.2%
Radio (linear) 12.7%
Internet 24.7%[2]
Weekly Papers (print) 10.1%[1]
Magazines (print) 4.6%
Out-of-Home 3.9%
TV (linear) 27.8%[1]

Notes:
[1]To avoid duplication, the TV and Papers figures exclude revenue generated from TV and Papers online properties.
[2]Internet revenue includes advertising, search, directories and production. All online revenue generated by "traditional" media is reported by the IAB as "Internet."

Source: Television Bureau of Canada, www.tvb.ca/pages/nav

16-4a Media Types

Advertising media are channels that advertisers use in mass communication. The major advertising media are newspapers, magazines, radio, television, outdoor media, direct response and the Internet. Exhibit 16.4 summarizes the advantages and disadvantages of

Exhibit 16.4
ADVANTAGES AND DISADVANTAGES OF MAJOR ADVERTISING MEDIA

Medium	Advantages	Disadvantages
Newspapers	Geographic selectivity and flexibility; short-term advertiser commitments; news value and immediacy; year-round readership; high individual market coverage; co-op and local tie-in availability; short lead time; highly credible	Little demographic selectivity; limited colour capabilities; low pass-along rate; may be expensive
Magazines	Good reproduction, especially for colour; demographic selectivity; regional selectivity; local market selectivity; relatively long advertising life; high pass-along rate	Long-term advertiser commitments; slow audience buildup; limited demonstration capabilities; lack of urgency; long lead time
Radio	Low cost; immediacy of message; can be scheduled on short notice; relatively no seasonal change in audience; highly portable; short-term advertiser commitments; entertainment carryover	No visual treatment; short advertising life of message; high frequency required to generate comprehension and retention; distractions from background sound; commercial clutter
Television	Ability to reach a wide, diverse audience; low cost per thousand; creative opportunities for demonstration; immediacy of messages; entertainment carryover; demographic selectivity with cable specialty stations; emotional medium	Short life of message; some consumer skepticism about claims; high campaign cost; little demographic selectivity with network stations; long-term advertiser commitments; long lead times required for production; commercial clutter
Outdoor Media	Repetition; moderate cost; flexibility; geographic selectivity; high creativity	Short message; lack of demographic selectivity; high "noise" level distracting audience
Direct Response	Geographic selectivity; one-to-one direct contact with audience; like a personal sales call; can be personalized; can contain multiple messages and offers	Low response rates; high cost per person reached; poor image, especially for direct mail and telemarketing
Internet and Mobile	Fastest-growing medium; ability to reach a narrow target audience; relatively short lead time required for creating Web-based advertising; moderate cost; ability to engage consumers through search engine marketing, social media, display advertising and mobile marketing	Ad exposure relies on "click-through" from banner ads; measurement for social media needs much improvement; not all consumers have access to internet and not all consumers use social media

these major channels. In recent years, however, alternative media channels have emerged that give advertisers innovative ways to reach their target audience and avoid advertising clutter.

NEWSPAPERS The advantages of newspaper advertising include geographic flexibility and timeliness. Because copywriters can usually prepare newspaper ads quickly and at a reasonable cost, local merchants can reach their target market almost daily. Because newspapers are generally a mass-market medium, they may not be the best vehicle for marketers trying to reach a very narrow market; however, newspapers have innovated by creating unique sections that target specific market segments. Newspaper advertising also encounters many distractions from competing ads and news stories. In response to consumer demand for real-time information, newspapers have their own websites that are constantly updated to bring news as it happens and allow for consumer dialogue. Newspapers have embraced Twitter and Facebook, with writers establishing their own Twitter handles and Facebook pages that readers can follow to get up-to-the-minute news.

The main sources of newspaper ad revenue are local retailers, classified ads, and cooperative advertising. In **cooperative advertising**, the manufacturer and the retailer split the costs of advertising the manufacturer's brand. Cooperative advertising encourages retailers to devote more effort to the manufacturer's lines.

MAGAZINES One of the main advantages of magazine advertising is its target market selectivity. Magazines are published for virtually every market segment, offering meaningful target market engagement. Consumers choose to read magazines and spend considerable time doing so. Readers have high acceptance of the advertisements they see in a magazine, and readers are often driven to websites

to seek additional information. Canadian magazine readers still prefer reading magazines on the printed page, but magazines have embraced the digital environment and now provide readers with digital editions. Younger readers who own smartphones often access or download magazines' branded apps. Reading digital magazine content on a smartphone tends to drive the reader to the magazine's website.

RADIO As an advertising medium, radio offers selectivity and audience segmentation, a large out-of-home audience, low unit and production costs, timeliness, and geographic flexibility. Local advertisers are the most frequent users of radio advertising. Like newspapers, radio lends itself well to cooperative advertising.

The ability to target specific demographic groups is a major selling point for radio stations. Radio listeners tend to listen habitually and at predictable times. The most popular listening time is drive-time, when commuters form a vast captive audience. Radio is thus a highly effective medium for retailers, automobiles, and impulse products. Radio often enhances a media plan that combines other mediums because of the ability to inexpensively increase reach and frequency, particularly among commuters. Internet radio may be the next trend to watch. Slacker Radio is an interactive Internet radio service available in Canada. Listeners can create and share personalized music playlists that are considered personalized music stations or access one of many already created music stations. Slacker was launched for the Web in 2004 and is now also available for listening on mobile devices. Slacker is free to use, can be listened to on the iPhone/iPod Touch and iPad as well as Android phones, and offers an application for Windows-only computers. The free service includes advertisements, but users can upgrade for a monthly fee and receive the service without advertisements and with some additional listening functionality.[12]

TELEVISION Television broadcasters include national, regional, and specialty and digital networks, independent stations, cable television, and satellite television. As a result of the significant increase in commercial television stations, the television audience is highly fragmented.

In today's digital world, some are questioning the role of television. However, as consumers embrace new media, it appears that rather than turning away from television, they are combining their viewership.

© Pixellover RM 4/Alamy

infomercial a 30-minute or longer advertisement that looks more like a TV talk show than a sales pitch

"It's clear that advertisers are wisely MAXIMIZING THEIR OPPORTUNITIES *to reach consumers across platforms with TV ad dollars showing no signs of slowing and noteworthy* INCREASES IN INTERNET AD SPEND.*"*[14]

—Randal Beard (global head, Advertiser Solutions for Nielsen)

Canadians continue to spend more time with television than any other media, and time spent online has grown to second place. Canadians still prefer watching television on their larger television screens rather than their computer screens because this offers the best overall sound and visual experience, making it a highly engaging and influential medium. While viewing television in the traditional sense, however, the viewer is often multitasking online. Online viewing extends the reach of a television program as it allows viewers who missed a regularly scheduled program to watch it at their convenience. Creative advertisers are driving people to websites, knowing that viewers are likely online while their advertisement airs.

For those consumers who do skip the ads, research indicates that they are aware of the product or service being featured in the commercials. PVRs have made television more user-friendly insofar as consumers are in control of when they watch their favourite shows.[13]

Advertising time on television can be very expensive, especially for network and popular cable channels. Specials events and first-run prime-time shows for top-ranked TV programs command the highest rates for a typical 30-second spot, with the least-expensive ads costing about $300,000 and the more expensive ones $500,000. **Infomercials** continue to be a successful television format as they are relatively inexpensive to produce and air. Advertisers use infomercials when the information to be presented to the consumer is relatively complicated.

OUT-OF-HOME MEDIA Outdoor, or out-of-home, advertising is a flexible, low-cost medium that may take a variety of forms. Examples include billboards, skywriting, giant inflatables, mini

GOOGLE GLASS

Google currently plays a huge role in online advertising in large part because its ads appear on many websites and its search engine is one of the most popular. In addition, Google has become a mobile giant with its Android operating system. But now Google is hoping to become even more ubiquitous with its new product—Google Glass. The specs are designed to unify Google's myriad offerings by streaming real-time information right to the viewer's eyes. Wearers can look at a poster for a movie, and ticket sales will pop up. Voice interaction enables users to ask for directions and have a course plotted on Google Maps. A small camera allows users to share what they are looking at and take photos. Calls can be made, emails and texts sent, locations shared, and places checked into—all through a streamlined, wraparound frame with one small, clear lens. What does this mean for marketers? It means a whole new level of contact. While Google says the glasses are not meant to be worn constantly, being able to display ads for

Peter Foley/Bloomberg via Getty Images

a search, on a map, or even through Facebook or Twitter to a user's eye might be the ultimate in alternative media marketing.

Source: Nick Bilton, "Google Begins Testing Its Augmented-Reality Glasses," *New York Times*, April 4, 2012, http://bits.blogs.nytimes.com/2012/04/04/google-begins-testing-its-augmented-reality-glasses (accessed April 20, 2012).

THE ELECTRONIC MUSIC DUO DAFT PUNK USED THIS EYE-CATCHING SUPERBOARD TO RAISE AWARENESS OF THEIR NEW ALBUM.

Courtesy of PATTISON Outdoor Advertising

billboards in malls and on bus stop shelters, signs in sports arenas, lighted moving signs in bus terminals and airports, and ads painted on cars, trucks, buses, water towers, manhole covers, drinking glass coasters, and even people (referred to as *living advertising*). Pattison Outdoor Advertising is Canada's largest out-of-home advertising company with a presence in over 100 cities in Canada. To meet the evolving needs of marketers, Pattison is always developing new out-of-home advertising products, such as the one seen above advertising Daft Punk.

One of the fastest-growing areas of out-of-home media is place-based media. Place-based media communicates to consumers where they live, work, and play. Its content is created to be personalized and relevant. A variety of place-based media allow marketers to reach the right consumer at the right place at the right time, such as washroom ads in bars, restaurants, schools, and fitness facilities. When you consider that approximately 70 percent of all decisions are made at the point of purchase, place-based media is critical to include in the media mix. Some other examples of place-based media include ads on pizza boxes, golf course hospitality carts, dry-cleaning bags and hangers, and food carriers used in stadiums, arenas, and movie theatres.

Outdoor advertising reaches a broad and diverse market, making it ideal both for promoting convenience products and services and for directing consumers to local

businesses. One of the main advantages of outdoor media over other media is its very high exposure frequency and very low clutter from competing ads. Outdoor advertising can also be customized to local marketing needs, which is why local businesses are often the leading outdoor advertisers in any given region.

THE INTERNET AND MOBILE ADVERTISING
Internet advertising revenue in 2012 hit $3.1 billion, or 27.5 percent of total advertising revenues (second only to television). Exhibit 16.5 shows that Internet advertising continues to grow at the expense of the other major advertising tools. Sixty-one percent of Internet ad revenue is derived from listings, such as search and classified and directories. Online video and display advertising represent 33 percent of online revenue, or $1.0 billion. The remaining 6 percent of online revenue is derived from mobile, gaming, and email.[15] Internet advertising provides an interactive, versatile medium that is able to target specific groups and that offers rich data on consumer usage and measurable results.[16]

Canada is one of the top countries globally in terms of online usage (eight in ten Canadians are online and most of those are daily users).[17] This ranking includes the number of hours spent online, engagement levels, social media adoption, and accessing of video online. Advertisers in Canada, however, lag in terms of their investment in the adoption of digital media options in media plans. Given increasing mobile adoption rates, the increasing supply of video options, and the increasing number of Canadians who use multiple screens in their living rooms simultaneously (88 percent of families), advertisers must increase

Exhibit 16.5

AD REVENUE GROWTH BY MAJOR MEDIA IN CANADA, 2011–2012

Rank		2011 $ Millions	% of Total	2012 $ millions	% of Total
1	Television	3,552	32.7%	3,467	30.9%
2	Internet	2,674	24.6%	3,085	27.5%
3	Daily newspapers	1,971	18.2%	2,019	18.0%
4	Radio	1,576	14.5%	1,585	14.1%
5	Magazines	593	5.5%	573	5.1%
6	Out of home	484	4.5%	486	4.3%
	Total	**10,850**	**100%**	**11,215**	**100.00**

Source: IAB Canda *2012 Actual + 2013 Estimated Canadian INTERNET Advertising Revenue Survey DETAILED REPORT*, September 18, 2013, http://iabcanada.com/files/Canadian_Internet_Advertising_Revenue_Survey_2012-13English.pdf

Canadians spend more time online than anybody else in the world—AN AVERAGE OF 45 HOURS/MONTH.

their investment in digital.[18] Online formats include search engine marketing, display advertising (banner ads), social media advertising (such as Facebook ads), email marketing, and mobile marketing. Search and display accounted for over 70 percent of all 2012 Internet revenue, with search advertising the key driver. Mobile advertising revenue grew significantly, almost doubling to $160 million in 2012.

Marketers' primary objective in using search engine ads is to enhance brand awareness. They do this through paid placement of ads tied to key words used in search engines searches—when someone clicks on the ad, the advertiser pays the search engine a fee. Search engine advertising accounts for just under half of all money spent on Internet advertising.

Display advertising is ad space bought on websites in a variety of formats. The ad space can be purchased directly from a website or media buyers can buy on networks that represent a variety of websites. This form of advertising can be highly effective, as Web analytics provide excellent information on website visitors, ensuring the opportunity for precise targeting.

Mobile advertising has exhibited significant growth because of increasing penetration of smartphones and tablets, faster connection speeds, increasing use of social media, and advances in ad integration into mobile apps and websites.[19]

Another popular Internet advertising format is **advergaming**, in which companies put ad messages in Web-based or video games (on PlayStation or Wii) to advertise or promote a product, a service, an organization, or an issue. Sometimes the entire game amounts to a virtual commercial; in other cases, advertisers sponsor games or buy ad space for a product placement in them. Many of these are social games played on Facebook or similar sites, where players can interact with one another. Social gaming has an audience of over 173 million people worldwide, and as more and more Canadians access social networks, advertisers need to consider this form of engagement.[20]

ALTERNATIVE MEDIA To cut through the clutter of traditional advertising media, adver-

To reach young audiences, Pattison developed a specialty vinyl poster put on display in LRT stations all over Calgary for Showcase's campaign.

tisers are developing new media vehicles, including shopping carts in grocery stores, computer screen savers, DVDs, interactive kiosks in department stores, advertisements run before movies, and *advertainments*—mini movies that promote a product and are shown via the Internet. Canadians have one of the highest per capita YouTube consumption rates. Slowly, Canadian marketers are coming to recognize the potential of YouTube as a vehicle that combines the powerful entertainment elements of television with social engagement.[21]

Marketers are looking for more innovative ways to reach captive and often bored commuters. For instance, subway systems now show ads via lighted boxes installed along tunnel walls.

16-4b Media Selection Considerations

An important element in any advertising campaign is the **media mix**, the combination of media to be used. Media mix decisions are typically based on several factors: cost per contact, reach, frequency, target audience considerations, flexibility of the medium, noise level, and the lifespan of the medium.

Cost per contact is the cost of reaching one member of the target market. Naturally, as the size of the audience increases, so does the total cost. Cost per contact enables an advertiser to compare media vehicles, such as television versus radio, magazine versus newspaper, or, more specifically, *Chatelaine* versus *Flare*. The advertiser might then pick the vehicle with the lowest cost per contact to maximize advertising punch for the money spent.

Reach is the number of different target consumers who are exposed to a commercial at least once during a specific period, usually four weeks. Media plans for product introductions and attempts at increasing brand awareness usually emphasize reach. For example, an advertiser might try to reach 70 percent of the target audience during the first three months of the campaign. Reach is related to a medium's ratings, generally referred to in the industry as *gross ratings points*, or GRP. A television program with a higher GRP means that more people are tuning in to the show and the reach is higher. Accordingly, as GRP increases for a particular medium, so does cost per contact.

Because the typical ad is short-lived and because often only a small portion of an ad may be perceived at one time, advertisers repeat their ads so that consumers will remember the message. **Frequency** is the number of times an individual is exposed to a message during a specific period. Advertisers use average frequency to measure the intensity of a specific medium's coverage. For example, Red Bull GmbH, the Austrian company selling the energy drink Red Bull, might want an average exposure frequency of five for its Red Bull television ads to ensure the Red Bull company slogan, "Red Bull gives you wings," is well entrenched in the target consumers' minds. In other words, Red Bull wants each television viewer to see the ad an average of five times.

Media selection is also a matter of matching the advertising medium with the product's target market. If marketers are trying to reach teenage females, they might select advertising on the retailer Sephora's website. A medium's ability to reach a precisely defined market is its **audience selectivity**. Some media vehicles, such as general newspapers and network television, appeal to a wide cross-section of the population. Others—such as Zoomer, Runners World, TSN, HGTV, OLN, and Christian radio stations— appeal to very specific groups.

The *flexibility* of a medium can be extremely important to an advertiser. For example, because of layouts and design, the lead time for magazine advertising is considerably longer than for other media types and so is less flexible. By contrast, radio and Internet advertising provide maximum flexibility. If necessary, an advertiser can change a radio ad on the day it is to air.

Noise level is the level of distraction of the target audience in a medium. Noise can be created by competing ads, as when a street is lined with billboards or when a television program is cluttered with competing ads. Whereas newspapers and magazines have a high noise level, direct mail is a private medium with a low noise level. Typically, no other advertising media or news stories compete for direct-mail readers' attention.

Media have either a short or a long *lifespan*, which means that messages can either quickly fade or persist as tangible copy to be carefully studied. A radio commercial may last less than a minute, but advertisers can overcome this short lifespan by repeating radio

cost per contact the cost of reaching one member of the target market

reach the number of target consumers exposed to a commercial at least once during a specific period, usually four weeks

frequency the number of times an individual is exposed to a given message during a specific period

audience selectivity the ability of an advertising medium to reach a precisely defined market

To build demand for their limited edition 625 ML Victory Bottles, Molson Canadian created a campaign featuring the true story of two Ottawa friends who bring a Molson Beer Fridge and a satellite to their friend who is living in Indonesia so they can all watch the 2013 World Junior Hockey Championship together. The campaign launched with a 2:45-minute video during Canada's first game in the 2013 series.

Courtesy of Molson Canada

ads often. In contrast, a magazine has a relatively long lifespan, which is further increased by a high pass-along rate.

Media planners have traditionally relied on the factors we've just discussed for selecting an effective media mix, with reach, frequency, and cost often being the overriding criteria. Well-established brands with familiar messages probably need fewer exposures to be effective, whereas newer or unfamiliar brands likely need more exposures to become familiar. In addition, today's media planners have more media options than ever before.

The proliferation of media channels is causing *media fragmentation* and forcing media planners to pay as much attention to where they place their advertising as to how often the advertisement is repeated. That is, marketers should evaluate reach

and frequency when assessing the effectiveness of advertising. In certain situations, it may be important to reach potential consumers through as many media vehicles as possible. When this approach is considered, however, the budget must be large enough to achieve sufficient levels of frequency to have an impact. In evaluating reach versus frequency, therefore, the media planner ultimately must select an approach that is most likely to result in the ad being understood and remembered when a purchase decision is being made.

Advertisers also evaluate the qualitative factors involved in media selection, including attention to the commercial and the program, involvement, program liking, lack of distractions, and other audience behaviours that affect the likelihood that a commercial message is being seen and, ideally, absorbed. While advertisers can advertise their product in as many media as possible and repeat the ad as many times as they like, the ad still may not be effective if the audience is not paying attention. Research on audience attentiveness for television, for example, shows that the longer viewers stay tuned to a particular program, the more memorable they find the commercials. Contrary to long-held assumptions, when selecting media vehicles, *holding power* can be more important than ratings (the number of people tuning in to any part of the program).

16-4c Media Scheduling

After choosing the media for the advertising campaign, advertisers must schedule the ads. A **media schedule** designates the media to be used (such as magazines, television, or radio), the specific vehicles (such as *Flare* magazine, the TV show *The Blacklist*, or the radio show *On Air with Ryan Seacrest*), and the insertion dates of the advertising.

Media schedules are divided into three basic types:

▸▸ Products in the later stages of the product life cycle, which are advertised on a reminder basis, use a **continuous media schedule**. A continuous schedule allows the advertising to run steadily throughout the advertising period. Examples include Boston Pizza, which may have a television commercial on Global every Wednesday at 7:30 and billboards in 14 major cities across Canada over a 12-week period.

▸▸ With a **flighted media schedule**, the advertiser may schedule the ads heavily every other month or every two weeks to achieve a greater impact with

Artpose Adam Borkowski/Shutterstock.com

Courtesy of GoodLife Fitness

pulsing media schedule a media scheduling strategy that uses continuous scheduling throughout the year coupled with a flighted schedule during the best sales periods

seasonal media schedule a media scheduling strategy that runs advertising only during times of the year when the product is most likely to be purchased

an increased frequency and reach at those times. Movie studios might schedule television advertising on Wednesday and Thursday nights, when moviegoers are deciding which films to see that weekend.

▸▸ A **pulsing media schedule** combines continuous scheduling with a flighted media schedule. Continuous advertising is simply heavier during the best sale periods. A retail department store may advertise year-round but place more advertising during certain sale periods, such as Thanksgiving, Christmas, and back to school.

▸▸ Certain times of the year call for a **seasonal media schedule**. GoodLife Fitness and other fitness facilities tend to follow a seasonal strategy, placing greater emphasis on January as New Year's resolutions are being made.

New research comparing continuous media schedules versus flighted ones finds that continuous schedules for television advertisements are more effective in driving sales than flighted schedules. The research suggests that it may be more important to get exposure as close as possible to the time when a consumer makes a purchase. Therefore, the advertiser should maintain a continuous schedule over as long a period as possible. Often called *recency planning*, this theory of scheduling is now commonly used for scheduling television advertising for frequently purchased products, such as Coca-Cola or Tide detergent. Recency planning's main premise is that advertising works by influencing the brand choice of people who are ready to buy.

16-5 PUBLIC RELATIONS

Public relations is the element in the promotional mix that evaluates public attitudes, identifies issues that may elicit public concern, and executes programs to gain public understanding and acceptance. Public relations is a vital link in a progressive company's marketing communication mix. Marketing managers plan solid public relations campaigns that fit into overall marketing plans and focus on targeted audiences. These campaigns strive to maintain a positive image of the corporation in the eyes of the public. As such, they should capitalize on the factors that enhance the firm's image and minimize the factors that could generate a negative image. In Canada, public relations practitioners can become members of the Canadian Public Relations Society (CPRS) **www .cprs.ca/aboutus,** which oversees the practice of public relations for the benefit and protection of public interest.

Publicity is the effort to capture media attention—for example, through articles or editorials in publications or through human-interest stories on radio or television programs. Corporations usually initiate publicity by issuing a media release that furthers their public relations plans. A company that is about to introduce a new product or open a new store may send out media releases in the hope that the story will be published or broadcast. Savvy publicity can often create overnight sensations or build up a reserve of goodwill with consumers. Corporate donations and sponsorships can also create favourable publicity.

Public relations departments may perform any or all of the following functions:

▸▸ **MEDIA RELATIONS:** placing positive, newsworthy information in the news media to attract attention to a product, a service, or a person associated with the firm or institution

▸▸ **PRODUCT PUBLICITY:** publicizing specific products or services

▸▸ **CORPORATE COMMUNICATION:** creating internal and external messages to promote a positive image of the firm or institution

▸▸ **PUBLIC AFFAIRS:** building and maintaining national or local community relations

▸▸ **LOBBYING:** influencing legislators and government officials to promote or defeat legislation and regulation

▸▸ **EMPLOYEE AND INVESTOR RELATIONS:** maintaining positive relationships with employees, shareholders, and others in the financial community

▸▸ **CRISIS MANAGEMENT:** responding to unfavourable publicity or a negative event

product placement a public relations strategy that involves getting a product, service, or company name to appear in a movie, television show, radio program, magazine, newspaper, video game, video or audio clip, book, or commercial for another product; on the Internet; or at special events

16-5a Major Public Relations Tools

Public relations professionals commonly use several tools, many of which require an active role on the part of the public relations professional, such as writing media releases and engaging in proactive media relations. Sometimes, however, these techniques create their own publicity.

PRODUCT PUBLICITY Publicity is instrumental in introducing new products and services. Publicity can help advertisers explain the special features of their new product by prompting free news stories or positive word of mouth. During the introductory period, an especially innovative new product often needs more exposure than conventional paid advertising affords. Public relations professionals write media releases or develop videos in an effort to generate news about their new product. They also jockey for exposure of their product or service at major events, on popular television and news shows, or in the hands of influential people. Publicity is sometimes created quite unintentionally. For example, in November 2013, a Walmart location in Canton, Ohio, made the news for holding a food drive for its own employees. The story was picked up by multiple media outlets and social media, ensuring that within minutes people would begin online and offline chatting about the poor wages

Walmart pays its employees. While the low wages are an issue in the United States more so than in Canada, the negative publicity impacted Walmart's reputation in Canada as well.[22]

PRODUCT PLACEMENT Marketers are increasingly using product placement to reinforce brand awareness and create favourable attitudes. **Product placement** is a strategy that involves getting a product, service, or company name to appear in a movie, television show, radio program, magazine, newspaper, video game, video or audio clip, book, or commercial for another product; on the Internet; or at special events. Good product placement—that is, product placement that reinforces brand personality and positioning—is placement whereby the brand is used in an appropriate context and by those that represent the brand's target group. The acclaimed series *Breaking Bad* had much product placement. The whole premise of the series (a teacher who becomes a meth manufacturer) would lead one to believe that companies would shy away from associating their product with Walt, Jesse, or other characters in the series. Quite the opposite ended up happening; deals were made with Chrysler (and other companies) and Walt ended up driving a 300c and his son Walt, Jr., another Chrysler model. Maybe, then, good product placement isn't about matching product attributes to personality and context but is rather about brand exposure. In the highly cluttered media environment of today, effective brand exposure

A TRULY INTEGRATED CAMPAIGN!

In January 2014, Bell launched its fourth annual Let's Talk campaign for mental health. This integrated marketing communications program combines strong cause marketing with traditional advertising and social media. Bell promoted Let's Talk Day with an advertising campaign and a number of PR initiatives that highlighted Clara Hughes, a six-time Olympic medalist, as the national spokesperson, with CTV national correspondent Seamus O'Regan, musician Stefie Shock, comedian Michel Mpambara, and other celebrities, including CFL veteran Shea Emry and NHL star Joe Juneau. The cornerstone of the program was Bell Let's Talk Day on January 28. On that day, for every text message and long distance call made by Bell customers, every tweet, that used #BellLetsTalk or @Bell_LetsTalk, and every

Courtesy of Bell Canada

Facebook share of the Bell Let's Talk Day image at Facebook.com/BellLetsTalk, Bell donated five cents to mental health programs. In 2014, 109,451,718 text messages, mobile calls, long distance calls, tweets, and Facebook shares were sent by people across Canada in support of Bell Let's Talk Day, resulting in an additional $5,472,585.90 in contributions to mental health programs across the country.

© AF archive/Alamy

is hard to come by. Product placement in a highly rated series, program, or movie, achieves exposure. In addition, *Breaking Bad* was a series that held viewers' attention from start to finish. That level of attention could not be achieved with a traditional commercial for the Chrysler 300c. A character like Walt is not likely who Chrysler wants associated with the 300c, but the series itself was an award winner, which likely ensured a favourable attitude for the 300c.[23]

SPONSORSHIP Sponsorships are increasing both in number and as a proportion of companies' marketing budgets, with worldwide sponsorship spending reached over US$53 billion in 2013. North American sponsorship spending for 2013 reached almost US$20 billion, increasing slightly more in 2013 than the total worldwide year-to-year increase.[24] Probably the biggest reason for the increasing use of sponsorships is the difficulty of reaching audiences and differentiating a product from competing brands in today's highly fragmented media environment.

sponsorship a public relations strategy in which a company spends money to support an issue, a cause, or an event that is consistent with corporate objectives, such as improving brand awareness or enhancing corporate image

With **sponsorship**, a company spends money to support an issue, a cause, or an event that is consistent with corporate objectives, such as improving brand awareness or enhancing corporate image. Most commonly, companies sponsor events, such as festivals and fairs, conventions, expositions, sporting events, arts and entertainment spectaculars, and charity benefits. Sports and entertainment sponsorship are the top two areas where dollars are being spent. In December 2013, the Sponsorship Marketing Council of Canada awarded Gold in the Sustained Success category to BMO Financial Group's sponsorship of soccer at the national, professional, and local levels. By taking sponsorship to the local level, individual branch managers are able to connect where their customers are, handing out branded soccer balls to hundreds of local soccer teams—great brand advertising!

Although the most popular sponsorship events continue to be those involving sports, music, or the arts, companies have recently been turning to more specialized events, such as tie-ins with schools, charities, and other community service organizations. Marketers sometimes even create their own events tied to their product.

When an advertiser attempts to position itself with an event but has not been sanctioned as an official sponsor, the advertiser is participating in ambush marketing. There are plenty of examples of ambush marketing surrounding the Olympics because of the strong reach of the Olympic games coverage, yet the high cost of being an official Olympic sponsor.

Corporations also sponsor issues. Sponsorship issues are quite diverse, but the three most popular are education, healthcare, and social programs. Firms

ZIPPO SAVES THE DAY

During the parade of the Olympic torch through Russia before the start of the Sochi 2014 Winter Games, the flame was unexpectedly extinguished. Someone came forward and relit it with a Zippo lighter. The next day Zippo posted on their Facebook page and tweeted "Zippo saves the Olympics." The IOC forced Zippo to remove the posts and cease tweeting, but the company then changed the communication to say, "Zippo. Perfect for all winter games. Wink-wink."

Kommersant/Getty Images

Chapter 17

Sales Promotion and Personal Selling

© iStockphoto.com/OSTILL

Learning Outcomes

"It's better to be first in the mind than to be first in the marketplace."

—Al Ries and Jack Trout

After you finish this chapter, go to www.nelson.com/student *for* **STUDY TOOLS**. 💼- - - - - ->

17-1 WHAT IS SALES PROMOTION?

Is it really best to be first in the mind? If you were first to market, wouldn't you be more likely to win? Remington Rand was the first mainframe computer manufacturer, but we certainly don't hear about them today. Kodak used to be number one in the market, but where are they now? Marketing managers must use an arsenal of tools to stay "first in the mind" of consumers. Advertising and publicity, as we learned in Chapter 16, can help create and maintain awareness, but to *stay first in mind*, the consumer has to use the product, like the product, and want to buy it again and again. With today's plethora of products and services, how can marketers increase the likelihood that the consumer will buy repeatedly? They add sales promotion tools into the communications mix. While advertising is designed to offer the consumer a reason to buy, sales promotion offers an incentive to buy. Sales promotion is a communications tool that provides a short-term incentive to the consumer or members of the distribution channel as a motivation to purchase a good or service immediately. Sales promotion methods either reduce the price of purchase or add value to the good or service (over a defined period), thereby creating a time-sensitive incentive.

Sales promotion is a key element in an integrated marketing communications program because when used strategically, it can ensure the product or service is available for purchase and it can close the sale. Sales promotion, in contrast to advertising, is easy to measure. While it is very difficult to determine how many people buy a product or service as a result of radio or TV ads, marketers know the precise number of coupons redeemed, the number of clicks through to a website, or the number of contest entries received. These can then quite accurately measure the effectiveness of the sales promotion campaign. Blogs, Facebook, Twitter, and other social media sites are being used to deliver sales promotion offers, providing instant two-way communication. Microsites (separate pages of a website with a separate URL from the home page) provide online locations for contests and sweepstakes engagement.

17-1a The Sales Promotion Target

Sales promotion is usually targeted toward either of two distinctly different markets. **Consumer sales promotion** is targeted to the ultimate consumer market. **Trade sales promotion** is directed to members of the marketing channel, such as wholesalers and retailers. Sales promotion expenditures have been steadily increasing over the last several years as a result of increased competition, the ever-expanding array of available media choices, new creative form's of sales promotion on the Internet, consumers and retailers demanding more deals from manufacturers, and the continued reliance on accountable and measurable marketing strategies. In addition, those product and service marketers that have traditionally ignored sales promotion activities have discovered the marketing power of sales promotion. In fact, annual expenditures on promotion marketing in North America are now estimated to be more than US$700 billion.

17-1b The Objectives of Sales Promotion

Sales promotion usually has more effect on behaviour than on attitudes. Immediate purchase is the goal of sales promotion, regardless of the form it takes. The objectives of a promotion depend on the general behaviour of target consumers (see Exhibit 17.1). For example, marketers who are targeting loyal users of their product need to reinforce existing behaviour or increase product usage. Starbucks' loyalty program is a perfect example of a program that reinforces existing behaviour but at the same time increases product usage. The My Starbucks Rewards loyalty program is a cross-channel multibrand loyalty program. Consumers can earn My Starbucks Rewards Stars for purchases of Starbucks packaged coffee in grocery stores. The

FIAT is a registered trademark of Fiat Group Marketing & Corporate Communications S.p.A., used under license by Chrysler Group LLC.

A MICROSITE FOR THE FIAT ATTEMPTS TO ENGAGE THE CONSUMER BY ALLOWING THEM TO CREATE THE CAR OF THEIR SPECIFIC LIKING ONLINE.

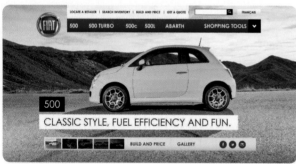

Exhibit 17.1

TYPES OF CONSUMERS AND SALES PROMOTION GOALS

Type of Buyer	Desired Results	Sales Promotion Examples
Loyal customers People who buy a particular brand most of the time or all of the time	Reinforce behaviour, increase consumption, change purchase timing	• Loyalty marketing programs, such as frequent-buyer cards or frequent-shopper clubs • Bonus packs that give loyal consumers an incentive to stock up or offer premiums in return for proof of purchase
Competitor's customers People who buy a competitor's product most of the time or all of the time	Break loyalty, persuade to switch to another brand	• Sampling to introduce another brand's superior qualities compared with competing brands • Sweepstakes, contests, or premiums that create interest in the product
Brand switchers People who buy a variety of products in the category	Persuade to buy one brand more often	• Any promotion that lowers the price of the product, such as coupons, price-off packages, and bonus packs • Trade deals that help make the product more readily available than competing products
Price buyers People who consistently buy the least expensive brand	Appeal with low prices or supply added value that makes price less important	• Coupons, price-off packages, refunds, or trade deals that reduce the price of the brand to match or undercut the price of the brand that would have otherwise been purchased

Source: From *Sales Promotion Essentials*, 3rd ed., by Don E. Schulz, William A. Robinson, and Lisa A. Petrison. © McGraw-Hill Education.

stars can then be used in Starbucks retail stores for free food or beverages.[1]

Once marketers understand the dynamics occurring within their product category and have determined the particular consumers and consumer behaviours they want to influence, they can then select the appropriate promotional tools to achieve these goals.

17-2 TOOLS FOR CONSUMER SALES PROMOTION

Marketing managers must decide which consumer sales promotion devices to use in a specific campaign. The methods chosen must suit the objectives to ensure success of the overall promotion plan.

17-2a Coupons

A **coupon** is a certificate that entitles consumers to an immediate price reduction when they buy the product. Coupons are a particularly good way to encourage product trial and repurchase. They are also likely to increase the amount of a product bought.

Almost 7 billion coupons were distributed in Canada in 2012, and the number continues to grow. Over the past few years, however, there has been a consistent decline in the number of coupons redeemed. While over 70 percent of Canadians claim to buy on sale, the decline in

coupon redemption is a result of an abundance of other forms of savings offered to the consumer, such as daily deals, online and mobile offers, savings cards, and loyalty programs. The continued increase in the number of coupons distributed in Canada is attributed to the intense competition in the consumer packaged-goods category, the annual introduction of more than 1200 new products, and the growth of companies that aggregate coupon offers to one online portal for easy consumer access. Such companies include Retailmenot, Living Social, TeamBuy.ca, and Red Flag Deals.[2] The key to the long-term success of the online coupon sites will be how marketers use the information they capture and store in their databases to deliver other marketing programs.

Mobile and social media are making it easy for consumers to receive coupons and are increasingly used by companies as a method of coupon distribution. Over 50 percent of Canadians claim to search for deals and coupons on their mobile phone, over 53 percent like pages on Facebook to receive deals or coupons, and over 40 percent follow brands or retailers on Twitter to receive immediate information on deals and coupons.[3]

In-store coupons are still popular because they are likely to influence customers' buying decisions. Instant coupons on product packages and electronic coupons issued at the counter now achieve much higher redemption rates because consumers are making more in-store purchase decisions.

17-2b Rebates

Rebates are cash refunds given for the purchase of a product during a specific period. They are similar to coupons in that they offer the purchaser a price reduction; however, because the purchaser must usually mail in a rebate form and some proof of purchase, the reward is

coupon a certificate that entitles consumers to an immediate price reduction when they buy the product

rebates cash refunds given for the purchase of a product during a specific period

want to take a long time building a personal relationship with their suppliers. With Canada's continued low economic growth, companies need to develop business outside Canada. While there has been a focus on the countries of Brazil, Russia, India, and China (BRIC) of late, companies also need to recognize the opportunities in Middle Eastern countries. The cultural, language, and religious differences in doing business in different countries can be learned and hence should not be a barrier to effective business development. A growing number of business schools, recognizing the importance of doing business abroad, are working to expose graduates to these markets and the cultural nuances that will increase the success of business relationships.[10]

17-6c The Impact of Technology on Personal Selling

Will the increasingly sophisticated technology now available at marketers' fingertips eliminate the need for salespeople? Experts agree that a relationship between the salesperson and customer will always be necessary. Technology, however, can certainly help to improve that relationship. Smartphones, netbooks, iPads, laptops, email, and mobile communication allow salespeople to be more accessible to both clients and the company. Moreover, the Internet provides salespeople with vast resources of information on clients, competitors, and the industry. All these new technologies, if used properly, can improve the effectiveness and efficiency of the salesperson.

E-commerce, or buying, selling, marketing, collaborating with partners, and servicing customers electronically using the Internet, has had a significant impact on personal selling. Virtually all companies are involved in e-commerce and consider it to be necessary to compete in today's marketplace. For customers, the Web has become a powerful tool, providing accurate and up-to-date information on products, pricing, and order status. The Internet also cost-effectively processes orders and services requests. Although on the surface the Internet might look like a threat to the job security of salespeople, it actually releases sales reps from tedious administrative tasks, resulting in more time to focus on the needs of their clients.

80%
Percentage of retail purchase decisions made in-store

97.3%
The number of staffing professionals (in a survey by Bullhorn) who claim to have used LinkedIn as a recruiting tool in 2012

65%
The percentage of Canadians who are aware of online group coupon sites

1958
The year Canadian Tire introduced Canadian Tire money

1986
The year of the first Roll Up the Rim contest for Tim Hortons

Built for the way you learn.

MKTG

Chapter 18

Social Media and Promotion

© iStockphoto.com/Valerie Loiseleux

For most people, social media is meant to be a social experience, not a marketing experience.

After you finish this chapter, go to www.nelson.com/student *for* **STUDY TOOLS**.

18-1 WHAT IS SOCIAL MEDIA?

Social media has changed the way that marketers can communicate with their brands—from mass messages to intimate conversations. While traditional media offer a mass-media method of interacting with consumers, social media offers more one-to-one ways to engage with consumers. Social media has changed how and where conversations take place, making human interaction global through popular technology. In 2013, Canadian astronaut Chris Hadfield's pictures from the International Space Station were viewed by people all around the world, his daily tweets were followed by over a million people, and his rendition of David Bowie's "Space Oddity" had 15 million views on YouTube in two weeks. Chris Hadfield connected with people around the world.[1] In November 2013, "Batkid" saved the City of San Francisco, after Make-A-Wish Greater Bay Area teamed up with the city of San Francisco to fulfill the wish of a five-year-old battling leukemia. Young Miles Scott's dream became a reality with the help of more than 20,000 volunteers from the San Francisco area, but people everywhere joined in. The hashtag #SFBatkid went around the world. Batkid was one of the most popular topics on Twitter on that day in November, with over 50,000 tweets per hour.[2] Batkid was discussed in 117 countries, with 13 percent of all tweets coming from outside the United States.[3]

Social media has also changed the way that marketers communicate—from mass messages locally to intimate conversations globally. As marketers continue to invest in social media, they must remember that social media is meant to be a social experience, not a marketing experience. Marketers must see and use social media as an opportunity to engage in conversation, create community, and connect with their audience to build and

social media collection of online communication tools that facilitate conversations online; when used by marketers, social media tools encourage consumer empowerment

Barack Obama ✓
@BarackObama

#FollowFriday RT @SFWish: **Here he comes!!!!** #SFBatkid
pic.twitter.com/pMn3gRHcLo

↩ Reply ↻ Retweet ★ Favorite ••• More

RETWEETS	FAVORITES
8,833	5,629

3:10 PM - 15 Nov 2013   Flag media

© Twitter/Make-A-Wish® Greater Bay Area

EVEN THE PRESIDENT OF THE UNITED STATES RETWEETED #SFBATKID!

nurture relationships. Marketers must remember, however, that the social and interactive nature of social media means that messages are shared across peer groups and that marketers are not always in control of the content that is being shared. The ability to share conversations quickly and with large numbers of people amplifies the word-of-mouth influence (positive and negative) of social media. Marketing consultant John Haydon said, "The real value of social media is that it exponentially leverages word-of-mouth."[4]

Marketers who understand the power of social media are vigilant in observing consumer behaviour

online and respond immediately to negative situations, mitigating the adverse influence on the brand.

Social media as a communication tool provides marketers with the opportunity not only to respond immediately but also to listen. Marketers who listen can tap into co-marketing—capitalizing on consumer input to create message content. Co-marketing relies on a continual dialogue with the consumer, who is empowered to vocalize likes and dislikes. Astute marketers use this information for continual improvement, as a source for message content, and to get ideas for mass-market campaigns.[5] Indeed, the culture of participation offered by social media may well prove to be the fifth P for marketing.

Social media offers more sophisticated methods of measuring the impact and effectiveness of the conversations, which is critical for the creation of new and innovative marketing communication campaigns. Facebook likes and shares can be measured, and the number of tweets and retweets on Twitter can be easily determined. It is necessary, however, as with traditional communication tools, that objectives be set at the start of the campaign. Marketers need to conduct research to determine the influence of social media activity on revenue, market share, and other marketing goals.

Currently, social media includes tools and platforms like social networks, blogs, microblogs, and media-sharing sites, which can be accessed through a growing number of devices, including computers, smartphones, ereaders, tablets, and netbooks. This technology changes daily, offering consumers new ways to experience social media platforms, which must constantly innovate to keep up with consumer demands.

Canadians rank second globally in terms of time spent online. Over 86 percent of Canadians have Internet access and almost 40 percent now access the Internet from their mobile devices, such as smartphones and tablets.[6] The digital universe that Canadians can access continues to explode, with online video playing an increasingly important role. As a result, more and more Canadians are engaging with social media, and marketers are effectively using social media to capture consumer attention.

"Social media will help you build up LOYALTY of your current customers to the point that they will WILLINGLY, and for FREE, tell others about you."
—Bonnie Sainsbury (founder and CEO of Social Media Smarter)

WHAT'S EXPECTED OF CANADIAN MARKETERS

Brandon Stranton, a photographer and the creative genius behind the Tumblr art project entitled Humans of New York, was approached by DKNY to purchase 300 of these photos. DKNY wanted to use the pictures in window displays around the world, promoting their Spring 2013 collection, which was inspired by New York—the city in the DKNY name. The money offered wasn't sufficient, so the deal was never solidified.

However, sometime later a friend of Stranton's sent him a picture of a store window in Bangkok full of his New York photos. Stranton immediately posted the picture on Facebook with an explanation and the request that, because the pictures had not been paid for and were being used without permission, DKNY donate $100,000 to the YMCA in Brooklyn. He also asked that readers who agreed with him share the post. It was shared over 36,000 times and received

AP Photo/Kathy Willens

over 34,000 likes. Within four hours, DKNY responded with an apology, an explanation of why that store had used the photos, and a donation of $25,000, which Brandon agreed to. The swift and honest response was well received by DKNY target customers and Brandon Stranton's followers.

Source: David Cohen, "DKNY Responds Quickly, Decisively to Facebook Crisis," AllFacebook, February 25, 2013, http://allfacebook.com/dkny-humans-of-new-york_b111521 (accessed January 2014).

18-1a How Canadians Use Social Media

Canadians are social media–savvy and are highly engaged. Almost 70 percent of Canadians claim to be active on social media, with over 63 percent of users accessing Facebook, Twitter, and/or LinkedIn every day.[7] Facebook remains the most popular site, with 93 percent of social media users saying they are on Facebook. Pinterest is the fastest-growing social media platform, and Canadians are second only to Americans in terms of the number of Pinterest users. While Facebook and Twitter dominate in terms of online sharing, Pinterest's growth is challenging both as it provides a highly visual tool for sharing content online.[8] And while Pinterest's growth is dominant, Twitter users are more frequent users, logging in often (multiple times per day) for short periods to get quick hits of information. The image-focused blogging platform Tumblr, purchased by Yahoo in 2013, is also popular with Canadians, particularly young Canadians. Canadians also have one of the highest per-capita YouTube consumption rates in the world. We love the ability to watch what we want, when we want to. In terms of video and photo sharing sites, YouTube is still the dominant player, but, interestingly, Snapchat and Instagram are outpacing Facebook in

terms of the number of photos and videos uploaded and shared daily. The key difference between Snapchat and Instagram is Snapchat's ability to let users determine how long the image or video remains visible and control whom the image is shared with. However, Instagram is challenging Snapchat's competitive advantage with its launch of Instagram Direct.

The sites just discussed are only a few of the many social media sites available One of the key drivers for the growth of social media usage and multisite usage by Canadians has been the rapid acceptance of smartphones. Smartphone penetration in Canada is close to 60 percent, and it is clearly the most popular way to access social media sites. Smartphones have become an indispensable part of day to day living. Many people will not leave home without their smartphones, using them frequently throughout the day for many activities beyond phone conversation, thus transforming behaviour. While viewing traditional media, consumers are doing other things such as watching a twiter feed on their smartphones. Over 50 percent of television viewers claim to use their smartphones to access additional information on a product or service immediately after seeing the product or service in a television advertisement. And they don't just search for the product—many people often make purchases using their smartphones. Smartphone research influences buyer decisions and purchases, with 27 percent of smartphone users making a purchase on their phone after having used it to research a product or service.[9]

The unprecedented penetration of smartphones and the continual advances in digital devices and social media tools have resulted in consumers who are willing to use a variety of media platforms. Today's consumer may have started watching a program on TV, continued watching it on a smartphone on the way home from school, and finished watching it in bed on a tablet. Therefore, marketers must create campaigns that deliver content in a multi-platform fashion. For example, TSN used multi-platform coverage for the 2014 IIHF World Junior Hockey Championship. Coverage was on TSN, TSN Radio, and TSN Digital, including TSN.ca and the TSN app for iPhone, iPad, BlackBerry, and Android. TSN's Twitter account @ TSN_Sports had exclusive embedded video content from the World Juniors. Through Twitter Amplify and sponsorship by McDonald's Canada, hockey fans and TSN followers received in-tweet video clips and instant replays.[10] However, this multi-platform usage, which puts consumer convenience ahead of all else, makes it increasingly difficult for marketers to measure the effectiveness of their campaigns and places the need for multi-platform measurement high on the priority list.[11]

Twitter Canada ✓
@TwitterCanada

▲ Follow

Watch 2014 World Junior Hockey Championship action on Twitter - @TSN_Sports partners w @TwitterCanada & @McD_Canada
bellmediapr.ca/Network/TSN/Pr...

↞ Reply ⇄ Retweet ★ Favorite ••• More

RETWEET	FAVORITES	
1	2	

2:56 PM - 19 Dec 2013

© Twitter

With online spending by marketers poised to outpace TV spending in 2014, one can see that marketers today are embracing online and social media alongside traditional media. The resulting shift from one-to-many communication to many-to-many communication provides tremendous opportunity but also tremendous risk. Social media transfers control to the audience. Thus, the audience can be in control of the message, the medium, and the response—or all three. This distribution of control is difficult for some companies to adjust to, but for those that do and for those that listen, influence and consumer engagement can be significantly more successful.

Embracing this redistribution of control and using consumers to develop and market products is called **crowdsourcing**. Crowdsourcing describes how the

DO US A FLAVOUR

A very good example of crowdsourcing is the campaign by PepsiCo Foods Canada and their *Lay's®* potato chip brand. The "*Do Us a Flavour*" campaign was launched in Canada in 2013 and was quickly embraced by Canadians who wanted a hand in creating the next *Lay's®* potato chip flavour. In 2013, the contest received over 600,000 submissions, many of which reflected the cultural diversity of Canada.

A panel of qualified judges narrowed the submissions down to four finalist flavours, which were made available in stores nationwide, and Canadians voted for their favourite. The grand prize winner received $50,000 plus

Courtesy of PepsiCo Foods Canada

1 percent of their flavour's future sales (after voting). The campaign was so successful at engaging Canadians that it was launched again in February 2014, and this time Canadians were encouraged to submit their flavour idea and choose a chip to pair with it—*Lay's®* Original, *Lay's®* Kettle Cooked, or *Lay's®* Wavy.

Source: "The Lay's Do Us A Flavour Contest Returns: Canadian Fans Invited to Pick Favorite Food to be Yummy as a Chip," CNW A PR Newswire Company, February 27, 2014, www.newswire.ca/en/story/1314023/the-lay-s-do-us-a-flavourtm-contest-returns-canadian-fans-invited-to-pick-favourite-foods-to-be-yummy-as-a-chip (accessed January 2014).

input of many people can be leveraged to make decisions that used to be based on the input of only a few people.[12] Asking consumers to provide feedback on marketing campaigns and products and responding to the feedback increases the chances of success and also creates brand advocates. Crowdsourcing is the foundation of co-branding.

SOCIAL COMMERCE As mentioned earlier, consumers are not just seeking product and service information on their digital platforms, but they are increasingly making online purchases. **Social commerce** is a subset of e-commerce that involves the interaction and user contribution aspects of social media to assist in the online buying and selling of products and services.[13] Basically, social commerce relies on user-generated content on websites to help consumers with purchases. The current social commerce darling is Pinterest. With a Pinterest account, users collect ideas and products from all over the Web and pin favourite items to individually curated pinboards. Other users browse boards by theme, keyword, or product; click on what they like; and are then either taken to the original site, or are able to re-pin the item on their own pinboard. Another social commerce site gaining in popularity is Etsy. Etsy is a marketplace where people around the world connect to buy and sell unique goods. Etsy gives users the opportunity to share on Facebook, Twitter, and Pinterest boards. Social commerce sites often include ratings and recommendations (like Amazon.ca) and social shopping tools (like Groupon). In general, social commerce sites are designed to help consumers make more informed decisions on purchases.

Courtesy of Etsy, Inc.

TREND TRUNK

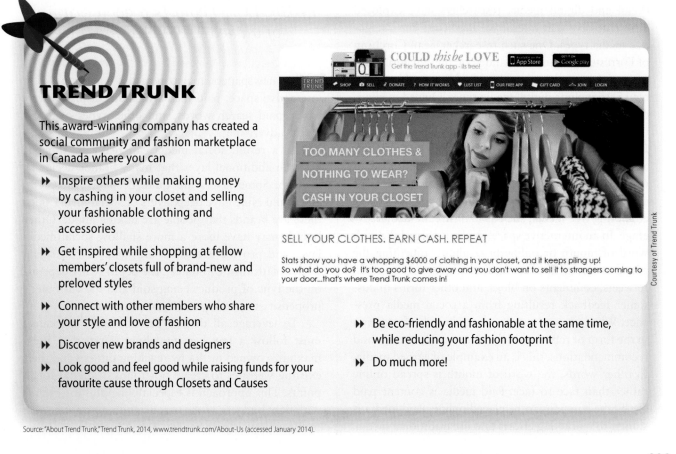

Courtesy of Trend Trunk

This award-winning company has created a social community and fashion marketplace in Canada where you can

▸▸ Inspire others while making money by cashing in your closet and selling your fashionable clothing and accessories

▸▸ Get inspired while shopping at fellow members' closets full of brand-new and preloved styles

▸▸ Connect with other members who share your style and love of fashion

▸▸ Discover new brands and designers

▸▸ Look good and feel good while raising funds for your favourite cause through Closets and Causes

▸▸ Be eco-friendly and fashionable at the same time, while reducing your fashion footprint

▸▸ Do much more!

Source: "About Trend Trunk," Trend Trunk, 2014, www.trendtrunk.com/About-Us (accessed January 2014).

18-2 CREATING AND LEVERAGING A SOCIAL MEDIA CAMPAIGN

Social media is an exciting new field, and its potential for expanding a brand's impact is enormous. Because social media's costs are often minimal and its learning curve is relatively low, some organizations are tempted to dive headfirst into it. However, as with any marketing campaign, it is always important to start with a strategy. For most organizations, this means starting with a marketing or communications plan, as covered in Chapter 3. Important evaluative areas, such as situation analysis, objectives, and evaluations, are still essential. It is important to link communication objectives (for example, improving customer service) to the most effective social media tools (for example, Twitter) and to be able to measure the results to determine whether the objectives were met. It is also important to understand the various types of media involved.

The new communication paradigm created by a shift to social media marketing raises questions about categorization. In light of the convergence of traditional and digital media, researchers have explored different ways that interactive marketers can categorize media types. One such researcher, Sean Corcoran of Forrester Research, expanded on the categorization of owned, earned, and paid media (discussed in Chapter 15) to include digital media types. Owned media is online content that an organization creates and controls. Owned media includes a brand's blogs, websites, Facebook pages, Twitter presence, YouTube channel, and other social media presences. The purpose of owned media is to develop deeper relationships with customers. *Earned media* is a public relations term connoting free media, such as mainstream media coverage. In an interactive space, media is earned through word of mouth or online buzz about something the brand is doing. Earned media includes viral videos, retweets, comments on blogs, and other forms of customer feedback resulting from a social media presence. When consumers pass along brand information in the form of retweets, blog comments, or ratings and recommendations, this is an example of earned media. In other words, the word of mouth is spread online rather than face to face. Paid media is content paid for by the company to be placed online. Paid media is similar to marketing efforts that use traditional media,

The LCBO magazine, distributed in LCBO stores in Ontario, is a good example of owned TRADITIONAL *media. LCBO.com is a good example of owned* DIGITAL *media.*

such as newspapers, magazines, and television. In an interactive space, paid media includes display advertising, paid search words, and other types of direct online advertising.[14]

As a result, social media can really be thought of as an additional layer that many brands decide to develop. Some layers are quite deep—Doritos, Old Spice, and Nike have deep layers of social media since these are brands that people are talking about. Other brands may have more a more shallow social media layer and provide access on only one or two social media platforms. Ultimately, the depth really depends on the type of product being sold and the customer's propensity to participate in social media.

To leverage all three types of media, marketers must follow a few key guidelines. First, they must maximize owned media by reaching out beyond their existing websites to create portfolios of digital touch points. This approach is especially helpful for brands with tight budgets, as the organization may not be able to afford much paid media. Second, marketers must

Ni ni/Imaginechina/AP Images

recognize that aptitude at public and media relations no longer translates into earned media. Instead, markets must learn how to listen and respond to stakeholders. This will stimulate word of mouth. Finally, marketers must understand that paid media is not dead but should serve as a catalyst to drive customer engagement.[15] If balanced correctly, all three types of media can be powerful tools for interactive marketers.

Consider the case of Tweet-a-Coffee, which has recently come to Canada. Tweet-a-Coffee allows consumers to give a coffee to another Twitter user with a tweet. After synching their Twitter account to their Starbucks account, consumers tweet to @tweetacoffee and include the Twitter handle of the user they want to send a coffee to. That person then receives a five-dollar electronic gift card, charged to the sender's Starbucks account, that they can redeem in store by printing it, showing it on their phone, or loading it on the Starbucks app. Starbucks as a brand is all about consumer engagement, and this program provides customers with a unique way to spread kindness. For Starbucks, the program in the United States generated increased sales, but more importantly, by synching

their Twitter account to their Starbucks account, consumers were voluntarily linking their social activity, their phone, and their credit card, providing Starbucks with a more robust picture of who the consumer is and how they spend. In addition, this example shows that social media can have a direct impact on a firm's return on investment.[16]

18-2a The Listening System

The first action a marketing team should take when initiating a social media campaign is simple—it should just listen. Developing an effective listening system is necessary to both understanding and engaging an online audience. Marketers must not only hear what is being said about the brand, the industry, the competition, and the customer—they must pay attention to who is saying what. The specific ways that customers and noncustomers rate, rank, critique, praise, deride, recommend, snub, and generally discuss brands are all important. Negative comments and complaints are of particular importance, both because they can illuminate unknown brand flaws and because they are the comments that tend to go viral. Thus, social media has created a new method of market research: customers telling marketers what they want and need (and don't want and need). Online tools, such as Google Alerts, Google Blog Search, Twitter Search, SiteVolume, Social Mention, and Socialcast, are extremely helpful in the development of efficient, effective listening. In Exhibit 18.1, social media strategist Jeremiah Owyang outlines eight stages of effective listening. Listening to customers communicate about one's own brand can be very revealing, but using social media is also a great way to monitor competitors' online presences, fans, and followers. Paying attention to the ways that competing brands attract and engage with their customers can be particularly enlightening for both small businesses and global brands.

18-2b Social Media Objectives

After establishing a listening platform, the organization should develop a list of objectives for its social media team to accomplish. These objectives must be developed with a clear understanding of how social media changes the communication dynamic with and for customers. Remember—attempting to reach a mass audience with a static message will never be as successful as influencing people through conversation.

Exhibit 18.1
EIGHT STAGES OF EFFECTIVE LISTENING

Stage	Description	Resources Required	Purpose
Stage 1: Being without an objective	The organization has established a listening system but has no goals.	Social media notification tools (Google Alerts)	To keep up with brand and competitor information
Stage 2: Tracking brand mentions	The organization tracks mentions in social space but has no guidance on next steps.	A listening platform with key word report capabilities (Radian6)	To track discussions, understand sentiment, and identify influencers to improve overall marketing strategy
Stage 3: Identifying market risks and opportunities	The organization seeks discussions online that may result in identification of problems and opportunities.	A listening platform with a large staff dedicated to the client (Converseon)	To seek out discussions and report to other teams, such as product development and sales; these teams then engage the customers directly or conduct further research.
Stage 4: Improving campaign efficiency	The organization uses tools to acquire real-time data on marketing efficiency.	Web analytics software (Google Analytics)	To gather a wealth of information about consumers' behaviour on their websites (and social media)
Stage 5: Measuring customer satisfaction	The organization collects information about satisfaction, including measures of sentiment.	Insight platforms that offer online focus group solutions	To measure the impact of satisfaction or frustration during interaction
Stage 6: Responding to customer inquiry	The organization identifies customers where they are (e.g., Twitter).	A customer service team is allowed to make real-time responses	To generate a high sense of satisfaction for customers
Stage 7: Understanding customers better	The organization adds social information to demographics and psychographics to gain better consumer profiles.	Social customer relationship management (CRM) systems to sync data	To create a powerful analytical tool by marrying the organization's database and social media (See Chapter 19 for more on CRM.)
Stage 8: Being proactive and anticipating customer demands	The organization examines previous patterns of data and social behaviour to anticipate needs.	Advanced customer database with predictive application (yet to be created)	To modify the social media strategy to preempt consumer behaviour modifications on the basis of trends

Sources: Jeremiah Owyang, "Web Strategy Matrix: The Eight Stages of Listening", *Web Strategy*, November 10, 2009; and Jim Sterne, *Social Media Metrics* (Hoboken, NJ: John Wiley & Sons, 2010).

Marketing managers must set objectives that reflect this reality. Here are some practical ideas that marketing managers should consider when setting social media objectives:

» **LISTEN AND LEARN:** Monitor what is being said about the brand and competitors, and glean insights about audiences. Use online tools and do research to implement the best social media practices. If you have established a listening strategy, this objective should have already been accomplished.

» **BUILD RELATIONSHIPS AND AWARENESS:** Open dialogues with stakeholders by giving them compelling content across a variety of media. Engage in conversations and answer customers' questions candidly, which will both increase Web traffic and boost your search engine ranking.

» **PROMOTE PRODUCTS AND SERVICES:** The clearest path to increasing the bottom line by using social media is to get customers talking about products and services, which ultimately translates into sales.

» **MANAGE YOUR REPUTATION:** Develop and improve the brand's reputation by responding to comments and criticism that appear on blogs and forums. Additionally, organizations can position themselves as helpful and benevolent by participating in other forums and discussions.

» **IMPROVE CUSTOMER SERVICE:** Customer comments about products and services will not always be positive. Use social media to search out displeased customers and engage them directly to solve their service issues.

18-3 EVALUATION AND MEASUREMENT OF SOCIAL MEDIA

Social media has the potential to revolutionize the way organizations communicate with stakeholders. Given the relative ease and efficiency with which organizations can use social media, a positive return on investment (ROI) is likely for many—if not most—organizations.

BUILDING TRUST ONLINE

The secret to a good relationship is trust. Cultivating trust online takes work, but it can be done.

1. *Acknowledge with empathy.* How you answer is key. Listen to your consumers and respond in an empathetic, emotionally intelligent way. If they are frustrated, acknowledge their frustration. If they are having a good experience with your brand, thank them and then share their feedback so as to amplify the positive word of mouth.

2. *Enable the right outcomes.* Use a variety of social media platforms so your consumers can connect with you and others in a location that is convenient to them.

3. *Educate through experience: Enable community.* Create an opportunity for your customers to share and create a space for conversations that are shared, to be organized and archived. Of course, you should be blogging and sending your own tweets and posts, but facilitate your customers doing so as well.

4. *Keep the momentum going.* Relationships are a two-way street, and trust once earned must be nurtured. Keep the customers engaged with your brand and trust them to be your brand advocate.

Source: Wendy Lea, "4 Steps to Cultivating Trust Online" *Mashable*, May 15, 2012.

A Forrester Research report found that 95 percent of marketers planned to increase or maintain their investments in social media. However, though they understand that it is a worthwhile investment, most marketers have not been able to figure out how to measure the benefits of social media. In fact, while over 80 percent of marketers claim that social media is important for their business, only one in four agreed that they were able to measure the ROI for their social media activities.[17]

Some marketers accept that this unknown variable and focus on social media is less about ROI than about deepening relationships with customers; others work tirelessly to better understand the measurement of social media's effectiveness. While literally hundreds of metrics have been developed to measure social media's value, these metrics are meaningless unless they are tied to key performance indicators.[18] For example, a local coffee shop manager may measure the success of her social media presence by her accumulated number of friends on Facebook and followers on Twitter. But these numbers depend entirely on context. The rate of accumulation, investment per fan and follower, and comparison to similarly sized coffee shops are all important variables to consider. Without context, measurements are meaningless.

Some social media metrics to consider include the following:

1. *Buzz:* Volume of consumer-related buzz for a brand based on posts and impression, by social channel, by stage in the purchase channel, by season, and by time of day

2. *Interest:* Number of likes, fans, followers, and friends; growth rates; rate of virality or pass-along; and change in pass-along over time

3. *Participation:* Number of comments, ratings, social bookmarks, subscriptions, page views, uploads, downloads, embeds, retweets, Facebook posts, pins, and time spent with social media platforms

4. *Search engine ranks and results:* Increases and decreases on searches and changes in key words

5. *Influence:* Media mentions, influences of bloggers reached, influences of customers reached, and second-degree reach based on social graphs

6. *Sentiment analysis:* Positive, neutral, and negative sentiment; trends of sentiment; and volume of sentiment

7. *Website metrics:* Clicks, click-through rates, and percentage of traffic. The main issue is to start with good measurable objectives, determine what needs to be measured, and figure it out.

18-4 CONSUMER BEHAVIOUR ON SOCIAL MEDIA

Online activity has changed the way people learn and the way they interact with companies and with each other in their daily lives. Consumers are online seeking

BATKID BY THE NUMBERS

We started this discussion on social media with a heart-warming story about Batkid. Here are the numbers that were achieved as presented by the San Francisco Make-A-Wish Foundation Chapter:

➡ **People who RSVP'd to volunteer via our website:** 16,077

➡ **Estimated size of the crowd at City Hall:** approximately 20,000

➡ **Number of #SFBatkid/#Batkid tweets generated (through Sunday 11/17):** 545,576

➡ **% of all tweets coming from outside US:** 13%

➡ **Number of countries where Batkid was discussed:** 117

➡ **% of all tweets that were deemed "positive":** 96%

➡ **Total Twitter potential reach:** 777,453,544

➡ **Total Twitter potential impressions:** 1,816,783,718

➡ **Number of Instagram photos with #SFBatkid:** 16,000

➡ **Total Instagram potential reach:** 19.5 million

➡ **Total Instagram potential impressions:** 23.6 million

Miikka Skaffari/Getty Images

➡ **Number of hits per second to all Make-A-Wish websites during peak:** 1,400

➡ **Number of staff in the Make-A-Wish Greater Bay Area office:** 23 full time; 4 part time

➡ **Number of wishes granted by our chapter each year:** approximately 350

Source: Make-A-Wish Foundation, "Batkid Miles saves San Francisco!" http://sf.wish.org/wishes/wish-stories/i-wish-to-be/wish-to-be-batkid

news from a variety of sources as the news is happening. Consumers are online building relationships and interacting with each other and with companies through social media. Consumers are online banking, investing, and purchasing. Social media has reinvented politics and civic engagement (e.g., the Aboriginal movement known as Idle No More grew nationwide attention through Twitter).

But who is using social media? How often are they online? How much time do they spend online? What types of social media do they use? How do they use social media? Do Twitter users retweet viral videos? How often do they post online? Are they just reading content or are they actually creating it? Does Facebook attract younger users? Why do consumers read blogs? These types of questions must be considered because

they determine not only which tools will be most effective but also, more importantly, whether launching a social media campaign even makes sense for a particular organization.

Understanding an audience necessitates understanding how that audience uses social media. In *Groundswell*, Charlene Li and Josh Bernoff of Forrester Research identify six categories of social media users:

1. *Creators:* Those who produce and share online content, such as blogs, websites, articles, and videos

2. *Critics:* Those who post comments, ratings, and reviews of products and services on blogs and forums

3. *Collectors:* Those who use RSS feeds to collect information and vote for websites online

4. *Joiners:* Those who maintain a social networking profile and visit other sites

5. *Spectators:* Those who read blogs, listen to podcasts, watch videos, and generally consume media

6. *Inactives:* Those who do none of these things[19]

A more recent study by the U.S. firm Aimia identified six segments as well:

1. *No Shows:* Those that haven't logged on to a social network in 60 days. They exhibit low degrees of trust and have no interest in sharing their world online with others.

2. *Newcomers:* Typically passive users of a single social media network who use it simply to enhance their online relationships.

3. *Onlookers:* Lurkers who post infrequently and are online to keep up to date on others. They limit their own postings as they want control of their online information.

4. *Cliquers:* These are active, single-network users who use primarily Facebook for the purpose of posting photos, comments, and status updates. They are influential in their small network of close friends.

5. *Mix-n-Minglers:* They participate actively on multiple platforms. They follow brands to receive offers and stay ahead of the curve. They meet friends online and are influential online.

6. *Sparks:* This group is the most active online. Social media is a way for them to express themselves, and they are active on a number of sites. They too are influential and are key influencers with respect to the brands they follow.

Exhibit 18.2 illustrates where each of these segments fits on measures of exposure and participation.

As marketers come to understand how consumers engage with social media to the same extent that they understand consumer engagement with traditional media, they will be able to create integrative marketing communication campaigns that combine traditional and online tools more effectively with greater chances for success.

Exhibit 18.2
SOCIAL MEDIA USAGE FRAMEWORK

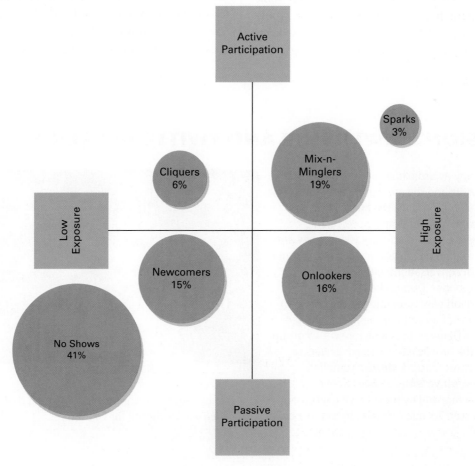

Courtesy of Aimia, Inc.

blogs publically accessible Web pages that function as interactive journals, whereby readers can post comments on the authors' entries

corporate or professional blogs blogs that are sponsored by a company or one of its brands and maintained by one or more of the company's employees

noncorporate blogs independent blogs that are not associated with the marketing efforts of any particular company or brand

18-5 SOCIAL MEDIA TOOLS: CONSUMER- AND CORPORATE- GENERATED CONTENT

It is important for marketers to engage with customers on social media for the reasons mentioned throughout this chapter, and a number of tools and platforms can be employed as part of an organization's social media strategy. Blogs, microblogs, social networks, media creation and sharing sites, social news sites, location-based social networking sites, review sites, and virtual worlds and online gaming all have their place in a company's social marketing plan. These are all tools in a marketing manager's toolbox, available when applicable to the marketing plan but not necessarily to be used all at once. Because of the breakneck pace at which technology changes, this list of resources will surely look markedly different five years from now. More tools emerge every day, and branding strategies must keep up with the ever-changing world of technology. For now, the resources highlighted in this section remain a marketer's strongest set of platforms for conversing and strengthening relationships with customers.

18-5a Blogs

Blogs have become staples in many social media strategies and are often a brand's social media centrepiece. Blogs allow marketers to create content in the form of posts, which ideally build trust and a sense of authenticity in customers. Once posts are made, audience members can provide feedback through comments. Because the comments section of a blog post opens a dialogue and gives customers a voice, it is one of the most important avenues of conversation between brands and consumers.

Blogs can be divided into two broad categories: **corporate or professional blogs** and **noncorporate blogs**, such as personal blogs. Corporate blogs are sponsored by a company and have become a critical element in reinforcing corporate image, for communicating with customers, and for adding value. Whole Foods Market Inc. has a blog that does all of that. It features recipes, product information, how-to articles, and much more. The blog features a number of different writers, as well as the CEO. The blog allows the company to communicate Whole Foods Market Inc.'s image. In contrast, noncorporate blogs are independent and not associated with the marketing efforts of any particular

TELEVISION VIEWERSHIP AND TWITTER COLLIDE

The 2014 Academy Awards show was the most-watched since 2004 and the most popular entertainment event on television since the finale of *Friends*. Big event programs are increasing in viewership because viewers are multi-platform-tasking. They are watching the program on television while at the same time engaging in conversations with friends on their tablets or smartphones. During the 2014 Academy Awards, 14.7 million tweets mentioned the Oscars or prominent actors or films during the telecast. When the host, Ellen DeGeneres, took a picture with a group of stars during the broadcast and asked viewers to help her set a retweet record, viewers complied. Twitter was in overdrive with 254,644 tweets per minute of the picture and by the following afternoon it had been retweeted 2.8 million times. In fact, the crush

Ellen DeGeneres/Twitter/Getty Images

of engagement was so overwhelming that Twitter service was disrupted for 20 minutes.

Source: Steven Musil, "DeGeneres' Oscar selfie tweet captures retweet crown" *CNET*, March 2, 2014, http://news.cnet.com/8301-1023_3-57619793-93/degeneres-oscar-selfie-tweet-captures-retweet-crown/ (accessed March 5, 2014).

company or brand. Because these blogs contain information not controlled by marketers, they are perceived to be more authentic than corporate blogs. Mommy bloggers—women who review children's products and discuss family-related topics on their personal blogs—are an example of noncorporate blogs. Because of the popularity of these and other types of blogs, many bloggers receive products and money from companies in exchange for a review. Whether bloggers are reviewing a product they have sourced themselves or a sampled product, the review can be a critical influencer to purchase for those reading it.

18-5b Microblogs

Microblogs are blogs with strict limits on the length of posts. Twitter, the most popular microblogging platform, requires that posts be no more than 140 characters. Other microblogging platforms include Tumblr, Google Buzz, and Qaiku.

While Tumblr is growing rapidly, Twitter is already wildly popular. Having become a social messaging tool, Twitter is effective for disseminating breaking news, promoting longer blog posts and campaigns, sharing links, keeping in touch, announcing events, and promoting sales. When a company follows, retweets, responds to potential customers' tweets, and tweets content that inspires customers to engage with the brand or the company, Twitter users will quickly and efficiently lay a foundation for meaningful two-way conversation. Research has found that when operated correctly, corporate Twitter accounts are well respected and well received. Twitter can be used to build communities; aid in customer service; gain prospects; increase awareness; and, in the case of nonprofits, raise funds.

During the People's Choice Awards in January 2014, Cover Girl tweeted out bonus video content from the awards show. The content included winners' reactions, hosts' jokes, and other can't-miss moments that consumers shared among themselves. The content originated from Global TV's Twitter account and then was amplified through Twitter Amplify to a custom targeted list created by Twitter. Twitter Amplify is a Twitter ad unit that allows advertisers to share content, such as sports replays or interviews with TV actors, at the same time as a TV broadcast. Cover Girl also shared the clips by using their own Twitter account. Global TV captured and cut the live video as the award show was airing and then delivered the real-time content based on what was trending online.[20]

Continuing the strategy that was started with the Vancouver Olympics, the Canadian Olympic Committee employed Twitter as its "exclusive Social Media Partner" to help Canadians to feel connected to the athletes competing for gold for Canada. Canadian Olympic partners were given the opportunity to promote Canadian Olympic tweets from approved athletes' handles and the official team handles.[21]

18-5c Social Networks

Social networking sites allow individuals to connect—or network—with friends, peers, and business associates. Connections may be made around shared interests, shared environments, or personal relationships. Depending on the site, connected individuals may be able to send each other messages, track each other's activity, see each other's personal information, share multimedia, or comment on each other's blog and microblog posts. Depending on its goals, a marketing team might engage several social networks as part of its social media strategy: Facebook is the largest social network; LinkedIn is geared toward professionals and businesses; Google+ is challenging Facebook as the second-largest social network with such unique features as Hangouts and Communities; and niche networks like MapMyRide and Match.com cater to specialized markets. Given the right strategy, increasing awareness, targeting audiences, promoting products, forging relationships, highlighting expertise and leadership, attracting event participants, performing research, and generating new business are attainable marketing goals on any social network.

Facebook has hundreds of millions of users, making it the most popular social networking site. While individual Facebook users create profiles, brands, organizations, and nonprofit causes operate as pages (see Exhibit 18.3). As opposed to individual profiles, all pages are public and are thus subject to search engine indexing. By maintaining a popular

Exhibit 18.3
FACEBOOK LINGO

Non-individual (Usually Corporate)	Individual
Page	Profile
Fan of a page; tells fan's friends that the user is a fan; creates mini viral campaign	Friend a person; send private messages; write on the Timeline; see friend-only content
Public; searchable	Privacy options; not searchable unless user enabled

Facebook page, a brand not only increases its social media presence but also helps to optimize search engine results. Pages often include photo and video albums, brand information, and links to external sites. The most useful page feature, however, is the Timeline. The Timeline allows a brand to communicate directly with fans via status updates, which enables marketers to build databases of interested stakeholders. When an individual becomes a fan of your organization or posts on your Timeline, that information is shared with the individual's friends, creating a mini viral marketing campaign. Facebook is an extremely important platform for marketers and is becoming an integral part of marketing campaigns.

LinkedIn is used primarily by professionals who want to build their personal brand online and by businesses as a tool to assist in recruitment and selection. LinkedIn features many of the same services as Facebook (profiles, status updates, private messages, company pages, and groups) but is oriented around business and professional connections—it is designed to be information-rich rather than multimedia-rich.

To demonstrate the effectiveness of the Canadian Tire Motomaster Eliminator battery, Canadian Tire truly put it to the test by placing the battery in a custom-made ice truck. To create awareness of the ice truck, a 60-second television ad was created that was played during the NHL Winter Classic game. But to create awareness of the ad, previews of it were posted on Facebook. Everyone over 25 saw the ice truck ad in their newsfeed on Facebook the day before the ad broke during the hockey game. In addition to using Facebook, Canadian Tire promoted the ad on Twitter and YouTube.

The challenge with social networks is the fickle nature of consumers' social media consumption. Myspace was the virtual hub for the social media generation until Facebook usurped its title and wooed away its youthful contingent with a cleaner interface. Myspace reached its peak in December 2008, when it was attracting nearly 76 million unique visitors each month. Since late 2009, however, Myspace has lost more than 1 million users a month. Myspace grew too quickly without understanding what consumers wanted. Parents came to mistrust it and perceived it as seedy. Users, once exposed to Facebook, wanted what Facebook offered: a safe, uncluttered, user-friendly place where they could interact with the people they wanted to interact with.

Users abandoned their Myspace pages and migrated to Facebook, and when they did, the advertisers left too. In 2009, Myspace generated US$470 million in advertising; the projection for 2011 was

only US$184 million. In 2011, Myspace was sold to Specific Media for US$35 million, a far cry from the 2005 sale to News Corporation for US$580 million. A social media site grows quickly, as influencers pull in all their peers, but they also pull them away at the first sign of trouble or something new on the horizon—a trend that current social media darlings, such as Twitter and LinkedIn, should notice. It took only one year for Facebook to eclipse Myspace, and it has taken less than two years for Myspace to lose hundreds of millions of dollars and users.[22]

18-5d Media-Sharing Sites

Media-sharing sites allow users to upload and distribute multimedia content, such as videos and photos. Sites such as YouTube, Flickr, and Pinterest are particularly useful to brands' social marketing strategies because they add an interactive channel on which to distribute content. Today, organizations can tell compelling brand stories through videos, photos, and audio.

Photo sharing sites allow users to archive and share photos. Flickr, Picasa, Snapchat, Vine, Instagram, and even Facebook all offer free photo hosting services that can be used by individuals and businesses alike.

Video creation and distribution have also gained popularity among marketers because of video's rich ability to tell stories. YouTube, the high-traffic video-based website, allows users to upload and stream their videos. YouTube dominates business video sharing with over 90 percent of marketers who share video saying they do so through YouTube. Creative marketers wanting to increase consumer engagement develop campaigns that encourage consumers to create product usage videos. Such user-generated content, if used strategically, can be a powerful tool for brands.

In an effort to extend the success of the 2012 awareness campaign Together We Will for the SickKids Foundation, SickKids created an in-cinema ad that was a faux superhero movie trailer featuring Antonio, one of the patients featured in the 2012 campaign who had been treated for acute lymphoblastic leukemia at SickKids Hospital. After the ad was shown in the movie theatre, the marketers revealed to the audience that Antonio, "the real-life hero," was in the audience with them. The audience rose to their feet to applaud Antonio. The emotional theatre experience was captured on video and debuted on YouTube as part of SickKids' digital marketing plan.

The idea was to show viewers the patients a year later, with the hope that such an emotional advertisement would not only connect with them but, because of the placement on YouTube, would be shared virally.[23]

In a similar fashion, WestJet emotionally engaged viewers during Christmas 2013 with a holiday YouTube video showing WestJet employees making the wishes of travellers come true. After passengers checked in at Toronto Pearson and Hamilton airports for flights to Calgary, they were asked by a virtual Santa what they wanted for Christmas, after scanning their boarding passes at kiosks. Responses ranged from computers to socks, from a flight home to see family to a big-screen TV. What passengers didn't know was that during their five-hour flight to Calgary, a team of more than 150 WestJet staff went shopping, wrapped presents, and delivered the gifts to the Calgary airport. When the passengers went to collect their baggage, wrapped presents addressed to them came down the carousel. The action by WestJet and their employees was wonderful, in the truest sense of the Christmas spirit, and the resulting video was gripping and emotional. The video hit 1 million viewers the first day it was posted, and within two days attracted over 7.5 million views. With the video, WestJet created brand engagement that would have been hard to achieve with a traditional television ad—and it would have been unaffordable.[24]

A podcast, another type of user-generated media, is a digital audio or video file that is distributed serially for other people to listen to or watch. Podcasts can be streamed online, played on a computer, uploaded to a portable media player (like an iPod), or downloaded onto a smartphone. Podcasts are like radio shows that are distributed through various means and not linked to a scheduled time slot.

18-5e Social News Sites

Social news sites allow users to post news stories and multimedia on a platform, such as Reddit or Digg, for readers to then vote on. The more interest from readers, the more votes the post gets, and thus the higher it is ranked. Marketers have found that these sites are great for promoting campaigns. If marketing content posted to a social news site is voted up, discussed, and shared enough to be listed among the most popular topics of the day, it can go viral. Social bookmarking sites,

media-sharing sites websites that allow users to upload and distribute multimedia content, such as videos and photos

social news sites websites that allow users to decide which content is promoted on a given website by voting that content up or down such as Digg and StumbleUpon, are similar to social news sites but the objective of their users is to collect, save, and share interesting and valuable links. The result is the creation of peer networks that are linked by a common interest.

18-5f Location-Based Social Networking Sites

Location-based social networking sites combine the fun of social networking with the utility of location-based GPS technology. Foursquare, one of the most popular location sites, treats location-based micro networking as a game: users earn badges and special statuses that are based on their number of visits to particular locations. Users can write and read short reviews and tips about businesses, organize meet-ups, and see which Foursquare-using friends are nearby. Foursquare updates can also be posted to linked Twitter and Facebook accounts for followers and friends to see. In a recent survey, less than 20 percent of people claimed to use the location-based social platforms, while almost all of them use other social channels like Facebook. The added value offered by location-based sites like Foursquare just isn't there. Facebook provides the ability to share your location with your network, and Facebook, Twitter, Instagram, Pinterest, and other more robust sites provide all that Foursquare offers and more.

18-5g Review Sites

Individuals tend to trust other people's opinions when it comes to purchasing. According to Nielsen Media

© NetPics/Alamy

Research, more than 70 percent of consumers said that they trusted online consumer opinions. This percentage is much higher than that of consumers who trust traditional advertising. Based on the early work of Amazon and eBay to integrate user opinions into product and seller pages, countless websites have sprung up that allow users to voice their opinions across every segment of the Internet market. **Review sites** allow consumers to post, read, rate, and comment on opinions regarding all kinds of products and services. Review sites can enhance consumer engagement opportunities for those marketers who follow and respond to consumer posts about their products or services.

18-5h Virtual Worlds and Online Gaming

Virtual worlds and online gaming present additional opportunities for marketers to engage with consumers. These include massive multiplayer online games (MMOGs), such as World of Warcraft and The Sims Online, as well as online communities. Consultancy firm KZero Worldwide reported that almost 800 million people have participated in some sort of virtual world experience, and the sector's annual revenue is approaching $1 billion. Growth is expected to continue in this area as consumer devices, such as virtual reality headsets, start to become more mainstream. While unfamiliar to and even intimidating for many traditional marketers, the field of virtual worlds is an important, viable, and growing consideration for social media marketing.

One area of growth is social gaming. A growing number of people are playing games within social networking sites like Facebook or on their mobile devices by downloading game apps. Some of the more popular games on Facebook and available for download on smartphones include Candy Crush, Angry Birds, Words with Friends, TexasHoldEm Poker, Pet Rescue Saga, and FarmVille, and new and exciting games are continually being made available. Such games are attractive because they can be played in just five minutes, perhaps while commuting home from school or work. A growing trend among mobile games is to use mobile ads to generate revenue for the game-makers.

18-6 SOCIAL MEDIA AND MOBILE TECHNOLOGY

While much of the excitement in social media has been based on websites and new technology uses, much of the growth lies in new platforms. These platforms include smartphones and tablets. The major implication of this development is that consumers now have a multitude of access points for websites.

18-6a Mobile and Smartphone Technology

Almost 70 percent of Canadians own a smartphone[25] and the usage figures suggest that they have become a necessary tool for everyday living. Sixty-six percent of Canadians access the Internet every day from their smartphone and very few smartphone users ever leave their home without them. Canadians use their smartphones to search for information, to watch videos, for social networking, and for traditional communication. Canadians download and use apps on their smartphones for a multitude of reasons, and they often multimedia-task; almost 50 percent of Canadians claim to use their phone while doing other things, such as watching television.[26]

In 2012, mobile advertising revenue was $160 million, representing a 1.3 percent share of reported media, and in 2013 it more than doubled to $290 million. Short Message Service (SMS) advertising was the number one form of mobile advertising in 2012, and while it is expected to continue to be a major player in the future, search and display advertising options are expected to dominate in the coming years.[27]

Tablet penetration has been precipitous. The most likely type of advertising winner as a result of tablet penetration is video, and Canadians lead the way in terms online video viewership growth, offering marketers a highly engaging communication opportunity.

The low barriers to entry that have been created by the standardization of mobile platforms, the seemingly reduced concerns over the once-worrisome privacy issues (especially among the younger population, who are the largest mobile users), and the portability of the smartphones are all reasons for the popularity and growth of mobile marketing. In addition, mobile marketing is measurable; metrics and usage statistics make it an effective tool for gaining insight into consumer behaviour, and mobile marketing's response rate is higher than that of traditional media types, further fuelling its popularity and growth.

One use for barcode scanning apps is the reading and processing of Quick Response (QR) codes. When scanned by a smartphone's QR reader app, a QR code takes the user to a specific site with content about or a discount for products or services.

The smartphone trend called *near field communication* (NFC) uses small chips hidden in or behind products that, when touched by compatible devices, will transfer the information on the chip to the device. In Canada, NFC offers the opportunity for mobile payments via your smartphone.

18-6b Applications and Widgets

Millions of applications or **apps** have been developed for the mobile market. These apps allow you to listen to music, track your calorie intake, play games, book a hotel, practise yoga, or find your way home. The CBC Olympic app, created for the 2014 Sochi Winter Olympic Games, drew 380 million views over the course of the Games, which is significantly higher than the app for the Vancouver Games in 2010.[28] Whether offering new or existing content, when an app is well branded and integrated into a company's overall marketing strategy, it can create buzz and generate customer engagement.

While some marketers focus their apps on connectivity, Nike created Nike+ to provide both utility and connectivity. Using an iPhone's GPS capabilities, users can track their jogging and cycling routes, and examine mapping and details of their pace and

COMMON MOBILE MARKETING TOOLS

» **SMS (SHORT MESSAGE SERVICE):**
160 character text messages sent to and from
cell phones. SMS is typically integrated with
other tools.

» **MMS (MULTIMEDIA MESSAGING
SERVICE):** Similar to SMS but allows
for the attachment of images, video,
ringtones, and other multimedia to text
messages.

» **MOBILE WEBSITES (MOBI AND
WAP WEBSITES):** Websites designed
specifically for viewing and navigation on
mobile devices.

» **MOBILE ADS:** Visual advertisements integrated into text messages, applications, and
mobile websites. Mobile ads are often sold on
a cost-per-click basis.

» **BLUETOOTH MARKETING:** A signal is
sent to Bluetooth-enabled devices that allows
marketers to send targeted messages to users
based on their geographic locations.

» **SMARTPHONE APPLICATIONS
(APPS):** Software designed specifically for
mobile and tablet devices. Theses apps include
software to turn phones into scanners for
various types of barcodes.

calories burned. Information on treadmill runs and other exercise details can be entered manually as well, so as a training tool this app can provide powerful information to the user. In addition, activities can be shared online with other runners and joggers.

Web widgets, also known as gadgets and badges, are software applications that run entirely within existing online platforms. Essentially, a Web widget allows a developer to embed a simple application, such as a weather forecast, horoscope, or stock market ticker, into a website, even if the developer did not write (or does not understand) the application's source code. From a marketing perspective, widgets allow customers to display company information (such as current promotions, coupons, news, or countdown clocks) on their own websites.

Oleg Pchelov/Shutterstock.com

18-7 THE SOCIAL MEDIA PLAN

To effectively use the tools in the social media toolbox, marketers need a clearly outlined social media plan. The social media plan is linked to larger plans, such as a promotional plan or marketing plan, and should fit appropriately into the objectives and steps in those plans (for more information, review Chapters 3 and 15). It is important to research throughout the development of the social media plan to keep abreast of the rapidly changing social media world. Creating an effective social media plan has six stages:

1. *The listening stage:* This stage is covered in the discussion entitled The Listening System earlier in the chapter.

2. *Set social media objectives:* Set objectives that can be specifically accomplished through social media, with special attention to how to measure the results. Numerous metrics are available, some of which are mentioned throughout the chapter.

3. *Identify the target audience:* This should line up with the target market defined in the marketing plan, but in the social media plan, pay special attention to how that audience participates and behaves online.

4. *Define strategies:* Once trends and best practices in the industry have been reviewed and an understanding of the target audience has been achieved, you can establish the strategies to reach the target.

HUMANITARIAN TEXTING

Rogers Wireless and Fido customers were able to immediately and easily contribute to those in southern Alberta who were hit hard by devastating flooding in June 2013. By texting ABHELP to shortcode 4664, customers were able to donate $5, with 100 percent of the proceeds going to the Canadian Red Cross. Today, research by the Huffington Post reports that donors want to give way more than just pocket change when they make contributions via text message.

After interviewing more than 20,000 mobile donors, the mGive Foundation found that 85 percent of the people surveyed would like to give $25 to $50 to charity just by tapping on their phones. The current limit is set at $10. Donors who use text message donations do so because of the convenience and because of the immediacy—the donation can be made right at the time of the request when the emotion is the highest.

The strategies answer the question, How can we best reach and engage our target audience? In addition, your strategies should include the identification of your unique selling proposition (USP). It is with an understanding of your USP that you can create a list of key phrases around which you can build the content for your social media strategies.

5. *Select the tools and platforms:* Based on the result of step 4, choose the social media tools and platforms that will be most relevant. These choices are based on the knowledge of where the target audience participates on social media.

6. *Implement and monitor the strategy:* Social media campaigns can be fluid, so it is important to keep a close eye on what is successful and what isn't. Based on the observations, make changes as needed. It becomes important, therefore, to go back to the listening stage to interpret how consumers are perceiving the social media campaign.

Listening to customers and industry trends and continually revising the social media plan to meet the needs of the changing social media market are keys to successful social media marketing. Numerous industry leaders are sharing some of their best practices, and sources such as *Marketing Magazine* and *The Globe and Mail* report regularly on how large and small companies are successfully using social media to gain market share and sales. A good example of using social media strategies is HubSpot, which is a company that practises what it preaches, namely the benefits of building valuable content online and then using social media to pull customers to its website. Social engine profiles have increased HubSpot's website traffic, which has made its lead-generation program much more effective.

18-7a The Changing World of Social Media

As you read through the chapter, some of the trends that are noted may already seem ancient to you.

> "INTERACTION *and* ENGAGEMENT *[on social media] is something that you don't necessarily see in traditional media. That's why we [at Ford] continue to accelerate our digital advertising investment to* MORE THAN 25 PERCENT *of our media dollars.*"
>
> —Jim Farley

The rate of change in social media is astounding—usage statistics change daily for sites like Facebook and Twitter. Some things that are in the rumour mill as we write this may have exploded in popularity; others may have fizzled out without even appearing on your radar. Given the speed at which social media changes, marketers are obliged to stay on top of current tools and keep tabs on rumoured new entrants. Doing so may result in a competitive advantage because of the ability to understand and invest in the next big social media site or tool.

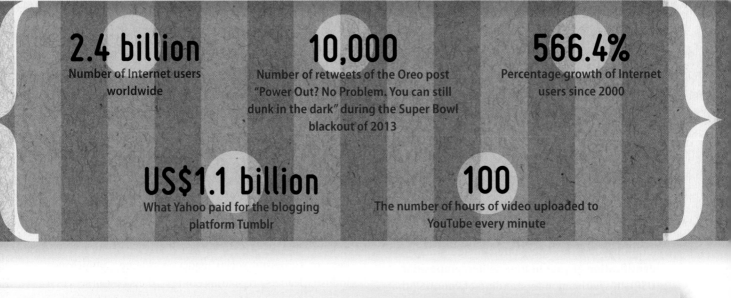

2.4 billion
Number of Internet users worldwide

10,000
Number of retweets of the Oreo post "Power Out? No Problem. You can still dunk in the dark" during the Super Bowl blackout of 2013

566.4%
Percentage growth of Internet users since 2000

US$1.1 billion
What Yahoo paid for the blogging platform Tumblr

100
The number of hours of video uploaded to YouTube every minute

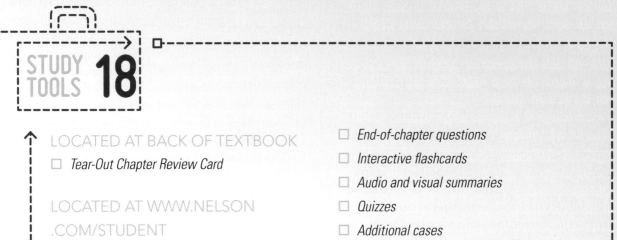

STUDY TOOLS **18**

LOCATED AT BACK OF TEXTBOOK
☐ *Tear-Out Chapter Review Card*

LOCATED AT WWW.NELSON .COM/STUDENT

☐ *End-of-chapter questions*
☐ *Interactive flashcards*
☐ *Audio and visual summaries*
☐ *Quizzes*
☐ *Additional cases*

Promotion Decisions Part 6 Case

Trend Trunk—Whose Closet Would You Like to Raid?

Courtesy of Trend Trunk

How many times have you bought something, brought it home, and then thought, "*Seriously … why did I do that?*" How many times have you bought something for a special occasion, worn it once, and then thought, "*Well, that is never going to see the light of day again!*"? How many times have you stood in front of your closet and lamented that you don't have anything to wear, yet there isn't room in your closet for the addition of even one more item?

Sean Snyder and his team have a solution, and it is a solution that could make you money.

In September 2012, Sean launched Trend Trunk, a specialty online marketplace that offers consumers a venue to *sell* their unwanted mid- to high-end clothing and accessories, and to *buy* either brand new with tags or pre-loved high-quality clothing and accessories. Sean previously owned Swapopolis, a Canadian online gift card exchange. Over his two years of running Swapopolis, Sean noted that the majority of gift cards swapped were fashion cards. His research into Canadians' fashion shopping behaviour identified that almost 6 percent of Canadians' yearly budget is spent on clothing.[1] In addition, he learned that the average Canadian has in excess of $6000 worth of clothing sitting idle in the closet.[2] This knowledge, plus his knowledge that Canadians were becoming increasingly comfortable with online shopping, led to the birth of Trend Trunk.

Becoming a Trend Trunk member is simple and can be done through Facebook or Twitter or directly on the website. Once you are a Trend Trunk member, selling and buying is simple and fun. Take a few pictures of your preloved but now unwanted items, upload the pictures, enter a description, and set your selling price. This is all made extremely user-friendly through Trend Trunk's simple-to-follow and prescriptive selling instruction page. After this process is complete, you have an online *closet* within which your new or preloved clothes are available for purchase. Buyers can ask you questions about the clothes you have in your closet and even negotiate price. Once a buyer has agreed to purchase an item in your closet, Trend Trunk takes care of everything else. A Canada Post trackable, prepaid, pre-addressed shipping label is emailed, so you just print, pack, and ship. Upon confirmation of delivery, Trend Trunk deposits 80 percent of the selling price in your Trend Trunk account, which you can then transfer to your bank account or use to go on your own shopping spree in any closets you have added to your Trend Trunk Lust List. Trend Trunk's online platform incorporates social features to let shoppers see what closets their friends are shopping in and what they are liking and buying. Trend Trunk is integrated with Facebook, Twitter, and Pinterest to help build awareness of the service in the marketplace and to keep users engaged.

Trend Trunk is focused on fashionable and trendy women ages 18 to 40. This is a tough segment to market to and an even tougher segment to convert to online shopping. Many in this group have an inherent fear of online shopping, particularly as it relates to online payment, and a belief that participating as a seller in an online marketplace requires time and tech-savviness.

Trend Trunk is dealing with a dual marketplace; it is dependent on sellers for their inventory and needs buyers to stay engaged. Trend Trunk must keep sellers involved to have them keep their clothing and accessories up long enough for buyers to browse, compare, discuss, and buy. In addition, Trend Trunk is dependent on the sellers not just for the quantity of merchandise that is uploaded for sale but also for the quality of that merchandise. As in bricks-and-mortar stores, the quality of the inventory and the inventory turnover rate are key to keeping the customer engaged and loyal.

Competition is strong for online shopping in Canada, with sites such as Amazon.ca, eBay, and Etsy, to name a few. Online shopping in Canada is expected to grow significantly over the next few years as bricks-and-mortar retailers concentrate on their online strategies, integrating online and in-store retailing into a seamless shopping experience. This change will increase competition for Trend Trunk but will also increase consumers' confidence in this form of shopping.

Trend Trunk wants to ensure the customer experience is satisfactory in both the buyer and seller marketplace so that the consumers will stay loyal.

To enhance the *seller* experience, Trend Trunk launched Runway Valet, **www.trendtrunk.com/RunwayValet**, a nationwide network of stylists who are also independent business owners. They offer the service of selling Trend Trunk members' clothing and accessories for them for a percentage of each sale. Trend Trunk members choose from among local stylists listed on the Trend Trunk website, contact the stylist, and establish a working relationship. Because they are independent business owners, it is in the stylists' best interests to become experts at their craft. They become proficient at merchandising; they understand how to take pictures of the clothing to enhance its saleability; and they quickly learn what will sell and what won't sell. In essence, they become inventory managers, ultimately helping to manage the inventory-quality issue for Trend Trunk.

The perceived value of Trend Trunk as a shopping destination and the engagement of the *buyer* are driven by the "freshness" of the merchandise. To this end, Trend Trunk launched Shoppes at Trend Trunk, **www.trendtrunk.com/shoppes**, a featured selection of co-branded boutiques from unique designers. The Shoppes at Trend Trunk ensure new and unique merchandise is available for shoppers and give designers an easy option for marketing their designs

Canadian women are by nature slightly more philanthropic than men. Giving to charities is positively influenced by the convenience of giving.[3] Trend Trunk makes it very simple for the buyer to make a charitable donation through Closets and Causes, **www.trendtrunk.com/fundraising**. Closets and Causes is crowdfunding with clothing, allowing the seller to choose from any charity in Canada to donate up to 100 percent of the proceeds of the sale to the charity.

Like any startup, Trend Trunk is resource and capital strapped. Growing the business through attracting more shoppers within the target market takes marketing money. Trend Trunk has been featured on *Dragons' Den*, **(www.cbc.ca/dragonsden/pitches/trend-trunk)** and was able to leverage that into great publicity. The company also won marketing and strategic services from Lion's Lair 2013 **(http://lionslair.ca)**, but actual cash to invest in marketing is in short supply.

Fashion is heavily influenced by perceived experts. Women devour fashion magazines in an attempt to learn about coming trends. Fashion magazines are key influences on fashion purchases but advertising in such magazines is prohibitively expensive for Trend Trunk. How do they reach fashion-conscious women, and how can they reach key influencers? In the social marketplace in which Trend Trunk operates, fashion bloggers are highly influential and have access to a large social network. Trend Trunk saw these bloggers as a key opportunity area and participated in a blogger trade show that exposed them to many bloggers. Like Trend Trunk, bloggers want enhanced engagement by their target audience, more subscribers, and compensation for promotion on their blog. Trend Trunk did not have the money, but they did have a way for the bloggers to increase engagement. The result was the launch of Trend Trunk Blogger Fashion Week, a seven-day online event in which established and emerging fashion bloggers had a chance to feature their clothing styles and blog to their community. Blogger Fashion Week featured 10 bloggers each day who showcased their personal styles to Trend Trunk members, while at the same time earning money by selling their own preloved items. The result was that Trend Trunk was featured on over 70 blogs during that week and received media attention from *Fashion* magazine (**www.fashionmagazine.com/fashion/2013/12/13/ trend-trunk-blogger-fashion-week/**).

While Trend Trunk has creatively solved key issues in their competitive marketplace, such creativity must continue. For Trend Trunk, it is the classic "how to be a bigger fish in a very large pond"—a pond that is projected to grow exponentially. How can Trend Trunk continue to meet the needs of this dual marketplace, build awareness of its product, and grow the business in the future?

QUESTIONS

1. **Complete a SWOT analysis for Trend Trunk.**

2. **Complete some research on your own to better understand the segment of the market that Trend Trunk is appealing to.**

3. **Based on your SWOT and segment analyses, recommend an integrated communications plan for Trend Trunk to build awareness of the business and sustain the target consumers' interest.**

4. **Trend Trunk innovatively line-extended to solve key issues and to keep the service unique. Closets for Causes is a creative solution, but it isn't achieving the level of donations for charities that Trend Trunk thought it would. Recommend a plan to increase the Closets for Causes participation rate and donation amount.**

Chapter 19

Customer Relationship Management (CRM)

iStock/Thinkstock

"There is only one boss. The customer. And he can fire everybody in the company from the chairman down, simply by spending his money somewhere else."[1]

—Sam Walton (founder of Walmart)

After you finish this chapter, go to www.nelson.com/student *for* **STUDY TOOLS**. ☐ - - - - - →

19-1 WHAT IS CUSTOMER RELATIONSHIP MANAGEMENT?

Customer relationship management (CRM) is not a new term or trend. If done right, it is not a gimmick or a fad. *CRM* is a term that is often buried in a marketing textbook, somewhere in the middle or as part of another chapter. But if understood properly, CRM can provide needed context for understanding how everything you have read so far fits together.

If we go back to Chapter 1, you will recall that marketing is about meeting the needs of customers. To do this, you must learn more about your customer by doing research, learning about customers' behaviours, segmenting them, and delivering something of value (the four Ps) to them. In the previous chapters we have discussed the tools that help us better understand the customer. What is left now is to bring those tools together into one focused objective. And that objective is customer relationship management. CRM is about building customer loyalty and retaining those valued customers. It is about delivering on the promises made and establishing a system that will continue to deliver over time. To return to another concept we've looked at in this book, CRM is about *interaction* with your customer over the long term, not just tracking transactions over the short term.

This leads us to an important statement: CRM is not just about tracking customer information. If you were to do an Internet search for "customer relationship management," you might get the impression that CRM is about building a computer system that captures information about your customers. In fact, in the 1990s and early 2000s, companies created information

customer relationship management (CRM) a system that gathers information about customers that can help to build customer loyalty and retain those loyal customers

systems that were referred to as "CRM systems." These systems were costly, and most firms could not find the value in using IT systems to create better customer relationships. Faith in IT-based CRM solutions wavered as sales of CRM systems were drastically reduced in the early 2000s. Some saw CRM as just "another overhyped IT investment."[2]

While IT is part of the development of a strong CRM program, information about customers is useless without knowing how to attract and keep those customers over the long term. In the end, the value is not how much you can squeeze out of each customer through a computer program—the value is in developing a customer who will be investing in maintaining a mutually beneficial interaction.

19-1a The Other CRM

As mentioned, there is an emphasis in customer relationship management on the hardware and software needed to gather consumer information. In fact, this focus on database creation is another CRM abbreviation—customer relationship *marketing*.

The two CRMs have seemingly been melded together by most companies; however, it is important to understand the difference between the two. Customer relationship marketing is more focused on acquiring the necessary hardware and software to create a database or system to gather and track customer information. Customer relationship management is an overall company strategy that a firm employs to understand the needs of customers, keep updated on their needs, and satisfy them over the long term. The heavy emphasis on technology in customer relationship management is understandable given the goals of trying to track customers down to an individual level, but it is still important to remember that this process has to be managed and assessed.

19-2 THE CRM CYCLE

In its 2010 report on CRM, *State of Customer Relationship Management*, the Government of Canada presented a three-step CRM cycle: (1) marketing and market research, (2) business development, and (3) customer feedback (Exhibit 19.1). This comprehensive assessment of a CRM system was based on a seminal article in the *Harvard Business Review* on CRM in 2004, right after the downfall of IT-based CRM systems in the early 2000s.

CRM has often been described as a closed-loop system that builds relationships with customers. However, too often CRM has been reduced to a tool for selling software that promises to identify customers and provide information at a microscopic level. Little thought was given to using

CRM—THE "WHOLE" SALE

In 2010, the Government of Canada released a report entitled *State of Customer Relationship Management*. The report focused on CRM being a "technology-driven" process but also presented CRM as a "valuable core business function" and highlighted the investment made in CRM in a given year ($106 billion in 2009) and the related employment for CRM-related services (502,000 people). What industry uses CRM the most? Wholesaling. This finding makes sense. As you will recall from Chapter 13, wholesalers are tasked with representing manufacturers' products,

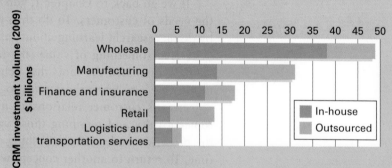

so they need to search for channels in which to do so. Identifying potential customers at the individual level (CRM) is clearly a valuable tool for wholesalers.

Industry Canada, *State of Customer Relationship Management: The Canadian Report 2010*, www.ic.gc.ca/eic/site/si-is.nsf/vwapj/ai00001_eng.pdf/$FILE/ai00001_eng.pdf. Reproduced with the permission of the Minister of Industry, 2014.

Exhibit 19.1

THE CRM CYCLE

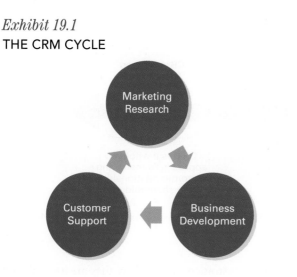

CRM as a tool to build long-term relationships with customers.

At its core, CRM is a relationship-building tool, and the sections that follow explain each stage of the CRM cycle. Stage 1 requires that companies understand what they have to offer to their customers and the marketing and market research tools that can help them use the four Ps. Stage 2 focuses on the use of technology to systematically identify customers, gather information on them, and store that information. Finally, in Stage 3 companies look at ways to use the information about customers to retain them in the long term by satisfying their needs.

Stage 2 of the CRM cycle includes many of the CRM tools and concepts a firm offering these types of solutions to companies would use. However, without an understanding of the context in Stage 1 and the ramifications of those CRM tools in Stage 3, CRM is a one-sided effort that lacks cooperation and inclusion of a most vital component—the customer.

19-3 THE CRM CYCLE—STAGE 1 (MARKETING RESEARCH)

During the first stage of creating a CRM system, companies must create an offering. This can be a product or service (or some combination of the two) that satisfies a customer need. Here is where marketing research can be helpful. As you recall from Chapter 5, conducting marketing research can help to identify customer needs, helping the marketer better understand the external marketplace where the company's offering will be sold.

Tools such as surveys, customer panels, and competitive intelligence are all helpful devices during this first stage for understanding the consumer and the marketplace. Product development and design (see Chapters 9 and 10) are also part of this initial stage, as companies develop ideas and concepts to prepare them for commercialization.

Companies should collect as much information as possible about the market and customer during this process. This will ensure that the offering supplied by the company reflects the current needs of customers. Companies can then make the right decisions about price (Chapter 12), place (Chapters 13 and 14), and promotion (Chapters 15 to 18) to provide an offering with the greatest opportunity for success in the marketplace.

Essentially, the first stage of developing a proper CRM system involves using the tools and techniques you learned about in the previous chapters. By creating an offering that reflects and satisfies customer needs, a company will develop a wholistic CRM system. The data acquired through various IT methods (discussed in the section on Stage 2) will only be as useful as the marketing strategies created by a firm that truly understands what marketing is about.

An article in the *Journal of Marketing* identified the qualities necessary for an effective CRM program: "CRM provides enhanced opportunities to use data and information to both understand customers and co-create value with them. This requires a cross-functional integration of processes, people, operations, and marketing capabilities that is enabled through information, technology, and applications."[3] The article also provided a continuum of CRM programs similar to the one shown in Exhibit 19.2.

The continuum highlights the importance of developing a CRM system that not only is technology based but also considers strategy and marketing. By using what is known about marketing, from marketing research through to the four Ps, companies can establish the foundation for an effective CRM program. Once these foundations are created, the technology can be introduced. And that is what the second stage of the CRM cycle is all about.

Exhibit 19.2

THE CRM CONTINUUM

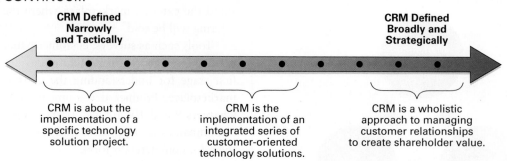

CRM Defined Narrowly and Tactically

CRM Defined Broadly and Strategically

CRM is about the implementation of a specific technology solution project.

CRM is the implementation of an integrated series of customer-oriented technology solutions.

CRM is a wholistic approach to managing customer relationships to create shareholder value.

Republished with permission of the American Marketing Association, from Adrian Payne, Pennie Frow (2005) A Strategic Framework for Customer Relationship Management. *Journal of Marketing*: October 2005, Vol. 69, No. 4, pp. 167–176; permission conveyed through Copyright Clearance Center, Inc.

19-4 THE CRM CYCLE—STAGE 2 (BUSINESS DEVELOPMENT)

Now that an offering has been developed that satisfies an identified customer need, the technology tools can be unleashed to seek out more detailed information on these customers. Exhibit 19.3 provides a flow model of the process of the technology stage of the CRM cycle.

To initiate Stage 2 of CRM cycle, a company must first *identify customer relationships with the organization*. This step may simply involve learning who the

Exhibit 19.3

A SIMPLE FLOW MODEL OF THE CUSTOMER RELATIONSHIP MANAGEMENT SYSTEM

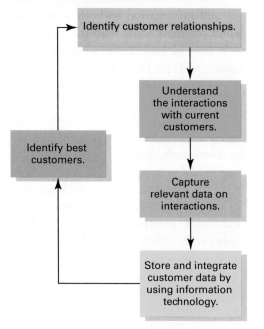

Identify customer relationships.

Understand the interactions with current customers.

Identify best customers.

Capture relevant data on interactions.

Store and integrate customer data by using information technology.

company's customers are or where they are located, or it may require more detailed information about the products and services these customers are using. Bridgestone Canada Inc., a tire service company that produces Firestone tires, uses a CRM system called OnDemand5, which initially gathers data from a point-of-sale interaction.[4] The information includes basic demographic information, the frequency of consumers' purchases, how much they purchase, and how far they drive.

Next, the company must *understand its interactions with current customers*. Companies accomplish this task by collecting data on all types of communications a customer has with the company. Using its OnDemand5 system, Bridgestone Canada Inc. can add information that is based on additional interactions with the consumer, such as multiple visits to a physical store location and purchasing history. In this phase, companies build on the initial information collected and develop a more useful database.

Using this knowledge of its customers and their interactions, the company then *captures relevant customer data on interactions*. As an example, Bridgestone/Firestone can collect such relevant information as the date of the last communication with a customer, how often the customer makes purchases, and whether the customer has redeemed coupons sent through direct mail.

How can marketers realistically analyze and communicate with individual customers? The answer lies in how information technology is used to implement the CRM system. Fundamentally, a CRM approach is no more than the relationship cultivated by a salesperson with the customer. A successful salesperson builds a relationship over time, constantly thinks about what the customer needs and wants, and is mindful of the trends and patterns in the customer's purchase history. The salesperson may also inform,

"How you GATHER, MANAGE *and* USE *information will determine whether you win or lose."*[5]

—Bill Gates

data mining an analytical process that compiles actionable data on the purchase habits of a firm's current and potential customers

customer-centric a philosophy under which the company customizes its product and service offerings based on data generated through interactions between the customer and the company

educate, and instruct the customer about new products, technology, or applications in anticipation of the customer's future needs or requirements.

This kind of thoughtful attention is the basis of successful IT CRM flow systems. Information technology is used not only to enhance the collection of customer data but also to *store and integrate customer data* throughout the company and, ultimately, to get to know customers on a personal level. Customer data are the first-hand responses obtained from customers through investigation or by asking direct questions. These initial data, which might include individual answers to questionnaires, responses on warranty cards, or lists of purchases recorded by electronic cash registers, have not yet been analyzed or interpreted.

The value of customer data depends on the system that stores the data and the consistency and accuracy of the data captured. Obtaining high-quality, actionable data from various sources is a key element in any CRM system. Bridgestone Canada Inc. accomplishes this task by managing all information in a central database accessible by marketers. Different kinds of database management software are available, from extremely high-tech, expensive, custom-designed databases to standardized programs.

Every customer wants to be a company's main priority, but not all customers are equally important in the eyes of a business. Consequently, the company must identify *its profitable and unprofitable customers*. The Pareto principle (the 80/20 rule mentioned in Chapter 8) indicates that 80 percent of a business's profit comes from 20 percent of its customers.

Data mining is an analytical process that compiles actionable data on the purchase habits of a firm's current and potential customers. Essentially, data mining transforms customer data into customer information that a company can use to make managerial decisions. Bridgestone Canada Inc. uses OnDemand5 to analyze its data to determine which customers qualify for the MasterCare Select program.

Once customer data are analyzed and transformed into usable information, the information must be *leveraged*. The CRM system sends the customer information to all areas of a business because the ultimately customer interacts with all aspects of the business. Essentially, the company is trying to enhance customer relationships by getting the right information to the right person in the right place at the right time.

Bridgestone Canada Inc. uses the information in its database to develop different marketing campaigns for each type of customer. Customers are also targeted with promotions aimed at increasing their store visits, upgrading their tires to higher-end models, and encouraging their purchases of additional services. Since the company customized its mailings to each type of customer, visits to stores have increased by more than 50 percent.[6]

19-4a Identify Customer Relationships

Companies that have a CRM system follow a customer-centric focus or model. Being **customer-centric** refers to an internal management philosophy similar to the marketing concept discussed in Chapter 1. Under this philosophy, the company customizes its product and service offerings based on data generated through interactions between the customer and the company. This philosophy transcends all functional areas of the business, producing an internal system where all of the company's decisions and actions are a direct result of customer information.

A customer-centric company builds long-lasting relationships by focusing on what satisfies and retains valuable customers. For example, Sony PlayStation's website (**www.playstation.ca**) focuses on learning, customer knowledge management, and empowerment to market its PlayStation gaming entertainment systems. The website offers online shopping, opportunities to try new games, customer support, and information on news, events, and promotions. The interactive features include online gaming and message boards.

The PlayStation site is designed to support Sony's CRM system. When PlayStation users want to access amenities on the site, they are required to log in and supply information, such as their name, email address, and birthdate. Users can opt to fill out a survey that asks questions about the types of computer entertainment systems they own, how many games are owned for each console, expected future game purchases, time spent playing games, types of games played, and level of Internet connectivity. Armed with this information, Sony marketers are then able to tailor the site, new games, and PlayStation hardware to the players' replies to the survey and their use of the website.[7]

Customer-centric companies continually learn ways to enhance their product and service offerings. **Learning** in a CRM environment involves the informal process of collecting customer information through comments and feedback on product and service performance.

Each unit of a business typically has its own way of recording what it learns and may even have its own customer information system. The departments' different interests make it difficult to pull all the customer information together in one place using a common

Barone Firenze/Shutterstock.com

format. To overcome this problem, companies using CRM rely on **knowledge management**, a process by which learned information from customers is centralized and shared to enhance the relationship between customers and the organization. Information collected includes experiential observations, comments, customer actions, and qualitative facts about the customer.

Empowerment involves delegating authority to solve customers' problems quickly, usually by the first person who learns of the problem. In other words, **empowerment** is the latitude organizations give their representatives to negotiate mutually satisfying commitments with customers. Usually, organizational representatives are able to make changes during interactions with customers through email or by phone, or face to face.

An **interaction** occurs when a customer and a company representative exchange information and develop learning relationships. With CRM, the customer, and not the organization, defines the terms of the interaction, often by stating his or her preferences. The organization responds by designing products and services around customers' desired experiences. For example, students in Canada can purchase the Student Price Card, a loyalty card, for a nominal fee and use it to obtain discounts from affiliated retailers, such as Aéropostale, Foot Locker, Puma, and Forever 21. Student Advantage tracks the cardholders' spending patterns and behaviours to gain a better understanding of what student customers want. Student Advantage then communicates this information to the affiliated retailers, who can tailor their discounts to meet students' needs.[8]

The success of CRM—building lasting and profitable relationships—can be directly measured by the effectiveness of the interaction between the customer

EMPOWERMENT *involves* DELEGATING AUTHORITY *to solve customers' problems quickly.*

and the organization. In fact, CRM is further differentiated from other strategic initiatives by the organization's ability to establish and manage interactions with its current customer base. The more latitude (empowerment) a company gives its representatives, the more likely the interaction will conclude in a way that satisfies the customer.

19-4b Understand Interactions of the Current Customer Base

The *interaction* between the customer and the organization is the foundation on which a CRM system is built. Only through effective interactions can organizations learn about the expectations of their customers, generate and manage knowledge about customers, negotiate mutually satisfying commitments, and build long-term relationships.

Exhibit 19.4 illustrates the customer-centric approach for managing customer interactions. Following a customer-centric approach, an interaction can occur through a formal or direct communication channel, such as a phone, the Internet, or a salesperson. Any activity or touch point a customer has with an organization, either directly or indirectly, constitutes an interaction.

Companies that effectively manage customer interactions recognize that customers provide data to

touch points all possible areas of a business where customers have contact with that business

point-of-sale interactions communications between customers and organizations that occur at the point of sale, usually in a store

the organization that affect a wide variety of touch points. In a CRM system, **touch points** are all possible areas of a business where customers have contact with that business and data might be gathered. Touch points might include a customer registering for a particular service; a customer communicating with customer service for product information; a customer making direct contact electronically via QR code, email, or website visit; a customer completing and returning the warranty information card for a product; or a customer talking with salespeople, delivery personnel, and product installers. Data gathered at these touch points, once interpreted, provide information that affects touch points inside the company. Interpreted information may be redirected to marketing research to develop profiles of extended warranty purchasers; to production to analyze recurring problems and repair components; and to accounting to establish cost-control models for repair service calls.

Web-based interactions are an increasingly popular touch point for customers to communicate with companies on their own terms. Web users can evaluate and purchase products, make reservations, input preferential data, and provide customer feedback on services and products. Data from these Web-based interactions are then captured, compiled, and used to segment customers, refine marketing efforts, develop new products, and deliver a degree of individual customization to improve customer relationships.

Another touch point is **point-of-sale interactions**, communications between customers and organizations that occur at the point of sale, usually in a store but also at information kiosks. Many point-of-sale software packages enable customers to easily provide information about themselves without feeling violated. The information is then used in two ways: for marketing and merchandising activities, and for accurately identifying the store's best customers and the types of products they buy. Data collected at point-of-sale interactions is also used to increase customer satisfaction through the development of in-store services and customer recognition promotions.

Exhibit 19.4

CUSTOMER-CENTRIC APPROACH FOR MANAGING CUSTOMER INTERACTIONS

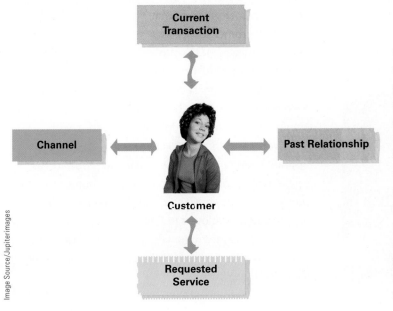

Image Source/Jupiterimages

POINT-OF-SALE INTERACTIONS ENABLE CUSTOMERS TO PROVIDE INFORMATION ABOUT THEMSELVES.

Digital Vision/Getty Images

19-4c Capture Customer Data

Vast amounts of data can be obtained from the interactions between an organization and its customers. Therefore, in a CRM system, the issue is not how much data can be obtained, but rather what types of data should be acquired and how the data can effectively be used for relationship enhancement.

The traditional approach for acquiring data from customers is through channel interactions. Channel interactions include store visits, conversations with salespeople, interactions via the Web, traditional phone conversations, and wireless communications. In a CRM system, channel interactions are viewed as prime information sources that are based on the channel selected to initiate the interaction rather than on the data acquired. For example, if a consumer logs on to the Sony website to find out why a Sony device is not functioning properly and the answer is not available online, the consumer is then referred to a page where he or she can describe the problem. The website then emails the problem description to a company representative, who will research the problem and reply via email. Sony continues to use the email mode of communication because the customer has established email as the preferred method of contact.[9]

Interactions between the company and the customer facilitate the collection of large amounts of data. Companies can obtain not only simple contact information (name, address, phone number) but also

MEMBERSHIP HAS ITS PRIVILEGES

The British Columbia Automobile Association (BCAA) offers its members a wide variety of services, such as insurance, roadside assistance, travel planning, and savings and rewards. To offer its services effectively, BCAA asks for and collects basic information from its members, including name, address, and age. But BCAA goes beyond this basic contact information to acquire client information related to life-stage and behavioural patterns, which can include information related to past trips, services used, and level of satisfaction. This information led BCAA to develop a Voice of the Customer program that includes customer service as one of its metrics. BCCA also integrates these measures into its employee compensation program. The result has been both greater focus on customer centricity among employees and greater employee satisfaction with their workplace. In both 2012 and 2013, BCAA Home Insurance was ranked by J.D. Power and Associates as "highest in customer satisfaction among home insurance providers in Western Canada." BCAA was named as one of the 50 best employers in Canada for five years in a row (2007–2011) by international human resources consultants Hewitt Associates and *The Globe and Mail's Report on Business* magazine.

Courtesy of J.D Power and Associates

Courtesy of British Columbia Automobile Association

Sources: "BCAA Recognized as One of Canada's 50 Best Employers," BCCA, October 20, 2011, www.bcaa.com/learning-centre/bcaa-newsroom/news-releases/10-20-2011-bcaa-50-best-employers (accessed August 24, 2014); and "Bringing It Home, 3 Times in a Row," BCCA, 2014, www.bcaa.com/insurance/rd/jd-power-award (accessed August 24, 2014).

data pertaining to the customer's current relationship with the organization—past purchase history, quantity and frequency of purchases, average amount spent on purchases, sensitivity to promotional activities, and so forth.

In this manner, much information can be captured from one individual customer across several touch points. Multiply this information by the thousands of customers across all the touch points within an organization, and the volume of data that company personnel deal with can rapidly become unmanageable. The large volumes of data resulting from a CRM initiative can be managed effectively only through technology. Once customer data are collected, the question of who owns those data becomes extremely salient. In its privacy statement, Toysmart.com declared it would never sell information registered at its website, including children's names and birthdates, to a third party. However, when the company filed for bankruptcy protection in the United States, it said the information collected constituted a company asset that needed to be sold to pay creditors. Despite the outrage at this announcement, many dot-com companies closing their doors found they had little in the way of assets and followed Toysmart's lead. In Canada, the Personal Information Protection and Electronic Documents Act (PIPEDA), which deals with the protection of personal information, specifies only that disclosure must be made when third parties have access to personal information. PIPEDA does not address the selling of the information as a business asset (see the box for more information on PIPEDA).

19-4d Store and Integrate Customer Data

Customer data are only as valuable as the system in which they are stored and their consistency and

PIPEDA—PERCEPTION OF PRIVACY?

PIPEDA (the Personal Information Protection and Electronic Documents Act) is not a well-known acronym, but it is an important piece of legislation that affects all Canadians. Signed into law in 2001 with much fanfare, PIPEDA sets out the rules for companies on how they can use information customers supply when they buy something or enter a contest or other promotion. The act was brought in to deal with the ever-increasing volume of Canadians' personal information online. Through PIPEDA, you can request to see what personal information about you is possessed by an organization with which you have had dealings, and even launch a complaint if a company violates the terms of PIPEDA. In 2013, the Privacy Commissioner of Canada (OPC) wrote a report that stated that most Canadian firms do not have the necessary tools to protect the personal information that falls under PIPEDA. The OPC noted that there is not enough enforcement and reporting of information breaches by companies, and it is pushing for legislation to strengthen PIPEDA. However, Parliament did not pass a bill in fall 2013 that would have required notification of a breach of personal information. In December 2013, Jennifer Stoddart

"OF COURSE I VALUE MY PRIVACY...THAT'S WHY I ONLY SHARE MY PERSONAL INFORMATION WITH 700 OF MY CLOSEST FRIENDS! "

Office of the Privacy Commissioner of Canada, https://www.priv.gc.ca/information/illustrations/illust_06_e.asp.

stepped down from her position as federal privacy commissioner. Coincidence? There is no information to prove or disprove it.

Sources: "A Guide for Individuals: Protecting Your Privacy: An Overview of the Office of the Privacy Commissioner of Canada and Federal Privacy Legislation," Office of the Privacy Commissioner of Canada, March 2014, www.priv.gc.ca/information/02_05_d_08_e.asp (accessed August 24, 2014); "The Case for Reforming the Personal Information Protection and Electronic Documents Act," Office of the Privacy Commissioner of Canada, May 2013, www.priv.gc.ca/parl/2013/pipeda_r_201305_e.asp (accessed August 24, 2014); Gonzalo S. Zeballos, James A. Sherer, and Alan M. Pate, "Canada: International Privacy—2013 Year in Review," Mondaq, January 6, 2014, www.mondaq.com/canada/x/284326/data+protection/International+Privacy+2013+Year+in+Review+Canada (accessed August 24, 2014).

accuracy. Gathering data is complicated because data needed by one unit of the organization, such as sales and marketing, are often generated by another area of the business or even a third-party supplier, such as an independent marketing research firm. Thus, companies must use information technology to capture, store, and integrate strategically important customer information. This process of centralizing data in a CRM system is referred to as data warehousing.

A **data warehouse** is a central repository (*database*) of data collected by an organization. Essentially, it is a large computerized file of all information collected in the previous stage of the CRM process, for example, information collected in channel, transaction, and product or service touch points. The core of the data warehouse is the **database**, "a collection of data, especially one that can be accessed and manipulated by computer software."[10] The CRM database focuses on collecting vital statistics on consumers, their purchasing habits, transactions methods, and product usage in a centralized repository that is accessible by all functional areas of a company. By using a data warehouse, marketing managers can quickly access vast amounts of information to make decisions.

When a company builds its database, usually the first step is to develop a list. A **response list** is a customer list that includes the names and addresses of individuals who have responded to an offer of some kind, such as by mail, telephone, direct-response television, product rebates, contests or sweepstakes, or billing inserts. It can also be a compiled list, created by an outside company that has collected names and contact information for potential consumers. Response lists tend to be especially valuable because past behaviour is a strong predictor of future behaviour and because consumers who have indicated interest in the product or service are more likely to purchase in the future. **Compiled lists** usually are prepared by an outside company and are available for purchase. A compiled list is a customer list that was developed by gathering names and addresses gleaned

from telephone directories or membership rosters, sometimes enhanced with information from public records, such as census data, auto registrations, birth announcements, business startups, or bankruptcies. Lists range from those owned by large list companies, such as Dun & Bradstreet, for business-to-business data, and Cornerstone Group of Companies, for consumer lists, to small groups or associations that are willing to sell their membership lists. Data compiled by large data-gathering companies are usually very accurate.

In this phase, companies are usually collecting channel, transaction, product, and service information, such as stores, salespersons, communication channels, contacts in formation, relationships, and brands.

A customer database becomes even more useful to marketing managers when it is enhanced to include more than simply a customer's or prospect's name, address, telephone number, and transaction history. Database enhancement involves purchasing information on customers or prospects to better describe their needs or to determine how responsive they might be to marketing programs. Enhancement data typically include demographic, lifestyle, or behavioural information.

Database enhancement can increase the effectiveness of marketing programs. By learning more about their best and most profitable customers, marketers can maximize the effectiveness of their marketing communications and cross-selling. Database enhancement also helps a company find new prospects.

Multinational companies building worldwide databases often face difficult problems when pulling together internal data about their customers. Differences in language, computer systems, and data-collection methods can be huge obstacles to overcome. In spite of the challenges, many global companies are

committed to building databases. Bell Canada raised eyebrows in late 2013 with the announcement that Canada's largest telecommunications company would go mining for customer data. Specifically, Bell noted it will be tracking customer phone calls, app downloads, and television watching patterns. The reason? To create new profiles of customers that could then be used to entice advertisers with the opportunity to target specific Bell customers with promotional efforts. Then-privacy commissioner Jennifer Stoddart investigated Bell's move to see if it breached PIPEDA. In its defence, Bell noted it was following the lead of Google and Facebook in gathering customer information and tailoring ads for those customers. The difference? Google and Facebook don't charge for their services. Bell does. Big data is a big sell to companies, but not respecting consumer privacy could lead to big trouble.[11]

19-4e Identifying the Best Customers

CRM manages interactions between a company and its customers. To be successful, companies need to identify those customers who yield high profits or high potential profits. To identify these customers, significant amounts of data must be gathered from customers, stored and integrated in the data warehouse, and then analyzed and interpreted for common patterns that can identify homogeneous customers who differ from other customer segments. Because not all customers are the same, organizations need to develop interactions that target the top 20 percent high-value customers' wants and needs. Therefore, the question becomes how to identify these customers. In a CRM system, the answer is data mining.

DATA MINING Data mining is used to find hidden patterns and relationships in the customer data stored in the data warehouse. A data analysis approach identifies patterns of characteristics that

Donating is uplifting.

Much has been said about the privacy aspect of data mining and the potential impact on consumers and the security of their private information. But there are positive aspects of data mining, including helping nonprofit organizations. Manifold Data Mining, one of Canada's largest data-mining companies, has worked with nonprofit groups like the Red Cross and Centraide (United Way in Québec) to help them create more effective direct mail campaigns.

relate to particular customers or customer groups. Although businesses have been conducting such analyses for many years, the procedures typically were performed on small data sets containing as few as 300 to 400 customers. Today, with the development of sophisticated data warehouses, millions of customers' shopping patterns can be analyzed.

Using data mining, marketers can search the data warehouse, capture relevant data, categorize significant characteristics, and develop customer profiles. When using data mining, it is important to remember that the real value is in the company's ability to transform its data from operational bits and bytes into information marketers' need for successful marketing strategies. Companies must analyze the data to identify and profile the best customers, calculate their lifetime value, and ultimately predict purchasing behaviour through statistical modelling. London Drugs uses data mining to identify commonly purchased items that should be displayed together on shelves and to learn what pop sells best in different parts of the country.

Before the information is leveraged, several types of analysis are often run on the data. These analyses include customer segmentation, recency-frequency-monetary (RFM) analysis, lifetime value (LTV) analysis, and predictive modelling.

CUSTOMER SEGMENTATION
Recall that *customer segmentation* is the process of breaking large groups of customers into smaller, more homogeneous groups. This type of analysis generates a profile, or picture, of the customers' similar demographic, geographic, and psychographic traits, in addition to their previous purchase behaviour; it focuses particularly on the best customers. Profiles of the best customers can be compared and contrasted with other customer segments. For example, a bank can segment consumers on their frequency of usage, credit, age, and turnover.

Once a profile of the best customer is developed by using these

recency-frequency-
monetary (RFM)
analysis the analysis of
customer activity by recency,
frequency, and monetary value

lifetime value
(LTV) analysis
a data manipulation technique
that projects the future value of
the customer over a period of
years by using the assumption
that marketing to repeat customers is more profitable than
marketing to first-time buyers

predictive model-
ling a data manipulation
technique in which marketers
try to determine, based on
some past set of occurrences,
the odds that some other
occurrence, such as an inquiry
or a purchase, will take place
in the future

*"To write it, it took three months; to conceive it three minutes;
to* COLLECT THE DATA *in it all my life."*[12]

—F. Scott Fitzgerald (author of *The Great Gatsby*)

criteria, this profile can be used to screen other potential consumers. Similarly, customer profiles can be used to introduce customers selectively to specific marketing actions. For example, young customers with an open mind can be introduced to online banking. See Chapter 8 for a detailed discussion of segmentation.

RECENCY-FREQUENCY-MONETARY (RFM) ANALYSIS Recency-frequency-monetary (RFM) analysis

allows firms to identify customers who have purchased recently and often and who have spent considerable money, because they are most likely to purchase again (see Exhibit 19.5). Firms develop equations to identify their best customers (often the top 20 percent of the customer base) by assigning a score to their customer records in the database based on how often, how recently, and how much customers have spent. Customers are then ranked to determine which will move to the top of the list and which will fall to the bottom. The ranking provides the basis for maximizing profits by enabling the firm to use the information to select those persons who have proved to be good sources of revenue.

LIFETIME VALUE (LTV) ANALYSIS Recency,

frequency, and monetary data can also be used to create a lifetime value model on customers in the database. Whereas RFM looks at how valuable a customer currently is to a company, **lifetime value (LTV) analysis** projects the future value of the customer over a period of years. An example of LTV for a female 20 to 30 years old who has her hair done four times a year at an average cost of $120 per visit, given data-mined information of an average typical patronage life of five years, is $2400 ($120/visit × 4 visits/year × 5 years). One of the basic assumptions in any LTV calculation is that marketing to repeat customers is more profitable than marketing to first-time buyers. That is, it costs

more to find a new customer, in terms of promotion and gaining trust, than to sell more to a customer who is already loyal.

Customer lifetime value has numerous benefits. It shows marketers how much they can spend to *acquire* new customers, it tells them the level of spending to *retain* customers, and it facilitates targeting new customers who are identified as likely to be profitable. While these are strong benefits, LTV can be problematic if companies treat customers like the numbers that appear on the screen. While keeping customers is a noble goal, the reasons should go beyond the numbers, and companies should remember that they need specific systems in place (e.g., customer satisfaction measurement) to maintain a relationship over time.

PREDICTIVE MODELLING The ability to reasonably predict future customer behaviour gives marketers a significant competitive advantage. Through **predictive modelling**, a data manipulation technique, marketers try to determine, using a past set of occurrences, the odds that some other occurrence, such as an inquiry or a purchase, will take place in the future. SPSS Predictive Marketing is one tool marketers can use to answer questions about their consumers. The software requires minimal knowledge of statistical analysis. Users oper-

Exhibit 19.5

RFM ANALYSIS: ALL CUSTOMERS ARE NOT THE SAME

Best Customers	Average Customers	Poor Customers
High profit	Average profit	Low profit
Spent >$1500	Spent approximately $400	Spent <$100
Multiple purchases	Two purchases	One purchase
Purchase in past 6 months	Purchase in past 18 months	Purchase in past two years
Lifetime value = high	Lifetime value = average	Lifetime value = low
N = 2500 (18.5%)*	N = 4000 (29.6%)*	N = 7000 (51.9%)*
Total annual sales = $2.4 million	Total annual sales = $1.1 million	Total annual sales = $800,000

* *N* = number of customers in a category. The total number of customers is 13,500, and total annual sales are $4.3 million.
Source: From LAMB/HAIR/MCDANIEL/FARIA/WELLINGTON. *Marketing*, 4E. © 2008 Nelson Education Ltd. Reproduced by permission. www.cengage.com/permissions

*Marketing to repeat customers is more profitable than
marketing to first-time buyers.*

ate from a prebuilt model, which generates profiles in three to four days. SPSS also has an online product that predicts website users' behaviour.

19-5 THE CRM CYCLE— STAGE 3 (CUSTOMER FEEDBACK)

As is clear from Stage 2 of the CRM Cycle, technology is an important driver of a successful CRM system. However, an overreliance on technology and data down to the individual customer level can lead to companies losing sight of the real goal of customer relationship management—maintaining long-term relationships with those who buy the products and services.

As long as firms can see CRM as a means to build a relationship with customers, and not as a sales tool or technology solution, they will see the need to complete the cycle. This is done by implementing measures of customer satisfaction to establish whether what the firm is doing is meeting the needs of those customers.

In the *MIT Sloan Management Review*, an article entitled "Putting the 'Relationship' Back into CRM" highlighted some of the concerns over how firms use CRM. The authors came up with three ways the current practice of CRM is failing companies:[13]

1. **CRM programs focus too much on transactions and not on other aspects of the customer's life.**

2. **Relationships cannot be solely about achieving loyalty, and companies need to find multiple ways to retain their customers.**

BLACKBERRY—FIELD OF DREAMS

If you were to look at any business textbook written between 2004 and 2011, you would see at least some mention of Research In Motion and BlackBerry. The company was touted as an unbelievable success story. BlackBerrys were omnipresent, seen in the hands of world leaders (e.g., Barack Obama) and celebrities (e.g., Kim Kardashian). With a security system beyond reproach and a messaging system that was as simple as it was addictive, the BlackBerry and Research In Motion (RIM) had arrived. But now, look at the magazine photo showing a BlackBerry as another ancient relic. What went wrong? Among other things was RIM's lack of interest in researching and understanding customer needs. The BlackBerry was created to provide security and messaging—but what did consumers want? In 2007, research showed that consumers were looking for "candy bar phones" that would have a simple user interface and a single touchscreen. What did BlackBerry put out to market? The Pearl Flip—a flip phone that consumers were no longer interested in. A member of RIM's customer base management team noted the interaction

between the sales team that wanted the candy bar phone and the company's development team: "All the sales guys were like ... 'We asked you for big screens, touchscreens, more of these candy bar

styles.' And they were like 'Yeah, but we came up with this really cool technology about the hinge. Look at how this works!' There is probably still a warehouse full of them." In the end, customers stopped buying BlackBerrys, and app makers stopped producing applications for BlackBerry devices. There was never an attempt to evolve with customers and their changing needs. BlackBerry suffered from the "field of dreams" belief described in Chapter 1—if you build it, they will come. Soon customers might have to visit a museum to see what a BlackBerry looks like.

Source: Felix Gillette, Diane Brady, and Caroline Winter, "The Rise and Fall of BlackBerry: An Oral History," *BusinessWeek*, December 5, 2013, www.businessweek.com/articles/2013-12-05/the-rise-and-fall-of-blackberry-an-oral-history (accessed August 4, 2014)..

campaign management developing product or service offerings customized for the appropriate customer segment and then pricing and communicating these offerings to enhance customer relationships

3. A relationship is dynamic and two sided. It is not enough to get a list of customers and their spending habits. The relationship will evolve with each transaction, and CRM systems must as well.

This third concern is the most serious. If marketing is about understanding and meeting customer needs, it is important to appreciate that those needs and how to meet them will change over time. Any relationship (whether it's between a business and a consumer, a business and another business, or even between family members) involves a series of interactions. The relationship builds over time with more of these interactions. The needs of both parties change, and the other party has to be willing to adjust to those changes to be successful. Companies that ignore this do so at their own peril.

To create a two-sided relationship that focuses on more than just loyalty, companies must leverage the customer information they have gathered. While there is an adage that states keeping an existing customer is cheaper than finding a new customer, a CRM system has to have the ability to move beyond just finding those loyal customers. A company can undertake to best leverage the information gathered through the database and IT solutions from Stage 2. Some of the benefits that can be gained by gathering this information can be seen in Exhibit 19.6.

19-5a Leverage Customer Information

Data mining identifies the most profitable customers and prospects. Managers can then design tailored marketing strategies to best appeal to the identified segments. In CRM, this activity is commonly referred to as leveraging customer information to facilitate enhanced relationships with customers.

CAMPAIGN MANAGEMENT Through campaign management, all areas of the company participate in the development of programs targeted to customers. **Campaign management** refers to developing product or service offerings customized for the appropriate customer segment and then pricing and communicating these offerings to enhance customer relationships. It involves monitoring and leveraging

Exhibit 19.6

COMMON CRM MARKETING DATABASE APPLICATIONS

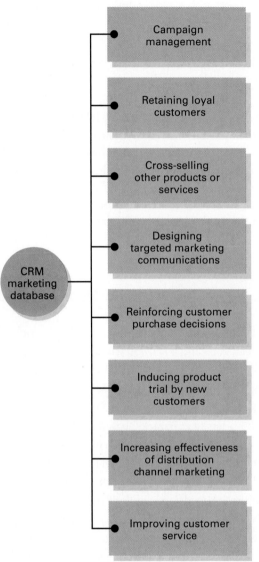

customer interactions to sell a company's products and to improve customer service. Campaigns are based directly on data obtained from customers through various interactions. Campaign management includes monitoring the success of the communications on the basis of customer reactions, such as customer inquiries, sales, orders, callbacks to the company, and the like. If a campaign appears unsuccessful, it is evaluated and changed to better achieve the company's desired objective.

Campaign management involves customizing product and service offerings, which requires managing multiple interactions with customers and giving priority to those products and services that are viewed as most desirable for a specifically designated customer. Even within a highly defined market segment, individual customer differences will emerge. Therefore, interactions among customers must focus on individual experiences, expectations, and desires.

RETAINING LOYAL CUSTOMERS
After a company has identified its best customers, it should make every effort to maintain and increase their loyalty. Loyalty programs reward loyal customers for making multiple purchases. The objective is to build long-term mutually beneficial relationships between a company and its key customers. Marriott, Hilton, and Starwood Hotels, for instance, reward their best customers with special perks not available to customers who stay less frequently. Travellers who spend a specified number of nights per year receive reservation guarantees, welcome gifts such as fruit baskets and wine in their rooms, and access to concierge lounges. Loyal members who sign up to collect points can use their accumulated points to receive discounts at hotels in exotic locations, free nights, free flights, and reduced rates on car rentals.

In addition to rewarding good customers, loyalty programs provide businesses with a wealth of information about their customers and shopping trends that can be used to make future business decisions. One of Canada's most successful loyalty programs is Shoppers Optimum, a membership program designed by retailer Shoppers Drug Mart. With over 9 million members, the Shoppers Optimum program allows customers to collect 10 points for every $1 spent. There are special sales where there are 20 times the points promotions on specific products, like fragrances and baby products. Customers can then redeem points to be used on future purchases

(e.g., 8000 points accrued can be turned into $10 off a future purchase). In late 2013, Shoppers Drug Mart teamed up with Montreal-based online retailer Beyond the Rack to create a new website devoted to Shoppers Optimum members. Those members who visit the site will have access to weekly offers that are exclusive to Shoppers Optimum members. As well, for every $1 spent at Beyond the Rack, Shoppers Optimum members will get 10 Optimum points.

CROSS-SELLING OTHER PRODUCTS AND SERVICES
CRM provides many opportunities to cross-sell related products. Marketers can use the database to match product profiles with consumer profiles, enabling the cross-selling of products that match consumers' demographic, lifestyle, or behavioural characteristics. Ingersoll Rand, a global manufacturer of everything from air compressors to refrigeration units, saw the benefits of cross selling. One of Ingersoll Rand's business units, Club Car, sells golf carts. The company soon found out that Club Car's customers were also potential customers in other areas, such as for excavators and loaders. Ingersoll Rand began to share information about customers across all of the more than 30 business units of the organization. In the first year of doing this, Ingersoll Rand brought in $6.2 million in incremental cross-selling revenue.[14]

Online firms use product and customer profiling to reveal cross-selling opportunities while a customer is surfing their site. Past purchases on a particular website and the website a surfer comes from provide online marketers with clues about the surfer's interests and what items to cross-sell. Similarly, profiles on customers enable sales representatives or customer service people to personalize their communications while the customer is shopping. Knowing a customer's past purchases and preferences can enable the employee to provide more advice or suggestions that fit with the customer's tastes.

DESIGNING TARGETED MARKETING COMMUNICATIONS
By using transaction and purchase data, a database allows marketers to track customers' relationships to the company's products and services and to then modify their marketing message accordingly. Kraft Foods teamed with a

Courtesy of Beyond The Rack

LOYAL CUSTOMERS CAN RECEIVE SPECIAL REWARDS!

supermarket chain to determine which advertising campaigns were most effective for frequent buyers of Kraft Macaroni & Cheese.[15]

Customers can also be segmented into infrequent users, moderate users, and heavy users. A segmented communications strategy can then be developed to target the customer segment. Communications to infrequent users might encourage repeat purchases through a direct incentive, such as a limited-time coupon or price discount. Communications to moderate users may use fewer incentives and more reinforcement of their past purchase decisions. Communications to heavy users would be designed around loyalty and reinforcement of the purchase rather than price promotions.

REINFORCING CUSTOMER PURCHASE DECISIONS

As you learned in Chapter 6, cognitive dissonance is the feeling consumers get when they recognize an inconsistency between their values and opinions and their purchase behaviour. In other words, they doubt the soundness of their purchase decision and feel anxious. CRM offers marketers an excellent opportunity to reach out to customers to reinforce the purchase decision. By thanking customers for their purchases and telling customers they are important, marketers can help cement a long-term, profitable relationship.

Updating customers periodically regarding the status of their order reinforces purchase decisions. Postsale emails also afford the chance to provide more customer service or cross-sell other products.

Campion Boats of Kelowna, British Columbia, builds custom pleasure and recreational sport fishing boats that can cost upward of $200,000 each. The company uses its website to monitor customer profiles, broadcast company information, and communicate with its dealers and customers worldwide. For example, it can post pictures of a purchaser's boat in progress, thus both reinforcing the buyer's decision and perception of the quality of the craftsmanship and reducing the customer's likelihood of having feelings of cognitive dissonance.[16]

INDUCING PRODUCT TRIAL BY NEW CUSTOMERS

Although significant time and money are expended on encouraging repeat purchases by the best customers, a marketing database is also used to identify new customers. Because a firm using a marketing database already has a profile of its best customers, it can easily use the results of modelling to profile potential customers. Bell Canada uses modelling to identify prospective residential and commercial telephone customers and successfully attract their business.

Marketing managers generally use demographic and behavioural data overlaid on existing customer data to develop a detailed customer profile that is a powerful tool for evaluating lists of prospects. For instance, if a firm's best customers are 35 to 50 years of age, live in suburban areas, and enjoy mountain climbing, the company can match this profile to prospects already in its database or to customers currently identified as using a competitor's product.

INCREASING EFFECTIVENESS OF DISTRIBUTION CHANNEL MARKETING
In Chapter 13, you learned that a marketing channel is a business structure of interdependent organizations, such as wholesalers and retailers, which move a product from the producer to the ultimate consumer. Most marketers rely on indirect channels to move their products to the end user. Thus, marketers often lose touch with customers as individuals because the relationship is really between the retailer and the consumers. Marketers in this predicament often view their customers as aggregate statistics because specific customer information is difficult to gather.

Using CRM databases, manufacturers now have a tool to gain insight into who is buying their products. Instead of simply unloading products into the distribution channel and leaving marketing and relationship building to dealers, auto manufacturers today are using websites to keep in touch with customers and prospects, to learn about their lifestyles and hobbies, to understand their vehicle needs, and to develop relationships in hopes these consumers will reward them with brand loyalty in the future. BMW and other vehicle manufacturers have databases filled with contact information on the millions of consumers who have expressed an interest in their products.

With many bricks-and-mortar stores setting up shop online, companies are now challenged to monitor the purchases of customers who shop both in-store and online. This concept is referred to as multichannel marketing. After Lands' End determined that multichannel customers are the most valuable, the company targeted marketing campaigns toward retaining these customers and increased sales significantly.

Companies are also using radio-frequency identification (RFID) technology to improve distribution.

Olay, a brand of Procter & Gamble, invites customers to join Club Olay, which offers special discounts, free samples, and the opportunity to purchase products before they are available in stores. But members are also able to communicate with the company by sharing their beauty secrets and entering various sweepstakes.

This technology uses a microchip with an antenna that tracks anything from a pop can to a car. A computer can locate the product usually within two metres of a scanner but new technology and applications can, in some situations, enable detection up to 20 metres. The main implication of this technology is that companies will enjoy a reduction both in theft and in loss of merchandise shipments and will always know where merchandise is in the distribution channel. Moreover, as this technology is further developed, marketers will be able to gather essential information related to product usage and consumption.[17]

IMPROVING CUSTOMER SERVICE CRM marketing techniques are increasingly being used to improve customer service. Many companies are using information and training webinars for their product or service to make personal contact with interested customers. Those interested in a topic are asked to register and provide a bit of information about themselves and their company's needs. Before or immediately after the webinar, a representative will contact them to answer questions and provide further information. Other companies, such as Canadian Tire, follow up customers' visits to the store with a call and a short survey to determine each customer's level of service satisfaction and whether any additional service is needed.

Albert Lozano/Shutterstock.com

19-6 PRIVACY CONCERNS AND CRM

Before rushing out to invest in a CRM system and build a database, marketers should consider consumers' reactions to the growing use of databases. Many customers are concerned about databases because of the potential for invasion of privacy. The sheer volume of information that is aggregated in databases makes this information vulnerable to unauthorized access and use. A fundamental aspect of marketing using CRM databases is providing valuable services to customers based on knowledge of what customers really value. It is critical, however, that marketers remember that these relationships should be built on trust. Although database technology enables marketers to compile ever-richer information about their customers that can be used to build and manage relationships, if these customers feel their privacy is being violated, then the relationship becomes a liability.

The popularity of the Internet for customer data collection and as a repository for sensitive customer data has alarmed privacy-minded customers. Online users complain loudly about being spammed, and Web surfers, including children, are routinely asked to divulge personal information to access certain screens or to purchase goods or services. Internet users are disturbed by the amount of information businesses collect on them as they visit various sites in cyberspace. Indeed, many users are unaware of how personal information is collected, used, and distributed. The government actively sells huge amounts of personal information to list companies. Consumer credit databases are often used by credit-card marketers to prescreen targets for solicitations. Online and off-line privacy concerns are growing and ultimately will have to be dealt with by businesses and regulators.

As we have discussed, privacy policies for Canadian companies are regulated by PIPEDA and the Privacy Act. But collecting data on consumers outside Canada is a different matter. For database marketers venturing beyond our borders, success requires careful navigation of foreign privacy laws. For example, under the European Union's European Data Protection Directive, any business that trades with a European organization must comply with the EU's rules for handling information about individuals or risk prosecution. More than 50 nations have developed, or are developing, privacy legislation. The EU nations have the strictest legislation regarding the collection and use of customer data, and other countries look to that legislation when formulating their policies.

GIGYA THINK YOU'D GET AWAY WITH IT?

Gigya is a California-based high-tech company that you have likely not heard of. The company offers what they call a "Consumer Management Suite" of services that help top brands (Pepsi and ABC are among their clients) connect with social media users. Essentially, Gigya lets customers easily register for an account on a company site or mobile app by using one or more of their existing social media identities. After a customer logs in socially, Gigya is able to help their clients gather information about consumers, which the client can then use to better understand its customer base and personalize brand experiences and marketing communications. But instead of trying to allay only social media and privacy concerns, Gigya has taken a much bolder step. In December 2012, Gigya rolled out its Social Privacy Certification program, which allows companies to assure consumers that they are following the industry best practices for managing consumer data mined from social media. Firms must pass a certification process to be able to display Gigya's SocialPrivacy™ Certification Seal. Specifically, Gigya lays out four Social Privacy™ principles that it requires all program participants to adhere to:

SocialPrivacy™
CERTIFIED by GIGYA

www.website.com adheres to the following with respect to your Social Login data and permissions:

✔ We will not sell your data or your friends' data
✔ We will not post on your behalf without your permission
✔ We will not send messages to your friends without your permission
✔ We will not spam you with unsolicited emails

Certified by GIGYA   Learn more

Courtesy of Gigya, Inc.

1. Companies will not sell social profile data of users or their friends to third parties.

2. Websites will not send private messages to friends of users.

3. Companies will not post social media network account details without written consent from users.

4. Companies will not engage in social media email campaigns without user permission.

10%
Percentage decrease in costs resulting from a 2 percent increase in customer retention

1.5 billion
Number of unique users per month that are connected through Gigya products[18]

90%
Percentage reduction in Research In Motion (BlackBerry) stock since 2009[19]

18 months
The time it takes companies to double the amount of customer information collected[20]

$332,000
Lifetime value of a loyal Cadillac customer

Managing the Customer Part 7 Case

DIY—NOT? Case

This is not your typical case. It is not going to be about you spending the next ten minutes reading a series of paragraphs on a company and then answering the required series of questions. It is not about sitting and pondering this case, wondering if it will be on your next exam. Nor is it about sitting in class and waiting (anxiously or not) to see if you will be called on.

This is a do-it-yourself (DIY) case: you will be asked to make decisions and fill in the information gaps. This is a case where you do some of the work while reading the case, gathering the pieces you will then use to help solve the case. Doing it yourself now will give you an idea of what it will be like when you move from the textbook world to the work world.

The scenario is as follows: you have been asked by a group of investors to help with a new business venture: a new airline in Canada. The group is working through yield management programs to handle flight scheduling. It has hired a firm to handle the necessary legal and accounting resources. Funding is being arranged through a network of investors and funding agencies.

But the marketing is where this group is lagging. You need to make some decisions right now to help give this group a better sense of the decisions to be made and the challenges ahead.

To better understand the industry, the investors have tasked you with researching the external trends that will impact their new venture. Use the lines below to research two significant trends. One source can be from the Internet; the other source must be a database at your school:

Trend #1: _____

_____

(Internet source: _____

_____)

Trend # 2: _____

_____

(Database source: _____

_____)

Next, in the space below, come up with a brand name and brandmark for this airline. The company wants to incorporate some element of Canada in the branding. (And Beaver Airlines and Moose Air are not feasible options!). Use the outline of the airplane below and add your brand name and brandmark:

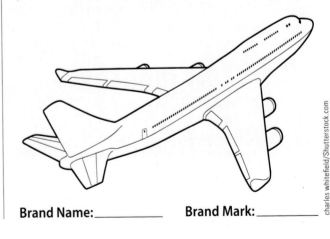

charles whitefield/Shutterstock.com

Brand Name: _____ **Brand Mark:** _____

The next step is to determine how to position this firm in the marketplace. The investor group is trying to find a niche in the Canadian market, buying locally made smaller airplanes and flying routes that larger firms might shy away from. While they are not willing to fly between two local airstrips, the group does want to find a way to fly between markets in Canada.

Your next task is to research flights between the airport closest to where you attend school and the next largest metropolitan area in Canada. Go onto the websites of at least two competitors in Canada and see what prices they charge for a flight leaving next Friday and returning on Sunday afternoon.

Price of competitor #1 (Name: _____):

$_____ [including all taxes]

Price of competitor #2 (Name: _____):

$_____ [including all taxes]

Now you are asked to set the price you would like to charge at your new airline. This cannot be arbitrary; it has to fit in with a pricing strategy and use one pricing tactic from your textbook.

Your price: $ _____

Name the pricing strategy used: _____

_____

Name the pricing tactic used: _____

_____

The investors are concerned about the proliferation of online travel booking websites and have asked you to come up with an argument for not using any intermediaries, like travel sites or travel agents. You will need to go back to your text and find two reasons from the material in Chapter 13 to justify this approach and two potential reasons not use a direct channel.

	Reason For	Reason Against
Direct Channel		
Indirect Channel		

Discussing the channels with the investment group later on raised the issue of the importance of a strategic social media presence, including websites, blogs, and networking sites. Before the group went too far down that path, you warned them that there was more to promotion than just an online presence.

You mention the promotional mix that would need to be created and that all six elements of this mix must be included. For each element in the chart below, write a 20-word description as it relates to your airline. Make sure that each description includes concrete actions you would take. To best fill in each box below, be sure to refer back to Chapters 15 through 18 and the details on each element of the promotional mix.

Advertising
Public Relations
Sales Promotion
Personal Selling
Direct Response
Social Media

Now that you have put in the time and researched all four Ps, you are ready to make some real decisions based on this case. The choices made above will determine how you create a SWOT analysis to better understand and analyze the new airline. Your choices in branding, pricing, channels, and promotion will help you to build a four-P strategy framework you can use to create alternative marketing opportunities.

Apply the questions below to the decisions you have made in this case.

QUESTIONS

1. **Complete a SWOT analysis by using the information provided in the case for the strengths and weaknesses, and then use the two trends you developed to create your opportunities and threats. Use no more than two points for each area of the SWOT.**

2. Given the focus of your new airline, create two market segments that could be targeted. Create the first segment as your present market, which is the group that you feel would be a significant user of your service. Your second segment should be a new market segment that you may not have thought of immediately when making decisions about your airline.

3. Use Ansoff's strategic opportunity matrix (Exhibit 3.3 in Chapter 3) to develop an alternative market for this case. Create a market penetration strategy by using your current market segment created in Question 2 and the airline as the present product. Next create market development strategy by using the new market segment created in Question 2, using the airline as the present product. When discussing these alternatives, be sure to use the four-P decisions you made while developing the case.

4. Based on the decisions you made during the case and your answers to Questions 1 through 3, you can now put together a customer relationship management (CRM) system for your airline. Use the three-stage CRM cycle model in this chapter as the structure for your CRM program. Use at least one tool from each of the cycle stages in developing a CRM program for your airline.

adopter a consumer who was happy enough with his or her trial experience with a product to use it again. p. 175

advergaming placing advertising messages in Web-based or video games to advertise or promote a product, a service, an organization, or an issue. p. 308

advertising impersonal, one-way mass communication about a product or an organization that is paid for by a marketer. p. 282

advertising appeal a reason for a person to buy a product. p. 301

advertising campaign a series of related advertisements focusing on a common theme, slogan, and set of advertising appeals. p. 300

advertising objective a specific communication task that a campaign should accomplish for a specified target audience during a specified period. p. 301

advertising response function a phenomenon in which spending for advertising and sales promotion increases sales or market share up to a certain level but then produces diminishing returns. p. 298

advocacy advertising a form of advertising in which an organization expresses its views on a particular issue or cause. p. 299

AIDA concept a model that outlines the process for achieving promotional goals in terms of stages of consumer involvement with the message; the acronym stands for *attention, interest, desire,* and *action.* p. 288

applied research an attempt by marketers to use research to develop new or improved products. p. 24

apps short for applications; free or purchased software programs that are downloaded to run on smartphones, tablet computers, and other mobile devices. p. 351

aspirational reference groups groups that an individual would like to join. p. 100

assurance the knowledge and courtesy of employees and their ability to convey trust. p. 185

atmosphere the overall impression conveyed by a store's physical layout, decor, and surroundings. p. 269

attitude a learned tendency to respond consistently toward a given object. p. 108

audience selectivity the ability of an advertising medium to reach a precisely defined market. p. 309

automatic vending the use of machines to offer goods for sale. p. 262

baby boomers people born between 1947 and 1965. p. 19

bait pricing a price tactic that tries to get consumers into a store through false or misleading price advertising and then uses high-pressure selling to persuade consumers to buy more expensive merchandise instead. p. 216

base price the general price level at which the company expects to sell the good or service. p. 210

basic research pure research that aims to confirm an existing theory or to learn more about a concept or phenomenon. p. 23

basing-point pricing charging freight from a given (basing) point, regardless of the city from which the goods are shipped. p. 212

belief an organized pattern of knowledge that an individual holds as true about his or her world. p. 108

benefit segmentation the process of grouping customers into market segments according to the benefits they seek from the product. p. 138

blogs publicly accessible Web pages that function as interactive journals, whereby readers can post comments on the authors' entries. p. 346

brainstorming the process of getting a group to think of unlimited ways to vary a product or solve a problem. p. 171

brand a name, term, symbol, design, or combination thereof that identifies a seller's products and differentiates them from competitors' products. p. 157

brand equity the value of company and brand names. p. 158

brand loyalty a consistent preference for one brand over all others. p. 158

brand mark the elements of a brand that cannot be spoken. p. 158

brand name that part of a brand that can be spoken, including letters, words, and numbers. p. 158

break-even analysis a method of determining what sales volume must be reached before total revenue equals total costs. p. 228

business analysis the second stage of the screening process, where preliminary figures for demand, cost, sales, and profitability are calculated. p. 171

business product a product used to manufacture other goods or services, to facilitate an organization's operations, or to resell to other customers. p. 152

business services complementary and ancillary actions that companies undertake to meet business customers' needs. p. 119

business-to-business (B2B) marketing the process of matching capabilities between two nonconsumer entities to create value for both organizations and the "customer's customer"; also referred to as *business marketing*. p. 111

buyer a department head who selects the merchandise for his or her department and may also be responsible for promotion and for personnel. p. 258

buyer for export an intermediary in the global market that assumes all ownership risks and sells globally for its own account. p. 58

buying centre all those people in an organization who become involved in the purchase decision. p. 122

campaign management developing product or service offerings customized for the appropriate customer segment and then pricing and communicating these offerings to enhance customer relationships. p. 372

cannibalization a situation that occurs when sales of a new product cut into sales of a firm's existing products. p. 142

capital intensive using more capital than labour in the production process. p. 50

cash cow in the portfolio matrix, a business unit that usually generates more cash than it needs to maintain its market share. p. 37

cash discount a price reduction offered to a consumer, an industrial user, or a marketing intermediary in return for prompt payment of a bill. p. 211

category killers specialty discount stores that heavily dominate their narrow merchandise segment. p. 261

causal research a type of conclusive research that focuses on the cause and effect of two variables and attempts to find some correlation between them. p. 71

cause-related marketing a type of sponsorship involving the association of a for-profit company with a nonprofit organization; through the sponsorship, the company's product or service is promoted, and money is raised for the nonprofit. p. 314

central-location telephone (CLT) facility a specially designed phone room used to conduct telephone interviewing. p. 77

chain stores stores owned and operated as a group by a single organization. p. 256

channel a medium of communication—such as a voice, radio, or newspaper—used for transmitting a message. p. 280

channel conflict a clash of goals and methods among distribution channel members. p. 246

channel control one marketing channel member intentionally affects another member's behaviour. p. 246

channel leader (channel captain) a member of a marketing channel who exercises authority and power over the activities of other channel members. p. 246

channel members all parties in the marketing channel that negotiate with one another, buy and sell products, and facilitate the change of ownership between buyer and seller

as they move the product from the manufacturer into the hands of the final consumer. p. 236

channel partnering (channel cooperation) the joint effort of all channel members to create a supply chain that serves customers and creates a competitive advantage. p. 247

channel power a marketing channel member's capacity to control or influence the behaviour of other channel members. p. 246

closed-ended question an interview question that asks the respondent to make a selection from a limited list of responses. p. 78

cobranding placing two or more brand names on a product or its package. p. 160

code of ethics a guideline to help marketing managers and other employees make better decisions. p. 30

cognitive dissonance the inner tension that a consumer experiences after recognizing an inconsistency between behaviour and values or opinions. p. 93

cold calling a form of lead generation in which the salesperson approaches potential buyers without any prior knowledge of the prospects' needs or financial status. p. 328

commercialization the decision to market a product. p. 174

communication the process by which we exchange or share meanings through a common set of symbols. p. 278

comparative advertising a form of advertising that compares two or more competing brands on one or more specific attributes. p. 300

Competition Bureau the federal department charged with administering most marketplace laws. p 24

competitive advantage the set of unique features of a company and its products that are perceived by the target market as significant and superior to the competition. p. 39

competitive advertising a form of advertising designed to influence demand for a specific brand. p. 300

compiled lists customer lists that are developed by gathering names and addresses gleaned from telephone directories and membership rosters, sometimes enhanced with information from public records, such as census data, auto registrations, birth announcements, business start-ups, or bankruptcies. p. 368

component lifestyles modes of living that involve choosing goods and services that meet one's diverse needs and interests rather than conforming to a single, traditional lifestyle. p. 16

computer-assisted personal interviewing technique in which the interviewer reads the questions from a computer screen and enters the respondent's data directly into a computer. p. 77

computer-assisted self-interviewing technique in which the respondent reads questions on a computer screen and directly keys his or her answers into a computer. p. 77

concentrated targeting strategy a strategy used to select one segment of a market to target marketing efforts. p. 141

concept test evaluation of a new-product idea, usually before any prototype has been created. p. 171

conclusive research a more specific type of research that attempts to provide clarity to a decision maker by identifying specific courses of action. p. 71

consumer behaviour how consumers make purchase decisions and how they use and dispose of purchased goods or services; also includes the factors that influence purchase decisions and product use. p. 89

consumer decision-making process a five-step process used by consumers when buying goods or services. p. 90

consumer product a product bought to satisfy an individual's personal wants. p. 152

consumer sales promotion sales promotion activities targeting the ultimate consumer. p. 320

consumer-generated content any form of publicly available online content created by consumers; also referred to as user-generated content. p. 286

continuous media schedule a media scheduling strategy in which advertising is run steadily throughout the advertising period; used for products in the later stages of the product life cycle. p. 310

contract manufacturing private-label manufacturing by a foreign company. p. 58

control provides the mechanisms both for evaluating marketing results in light of the plan's objectives and for correcting actions that do not help the organization reach those objectives within budget guidelines. p. 45

convenience product a relatively inexpensive item that merits little shopping effort. p. 152

convenience sample a form of nonprobability sample using respondents who are convenient, or readily accessible, to the researcher—for example, employees, friends, or relatives. p. 81

convenience store a miniature supermarket, carrying only a limited line of high-turnover convenience goods. p. 260

cooperative advertising an arrangement in which the manufacturer and the retailer split the costs of advertising the manufacturer's brand. p. 305

core competencies key unique strengths that are hard to imitate and underlie the functioning of an organization. p. 38

core service the most basic benefit the consumer is buying. p. 188

corporate or professional blogs blogs that are sponsored by a company or one of its brands and maintained by one or more of the company's employees. p. 346

corporate social responsibility a business's concern for society's welfare. p. 26

cost competitive advantage being the low-cost competitor in an industry while maintaining satisfactory profit margins. p. 39

cost per contact the cost of reaching one member of the target market. p. 309

countertrade a form of trade in which all or part of the payment for goods or services is in the form of other goods or services. p. 63

coupon a certificate that entitles consumers to an immediate price reduction when they buy the product. p. 321

coverage ensuring product availability in every outlet where potential customers might want to buy it. p. 245

credence quality a characteristic that consumers may have difficulty assessing even after purchase because they do not have the necessary knowledge or experience. p. 184

crisis management a coordinated effort to handle all the effects of either unfavourable publicity or an unexpected unfavourable event. p. 314

cross-tabulation a method of analyzing data that shows the analyst the responses to one question in relation to the responses to one or more other questions. p. 82

crowdsourcing the use of consumers to develop and market products. p. 338

culture the set of values, norms, attitudes, and other meaningful symbols that shape human behaviour and the artifacts, or products, of that behaviour as they are transmitted from one generation to the next. p. 96

cumulative quantity discount a deduction from list price that applies to the buyer's total purchases made during a specific period. p. 211

customer relationship management (CRM) a system that gathers information about customers that can help to build customer loyalty and retain those loyal customers. p. 359

customer satisfaction customers' evaluation of a good or service in terms of whether it has met their needs and expectations. p. 8

customer value the relationship between benefits and the sacrifice necessary to obtain those benefits. p. 9

customer-centric a philosophy under which the company customizes its product and service offering based on data generated through interactions between the customer and the company. p. 363

data mining an analytical process that compiles actionable data on the purchase habits of a firm's current and potential customers. p. 363

data warehouse a central repository of data from various functional areas of the organization that are stored and inventoried on a centralized computer system so that the information can be shared across all functional departments of the business. p. 368

database an organized system of data collection that allows for assessment, usually by computer. p. 368

deceptive pricing promoting a price or price saving that is not actually available. p. 216

decision confirmation the reaffirmation of the wisdom of the decision a consumer has made. p. 93

decline stage a long-run drop in sales. p. 180

decoding interpretation of the language and symbols sent by the source through a channel. p. 280

demographic segmentation segmenting markets by age, gender, income, ethnic background, and family life cycle. p. 133

demography the study of people's vital statistics, such as their age, race and ethnicity, and location. p. 17

department store a store housing several departments under one roof. p. 258

depth interview an interview that involves a discussion between a well-trained researcher and a respondent who is asked about attitudes and perspectives on a topic. p. 75

derived demand demand in the business market that comes from demand in the consumer market. p. 116

descriptive research a type of conclusive research that attempts to describe marketing phenomena and characteristics. p. 71

destination stores stores that consumers purposely plan to visit. p. 269

development the stage in the product development process in which a prototype is developed and a marketing strategy is outlined. p. 172

diffusion the process by which the adoption of an innovation spreads. p. 175

direct channel a distribution channel in which producers sell directly to customers. p. 240

direct foreign investment active ownership of a foreign company or of overseas manufacturing or marketing facilities. p. 59

direct mail a printed form of direct-response communication that is delivered directly to consumers' homes. p. 316

direct marketing (direct-response marketing) techniques used to get consumers to make a purchase from their home, office, or another nonretail setting. p. 263

direct retailing the selling of products by representatives who work door-to-door, office-to-office, or at-home parties. p. 262

direct-response broadcast advertising that uses television or radio and includes a direct call to action asking the consumer to respond immediately. p. 315

direct-response communication communication of a message directly from a marketing company and directly to an intended individual target audience. p. 285

direct-response print advertising in a print medium that includes a direct call to action. p. 315

direct-response television (DRTV) advertising that appears on television and encourages viewers to respond immediately. p. 315

discount store a retailer that competes on the basis of low prices, high turnover, and high volume. p. 260

discrepancy of assortment the lack of all the items a customer needs to receive full satisfaction from a product or products. p. 237

discrepancy of quantity the difference between the amount of product produced and the amount an end-user wants to buy. p. 236

distribution resource planning (DRP) an inventory control system that manages the replenishment of goods from the manufacturer to the final consumer. p. 251

diversification a strategy of increasing sales by introducing new products into new markets. p. 38

Do Not Call List (DNCL) a free service whereby Canadians register their telephone number to reduce or eliminate phone calls from telemarketers. p. 316

dog in the portfolio matrix, a business unit that has low growth potential and a small market share. p. 37

drugstores retail stores that stock pharmacy-related products and services as their main draw. p. 259

dual distribution (multiple distribution) the use of two or more channels to distribute the same product to target markets. p. 243

dumping the sale of an exported product at a price lower than that charged for the same or a like product in the home market of the exporter. p. 62

earned media a category of promotional tactic based on a public relations model that gets customers talking about products or services. p. 287

80/20 principle a principle holding that 20 percent of all customers generate 80 percent of the demand. p. 138

electronic data interchange (EDI) information technology that replaces the paper documents that usually accompany business transactions, such as purchase orders and invoices, with electronic transmission of the needed information to reduce inventory levels, improve cash flow, streamline operations, and increase the speed and accuracy of information transmission. p. 251

electronic distribution a distribution technique that includes any kind of product or service that can be distributed electronically, whether over traditional forms, such as fibre-optic cable, or through satellite transmission of electronic signals. p. 252

empathy caring, individualized attention paid to customers. p. 186

empowerment delegation of authority to solve customers' problems quickly—usually by the first person who learns of the customer's problem. p. 364

encoding the conversion of the sender's ideas and thoughts into a message, usually in the form of words or signs. p. 278

environmental management when a company implements strategies that attempt to shape the external environment within which it operates. p. 16

environmental scanning the collection and interpretation of information about forces, events, and relationships in the external environment that may affect the future of the organization or the implementation of the marketing plan. p. 36

ethics the moral principles or values that generally govern the conduct of an individual or a group. p. 28

ethnographic research the study of human behaviour in its natural context; involves observation of behaviour and physical setting. p. 79

European Union a free trade zone encompassing 28 European countries. p. 55

evaluation gauging the extent to which the marketing objectives have been achieved during the specified period. p. 45

evoked set (consideration set) a group of the most preferred alternatives resulting from an information search, which a buyer can further evaluate to make a final choice. p. 92

exchange people giving up one thing to receive another thing they would rather have. p. 9

exclusive distribution a form of distribution that involves only one or a few dealers within a given area. p. 245

experience curves curves that show costs declining at a predictable rate as experience with a product increases. p. 40

experience quality a characteristic that can be assessed only after use. p. 184

experiential marketing a form of advertising that focuses on helping consumers experience a brand such that a memorable and emotional connection is formed between the consumer and the brand. p. 314

experiment a method a researcher uses to gather primary data to determine cause and effect. p. 79

exploratory research an informal discovery process that attempts to gain insights and a better understanding of the management and research problems. p. 71

export agents intermediaries who act like manufacturers' agents for exporters; the export agents live in the foreign market. p. 58

export broker an intermediary who plays the traditional broker's role by bringing buyer and seller together. p. 58

exporting selling domestically produced products to buyers in another country. p. 58

express warranty a written guarantee. p. 164

extensive decision making the most complex type of consumer decision making, used when considering the purchase of an unfamiliar, expensive product or an infrequently purchased item; requires the use of several criteria for evaluating options and much time for seeking information. p. 94

external information search the process of seeking information in the outside environment. p. 91

factory outlet an off-price retailer that is owned and operated by a manufacturer. p. 261

family brand the marketing of several different products under the same brand name. p. 160

family life cycle (FLC) a series of stages determined by a combination of age, marital status, and the presence or absence of children. p.136

feedback the receiver's response to a message. p. 280

flexible pricing (variable pricing) different customers pay different prices for essentially the same merchandise bought in equal quantities. p. 213

flighted media schedule a media scheduling strategy in which ads are run heavily every other month or every two weeks, to achieve a greater impact with an increased frequency and reach at those times. p. 310

floating exchange rates prices of different currencies move up and down based on the demand for and the supply of each currency. p. 62

FOB origin pricing the buyer absorbs the freight costs from the shipping point ("free on board"). p. 212

focus group a small group of recruited participants engaged in a nonstructured discussion in a casual environment. p. 75

follow-up the final step of the selling process, in which the salesperson ensures that delivery schedules are met, that the goods or services perform as promised, and that the buyers' employees are properly trained to use the products. p. 331

four Ps product, place, promotion, and price, which together make up the marketing mix. p. 43

frame error a sample drawn from a population differs from the target population. p. 81

franchisee an individual or a business that is granted the right to sell a franchiser's product. p. 265

franchiser the originator of a trade name, product, methods of operation, and so on, that grants operating rights to another party to sell its product. p. 265

franchises relationships in which the business rights to operate and sell a product or service are granted by the franchiser to the franchisee. p. 256

freight absorption pricing the seller pays all or part of the actual freight charges and does not pass them on to the buyer. p. 212

frequency the number of times an individual is exposed to a given message during a specific period. p. 309

frequent-buyer program a loyalty program in which loyal consumers are rewarded for making multiple purchases of a particular good or service. p. 322

full-line discount stores retailers that offer consumers very limited service and carries a broad assortment of well-known, nationally branded hard goods. p. 260

functional discount (trade discount) a discount to wholesalers and retailers for performing channel functions. p. 211

gap model a model identifying five gaps that can cause problems in service delivery and influence customer evaluations of service quality. p. 186

General Agreement on Tariffs and Trade (GATT) a trade agreement that contained loopholes that enabled countries to avoid trade-barrier reduction agreements. p. 54

Generation X people born between 1966 and 1978. p. 19

Generation Y people born between 1979 and 1994. p. 18

generic product a no-frills, no-brand-name, low-cost product that is simply identified by its product category. p. 158

generic product name a term that identifies a product by class or type and cannot be trademarked. p. 161

geodemographic segmentation segmenting potential customers into neighbourhood lifestyle categories. p. 137

geographic segmentation segmenting markets by region of a country or the world, market size, market density, or climate. p. 132

global brand a brand where at least 20 percent of the product is sold outside its home country or region. p. 158

global marketing marketing that targets markets throughout the world. p. 47

global marketing standardization production of uniform products that can be sold the same way all over the world. p. 51

global vision a recognition of and reaction to international marketing opportunities using effective global marketing strategies and being aware of threats from foreign competitors in all markets. p. 47

green marketing the development and marketing of products designed to minimize negative effects on the physical environment. p. 27

gross domestic product (GDP) the total market value of all goods and services produced in a country for a given period. p. 48

gross margin the amount of money the retailer makes as a percentage of sales after the cost of goods sold is subtracted. p. 258

gross national income (GNI per capita) one measure of the ability of a country's citizens to buy various goods and services. p. 52

growth stage the second stage of the product life cycle when sales typically grow at an increasing rate, many competitors enter the market, large companies may start to acquire small pioneering firms, and profits are healthy. p. 179

horizontal conflict a channel conflict that occurs among channel members on the same level. p. 247

ideal self-image the way an individual would like to be. p. 104

implementation the process that turns a marketing plan into action assignments and ensures that these assignments are executed in a way that accomplishes the plan's objectives. p. 44

implied warranty an unwritten guarantee that the good or service is fit for the purpose for which it was sold. p. 164

inconsistency the inability of service quality to be consistent each time it is delivered because the service depends on the people that provide it. p. 184

independent retailers retailers owned by a single person or partnership and not operated as part of a larger retail institution. p. 256

individual branding the use of different brand names for different products. p. 160

inflation a measure of the decrease in the value of money, expressed as the percentage reduction in value since the previous year. p. 22

infomercial a 30-minute or longer advertisement that looks more like a TV talk show than a sales pitch. p. 306

informational labelling package labelling designed to help consumers make proper product selections and to lower their cognitive dissonance after the purchase. p. 163

innovation a product perceived as new by a potential adopter. p. 175

inseparability the inability of the production and consumption of a service to be separated; consumers must be present during the production. p. 184

institutional advertising a form of advertising designed to enhance a company's image rather than promote a particular product. p. 299

intangibility the inability of services to be touched, seen, tasted, heard, or felt in the same manner that goods can be sensed. p. 184

integrated marketing communications (IMC) the careful coordination of all promotional messages for a product or a service to ensure the consistency of messages at every contact point where a company meets the consumer. p. 294

intensive distribution a form of distribution aimed at having a product available in every outlet where target customers might want to buy it. p. 245

interaction the point at which a customer and a company representative exchange information and develop learning relationships. p. 364

internal information search the process of recalling information stored in one's memory. p. 91

internal marketing treating employees as customers and developing systems and benefits that satisfy their needs. p. 193

International Monetary Fund (IMF) an international organization that acts as a lender of last resort, providing loans to troubled nations, and also works to promote trade through financial cooperation. p. 56

interpersonal communication direct, face-to-face communication between two or more people. p. 278

introductory stage the full-scale launch of a new product into the marketplace. p. 178

inventory the inability of services to be stored for future use. p. 185

inventory control system a method of developing and maintaining an adequate assortment of materials or products to meet a manufacturer's or a customer's demand. p. 251

inventory turnover measures the number of times a firm "turns" its inventory each year. p. 230

involvement the amount of time and effort a buyer invests in the search, evaluation, and decision processes of consumer behaviour. p. 94

joint demand the demand for two or more items used together in a final product. p. 117

joint venture a domestic firm's purchase of part of a foreign company or a domestic firm joining with a foreign company to create a new entity. p. 59

just-in-time production (JIT) a process that redefines and simplifies manufacturing by reducing inventory levels and delivering raw materials just when they are needed on the production line. p. 250

knowledge management the process by which learned information from customers is centralized and shared for the purpose of enhancing the relationship between customers and the organization. p. 364

lead generation (prospecting) identification of those firms and people most likely to buy the seller's offerings. p. 328

lead qualification determination of a sales prospect's (1) recognized need, (2) buying power, and (3) receptivity and accessibility. p. 329

leader pricing (loss-leader pricing) a product is sold near or even below cost in the hope that shoppers will buy other items once they are in the store. p. 213

learning a process that creates changes in behaviour, immediate or expected, through experience and practice. p. 107

learning (CRM) in a CRM environment, the informal process of collecting customer data through customer comments and feedback on product or service performance. p. 364

licensing the legal process whereby a licensor agrees to let another firm use its manufacturing process, trademarks, patents, trade secrets, or other proprietary knowledge. p. 58

lifestyle a mode of living as identified by a person's activities, interests, and opinions. p. 104

lifetime value (LTV) analysis a data manipulation technique that projects the future value of the customer over a period of years by using the assumption that marketing to repeat customers is more profitable than marketing to first-time buyers. p. 370

limited decision making the type of decision making that requires a moderate amount of time for gathering information and deliberating about an unfamiliar brand in a familiar product category. p. 94

location-based social networking sites websites that combine the fun of social networking with the utility of location-based GPS technology. p. 350

logistics the process of strategically managing the efficient flow and storage of raw materials, in-process inventory, and finished goods from point of origin to point of consumption. p. 248

logistics information system the link that connects all the logistics functions of the supply chain. p. 248

loyalty marketing program a promotional program designed to build long-term, mutually beneficial relationships between a company and its key customers. p. 322

mall intercept interview interviewing people in the common areas of shopping malls. p. 76

manufacturer's brand the brand name of a manufacturer. p. 158

market people or organizations with needs or wants and the ability and willingness to buy. p. 131

market development a marketing strategy that involves attracting new customers to existing products. p. 38

market opportunity analysis (MOA) the description and estimation of the size and sales potential of market segments that are of interest to the firm and the assessment of key competitors in these market segments. p. 43

market penetration a marketing strategy that tries to increase market share among existing customers. p. 38

market segment a subgroup of people or organizations sharing one or more characteristics that cause them to have similar product needs. p. 131

market segmentation the process of dividing a market into meaningful, relatively similar, and identifiable segments or groups. p. 131

market share a company's product sales as a percentage of total sales for that industry. p. 206

marketing the activities that develop an offering in order to satisfy a customer need. p. 3

marketing audit a thorough, systematic, periodic evaluation of the objectives, strategies, structure, and performance of the marketing organization. p. 45

marketing channel (channel of distribution) a set of interdependent organizations that ease the transfer of ownership as products move from producer to business user or consumer. p. 236

marketing company orientation a strong emphasis on the marketing concept and development of a more comprehensive approach to understanding the customer. p. 5

marketing mix a unique blend of product, place, promotion, and pricing strategies designed to produce mutually satisfying exchanges with a target market. p. 43

marketing myopia defining a business in terms of goods and services rather than in terms of the benefits that customers seek. p. 35

marketing objective a statement of what is to be accomplished through marketing activities. p. 42

marketing research the process of planning, collecting, and analyzing data relevant to a marketing decision. p. 69

marketing research objective specific statement about the information needed to solve the research question. p. 71

marketing strategy the activities of selecting and describing one or more target markets and developing and maintaining a marketing mix that will produce mutually satisfying exchanges with target markets. p. 42

marketing-controlled information source a product information source that originates with marketers promoting the product. p. 91

markup the dollar amount added to the cost of sales to get to the selling price. p. 225

Maslow's hierarchy of needs a method of classifying human needs and motivations into five categories in ascending order of importance: physiological, safety, social, esteem, and self-actualization. p. 106

mass communication the communication of a concept or message to large audiences. p. 278

mass customization (build-to-order) a production method whereby products are not made until an order is placed by the customer; products are made according to customer specifications. p. 249

mass merchandising a retailing strategy using moderate to low prices on large quantities of merchandise and lower levels of service to stimulate high turnover of products. p. 260

materials requirement planning (MRP) (materials management) an inventory control system that manages the replenishment of raw materials, supplies, and components from the supplier to the manufacturer. p. 251

maturity stage a period during which sales increase at a decreasing rate. p. 179

measurement error an error that occurs when the information desired by the researcher differs from the information provided by the measurement process. p. 81

media mix the combination of media to be used for a promotional campaign. p. 308

media planning the series of decisions advertisers make regarding the selection and use of media, allowing the marketer to optimally and cost-effectively communicate the message to the target audience. p. 303

media schedule designation of the media, the specific publications or programs, and the insertion dates of advertising. p. 310

media-sharing sites websites that allow users to upload and distribute multimedia content, such as videos and photos. p. 349

medium the channel used to convey a message to a target market. p. 303

Mercosur the largest Latin American trade agreement, which includes Argentina, Bolivia, Brazil, Chile, Colombia, Ecuador, Paraguay, Peru, Uruguay, and Venezuela. p. 54

microblogs blogs with strict post-length limits. p. 347

mission statement a statement of the firm's business based on a careful analysis of benefits sought by present and potential customers and an analysis of existing and anticipated environmental conditions. p. 34

mobile advertising advertising that displays text, images, and animated ads via mobile phones or other mobile devices that are data enabled. p. 308

modified rebuy a situation where the purchaser wants some change in the original good or service. p. 124

morals the rules people develop as a result of cultural values and norms. p. 28

motives driving forces that cause a person to take action to satisfy specific needs. p. 106

multiculturalism peaceful and equitable coexistence of different cultures, rather than one national culture, in a country. p. 21

multinational corporations companies that are heavily engaged in international trade, beyond exporting and importing. p. 50

multiplier effect (accelerator principle) the phenomenon in which a small increase or decrease in consumer demand can produce a much larger change in demand for the facilities and equipment needed to make the consumer product. p. 117

multisegment targeting strategy a strategy that chooses two or more well-defined market segments and develops a distinct marketing mix for each. p. 142

mystery shoppers researchers posing as customers who gather observational data about a store. p. 79

need a state of being where we desire something that we do not possess but yearn to acquire. p. 3

need recognition the result of an imbalance between actual and desired states. p. 90

needs assessment a determination of the customer's specific needs and wants and the range of options the customer has for satisfying them. p. 329

negotiation the process during which both the salesperson and the prospect offer concessions in an attempt to arrive at a sales agreement. p. 331

networking the use of friends, business contacts, coworkers, acquaintances, and fellow members in professional and civic organizations to identify potential clients. p. 329

new product a product new to the world, new to the market, new to the producer or seller, or new to some combination of these. p. 167

new task buy a situation requiring the purchase of a product for the first time. p. 124

new-product strategy a plan that links the new-product development process with the objectives of the marketing department, the business unit, and the corporation. p. 169

niche one segment of a market. p. 141

niche competitive advantage the advantage achieved when a firm seeks to target and effectively serve a single segment of the market. p. 41

noise anything that interferes with, distorts, or slows down the transmission of information. p. 280

nonaspirational reference groups (dissociative groups) groups that influence our behaviour because we try to maintain distance from them. p. 101

noncorporate blogs independent blogs that are not associated with the marketing efforts of any particular company or brand. p. 346

noncumulative quantity discount a deduction from list price that applies to a single order rather than to the total volume of orders placed during a certain period. p. 211

nonmarketing-controlled information source a product information source not associated with advertising or promotion. p. 91

nonprobability sample any sample in which little or no attempt is made to have a representative cross-section of the population. p. 80

nonprofit organization an organization that exists to achieve some goal other than the usual business goals of profit, market share, or return on investment. p. 193

nonprofit organization marketing the effort by nonprofit organizations to bring about mutually satisfying exchanges with target markets. p. 193

nonstore retailing shopping without visiting a store. p. 262

norms the values and attitudes deemed acceptable by a group. p. 100

North American Free Trade Agreement (NAFTA) an agreement among Canada, the United States, and Mexico that created the world's largest free trade zone at that time. p. 54

North American Industry Classification System (NAICS) an industry classification system developed by the United States, Canada, and Mexico to classify North American business establishments by their main production processes. p. 122

observation research a research method that relies on four types of observation: people watching people, people watching an activity, machines watching people, and machines watching an activity. p. 78

odd–even pricing (psychological pricing) odd-numbered prices connote bargains, and even-numbered prices imply quality. p. 214

off-price retailer a retailer that sells brand-name merchandise at considerable discounts. p. 261

omni channel retailing an approach that combines the advantages of the physical store experience with the information-rich experience of online shopping, providing the consumer with a seamless experience through all available shopping channels. p. 264

one-to-one marketing an individualized marketing method that uses customer information to build long-term, personalized, and profitable relationships with each customer. p. 142

online marketing two-way communication of a message delivered through the Internet to the consumer. p. 285

online retailing a type of shopping available to consumers who have personal computers and access to the Internet. p. 264

open-ended question an interview question that encourages an answer phrased in the respondent's own words. p. 78

opinion leader an individual who influences the opinions of others. p. 101

optimizers business customers who consider numerous suppliers, both familiar and unfamiliar, solicit bids, and study all proposals carefully before selecting one. p. 139

order processing system a system whereby orders are entered into the supply chain and filled. p. 250

original equipment manufacturers (OEMs) individuals and organizations that buy business goods and incorporate them into the products that they produce for eventual sale to other producers or to consumers. p. 120

outsourcing (contract logistics) a manufacturer's or supplier's use of an independent third party to manage an entire function of the logistics system, such as transportation, warehousing, or order processing. p. 252

owned media a category of promotional tactic based on brands becoming publishers of their own content to maximize the brands' value to consumers. p. 287

paid media a category of promotional tactic based on the traditional advertising model whereby a brand pays for advertising space. p. 287

penetration pricing a relatively low price for a product initially as a way to reach the mass market. p. 209

perception the process by which people select, organize, and interpret stimuli into a meaningful and coherent picture. p. 105

perceptual mapping a means of displaying or graphing, in two or more dimensions, the location of products, brands, or groups of products in customers' minds. p. 144

personal selling a purchase situation involving a personal, paid-for communication between two people in an attempt to influence each other. p. 284

personality a way of organizing and grouping the consistency of an individual's reactions to situations. p. 104

persuasive labelling package labelling that focuses on a promotional theme or logo, and on which consumer information is secondary. p. 163

pioneering advertising a form of advertising designed to stimulate primary demand for a new product or product category. p. 299

planned obsolescence the practice of modifying products so those that have already been sold become obsolete before they actually need replacement. p. 155

planning the process of anticipating future events and determining strategies to achieve organizational objectives in the future. p. 33

point-of-sale interactions communications between customers and organizations that occur at the point of sale, usually in a store. p. 364

portfolio matrix a tool for allocating resources among products or strategic business units on the basis of relative market share and market growth rate. p. 36

position the place a product, brand, or group of products occupies in consumers' minds relative to competing offerings. p. 144

positioning a process that influences potential customers' overall perception of a brand, a product line, or an organization in general. p. 143

preapproach a process that describes the research a salesperson must do before contacting a prospect. p. 329

predatory pricing the practice of charging a very low price for a product with the intent of driving competitors out of business or out of a market. p. 217

predictive modelling a data manipulation technique in which marketers try to determine, based on some past set of occurrences, the odds that some other occurrence, such as an inquiry or a purchase, will take place in the future. p. 370

premium an extra item offered to the consumer, usually in exchange for some proof of purchase of the promoted product. p. 322

price that which is given up in an exchange to acquire a good or service. p. 203

price bundling marketing two or more products in a single package for a special price. p. 214

price fixing an agreement between two or more firms on the price they will charge for a product. p. 216

price lining offering a product line with several items at specific price points. p. 213

price skimming a high introductory price, often coupled with heavy promotion. p. 209

price strategy a basic, long-term pricing framework that establishes the initial price for a product and the intended direction for price movements over the product life cycle. p. 208

primary data information that is collected for the first time and is used for solving the particular problem under investigation. p. 74

primary membership groups groups with which individuals interact regularly in an informal, face-to-face manner. p. 100

private brand a brand name owned by a wholesaler or a retailer. p. 159

probability sample a sample in which every element in the population has a known statistical likelihood of being selected. p. 80

problem child (question mark) in the portfolio matrix, a business unit that shows rapid growth but poor profit margins. p. 37

product anything, both favourable and unfavourable, received by a person in an exchange for possession, consumption, attention, or short-term use. p. 151

product advertising a form of advertising that promotes the benefits of a specific good or service. p. 299

product category all brands that satisfy a particular type of need. p. 178

product development a marketing strategy that entails the creation of new products for current customers. pp. 38, 170

product differentiation a positioning strategy that some firms use to distinguish their products from those of competitors. p. 144

product item a specific version of a product that can be designated as a distinct offering among an organization's products. p. 153

product life cycle (PLC) a concept that traces the stages of a product's acceptance, from its introduction (birth) to its decline (death). p. 177

product line a group of closely related product items. p. 153

product line depth the different version of a product item in a product line. p. 154

product line extension adding additional products to an existing product line to compete more broadly in the industry. p. 156

product line length the number of product items in a product line. p. 154

product mix all products that an organization sells. p. 153

product mix width the number of product lines an organization offers. p. 154

product modification changing one or more of a product's characteristics. p. 155

product offering the mix of products offered to the consumer by the retailer; also called the product assortment or merchandise mix. p. 267

product placement a public relations strategy that involves getting a product, service, or company name to appear in a movie, television show, radio program, magazine, newspaper, video game, video or audio clip, book, or commercial for another product; on the Internet; or at special events. p. 312

product/service differentiation competitive advantage the provision of a unique benefit that is valuable to buyers beyond simply offering a low price. p. 40

production orientation a focus on manufacturing and production quantity in which customers are meant to choose based on what is most abundantly available. p. 4

profit revenue minus expenses. p. 204

promotion communication by marketers that informs, persuades, reminds, and connects potential buyers to a product for the purpose of influencing an opinion or eliciting a response. p. 277

promotional mix the combination of promotional tools—including advertising, publicity, sales promotion, personal selling, direct-response communication, and social media—used to reach the target market and fulfill the organization's overall goals. p. 282

promotional strategy a plan for the use of the elements of promotion: advertising, public relations, personal selling, sales promotion, direct-response communication, and social media. p. 277

psychographic segmentation market segmentation on the basis of personality, motives, lifestyles, and geodemographics categories. p. 137

psychological factors tools that consumers use to recognize, gather, analyze, and self-organize to aid in decision making. p. 104

public relations the marketing function that evaluates public attitudes, identifies areas within the organization the public may be interested in, and executes a program of action to earn public understanding and acceptance. p. 283

public service advertisement (PSA) an announcement that promotes a program of a nonprofit organization or of a federal, provincial or territorial, or local government. p. 196

publicity public information about a company, a product, a service, or an issue appearing in the mass media as a news item. p. 283

pull strategy a marketing strategy that stimulates consumer demand to obtain product distribution. p. 293

pulsing media schedule a media scheduling strategy that uses continuous scheduling throughout the year coupled with a flighted schedule during the best sales periods. p. 311

purchasing power a comparison of income versus the relative cost of a set standard of goods and services in different geographic areas. p. 22

push money money offered to channel intermediaries to encourage them to push products—that is, to encourage other members of the channel to sell the products. p. 325

push strategy a marketing strategy that uses aggressive personal selling and trade advertising to convince a wholesaler or a retailer to carry and sell particular merchandise. p. 293

pyramid of corporate social responsibility a model that suggests corporate social responsibility is composed of economic, legal, ethical, and philanthropic responsibilities and that the firm's economic performance supports the entire structure. p. 27

quantity discount a unit price reduction offered to buyers buying either in multiple units or at more than a specified dollar amount. p. 211

random error type of sampling error in which the selected sample is an imperfect representation of the overall population. p. 81

random sample a sample arranged in such a way that every element of the population has an equal chance of being selected as part of the sample. p. 80

reach the number of target consumers exposed to a commercial at least once during a specific period, usually four weeks. p. 309

real self-image the way an individual actually perceives himself or herself to be. p. 104

rebates cash refunds given for the purchase of a product during a specific period. p. 321

receivers the people who decode a message. p. 280

recency-frequency-monetary (RFM) analysis the analysis of customer activity by recency, frequency, and monetary value. p. 370

recession a period of economic activity characterized by negative growth, which reduces demand for goods and services. p. 23

reciprocity a practice where business purchasers choose to buy from their own customers. p. 118

reference group a group in society that influences an individual's purchasing behaviour. p. 100

referrals recommendations to a salesperson from a customer or business associate. p. 329

relationship commitment a firm's belief that an ongoing relationship with another firm is so important that the relationship warrants maximum efforts at maintaining it indefinitely. p. 113

relationship marketing a strategy that focuses on keeping and improving relationships with current customers. p. 8

relationship selling (consultative selling) a multistage sales process that involves building, maintaining, and enhancing interactions with customers for the purpose of developing long-term satisfaction through mutually beneficial partnerships. p. 326

reliability the ability to perform a service dependably, accurately, and consistently. p. 185

repositioning changing consumers' perceptions of a brand in relation to competing brands. p. 145

resale price maintenance attempts by a producer to control a store's retail price for the product. p. 217

research design a plan that specifies how to answer the research question and achieve the research objectives by laying out the research tools and techniques necessary to collect and analyze data. p. 71

response list a customer list that includes the names and addresses of individuals who have responded to an offer of some kind, such as by mail, telephone, direct-response television, product rebates, contests or sweepstakes, or billing inserts. p. 368

responsiveness the ability to provide prompt service. p. 185

retailer the market intermediary that sells goods and services to the final consumer. pp. 239, 255

retailing all the activities directly related to the sale of goods and services to the ultimate consumer for personal, nonbusiness use. p. 255

retailing mix a combination of the six Ps—product, place, promotion, price, presentation, and personnel—to sell goods and services to the ultimate consumer. p. 267

return on assets (ROA) measures the firm's efficiency in generating sales and profits from the total amount invested in the company. p. 230

return on investment (ROI) net profits divided by the investment. pp. 206, 231

return on marketing investment (ROMI) the contribution attributable to marketing spending (net). p. 231

revenue the price charged to customers multiplied by the number of units sold. p. 203

review sites websites that allow consumers to post, read, rate, and comment on opinions regarding all kinds of products and services. p. 350

routine response behaviour the type of decision making exhibited by consumers buying frequently purchased, low-cost goods and services; requires little search and decision time. p. 94

sales orientation hard selling to the customer, who has greater choice thanks to more competition in the marketplace. p. 5

sales presentation a formal meeting in which the salesperson presents a sales proposal to a prospective buyer. p. 330

sales process (sales cycle) the set of steps a salesperson goes through to sell a particular product or service. p. 327

sales promotion marketing activities—other than personal selling, advertising, direct-response marketing, and public relations—that stimulate consumer buying and dealer effectiveness. p. 284

sales proposal a formal written document or professional presentation that outlines how the salesperson's product or service will meet or exceed the prospect's needs. p. 330

sample a subset from a larger population. p. 80

sampling a promotional program that allows the consumer the opportunity to try a product or service for free. p. 323

sampling error error that occurs when a sample that does not represent the target population. p. 81

satisficers business customers who place their order with the first familiar supplier to satisfy their product and delivery requirements. p. 139

scaled-response question a closed-ended question designed to measure the intensity of a respondent's answer. p. 78

scrambled merchandising the tendency to offer a wide variety of nontraditional goods and services under one roof. p. 259

screening the first filter in the product development process, which eliminates ideas that are inconsistent with the organization's new-product strategy or are obviously inappropriate for some other reason. p. 171

search quality a characteristic that can be easily assessed before purchase. p. 184

seasonal discount a price reduction for buying merchandise out of season. p. 211

seasonal media schedule a media scheduling strategy that runs advertising only during times of the year when the product is most likely to be purchased. p. 311

secondary data data previously collected for any purpose other than the one at hand. p. 72

secondary membership groups groups with which individuals interact less consistently and more formally than with primary membership groups. p. 100

segmentation bases (variables) characteristics of individuals, groups, or organizations. p. 132

selective distortion a process whereby consumers change or distort information that conflicts with their feelings or beliefs. p. 105

selective distribution a form of distribution achieved by screening dealers to eliminate all but a few in any single area. p. 245

selective exposure the process whereby a consumer decides which stimuli to notice and which to ignore. p. 105

selective retention a process whereby consumers remember only information that supports their personal beliefs. p. 105

self-concept how consumers perceive themselves in terms of attitudes, perceptions, beliefs, and self-evaluations. p. 104

self-regulation programs voluntarily adopted by business groups to regulate the activities of their members. p. 25

sender the originator of the message in the communication process. p. 278

service the result of applying human or mechanical efforts to people or objects. p. 183

service mark a trademark for a service. p. 161

shopper marketing promotion set up at the retailer's location to build traffic, advertise the product, or induce impulse buying. p. 324

shopping product a product that requires comparison shopping because it is usually more expensive than a convenience product and is found in fewer stores. p. 152

simulated (laboratory) market testing the presentation of advertising and other promotion materials for several products, including a test product, to members of the product's target market. p. 174

simultaneous product development a team-oriented approach to new-product development. p. 172

single-price tactic offering all goods and services at the same price (or perhaps two or three prices). p. 212

situation (SWOT) analysis identifying internal strengths (S) and weaknesses (W) and also examining external opportunities (O) and threats (T). p. 35

social class a group of people who are considered nearly equal in status or community esteem, who regularly socialize among themselves both formally and informally, and who share behavioural norms. p. 98

social commerce a subset of e-commerce that involves the interaction and user contribution aspects of social media to assist in the online buying and selling of products and services. p. 339

social media a collection of online communication tools that facilitate conversations online; when used by marketers, social media tools encourage consumer empowerment. pp. 285, 335

social networking sites websites that allow individuals to connect—or network—with friends, peers, and business associates. p. 347

social news sites websites that allow users to decide which content is promoted on a given website by voting that content up or down. p. 349

socialization process the passing down of cultural values and norms to children. p. 102

societal marketing orientation looking not only at the customer but expanding marketing efforts to include aspects from the external environment. p. 6

sociometric leader a low-profile, well-respected collaborative professional who is socially and professionally well connected. p. 101

spatial discrepancy the difference between the location of a producer and the location of widely scattered markets. p. 237

specialty discount stores retail stores that offer a nearly complete selection of single-line merchandise and use self-service, discount prices, high volume, and high turnover. p. 260

specialty product a particular item with unique characteristics for which consumers search extensively and for which they are very reluctant to accept substitutes. p. 153

specialty store a retail store specializing in a given type of merchandise. p. 259

sponsorship a public relations strategy in which a company spends money to support an issue, a cause, or an event that is consistent with corporate objectives, such as improving brand awareness or enhancing corporate image. p. 313

star in the portfolio matrix, a business unit that is a fast-growing market leader. p. 37

status quo pricing a pricing objective that maintains existing prices or meets the competition's prices. p. 207

stimulus any unit of input affecting one or more of the five senses: sight, smell, taste, touch, hearing. p. 90

straight rebuy a situation in which the purchaser reorders the same goods or services without looking for new information or new suppliers. p. 124

strategic business unit (SBU) a subgroup of a single business or a collection of related businesses within the larger organization. p. 34

strategic channel alliances cooperative agreements between business firms to use one of the manufacturer's already established distribution channels. p. 243

strategic planning the managerial process of creating and maintaining a fit between the organization's objectives and resources and evolving market opportunities. p. 33

subculture a homogeneous group of people who share elements of the overall culture and also have their own unique cultural elements. p. 98

supercentres retail stores that combine groceries and general merchandise goods with a wide range of services. p. 260

supermarkets large, departmentalized, self-service retailers that specialize in food and some nonfood items. p. 259

supplementary services a group of services that support or enhance the core service. p. 188

supply chain the connected chain of all the business entities, both internal and external to the company, that perform or support the marketing channel functions. p. 236

supply chain management a management system that coordinates and integrates all the activities performed by supply chain members into a seamless process, from the source to the point of consumption, resulting in enhanced customer and economic value. p. 247

supply chain team an entire group of individuals who orchestrate the movement of goods, services, and information from the source to the consumer. p. 249

survey research the most popular technique for gathering primary data, in which a researcher interacts with people to obtain facts, opinions, and attitudes. p. 76

sustainability the idea that socially responsible companies will outperform their peers by focusing on the world's social problems and viewing them as opportunities to build profits and help the world at the same time. p. 26

sustainable competitive advantage an advantage that cannot be copied by the competition. p. 41

tangibles the physical evidence of a service, including the physical facilities, tools, and equipment used to provide the service. p. 186

target market a group of people or organizations for which an organization designs, implements, and maintains a marketing mix intended to meet the needs of that group, resulting in mutually satisfying exchanges. pp. 15, 140

telemarketing the use of telecommunications to sell a product or service; involves both outbound and inbound calls. pp. 264, 315

temporal discrepancy a product is produced but a customer is not ready to buy it. p. 237

test marketing the limited introduction of a product and a marketing program to determine the reactions of potential customers in a market situation. p. 173

touch points all possible areas of a business where customers have contact with that business. p. 364

trade allowance a price reduction offered by manufacturers to intermediaries, such as wholesalers and retailers. p. 325

trade sales promotion sales promotion activities targeting a marketing channel member, such as a wholesaler or retailer. p. 320

trademark the exclusive right to use a brand or part of a brand. p. 161

trust confidence in an exchange partner's reliability and integrity. p. 113

two-part pricing charging two separate amounts to consume a single good or service. p. 215

unbundling reducing the bundle of services that comes with the basic product. p. 214

undifferentiated targeting strategy a marketing approach that views the market as one big market with no individual segments and thus uses a single marketing mix. p. 141

uniform delivered pricing the seller pays the actual freight charges and bills every purchaser an identical, flat freight charge. p. 212

unique selling proposition a desirable, exclusive, and believable advertising appeal selected as the theme for a campaign. p. 301

universal product codes (UPCs) a series of thick and thin vertical lines (bar codes), readable by computerized optical scanners that match the codes to brand names, package sizes, and prices. p. 163

unsought product a product unknown to the potential buyer or a known product that the buyer does not actively seek. p. 153

Uruguay Round an agreement created by the World Trade Organization to dramatically lower trade barriers worldwide. p. 54

usage-rate segmentation dividing a market by the amount of product bought or consumed. p. 138

value the enduring belief shared by a society that a specific mode of conduct is personally or socially preferable to another mode of conduct. p. 97

value-based pricing setting the price at a level that seems to the customer to be a good price compared with the prices of other options. p. 211

vertical conflict a channel conflict that occurs between different levels in a marketing channel, most typically between the manufacturer and wholesaler or between the manufacturer and retailer. p. 247

want a particular product or service that the consumer believes could satisfy an unfulfilled need. p. 90

warehouse membership clubs limited-service merchant wholesalers that sell a limited selection of brand-name appliances, household items, and groceries to members, small businesses, and groups. p. 261

warranty a confirmation of the quality or performance of a good or service. p. 164

World Bank an international bank that offers low-interest loans, advice, and information to developing nations. p. 56

World Trade Organization (WTO) a trade organization that replaced the old General Agreement on Tariffs and Trade (GATT). p. 54

zone pricing a modification of uniform delivered pricing that divides the total market into segments or zones and charges a flat freight rate to all customers in a given zone. p. 212

Chapter 1

1. "W. Brett Wilson's Top 10 Tips for Small Businesses and Startups," CBC News, October 9, 2009, www.cbc.ca/news/business/w-brett-wilson-s-top-10-tips-for-small-businesses-and-startups-1.859309 (accessed September 2013).

2. Andrew Hampp, "Saatchi CEO Kevin Roberts Declares Death of Marketing, Future of Movements @ MIDEM," Billboard, January 30, 2012, www.billboard.com/biz/articles/news/branding/1099158/saatchi-ceo-kevin-roberts-declares-death-of-marketing-future-of (accessed September 14, 2014).

3. Ibid.

4. Seth Godin's comment is in the comments section of Fred Wilson, "Marketing," AVC, February 25, 2011, www.avc.com/a_vc/2011/02/marketing.html#comment-155823042 (accessed September 2013).

5. SAP, "What Is Marketing?", Forbes, September 8, 2012, www.forbes.com/sites/sap/2012/08/09/what-is-marketing/ (accessed September 14, 2014).

6. Scott Adams, "Dilbert," Dilbert, October 1, 2010, http://search.dilbert.com/comic/Marketing (accessed September 14, 2014).

7. William L. Wilkie and Elizabeth S. Moore, "Scholarly Research in Marketing: Exploring the '4 Eras' of Thought Development," Journal of Public Policy & Marketing, 22, 2, 2003, 116–146.

8. Internet Movie Database, Mad Men, "For Those Who Think Young (2008)," www.imdb.com/title/tt1118051/quotes (accessed September 2013).

9. Peter F. Drucker, Management: Tasks, Responsibilities, Practices. (Piscataway, NJ: Transaction Publishers, 2007).

10. Andrew Hampp, "Saatchi CEO Kevin Roberts Declares Death of Marketing, Future of Movements @ MIDEM," Billboard, January 30, 2012, www.billboard.com/biz/articles/news/branding/1099158/saatchi-ceo-kevin-roberts-declares-death-of-marketing-future-of (accessed September 14, 2014).

11. Valarie A. Zeithaml, Mary Jo Bitner, and Dwayne D. Gremler, Services Marketing, 4th ed. (New York: McGraw-Hill Irwin, 2006), 110.

12. "Building Business around Customers: Know Thy Customer," BusinessWeek, September 12, 2005, 8.

13. Vadim Kotelnikov, "Customer Retention: Driving Profits through Giving Customers Lots of Reasons to Stay," e-COACH, www.1000ventures.com/business_guide/crosscuttings/customer_retention.html (accessed September 26, 2010).

14. Christine Moorman, "Why Apple Is a Great Marketer," Forbes, October 7, 2012, www.forbes.com/sites/christinemoorman/2012/07/10/why-apple-is-a-great-marketer/ (accessed September 2013).

15. "Marketing Salary in Canada," Wowjobs, www.wowjobs.ca/salary-marketing (accessed September 2013).

16. W. Brett Wilson, "Best Business Advice from W. Brett Wilson," Financial Post, June 10, 2013, http://business.financialpost.com/2013/06/10/best-business-advice-from-w-brett-wilson/ (accessed September 2013).

17. "Subscriber Stats," Canadian Wireless Telecommunications Association, http://cwta.ca/wordpress/wp-content/uploads/2011/08/SubscribersStats_en_2013_Q2.pdf (accessed September 2013).

18. Morgan Campbell, "Canadians Still Love TV, but Online Viewing Growing in Popularity," Toronto Star, September 26, 2013, www.thestar.com/business/2013/09/26/canadians_still_love_tv_but_online_viewing_growing_in_popularity.html (accessed September 2013).

Chapter 2

1. "Definition of Family," The Vanier Institute of the Family, www.vanierinstitute.ca/definition_of_family#.Umhz7Pkqhng (accessed October 22, 2013).

2. "Thinking about Families: An Interview with Katherine Scott, Director of Programs, Vanier Institute of the Family," Transition Magazine, Winter 2010, 5–7, http://vanierinstitute.ca/include/get.php?nodeid=220 (accessed October 21, 2013).

3. Ibid.

4. Karen Mazurkewich, "Tweens & Technology," National Post, August 10, 2010, www.mhoneill.com/106B/articles/tween%20power.pdf (accessed August 29, 2011).

5. Michael Oliveira, "Facebook Says Opening Site to Preteens 'Is Something We Think About,'" Calgary Herald, October 21, 2013, www.calgaryherald.com/technology/Facebook+says+opening+site+preteens+something+think+about/9060860/story.html (accessed October 21, 2013).

6. "Despite Economic Upheaval Generation Y Is Still Feeling Green: RSA Canada Survey," CNW, October 28, 2010, www.newswire.ca/en/releases/archive/October2010/28/c6663.html (accessed October 23, 2013).

7. Ashante Infantry, "Gen Y Canadians Splurging on Luxury Items, Despite High Unemployment," Toronto Star, June 19, 2013, www.thestar.com/business/2012/06/19/gen_y_canadians_splurging_on_luxury_items_despite_high_unemployment.html (accessed October 23, 2013).

8. Karen Akers, "Generation Y: Marketing to the Young and the Restless," Successful Promotions, January/February 2005, 33–38.

9. Ashante Infantry, "Gen Y Canadians Splurging on Luxury Items, Despite High Unemployment," Toronto Star, June 19, 2013, www.thestar.com/business/2012/06/19/gen_y_canadians_splurging_on_luxury_items_despite_high_unemployment.html (accessed February 18, 2014).

10. Layton Han, "Gen X: The New Luxury Buyers and How to Reach Them," MediaPost, May 30, 2012, www.mediapost.com/publications/article/175754/gen-x-the-new-luxury-buyers-and-how-to-reach-them.html (accessed February 18, 2014).

11. Julian Beltrame, "Unemployed Kids a Burden for Boomer Parents: Report," HuffPost Business, July 5, 2013, www.huffingtonpost.ca/2013/05/07/baby-boomers-children-money_n_3230204.html (accessed October 23, 2012).

12. Ibid.

13. "Census Metropolitan Area and Census Agglomeration Definitions," Statistics Canada, September 17, 2010, www.statcan.gc.ca/pub/93-600-x/2010000/definitions-eng.htm (accessed October 23, 2013).

14. Martin Turcotte and Mireille Vézina, "Migration from Central to Surrounding Municipalities in Toronto, Montréal and Vancouver," Canadian Social Trends, Statistics Canada catalogue no. 11-008-X, 90, Winter 2010, www.statcan.gc.ca/pub/11-008-x/2010002/article/11159-eng.pdf (accessed October 23, 2013).

15. "Young, Suburban and Mostly Asian: Canada's Immigrant Population Surges," National Post, May 8, 2013, http://news.nationalpost.com/2013/05/08/young-suburban-and-mostly-asian-canadas-immigrant-population-surges/ (accessed October 25, 2013).

16. Statistics Canada, "Population Projections of Visible Minority Groups, Canada, Provinces and Regions," Catalogue no. 91-541-XIE.

17. Ibid.

18. "Bilingualism Is Growing, But Not in English and French," CBC News, October 24, 2012, www.cbc.ca/news/canada/bilingualism-growing-but-not-in-french-and-english-1.1176469 (accessed October 25, 2013).

19. "Diversity," City of Toronto, 2007 www.toronto.ca/quality_of_life/diversity.htm (accessed October 25, 2013).

20. Duane Stanford, "Coke's World Cup Song Is a Marketing Winner," Bloomberg Business Week, July 15, 2010, www.businessweek.com/magazine/content/10_30/b4188024314746.htm (accessed September 4, 2010).

21. Heather Scoffield, "Median Family Income in Canada Is $76,000, StatsCan Survey Shows," CTV News, September 11, 2013, www.ctvnews.ca/canada/median-family-income-in-canada-is-76-000-statscan-survey-shows-1.1449641#ixzz2iezg6lk4 (accessed October 25, 2013).

22. "Special Reports—What Difference Does Learning Make to Financial Security?", Employment and Social Development Canada, January 2008, www4.hrsdc.gc.ca/.3ndic.1t.4r@-eng.jsp?iid=54 (accessed August 28, 2011).

23. "Canadians' Household Debt Reaches New High: $1.63 for Every Dollar Earned," *HuffPost Business*, October 2, 2013, www.huffingtonpost.ca/2013/09/13/household-mortgage-debt-canada_n_3920887.html (accessed October 25, 2013).

24. Matthew McClearn, "Prediction: Canada will Slip Back into Recession in 2013," *Canadian Business*, January 28, 2013, www.canadianbusiness.com/economy/canada-will-slip-back-into-recession-in-2013/ (accessed October 24, 2013).

25. Bertrand Marotte, "Majority of Rich Canadians Feel Better Off than Before the Recession," *The Globe and Mail*, October 3, 2013, www.theglobeandmail.com/report-on-business/majority-of-rich-canadians-feel-better-off-than-before-the-recession/article14660866/ (accessed October 24, 2013).

26. Robert Hof, "The Top 10 Tech Trends, Straight from 5 Top Tech VCs," Forbes, May 22, 2012, www.forbes.com/sites/roberthof/2012/05/22/the-top-10-tech-trends-according-to-5-top-tech-vcs/ (accessed October 27, 2013).

27. Competition Bureau, www.competition bureau.gc.ca (accessed September 15, 2014).

28. "The 14 Clauses of the Canadian Code of Advertising Standards," Advertising Standards Canada, www.adstandards.com/en/standards/the14Clauses.aspx#bait (accessed October 25, 2013).

29. Emma Thomasson, "Insight—At Nestle, Interacting with the Online Enemy," Reuters, October 26, 2012, http://uk.reuters.com/article/2012/10/26/uk-nestle-online-water-idUKBRE89P07Q20121026 (accessed October 25, 2013).

30. Marc Gunther, "Will Social Responsibility Harm Business?", *The Wall Street Journal*, May 18, 2005, A2.

31. This section is adapted from Archie B. Carroll, "The Pyramid of Corporate Social Responsibility: Toward the Moral Management of Organizational Stakeholders," *Business Horizons*, July-August 1991, 39–48. See also Kirk Davidson, "Marketers Must Accept Greater Responsibilities," *Marketing News*, February 2, 1998, 6.

32. "Sustainability on the Rise in Corporate Agendas," The British Assessment Bureau, February 23, 2012, www.british-assessment.co.uk/news/sustainability-on-the-rise-in-corporate-agendas/ (accessed October 25, 2013).

33. "Greenlist™," S. C. Johnson, www.scjohnson.ca/en/scj_greenlist.aspx (accessed October 25, 2013).

34. Based on Edward Stevens, *Business Ethics*. (New York: Paulist Press, 1979). Used with permission of Paulist Press.

35. Anusorn Singhapakdi, Scott J. Vitell, and Kenneth L. Kraft, "Moral Intensity and Ethical Decision-Making of Marketing Professionals," *Journal of Business Research*, 36, 3, 1996, 245–255; and Ishmael P. Akaah and Edward A. Riordan, "Judgments of Marketing Professionals about Ethical Issues in Marketing Research: A Replication and Extension," *Journal of Marketing Research*, XXVI, 1989, 112–120.

36. Katie Keir, "Women: The Next Emerging Market," Advisor.ca, March 7, 2013, www.advisor.ca/news/industry-news/women-the-next-emerging-market-86118 (accessed September 15, 2014).

Chapter 3

1. "Procter & Gamble Announces Agreement to Divest Pringles to The Kellogg Company for $2.7 Billion," Procter & Gamble, February 15, 2012, http://news.pg.com/press-release/pg-corporate-announcements/procter-gamble-announces-agreement-divest-pringles-kellogg- (accessed October 27, 2013).

2. "Duracell Quantum," Procter & Gamble, www.pg.com/en_US/downloads/innovation/factsheet_Duracell_Quantum_final.pdf (accessed October 28, 2013).

3. "Loblaw to Buy Shoppers Drug Mart for $12.4B," CBC News, July 15, 2013, www.cbc.ca/news/business/loblaw-to-buy-shoppers-drug-mart-for-12-4b-1.1342108 (accessed October 28, 2013).

4. "Apple Profits Decline Despite iPhone Sales Boost," BBC News Business, October 28, 2013, www.bbc.co.uk/news/business-24719728 (accessed October 28, 2013).

Chapter 4

1. "Trade to Remain Subdued in 2013 after Sluggish Growth in 2012 as European Economies Continue to Struggle," World Trade Organization, April 10, 2013, www.wto.org/english/news_e/pres13_e/pr688_e.htm (accessed September 15, 2014).

2. "About Harlequin," Harlequin, www.harlequin.com/articlepage.html?articleId=36&chapter=0 (accessed September 15, 2014).

3. "Our Business," McCain, www.mccain.com/GoodBusiness/business/Pages/default.aspx (accessed September 15, 2014).

4. Sean Silcoff, Jacquie McNish, and Steve Ladurantaye, "Inside the Fall of BlackBerry: How the Smartphone Inventor Failed to Adapt," *The Globe and Mail*, September 27, 2013, www.theglobeandmail.com/report-on-business/the-inside-story-of-why-blackberry-is-failing/article14563602/?page=all (accessed September 15, 2014).

5. Alexandre Gauthier and Katie Meredith, "Canada's Merchandise Trade with the World: 2011," Parliament of Canada, July 13, 2012, www.parl.gc.ca/Content/LOP/ResearchPublications/2012-41-e.htm (accessed September 15, 2014).

6. "Welcome to Toronto Star Replica Edition: Toronto Star," *Toronto Star*, http://torontostar.newspaperdirect.com/epaper/viewer.aspx (accessed September 15, 2014).

7. "Mistakes in Advertising," LEO Network, www.learnenglish.de/mistakes/Horror Mistakes.html (accessed September 15, 2014).

8. "World Development Indicators: Size of the Economy," The World Bank, http://wdi.worldbank.org/table/1.1 (accessed September 15, 2014).

9. Rajeshni Naidu-Ghelani, "The World's Most Expensive Places to Live 2012," Yahoo Finance, June 12, 2012, http://finance.yahoo.com/news/the-world-s-most-expensive-places-to-live-2012.html?page=all (accessed September 15, 2014).

10. Yuval Atsmon, Vinay Dixit, and Cathy Wu, "Tapping China's Luxury-goods Market," McKinsey & Company, April 2011, www.mckinsey.com/insights/marketing_sales/tapping_chinas_luxury-goods_market (accessed September 15, 2014).

11. "What Does Canada Trade with China?", CBC News, July 12, 2012, www.cbc.ca/news/canada/what-does-canada-trade-with-china-1.1262424 (accessed September 15, 2014).

12. "Canada's Free Trade Agreements," Foreign Affairs, Trade and Development Canada, www.international.gc.ca/trade-agreements-accords-commerciaux/agr-acc/fta-ale.aspx?lang=eng#ongoing (accessed September 15, 2014).

13. "A Canadian Success Story: Icewine Exports to China," Foreign Affairs, Trade and Development Canada, April 16, 2013, www.international.gc.ca/media_commerce/release_photo_distribution/2013/04/16b.aspx?lang=eng (accessed September 15, 2014).

14. "Walmart and Bharti End Joint Venture," *Bangkok Post*, October 9, 2013, www.bangkokpost.com/breakingnews/373833/us-giant-walmart-and-india-bharti-end-joint-venture (accessed September 15, 2014).

15. Jonathan Asher, "Capturing a Piece of the Global Market," *Brandweek*, June 20, 2005, 20.

16. "If Only 'Krispy Kreme' Meant Makes You Smarter," *Business 2.0*, August 2005, 108.

Part 1 Case

1. Marsha Lederman, "Bill Clinton Sings the Praises of Sarah McLachlan's Music School at Fundraiser," *The Globe and Mail*, September 16, 2012, www.theglobeandmail.com/news/british-columbia/bill-clinton-sings-the-praises-of-sarah-mclachlans-music-school-at-fundraiser/article4547898/ (accessed September 15, 2014).

2. Niall O'Dowd, "Bill Clinton and Bono Reveal How Music Changed Their Lives," IrishCentral, May 6, 2010, www.irishcentral.com/opinion/niallodowd/bill-clinton-and-bono-reveal-how-music-changed-their-lives-93047739-238032671.html (accessed February 2014).

3. "Music Canada: Economic Impact Analysis of the Sound Recording Industry in Canada," PriceWaterhouseCoopers, April 12, 2012, http://musiccanada.com/wp-content/

uploads/2014/06/Music-Canada-Economic
-Impact-Analysis-of-the-Sound-Recording
-Industry-in-Canada.pdf (accessed
September 15, 2014).

4. "The Next Big Bang," Music Canada, http://
musiccanada.com/resources/research/the
-next-big-bang/ (accessed February 2014).

5. "Why Is Music Education Important?",
Spirit of Harmony Foundation, www
.spiritofharmony.org/music.html (accessed
February, 2014).

6. "Frequently Asked Questions," Jammit,
www.jammit.com/faq (accessed February
2014).

7. Rip Empson, "Jammit Lets Budding Rock
Stars Play Along With, Isolate, and Record
Over The 'Masters'," TechCrunch, January
25, 2012, http://techcrunch.com/2012/01/25/
jammit-lets-budding-rock-stars-play-along
-with-isolate-and-record-over-multi-track
-tunes/ (accessed February, 2014).

Chapter 5

1. "Research Quotes," QFINANCE, www
.qfinance.com/finance-and-business-quotes/
research (accessed September 15, 2014).

2. "Definition of Marketing: About AMA,"
American Marketing Association, www
.ama.org/AboutAMA/Pages/Definition-of
-Marketing.aspx (accessed August 5, 2014).

3. Scott M. Smith and Gerald S. Albaum, Basic
Marketing Research: Volume 1, Handbook
for Research Professionals Official Training
Guide from Qualtrics. Provo, UT: Qualtrics
Labs, 2012, http://cloudfront.qualtrics
.com/q1/wp-content/uploads/2012/02/
BasicMarketingResearch.pdf (accessed
August 2, 2014); and Avery M. Abernethy,
George R. Franke, "FTC Regulatory Activity
and the Information Content of Advertising," Journal of Public Policy & Marketing,
17, Fall 1998, 239–256, www.jstor.org/
stable/30000774 (accessed August 2,
2014).

4. "City of Kelowna: 2006 Citizen Survey
Detailed Report," Kettle Valley Research,
1–2, 2007, www.city.kelowna.bc.ca/
CityPage/Docs/PDFs/Communications/
2006%20Citizen%20Survey%20Report.pdf
(accessed July 2008).

5. Alison Stein Wellner, "Watch Me Now,"
American Demographics, October 2002,
S1–S8.

6. "Individual Internet Use and E-commerce,
2012," Statistics Canada, October 28, 2013,
www.statcan.gc.ca/daily-quotidien/131028/
dq131028a-eng.htm (accessed September 15,
2014).

7. "Online Panels," TNS Canada, 2009, www
.tnscanada.ca/our-expertise/onlinepanels
.html (accessed July 2010).

8. "Our Mobile Planet: Canada—Understanding
the Mobile Consumer," Google, May 2013,
http://services.google.com/fh/files/misc/omp
-2013-ca-en.pdf (accessed September 15,
2014); and Kamila Hinkson, "Smartphones:
Canadians Increasingly Attached to Their
Mobile Devices," Toronto Star, July 29,
2013, www.thestar.com/business/tech_news/
2013/07/29/canadians_addicted_to
_smartphones_ownership_zooms_study
_says.html (accessed September 15, 2014).

9. Jasper Lim, "Challenges and Opportunities
Facing Mobile Research on a Global Scale,"
HeraldBoy News, October 20, 2013, www
.heraldboy.com/challenges-and-opportunities
-facing-mobile-research-on-a-global-scale/
(accessed September 15, 2014).

10. Knowlton Thomas, "Canadians Can't Go
One Day without Checking Social Media,
Study Says," Techvibes, May 8, 2013, www
.techvibes.com/blog/canadians-cant-go-one
-day-without-checking-social-media-study
-says-2013-05-08 (accessed September 15,
2014).

11. "Our Mobile Planet: Canada—Understanding
the Mobile Consumer," Google, May 2013,
http://services.google.com/fh/files/
misc/omp-2013-ca-en.pdf (accessed
September 15, 2014).

12. "Deming Quotes," Deming Collaboration,
http://demingcollaboration.com/deming
-quotes/ (accessed September 15, 2014).

13. "Research Is Creating New Knowledge," C3
Metrics, http://c3metrics.com/research-is
-creating-new-knowledge/ (accessed
September 15, 2014).

Chapter 6

1. "What's Hot in the Living Spaces of Young
Adults?", American Demographics, 25, 7,
2003, 14.

2. Ronald Alsop, "The Best Corporate Reputa-
tions in America: Johnson & Johnson
(Think Babies!) Turns Up Tops," The Wall
Street Journal, September 23, 1999, B1; and
Alsop, "Survey Rates Companies' Reputa-
tions, and Many are Found Wanting," The
Wall Street Journal, February 7, 2001, B1.

3. Mystic Tan, www.mystictan.com (accessed
February 2006).

4. "Yogurt Consumption in Canada," Alberta
Agriculture and Rural Development, June
2014, www1.agric.gov.ab.ca/$department/
deptdocs.nsf/all/sis14591/$file/jeewani
_yogurt_market_revised_june%2011_2014
.pdf?OpenElement (accessed July 20, 2014).

5. Cathleen Egan, "Kellogg, General Mills
Battle over Bars," The Wall Street Journal,
March 26, 2001, B10.

6. "Bilingualism is Growing, But Not in English and French," CBC News, October 24,
2012, www.cbc.ca/news/canada/bilingualism
-growing-but-not-in-french-and-english
-1.1176469 (accessed November 8, 2013).

7. "LeBron James Hits $90M Jackpot," CBS
News, February 11, 2009.

8. "The Buzz Starts Here: Finding the
First Mouth for Word-of-Mouth Marketing," Knowledge@Wharton, March 4, 2009.

9. "Nintendo's Women Gamers Could
Transform Market," Times Online, October
10, 2007.

10. "2013 Sales, Demographic and Usage Data:
Essential Facts about the Computer and
Video Game Industry," Entertainment Soft-
ware Association (ESA), www.theesa
.com/facts/pdfs/ESA_EF_2013.pdf (accessed
November 9, 2013).

11. "Nintendo's Women Gamers Could Transform Market," Times Online, October 10,
2007.

12. Jack Neff, "Time to Rethink Your Message:
Now the Cart Belongs to Daddy," Advertising Age, January 17, 2011, 1.

13. Linda Crane, "YouthPulseSM 2010," Trends
& Tudes, November 2010.

14. Nora J. Rifon and Molly Catherine Ziske,
"Using Weight Loss Products: The Roles of
Involvement, Self-Efficacy and Body Image,"
in 1995 AMA Educators' Proceedings, ed.
Barbara B. Stern and George M. Zinkhan.
(Chicago: American Marketing Association,
1995), 90–98.

15. Keith Naughton, "In Car Buying, Baby
Boomers Surpass the Young," Bloomberg
Business Week, August 29, 2013, www
.businessweek.com/articles/2013-08-29/
in-car-buying-baby-boomers-surpass-the
-young (accessed November 9, 2013).

16. "PRIZM$_{C2}$ Segmentation," Environics Analytics, www.environicsanalytics.ca/environics
-analytics/data/consumer-segmentation/
prizmc2 (accessed November 9, 2013).

17. Sarah Hall, "What Color Is Your Cart?" Self,
September 1999, www.godiva.com
(accessed January 2006).

18. Joshua Rosenbaum, "Guitar Maker Looks
for a New Key," The Wall Street Journal,
February 11, 1998, B1, B5.

19. Elizabeth J. Wilson, "Using the Dollarmet-
ric Scale to Establish the Just Meaningful
Difference in Price," in 1987 AMA Educators' Proceedings, ed. Susan Douglas et al.
(Chicago: American Marketing Association,
1987), 107.

20. Sunil Gupta and Lee G. Cooper, "The
Discounting of Discounts and Promotion
Thresholds," Journal of Consumer Research,
December 1992, 401–411.

21. Mark Stiving and Russell S. Winer, "An
Empirical Analysis of Price Endings with
Scanner Data," Journal of Consumer
Research, June 1997, 57–67; and Robert M.
Schindler and Patrick N. Kirby, "Patterns of
Rightmost Digits Used in Advertised Prices:
Implications for Nine-Ending Effects," Jour-
nal of Consumer Research, September 1997,
192–201.

Chapter 7

1. "The Henry Ford: America's Greatest History Attraction—Annual Report 2004,"
The Henry Ford, 2, www.thehenryford
.org/images/AnnualReport04.pdf (accessed
September 15, 2014).

2. Industry Canada, "Consumer Trends:
Chapter 2—Consumers and Changing Retail
Markets," July 27, 2012, www.ic.gc.ca/eic/
site/oca-bc.nsf/eng/ca02096.html (accessed
August 9, 2014).

3. "Shaping the Future of Marketing: B2B,"
Canadian Marketing Association, www
.the-cma.org/disciplines/b2b (accessed September 15, 2014).

4. Robert M. Morgan and Shelby D. Hunt,
"The Commitment-Trust Theory of Relationship Marketing," Journal of Marketing,
58, 3, 1994, 23.

5. Ibid.

6. Leila Abboud, "How Eli Lilly's Monster
Deal Faced Extinction—But Survived,"
The Wall Street Journal, April 27,
2005, http://online.wsj.com/articles/
SB111455716131617636 (accessed
September 16, 2014).

7. Andrew Hampp, "Saatchi CEO Kevin Roberts Declares Death of Marketing, Future of Movements @ MIDEM," Billboard, January 30, 2012, www.billboard.com/biz/articles/news/branding/1099158/saatchi-ceo-kevin-roberts-declares-death-of-marketing-future-of (accessed September 16, 2014).

8. "About the IMP Group," Industrial Marketing and Purchasing Group, www.impgroup.org/about.php (accessed September 16, 2014).

9. Alan Greenspan, "Financial Literacy," The Federal Reserve Board, May 13, 2004, www.federalreserve.gov/Boarddocs/Speeches/2004/20040513/ (accessed September 16, 2014).

10. Scott C. Hammond and Lowell M. Glenn, "The Ancient Practice of Chinese Social Networking: Guanxi and Social Network Theory," E:CO, 6, 1–2, 2004, 24–31, http://emergentpublications.com/ECO/eco_other/issue_6_1-2_6_ac.pdf?AspxAutoDetectCookieSupport=1 (accessed September 16, 2014).

11. "Delivering Results That Matter to Canadians," Network of Centres of Excellence of Canada, 2012, www.nce-rce.gc.ca/_docs/reports/annual-annuel/Annual_Report_2011-2012_Rapport_Annuel_eng.pdf (accessed September 16, 2014).

12. Lin Ai and Michael Burt, "Walking the Silk Road: Understanding Canada's Changing Trade Patterns," The Conference Board of Canada, December 2012, www.conferenceboard.ca/e-library/abstract.aspx?did=5266 (accessed September 16, 2014).

13. "Goods and Services," Buyandsell.gc.ca Public Works and Government Services Canada, September 2, 2014, https://buyandsell.gc.ca/goods-and-services (accessed September 16, 2014).

14. Ibid.

15. "Public Sector Employment, Wages and Salaries, by Province and Territory (Newfoundland and Labrador)," Statistics Canada, May 30, 2012, www.statcan.gc.ca/tables-tableaux/sum-som/l01/cst01/govt62a-eng.htm (accessed September 16, 2014).

16. Matevž Rašković and Barbara Mörec, "Determinants of Supplier-Buyer Relationship Competitiveness in Transnational Companies," Economic and Business Review, 15 (1), 2013, 5–31, www.ebrjournal.net/ojs/index.php/ebr/article/download/211/pdf (accessed August 9, 2013).

17. "E-commerce Doubles in 5 Years but Still a Fraction of Sales," CBC News, June 12, 2013, www.cbc.ca/news/business/e-commerce-doubles-in-5-years-but-still-a-fraction-of-sales-1.1390340 (accessed September 16, 2014).

18. David Sweet, M.P., Chair, "E-commerce in Canada: Pursuing the Promise—Report of the Standing Committee on Industry, Science and Technology," May 2012, www.parl.gc.ca/content/hoc/Committee/411/INDU/Reports/RP5535392/indurp01/indurp01-e.pdf (accessed September 16, 2014).

19. Ibid.

20. "2013 B2B Commerce Trends," Oracle, April 2013, www.oracle-downloads.com/b2b_commercetrends.pdf (accessed September 16, 2014).

21. "2014 B2B Content Marketing Benchmarks, Budgets, and Trends," MarketingProfs, October 1, 2013, www.marketingprofs.com/charts/2013/11759/2014-b2b-content-marketing-benchmarks-budgets-and-trends (accessed September 16, 2014).

22. Dom Nicastro, "B2B Marketing Stats: CEOs Don't Trust CMOs, Social Doesn't Work, Banner Ads Aren't Dead," CMSWire.com, October 17, 2013, www.cmswire.com/cms/digital-marketing/b2b-marketing-stats-ceos-dont-trust-cmos-social-doesnt-work-banner-ads-arent-dead-022832.php (accessed September 16, 2014).

23. Barry Levine, "Forrester Report: The Social Media Habits of B2B Customers," CMSWire.com, July 18, 2013, www.cmswire.com/cms/customer-experience/forrester-report-the-social-media-habits-of-b2b-customers-021777.php (accessed September 16, 2014).

Chapter 8

1. "How Marketers Target Kids," Media Smarts, http://mediasmarts.ca/marketing-consumerism/how-marketers-target-kids (accessed November 8, 2013).

2. "Population by Sex and Age Group," Statistics Canada, November 25, 2013, www.statcan.gc.ca/tables-tableaux/sum-som/l01/cst01/demo10a-eng.htm (accessed November 8, 2013).

3. "Canadian Teenagers are Leading the Online Revolution? Maybe Not…," Ipsos, February 27, 2008, www.ipsos-na.com/news-polls/pressrelease.aspx?id=3829 (accessed February 6, 2011).

4. "Magazines for Teens—Online!", This IS Literacy, www.thisisliteracy.ca/teenagers/resources/407 (accessed November 9, 2013).

5. Ibid.

6. "Generations in Canada," Statistics Canada, December 18, 2013, www12.statcan.gc.ca/census-recensement/2011/as-sa/98-311-x/98-311-x2011003_2-eng.cfm (accessed November 9, 2013).

7. Bill Curry, "Highlights: Canada's Baby Boom Larger than in Other G8 Countries," The Globe and Mail, June 19, 2012, www.theglobeandmail.com/news/politics/highlights-canadas-baby-boom-larger-than-in-other-g8-countries/article4217072/ (accessed November 9, 2013).

8. Romina Maurino, "Boomers Tough Marketing Target," Winnipeg Free Press, September 9, 2013, www.winnipegfreepress.com/canada/boomers-tough-marketing-target-222921831.html (accessed November 9, 2013).

9. Mark Kennedy, "Canada's Aging Boomers Place New Strain on Pensions, Health Care: Census," National Post, May 29, 2012, http://news.nationalpost.com/2012/05/29/canadas-aging-boomers-are-placing-new-strain-on-business-government/ (accessed November 8, 2013).

10. "Dentures get Sexed Up," Marketing Magazine, September 9, 2002, 16.

11. "Canadian Baby Boomers Testing the Waters of New Technology," Ipsos, November 20, 2012, www.ipsos-na.com/news-polls/pressrelease.aspx?id=5903 (accessed November 8, 2013).

12. Jen Weigel, "Grooms getting Involved," Chicago Tribune, February 23, 2012, http://articles.chicagotribune.com/2012-02-23/features/ct-tribu-weigel-grooms-20120223_1_wedding-dress-grooms-wedding-planning (accessed November 9, 2013).

13. "Nivea for Men," www.casestudiesonline.com/nivea-for-men-targeted-women-partners-to-market-their-products/ (accessed November 9, 2013).

14. "2013 Sales, Demographic and Usage Data: Essential Facts about the Computer and Video Game Industry," Entertainment Software Association (ESA), www.theesa.com/facts/pdfs/ESA_EF_2013.pdf (accessed November 9, 2013).

15. "Holiday Proposal Dos and Don'ts," Wedding Channel, http://weddings.weddingchannel.com/wedding-planning-ideas/proposals-engagement-advice/articles/holiday-proposal-dos-and-donts.aspx (accessed November 9, 2013).

16. "Bilingualism Is Growing, but Not in English and French," CBC News, October 24, 2012, www.cbc.ca/news/canada/bilingualism-growing-but-not-in-french-and-english-1.1176469 (accessed November 8, 2013).

17. Misty Harris, "Oh, Canada! Ethnic Marketing Giving Way to 'Post-Multiculturalism'," Canada.com, October 25, 2013, http://o.canada.com/news/oh-canada-ethnic-marketing-giving-way-to-post-multiculturalism/ (accessed November 9, 2013).

18. Heather Scoffield, "Median Family Income in Canada Is $76,000, StatsCan Survey Shows," CTV News, September 11, 2013, www.ctvnews.ca/canada/median-family-income-in-canada-is-76-000-statscan-survey-shows-1.1449641#ixzz2iezg6lk4 (accessed November 9, 2013).

19. Michael Babad, "One-Quarter of Canadian Families Spend More than They Should on Housing," The Globe and Mail, September 11, 2013, www.theglobeandmail.com/report-on-business/top-business-stories/one-quarter-of-canadian-families-spend-more-than-they-should-on-housing/article14241564/ (accessed November 9, 2013).

20. Bruce Campion-Smith, "Canadian Families Growing More Diverse, Census Data Shows," Toronto Star, September 20, 2012, www.thestar.com/news/canada/2012/09/20/canadian_families_growing_more_diverse_census_data_shows.html (accessed November 9, 2013).

21. Ibid.

22. Charles W. Lamb, Jr., Joe F. Hair, Jr., Carl McDaniel, A. J. Faria and William J. Wellington, Marketing, Fourth Canadian Edition. (Toronto: Nelson Education Ltd., 2009), 169–170.

23. "PRIZM$_{C2}$ Segmentation," Environics Analytics, www.environicsanalytics.ca/environics-analytics/data/consumer-segmentation/prizmc2 (accessed November 9, 2013).

24. "Luna Protein FAQs," LUNA, www.lunabar.com/products/faqs/luna-protein (accessed September 16, 2014).

25. "Canadian Food Trends to 2020: A Long Range Consumer Outlook," Agriculture and Agri-Food Canada, July 2005, www.weldenscott.ca/pdf/ft-ta_e.pdf (accessed November 8, 2013).

26. "About," The Chickenburger, www .thechickenburger.com/content/about (accessed November 9, 2013).

27. Danny Kucharsky, "Mega Bloks Target Kids at Retail," *Marketing Magazine*, November 12, 2001, 4.

28. "Brands," Gap Inc., www.gapinc.com/ content/gapinc/html/aboutus/ourbrands .html (accessed April 18, 2012).

29. "Rihanna Tops the Charts with Milk— Video!", All Women Stalk, http:// allwomenstalk.com/rihanna-tops-the-charts -with-milk-video/ (accessed September 1, 2011).

30. Vijay Mahajan and Yoram Wind, "Get Emotional Product Positioning," *Marketing Management*, May/June 2002, 36–41.

31. John Ellett, "Being Transparent to Revitalize a Brand—The Domino's Story," *Forbes*, August 25, 2011, www.forbes.com/sites/ johnellett/2011/08/25/being-transparent -to-revitalize-a-brand-the-dominos-story/ (accessed November 9, 2013).

32. Alice Tybout and Brian Sternthal, "Brand Positioning," in *Kellogg on Branding: The Marketing Faculty of The Kellogg School of Management*, ed. Tim Calkins et al. (Hoboken, NJ: John Wiley & Sons, Inc., 2005).

33. Ibid.

Part 2 Case

1. "Analyzing the Cosmetics Industry in Canada," Research and Markets, August 2014, www.researchandmarkets.com/reports/ 546301/analyzing_the_cosmetics_industry _in_canada (accessed August, 2014).

2. Ibid.

3. Ibid.

4. "The Industry: Profile of Direct Sellers," Direct Sellers Association of Canada, http:// dsa.ca/the-industry/industry-stats/ (accessed June 5, 2014).

5. Ibid.

6. Mary Kay home page, www.marykay.ca (accessed June 5, 2014).

7. "Mary Kay Targets Millennials," Household and Personal Products Industry, December 6, 2013, www.happi.com/contents/view _breaking-news/2013-12-06/mary-kay -targets-millennials/ (accessed June 5, 2014).

8. Ibid.

9. Ibid.

10. Lauri Dodd, "Youthful (R)evolution," *Direct Selling News*, December 6, 2010, http://directsellingnews.com/index.php/view/ youthful_revolution#.U6GAZ_ldWSo (accessed June 5, 2014).

Chapter 9

1. Todd Wasserman, "P&G Tries to Absorb More Low-End Sales," *BrandWeek*, September 26, 2005, 4.

2. Todd Wasserman, "P&G Seeks Right Ingredient to Wash Out Laundry Woes," *BrandWeek*, August 8, 2005, 5.

3. Kenneth Hein, "Parade of Drinks May Clog Channel," *BrandWeek*, February 7, 2005, 4.

4. Janet Adamy, "Heinz Sets Overhaul Plans in Motion," *The Wall Street Journal*, September 20, 2005, A4.

5. "Dictionary," American Marketing Association, www.marketingpower.com/_layouts/ dictionary.aspx?dLetter=B (accessed, January 5, 2014).

6. "Nielsen: Store Brand Consumers Evolving in Canada," www.pgstorebrands.com/ top-story-nielsen__store_brand_consumers _evolving_in_canada-709.html (accessed February 9, 2011).

7. Chris Powell, "Store Brands Losing Their Lustre: Study," *Marketing*, July 22, 2011, www.marketingmag.ca/news/marketer-news/ store-brands-losing-their-lustre-study-32536 (accessed January 2, 2014).

8. Ibid.

9. Deborah L. Vence, "Product Enhancement," *Marketing News*, May 1, 2005, 19.

10. Ibid.

11. Erin White, "Burberry Wants the Knockoffs to Knock it Off," *Fort Worth Star Telegram*, May 28, 2003, 6F.

12. Deborah Ball, "The Perils of Packaging: Nestlé Aims for Easier Openings," *The Wall Street Journal*, November 17, 2005, B1.

Chapter 10

1. Marsha Lindsay, "8 Ways to Ensure Your New-Product Launch Succeeds," Fast Company, www.fastcompany.com/1829483/8 -ways-ensure-your-new-product-launch -succeeds (accessed January 7, 2014).

2. Patricia Sellers, "P&G: Teaching an Old Dog New Tricks," *Fortune*, May 31, 2004, 168–178.

3. Elaine Watson, "J M Smucker: 'Our Innovation Success Rate Exceeds Industry Norms'," FoodNavigator-USA.com, September 4, 2013, www.foodnavigator-usa.com/ Manufacturers/J-M-Smucker-Our -innovation-success-rate-exceeds-industry -norms (accessed January 9, 2014).

4. Ibid.

5. Sellers, "P&G: Teaching an Old Dog New Tricks," 168.

6. Barbara Keller, "McDonald's #1 Repositioning Method," barbarakeller, November 22, 2011, http://barbarakeller.wordpress .com/2011/11/22/mcdonalds-1-repositioning -method/ (accessed January 10, 2014).

7. Renee Hopkins Callahan et al., "The Case for In-the-Box Innovation," Decision Analyst, www.decisionanalyst.com/Downloads/ IntheBoxInnovation.pdf (accessed September 16, 2014).

8. Gary Fraser and Bryan Mattimor, "Slow Down, Speed Up New Product Growth," *Brandweek*, January 10, 2005, 18.

9. Rachel Emma Silverman, "For Bright Ideas, Ask the Staff," *The Wall Street Journal*, October 17, 2011, http://online.wsj.com/ news/articles/SB10001424052970204774604576631063939483984 (accessed January 10, 2014).

10. Sellers, "P&G: Teaching an Old Dog New Tricks," 174.

11. Ryan Tate, "Google Couldn't Kill 20 Percent Time Even if it Wanted To," Wired, August 21, 2013, www.wired.com/ business/2013/08/20-percent-time-will -never-die/ (accessed February 20, 2014).

12. Sellers, "P&G: Teaching an Old Dog New Tricks," 174.

13. Chris Penttila, "Keeping it Fresh," *Entrepreneur*, April 2005, 88.

14. Adam Hartung, "Top 20 R&D Spenders— Not Good Investments," *Forbes*, November, 5, 2012, www.forbes.com/sites/adamhartung/ 2012/11/05/top-20-rd-spenders-not-good -investments/ (accessed January 12, 2014).

15. Aaron Tilley, "Google Acquires Smart Thermostat Maker Nest for $3.2 Billion," *Forbes*, January 13, 2014, www.forbes.com/sites/ aarontilley/2014/01/13/google-acquires -nest-for-3-2-billion/ (accessed January 14, 2014).

16. Sarah Ellison and Charles Forelle, "Gillette's Smooth Bet: Men Will Pay More for Five-Blade Razor," *The Wall Street Journal*, September 15, 2005, B1, B5.

17. Paul Lukas, "How Many Blades Is Enough?," *Fortune*, October 31, 2005, 40.

18. Pete Engardio, "Scouring the Planet for Brainiacs," *BusinessWeek*, October 11, 2004, 106.

19. Kevin J. Clancy and Peter C. Krieg, "Product Life Cycle: A Dangerous Idea," *Brandweek*, March 1, 2004, 26.

20. "When Will it Fly?", *The Economist*, August 9, 2003, 332.

21. James Daly, "Restart, Redo, Recharge," *Business 2.0*, May 1, 2001, 11.

Chapter 11

1. "What Canadians Think about Their Banks," Canadian Bankers Association, www.cba .ca/en/media-room/50-backgrounders-on -banking-issues/480-what-canadians -think-about-their-banks (accessed December 2013).

2. "Employment by Industry and Sex," Statistics Canada, www.statcan.gc.ca/tables -tableaux/sum-som/l01/cst01/labor10a-eng .htm (accessed December 2013).

3. The Canadian Services Coalition, www .chamber.ca/advocacy/canadian-services -coalition/CSC-brochure.pdf (accessed December 2013).

4. Megan Haynes, "Brands of the Year: Davids Tea Brews Up Growth," *Strategy*, October 3, 2013, http://strategyonline.ca/2013/10/03/ brands-of-the-year-davidstea-brews-up -growth/ (accessed September 17, 2014).

5. Valarie A. Zeithaml, Mary Jo Bitner, and Dwayne D. Gremler, *Services Marketing: Integrating Customer Focus across the Firm*, 4th ed. (New York: McGraw Hill, 2006).

6. "About Us," Starbucks, www.starbucks.ca/ about-us (accessed December 2013).

7. Valarie A. Zeithaml, Mary Jo Bitner, and Dwayne D. Gremler, *Services Marketing: Integrating Customer Focus across the Firm*, 4th ed. (New York: McGraw Hill, 2006).

8. "Working at Starbucks," Starbucks, www .starbucks.ca/careers/working-at-starbucks (accessed December 2013).

9. Much of the material in this section is based on Christopher H. Lovelock and Jochen Wirtz, *Services Marketing*, 5th ed. (Upper Saddle River, NJ: Prentice Hall, 2004).

10. "About the Grounds Guys," The Grounds Guys, www.groundsguys.ca/about/ (accessed December 2013).

11. "The 7 Pillars," Moksha Yoga International, www.mokshayoga.ca/about/the_7_pillars/ (accessed December 2013).

12. "Family Healthcare Delivered to You," Ronald McDonald House Southern Alberta, www.ahomeawayfromhome.org/southern/welcome/programs/the-care-mobile/schedule.html#.Ung6gHBJOAg (accessed December 2013).

13. "Changes at Hamilton Health Sciences Enhance Care, Improve System Sustainability," Hamilton Health Sciences, April 4, 2011, www.mcmasterchildrenshospital.ca/workfiles/PR/ABC%20-%20April%204,%202011%20News%20Release%20and%20Backgrounder.doc (accessed April 19, 2011).

14. "About Medavie EMS," Medavie EMS, www.medaviems.com/Pages/default.aspx (accessed December 2013).

15. Lovelock and Wirtz, *Services Marketing*.

16. Much of the material in this section is based on Leonard L. Berry and A. Parasuraman, *Marketing Services: Competing through Quality*. New York: The Free Press, 1991, 132–150.

17. James Christie, "Onsite Gyms Show Firms' Commitment to Health," *The Globe and Mail*, October 9, 2012, www.theglobeandmail.com/report-on-business/careers/top-employers/onsite-gyms-show-firms-commitment-to-health/article4598606/ (accessed September 17, 2014).

18. "International Commerce—By Country," Foreign Affairs, Trade and Development Canada, October 8, 2013, http://w03.international.gc.ca/Commerce_International/Commerce_Country-Pays.aspx?lang=eng (accessed December 2013).

19. "Sector Impact," Imagine Canada, http://sectorsource.ca/research-and-impact/sector-impact (accessed December 2013).

20. Ibid.

Part 3 Case

1. "Get the Rest of the Story," Harley-Davidson Museum, www.harley-davidson.com/content/h-d/en_US/home/museum/explore/hd-timeline.html (accessed June 7, 2014).

2. Ibid.

3. "Best Global Brands 2013," Interbrand, www.interbrand.com/en/best-global-brands/2013/Harley-Davidson (accessed June 7, 2014).

4. "The Canadian Annual Industry Statistics Report Summary from MMIC and COHV, January 1st, 2013 to December 31st, 2013," The Motorcycle & Moped Industry Council, www.mmic.ca/content.asp?ContentId=1058 (accessed June 7, 2014).

5. Ibid.

6. Ibid.

7. Cyril Huze, "In 2013 What Is the Average Age of a Harley-Davidson Buyer?," Cyril Huze Post, June 27, 2013, http://cyrilhuzeblog.com/2013/06/27/in-2013-what-is-the-average-age-of-a-harley-davidson-buyer-2/ (accessed June 7, 2014).

8. Ibid.

9. "Why Harley-Davidson Can't Break through the Wall of China," *Forbes*, January 31, 2014, www.forbes.com/sites/greatspeculations/2014/01/31/why-harley-davidson-cant-break-through-the-wall-of-china/ (accessed June 8, 2014).

10. Ibid.

Chapter 12

1. Richard Meyer, "More 2014 Marketing Predictions…," New Media and Marketing, "www.newmediaandmarketing.com/more-2014-marketing-predictions/ (accessed September 18, 2014).

2. "Market Share Quotes," BrainyQuote, www.brainyquote.com/quotes/keywords/market_share.html (accessed September 18, 2014).

3. Brian Karlovsky, "Samsung, Apple, Microsoft Fight for Share of Booming Tablet Market," Computerworld, November 27, 2013, http://news.idg.no/cw/art.cfm?id=01809FBF-A27A-6E21-9F8C2220919108FA (accessed September 18, 2014).

4. Kent B. Monroe and Jennifer L. Cox, "Pricing Practices that Endanger Profits," *Marketing Management*, 10, 3, 2001, 42–46.

5. Thomas T. Nagle and George Cressman, "Don't Just Set Prices, Manage Them," *Marketing Management*, November/December 2002, 29–33; Jay Klompmaker, William H. Rogers, and Anthony Nygren, "Value, Not Volume," *Marketing Management*, June 2003, 45–48; and Alison Wellner, "Boost Your Bottom Line by Taking the Guesswork Out of Pricing," *Inc.*, June 2005, 72–82.

6. John Kirk, "Android's Penetration vs. Apple's Skimming Marketing Strategies," Tech.pinions, March 21, 2013, http://techpinions.com/androidss-penetration-vs-apples-skimming-marketing-strategies/15255 (accessed September 18, 2014).

7. "Out-Discounting the Discounter," *Business-Week*, May 9, 2004, 78–79; an interesting article on shoppers who use penetration pricing to their advantage is Edward J. Fox and Stephen J. Hoch, "Cherry-Picking," *Journal of Marketing*, 69, 1, 2005, 46–62.

8. Bruce Alford and Abhijit Biswas, "The Effects of Discount Level, Price Consciousness, and Sale Proneness on Consumers' Price Perception and Behavioral Intention," *Journal of Business Research*, September 2002, 775–783. See also V. Kumar, Vibhas Madan, and Srini Srinivasan, "Price Discounts or Coupon Promotions: Does It Matter?", *Journal of Business Research*, September 2004, 933–941.

9. "Price War in Aisle 3," *The Wall Street Journal*, May 27, 2003, B1, B16. See also Kathleen Seiders and Glenn Voss, "From Price to Purchase," *Marketing Management*, December 2004, 38–43; "Grocery Stores Cut Out the Weekly Specials," *The Wall Street Journal*, July 20, 2005, D1, D3; and Gerald E. Smith and Thomas Nagle, "A Question of Value," *Marketing Management*, July/August 2005, 39–44.

10. To learn more about pricing fairness, see Lan Xia, Kent B. Monroe, and Jennifer L. Cox, "The Price Is Unfair! A Conceptual Framework of Price Fairness Perceptions," *Journal of Marketing*, 68, 2004, 1–15.

11. David Bell, Ganesh Iyer, and V. Padmanabhar, "Price Competition under Stockpiling and Flexible Consumption," *Journal of Marketing Research*, 49, 2002, 292–303.

12. Dilip Soman and John Gourville, "Transaction Decoupling: The Effects of Price Bundling on the Decision to Consume," MSI Report, 2002, 98–131; Stefan Stremersch and Gerard J. Tellis, "Strategic Bundling of Products and Prices: A New Synthesis for Marketing," *Journal of Marketing*, January 2002, 55–71; and "Forget Prices and Get People to Use the Stuff," *The Wall Street Journal*, June 3, 2004, A2.

13. Dilip Soman and John Gourville, "Transaction Decoupling: How Price Bundling Affects the Decision to Consume," *Journal of Marketing Research*, 38, 2001, 30–44.

14. Patrick Brethour and Janet McFarland, "Forzani Agrees to Pay Record Fine," The *Globe and Mail*, July 7, 2004, B1, B22.

15. "Grafton-Fraser Pays $1.2 Million to Settle Misleading Advertising Case with Competition Bureau," Market Wired, July 27, 2006, www.marketwired.com/press-release/grafton-fraser-pays-12-million-settle-misleading-advertising-case-with-competition-bureau-605480.htm (accessed September 18, 2014).

16. "Gas Stations Busted for Price Fixing in Quebec," *Kelowna Daily Courier*, June 13, 2008, A1, A5; "Quebec Gas Companies Charged with Price Fixing," CTV News, June 12, 2008, www.ctvnews.ca/quebec-gas-companies-charged-with-price-fixing-1.301955 (accessed September 2008).

17. Nicolas Van Praet, "Profitable WestJet Accuses Air Canada of Using Court-Protection to Reduce Air Fares Below Cost," *CanWest News*, October 20, 2003, 1; "Small B.C. Airline Accuses Insolvent Air Canada of Predatory Pricing," *Canadian Press News-Wire*, April 16, 2003.

18. Phillip Dampier, "BC Supreme Court Tosses Out Novus Entertainment's Lawsuit against Shaw Cable," Stop the Cap!, August 18, 2010, http://stopthecap.com/2010/08/18/bc-supreme-courttosses-out-novus-entertainments-lawsuit-againstshaw-cable/ (accessed September 1, 2011).

19. "Charges Laid in a Price-fixing Cartel in the Chocolate Industry," Competition Bureau, June 6, 2013, www.competitionbureau.gc.ca/eic/site/cb-bc.nsf/eng/03569.html (accessed September 18, 2014). This is an excerpt from a June 6, 2013, statement regarding alleged price-fixing activities by Mars, Nestlé, and other chocolate manufacturers in Canada. Hershey Canada pled guilty a few weeks later.

20. "Phasing Out the Penny," Royal Canadian Mint, www.mint.ca/store/mint/about-the-mint/phasing-out-the-penny-6900002 (accessed September 18, 2014).

21. "Hershey Canada Fined $4M for Chocolate Price Fixing," CBC News, June 21, 2013, www.cbc.ca/news/business/hershey-canada-fined-4m-for-chocolate-price-fixing-1.1313336 (accessed September 18, 2014).

22. "'Country pricing' a Cause of Canada-U.S. Price Gaps," CBC News, February 8, 2013, www.cbc.ca/news/canada/country-pricing-a-cause-of-canada-u-s-price-gaps-1.1405894 (accessed September 18, 2014).

Chapter 12 Appendix

1. Tammo H. A. Bijmolt, Harald J. van Heerde, and Rik G. M. Pieters, "New Empirical Generalizations on the Determinants of Price Elasticity," *Journal of Marketing Research*, XLII, 2005, 141–156; Christian Homburg, Wayne D. Hoyer, and Nicole Koschate, "Customers' Reactions to Price Increases: Do Customer Satisfaction and Perceived Motive Fairness Matter?", *Journal of the Academy of Marketing Science*, 33, 1, 2005, 36–49; and Gadi Fibich, Arieh Gavious, and Oded Lowengart, "The Dynamics of Price Elasticity of Demand in the Presence of Reference Price Effects," *Journal of the Academy of Marketing Science*, 33, 1, 2005, 66–78.
2. Equation is from "Marketing Analytics_1" file from Ingrid Mueller.

Part 4 Case

1. Greg Sandoval, "Netflix's Lost Year: The Inside Story of the Price-hike Train Wreck," CNET, July 11, 2012, www.cnet.com/news/netflixs-lost-year-the-inside-story-of-the-price-hike-train-wreck/ (accessed September 18, 2014).
2. Chris Sorensen, "Video Stores Bring Back Late Charges," *Toronto Star*, November 23, 2007, www.thestar.com/business/2007/11/23/video_stores_bring_back_late_charges.html (accessed September 18, 2014).
3. Matt Phillips and Roberto A. Ferdman, "A Brief, Illustrated History of Blockbuster, Which Is Closing the Last of Its US Stores," Quartz, November 7, 2013, http://qz.com/144372/a-brief-illustrated-history-of-blockbuster-which-is-closing-the-last-of-its-us-stores/ (accessed September 18, 2014).
4. Jessie Becker, "A New Plan for Watching Instantly, Plus Price Changes to Existing Unlimited Plans," Netflix, November 22, 2010, http://blog.netflix.com/2010/11/new-plan-for-watching-instantly-plus.html (accessed September 18, 2014).
5. Jason O. Gilbert, "'How Could Netflix Do This to Me?': Netflix Users Lash Out," *HuffPost Tech*, September 13, 2011, www.huffingtonpost.com/2011/07/14/how-could-netflix-do-this-to-me_n_897763.html#s308542title=Carlos_Perez (accessed September 18, 2014).
6. Dan Frommer, "Netflix already Proves that Raising DVD Prices was the Right Move," *HuffPost Business*, September 25, 2011, www.huffingtonpost.com/dan-frommer/netflix-dvd-prices_b_909628.html (accessed September 18, 2014).
7. Michael Liedtke, "Netflix Kids Section Launches Amid Subscriber Backlash," *HuffPost Tech*, October 16, 2011, www.huffingtonpost.com/2011/08/16/netflix-just-for-kids-section_n_928026.html (accessed September 18, 2014).
8. Netflix, January 22, 2014, http://files.shareholder.com/downloads/NFLX/2561927671x7287565x720306/119321bc-89c3-4306-93ac-93c02da2354f/Q4 percent2013 percent20Letter percent20to percent20shareholders.pdf (accessed September 18, 2014).

Chapter 13

1. Nicole Harris, "'Private Exchanges' May Allow B-to-B Commerce to Thrive After All," *The Wall Street Journal*, March 16, 2001, B1; Michael Totty, "The Next Phase," *The Wall Street Journal*, May 21, 2001, R8.
2. "Pot Vending Machines Coming to Canada, Medbox Promises," *The Huffington Post*, October 17, 2013, www.huffingtonpost.ca/2013/10/17/pot-vending-machines-canada_n_4116533.html (accessed September 18, 2014).
3. "Pepsi, Starbucks Teaming Up," *Supermarket News*, October 31, 1994, 31; "Starbucks Corporation Fiscal 2006 Annual Report," Starbucks, 2006, http://media.corporate-ir.net/media_files/irol/99/99518/reports/StarbucksAnnualReport.pdf (accessed September 18, 2014).
4. Toyota Industrial Equipment, www.toyota-forklift.com (accessed September 18, 2014); www.toyotaforklift.com/about_us/company_profile/toyotaphilosophy.aspx; Elena Eptako Murphy, "Buying on Price Alone Can Lead to High Operating Costs," Purchasing.com, September 4, 2003.
5. "About Brokerhouse," Brokerhouse Distributors Inc., www.brokerhousedist.com/About.aspx (accessed September 18, 2014).
6. Cassie Howard, "How Does Dollarama get Name Brand Items?", DollarStoreHouse.com, www.dollarstorehouse.com/dollarama-name-brands/ (accessed September 18, 2014).
7. Leigh Muzslay, "Shoes that Morph from Sneakers to Skates are Flying Out of Stores," *The Wall Street Journal*, July 26, 2001, B1; Heelys, www.heelys.com (accessed January 2006).
8. Neil Hughes, "Apple Store Sales Fall 3% as iPhone, iPad Distribution Network Grows," Apple Insider, November 11, 2013, http://appleinsider.com/articles/13/11/11/apple-store-sales-fall-3-as-iphone-ipad-distribution-network-grows (accessed September 18, 2014).
9. "Angela Ahrendts to Join Apple as Senior Vice President of Retail and Online Stores," Apple Press Info, October 14, 2013, www.apple.com/pr/library/2013/10/15Angela-Ahrendts-to-Join-Apple-as-Senior-Vice-President-of-Retail-and-Online-Stores.html (accessed September 18, 2014).
10. Jonathan Welsh, "Auto Makers Now 'Slam' Cars Right in the Factory," *The Wall Street Journal*, October 30, 2001, B1.
11. Owen Keates, "Flow Control," *New Zealand Management*, 48, 2, 2001, 28.
12. Julie Schlosser, "Just Do It," *Fortune*, December 13, 2004, http://archive.fortune.com/magazines/fortune/fortune_archive/2004/12/13/8214244/index.htm (accessed September 18, 2014).
13. "Zara," Inditex, www.inditex.com/en/brands/zara (accessed August 4, 2014).
14. Amazon.com, www.amazon.com (accessed February 2006).
15. Glenn Bischoff, "Item-Level RFID Takes a Step Forward," IWCE's Urgent Communications, January 1, 2006, http://urgentcomm.com/mag/item-level-rfid-takes-step-forward (accessed January 2006); Mary Catherine O'Connor, "Walgreen to Use Tagged Displays," RFID Journal, December 7, 2005, www.rfidjournal.com/articles/view?2031 (accessed February 2006); and NCR, www.ncr.com (accessed February 2006).
16. "Leveraged Procurement," www.outsourcing-supply-chain-management.com/leveraged.html; and Sysco, www.sysco.ca (accessed September 18, 2014).
17. Toby Herscovitch, "Wide Range: Cutting the Cost of Crossing Borders," *ExportWise*, Winter 2006, 8–9.
18. Kevin Hogan, "Borderline Savings," *Business 2.0*, May 17, 2001, 34.
19. "Logistics Performance Index," The World Bank, http://lpi.worldbank.org (accessed September 18, 2014).
20. "State of Channel Study," CompTIA, May 1 2013, www.comptia.org/resources/state-of-channel-study-channel-conflict-deal-registration-trends (accessed June 2014).
21. Neil Hughes, "Apple Store Sales Fall 3% as iPhone, iPad Distribution Network Grows," Apple Insider, November 11, 2013, http://appleinsider.com/articles/13/11/11/apple-store-sales-fall-3-as-iphone-ipad-distribution-network-grows (accessed September 18, 2014).
22. Je' Czaja , "Examples of Successful Strategic Alliances," *Chron*, http://smallbusiness.chron.com/examples-successful-strategic-alliances-13859.html (accessed September 18, 2014).

Chapter 14

1. "The Structure of Retail in Canada: Statistical Appendix," www.retailcouncil.org/sites/default/files/documents/the-structure-of-retail-in-canada-statistical-appendix-2013.pdf (accessed September 18, 2014).
2. "Retail Sales, by Industry," Statistics Canada, www.statcan.gc.ca/tables-tableaux/sum-som/l01/cst01/trad15a-eng.htm (accessed October 2013).
3. "Canada's Changing Retail Market: Consumer Trends Update—Summer 2013," Industry Canada, August 2, 2013, www.ic.gc.ca/eic/site/oca-bc.nsf/eng/ca02854.html (accessed October 2013).
4. "Investor Relations," Hudson's Bay Company, http://investor.hbc.com/ (accessed October 2013).
5. Bertrand Marotte, "Loblaw to Buy Shoppers Drug Mart for $12.4-billion," July 15, 2013, *The Globe and Mail*, www.theglobeandmail.com/report-on-business/loblaw-to-buy-shoppers-drug-mart-for-124-billion/article13215651/ (accessed October 2013); and Marina Strauss and Steve Ladurantaye, "Sobeys Snaps Up Safeway in Western Push," *The Globe and Mail*, June 13, 2013, www.theglobeandmail.com/report-on-business/sobeys-to-buy-safeway-in-58-billion-deal/article12499648/ (accessed October 2013).
6. "Industry Fact Sheet," Canadian Convenience Stores Association, www.theccsa.ca/content/industry-fact-sheet?language=en (accessed October 2013).

7. "Shop Brilliantly," Toronto Premium Outlets, www.torontopremiumoutlets.ca/; and David Shum, "Toronto Premium Outlets open in Halton Hills," *Global BC*, August 1, 2013, http://globalnews.ca/news/754596/toronto-premium-outlets-open-in-halton-hills/ (accessed October 2013).

8. Olga Kharif, "Vending Machines Get Smart to Accommodate the Cashless," *Bloomberg BusinessWeek*, August 29, 2013, www.businessweek.com/articles/2013-08-29/vending-machines-get-smart-to-accommodate-the-cashless (accessed October 2013).

9. "2014 IKEA Catalogue Comes to Life with Augmented Reality," IKEA, August 12, 2013, www.ikea.com/ca/en/about_ikea/newsitem/2014catalogue (accessed October 2013).

10. Etan Vlessing, "Canada's The Shopping Channel Rebrands amid Digital Makeover," *The Hollywood Reporter*, September 6, 2013, www.hollywoodreporter.com/news/canadas-shopping-channel-rebrands-digital-623130 (accessed October 2013).

11. Hollie Shaw, "Online Retail Sales to Hit $34-billion in Canada by 2018," *Financial Post*, July 23, 2013, http://business.financialpost.com/2013/07/23/online-retail-sales-to-hit-40-billion-in-canada-by-2018/ (Acessed October 2013).

12. "MasterCard Tap & Go™ Contactless Technology Paves the Way for Mobile Payments in Canada," CNW, November 7, 2013, www.newswire.ca/en/story/1256601/mastercard-tap-gotm-contactless-technology-paves-the-way-for-mobile-payments-in-canada (accessed August 2014).

13. "Fast Franchise Facts," Canadian Franchise Association, www.cfa.ca/Publications_Research/FastFacts.aspx (accessed October 2013).

14. "Purchasing Your Franchise," McDonald's, www.mcdonalds.ca/ca/en/our_story/corporate_info/franchising/purchasing_your_franchise.html (accessed October 2013).

15. Hollie Shaw, "Hudson's Bay Co Bets on Saks Deal to Lift Luxury Shopping in Canada," *Financial Post*, September 12, 2013, http://business.financialpost.com/2013/09/12/hudsons-bay-co-cuts-dividend-to-help-pay-for-2-9-billion-saks-deal/ (accessed October 2013).

16. "About Us," Caterpillar Baby, www.caterpillarbaby.com/about-caterpillar-baby (accessed October 2014).

Part 5 Case

1. Malathi Nayak, "Take Two's GTA V Starts Strong with $800 mln in First-day Sales," Reuters, September 18, 2013, www.reuters.com/article/2013/09/18/us-taketwo-gta-idUSBRE98H0Z720130918 (accessed September 18, 2014).

2. "Annual Movie Chart—2013," The Numbers, www.the-numbers.com/market/2013/top-grossing-movies (accessed September 18, 2014).

3. Peter Nowak, "Perfect 'GTA V' May Be the Best Game Ever Made," *The Globe and Mail*, September 17, 2013, www.theglobeandmail.com/technology/gaming/perfect-gta-v-may-be-the-best-game-

ever-made/article14333923/?page=all (accessed September 18, 2014).

4. Matt Furtado, "'GTA 5' PC, PS4, and Xbox One Release Discussed by Take-Two," Examiner.com, February 8, 2014, www.examiner.com/article/gta-5-pc-ps4-and-xbox-one-release-discussed-by-take-two (accessed September 18, 2014).

5. "2013 Essential Facts about the Canadian Video Game Industry," Entertainment Software Association of Canada, http://theesa.ca/wp-content/uploads/2013/10/Essential-Facts-English.pdf (accessed September 18, 2014).

6. "DFC Intelligence Forecasts Worldwide Online Game Market to Reach $79 Billion by 2017," DFC Intelligence, June 4, 2013, www.dfcint.com/wp/?p=353 (accessed September 18, 2014).

7. Mike Jackson, "GTA 5: Don't Install 'Play' Disc, Advises Rockstar," CVG, September 16, 2013, www.computerandvideogames.com/429603/gta-5-dont-install-play-disc-advises-rockstar/ (accessed September 18, 2014).

8. "GTA Online: The Business Update Coming Next Week, Tuesday march 4th," Rockstar Games, February 27, 2014, www.rockstargames.com/newswire/article/52200/GTA-Online-The-Business-Update-Coming-Next-Week-Tuesday (accessed September 18, 2014).

Chapter 15

1. "A Taste of Stella Artois," Stella Artois, www.stellaartois.com/en/ca/home (accessed November 2013).

2. "Social Networking Dominates Time Spent Online in Canada," eMarketer, July 3, 2013, www.emarketer.com/Article/Social-Networking-Dominates-Time-Spent-Online-Canada/1010023 (accessed September 20, 2013).

3. "Canadian Ad Spending to Increase by Billions by 2016: Report," Designedge Canada, October 5, 2012, www.designedgecanada.com/news/2012/20121005641.shtml (accessed September 19, 2013).

4. "Giving Wings to People and Ideas," Red Bull, http://energydrink-ca.redbull.com/en (accessed November 2013).

5. "Mission to the Edge of Space," Red Bull Stratos, www.redbullstratos.com/ (accessed November 2013).

6. Leo Burnett, "IKEA—Human Coupons," Promo!Awards 2014, https://promoawards.strategyonline.ca/Winners/Winner/2013/?w=IKEA_Human_Coupons (accessed November 2013).

7. The AIDA concept is based on the classic research of E. K. Strong, Jr., as theorized in *The Psychology of Selling and Advertising* (New York: McGraw-Hill Book Co., 1925); and "Theories of Selling," *Journal of Applied Psychology*, 9, 1, 75–86.

8. Matthew Chung, "U-Be-Livin-Smart Goes Big on Nutrition," Strategy, September 19, 2013, http://strategyonline.ca/2013/09/19/u-be-livin-smart-goes-big-on-nutrition/ (accessed September 18, 2014).

9. Daniel J. Howard and Thomas E. Barry, "A Review and Critique of the Hierarchy of

Effects in Advertising," *International Journal of Advertising*, 9, 2, 1990, 121-135.

10. Janessa Mangone, "The Rise of the Brand Advocate," Social Media Today, September 12, 2013, http://socialmediatoday.com/janessa-mangone/1735176/rise-brand-advocate (accessed September 18, 2014).

11. Duncan MacLeod, "Nike Presents Possibilities," Inspiration Room, September 2, 2013, http://theinspirationroom.com/daily/2013/nike-presents-possibilities/ (accessed September 18, 2014).

Chapter 16

1. "Leo Burnett Quotes," BrainyQuote, www.brainyquote.com/quotes/authors/l/leo_burnett.html (accessed November 20, 2013).

2. Heidi Cohen, "Leo Burnett: 12 Advertising Tips that are Still Relevant Today," Heidi Cohen Actionable Marketing Guide, July 29, 2011, http://heidicohen.com/leo-burnett-12-advertising-tips/ (accessed November 20, 2013).

3. Michelle DiPardo, "Calder Bateman Shows How Much Booze Is 'Responsible'," *Marketing*, March 22, 2013, www.marketingmag.ca/news/marketer-news/calder-bateman-shows-how-much-booze-is-responsible-74927 (accessed November 20, 2013).

4. "Does Humor Make Ads More Effective?", Knowledge Point, www.millwardbrown.com/Libraries/MB_Knowledge_Points_Downloads/MillwardBrown_KnowledgePoint_HumorInAdvertising.sflb.ashx (accessed September 18, 2014).

5. Tom Duncan, *Integrated Marketing Communications*. (Burr Ridge, IL: McGraw-Hill, 2002), 257.

6. "Our Brands," Kellogg's, www.kelloggs.ca/en_CA/our-brands.html (accessed November 2013).

7. Wing Sze Tang, "Travel Manitoba's New Marketing Campaign Goes for the Heart," *Marketing*, December 12, 2013, www.marketingmag.ca/news/marketer-news/travel-manitoba%E2%80%99s-new-marketing-campaign-goes-for-the-heart-96552 (accessed December 13, 2013).

8. "Responsibility," Liquor Control Board of Ontario, www.lcbo.com/content/lcbo/en/responsibility/responsibility.html#.U__Bh8VdW8A (accessed August 2014).

9. Tim Nudd, "Budweiser Taps 'Born of Fire' Director for Black Crown Super Bowl Spot—Samuel Bayer Crafts :30 for Amber Lager," *Adweek*, January 8, 2013, www.adweek.com/news/advertising-branding/budweiser-taps-born-fire-director-black-crown-super-bowl-spot-146369 (accessed December 1, 2013).

10. Zayda Rivera, "Scarlett Johansson's Uncensored SodaStream Super Bowl Ad Banned by Fox," *New York Daily News*, January 29, 2014, www.nydailynews.com/entertainment/tv-movies/scarlett-johansson-uncensored-sodastream-super-bowl-ad-banned-article-1.1595712 (accessed September 18, 2014).

11. "Net Advertising Revenue: Canada—Millions of Dollars," Television Bureau of Canada, www.tvb.ca/pages/nav (accessed December 2, 2013).

12. Bryan M. Wolfe, "The Best Streaming Music Services: Rdio, Spotify, Slacker Radio and More," AppAdvice, April 25, 2013, http://appadvice.com/appnn/2013/04/the-best-streaming-music-services-rdio-spotify-slacker-radio-and-more (accessed September 18, 2014).

13. "TVBasics 2013–2014," Television Bureau of Canada, 21, www.tvb.ca/page_files/pdf/InfoCentre/TVBasics.pdf (accessed January 10, 2014).

14. Wayne Friedman, "Global TV Ad Spend Up 4.2%, Internet Ads Skyrocket," MediaPost, October 22, 2013, www.mediapost.com/publications/article/211792/global-tv-ad-spend-up-42-internet-ads-skyrocket.html (accessed December 15, 2013).

15. "Net Advertising Revenue: Canada—Millions of Dollars," Television Bureau of Canada, www.tvb.ca/pages/nav (accessed December 2, 2013).

16. eMarketer, www.eMarketer.com (accessed January 29, 2007).

17. "CIRA Factbook 2013: 3 Canada Online," Canadian Internet Registration Authority, www.cira.ca/factbook/2013/canada-online.html (accessed December 15, 2013).

18. "Canadian Media Directors' Council Media Digest 2012/2013," Canadian Media Directors' Council, http://cmdccanada.wordpress.com/?attachment_id=821 (accessed December 15, 2013).

19. "2012 Actual + 2013 Estimated Canadian Internet Advertising Revenue Survey: Detailed Report," Interactive Advertising Bureau of Canada, September 18, 2013, http://iabcanada.com/files/Canadian_Internet_Advertising_Revenue_Survey_2012-13 English.pdf (accessed December 15, 2013).

20. Peter Czegledy, "Social Network Gaming: A Canadian Perspective," June 2013, www.airdberlis.com/Templates/Articles/articleFiles/808/Social%20Network%20Gaming%20-%20A%20Canadian%20Perspective.pdf (accessed September 18, 2014).

21. Dan Ovsey, "Canada's C-suite Slow to Use YouTube as Strategic Advertising Tool," Financial Post, March 13, 2014, http://business.financialpost.com/2013/04/23/canadas-c-suite-slow-to-use-youtube-as-strategic-advertising-tool/ (accessed September 18, 2014).

22. Rebecca Harris, "Walmart Faces Growing PR Nightmare over Low Wages," Marketing, November 26, 2013, www.marketingmag.ca/news/pr-news/walmart-faces-growing-pr-nightmare-over-low-wages-94867 (accessed September 18, 2014).

23. Jonathan Salem Baskin, "Anathema No More, 'Breaking Bad' Is Redefining Rules for Product Placement," Forbes, September 25, 2013, www.forbes.com/sites/jonathansalembaskin/2013/09/25/anathema-no-more-breaking-bad-is-redefining-rules-for-product-placement/ (accessed September 18, 2014).

24. "2013 Sponsorship Outlook: Spending Increase Is Double-edged Sword," IEGSR, January 7, 2013, www.sponsorship.com/iegsr/2013/01/07/2013-Sponsorship-Outlook—Spending-Increase-Is-Dou.aspx#.UxNkVuNdW8A (accessed September 18, 2014).

25. "Band-Aid® Brand Jingle Tour," Mosaic, www.mosaic.com/xm#!/case_studies/band-aid-sup-reg-sup-brand-jingle-tour (accessed November 2013).

26. "CRTC Fines Telemarketers for Do-not-call Violations," CBC News, October 3, 2012, www.cbc.ca/news/business/crtc-fines-telemarketers-for-do-not-call-violations-1.1142345 (accessed September 18, 2014).

Chapter 17

1. "Same Rewards—More Stores!", Starbucks: My Starbucks Idea, August 31, 2010, http://blogs.starbucks.com/blogs/customer/archive/2010/08/31/same-rewards-more-stores.aspx (accessed December 2013).

2. "Coupons First. Then Deals. Now Back to Coupon Crazy," Canadian Deals and Coupons Association, www.canadiandealsassociation.com/coupons-first-then-deals-now-back-to-coupon-crazy/ (accessed December 20, 2013).

3. "All New 2014 Deals & Coupon Ecosystem in Canada," Slideshare, www.slideshare.net/VillaKullaVentures/deals-ecosystem-in-canada-23738688 (accessed December 2013).

4. "Graduate Program," Volkswagen, www.vw.ca/en/shopping_tools/volkswagen_finance/graduate_program.html (accessed December 2013).

5. "Canadians Love Loyalty," The Globe and Mail, December 3, 2013, www.theglobeandmail.com/partners/advtarget1113/canadians-love-loyalty/article15613770/ (accessed December 20, 2013).

6. Michelle Warren, "Loblaws Takes PC Plus Canada-Wide," Marketing, November 19, 2013, www.marketingmag.ca/news/marketer-news/loblaws-pc-plus-gets-personal-with-canadians-94295 (accessed September 18, 2014).

7. Megan Haynes, "Pepsi Taste Challenge Exceeds Targets," Strategy, October 22, 2012, http://strategyonline.ca/2012/10/22/pepsis-taste-challenge-exceeds-targets/ (accessed September 18, 2014).

8. Michael Kolberg, "Jean Coutu Installs an e-Store Window," Strategy, December 4, 2013, http://strategyonline.ca/2013/12/04/jean-coutu-installs-e-store-window/ (accessed September 18, 2014).

9. Michael Beverland, "Contextual Influences and the Adoption and Practice of Relationship Selling in a Business-to-Business Setting: An Exploratory Study," Journal of Personal Selling and Sales Management, 21, 3, 2001, 207.

10. Denise Deveau, "Cultural Barriers, Perceptions Keeping Canadians from Exploring Hot Global Markets," Financial Post, October 28, 2013, http://business.financialpost.com/2013/10/28/cultural-barriers-perceptions-keeping-canadians-from-exploring-hot-global-markets/ (accessed September 18, 2014).

Chapter 18

1. Ned Potter, "How Chris Hadfield Conquered Social Media from Outer Space," Forbes, June 28, 2013, www.forbes.com/sites/forbesleadershipforum/2013/06/28/how-chris-hadfield-conquered-social-media-from-outer-space/ (accessed September 18, 2014).

2. Selena Larson, "3 Things San Francisco's #BatKid Teaches us about Twitter," ReadWrite, November 15, 2013, http://readwrite.com/2013/11/15/three-things-san-francisco-batkid-teaches-us-about-twitter#awesm=~orVgV4VL2MxlWs (accessed September 18, 2014).

3. "Miles' Wish to Be Batkid," Make-A-Wish Foundation of Greater Bay Area, 2013, http://sf.wish.org/wishes/wish-stories/i-wish-to-be/i-wish-to-be-batkid (accessed January 2014).

4. "Social Media Marketing, ForNonprofits," http://fornonprofits.wordpress.com/social-media-marketing/ (accessed January 2014).

5. Megan Haynes, "Trending in 2014," Strategy, December 12, 2013, http://strategyonline.ca/2013/12/12/trending-in-2014/ (accessed January 2014).

6. "The Ipsos Canadian Inter@ctive Reid Report 2012 Fact Guide," Ipsos, www.ipsos.ca/common/dl/pdf/Ipsos_InteractiveReidReport_FactGuide_2012.pdf (accessed January 2014).

7. "Two in Three Canadians Use Social Media," MacLean's, April 29, 2013, www.macleans.ca/education/uniandcollege/two-in-three-canadians-use-social-media/ (accessed January 2014).

8. Alison Griswold, "Pinterest Is Now the Fastest Growing Content-Sharing Platform," Business Insider, November 5, 2013, www.businessinsider.com/pinterest-is-fastest-growing-content-sharing-platform-2013-11 (accessed January 2014).

9. "Our Mobile Planet: Canada—Understanding the Mobile Consumer," Google, May 2013, http://services.google.com/fh/files/misc/omp-2013-ca-en.pdf (accessed January 2014).

10. "TSN Debuts Canada's First Live Sports Twitter Amplify Campaign for the World Juniors (#2014WJC)," Bell Media Press Room, December 19, 2013, www.bellmediapr.ca/Network/TSN/Press/TSN-Debuts-Canadas-First-Live-Sports-Twitter-Amplify-Campaign-for-the-World-Juniors-2014WJC- (accessed September 18, 2014).

11. "Canada Digital Future in Focus 2013: Key Insights from 2012 and What They Mean for the Coming Year," The Exchange Network, http://theexchangenetwork.ca/upload/docs/Canada's%20Digital%20Future%20in%20Focus%202013.pdf (accessed January 2014).

12. Jeff Howe, Crowdsourcing: Why the Power of the Crowd Is Driving the Future of Business (New York, NY: Three Rivers Press, 2009), 32.

13. "The 2010 Canada Digital Year in Review," comScore, March 8, 2011, www.comscore.com/Insights/Presentations-and-Whitepapers/2011/2010-Canada-Digital-Year-in-Review (accessed January 2014).

14. Sean Corcoran, "Defining Earned, Owned and Paid Media," Forrester, December 16, 2009, http://blogs.forrester.com/interactive_marketing/2009/12/defining-earned-owned-and-paid-media.html; and Brian Solis, "Why Brands are Becoming Media," Mashable, February 11, 2010, http://

mashable.com/2010/02/11/social-objects/ (accessed September 18, 2014).

15. Ibid.

16. Russ Martin, "After a Successful U.S. Launch, Starbucks' Tweet-A-Coffee Comes to Canada," *Marketing*, January 9, 2014, www.marketingmag.ca/news/media-news/after-a-successful-u-s-launch-starbucks-tweet-a-coffee-comes-to-canada-97906 (accessed January 2014).

17. Michael A. Stelzner, "2013 Social Media Marketing Industry Report," May 2013, www.socialmediaexaminer.com/SocialMediaMarketingIndustryReport2013.pdf (accessed January 2014).

18. David Berkowitz, "100 Ways to Measure Social Media," Marketers Studio, November 17, 2009, www.marketersstudio.com/2009/11/100-ways-to-measure-social-media-.html (accessed January 2014).

19. Charlene Li and Josh Bernoff, *Groundswell: Winning in a World Transformed by Social Technologies*, expanded and revised ed. (Boston: Harvard Business Press, 2011).

20. Russ Martin, "Shaw and CoverGirl to Offer Bonus Twitter Content during The People's Choice Awards," *Marketing*, January 7, 2014, www.marketingmag.ca/news/media-news/shaw-and-cover-girl-to-offer-bonus-twitter-content-during-the-peoples-choice-awards-97692 (accessed January 2014).

21. David Brown, "Canadian Olympic Committee Launches Large-Scale Sochi Campaign," *Marketing*, December 31, 2013, www.marketingmag.ca/news/marketer-news/canadian-olympic-committee-launches-large-scale-sochi-campaign-97425 (accessed January 2014).

22. Felix Gillette, "The Rise and Inglorious Fall of Myspace," *Bloomberg BusinessWeek*, June 27–July 3, 2011, 54–59; Brian Stelter, "News Corporation Sells Myspace for $35 Million," *New York Times*, June 29, 2011, http://mediadecoder.blogs.nytimes.com/2011/06/29/news-corp-sells-myspace-to-specific-media-for-35-million (accessed April 30, 2012).

23. Michael Kolberg, "SickKids Brings Cinema Audience to Their Feet," Strategy, November 20, 2013, http://strategyonline.ca/2013/11/20/sickkids-brings-cinema-audience-to-their-feet/ (accessed January 2014).

24. "WestJet Airlines Ltd. Performs Christmas Marketing Miracle with Viral Video," *Financial Post*, December 11, 2013, http://business.financialpost.com/2013/12/11/westjet-airlines-ltd-performs-christmas-marketing-miracle-with-viral-video/ (accessed January 2014).

25. "Canadian Media Directors' Council Media Digest 2013/2014," Canadian Media Directors' Council, http://cmdccanada.files.wordpress.com/2013/11/cmdc_onlinesm.pdf (accessed January 2014).

26. "Our Mobile Planet: Canada—Understanding the Mobile Consumer," Google, May 2013, http://services.google.com/fh/files/misc/omp-2013-ca-en.pdf (accessed January 2014).

27. "Canadian Media Directors' Council Media Digest 2013/2014," Canadian Media Directors' Council, http://cmdccanada.files.wordpress.com/2013/11/cmdc_onlinesm.pdf (accessed January 2014).

28. "Sochi Olympics: TV Ratings Down Compared to 2010 in Vancouver; Digital Viewing Soars," The Toronto Star, Bill Brioux, February 23, 2014, www.thestar.com/sports/sochi2014/2014/02/25/sochi_olympics_tv_ratings_down_compared_to_2010_in_vancouver_digital_viewing_soars.html, accessed October 25th, 2014.

Part 6 Case

1. Jon Haver, "How Do Canadian Consumers Spend Their Money?", Our Insurance Canada, June 18, 2013, http://ourinsurancecanada.com/canadian-consumers-spend-money/ (accessed September 18, 2014).

2. Ellen Roseman, "Make Money Online from Unwanted Clothes: Roseman," *Toronto Star*, January 7, 2014, www.thestar.com/business/personal_finance/2014/01/07/make_money_online_from_unwanted_clothes_roseman.html (accessed September 18, 2014).

3. Martin Turcotte, "Charitable Giving by Canadians," Statistics Canada, April 16, 2012, www.statcan.gc.ca/pub/11-008-x/2012001/article/11637-eng.pdf (accessed September 18, 2014).

Chapter 19

1. Nicola Brookes, "Customer Service Quotes to Inspire You," NewVoiceMedia Blog, August 28, 2013, www.newvoicemedia.com/blog/20-inspirational-customer-service-quotes/#sthash.zMgR3pwg.dpuf (accessed September 18, 2014).

2. Darrell K. Rigby and Dianne Ledingham, "CRM Done Right," *Harvard Business Review*, November 2004, 2, www.google.ca/url?sa=t&rct=j&q=&esrc=s&source=web&cd=2&ved=0CDQQFjAB&url=http%3A%2F%2Fdownload.microsoft.com%2Fdownload%2F8%2FB%2F8%2F8B8106EE-B72C-4B14-96B9-69633E92A0A4%2FCRM_Done_Right.pdf&ei=I776U5rnLseayATv6oHgCg&usg=AFQjCNHwVWxdo0IaIyYd7opiqhXw_4vkQg (accessed August 5, 2014).

3. Adrian Payne and Pennie Frow, "A Strategic Framework for Customer Relationship Management," *Journal of Marketing*, 69, 2005, 167-176, http://ns2.academicroom.com/sites/default/files/article/118/files_articles_Strategic%20Framework%20for%20Customer%20Relationship%20Management.pdf (accessed September 18, 2014).

4. OnDemand5.com, www.ondemand5.com (accessed September 18, 2014).

5. "Customer Relationship Management (CRM) Quotes,) SmallBizCRM, www.smallbizcrm.com/crm-quotes.html#sthash.DdnmhRvl.dpuf (accessed September 18, 2014).

6. Jeff Sweat, "Keep 'Em Happy," *Internet Week.com*, January 28, 2002.

7. Sony PlayStation, www.playstation.ca/; and "SAP Customer Success Story: Playstation.com Chooses mySAP CRM," http://h71028.www7.hp.com/enterprise/downloads/playstation.pdf (accessed August 3, 2011).

8. "Get the Card," Student Price Card, www.spccard.ca/about.aspx (accessed August 31, 2011).

9. Sony PlayStation, www.playstation.ca/; and "SAP Customer Success Story: Playstation.com Chooses mySAP CRM," http://h71028.www7.hp.com/enterprise/downloads/playstation.pdf (accessed August 3, 2011).

10. Random House, *Random House Webster's Unabridged Dictionary*, 2nd ed. (New York: Random House Reference, 2005).

11. Ian Munroe, "Bell Data Collection Part of 'Disturbing Trend,'" *CBC News*, October 30, 2013, www.cbc.ca/news/technology/bell-data-collection-part-of-disturbing-trend-1.2223949 (accessed August 4, 2014); and Ishmael N. Daro, "Questions Remain about Bell's New Data Mining Plan," Canada.com, October 23, 2013, http://o.canada.com/technology/questions-remain-about-bells-new-data-mining-plan/ (accessed August 4, 2014).

12. "6 Data-Driven Quotes to Inspire," Asking Smarter Questions, www.askingsmarterquestions.com/6-data-driven-quotes-to-inspire/ (accessed September 18, 2014).

13. Susan Fournier and Jill Avery, "Putting the 'Relationship' Back into CRM," *MIT Sloan Management Review*, March 23, 2011, http://sloanreview.mit.edu/article/putting-the-relationship-back-into-crm/ (accessed August 5, 2014).

14. "Ingersoll-Rand Company Limited Maximizes Customer Focus with Expanded CRM Capabilities," Oracle, June 2006, www.ediguys.net/pages/SCIS/ingersoll-rand-siebel-casestudy.pdf (accessed August 5, 2014); and Darrell K. Rigby and Dianne Ledingham, "CRM Done Right," *Harvard Business Review*, November 2004, 2, https://hbr.org/2004/11/crm-done-right (accessed August 5, 2014).

15. Karen Schwartz, "Kraft Data Mining Transforms Marketing and Margins," *Consumer Goods Technology*, September 2000, www.consumergoods.com (accessed September 18, 2014).

16. Insights taken from a conversation with Campion CEO Brock Elliot, June 13, 2008.

17. Kit Davis, "Track Star," *Consumer Goods Technology*, June 1, 2003, http://consumer-goods.edgl.com/old-magazine%5CTrack-Star52676 (accessed September 18, 2014).

18. "About Us," Gigya, www.gigya.com/company/ (accessed September 18, 2014).

19. Sam Gustin, "The Fatal Mistake that Doomed BlackBerry," *Time*, September 24, 2013, http://business.time.com/2013/09/24/the-fatal-mistake-that-doomed-blackberry/ (accessed September 18, 2014).

20. "Customer Loyalty Programs: Are Rules Needed?" Public Interest Advocacy Centre, November 13, 2013, www.piac.ca/files/customer_loyalty_programs_are_rules_needed_1.pdf (accessed August 3, 2014).

INDEX

customer satisfaction customers' evaluation of a good or service in terms of whether it has met their needs and expectations

customer value the relationship between benefits and the sacrifice necessary to obtain those benefits

exchange people giving up one thing to receive another thing they would rather have

marketing the activities that develop an offering in order to satisfy a customer need

marketing company orientation a strong emphasis on the marketing concept and development of a more comprehensive approach to understanding the customer

need a state of being where we desire something that we do not possess but yearn to acquire

production orientation a focus on manufacturing and production quantity in which customers are meant to choose based on what is most abundantly available

relationship marketing a strategy that focuses on keeping and improving relationships with current customers

sales orientation hard selling to the customer, who has greater choice thanks to more competition in the marketplace

societal marketing orientation looking not only at the customer but at expanding marketing efforts to include aspects from the external environment

1-1 Define *marketing* (p. 3–4). Marketing is about understanding the needs of the customer. No other aspect of business has this focus. Marketing helps to shape a firm's products and services based on an understanding of what the customer is looking for. Marketing is about engaging in a conversation with that customer and guiding the delivery of what is required to satisfy those needs.

1-2 Describe the evolution of marketing (p. 4–10). Marketing has been created by an evolution in the use and application of marketing techniques in firms over many decades. The five orientations of marketing are the production orientation, the sales orientation, the marketing company orientation, the societal marketing orientation, and the relationship marketing orientation. Each one developed a new aspect of what we now know as marketing and contributed to how many view marketing today.

1-3 Define key marketing terms (p. 10–12). An understanding of the following terms is fundamental for anyone learning about marketing:

▶▶ *Exchange*: people giving up one thing to receive another thing they would rather have

▶▶ *Customer value*: the relationship between benefits and the sacrifice necessary to obtain those benefits

▶▶ *Market segments*: groups of individuals, families, or companies that are placed together because it is believed that they share similar needs

▶▶ *Relationship building*: companies can expand their market share in three ways: attracting new customers, increasing business with existing customers, and retaining current customers

▶▶ *The marketing mix*: also known as the four Ps of marketing, these are product, price, place, and promotion. Each of the four Ps must be studied and developed to create a proper strategy to attract a market segment.

1-4 Explain why marketing matters (p. 12–13). Marketing is not just about sales and advertising within a firm; it permeates the whole firm. There are rewarding careers in marketing, with compensation that is competitive with other fields of business, along with opportunities that go well beyond the cubicle. Successfully understanding marketing means having an ability to analyze and communicate findings, important skill sets for anyone in business. An understanding of marketing allows people to be informed consumers, ones who are not afraid to demand more from the products and services they rely on every day.

Why Study Marketing?

Important to Society

Important to Business

Good Career Opportunities

Marketing affects you every day!

applied research an attempt by marketers to use research to develop new or improved products

baby boomers people born between 1947 and 1965

basic research pure research that aims to confirm an existing theory or to learn more about a concept or phenomenon

code of ethics a guideline to help marketing managers and other employees make better decisions

Competition Bureau the federal department charged with administering most marketplace laws

component lifestyles modes of living that involve choosing goods and services that meet one's diverse needs and interests rather than conforming to a single, traditional lifestyle

corporate social responsibility a business's concern for society's welfare

demography the study of people's vital statistics, such as their age, race and ethnicity, and location

environmental management when a company implements strategies that attempt to shape the external environment within which it operates

ethics the moral principles or values that generally govern the conduct of an individual or a group

Generation X people born between 1966 and 1978

Generation Y people born between 1979 and 1994

green marketing the development and marketing of products designed to minimize negative effects on the physical environment

inflation a measure of the decrease in the value of money, expressed as the percentage reduction in value since the previous year

morals the rules people develop as a result of cultural values and norms

2-1 Discuss the external environment of marketing, and explain how it affects a firm (p. 15–16). The external marketing environment consists of social, demographic, economic, technological, political, legal, and competitive variables. Marketers cannot control the external environment, but they must understand how it is changing and the effect on the target market. Marketing managers can then create a marketing mix to effectively meet the needs of target customers.

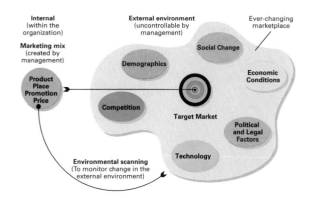

2-2 Describe the social factors that affect marketing (p. 16–17). Within the external environment, social factors are perhaps the most difficult for marketers to anticipate. Several major social trends are currently shaping marketing strategies. First, people of all ages have a broader range of interests, defying traditional consumer profiles. Second, changing gender roles are bringing more women into the workforce and increasing the number of men who shop. Third, having a greater number of dual-career families creates demand for time-saving goods and services.

2-3 Explain the importance to marketing managers of current demographic trends (p. 17–20). Today, several basic demographic patterns are influencing marketing mixes. Because the Canadian population is growing at a slower rate, marketers can no longer rely on profits from generally expanding markets. Marketers are also faced with increasingly experienced consumers among the younger generations, such as tweens and Gen-Yers. And because the population is also growing older, marketers are offering more products that appeal to middle-age and senior consumers.

2-4 Explain the importance to marketing managers of multiculturalism and growing ethnic markets (p. 20–21). Multiculturalism occurs when all major ethnic groups in an area are roughly equally represented. Growing multiculturalism makes the marketer's task more challenging. Many companies are now creating departments and product lines to effectively target multicultural market segments.

2-5 Identify consumer and marketer reactions to the state of the economy (p. 21–23). In recent years, many households have gone into debt as the rise in consumer spending has outpaced the growth in income. At the same time, the financial power of women has increased, and they are making the purchasing decisions for many products in traditionally male-dominated areas. During a time of inflation, marketers generally attempt to maintain level pricing to avoid losing customer brand loyalty. During times of recession, many marketers maintain or reduce prices to counter the effects of decreased demand; they also concentrate on increasing production efficiency and improving customer service.

multiculturalism peaceful and equitable coexistence of different cultures, rather than one national culture, in a country

purchasing power a comparison of income versus the relative cost of a set standard of goods and services in different geographic areas

pyramid of corporate social responsibility a model that suggests corporate social responsibility is composed of economic, legal, ethical, and philanthropic responsibilities and that the firm's economic performance supports the entire structure

recession a period of economic activity characterized by negative growth, which reduces demand for goods and services

self-regulation programs voluntarily adopted by business groups to regulate the activities of their members

sustainability the idea that socially responsible companies will outperform their peers by focusing on the world's social problems and viewing them as opportunities to build profits and help the world at the same time

target market a group of people or organizations for which an organization designs, implements, and maintains a marketing mix intended to meet the needs of that group, resulting in mutually satisfying exchanges

VISIBLE MINORITY POPULATION IN SELECTED MAJOR CANADIAN CITIES, 2011

Vancouver	45.2%
Toronto	47%
Calgary	28.1%
Ottawa	19.2%
Edmonton	22.4%
Montréal	20.3%
Winnipeg	19.7%
Hamilton	14.3%

Source: Adapted from Statistics Canada, "Visible Minority Population and Top Three Visible Minority Groups, Selected Census Metropolitan Areas, Canada, 2011," *National Household Survey 2011*, April 24, 2103, www12.statcan .gc.ca/nhs-enm/2011/as-sa/99-010-x/2011001/tbl/tbl2-eng.cfm (accessed September 24, 2014).

2-6 Identify the impact of technology on a firm (p. 23–24). Monitoring new technology is essential to keeping up with competitors in today's marketing environment. Canada excels in basic research and, in recent years, has dramatically improved its track record in applied research. Innovation is increasingly becoming a global process. Without innovation, Canadian companies can't compete in global markets.

2-7 Discuss the political and legal environment of marketing (p. 24–26). All marketing activities are subject to provincial, territorial, and federal laws and the rulings of regulatory agencies. Marketers are responsible for remaining aware of and abiding by such regulations. Many laws, including privacy laws, have been passed to protect the consumer.

2-8 Explain the basics of foreign and domestic competition (p. 26).
The competitive environment encompasses the number of competitors a firm must face, the relative size of the competitors, and the degree of interdependence within the industry. Declining population growth, rising costs, and shortages of resources have heightened domestic competition.

2-9 Discuss corporate social responsibility (p. 26–28). Responsibility in business refers to a firm's concern for the way its decisions affect society. Social responsibility has four components: economic, legal, ethical, and philanthropic. These components are intertwined, yet the most fundamental responsibility is earning a profit. Most business people believe they should do more than pursue profits. Although a company must consider its economic needs first, it must also operate within the law, do what is ethical and fair, and be a good corporate citizen. The concept of sustainability means that socially responsible companies will outperform their peers by focusing on the world's social problems and viewing them as an opportunity to earn profits and help the world at the same time.

2-10 Describe the role of ethics and ethical decisions in business (p. 28–31). Business ethics may be viewed as a subset of the values of society as a whole. The ethical conduct of business people is shaped by societal elements, including family, education, religion, and social movements. As members of society, business people are morally obligated to consider the ethical implications of their decisions.

Ethical decision making is approached in three basic ways. The first approach examines the consequences of decisions. The second approach relies on rules and laws to guide decision making. The third approach is based on a theory of moral development that places individuals or groups in one of three developmental stages: preconventional morality, conventional morality, or postconventional morality.

Many companies develop a code of ethics to help their employees make ethical decisions. A code of ethics can help employees identify acceptable business practices, be an effective internal control on behaviour, help employees avoid confusion when determining whether decisions are ethical, and facilitate discussion about what is right and wrong.

cash cow in the portfolio matrix, a business unit that usually generates more cash than it needs to maintain its market share

competitive advantage the set of unique features of a company and its products that are perceived by the target market as significant and superior to the competition

control provides the mechanisms both for evaluating marketing results in light of the plan's objectives and for correcting actions that do not help the organization reach those objectives within budget guidelines

core competencies key unique strengths that are hard to imitate and underlie the functioning of an organization

cost competitive advantage being the low-cost competitor in an industry while maintaining satisfactory profit margins

diversification a strategy of increasing sales by introducing new products into new markets

dog in the portfolio matrix, a business unit that has low growth potential and a small market share

environmental scanning the collection and interpretation of information about forces, events, and relationships in the external environment that may affect the future of the organization or the implementation of the marketing plan

evaluation gauging the extent to which the marketing objectives have been achieved during the specified period

experience curves curves that show costs declining at a predictable rate as experience with a product increases

four Ps product, place, promotion, and price, which together make up the marketing mix

implementation the process that turns a marketing plan into action assignments and ensures that these assignments are executed in a way that accomplishes the plan's objectives

3-1 Explain the importance of strategic planning (p. 33–34). Strategic marketing planning is the basis for all marketing strategies and decisions. The marketing plan acts as a guidebook of marketing activities for the marketing manager. By specifying objectives and defining the actions required to attain them, a marketing plan provides the basis on which actual and expected performance can be compared.

Although there is no set formula, a marketing plan should include such elements as stating the business mission, setting objectives, performing a situation analysis of internal and external environmental forces, selecting target markets, delineating a marketing mix (product, place, promotion, and price), and establishing ways to implement, evaluate, and control the plan.

3-2 Develop an appropriate business mission statement (p. 34–35). The mission statement is based on a careful analysis of benefits sought by present and potential customers and an analysis of existing and anticipated environmental conditions. The firm's mission statement establishes boundaries for all subsequent decisions, objectives, and strategies. It should focus on the market the organization is attempting to serve rather than on the good or service offered.

3-3 Describe how to conduct business portfolio analysis (p. 35–38). To determine the future cash contributions and cash requirements expected for each strategic business unit (SBU), managers can use the Boston Consulting Group's portfolio matrix. The portfolio matrix is a tool for allocating resources among products and SBUs on the basis of relative market share and market growth rate. Using the portfolio matrix requires classifying each SBU by its present or forecast growth and market share. The underlying assumption is that market share and profitability are strongly linked. The measure of market share used in the portfolio approach is relative market share: the ratio between the company's share and the share of the largest competitor. The use of this technique results in four types of business opportunities: (1) cash cows, (2) stars, (3) question marks, and (4) dogs.

3-4 Summarize how business planning is used for competitive advantage (p. 38–42). A competitive advantage is a set of unique features of a company and its products that are perceived by the target market as significant and superior to those of the competition. Competitive advantages can be divided into three types: cost, product/service differentiation, and niche strategies. Sources of cost competitive advantages include experience curves, efficient labour, no-frills goods and services, government subsidies, product design, re-engineering, product innovations, and new methods of service delivery. A product/service differentiation competitive advantage exists when a firm provides something unique that is valuable to buyers beyond just low price. Niche competitive advantages result from targeting unique segments that have specific needs and wants. The goal of all sources of competitive advantage is to be sustainable.

3-5 Discuss marketing planning and identification of target markets (p. 42–43). The target market strategy identifies which market segment or segments to focus on. A market opportunity analysis (MOA) describes and estimates the size and sales potential of market segments that are of interest to the firm. In addition, an assessment of key competitors in these market segments is performed. After the market segments are described, one or more may be targeted by the firm by (1) appealing to the entire market with one marketing mix, (2) concentrating on one segment, or (3) appealing to multiple market segments by using multiple marketing mixes.

market development a marketing strategy that involves attracting new customers to existing products

market opportunity analysis (MOA) the description and estimation of the size and sales potential of market segments that are of interest to the firm and the assessment of key competitors in these market segments

market penetration a marketing strategy that tries to increase market share among existing customers

marketing audit a thorough, systematic, periodic evaluation of the objectives, strategies, structure, and performance of the marketing organization

marketing mix a unique blend of product, place, promotion, and pricing strategies designed to produce mutually satisfying exchanges with a target market

marketing myopia defining a business in terms of goods and services rather than in terms of the benefits that customers seek

marketing objective a statement of what is to be accomplished through marketing activities

marketing strategy the activities of selecting and describing one or more target markets and developing and maintaining a marketing mix that will produce mutually satisfying exchanges with target markets

mission statement a statement of the firm's business based on a careful analysis of benefits sought by present and potential customers and an analysis of existing and anticipated environmental conditions

Target Market Options

Entire Market   **Multiple Markets**   **Single Market**

3-6 Describe the elements of the marketing mix (p. 43–44). The marketing mix (or four Ps) is a blend of product, place, promotion, and pricing strategies designed to produce mutually satisfying exchanges with a target market. The starting point of the marketing mix is the product offering. Products can be tangible goods, ideas, or services. Place (distribution) strategies are concerned with making products available when and where customers want them. Elements of the promotional mix include advertising, direct marketing, public relations, sales promotion, personal selling, and online marketing. Price is what a buyer must give up to obtain a product and is often the easiest to change of the four marketing mix elements.

3-7 Explain why implementation, evaluation, and control of the marketing plan are necessary (p. 44–45). Before a marketing plan can work, it must be implemented. The plan should also be evaluated to determine whether it has achieved its objectives. Poor implementation can be a major factor in a plan's failure. Control provides the mechanisms for evaluating marketing results in light of the plan's objectives and for correcting actions that do not help the organization reach those objectives within budget guidelines.

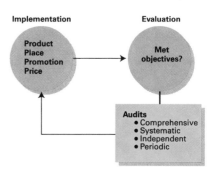

3-8 Identify several techniques that help make strategic planning effective (p. 45). First, management must realize that strategic planning is an ongoing process and not a once-a-year exercise. Second, good strategic planning involves a high level of creativity. The last requirement is top management's support and cooperation.

niche competitive advantage the advantage achieved when a firm seeks to target and effectively serve a single segment of the market

planning the process of anticipating future events and determining strategies to achieve organizational objectives in the future

portfolio matrix a tool for allocating resources among products or strategic business units on the basis of relative market share and market growth rate

problem child (question mark) in the portfolio matrix, a business unit that shows rapid growth but poor profit margins

product development a marketing strategy that entails the creation of new products for current customers

product/service differentiation competitive advantage the provision of a unique benefit that is valuable to buyers beyond simply offering a low price

situation (SWOT) analysis identifying internal strengths (S) and weaknesses (W) and also examining external opportunities (O) and threats (T)

star in the portfolio matrix, a business unit that is a fast-growing market leader

strategic business unit (SBU) a subgroup of a single business or a collection of related businesses within the larger organization

strategic planning the managerial process of creating and maintaining a fit between the organization's objectives and resources and evolving market opportunities

sustainable competitive advantage an advantage that cannot be copied by the competition

buyer for export an intermediary in the global market that assumes all ownership risks and sells globally for its own account

capital intensive using more capital than labour in the production process

contract manufacturing private-label manufacturing by a foreign company

countertrade a form of trade in which all or part of the payment for goods or services is in the form of other goods or services

direct foreign investment active ownership of a foreign company or of overseas manufacturing or marketing facilities

dumping the sale of an exported product at a price lower than that charged for the same or a like product in the home market of the exporter

European Union a free trade zone encompassing 28 European countries

export agents intermediaries who act like manufacturers' agents for exporters; the export agents live in the foreign market

export broker an intermediary who plays the traditional broker's role by bringing buyer and seller together

exporting selling domestically produced products to buyers in another country

floating exchange rates prices of different currencies move up and down based on the demand for and the supply of each currency

General Agreement on Tariffs and Trade (GATT) a trade agreement that contained loopholes that enabled countries to avoid trade-barrier reduction agreements

global marketing marketing that targets markets throughout the world

global marketing standardization production of uniform products that can be sold the same way all over the world

4-1 Discuss the importance of global marketing (p. 47–49). Business people who adopt a global vision are better able to identify global marketing opportunities, understand the nature of global networks, create effective global marketing strategies, and compete against foreign competition in domestic markets.

4-2 Discuss the impact of multinational firms on the world economy (p. 49–51). Multinational corporations are international traders that regularly operate across national borders. Because of their vast size and financial, technological, and material resources, multi-national corporations have a great influence on the world economy. They have the ability to overcome trade problems, save on labour costs, and tap new technology.

4-3 Describe the external environment facing global marketers (p. 51–57). Global marketers face the same environmental factors as they do domestically: cultural; economic and techno-logical development; political structure and actions; demography; and natural resources. Cultural consider-ations include societal values, attitudes and beliefs, language, and customary busi-ness practices. A country's economic and technological status depends on its stage of industrial development, which, in turn, affects average family incomes. The political structure is shaped by political ideology and such policies as tariffs, quotas, boycotts,

global vision a recognition of and reaction to international marketing opportunities using effective global marketing strategies and being aware of threats from foreign competitors in all markets

gross domestic product (GDP) the total market value of all goods and services produced in a country for a given period

gross national income (GNI) per capita one measure of the ability of a country's citizens to buy various goods and services

International Monetary Fund (IMF) an international organization that acts as a lender of last resort, providing loans to troubled nations, and also works to promote trade through financial cooperation

joint venture a domestic firm's purchase of part of a foreign company or a domestic firm joining with a foreign company to create a new entity

licensing the legal process whereby a licensor agrees to let another firm use its manufacturing process, trademarks, patents, trade secrets, or other proprietary knowledge

Mercosur the largest Latin American trade agreement, which includes Argentina, Bolivia, Brazil, Chile, Colombia, Ecuador, Paraguay, Peru, Uruguay, and Venezuela

multinational corporations companies that are heavily engaged in international trade, beyond exporting and importing

North American Free Trade Agreement (NAFTA) an agreement between Canada, the United States, and Mexico that created the world's largest free trade zone at that time

Uruguay Round an agreement created by the World Trade Organization to dramatically lower trade barriers worldwide

World Bank an international bank that offers low-interest loans, advice, and information to developing nations

World Trade Organization (WTO) a trade organization that replaced the old General Agreement on Tariffs and Trade (GATT)

exchange controls, trade agreements, and market groupings. Demographic variables include the size of a population and its age and geographic distribution.

4-4 Identify the various ways of entering the global marketplace (p. 57–60). Firms use the following strategies to enter global markets, in descending order of risk and profit: direct investment, joint venture, contract manufacturing, licensing and franchising, and exporting.

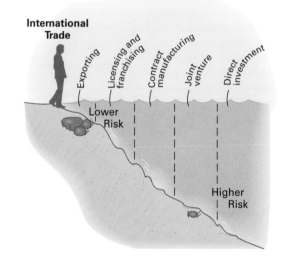

4-5 List the basic elements involved in developing a global marketing mix (p. 60–63). A firm's major consideration is how much it will adjust the four Ps—product, promotion, place (distribution), and price—within each country. One strategy is to use one product and one promotion message worldwide. A second strategy is to create new products for global markets. A third strategy is to keep the product basically the same but alter the promotional message. A fourth strategy is to slightly alter the product to meet local conditions.

Global Marketing Mix		
Product + Promotion	**Place (Distribution)**	**Price**
One product, one message	Channel choice	Dumping
Product invention	Channel structure	Countertrade
Product adaption	Country infrastructure	Exchange rates
Message adaption		Purchasing power

4-6 Discover how the Internet is affecting global marketing (p. 63). Simply opening a website can open the door to international sales. International carriers, such as UPS, can help solve logistics problems. Language translation software can help an e-commerce business become multilingual. Yet cultural differences and old-line rules, regulations, and taxes hinder rapid development of e-commerce in many countries.

CHAPTER REVIEW

causal research a type of conclusive research that focuses on the cause and effect of two variables and attempts to find some correlation between them

central-location telephone (CLT) facility a specially designed phone room used to conduct telephone interviewing

closed-ended question an interview question that asks the respondent to make a selection from a limited list of responses

computer-assisted personal interviewing technique in which the interviewer reads the questions from a computer screen and enters the respondent's data directly into a computer

computer-assisted self-interviewing technique in which the respondent reads questions on a computer screen and directly keys his or her answers into a computer

conclusive research a more specific type of research that attempts to provide clarity to a decision maker by identifying specific courses of action

convenience sample a form of nonprobability sample using respondents who are convenient, or readily accessible, to the researcher—for example, employees, friends, or relatives

cross-tabulation a method of analyzing data that shows the analyst the responses to one question in relation to the responses to one or more other questions

depth interview an interview that involves a discussion between a well-trained researcher and a respondent who is asked about attitudes and perspectives on a topic

descriptive research a type of conclusive research that attempts to describe marketing phenomena and characteristics

5-1 Explain the role of marketing research (p. 69–70). Marketing research is about using information-gathering processes to discover the needs of customers and how to better serve those needs.

Marketing research is a process, like any other kind of research, and it needs guidelines to follow and direction. Marketing research helps decision makers not by solving the problem but by providing information on which decisions can be made. In a firm, marketing research can take on any one of three roles: descriptive, diagnostic and predictive.

Why marketing research?	
☑	Improve quality of decision making
☑	Trace problems
☑	Focus on keeping existing customers
☑	Understand changes in marketplace

5-2 List the steps in the marketing research process (p. 70–83). Marketing research is a process of collecting and analyzing data to use in solving specific marketing problems. There are six steps in the process of properly gathering data and creating information used to make marketing decisions. The first step, the most important and strategic decision in the research process, is to identify the problem. The second step is to choose the research design and determine whether to use an exploratory, a descriptive or a causal approach. The third step is to decide how much secondary and primary data will be collected and then to collect the data. The

1 Identify the problem.

2 Design the research.

3 Collect the data.

4 Analyze the data.

5 Present the report.

6 Provide follow-up.

ethnographic research the study of human behaviour in its natural context; involves observation of behaviour and physical setting

experiment a method a researcher uses to gather primary data to determine cause and effect

exploratory research an informal discovery process that attempts to gain insights and a better understanding of the management and research problems

focus group a small group of recruited participants engaged in a nonstructured discussion in a casual environment

frame error an error that occurs when sample is drawn from a population that differs from the target population

mall intercept interview interviewing people in the common areas of shopping malls

marketing research objective specific statement about the information needed to solve the research question

marketing research the process of planning, collecting, and analyzing data relevant to a marketing decision

measurement error an error that occurs when the information desired by the researcher differs from the information provided by the measurement process

mystery shoppers researchers posing as customers who gather observational data about a store

nonprobability sample any sample in which little or no attempt is made to have a representative cross-section of the population

observation research a research method that relies on four types of observation: people watching people, people watching an activity, machines watching people, and machines watching an activity

fourth step is to analyze the data. Technology can provide a lot of help to researchers, and analysis goes well beyond the basic pie chart or bar graph. The fifth step is for researchers to present their report, taking the reams of data and turning them into something actionable for a company's decision makers. The last step is to follow-up, and because marketing research is about helping make decisions, it's important that marketing researchers be able to see how their data and information are used in those decisions.

5-3 Discuss the impact of technology on marketing research (p. 83–86). Technology has an impact on many aspects of our lives, both at home and at work. Marketing researchers are using technology to help make decisions at work and to gather information from people at home and on the go. Online surveys have become a staple of most companies' marketing research efforts because of the ease of implementation. There are also online research panels and online focus groups that provide access to respondents with just a click. Mobile technology tools allow people to answer questions on the go, and social networks have created excellent potential pools of respondents. Big data may sound intimidating, but technology has allowed companies to mine information about consumers long thought impossible or unreachable.

5-4 Describe when to conduct marketing research (p. 86–87). The marketing research process provides an overview of what to research. But the questions of when to research and even if research should be done are just as valuable. Technology has given many people the tools to write a great survey disseminate research quickly and easily, but it is still important to determine the right situation in which to take on the marketing research process.

open-ended question an interview question that encourages an answer phrased in the respondent's own words

primary data information that is collected for the first time and is used for solving the particular problem under investigation

probability sample a sample in which every element in the population has a known statistical likelihood of being selected

random error type of sampling error in which the selected sample is an imperfect representation of the overall population

random sample a sample arranged in such a way that every element of the population has an equal chance of being selected as part of the sample

research design a plan that specifies how to answer the research question and achieve the research objectives by laying out the research tools and techniques necessary to collect and analyze data

sample a subset from a larger population

sampling error an error that occurs when a sample that does not represent the target population

scaled-response question a closed-ended question designed to measure the intensity of a respondent's answer

secondary data data previously collected for any purpose other than the one at hand

survey research the most popular technique for gathering primary data, in which a researcher interacts with people to obtain facts, opinions, and attitudes

CHAPTER REVIEW

aspirational reference groups groups that an individual would like to join

attitude a learned tendency to respond consistently toward a given object

belief an organized pattern of knowledge that an individual holds as true about his or her world

cognitive dissonance the inner tension that a consumer experiences after recognizing an inconsistency between behaviour and values or opinions

consumer behaviour how consumers make purchase decisions and how they use and dispose of purchased goods or services; also includes the factors that influence purchase decisions and product use

consumer decision-making process a five-step process used by consumers when buying goods or services

culture the set of values, norms, attitudes, and other meaningful symbols that shape human behaviour and the artifacts, or products, of that behaviour as they are transmitted from one generation to the next

decision confirmation the reaffirmation of the wisdom of the decision a consumer has made

evoked set (consideration set) a group of the most preferred alternatives resulting from an information search, which a buyer can further evaluate to make a final choice

extensive decision making the most complex type of consumer decision making, used when considering the purchase of an unfamiliar, expensive product or an infrequently purchased item; requires the use of several criteria for evaluating options and much time for seeking information

external information search the process of seeking information in the outside environment

ideal self-image the way an individual would like to be

6-1 Explain why marketing managers should understand consumer behaviour (p. 89). Consumer behaviour describes how consumers make purchase decisions and how they use and dispose of the products they buy. An understanding of consumer behaviour reduces marketing managers' uncertainty when they are defining a target market and designing a marketing mix.

6-2 Analyze the components of the consumer decision-making process (p. 90–94). The consumer decision-making process begins with need recognition, when stimuli trigger awareness of an unfulfilled want. If additional information is required to make a purchase decision, the consumer may engage in an internal or external information search. The consumer then evaluates the additional information and establishes purchase guidelines. Finally, a purchase decision is made.

Consumer postpurchase evaluation is influenced by prepurchase expectations, the prepurchase information search, and the consumer's general level of self-confidence. Cognitive dissonance is the inner tension that a consumer experiences after recognizing a purchased product's disadvantages.

6-3 Identify the types of consumer buying decisions and discuss the significance of consumer involvement (p. 94–96). Consumer decision making falls into three broad categories. First, consumers

exhibit routine response behaviour for frequently purchased, low-cost items that require very little decision effort; routine response behaviour is typically characterized by brand loyalty. Second, consumers engage in limited decision making for occasional purchases or for unfamiliar brands in familiar product categories. Third, consumers practise extensive decision making when making unfamiliar, expensive, or infrequent purchases. The main factors affecting the level of consumer involvement are previous experience, interest, perceived risk of negative consequences (financial, social, and psychological), situation, and social visibility.

6-4 Identify and understand the cultural factors that affect consumer buying decisions (p. 96–100). Cultural influences on consumer buying decisions include culture and values, subculture, and social class. Culture is the essential character of a society that distinguishes it from other cultural groups. The underlying elements of every culture are the values, language, myths, customs, rituals, laws, and the artifacts, or products, transmitted from one generation to the next. The most defining element of a culture is its values—the enduring beliefs shared by a society that a specific mode of conduct is personally or socially preferable to another mode of conduct. A culture can be divided into subcultures on the basis of demographic characteristics, geographic regions, national and ethnic background, political beliefs, and religious beliefs.

6-5 Identify and understand the social factors that affect consumer buying decisions (p. 100–102). Social factors include such external influences as reference groups, opinion leaders, and family. Consumers seek out others' opinions for guidance on new products, on services and products with image-related attributes, or for those on which attribute information is lacking or uninformative. Consumers may use products or brands to identify with or become a member of a reference group. Opinion leaders are members of reference groups who influence others' purchase decisions. Family members also influence purchase decisions; children tend to shop in patterns similar to those of their parents.

internal information search the process of recalling information stored in one's memory

involvement the amount of time and effort a buyer invests in the search, evaluation, and decision processes of consumer behaviour

learning a process that creates changes in behaviour, either immediate or expected, through experience and practice

lifestyle a mode of living as identified by a person's activities, interests, and opinions

limited decision making the type of decision making that requires a moderate amount of time for gathering information and deliberating about an unfamiliar brand in a familiar product category

marketing-controlled information source a product information source that originates with marketers promoting the product

Maslow's hierarchy of needs a method of classifying human needs and motivations into five categories in ascending order of importance: physiological, safety, social, esteem, and self-actualization

motives driving forces that cause a person to take action to satisfy specific needs

need recognition the result of an imbalance between actual and desired states

nonaspirational reference groups (dissociative groups) groups that influence our behaviour because we try to maintain distance from them

nonmarketing-controlled information source a product information source not associated with advertising or promotion

norms the values and attitudes deemed acceptable by a group

opinion leader an individual who influences the opinions of others

perception the process by which people select, organize, and interpret stimuli into a meaningful and coherent picture

6-6 Identify and understand the individual factors that affect consumer buying decisions (p. 102–105). Individual factors that affect consumer buying decisions include gender, age, family life-cycle stage, personality, self-concept, and lifestyle. Beyond obvious physiological differences, men and women differ in their social and economic roles, which affects their consumer buying decisions. A consumer's age generally indicates what products he or she may be interested in purchasing. Marketers often define their target markets in terms of consumers' life-cycle stage, following changes in consumers' attitudes and behavioural tendencies as they mature. Finally, certain products and brands reflect consumers' personality, self-concept, and lifestyle.

6-7 Identify and understand the psychological factors that affect consumer buying decisions (p. 105–109). Psychological factors include perception, motivation, learning, values, beliefs, and attitudes. These factors allow consumers to interact with the world around them, recognize their feelings, gather and analyze information, formulate thoughts and opinions, and take action. Perception allows consumers to recognize their consumption problems. Motivation is what drives consumers to take action to satisfy specific consumption needs. Almost all consumer behaviour results from learning, which is the process that creates changes in behaviour through experience. Consumers with similar beliefs and attitudes tend to react alike to marketing-related inducements.

personality a way of organizing and grouping the consistency of an individual's reactions to situations

primary membership groups groups with which individuals interact regularly in an informal, face-to-face manner

psychological factors tools that consumers use to recognize, gather, analyze, and self-organize to aid in decision making

real self-image the way an individual actually perceives himself or herself to be

reference group a group in society that influences an individual's purchasing behaviour

routine response behaviour the type of decision making exhibited by consumers buying frequently purchased, low-cost goods and services; requires little search and decision time

secondary membership groups groups with which individuals interact less consistently and more formally than with primary membership groups

selective distortion a process whereby consumers change or distort information that conflicts with their feelings or beliefs

selective exposure the process whereby a consumer decides which stimuli to notice and which to ignore

selective retention a process whereby consumers remember only information that supports their personal beliefs

self-concept how consumers perceive themselves in terms of attitudes, perceptions, beliefs, and self-evaluations

social class a group of people who are considered nearly equal in status or community esteem, who regularly socialize among themselves both formally and informally, and who share behavioural norms

socialization process the passing down of cultural values and norms to children

sociometric leader a low-profile, well-respected collaborative professional who is socially and professionally well connected

stimulus any unit of input affecting one or more of the five senses: sight, smell, taste, touch, hearing

subculture a homogeneous group of people who share elements of the overall culture and also have their own unique cultural elements

value the enduring belief shared by a society that a specific mode of conduct is personally or socially preferable to another mode of conduct

want a particular product or service that the consumer believes could satisfy an unfulfilled need

business services complementary and ancillary actions that companies undertake to meet business customers' needs

business-to-business (B2B) marketing the process of matching capabilities between two nonconsumer entities to create value for both organizations and the "customer's customer"; also referred to as *business marketing*

buying centre all those people in an organization who become involved in the purchase decision

derived demand demand in the business market that comes from demand in the consumer market

joint demand the demand for two or more items used together in a final product

modified rebuy a situation where the purchaser wants some change in the original good or service

multiplier effect (accelerator principle) the phenomenon in which a small increase or decrease in consumer demand can produce a much larger change in demand for the facilities and equipment needed to make the consumer product

new task buy a situation requiring the purchase of a product for the first time

North American Industry Classification System (NAICS) an industry classification system developed by the United States, Canada, and Mexico to classify North American business establishments by their main production processes

original equipment manufacturers (OEMs) individuals and organizations that buy business goods and incorporate them into the products that they produce for eventual sale to other producers or to consumers

7-1 Describe business marketing (p. 111). Business-to-business (B2B) marketing is more than simply using the same aspects of consumer marketing and putting the word *business* in front of the concepts and terms. B2B marketing is about making matches between the capabilities of firms and focusing on active cooperation between parties.

7-2 Explain the differences between consumer and business marketing (p. 112). Business marketing is about an active buyer and active seller. Often consumer marketing focuses on a customer that passively waits for a business to develop an offering based on the 4Ps. The Canadian Marketing Association's definition of business marketing is particularly relevant to our understanding of B2B: "What makes B-to-B different than consumer marketing is the complex nature of *relationships* and *interactions* that form a buying process and customer lifecycle that lasts months or years. It involves a network of individuals from buyer, seller, and even third-party partners who have different needs and interests."

7-3 Summarize the network and relationship approach to business marketing (p. 112–116). Given the importance of relationships and interactions, it is important to stress that trust and commitment form the foundation of solid business to business relationships. We talk here about interaction, not transaction. Much of consumer marketing's focus is on getting customers to buy once and hoping they will buy again—a single transaction. With business marketing, the focus shifts to a series of transactions over time that build trust and establish commitment—an interaction. Traditional sales and marketing management approaches rely more on transactions, while a network model looks at interactions. The term *networks* has become a familiar one, given the growth of mobile technologies and social media. The network model in business marketing stresses the interaction among various parties looking for individual gain but not at the expense of the larger network of interconnected firms. Networks have been present in many cultures, including Japan and China, in various forms. What each incarnation of networks shows is the importance of firms working together for mutual gain while ensuring success at the company level.

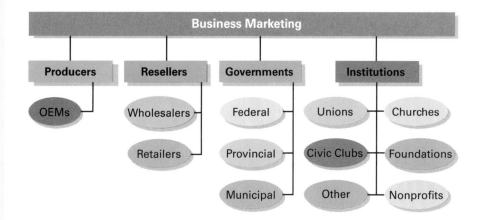

7-4 State the fundamental aspects of business marketing (p. 116–119). One of the most important and unique aspects of business marketing is how demand is treated, whether derived, inelastic, or joint. Compared with consumer marketing, in business marketing the number of customers is fewer, the location of businesses

reciprocity a practice where business purchasers choose to buy from their own customers

relationship commitment a firm's belief that an ongoing relationship with another firm is so important that the relationship warrants maximum efforts to maintain it indefinitely

straight rebuy a situation in which the purchaser reorders the same goods or services without looking for new information or new suppliers

trust confidence in an exchange partner's reliability and integrity

is strategic, negotiations are important, and understanding reciprocity is essential to learning about business relationships. Business products that are offered as part of a business relationship are varied, ranging from major equipment purchases to basic supplies. Services to business are unique and more prevalent than in consumer marketing.

7-5 Classify business customers (p. 120–122). To understand the customer landscape in business marketing, it is helpful to categorize business customers into different groups. Most businesses that would be considered major players in business marketing are producers and resellers. However, government, MASH, and nonprofits are also important in business marketing. A well-established system to classify companies in North America is the North American Industrial Classification System (NAICS). The NAICS provides a way to identify, analyze, segment, and target business and government markets. Organizations can be identified and compared by using the NAICS numeric codes, which indicates the business sector, subsector, industry group, industry, and country industry. NAICS is a valuable tool for analyzing, segmenting, and targeting business markets.

7-6 Identify aspects of business buying behaviour (p. 122–125). Business buying involves a much larger group of individuals working together to make a decision. While consumers can make decisions on their own or with the aid of the reference group, a business often will have a buying centre from which decisions are made. A buying centre has six types of members: initiator, influencer, gatekeeper, decider, purchaser, and user. Buying also involves understanding the situation in which a company is making a purchase. Companies may be in a new task buy situation: this is the first time they have made this type of purchase. Otherwise, business buyers are in a straight rebuy situation in which they are generally satisfied and buy the same offering again or in a modified rebuy in which some element of the previous offering was unsatisfactory and they are seeking some improvement. Finally, most business purchases are made based on the evaluative criteria of quality, service, and price.

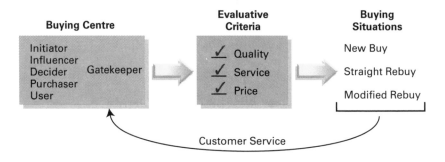

7-7 Describe the ways in which business marketing has gone online (p. 125–129). While much discussion of business marketing is focused on how it differs from consumer marketing, much of what is happening online is similar for both B2B and B2C. Mobile marketing and content marketing are strong trends for business marketers, providing opportunity for both new markets and new relationships but also making it necessary to understand the needs of a more informed marketplace. Social media is another area of growth for business marketing, as seen by the increased use of LinkedIn and other tools.

benefit segmentation the process of grouping customers into market segments according to the benefits they seek from the product

cannibalization a situation that occurs when sales of a new product cut into sales of a firm's existing products

concentrated targeting strategy a strategy used to select one segment of a market to target marketing efforts

demographic segmentation segmenting markets by age, gender, income, ethnic background, and family life cycle

80/20 principle a principle holding that 20 percent of all customers generate 80 percent of the demand

family life cycle (FLC) a series of stages determined by a combination of age, marital status, and the presence or absence of children

geodemographic segmentation segmenting potential customers into neighbourhood lifestyle categories

geographic segmentation segmenting markets by region of a country or the world, market size, market density, or climate market people or organizations with needs or wants and the ability and willingness to buy

market segment a subgroup of people or organizations sharing one or more characteristics that cause them to have similar product needs

market segmentation the process of dividing a market into meaningful, relatively similar, and identifiable segments or groups

multisegment targeting strategy a strategy that chooses two or more well-defined market segments and develops a distinct marketing mix for each

niche one segment of a market

one-to-one marketing an individualized marketing method that uses customer information to build long-term, personalized, and profitable relationships with each customer

8-1 Describe the characteristics of markets and market segments (p. 131–132). A market is composed of individuals or organizations that have both the ability and the willingness to make purchases to fulfill their needs or wants. A market segment is a group of individuals or organizations with similar product needs because of one or more common characteristics.

8-2 Explain the importance of market segmentation (p. 132). Before the 1960s, few businesses targeted specific market segments. Today, segmentation is a crucial marketing strategy for nearly all successful organizations. Market segmentation enables marketers to tailor marketing mixes to meet the needs of particular population segments. Segmentation helps marketers identify consumer needs and preferences, areas of declining demand, and new marketing opportunities.

8-3 Describe the bases commonly used to segment consumer markets (p. 132–138). Five bases are commonly used for segmenting consumer markets. Geographic segmentation is based on region, size, density, and climate characteristics. Demographic segmentation is based on age, gender, income level, ethnicity, and family life-cycle characteristics. Psychographic segmentation includes personality, motives, and lifestyle characteristics. Benefits sought is a type of segmentation that identifies customers according to the benefits they seek in a product. Finally, usage segmentation divides a market by the amount of product purchased or consumed.

8-4 Discuss criteria for successful market segmentation (p. 138–139). Successful market segmentation depends on four basic criteria: (1) a market segment must be substantial and have enough potential customers to be viable; (2) a market segment must be identifiable and measurable; (3) members of a market segment must be accessible to marketing efforts; and (4) a market segment must respond to particular marketing efforts in a way that distinguishes it from other segments.

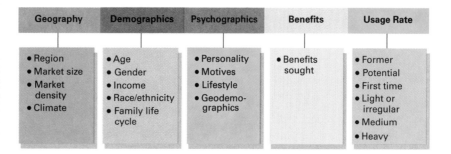

Geography	Demographics	Psychographics	Benefits	Usage Rate
• Region • Market size • Market density • Climate	• Age • Gender • Income • Race/ethnicity • Family life cycle	• Personality • Motives • Lifestyle • Geodemographics	• Benefits sought	• Former • Potential • First time • Light or irregular • Medium • Heavy

8-5 Describe the bases for segmenting business markets (p. 139–140). Business markets can be segmented on two general bases. First, businesses segment markets on the basis of company characteristics, such as customers' geographic location, type of company, company size, and product use. Second, companies may segment customers on the basis of the buying processes those customers use.

8-6 List the steps involved in segmenting markets (p. 140). Six steps are involved when segmenting markets: (1) selecting a market or product category for study; (2) choosing a basis or bases for segmenting the market; (3) selecting segmentation descriptors; (4) profiling and evaluating segments; (5) selecting target markets; and (6) designing, implementing, and maintaining appropriate marketing mixes.

optimizers business customers who consider numerous suppliers, both familiar and unfamiliar, solicit bids, and study all proposals carefully before selecting one

perceptual mapping a means of displaying or graphing, in two or more dimensions, the location of products, brands, or groups of products in customers' minds

position the place a product, brand, or group of products occupies in consumers' minds relative to competing offerings

positioning a process that influences potential customers' overall perception of a brand, a product line, or an organization in general

product differentiation a positioning strategy that some firms use to distinguish their products from those of competitors

psychographic segmentation market segmentation on the basis of personality, motives, lifestyles, and geodemographic categories

repositioning changing consumers' perceptions of a brand in relation to competing brands

satisficers business customers who place their order with the first familiar supplier to satisfy their product and delivery requirements

segmentation bases (variables) characteristics of individuals, groups, or organizations

target market a group of people or organizations for which an organization designs, implements, and maintains a marketing mix intended to meet the needs of that group, resulting in mutually satisfying exchanges

undifferentiated targeting strategy a marketing approach that views the market as one big market with no individual segments and thus uses a single marketing mix

usage-rate segmentation dividing a market by the amount of product bought or consumed

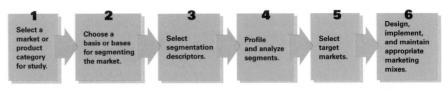

Note that steps 5 and 6 are actually marketing activities that follow market segmentation (steps 1 through 4).

8-7 Discuss alternative strategies for selecting target markets (p. 140–142). Marketers select target markets by using three different strategies: undifferentiated targeting, concentrated targeting, and multisegment targeting. An undifferentiated targeting strategy assumes that all members of a market have similar needs that can be met by using a single marketing mix. A concentrated targeting strategy focuses all marketing efforts on a single market segment. Multisegment targeting is a strategy that uses two or more marketing mixes to target two or more market segments.

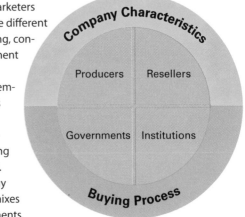

8-8 Explain one-to-one marketing (p. 142–143). One-to-one marketing is an individualized marketing method that uses customer information to build long-term, personalized, and profitable relationships with each customer. Successful one-to-one marketing comes from understanding customers and collaborating with them, rather than using them as targets for generic messages. Database technology makes it possible for companies to interact with customers on a personal, one-to-one basis.

8-9 Explain how and why firms implement positioning strategies and how product differentiation plays a role (p. 143–146). Positioning is used to influence consumer perceptions of a particular brand, product line, or organization in relation to competitors. The term *position* refers to the place that the offering occupies in consumers' minds. To establish a unique position, many firms use product differentiation, emphasizing the real or perceived differences between competing offerings. Products may be differentiated on the basis of attribute, price and quality, use or application, product user, product class, or competitor.

Each car occupies a position in consumers' minds.
Cars can be positioned according to attribute (sporty, conservative, etc.), to price/quality (affordable, classy, etc.), or other bases.
With edgier ads, Cadillac has repositioned itself as a car for younger drivers.

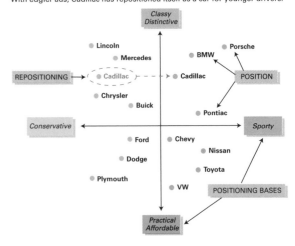

brand a name, term, symbol, design, or combination thereof that identifies a seller's products and differentiates them from competitors' products

brand equity the value of company and brand names

brand loyalty a consistent preference for one brand over all others

brand mark the elements of a brand that cannot be spoken

brand name that part of a brand that can be spoken, including letters, words, and numbers

business product a product used to manufacture other goods or services, to facilitate an organization's operations, or to resell to other customers

cobranding placing two or more brand names on a product or its package

consumer product a product bought to satisfy an individual's personal wants

convenience product a relatively inexpensive item that merits little shopping effort

express warranty a written guarantee

family brand the marketing of several different products under the same brand name

generic product a no-frills, no-brand-name, low-cost product that is simply identified by its product category

generic product name a term that identifies a product by class or type and cannot be trademarked

global brand a brand where at least 20 percent of the product is sold outside its home country or region

implied warranty an unwritten guarantee that the good or service is fit for the purpose for which it was sold

individual branding the use of different brand names for different products

9-1 Define the term *product* (p. 151). A product is anything, desired or not, that a person or organization receives in an exchange. The basic goal of purchasing decisions is to receive the tangible and intangible benefits associated with a product. Tangible aspects include packaging, style, colour, size, and features. Intangible qualities include service, the retailer's image, the manufacturer's reputation, and the social status associated with a product. An organization's product offering is the crucial element in any marketing mix.

9-2 Classify consumer products (p. 152–153). Consumer products are classified into four categories: convenience products, shopping products, specialty products, and unsought products. Convenience products are relatively inexpensive and require limited shopping effort. Shopping products are of two types: homogeneous and heterogeneous. Because of the similarity of homogeneous products, they are differentiated mainly by price and features. In contrast, heterogeneous products appeal to consumers because of their distinct characteristics. Specialty products possess unique benefits that are highly desirable to certain customers. Finally, unsought products are either new products or products that require aggressive selling because they are generally avoided or overlooked by consumers.

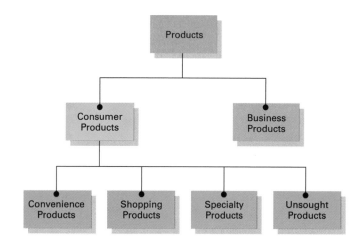

9-3 Define the terms *product item, product line,* and *product mix* (p. 153–156). A product item is a specific version of a product that can be designated as a distinct offering among an organization's products. A product line is a group of closely related products offered by an organization. An organization's product mix includes all the products it sells. Product mix width refers to the number of product lines an organization offers. Product line depth is the number of product items in a product line. Firms modify existing products by changing their quality, functional characteristics, or style. Product line extension occurs when a firm adds new products to existing product lines.

9-4 Describe marketing uses of branding (p. 156–162). A brand is a name, term, or symbol that identifies and differentiates a firm's products. Established brands encourage customer loyalty and help new products succeed. Branding strategies require decisions about individual, family, manufacturers', and private brands.

9-5 Describe marketing uses of packaging and labelling (p. 162–163). Packaging has four functions: containing and protecting products; promoting products; facilitating product storage, use, and convenience; and facilitating

informational labelling package labelling designed to help consumers make proper product selections and to lower their cognitive dissonance after the purchase

manufacturer's brand the brand name of a manufacturer

persuasive labelling package labelling that focuses on a promotional theme or logo, and consumer information is secondary

planned obsolescence the practice of modifying products so that those that have already been sold become obsolete before they actually need replacement

private brand a brand name owned by a wholesaler or a retailer

product anything, both favourable and unfavourable, received by a person in an exchange for possession, consumption, attention, or short-term use

product item a specific version of a product that can be designated as a distinct offering among an organization's products

product line a group of closely related product items

product line depth the different version of a product item in a product line

product line extension adding additional products to an existing product line to compete more broadly in the industry

product line length the number of product items in a product line

product mix all products that an organization sells

product mix width the number of product lines an organization offers

product modification changing one or more of a product's characteristics

service mark a trademark for a service

recycling and reducing environmental damage. As a tool for promotion, packaging identifies the brand and its features. It also serves the critical function of differentiating a product from competing products and linking it with related products from the same manufacturer. The label is an integral part of the package and has persuasive and informational functions. In essence, the package is the marketer's last chance to influence buyers before they make a purchase decision.

9-6 Discuss global issues in branding and packaging (p. 164).

In addition to brand piracy, international marketers must address a variety of concerns regarding branding and packaging, including choosing a brand-name policy, translating labels and meeting host-country labelling requirements, making packages aesthetically compatible with host-country cultures, and offering the sizes of packages preferred in host countries.

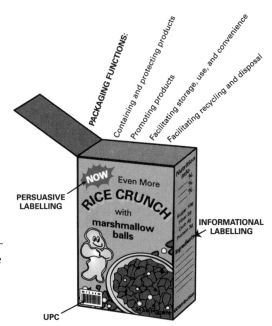

	Branding choices:	Packaging considerations:
	One name	Labelling
	Modify or adapt one name	Aesthetics
	Different names in different markets	Climate

9-7 Describe how and why product warranties are important marketing tools (p. 164–165).

Product warranties are important tools because they offer consumers protection and help them gauge product quality.

Express warranty = Written guarantee

Implied warranty = Unwritten guarantee

shopping product a product that requires comparison shopping because it is usually more expensive than a convenience product and is found in fewer stores

specialty product a particular item with unique characteristics that consumers search for extensively and for which they are very reluctant to accept substitutes

trademark the exclusive right to use a brand or part of a brand

universal product codes (UPCs) a series of thick and thin vertical lines (bar codes), readable by computerized optical scanners that match the codes to brand names, package sizes, and prices

unsought product a product unknown to the potential buyer or a known product that the buyer does not actively seek

warranty a confirmation of the quality or performance of a good or service

adopter a consumer who was happy enough with his or her trial experience with a product to use it again

brainstorming the process of getting a group to think of unlimited ways to vary a product or solve a problem

business analysis the second stage of the screening process, where preliminary figures for demand, cost, sales, and profitability are calculated

commercialization the decision to market a product

concept test evaluation of a new-product idea, usually before any prototype has been created

decline stage a long-run drop in sales

development the stage in the product development process in which a prototype is developed and a marketing strategy is outlined

diffusion the process by which the adoption of an innovation spreads

growth stage the second stage of the product life cycle when sales typically grow at an increasing rate, many competitors enter the market, large companies may start to acquire small pioneering firms, and profits are healthy

innovation a product perceived as new by a potential adopter

introductory stage the full-scale launch of a new product into the marketplace

maturity stage a period during which sales increase at a decreasing rate

new product a product new to the world, new to the market, new to the producer or seller, or new to some combination of these

new-product strategy a plan that links the new-product development process with the objectives of the marketing department, the business unit, and the corporation

product category all brands that satisfy a particular type of need

10-1 Explain the importance of developing new products and describe the six categories of new products (p. 167–168). New products are important to sustain growth and profits and to replace obsolete items. New products can be classified as new-to-the-world products (discontinuous innovations), new product lines, additions to existing product lines, improvements or revisions of existing products, repositioned products, or lower-priced products. To sustain or increase profits, a firm must innovate.

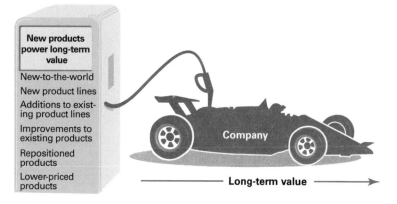

New products power long-term value
- New-to-the-world
- New product lines
- Additions to existing product lines
- Improvements to existing products
- Repositioned products
- Lower-priced products

Company — Long-term value →

10-2 Explain the steps in the new-product development process (p. 169–175). First, a firm forms a new-product strategy by outlining the characteristics and roles of future products. Then new-product ideas are generated by customers, employees, distributors, competitors, vendors, and internal R&D personnel. Once a product idea has survived initial screening by an appointed screening group, it undergoes business analysis to determine its potential profitability. If a product concept seems viable, it progresses into the development phase, in which the technical and economic feasibility of the manufacturing process is evaluated. The development phase also includes laboratory and use testing of a product for performance and safety. Following initial testing and refinement, most products are introduced in a test market to evaluate consumer response and marketing strategies. Finally, test market successes are propelled into full commercialization. The commercialization process involves starting up production, building inventories, shipping to distributors, training a sales force, announcing the product to the trade, and advertising to consumers.

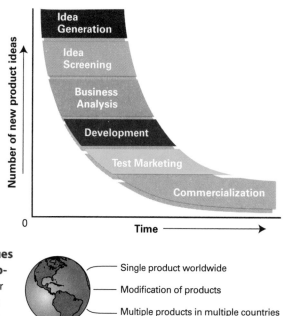

Number of new product ideas
- Idea Generation
- Idea Screening
- Business Analysis
- Development
- Test Marketing
- Commercialization

Time →

10-3 Discuss global issues in new-product development (p. 175). A marketer with global vision seeks to develop products that can

- Single product worldwide
- Modification of products
- Multiple products in multiple countries

product development a marketing strategy that entails the creation of new products for current customers

product life cycle (PLC) a concept that traces the stages of a product's acceptance, from its introduction (birth) to its decline (death)

screening the first filter in the product development process, which eliminates ideas that are inconsistent with the organization's new-product strategy or are obviously inappropriate for some other reason

simulated (laboratory) market testing the presentation of advertising and other promotion materials for several products, including a test product, to members of the product's target market

simultaneous product development a team-oriented approach to new-product development

test marketing the limited introduction of a product and a marketing program to determine the reactions of potential customers in a market situation

easily be adapted to suit local needs. The goal is not simply to develop a standard product that can be sold worldwide. Smart global marketers also look for good product ideas worldwide.

10-4 Explain the diffusion process through which new products are adopted (p. 175–177). The diffusion process is the spread of a new product from its producer to its ultimate adopters. Adopters in the diffusion process belong to five categories: innovators, early adopters, the early majority, the late majority, and laggards. Product characteristics that affect the rate of adoption include product complexity, compatibility with existing social values, relative advantage over existing substitutes, visibility, and trialability. The diffusion process is facilitated by word-of-mouth communication and communication from marketers to consumers.

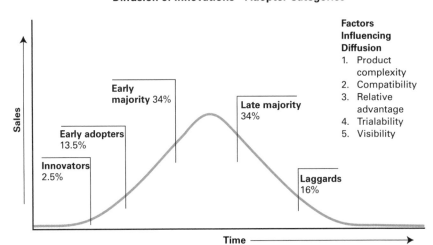

Diffusion of Innovations—Adopter Categories

Innovators 2.5%
Early adopters 13.5%
Early majority 34%
Late majority 34%
Laggards 16%

Factors Influencing Diffusion
1. Product complexity
2. Compatibility
3. Relative advantage
4. Trialability
5. Visibility

10-5 Explain the concept of product life cycles (p. 177–181). All brands and product categories have a life cycle with four stages: introduction, growth, maturity, and decline. The rate at which products move through these stages varies dramatically. Marketing managers use the product life-cycle concept as an analytical tool to forecast a product's future and devise effective marketing strategies.

Marketing Mix Strategy	Product Life Cycle Stage			
	Introductory	**Growth**	**Maturity**	**Decline**
Product Strategy	Limited number of models; frequent product modifications	Expanded number of models; frequent product modifications	Large number of models	Elimination of unprofitable models and brands
Distribution Strategy	Distribution usually limited, depending on product; intensive efforts and high margins often needed to attract wholesalers and retailers	Expanded number of dealers; intensive efforts to establish long-term relationships with wholesalers and retailers	Extensive number of dealers; margins declining; intensive efforts to retain distributors and shelf space	Unprofitable outlets phased out
Promotion Strategy	Develop product awareness; stimulate primary demand; use intensive personal selling to distributors; use sampling and couponing for consumers	Stimulate selective demand; advertise brand aggressively	Stimulate selective demand; advertise brand aggressively; promote heavily to retain dealers and customers	Phase out all promotion
Pricing Strategy	Prices are usually high to recover development costs (see the appendix to Chapter 12)	Prices begin to fall toward end of growth stage as result of competitive pressure	Prices continue to fall	Prices stabilize at relatively low level; small price rises are possible if competition is negligible

assurance the knowledge and courtesy of employees and their ability to convey trust

core service the most basic benefit the consumer is buying

credence quality a characteristic that consumers may have difficulty assessing even after purchase because they do not have the necessary knowledge or experience

empathy caring, individualized attention paid to customers

experience quality a characteristic that can be assessed only after use

gap model a model identifying five gaps that can cause problems in service delivery and influence customer evaluations of service quality

inconsistency the inability of service quality to be consistent each time it is delivered because the service depends on the people that provide it

inseparability the inability of the production and consumption of a service to be separated; consumers must be present during the production

intangibility the inability of services to be touched, seen, tasted, heard, or felt in the same manner that goods can be sensed

internal marketing treating employees as customers and developing systems and benefits that satisfy their needs

inventory the inability of services to be stored for future use

nonprofit organization an organization that exists to achieve some goal other than the usual business goals of profit, market share, or return on investment

nonprofit organization marketing the effort by nonprofit organizations to bring about mutually satisfying exchanges with target markets

11-1 Discuss the importance of services to the economy (p. 183–184). The service sector plays a crucial role in the Canadian economy, employing more than 78 percent of the workforce and accounting for a similar percentage of the gross domestic product.

11-2 Discuss the differences between services and goods (p. 184–185). Services are distinguished by four characteristics. Services are intangible performances because they lack clearly identifiable physical characteristics, making it difficult for marketers to communicate their specific benefits to potential customers. The production and consumption of services occur simultaneously. Services quality is inconsistent because the service depends on such elements as the service provider, individual consumer, location, and so on. Finally, services cannot be inventoried. As a result, synchronizing supply with demand is particularly challenging in the service industry.

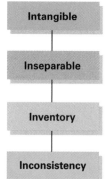

11-3 Describe the components of service quality and the gap model of service quality (p. 185–187). Service quality has five components: reliability (ability to perform the service dependably, accurately, and consistently), responsiveness (providing prompt service), assurance (knowledge and courtesy of employees and their ability to convey trust), empathy (caring, individualized attention), and tangibles (physical evidence of the service).

The gap model identifies five key discrepancies that can influence customer evaluations of service quality. When the gaps are large, service quality is low. As the gaps shrink, service quality improves. Gap 1, the knowledge gap, is found between customers' expectations and management's perceptions of those expectations. Gap 2, the standard gap, is found between management's perception of what the customer wants and the specifications for service quality. Gap 3, the delivery gap, is found between service quality specifications and delivery of the service. Gap 4, the communications gap, is found between service delivery and what the company promises to the customer through external communication. Gap 5, the perception gap, is found between customers' service expectations and their perceptions of service performance.

▸▸ **knowledge**

▸▸ **standards**

▸▸ **delivery**

▸▸ **communication**

▸▸ **perception**

11-4 Develop marketing mixes for services using the eight Ps of services marketing (p. 187–191).

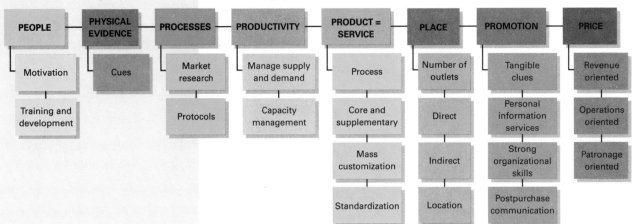

11-5 Discuss relationship marketing in services (p. 191–193). Relationship marketing in services involves attracting, developing, and retaining customer relationships. Relationship marketing has three levels: level 1 focuses on pricing incentives; level 2 uses pricing incentives and social bonds with customers; and level 3 uses pricing, social bonds, and structural bonds to build long-term relationships.

11-6 Explain internal marketing in services (p. 193). Internal marketing means treating employees as customers and developing systems and benefits that satisfy their needs. Employees who like their jobs and are happy with the firm they work for are more likely to deliver good service.

11-7 Discuss global issues in services marketing (p. 193). To be successful globally, service firms must adjust their marketing mix for the environment of each target country.

11-8 Describe nonprofit organization marketing (p. 193–197). Nonprofit organizations pursue goals other than profit, market share, and return on investment.

Nonprofit Organization Marketing

bait pricing a price tactic that tries to get consumers into a store through false or misleading price advertising and then uses high-pressure selling to persuade consumers to buy more expensive merchandise instead

base price the general price level at which the company expects to sell the good or service

basing-point pricing charging freight from a given (basing) point, regardless of the city from which the goods are shipped

cash discount a price reduction offered to a consumer, an industrial user, or a marketing intermediary in return for prompt payment of a bill

cumulative quantity discount a deduction from list price that applies to the buyer's total purchases made during a specific period

deceptive pricing promoting a price or price saving that is not actually available

flexible pricing (variable pricing) different customers pay different prices for essentially the same merchandise bought in equal quantities

FOB origin pricing the buyer absorbs the freight costs from the shipping point ("free on board")

freight absorption pricing the seller pays all or part of the actual freight charges and does not pass them on to the buyer

functional discount (trade discount) a discount to wholesalers and retailers for performing channel functions

leader pricing (loss-leader pricing) a product is sold near or even below cost in the hope that shoppers will buy other items once they are in the store

market share a company's product sales as a percentage of total sales for that industry

12-1 Explain the importance of price (p. 203–204). Of the four Ps, price is special. Price is a source of revenue for the firm, not a cost centre like many promotional activities. Price involves an understanding of revenues, expenses, and the resulting profit. Many economic factors go into pricing a product or service, but there are also many other factors that are more psychological.

12-2 Describe the four-step pricing process (p. 204–215). The four-step pricing process allows for a true understanding of the many factors included in and decisions that must be made in setting a price. The first step is to establish pricing goals. Companies must determine if they are profit oriented, focused on meeting a profit objective or a target return, or will look to sales as a way to create their pricing goals. The second step is to estimate demand, costs, and profit. This step is tied in with product and specifically the product life cycle. The third step is to establish a pricing strategy. Companies can decide to price higher (skimming), lower (penetration), or about the same (status quo) as the competition. Finally, the fourth step is to establish a pricing tactic. Pricing tactics tend to be used once the base price has been established. Tactics include discounts, geographic pricing, flexible pricing, price lining, loss leaders, and odd–even pricing (though that last one might be dying out).

12-3 Recognize the legalities and ethics of setting a price (p. 216–218). This darker side of pricing introduces us to the concepts of bait pricing, bait and switch, and other deceptive practices. Some firms try to influence the price of their products by making agreements with competitors or by using discriminatory practices to influence the price on the shelves. All of these methods are problematic, and some well-known firms have run afoul of these legal and ethical issues with pricing.

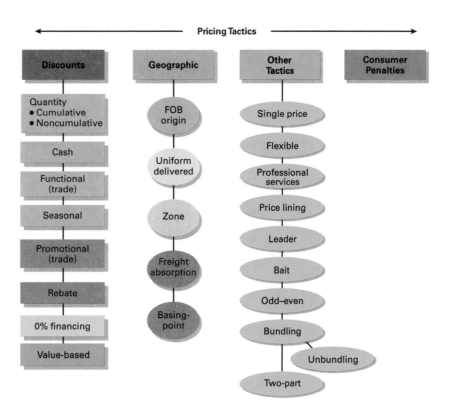

noncumulative quantity discount a deduction from list price that applies to a single order rather than to the total volume of orders placed during a certain period

odd–even pricing (psychological pricing) odd-numbered prices connote bargains, and even-numbered prices imply quality

penetration pricing a relatively low price for a product initially as a way to reach the mass market

predatory pricing the practice of charging a very low price for a product with the intent of driving competitors out of business or out of a market

price that which is given up in an exchange to acquire a good or service

price bundling marketing two or more products in a single package for a special price

price fixing an agreement between two or more firms on the price they will charge for a product

price lining offering a product line with several items at specific price points

price skimming a high introductory price, often coupled with heavy promotion

price strategy a basic, long-term pricing framework that establishes the initial price for a product and the intended direction for price movements over the product life cycle

profit revenue minus expenses

quantity discount a unit price reduction offered to buyers buying either in multiple units or at more than a specified dollar amount

resale price maintenance attempts by a producer to control a store's retail price for the product

return on investment (ROI) net profits divided by the investment

revenue the price charged to customers multiplied by the number of units sold

seasonal discount a price reduction for buying merchandise out of season

single-price tactic offering all goods and services at the same price (or perhaps two or three prices)

status quo pricing a pricing objective that maintains existing prices or meets the competition's prices

two-part pricing charging two separate amounts to consume a single good or service

unbundling reducing the bundle of services that comes with the basic product

uniform delivered pricing the seller pays the actual freight charges and bills every purchaser an identical, flat freight charge

value-based pricing setting the price at a level that seems to the customer to be a good price compared with the prices of other options

zone pricing a modification of uniform delivered pricing that divides the total market into segments or zones and charges a flat freight rate to all customers in a given zone

average fixed cost (AFC) total fixed costs divided by quantity of output

$$AFC = \frac{TFC}{Q}$$

average total cost (ATC) total costs divided by quantity of output

$$ATC = \frac{TC}{Q}$$

average variable cost (AVC) total variable costs divided by quantity of output

$$AVC = \frac{TVC}{Q}$$

break-even analysis a method of determining what sales volume must be reached before total revenue equals total costs

demand the quantity of a product that will be sold in the market at various prices for a specified period

elastic demand a situation in which consumer demand is sensitive to changes in price

elasticity of demand consumers' responsiveness or sensitivity to changes in price

fixed cost a cost that does not change as output is increased or decreased

floor price the lowest price to which a company will allow its price to drop

inelastic demand a situation in which an increase or a decrease in price will not significantly affect demand for the product

inventory turnover measures the number of times a firm "turns" its inventory each year

marginal cost (MC) the change in total costs associated with a one-unit change in output

$$MC = \frac{\text{Change in TC}}{\text{Change in Q}}$$

Elasticity of Demand

$$\text{Elasticity } (E) = \frac{\text{Percentage change in quantity demanded of good A}}{\text{Percentage change in price of good A}}$$

If E is greater than 1, demand is elastic.

If E is less than 1, demand is inelastic.

If E is equal to 1, demand is unitary.

Markup Pricing

$$\text{Dollar markup} = \text{Selling price} - \text{Cost}$$

$$\text{Percentage markup on cost} = \frac{\text{Dollar markup}}{\text{Cost}} \times 100$$

$$\text{Percentage markup on selling price} = \frac{\text{Dollar markup}}{\text{Selling price}} \times 100$$

Markup Conversions. To convert from percentage markup on cost to percentage markup on selling price:

$$\text{Percentage markup on selling price} = \frac{\text{Percentage markup on cost}}{100 + \text{Percentage markup on cost}} \times 100$$

To convert from percentage markup on selling price to percentage markup on cost:

$$\text{Percentage markup on cost} = \frac{\text{Percentage markup on selling price}}{100 - \text{Percentage markup on selling price}} \times 100$$

Break-Even Analysis. Determines the required sales volume to be reached before the company breaks even (its total costs equal total revenue) and no profits are earned. The formula for calculating break-even quantities is simple:

$$\text{Break-even (quantity)} = \frac{\text{Total fixed costs}}{\text{Price} - \text{Variable costs}}$$

or

$$\left(\frac{\text{Total fixed costs}}{\text{Fixed-costs contribution}} \right)$$

$$(\text{Fixed-cost contribution} = \text{Price} - \text{Average variable cost})$$

Performance Ratios. A variety of financial ratios to assess the performance of a firm. These ratios are calculated using data found on both the income statement and the balance sheet.

Return on Assets (ROA)

$$ROA = \frac{\text{Sales}}{\text{Average assets}} \times \frac{\text{Net income}}{\text{Sales}}$$

marginal revenue (MR) the extra revenue associated with selling an extra unit of output, or the change in total revenue as a result of a one-unit change in output

markup the dollar amount added to the cost of sales to get to the selling price

profit maximization a method of setting prices so that marginal revenue equals marginal cost

return on assets (ROA) measures the firm's efficiency in generating sales and profits from the total amount invested in the company

return on investment (ROI) net profits divided by the investment

return on marketing investment (ROMI) the contribution attributable to marketing spending (net)

supply the quantity of a product that will be offered to the market by a supplier at various prices for a specified period

unitary elasticity a situation in which total revenue remains the same when prices change

variable cost a cost that varies with changes in the level of output

Inventory Turnover

$$\frac{\text{Sales}}{\text{Average inventory}}$$

Accounts Receivable Turnover

$$\text{Accounts receivable turnover} = \frac{\text{Credit sales}}{\text{Average accounts receivable}}$$

Return on Investment (ROI)

$$\text{ROI (\%)} = \frac{\text{Net profit} \times 100}{\text{Investment}}$$

Return on Marketing Investment (ROMI)

$$\text{ROMI} = \frac{\text{Revenue attributable to marketing (\$)} \times \text{Contribution margin (\%)} - \text{Marketing spending (\$)}}{\text{Marketing spending (\$)}}$$

channel conflict a clash of goals and methods among distribution channel members

channel control one marketing channel member intentionally affects another member's behaviour

channel leader (channel captain) a member of a marketing channel who exercises authority and power over the activities of other channel members

channel members all parties in the marketing channel that negotiate with one another, buy and sell products, and facilitate the change of ownership between buyer and seller as they move the product from the manufacturer into the hands of the final consumer

channel partnering (channel cooperation) the joint effort of all channel members to create a supply chain that serves customers and creates a competitive advantage

channel power a marketing channel member's capacity to control or influence the behaviour of other channel members

coverage ensuring product availability in every outlet where potential customers might want to buy it

direct channel a distribution channel in which producers sell directly to customers

discrepancy of assortment the lack of all the items a customer needs to receive full satisfaction from a product or products

discrepancy of quantity the difference between the amount of product produced and the amount an end-user wants to buy

distribution resource planning (DRP) an inventory control system that manages the replenishment of goods from the manufacturer to the final consumer

dual distribution (multiple distribution) the use of two or more channels to distribute the same product to target markets

13-1 Explain the nature of marketing channels (p. 235–238). Sometimes referred to as the "forgotten P" of the four Ps, place is an important, albeit overshadowed, element of the marketing mix. The focus of place is on marketing channels (channels of distribution) that guide products from the companies producing them to the consumers or business customers purchasing and using them. The supply chain covers all companies that are responsible for some aspect of developing and distributing a product. Supply chains have intermediaries that end up performing a number of important tasks including specialization, division of labour, the overcoming of discrepancies, and contact efficiency.

13-2 Identify different channel intermediaries and their functions (p. 238–240). The intermediaries in a channel system and supply chain undertake important tasks that are key to a properly functioning distribution system. Intermediaries work with other firms while also ensuring their own firms' success. In determining what type of intermediary to use, a producer should look at a number of factors including product characteristics, buyer considerations, and market characteristics. Retailers sell mainly to customers. Wholesalers help move goods through the supply chain. Agents and brokers facilitate the exchange of ownership between buyers and sellers.

13-3 Describe the types of marketing channels (p. 240–243). Marketing channels are paths to move goods from producer to customer. The most straightforward is called the direct channel: a producer has direct contact with the end customer and does not have to rely on intermediaries. Business channels focus on B2B interactions. In multiple channels, two different types of channels are used to deliver the same product. Nontraditional channels, like vending machines, are intriguing options but with potential risk to the brand and company image. In strategic channel alliances, companies decide to work together to achieve certain supply chain goals.

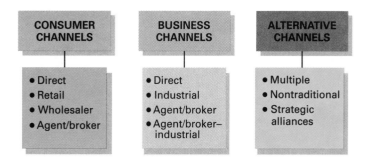

CONSUMER CHANNELS	BUSINESS CHANNELS	ALTERNATIVE CHANNELS
• Direct • Retail • Wholesaler • Agent/broker	• Direct • Industrial • Agent/broker • Agent/broker–industrial	• Multiple • Nontraditional • Strategic alliances

13-4 Summarize how to make channel strategy decisions (p. 243–246). To make the correct decisions when selecting the overall makeup of a channel, companies look at several important factors. The market factors relate to the customer to determine the likely behaviours and patterns that they will display. Product factors deal with the product on offer and, depending on the complexity of the product, will determine how the product moves through the channel system. Finally, producer factors connect to the company behind the product and whether it has the necessary size and capabilities to manage a certain type of channel system. Distribution intensity is another important consideration. The three main types of distribution intensity are intensive, selective, and exclusive; each has its own benefits and drawbacks.

13-5 Recognize how to handle channel relationships (p. 246–247). The importance of relationships was made evident in Chapter 7 in the discussion of business marketing. With place and distribution, we are once again talking about the need for businesses to work together. However, because business is focused on profit and

electronic data interchange (EDI) information technology that replaces the paper documents that usually accompany business transactions, such as purchase orders and invoices, with electronic transmission of the needed information to reduce inventory levels, improve cash flow, streamline operations, and increase the speed and accuracy of information transmission

electronic distribution a distribution technique that includes any kind of product or service that can be distributed electronically, whether over traditional forms, such as fibre-optic cable, or through satellite transmission of electronic signals

exclusive distribution a form of distribution that involves only one or a few dealers within a given area

horizontal conflict a channel conflict that occurs among channel members on the same level

intensive distribution a form of distribution aimed at having a product available in every outlet where target customers might want to buy it

inventory control system a method of developing and maintaining an adequate assortment of materials or products to meet a manufacturer's or a customer's demand

just-in-time production (JIT) a process that redefines and simplifies manufacturing by reducing inventory levels and delivering raw materials just when they are needed on the production line

logistics the process of strategically managing the efficient flow and storage of raw materials, in-process inventory, and finished goods from point of origin to point of consumption

logistics information system the link that connects all the logistics functions of the supply chain

marketing channel (channel of distribution) a set of interdependent organizations

growth-oriented goals, there is bound to be conflict when companies interact in a marketing channel. Issues of power and control are not surprising in channels and managing them, along with taking a leadership role, is an important step for any company in a channel. Conflict in a channel can be horizontal, meaning at the same level of intermediary (e.g., distributor versus distributor) between different channels. Conflict can also be vertical within a channel (e.g., distributor versus retailer). But with all of this conflict comes some positive cooperation, and firms work together to make things easier for the entire channel, which also benefits individual firms in the process.

13-6 Learn about supply chain management (p. 247–252). Supply chain management strives to coordinate and integrate all the activities involved in getting a product to market. This includes everything from raw materials all the way to the managing of the delivery of the final product to a customer. Logistics is often described as the grease in the wheels of supply chain management, offering the flow and storage necessary for supplies and products to make their way to the necessary points in a channel system. Purchasing and procuring the right items is a vital task in supply chain management.

13-7 List channel and distribution challenges in global markets (p. 252–253). Globalization of markets has led to innovations and changes in every market, and channels and distribution are certainly not immune. World markets continue to open up, and with more agreements being ratified by the World Trade Organization, companies now have access to markets and partners that can potentially provide improvements to the existing supply chain.

that ease the transfer of ownership as products move from producer to business user or consumer

mass customization (build-to-order) a production method whereby products are not made until an order is placed by the customer; products are made according to customer specifications

materials requirement planning (MRP) (materials management) an inventory control system that manages the replenishment of raw materials, supplies, and components from the supplier to the manufacturer

order processing system a system whereby orders are entered into the supply chain and filled

outsourcing (contract logistics) a manufacturer's or supplier's use of an independent third party to manage an entire function of the logistics system, such as transportation, warehousing, or order processing

retailer the market intermediary that sells goods and services to the final consumer

selective distribution a form of distribution achieved by screening dealers to eliminate all but a few in any single area

spatial discrepancy the difference between the location of a producer and the location of widely scattered markets

strategic channel alliances cooperative agreements between business firms to use one of the manufacturer's already established distribution channels

supply chain the connected chain of all the business entities, both internal and external to the company, that perform or support the marketing channel functions

supply chain management a management system that coordinates and integrates all the activities performed by supply chain members into a seamless process, from the source to the point of consumption, resulting in enhanced customer and economic value

supply chain team an entire group of individuals who orchestrate the movement of goods, services, and information from the source to the consumer

temporal discrepancy a product is produced but a customer is not ready to buy it

vertical conflict a channel conflict that occurs between different levels in a marketing channel, most typically between the manufacturer and wholesaler or between the manufacturer and retailer

CHAPTER REVIEW

atmosphere the overall impression conveyed by a store's physical layout, decor, and surroundings

automatic vending the use of machines to offer goods for sale

buyer a department head who selects the merchandise for his or her department and may also be responsible for promotion and personnel

category killers specialty discount stores that heavily dominate their narrow merchandise segment

chain stores stores owned and operated as a group by a single organization

convenience store a miniature supermarket, carrying only a limited line of high-turnover convenience goods

department store a store housing several departments under one roof

destination stores stores that consumers purposely plan to visit

direct marketing (direct-response marketing) techniques used to get consumers to make a purchase from their home, office, or another nonretail setting

direct retailing the selling of products by representatives who work door-to-door, office-to-office, or at-home parties

discount store a retailer that competes on the basis of low prices, high turnover, and high volume

drugstores retail stores that stock pharmacy-related products and services as their main draw

factory outlet an off-price retailer that is owned and operated by a manufacturer

franchisee an individual or a business that is granted the right to sell a franchiser's product

franchiser the originator of a trade name, product, methods of operation, and so on, that grants operating rights to another party to sell its product

14-1 Discuss the importance of retailing in the Canadian economy (p. 255). Retailing plays a vital role in the Canadian economy for two main reasons. First, retail businesses contribute to our high standard of living by providing a vast number and diversity of goods and services. Second, retailing employs a large portion of the Canadian working population.

14-2 Explain the dimensions by which retailers can be classified (p. 256–258). Many different kinds of retailers exist. A retail establishment can be classified according to its ownership, level of service, product assortment, and price. On the basis of ownership, retailers can be broadly differentiated as independent retailers, chain stores, or franchise outlets. The level of service retailers provide can be classified along a continuum of high to low. Retailers also classify themselves by the breadth and depth of their product assortments. Last, general price levels also classify a store, from discounters offering low prices to exclusive specialty stores where high prices are the norm.

14-3 Describe the major types of retail operations (p. 258–262). The major types of retail stores are department stores, specialty retailers, supermarkets, drugstores, convenience stores, discount stores, and restaurants. Department stores carry a wide assortment of shopping and specialty goods, are organized into relatively independent departments, and offset higher prices by emphasizing customer service and decor. Specialty retailers typically carry a narrower but deeper assortment of merchandise, emphasizing distinctive products and a high level of customer service. Supermarkets are large self-service retailers that offer a wide variety of food products and some nonfood items. Drugstores are retail formats that sell mostly prescription and over-the-counter medications, health and beauty aids, cosmetics, and specialty items. Convenience stores carry a limited line of high-turnover convenience goods. Discount stores offer low-priced general merchandise and consist of four types: full-line discounters, specialty discount retailers, warehouse clubs, and off-price retailers. Finally, restaurants straddle the line between the retailing and services industries; although restaurants sell a product, food and drink, to final consumers, they can also be considered service marketers because they provide consumers with the service of preparing food and providing table service.

14-4 Discuss nonstore retailing techniques (p. 262–265). Nonstore retailing, which is shopping outside a store setting, has three major categories: automatic vending machines, direct retailing, and direct marketing. The latest developments in retailing have occurred in the area of direct marketing, specifically electronic retailing such as home shopping channels and online retailing.

14-5 Define franchising and describe its two basic forms (p. 265). Franchising is a continuing relationship in which a franchiser grants to a franchisee the business rights to operate or to sell a product. Modern franchising takes two basic forms: product or trade-name franchising and business-format franchising.

14-6 List the major tasks involved in developing a retail marketing strategy (p. 266–272). Retail management begins with defining the target market, typically on the basis of demographic, geographic, or psychographic characteristics. After determining the target market, retail managers must develop the six variables of the retailing mix: product, promotion, place, price, presentation, and personnel.

franchises relationships in which the business rights to operate and sell a product or service are granted by the franchiser to the franchisee

full-line discount stores retailers that offer consumers very limited service and carry a broad assortment of well-known, nationally branded hard goods

gross margin the amount of money the retailer makes as a percentage of sales after the cost of goods sold is subtracted

independent retailers retailers owned by a single person or partnership and not operated as part of a larger retail institution

mass merchandising a retailing strategy using moderate to low prices on large quantities of merchandise and lower levels of service to stimulate high turnover of products

nonstore retailing shopping without visiting a store

off-price retailer a retailer that sells brand-name merchandise at considerable discounts

omni channel retailing an approach that combines the advantages of the physical store experience with the information-rich experience of online shopping, providing the consumer with a seamless experience through all available shopping channels

online retailing a type of shopping available to consumers who have personal computers and access to the Internet

product offering the mix of products offered to the consumer by the retailer; also called the product assortment or merchandise mix

retailer the market intermediary that sells goods and services to the final consumer

retailing all the activities directly related to the sale of goods and services to the ultimate consumer for personal, nonbusiness use

14-7 Describe new developments in retailing (p. 272). Both small retailers and national chains are using interactivity to involve customers and set themselves apart from the competition. M-commerce (mobile e-commerce) is gaining in popularity. M-commerce enables consumers to purchase goods and services by using wireless mobile devices, such as smartphones and tablets.

retailing mix a combination of the six Ps—product, place, promotion, price, presentation, and personnel—to sell goods and services to the ultimate consumer

scrambled merchandising the tendency to offer a wide variety of nontraditional goods and services under one roof

specialty discount stores retail stores that offer a nearly complete selection of single-line merchandise and use self-service, discount prices, high volume, and high turnover

specialty store a retail store specializing in a given type of merchandise

supercentres retail stores that combine groceries and general merchandise goods with a wide range of services

supermarkets large, departmentalized, self-service retailers that specialize in food and some nonfood items

telemarketing the use of telecommunications to sell a product or service; involves both outbound and inbound calls

warehouse membership clubs limited-service merchant wholesalers that sell a limited selection of brand-name appliances, household items, and groceries to members, small businesses, and groups

advertising impersonal, one-way mass communication about a product or an organization that is paid for by a marketer

AIDA concept a model that outlines the process for achieving promotional goals in terms of stages of consumer involvement with the message; the acronym stands for *attention*, *interest*, *desire*, and *action*

channel a medium of communication—such as a voice, radio, or newspaper—used for transmitting a message

communication the process by which we exchange or share meanings through a common set of symbols

competitive advantage the set of unique features of a company and its products that are perceived by the target market as significant and superior to the competition

consumer-generated content any form of publically available online content created by consumers; also referred to as user-generated content

decoding interpretation of the language and symbols sent by the source through a channel

direct-response communication communication of a message directly from a marketing company and directly to an intended individual target audience

earned media a category of promotional tactic based on a public relations model that gets customers talking about products or services

encoding the conversion of the sender's ideas and thoughts into a message, usually in the form of words or signs

feedback the receiver's response to a message

integrated marketing communications (IMC) the careful coordination of all promotional messages for a product or a service to ensure the consistency of messages at every contact point where a company meets the consumer

15-1 Discuss the role of promotion in the marketing mix (p. 277–278).
Promotion is communication by marketers that informs, persuades, reminds, and connects potential buyers of a product to influence their opinion or elicit a response. Promotional strategy is the plan for using the elements of promotion—advertising, public relations, sales promotion, direct response communication, personal selling, and social media—to meet the firm's overall objectives and marketing goals. Using these objectives, marketers combine the elements of the promotional strategy to form a coordinated promotion plan. The promotion plan then becomes an integral part of the total marketing strategy for reaching the target market, in addition to product, distribution, and price.

15-2 Describe the communication process (p. 278–281).
The communication process has several steps. It begins with encoding the message using language and symbols familiar to the receiver. The message is sent through a message channel to the receiver, who decodes the message and provides feedback to the source. Noise in the message channel can distort the message.

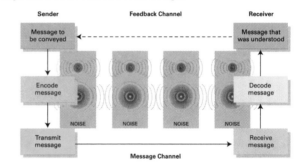

15-3 Outline the goals and tasks of promotion (p. 281–282).
The fundamental goals of promotion are to induce, modify, or reinforce behaviour by informing, persuading, reminding, and connecting Informative promotion explains a good's or service's purpose and benefits. Promotion that informs the consumer is typically used to increase demand for a general product category or to introduce a new good or service. Persuasive promotion is designed to stimulate a purchase or an action. Promotion that persuades the consumer to buy is essential during the growth stage of the product life cycle, when competition becomes fierce. Reminder promotion is used to keep the product and brand name in the public's mind. Promotions that remind are generally used during the maturity stage of the product life cycle. To create loyal consumers, promotion today makes a connection. Social media tools are perfect for creating connection.

15-4 Discuss the elements of the promotional mix (p. 282–287).
The elements of the promotional mix include advertising, public relations, sales promotion, personal selling, direct-response communication, and social media. Advertising is a form of impersonal, one-way mass communication paid for by the source. Public relations is concerned with a firm's public image. Sales promotion is typically used to back up other components of the promotional mix by stimulating immediate demand. Personal selling typically involves direct communication, in person or by telephone. Direct-response communication is targeted communications to a specific audience. Social media are promotional tools that facilitate conversations online and encourage consumer empowerment.

15-5 Discuss the AIDA concept and its relationship to the promotional mix (p. 288–290).
The AIDA model outlines the four basic stages in the purchase decision-making process, which are initiated and propelled by promotional activities:

interpersonal communication direct, face-to-face communication between two or more people

mass communication the communication of a concept or message to large audiences

noise anything that interferes with, distorts, or slows down the transmission of information

online marketing two-way communication of a message delivered through the Internet to the consumer

owned media a category of promotional tactic based on brands becoming publishers of their own content to maximize the brands' value to consumers

paid media a category of promotional tactic based on the traditional advertising model whereby a brand pays for advertising space

personal selling a purchase situation involving a personal, paid-for communication between two people in an attempt to influence each other

promotion communication by marketers that informs, persuades, reminds, and connects potential buyers to a product for the purpose of influencing an opinion or eliciting a response

promotional mix the combination of promotional tools—including advertising, publicity, sales promotion, personal selling, direct-response communication, and social media—used to reach the target market and fulfill the organization's overall goals

promotional strategy a plan for the use of the elements of promotion: advertising, public relations, personal selling, sales promotion, direct-response communication, and social media

public relations the marketing function that evaluates public attitudes, identifies areas within the organization the public may be interested in, and executes a program of action to earn public understanding and acceptance

(1) attention, (2) interest, (3) desire, and (4) action. The components of the promotional mix have varying levels of influence at each stage of the AIDA model.

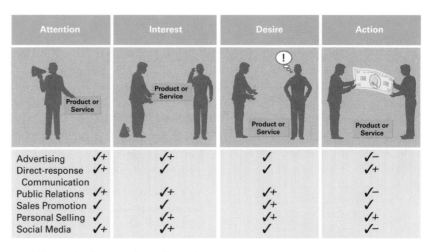

	Attention	Interest	Desire	Action
Advertising	✓+	✓+	✓	✓−
Direct-response Communication	✓+	✓	✓	✓+
Public Relations	✓+	✓+	✓+	✓−
Sales Promotion	✓	✓	✓+	✓
Personal Selling	✓	✓+	✓+	✓+
Social Media	✓+	✓+	✓	✓−

15-6 Know the factors that affect the promotional mix (p. 290–294). Promotion managers consider many factors when creating promotional mixes. These factors include the nature of the product, the product life-cycle stage, the target market characteristics, the type of buying decision involved, the availability of funds, and the feasibility of push or pull strategies.

15-7 Discuss the concept of integrated marketing communications (p. 294–295). Integrated marketing communications is the careful coordination of all promotional messages for a product or service to ensure the consistency of messages at every contact point at which a company meets the consumer—advertising, sales promotion, personal selling, public relations, as well as direct marketing, packaging, and other forms of communication. Marketing managers carefully coordinate all promotional activities to ensure that consumers see and hear one message. Integrated marketing communications has received more attention in recent years because of the proliferation of media choices, the fragmentation of mass markets into segmented niches, and the decrease in advertising spending in favour of promotional techniques that generate an immediate sales response.

publicity public information about a company, a product, a service, or an issue appearing in the mass media as a news item

pull strategy a marketing strategy that stimulates consumer demand to obtain product distribution

push strategy a marketing strategy that uses aggressive personal selling and trade advertising to convince a wholesaler or a retailer to carry and sell particular merchandise

receivers the people who decode a message

sales promotion marketing activities—other than personal selling, advertising, direct-response marketing, and public relations—that stimulate consumer buying and dealer effectiveness

sender the originator of the message in the communication process

social media a collection of online communication tools that facilitate conversations online; when used by marketers, social media tools encourage consumer empowerment

advergaming placing advertising messages in Web-based or video games to advertise or promote a product, a service, an organization, or an issue

advertising appeal a reason for a person to buy a product

advertising campaign a series of related advertisements focusing on a common theme, slogan, and set of advertising appeals

advertising objective a specific communication task that a campaign should accomplish for a specified target audience during a specified period

advertising response function a phenomenon in which spending for advertising and sales promotion increases sales or market share up to a certain level but then produces diminishing returns

advocacy advertising a form of advertising in which an organization expresses its views on a particular issue or cause

audience selectivity the ability of an advertising medium to reach a precisely defined market

cause-related marketing a type of sponsorship involving the association of a for-profit company with a nonprofit organization; through the sponsorship, the company's product or service is promoted, and money is raised for the nonprofit

comparative advertising a form of advertising that compares two or more competing brands on one or more specific attributes

competitive advertising a form of advertising designed to influence demand for a specific brand

continuous media schedule a media scheduling strategy in which advertising is run steadily throughout the advertising period; used for products in the later stages of the product life cycle

cooperative advertising an arrangement in which the manufacturer and the retailer split the costs of advertising the manufacturer's brand

cost per contact the cost of reaching one member of the target market

16-1 Define advertising and understand the effect of advertising (p. 297–299). Advertising is any form of impersonal, paid communication in which the sponsor or company is identified. Advertising helps marketers increase or maintain brand awareness and, subsequently, market share.

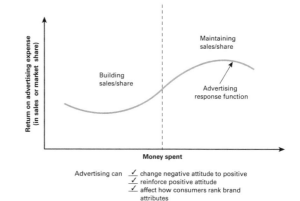

16-2 Identify the major types of advertising (p. 299–300). The two major types of advertising are institutional advertising and product advertising. The purpose of institutional advertising is to foster a positive company image with all stakeholders. Product advertising is designed mainly to promote goods and services, and it is classified into three main categories: pioneering, competitive, and comparative.

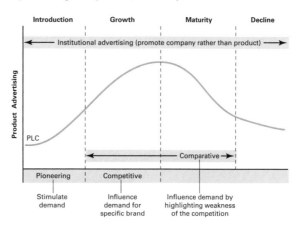

16-3 Discuss the creative decisions in developing an advertising campaign (p. 300–303). Once the goals and objectives of the advertising are defined, creative work can begin. Creative decisions include identifying the product's benefits, developing possible advertising appeals, evaluating and selecting the advertising appeals, executing the advertising message, and evaluating the effectiveness of the campaign.

16-4 Describe media evaluation and selection techniques (p. 303–311). Media evaluation and selection comprise a crucial step in the advertising campaign process. Major types of advertising media include newspapers; magazines; radio; television; outdoor advertising, such as billboards and bus panels; and the Internet. Promotion managers choose the advertising campaign's media mix on the basis of the following variables: cost per contact, reach, frequency, characteristics of the target audience, flexibility of the medium, noise level, and lifespan of the medium. After choosing the media mix, a media schedule designates when the advertisement will appear and the specific vehicles it will appear in.

crisis management a coordinated effort to handle all the effects of either unfavourable publicity or an unexpected unfavourable event

direct mail a printed form of direct-response communication that is delivered directly to consumers' homes

direct-response broadcast advertising that uses television or radio and includes a direct call to action asking the consumer to respond immediately

direct-response print advertising in a print medium that includes a direct call to action

direct-response television (DRTV) advertising that appears on television and encourages viewers to respond immediately

Do Not Call List (DNCL) a free service whereby Canadians register their telephone number to reduce or eliminate phone calls from telemarketers

experiential marketing a form of advertising that focuses on helping consumers experience a brand such that a memorable and emotional connection is formed between the consumer and the brand

flighted media schedule a media scheduling strategy in which ads are run heavily every other month or every two weeks, to achieve a greater impact with an increased frequency and reach at those times

frequency the number of times an individual is exposed to a given message during a specific period

infomercial a 30-minute or longer advertisement that looks more like a TV talk show than a sales pitch

institutional advertising a form of advertising designed to enhance a company's image rather than promote a particular product

media mix the combination of media to be used for a promotional campaign

media planning the series of decisions advertisers make regarding the selection and use of media, allowing the marketer to optimally and cost-effectively communicate the message to the target audience

16-5 Discuss the role of public relations in the promotional mix (p. 311–314). Public relations is a vital part of a firm's promotional mix. Popular public relations tools include new-product publicity, product placement, consumer education, event sponsorship, issue sponsorship, and websites. An equally important aspect of public relations is managing unfavourable publicity in a way that is least damaging to a firm's image.

16-6 Discuss the role of direct-response communication in the promotional mix (p. 314–317). Direct-response communication is often referred to as direct marketing. It involves the development of relevant messages and offers that can be tracked, measured, analyzed, stored, and leveraged. Popular direct-marketing tools include direct-response broadcast, direct-response print, telemarketing, and direct mail. Direct-response communication is designed to generate an immediate response from the consumer through the inclusion of a key element—the offer.

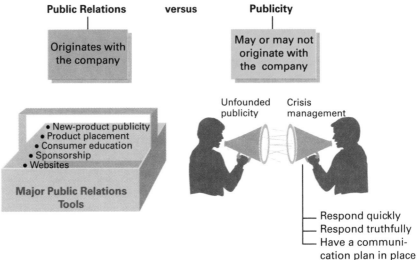

media schedule designation of the media, the specific publications or programs, and the insertion dates of advertising

medium the channel used to convey a message to a target market

mobile advertising advertising that displays text, images, and animated ads via mobile phones or other mobile devices that are data enabled

pioneering advertising a form of advertising designed to stimulate primary demand for a new product or product category

product advertising a form of advertising that promotes the benefits of a specific good or service

product placement a public relations strategy that involves getting a product, service, or company name to appear in a movie, television show, radio program, magazine, newspaper, video game, video or audio clip, book, or commercial for another product; on the Internet; or at special events

pulsing media schedule a media scheduling strategy that uses continuous scheduling throughout the year coupled with a flighted schedule during the best sales periods

reach the number of target consumers exposed to a commercial at least once during a specific period, usually four weeks

seasonal media schedule a media scheduling strategy that runs advertising only during times of the year when the product is most likely to be purchased

sponsorship a public relations strategy in which a company spends money to support an issue, a cause, or an event that is consistent with corporate objectives, such as improving brand awareness or enhancing corporate image

telemarketing the use of telecommunications to sell a product or service; involves both outbound and inbound calls

unique selling proposition a desirable, exclusive, and believable advertising appeal selected as the theme for a campaign

cold calling a form of lead generation in which the salesperson approaches potential buyers without any prior knowledge of the prospects' needs or financial status

consumer sales promotion sales promotion activities targeting the ultimate consumer

coupon a certificate that entitles consumers to an immediate price reduction when they buy the product

follow-up the final step of the selling process, in which the salesperson ensures that delivery schedules are met, that the goods or services perform as promised, and that the buyers' employees are properly trained to use the products

frequent-buyer program a loyalty program in which loyal consumers are rewarded for making multiple purchases of a particular good or service

lead generation (prospecting) identification of those firms and people most likely to buy the seller's offerings

lead qualification determination of a sales prospect's (1) recognized need, (2) buying power, and (3) receptivity and accessibility

loyalty marketing program a promotional program designed to build long-term, mutually beneficial relationships between a company and its key customers

needs assessment a determination of the customer's specific needs and wants and the range of options the customer has for satisfying them

negotiation the process during which both the salesperson and the prospect offer concessions in an attempt to arrive at a sales agreement

networking the use of friends, business contacts, co-workers, acquaintances, and fellow members in professional and civic organizations to identify potential clients

preapproach a process that describes the research a salesperson must do before contacting a prospect

17-1 Define and state the objectives of sales promotion (p. 319–321). Sales promotion consists of those marketing communication activities, in which a short-term incentive motivates consumers or members of the distribution channel to purchase a good or service immediately, through either by lowering the price or by adding value. The main objective of sales promotion is to increase trial purchases, consumer inventories, and repeat purchases. Sales promotion is also used to encourage brand switching and to build brand loyalty. Sales promotion supports advertising activities.

17-2 Discuss the most common forms of consumer sales promotion (p. 321–324). Consumer forms of sales promotion include coupons and rebates, premiums, loyalty marketing programs, contests and sweepstakes, sampling, and point-of-purchase displays. Coupons are certificates entitling consumers to an immediate price reduction when they purchase a product or service. Coupons are a particularly good way to encourage product trial and brand switching. Similar to coupons, rebates provide purchasers with a price reduction, although it is not immediate. Premiums offer an extra item or incentive to the consumer for buying a product or service. Loyalty programs are extremely effective at building long-term, mutually beneficial relationships between a company and its key customers. Contests and sweepstakes are generally designed to create interest, often to encourage brand switching. Sampling is an effective method of gaining new customers. Finally, point-of-purchase displays set up at the retailer's location build traffic, advertise the product, and induce impulse buying.

17-3 Discuss the most common forms of trade sales promotion (p. 325). Manufacturers use many of the same sales promotion tools used in consumer promotions, such as sales contests, premiums, and point-of-purchase displays. In addition, manufacturers and channel intermediaries use several unique promotional strategies: trade allowances, push money, training programs, free merchandise, store demonstrations, and meetings, conventions, and trade shows.

17-4 Describe personal selling (p. 325–326). Personal selling is direct communication between a sales representative and one or more prospective buyers in an attempt to influence each other in a purchase situation. Personal selling offers several advantages over other forms of promotion. Personal selling allows salespeople to thoroughly explain and demonstrate a product. Salespeople have the flexibility to tailor a sales proposal to the needs and preferences of targeted qualified prospects. Personal selling affords greater managerial control over promotion costs and is the most effective method of closing a sale and producing satisfied customers.

17-5 Discuss the key differences between relationship selling and traditional selling (p. 326–327). Relationship selling is the practice of building, maintaining, and enhancing interactions with customers to develop long-term satisfaction through mutually beneficial partnerships. Traditional selling, on the other hand, is transaction focused. That is, the salesperson is most concerned with making one-time sales and moving on to the next prospect. In contrast, salespeople who

premium an extra item offered to the consumer, usually in exchange for some proof of purchase of the promoted product

push money money offered to channel intermediaries to encourage them to push products—that is, to encourage other members of the channel to sell the products

rebates cash refunds given for the purchase of a product during a specific period

referrals recommendations to a salesperson from a customer or business associate

relationship selling (consultative selling) a multistage sales process that involves building, maintaining, and enhancing interactions with customers for the purpose of developing long-term satisfaction through mutually beneficial partnerships

sales presentation a formal meeting in which the salesperson presents a sales proposal to a prospective buyer

sales process (sales cycle) the set of steps a salesperson goes through to sell a particular product or service

sales proposal a formal written document or professional presentation that outlines how the salesperson's product or service will meet or exceed the prospect's needs

sampling a promotional program that allows the consumer the opportunity to try a product or service for free

shopper marketing promotion set up at the retailer's location to build traffic, advertise the product, or induce impulse buying

trade allowance a price reduction offered by manufacturers to intermediaries, such as wholesalers and retailers

trade sales promotion sales promotion activities targeting a marketing channel member, such as a wholesaler or retailer

practise relationship selling typically spend more time understanding a prospect's needs and developing solutions to meet those needs.

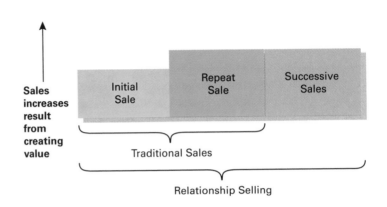

17-6 List the steps in the selling process and discuss key issues (p. 327–333). The selling process is composed of seven basic steps: (1) generating leads, (2) qualifying leads, (3) approaching the customer and probing needs, (4) developing and proposing solutions, (5) handling objections, (6) closing the sale, and (7) following up.

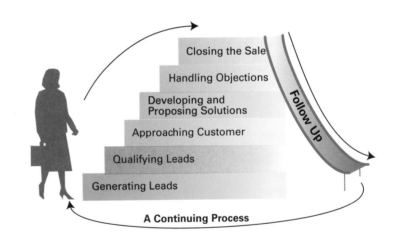

apps short for applications; free or purchased software programs that are downloaded to run on smartphones, tablet computers, and other mobile devices

blogs publicly accessible Web pages that function as interactive journals, whereby readers can post comments on the authors' entries

corporate or professional blogs blogs that are sponsored by a company or one of its brands and maintained by one or more of the company's employees

crowdsourcing the use of consumers to develop and market products

location-based social networking sites websites that combine the fun of social networking with the utility of location-based GPS technology

media-sharing sites websites that allow users to upload and distribute multimedia content, such as videos and photos

microblogs blogs with strict post-length limits

noncorporate blogs independent blogs that are not associated with the marketing efforts of any particular company or brand

review sites websites that allow consumers to post, read, rate, and comment on opinions regarding all kinds of products and services

social commerce a subset of e-commerce that involves the interaction and user contribution aspects of social media to assist in the online buying and selling of products and services

social media a collection of online communication tools that facilitate conversations online; when used by marketers, social media tools encourage consumer empowerment

social networking sites websites that allow individuals to connect—or network—with friends, peers, and business associates

18-1 Describe how social media is used in an integrated marketing communication plan (p. 335–339). Social media, commonly thought of as digital technology, is a way for marketers to communicate one on one with consumers and measure the effects of those interactions. Social media includes social networks, microblogs, and media-sharing sites, all of which are used by the majority of adults. Smartphones and tablet computers have given consumers greater freedom to access social media on the go, which has increased the use of social media sites. Many advertising budgets are allotting more money to online marketing, including social media, mobile marketing, and search marketing.

18-2 Explain how to create a social media campaign (p. 340–342). A social media campaign should take advantage of the three media categories: *owned media, earned media,* and *paid media.* To use these types of media in a social media campaign, first implement an effective listening system. Marketers can interact with negative feedback, make changes, and effectively manage their online presence. Paying attention to the ways that competing brands attract and engage with their customers can be particularly enlightening for both small businesses and global brands. Second, develop a list of objectives that reflects how social media dynamically communicates with customers and builds relationships.

CATEGORIES OF MEDIA TYPES

Owned Media	Earned Media	Paid Media
Blogs	Word of mouth	Newspapers
Websites	Online buzz	Television
Facebook Pages	Viral videos	Radio
	Retweets	Magazines
	Comments on blogs	Out of home
	Publicity	Direct mail
		Display
		Paid search
		Other direct online advertising

SOCIAL MEDIA OBJECTIVES

Listen and learn
Build relationships and awareness
Promote products and services
Manage reputation
Improve customer service

18-3 Evaluate the various methods of measurement for social media (p. 342–343). Hundreds of metrics have been developed to measure social media's value, but these metrics are meaningless unless they are tied to key performance indicators. The three areas of media measurement are social media measurement (track return on investment of each social media tool), public relations (PR) measurement (calculate the impact of social media on press coverage and other elements of PR), and social media monitoring (customer service improvement, brand management, and prospecting).

social news sites websites that allow users to decide which content is promoted on a given website by voting that content up or down

18-4 Explain consumer behaviour on social media (p. 343–345). To effectively leverage social media, marketers must understand who uses social media and how they use it. If a brand's target market does not use social media, a social media campaign might not be useful. There are six categories of social media users: creators, critics, collectors, joiners, spectators, and inactives. A new category is emerging called conversationalists, who post status updates on social networking sites or microblogs.

18-5 Describe the social media tools in a marketer's toolbox, and explain how they are useful (p. 346–351). A marketer has many tools to implement a social media campaign. However, new tools emerge daily, so these resources will change rapidly. Some of the strongest social media platforms are blogs, microblogs, social networks, media creation and sharing sites, social news sites, location-based social networking sites, and virtual worlds and online gaming. Blogs allows marketers to create content in the form of posts, which ideally build trust and a sense of authenticity in customers. Microblogs, such as Twitter, allow brands to follow, retweet, respond to potential customers' tweets, and to tweet content that inspires customers to engage the brand, laying a foundation for meaningful two-way conversation. Social networks allow marketers to increase awareness, target audiences, promote products, forge relationships, attract event participants, perform research, and generate new business. Media sharing sites give brands an interactive channel in which to disseminate content. Social news sites are useful to marketers to promote campaigns, create conversations, and build website traffic. Location-based social networking sites can forge lasting relationships and loyalty in customers. Review sites allow marketers to respond to customer reviews and comments about their brand. Virtual worlds are fertile ground for branded content, and online gaming allows marketers to integrate their message into a game platform.

- Blogs
- Microblogs
- Social networks
- Media creation and sharing sites
- Location-based social networking sites
- Virtual worlds and online gaming

18-6 Describe the impact of mobile technology on social media (p. 351–352). While much of the excitement in social media has been based on websites and new technology uses, much of the growth lies in new platforms. These platforms include smartphones and tablets. The major implication of this development is that consumers now have a multitude of access points for websites.

18-7 Understand the aspects of developing a social media plan (p. 352–354). The social media plan is linked to larger plans, such as a promotional plan or marketing plan, and should fit appropriately into the objectives and steps in those plans. There are six stages involved in creating an effective social media plan: (1) listen, (2) identify the target audience, (3) set social media objectives, (4) define strategies, (5) select the tools and platforms, and (6) implement and monitor the strategy.

campaign management developing product or service offerings customized for the appropriate customer segment and then pricing and communicating these offerings to enhance customer relationships

compiled lists customer lists that are developed by gathering names and addresses gleaned from telephone directories and membership rosters, sometimes enhanced with information from public records, such as census data, auto registrations, birth announcements, business startups, or bankruptcies

customer relationship management (CRM) a system that gathers information about customers that can help to build customer loyalty and retain those loyal customers

customer-centric a philosophy under which the company customizes its product and service offering based on data generated through interactions between the customer and the company

database an organized system of data collection that allows for assessment, usually by computer

data mining an analytical process that compiles actionable data on the purchase habits of a firm's current and potential customers

data warehouse a central repository of data from various functional areas of the organization that are stored and inventoried on a centralized computer system so that the information can be shared across all functional departments of the business

empowerment delegation of authority to solve customers' problems quickly—usually by the first person who learns of the customer's problem

interaction the point at which a customer and a company representative exchange information and develop learning relationships

19-1 Summarize customer relationship management (p. 359–360). In customer relationship management (CRM), a company gathers information about its customers and then uses that information to build loyalty and long-term commitments with those customers. CRM started out as a technology solution for companies looking for data on customers. Much of what was developed was strong from the technology side but did not have the loyalty focus necessary for a true CRM system. CRM must be differentiated from customer relationship marketing, which is more of a customer database than a comprehensive system of tracking and maintaining customer loyalty.

19-2 Explain the CRM cycle (p. 360–361). In 2010, the Government of Canada released an important report on CRM in Canada. The focus of the report was on developing a system of CRM that was not too strongly based in information technology but did use those tools to help create customer loyalty. What was developed was a three-stage CRM cycle. The first stage is focused on using marketing research and general marketing tools to help design and structure a system to keep track of customer information. The second stage is called business development, and here the IT tools are used to help track and establish an efficient system of data collection. Finally, the third stage takes action on the data collected and determines what systems of customer retention and loyalty could be established to not only track customers but begin a two-way interaction that will lead to long-term benefits for both parties.

19-3 Describe Stage 1 in the CRM cycle: marketing research (p. 361). In the first stage of the cycle, there is a renewed focus on marketing as part of CRM. Much of what had been developed for CRM concerned technology solutions and systems rather than what needed to go into these systems. Marketing research techniques, such as competitive intelligence, focus groups, and surveys, are all possible inputs to this first stage of the CRM cycle. As the CRM cycle begins, it becomes clear that CRM is about cross-functional integration of activities in a firm that will lead to customer loyalty. The drivers of this process are those with knowledge of marketing strategy.

19-4 Describe Stage 2 in the CRM cycle: business development (p. 362–371). Stage 2 begins with the assumption that we understand the needs of our customers and have developed an offering that should satisfy them. The first activity in this stage, then, is to identify customer relationships. Using such tools as learning and knowledge management, those relationships are identified, and the nature of the relationships and interactions is used to build a knowledge base. The action then moves to the technology side of CRM by tackling the data needs. Companies need to figure out at this stage how to capture data, store them, and determine which IT tools will best mine them.

knowledge management the process by which learned information from customers is centralized and shared for the purpose of enhancing the relationship between customers and the organization

learning (CRM) in a CRM environment, the informal process of collecting customer data through customer comments and feedback on product or service performance

lifetime value (LTV) analysis a data manipulation technique that projects the future value of the customer over a period of years by using the assumption that marketing to repeat customers is more profitable than marketing to first-time buyers

point-of-sale interactions communications between customers and organizations that occur at the point of sale, usually in a store

predictive modelling a data manipulation technique in which marketers try to determine, based on some past set of occurrences, the odds that some other occurrence, such as an inquiry or a purchase, will take place in the future

recency-frequency-monetary (RFM) analysis the analysis of customer activity by recency, frequency, and monetary value

response list a customer list that includes the names and addresses of individuals who have responded to an offer of some kind, such as by mail, telephone, direct-response television, product rebates, contests or sweepstakes, or billing inserts

touch points all possible areas of a business where customers have contact with that business

19-5 Describe Stage 3 in the CRM cycle: customer feedback (p. 371–376). Even after the data have been collected and mined, they will only get us so far in developing effective CRM. At this stage, companies need to look beyond the reams of data and see in there the people and companies that make up their customer base. CRM must be focused on relationship development, not just database development. Companies can use different methods and applications to build customer loyalty. Companies can develop campaigns and loyalty programs, they can try to cross-sell, and they can target their communications. They can look at a product trials and distribution channel marketing. All these tools must have one goal: to truly change the way in which customers are managed and build a loyal customer base from a foundation of customer service.

19-6 Identify privacy issues in CRM (p. 376–377). The three-stage process of CRM offers numerous options and great potential for data collection, but companies must incorporate strong policies on privacy to protect their customers. Online options are enticing, given the potential access to data, as discussed in Chapter 5 on marketing research, but big data and online options can be a dangerous mix if not managed properly. When developing CRM systems, companies should familiarize themselves with legislation such as the Personal Information Protection and Electronic Documents Act (PIPEDA) and the Privacy Act.